WITCH BUSTER

10

JUNG-MAN CHO

SEVEN SEAS ENTERTAINMENT PRESENTS

WITCH BUSTER

story and art by **JUNG-MAN CHO**

VOLUMES 9-10

TRANSLATION
ChanHee Grace Sung

ADAPTATION
Rebecca Scoble

LETTERING
Wacky Eloriaga-Dunglao
Roland Amago

LAYOUT
Bambi Eloriaga-Amago

COVER DESIGN
Nicky Lim

PROOFREADER
Danielle King

MANAGING EDITOR
Adam Arnold

PUBLISHER
Jason DeAngelis

Seven Seas books may be purchased in bulk for educational, business, or promotional use. For information on bulk purchases, please contact Macmillan Corporate & Premium Sales Department at 1-800-221-7945 (ext 5442) or write specialmarkets@macmillan.com.

ISBN: 978-1-937867-77-5

Printed in Canada

First Printing: March 2014

10 9 8 7 6 5 4 3 2 1

FOLLOW US ONLINE: ***www.gomanga.com***

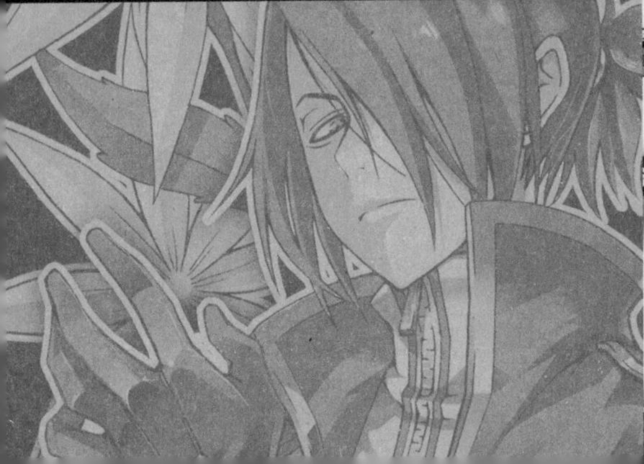

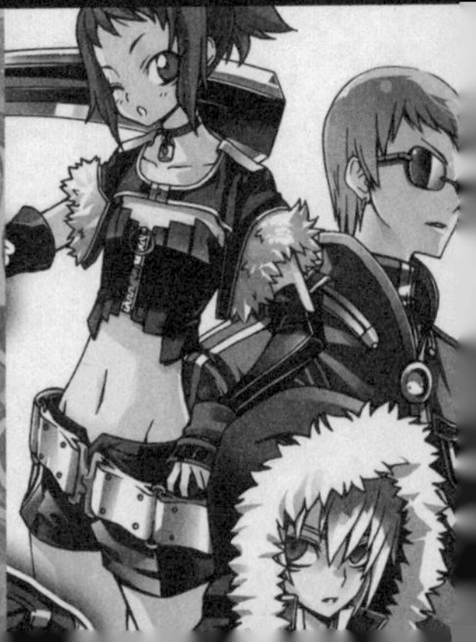

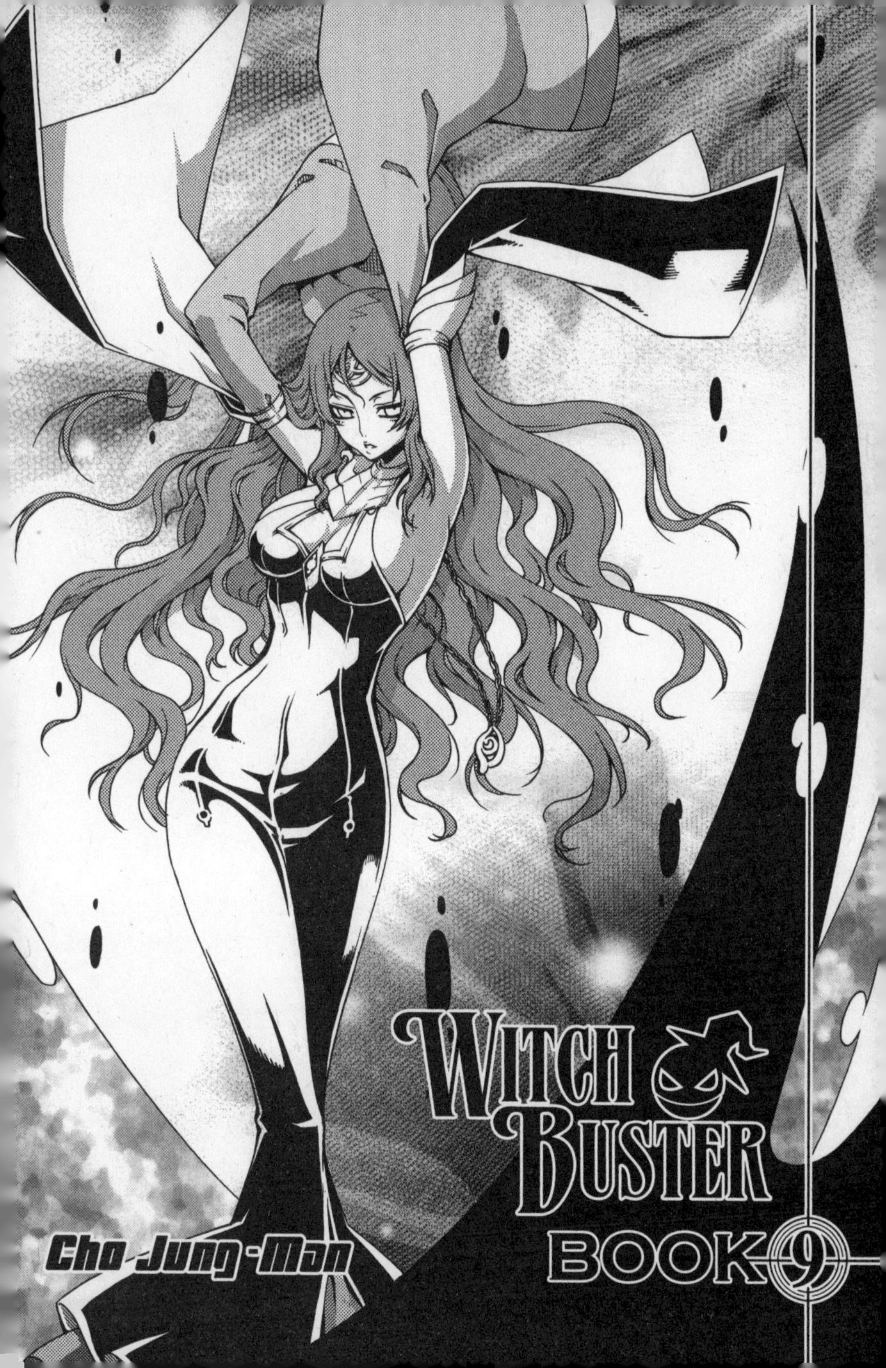
WITCH BUSTER
BOOK 9
Cho Jung-Man

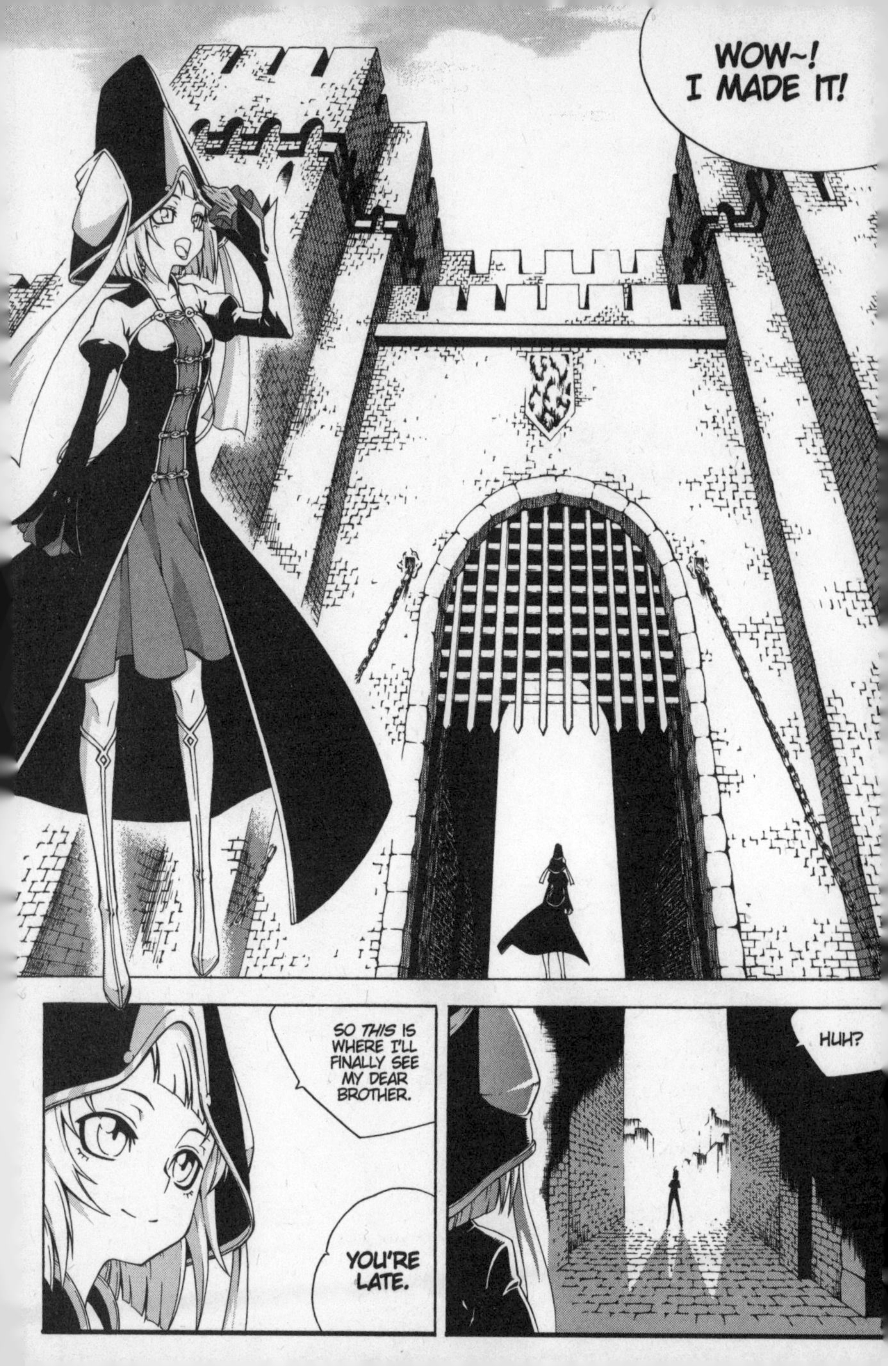
WOW~! I MADE IT!
SO THIS IS WHERE I'LL FINALLY SEE MY DEAR BROTHER.
YOU'RE LATE.
HUH?

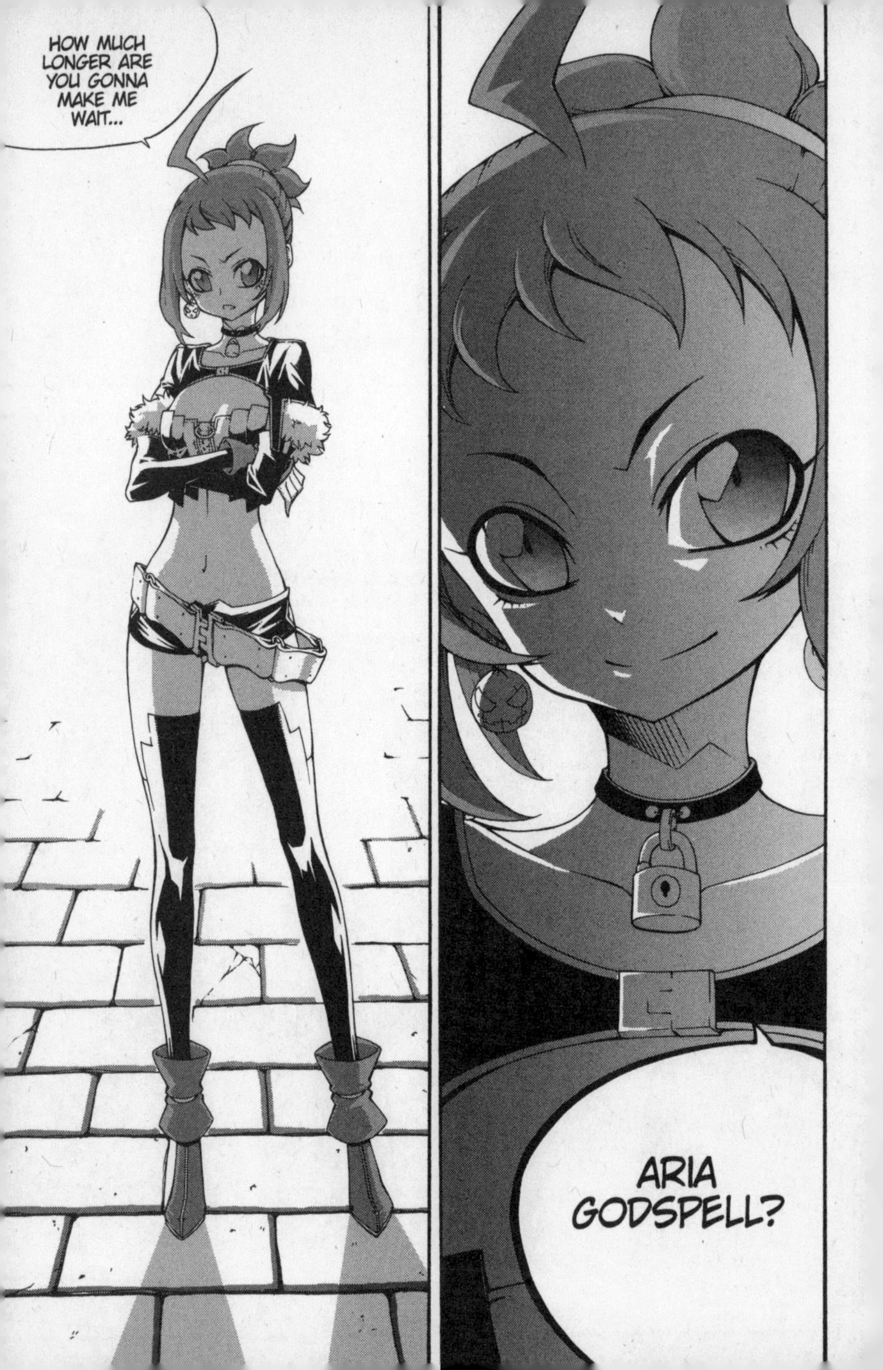
HOW MUCH LONGER ARE YOU GONNA MAKE ME WAIT...
ARIA GODSPELL?

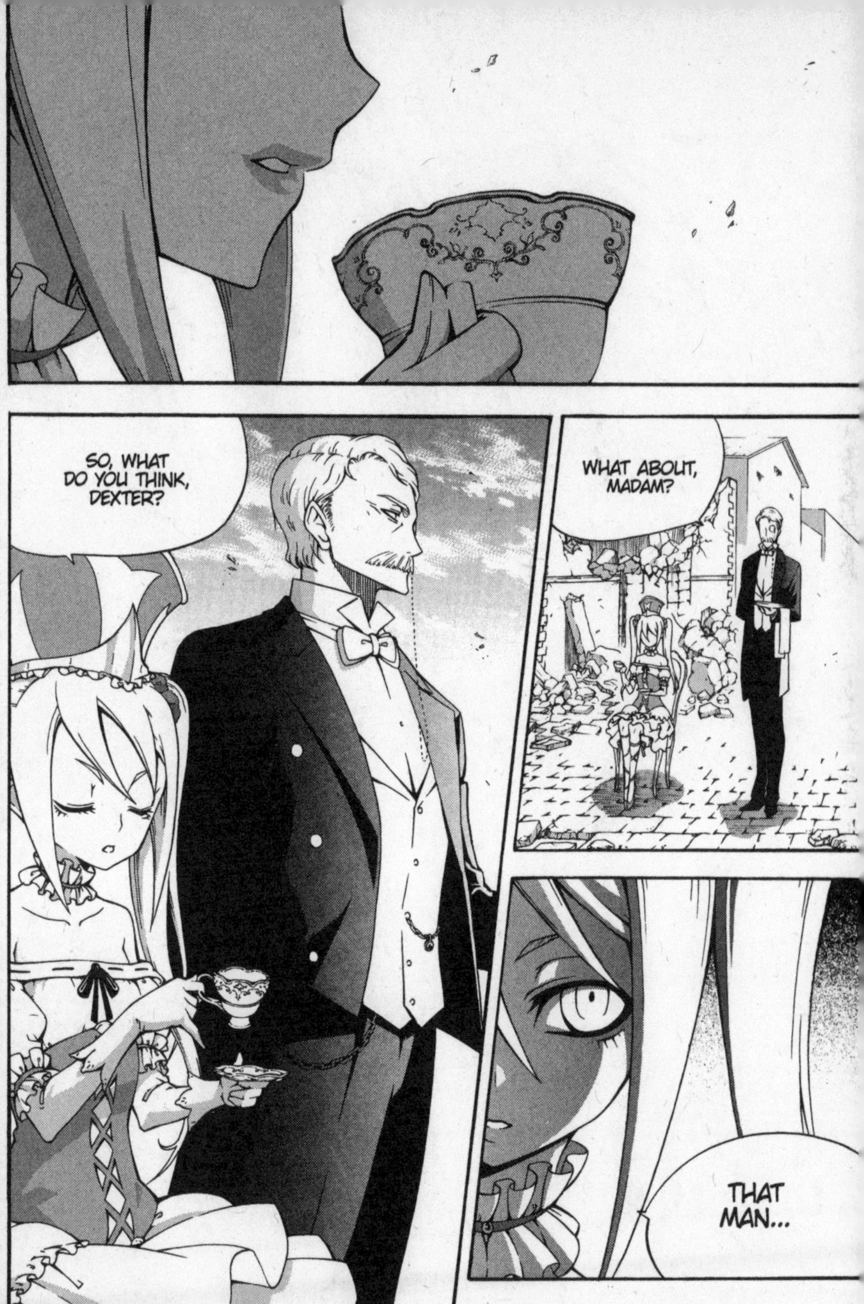
SO, WHAT DO YOU THINK, DEXTER?
WHAT ABOUT, MADAM?
THAT MAN...

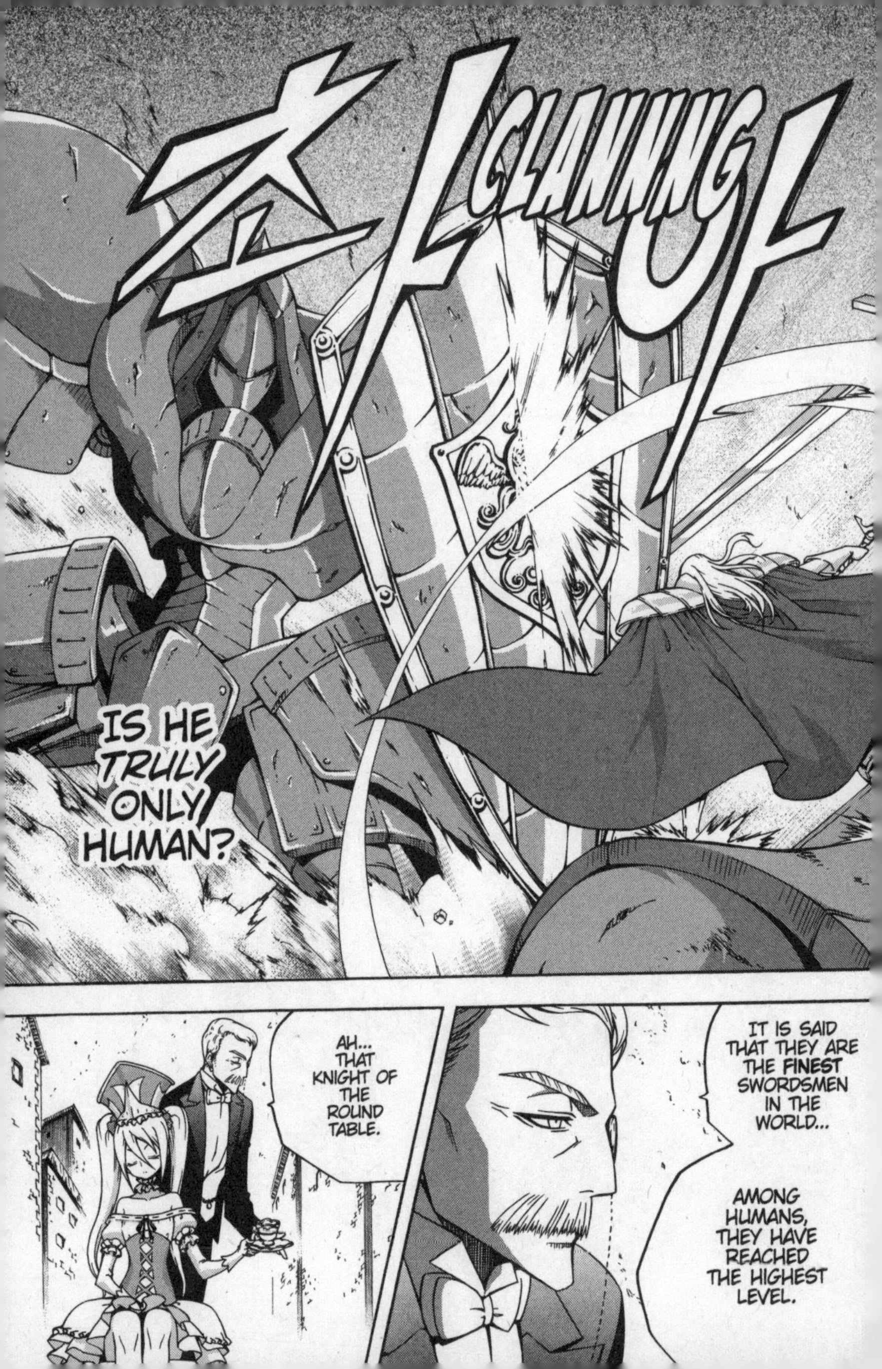
CLANNNG!
IS HE TRULY ONLY HUMAN?
AH... THAT KNIGHT OF THE ROUND TABLE.
IT IS SAID THAT THEY ARE THE FINEST SWORDSMEN IN THE WORLD...
AMONG HUMANS, THEY HAVE REACHED THE HIGHEST LEVEL.

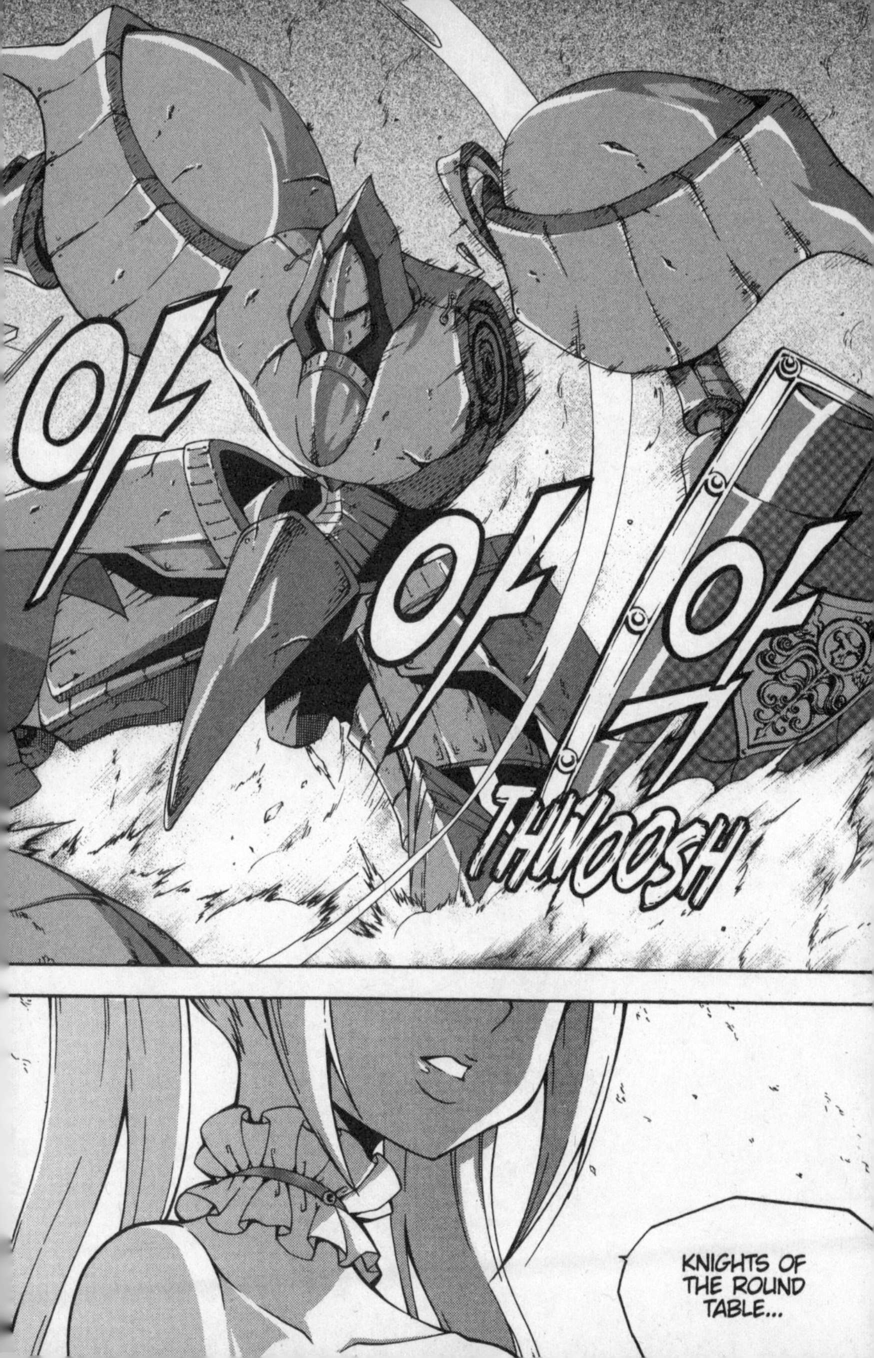
THWOOSH
KNIGHTS OF THE ROUND TABLE...

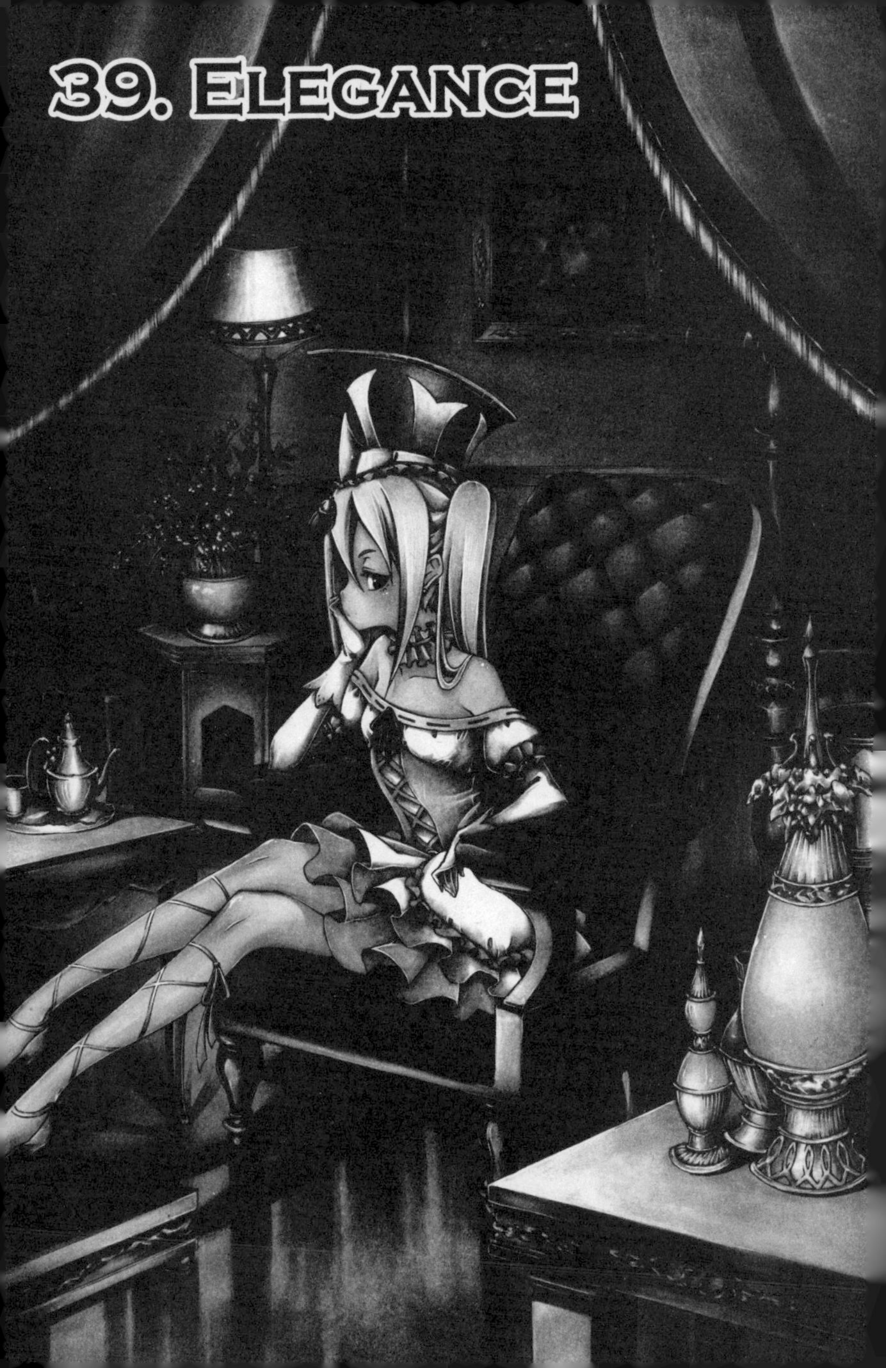
39. Elegance

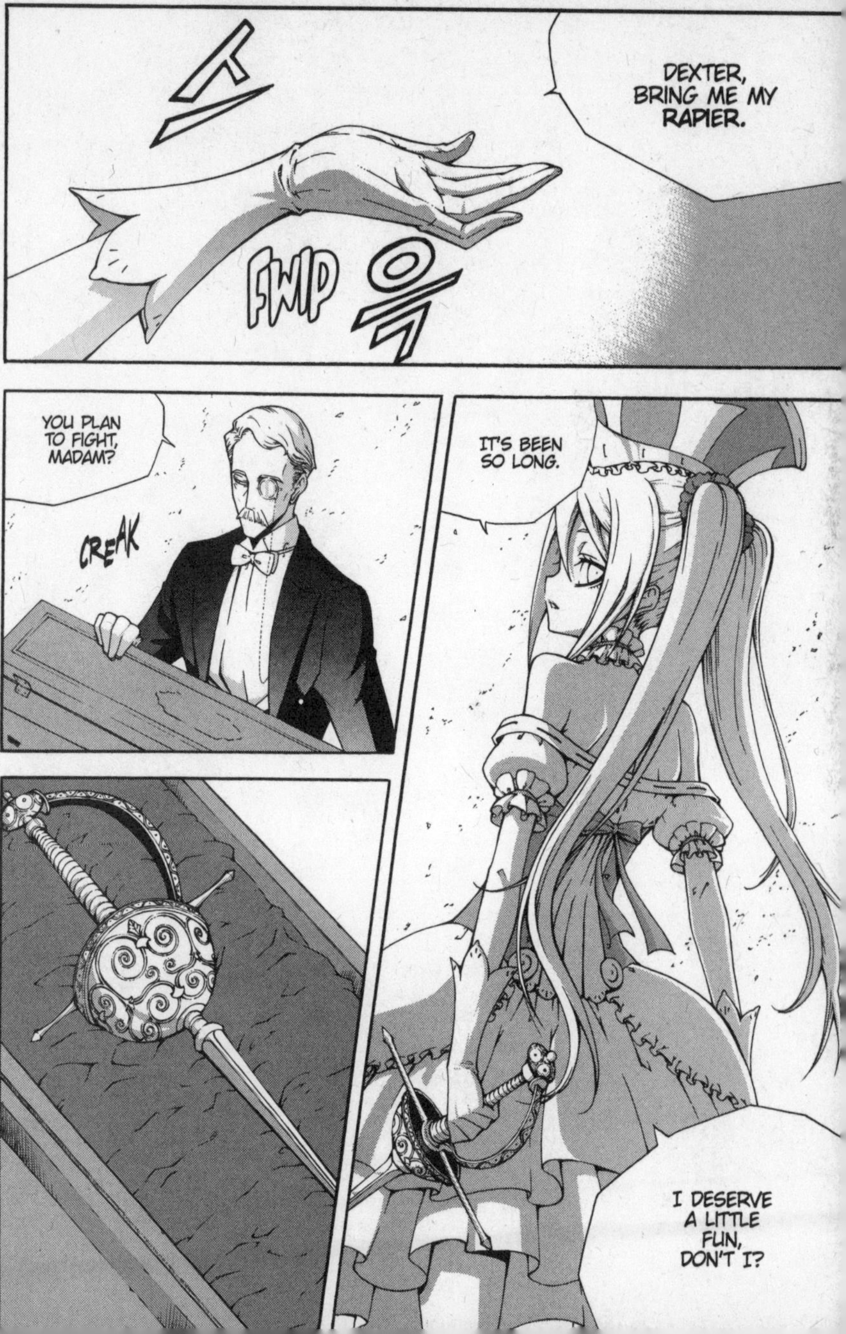
DEXTER, BRING ME MY RAPIER.
FWIP
YOU PLAN TO FIGHT, MADAM?
CREAK
IT'S BEEN SO LONG.
I DESERVE A LITTLE FUN, DON'T I?

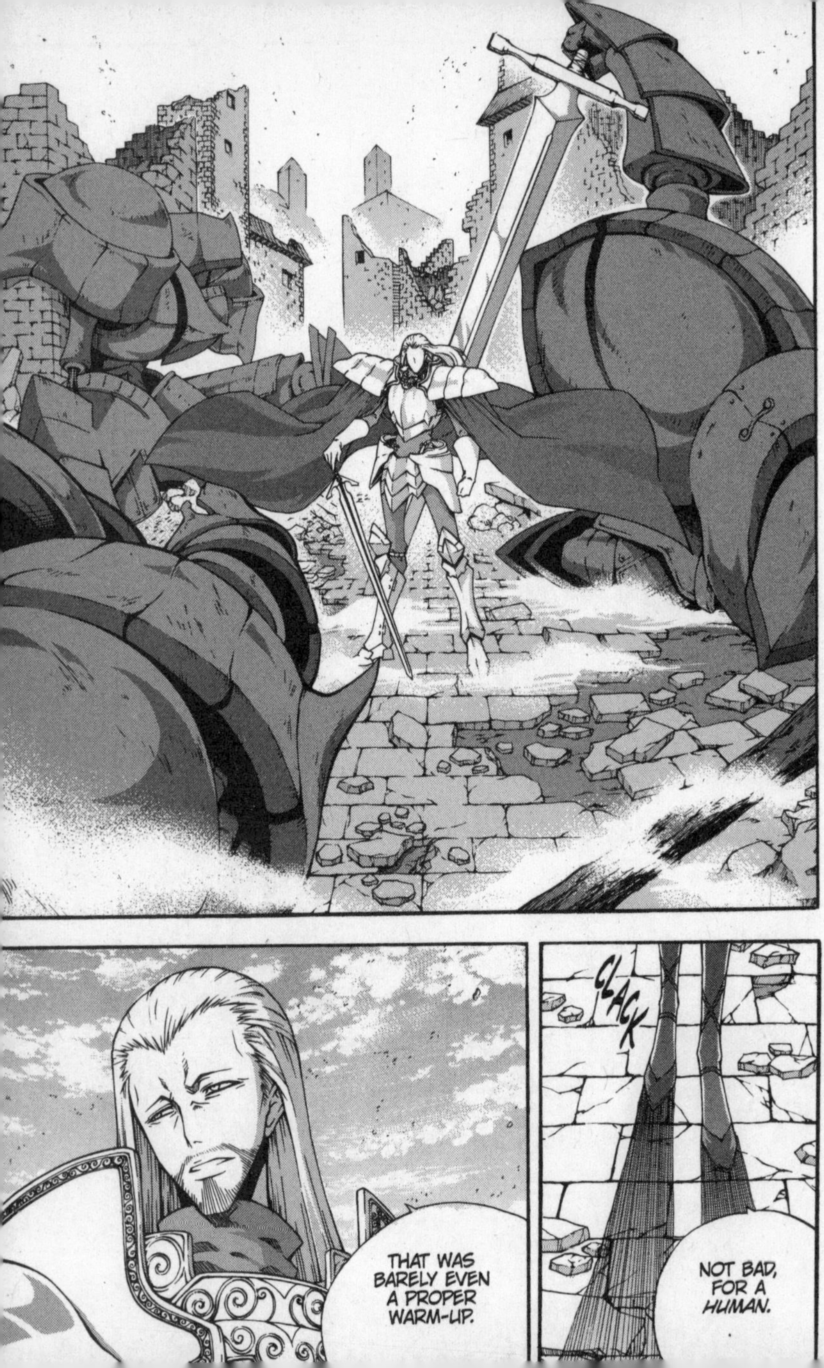
THAT WAS BARELY EVEN A PROPER WARM-UP.
CLACK
NOT BAD, FOR A *HUMAN.*

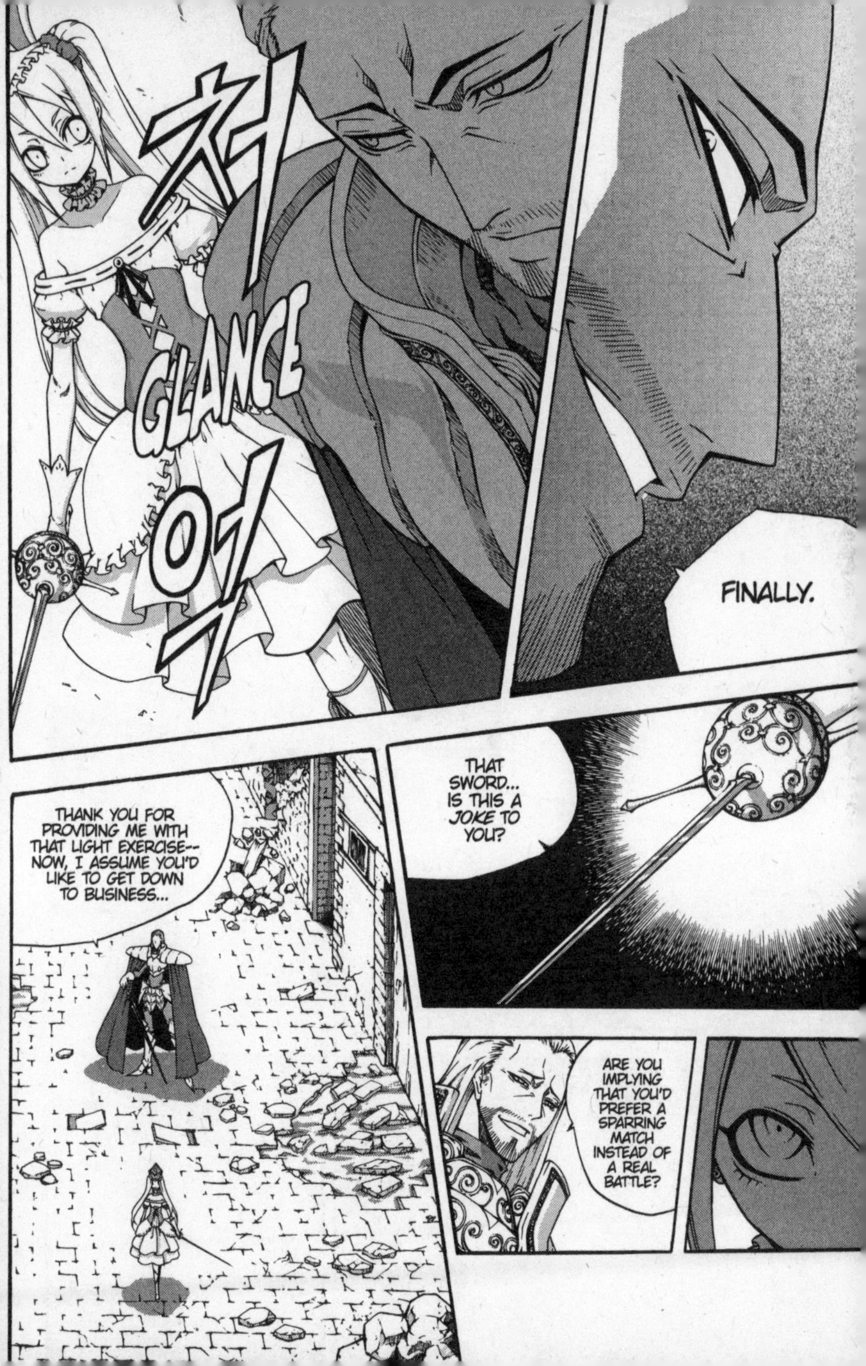
GLANCE
FINALLY.
THANK YOU FOR PROVIDING ME WITH THAT LIGHT EXERCISE-- NOW, I ASSUME YOU'D LIKE TO GET DOWN TO BUSINESS...
THAT SWORD... IS THIS A *JOKE* TO YOU?
ARE YOU IMPLYING THAT YOU'D PREFER A SPARRING MATCH INSTEAD OF A REAL BATTLE?

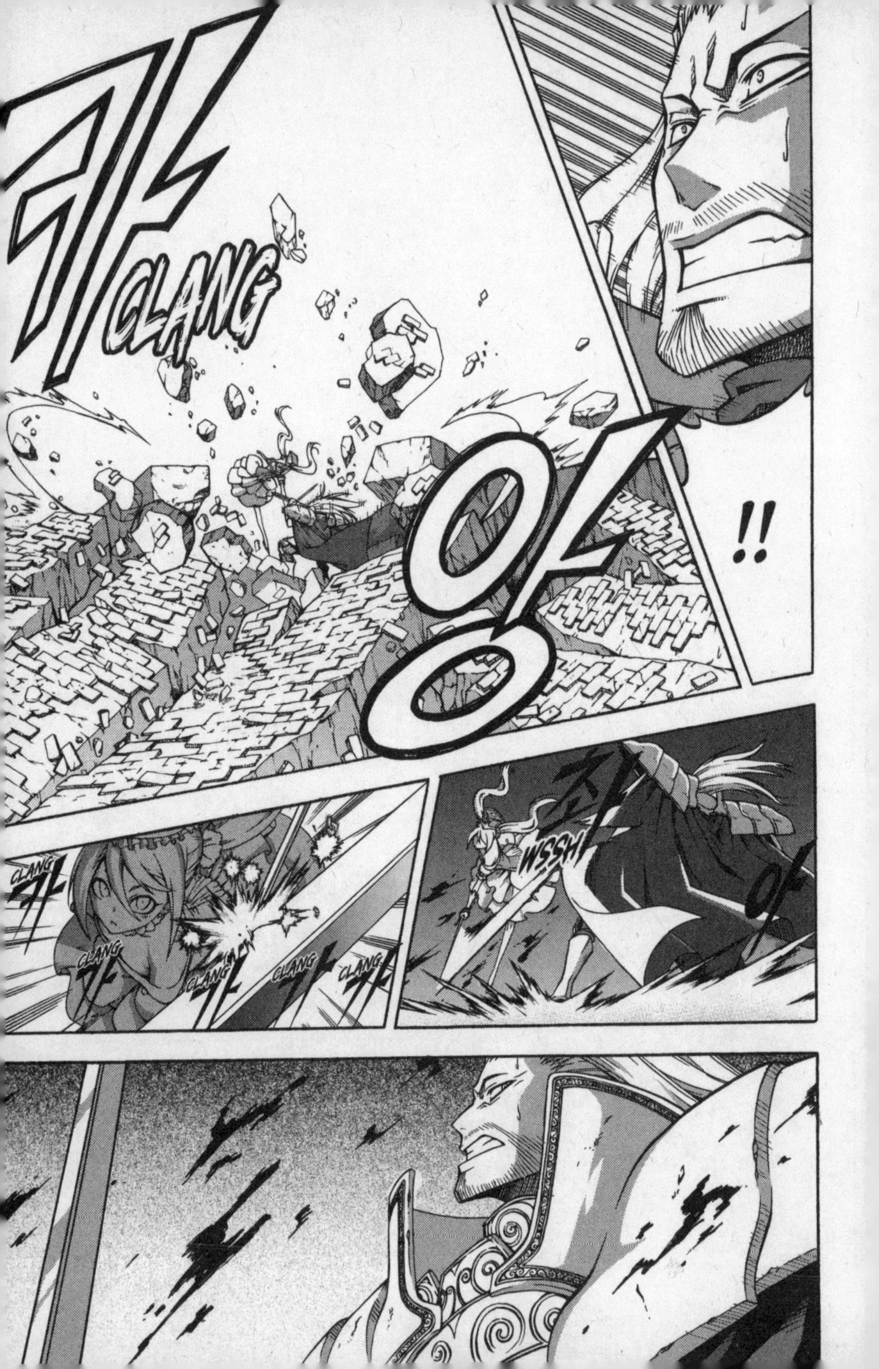

CLANG
!!
CLANG
CLANG
CLANG
CLANG
CLANG
WSSH

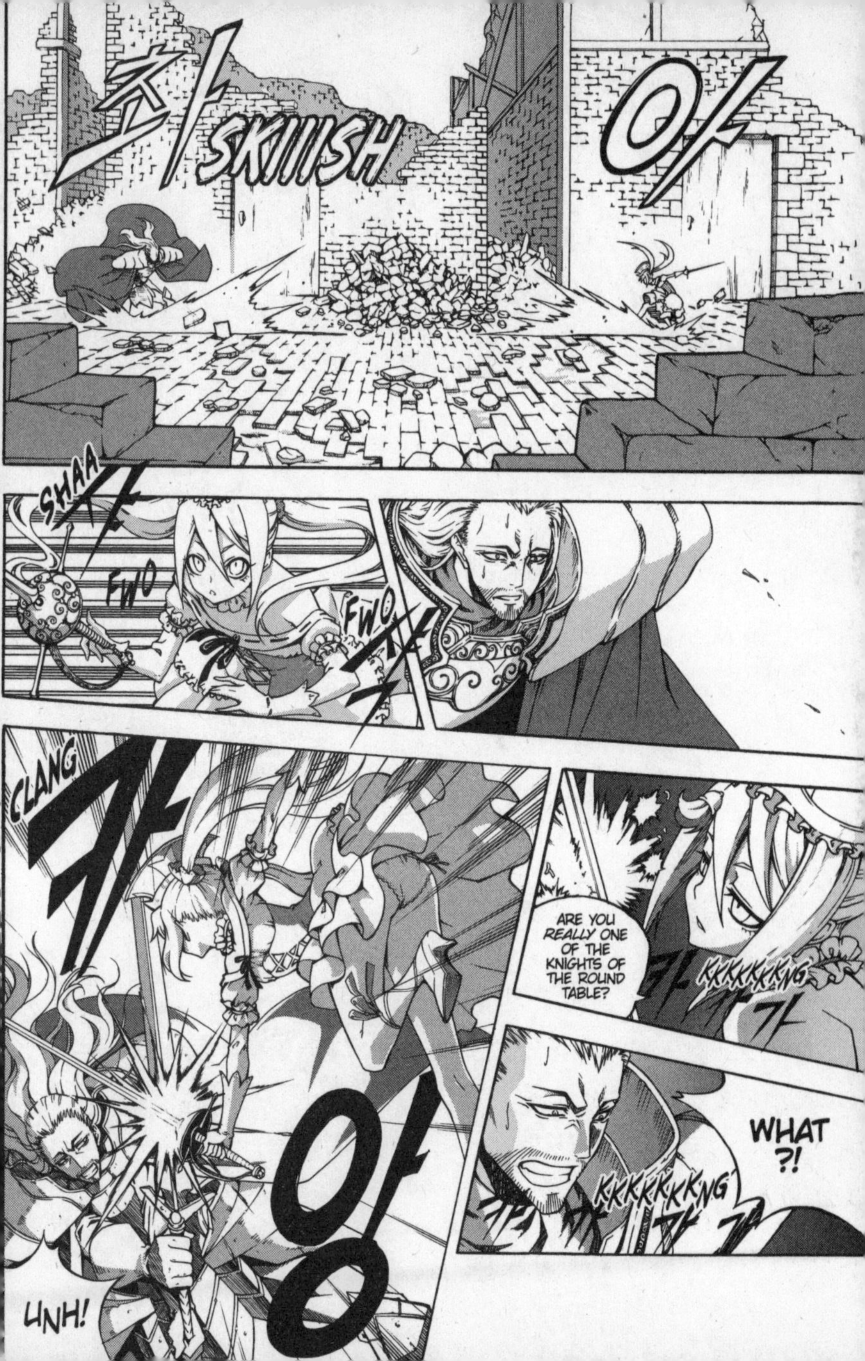
SKIIISH
SHAA
FWO
FWO
CLANG
UNH!
ARE YOU REALLY ONE OF THE KNIGHTS OF THE ROUND TABLE?
KKKKKKNG
KKKKKKNG
WHAT?!

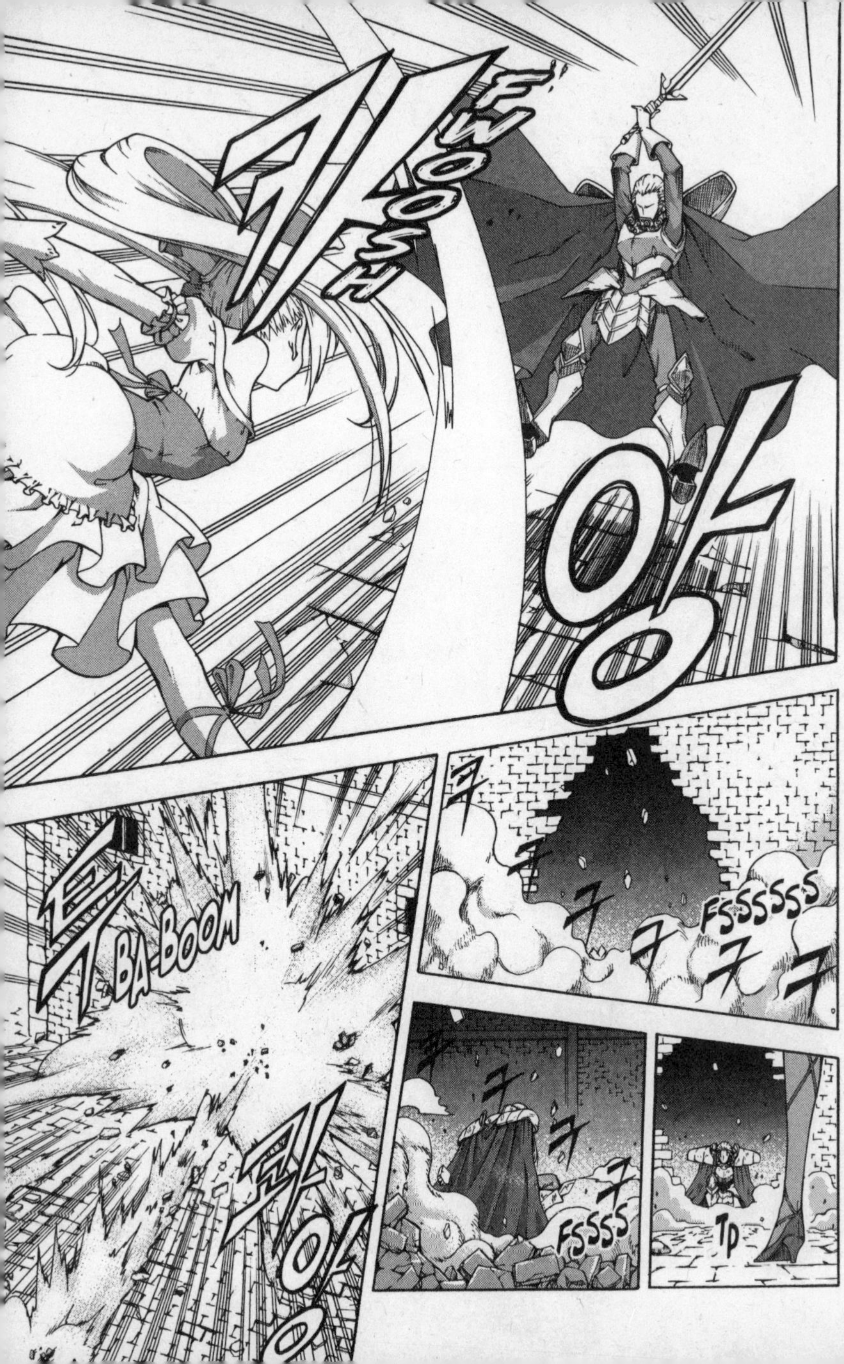
FWOOSH
BA-BOOM
FSSSSSS
FSSSS
TP

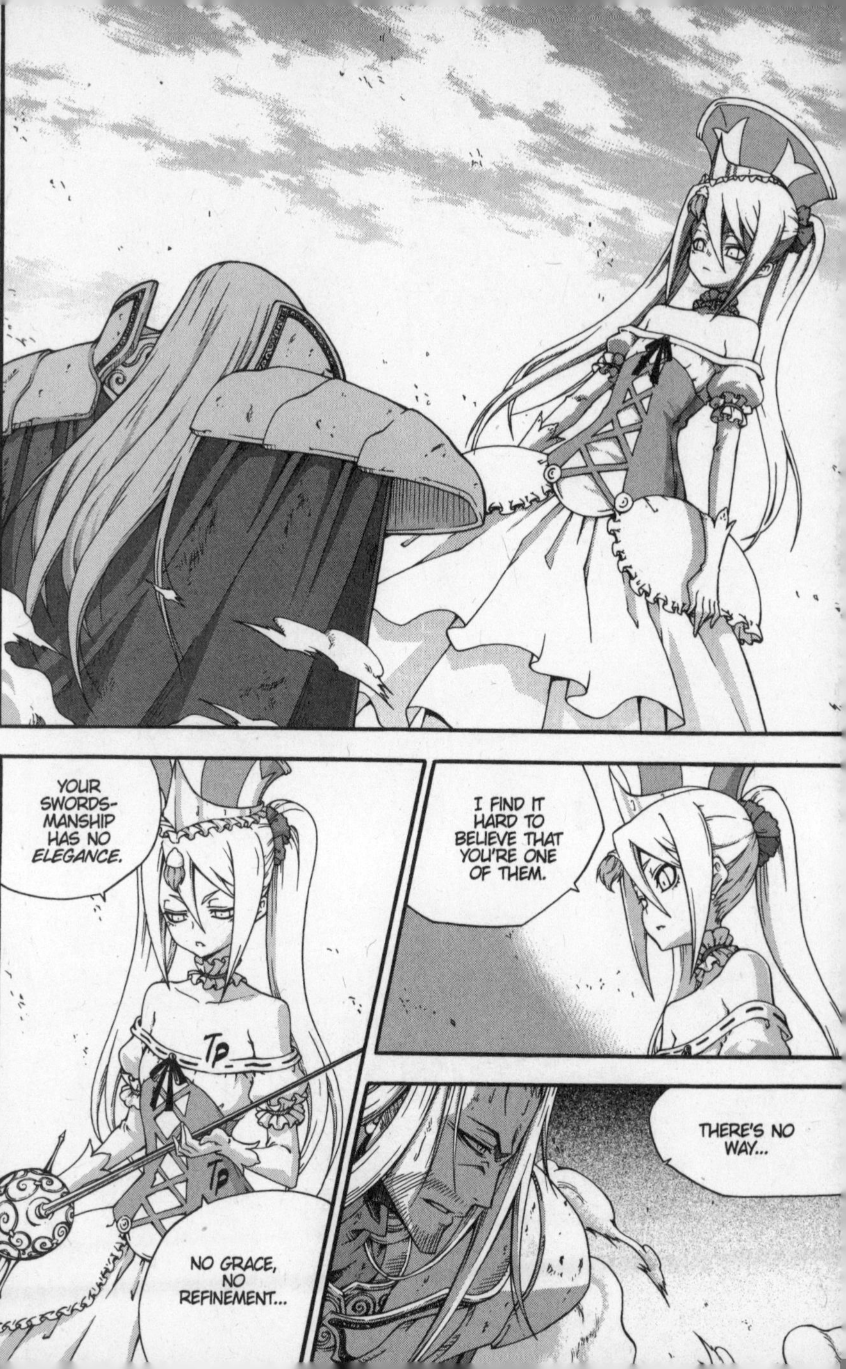
YOUR SWORDS-MANSHIP HAS NO ELEGANCE.
NO GRACE, NO REFINEMENT...
I FIND IT HARD TO BELIEVE THAT YOU'RE ONE OF THEM.
THERE'S NO WAY...

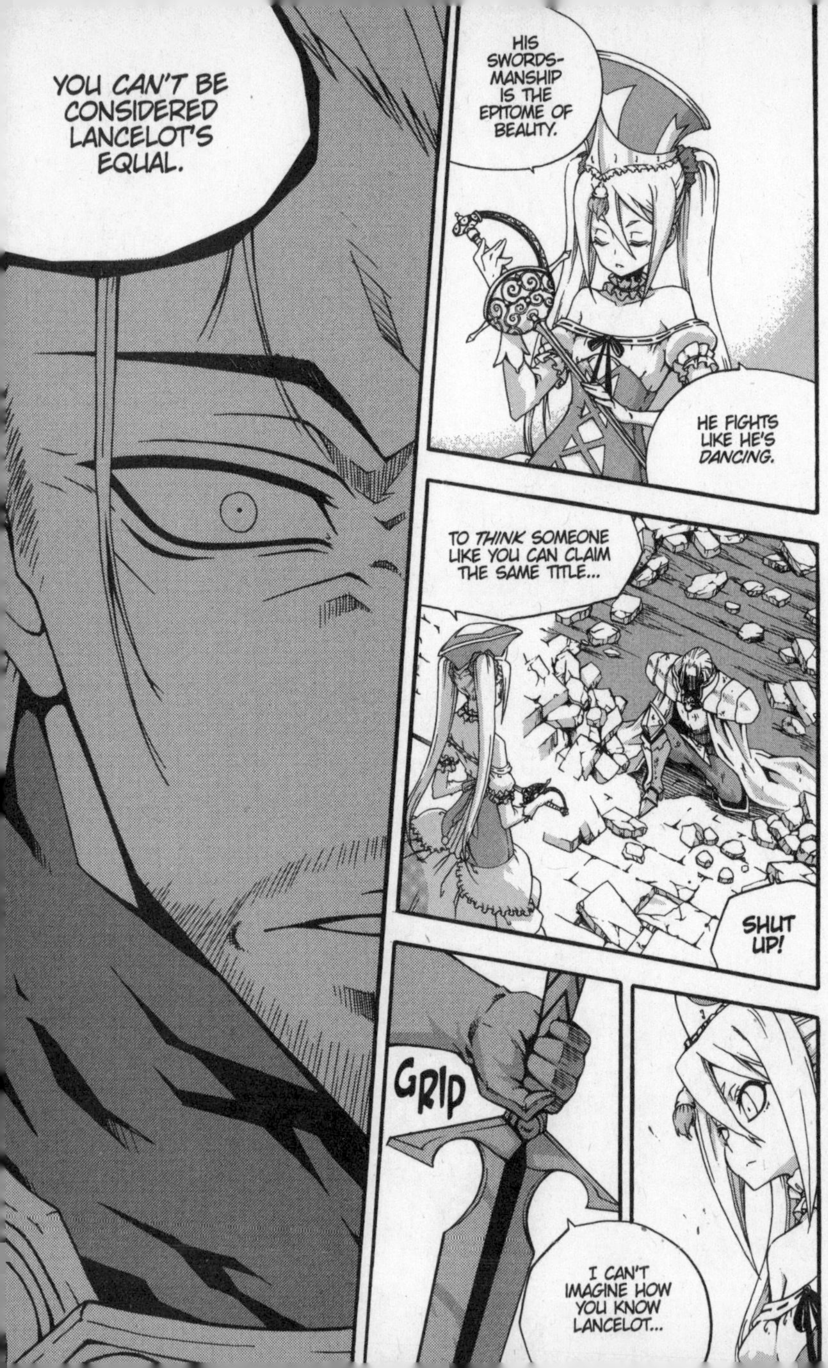
YOU *CAN'T* BE CONSIDERED LANCELOT'S EQUAL.
HIS SWORDS-MANSHIP IS THE EPITOME OF BEAUTY.
HE FIGHTS LIKE HE'S *DANCING.*
TO *THINK* SOMEONE LIKE YOU CAN CLAIM THE SAME TITLE...
SHUT UP!
GRIP
I CAN'T IMAGINE HOW YOU KNOW LANCELOT...

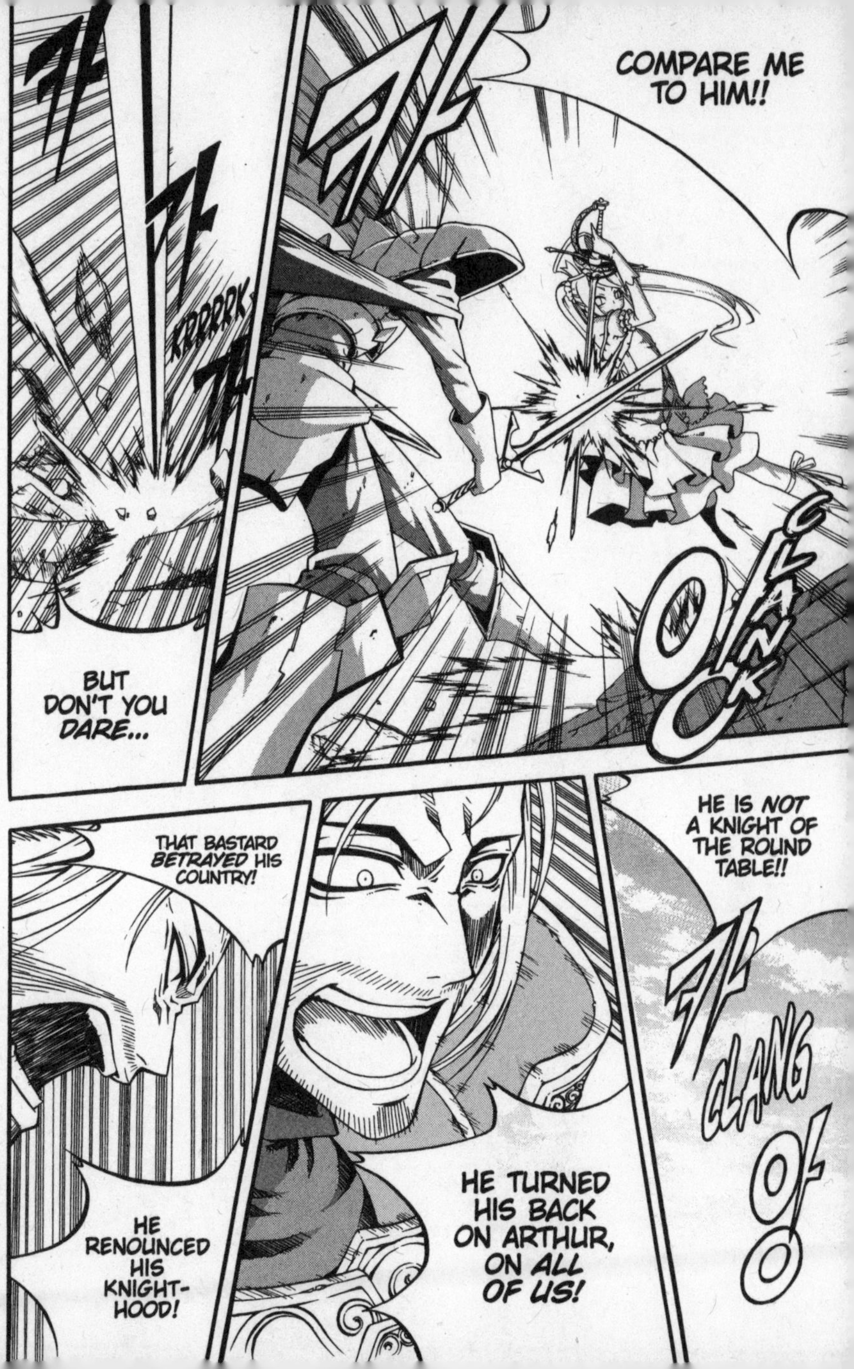
KRRRRK
BUT DON'T YOU *DARE*...
COMPARE ME TO HIM!!
CLANK
THAT BASTARD *BETRAYED* HIS COUNTRY!
HE RENOUNCED HIS KNIGHT-HOOD!
HE TURNED HIS BACK ON ARTHUR, ON *ALL* OF US!
HE IS *NOT* A KNIGHT OF THE ROUND TABLE!!
CLANG

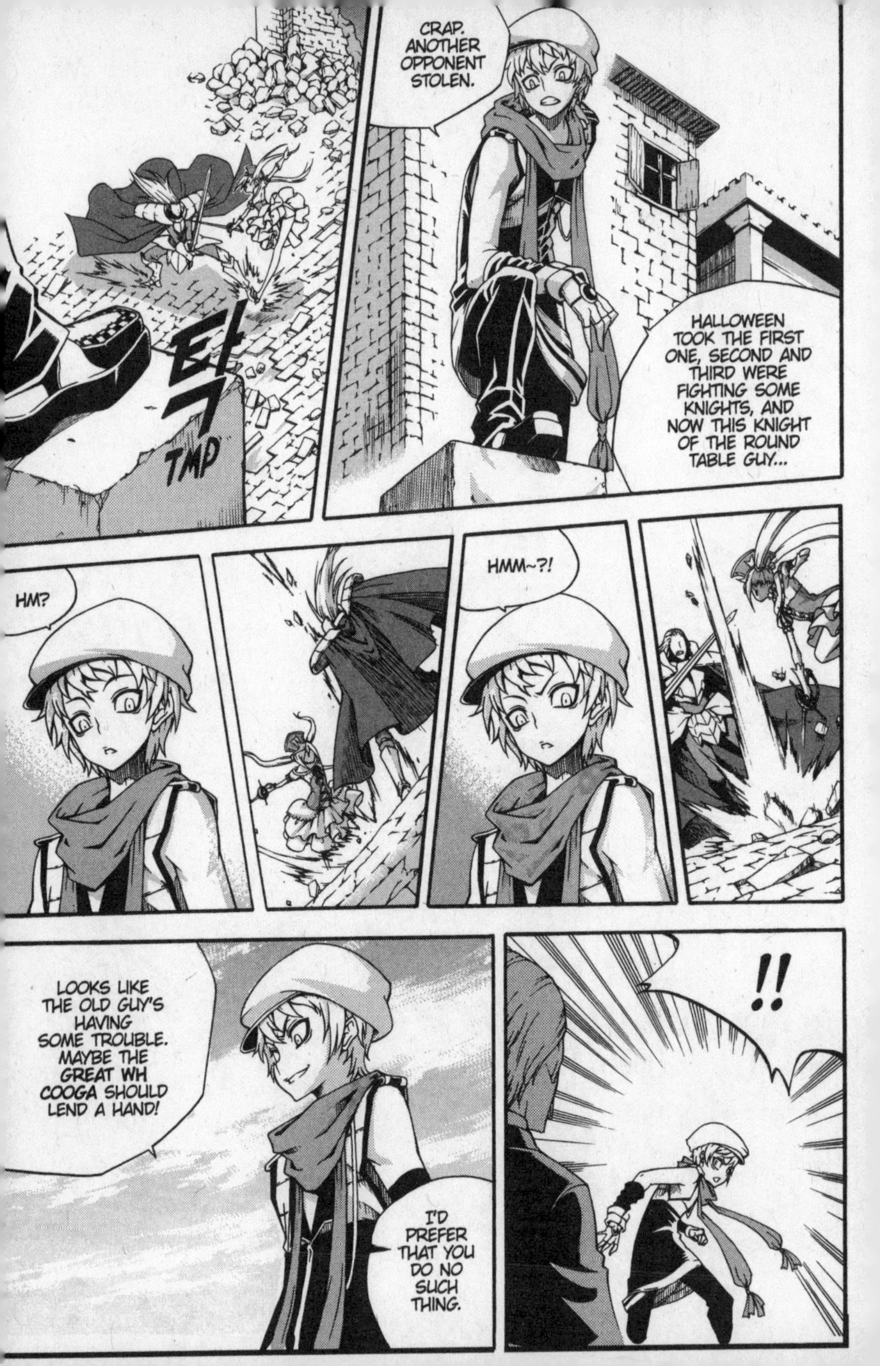
탁
TMP
CRAP. ANOTHER OPPONENT STOLEN.
HALLOWEEN TOOK THE FIRST ONE, SECOND AND THIRD WERE FIGHTING SOME KNIGHTS, AND NOW THIS KNIGHT OF THE ROUND TABLE GUY...
HM?
HMM~?!
LOOKS LIKE THE OLD GUY'S HAVING SOME TROUBLE. MAYBE THE GREAT WH COOGA SHOULD LEND A HAND!
I'D PREFER THAT YOU DO NO SUCH THING.
!!

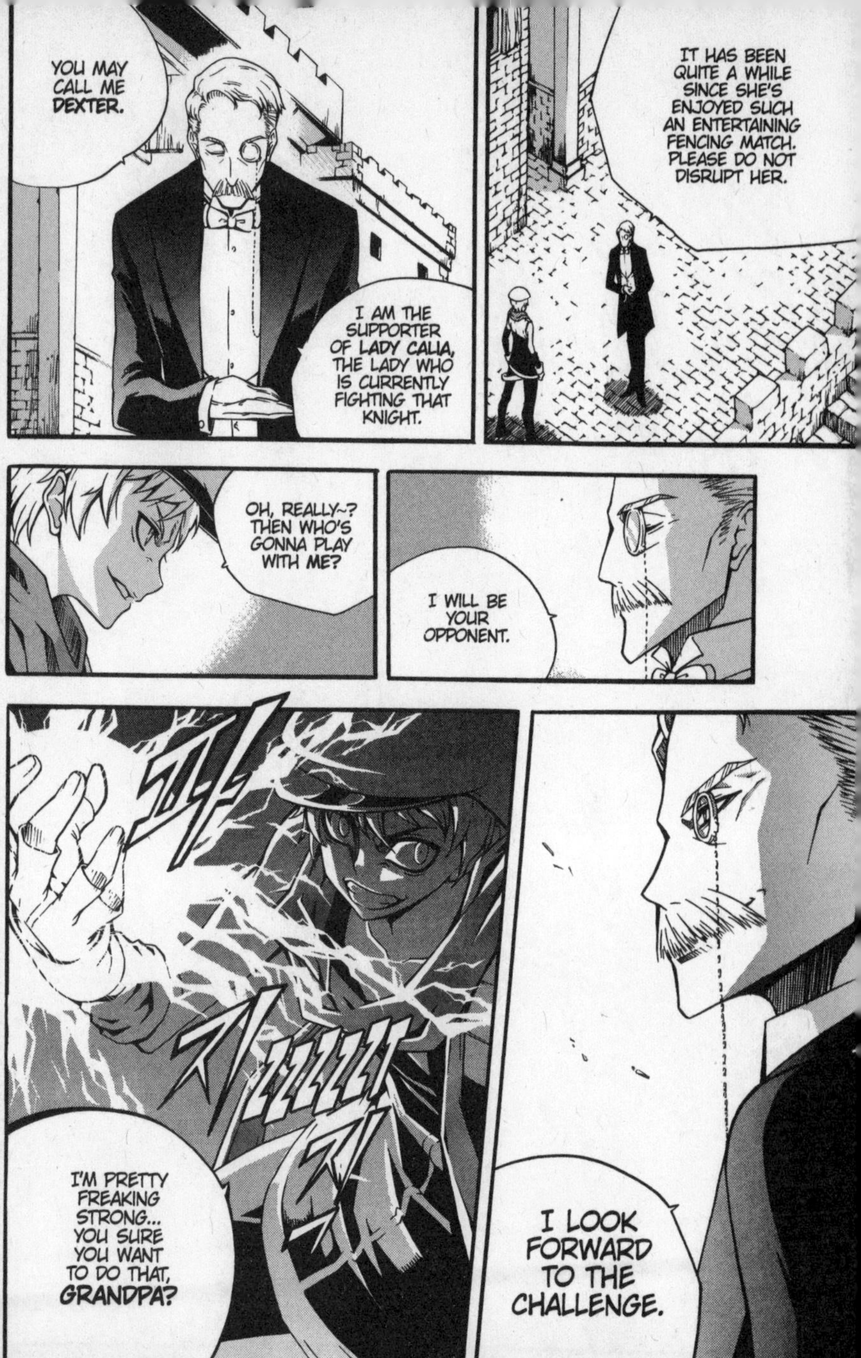
YOU MAY CALL ME DEXTER.
I AM THE SUPPORTER OF LADY CALIA, THE LADY WHO IS CURRENTLY FIGHTING THAT KNIGHT.
IT HAS BEEN QUITE A WHILE SINCE SHE'S ENJOYED SUCH AN ENTERTAINING FENCING MATCH. PLEASE DO NOT DISRUPT HER.
OH, REALLY~? THEN WHO'S GONNA PLAY WITH ME?
I WILL BE YOUR OPPONENT.
I'M PRETTY FREAKING STRONG... YOU SURE YOU WANT TO DO THAT, GRANDPA?
I LOOK FORWARD TO THE CHALLENGE.

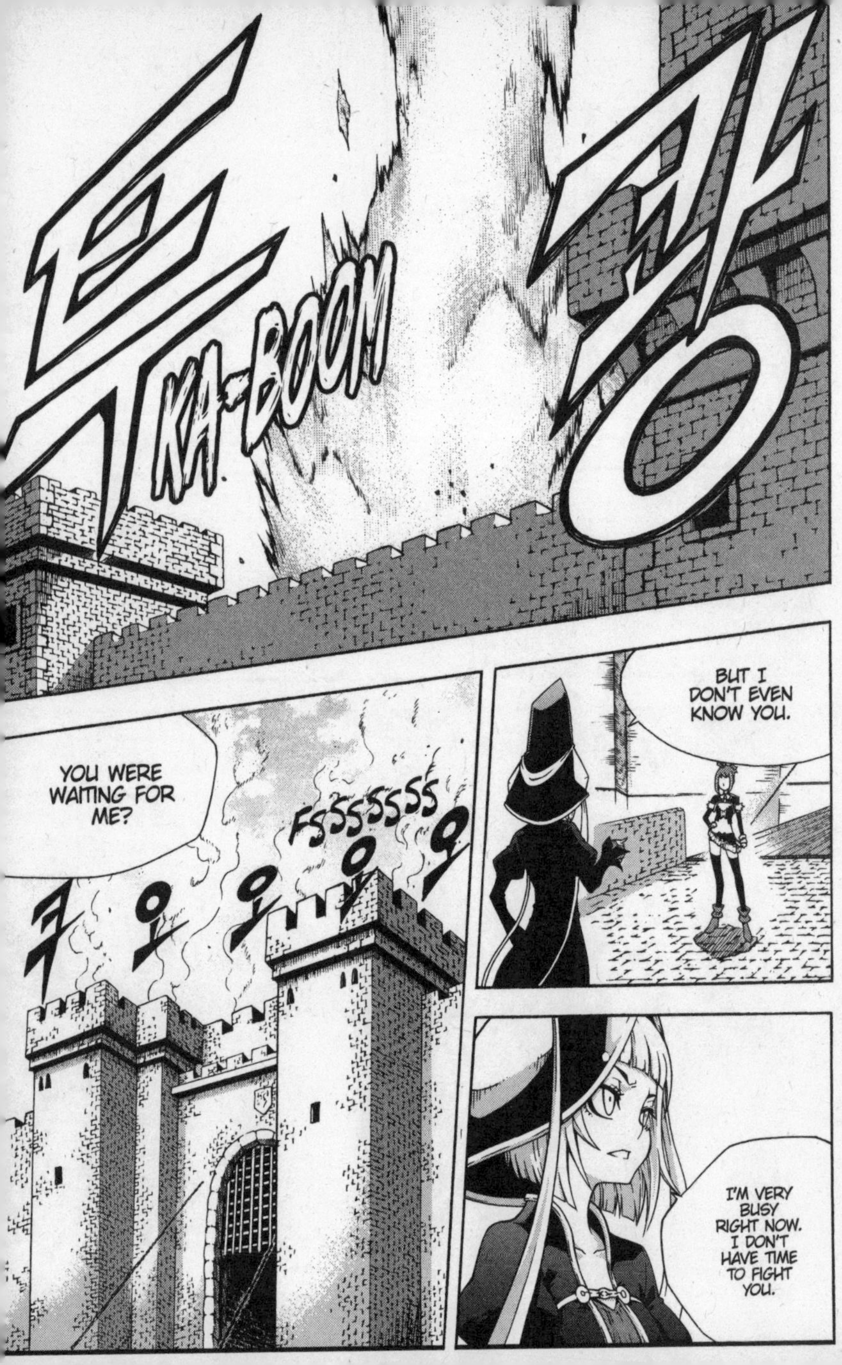
KA-BOOM
YOU WERE WAITING FOR ME?
FSSSSSSSS
BUT I DON'T EVEN KNOW YOU.
I'M VERY BUSY RIGHT NOW. I DON'T HAVE TIME TO FIGHT YOU.

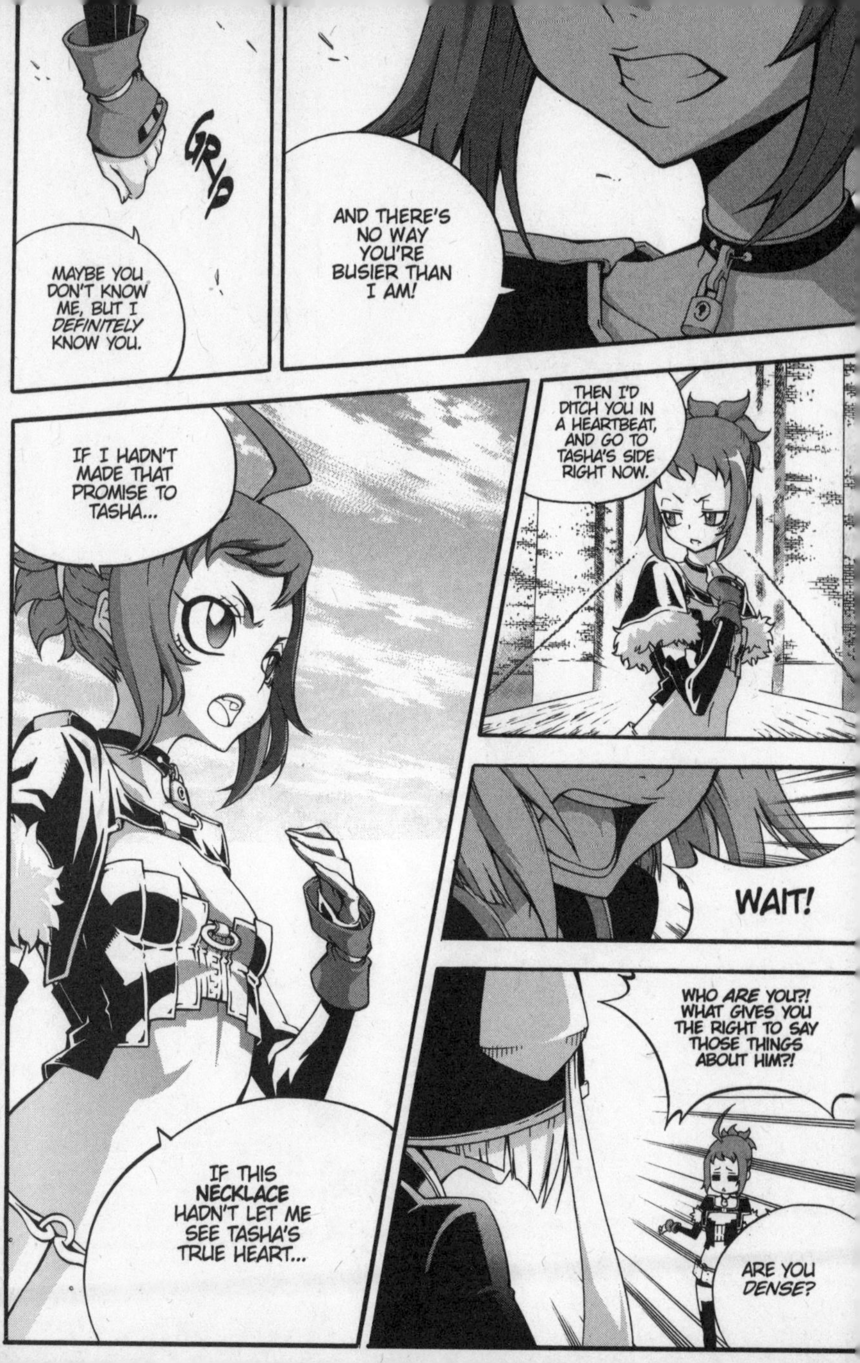
GRIP
MAYBE YOU DON'T KNOW ME, BUT I *DEFINITELY* KNOW YOU.
AND THERE'S NO WAY YOU'RE BUSIER THAN I AM!
IF I HADN'T MADE THAT PROMISE TO TASHA...
IF THIS NECKLACE HADN'T LET ME SEE TASHA'S TRUE HEART...
THEN I'D DITCH YOU IN A HEARTBEAT, AND GO TO TASHA'S SIDE RIGHT NOW.
WAIT!
WHO *ARE* YOU?! WHAT GIVES YOU THE RIGHT TO SAY THOSE THINGS ABOUT HIM?!
ARE YOU *DENSE?*

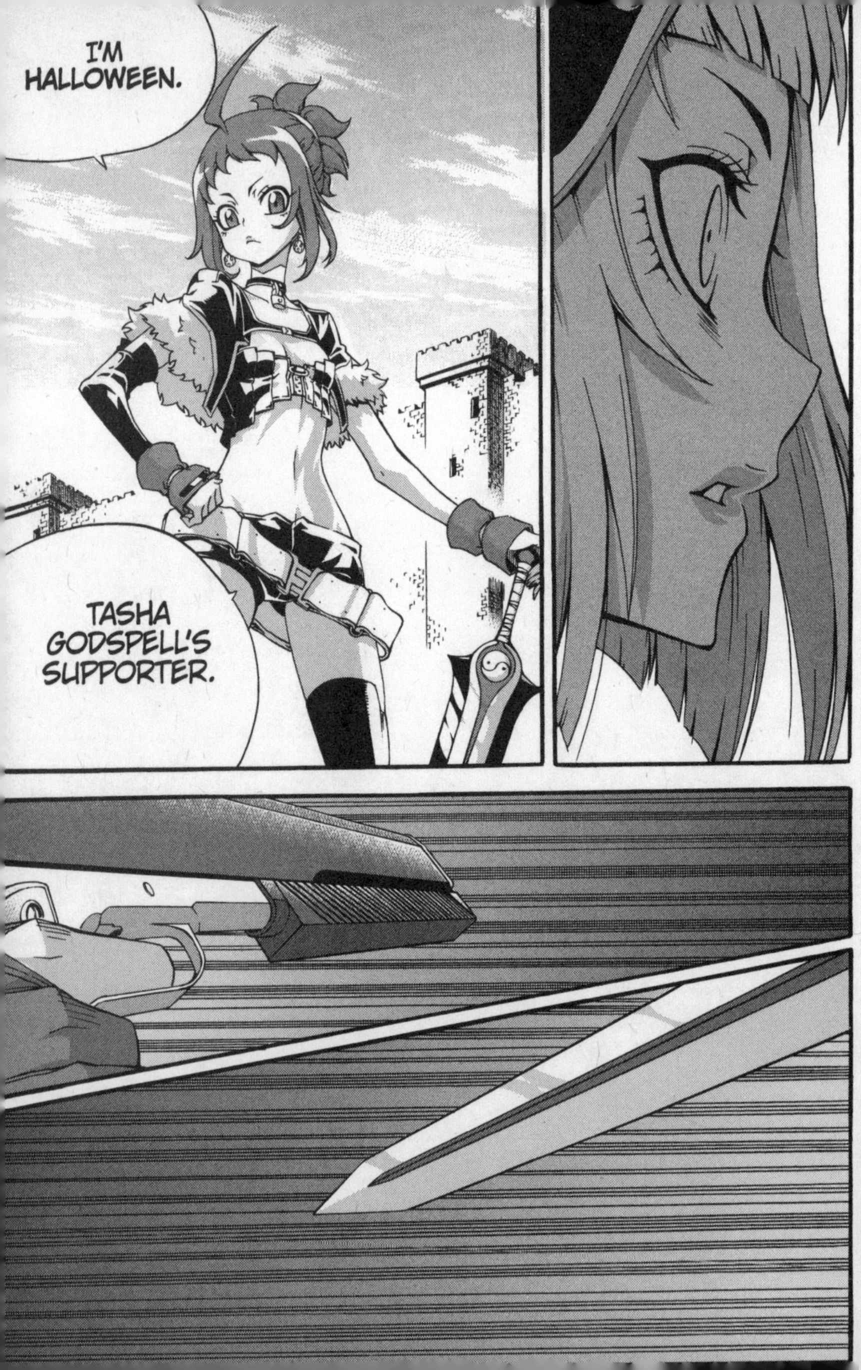
I'M HALLOWEEN.
TASHA GODSPELL'S SUPPORTER.

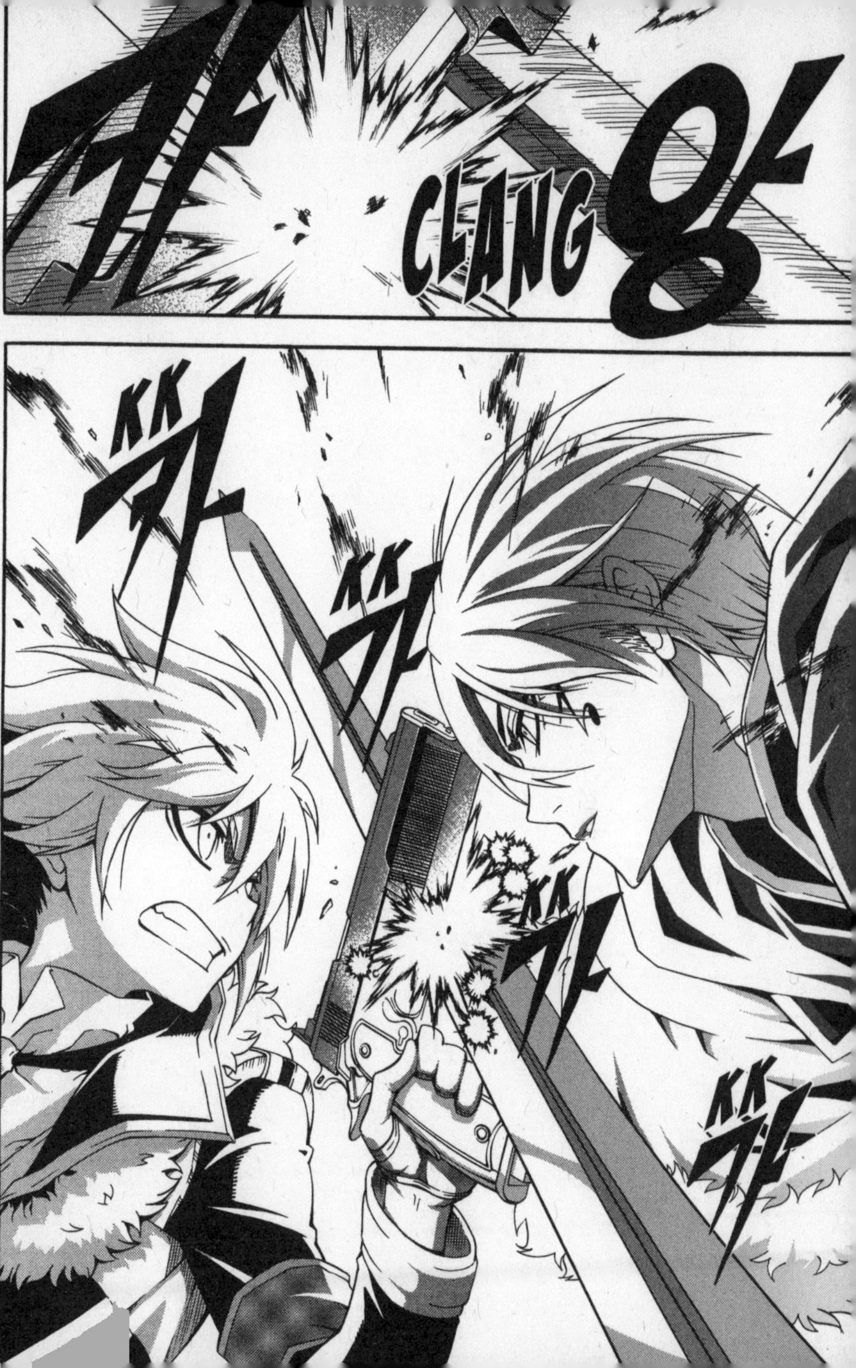
CLANG
KK
KK
KK
KK

FAN LETTER

BOSS~! SOMEONE SENT ME A FAN LETTER!
WHA ?!
FAN...
LEEEH--
TER~!

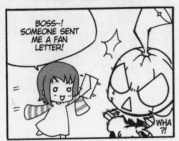

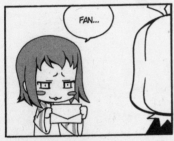

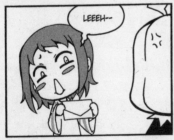

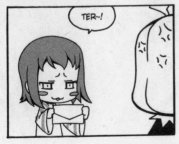

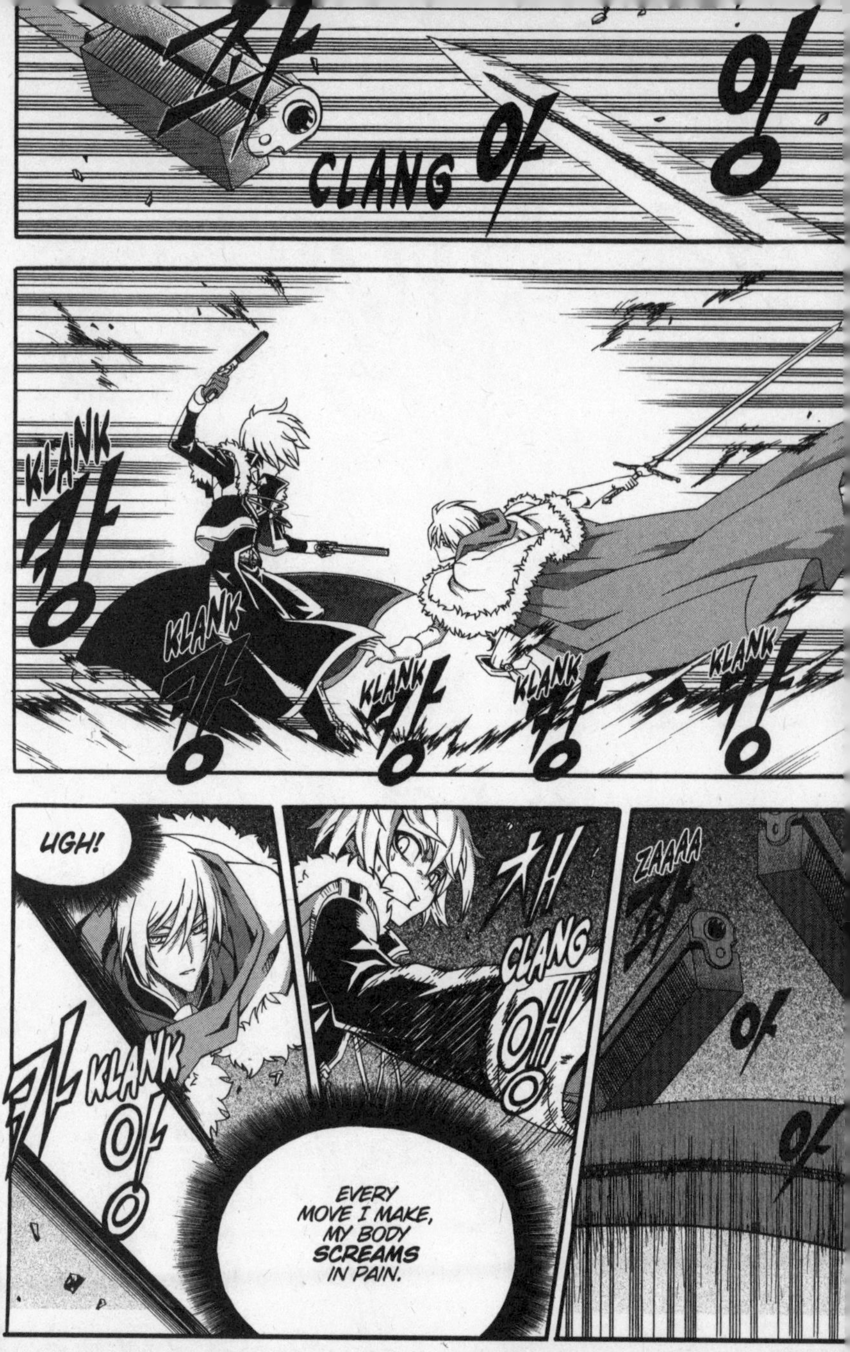
CLANG
KLANK
KLANK
KLANK
KLANK
KLANK
UGH!
KLANK
CLANG
ZAAAA
EVERY MOVE I MAKE, MY BODY SCREAMS IN PAIN.

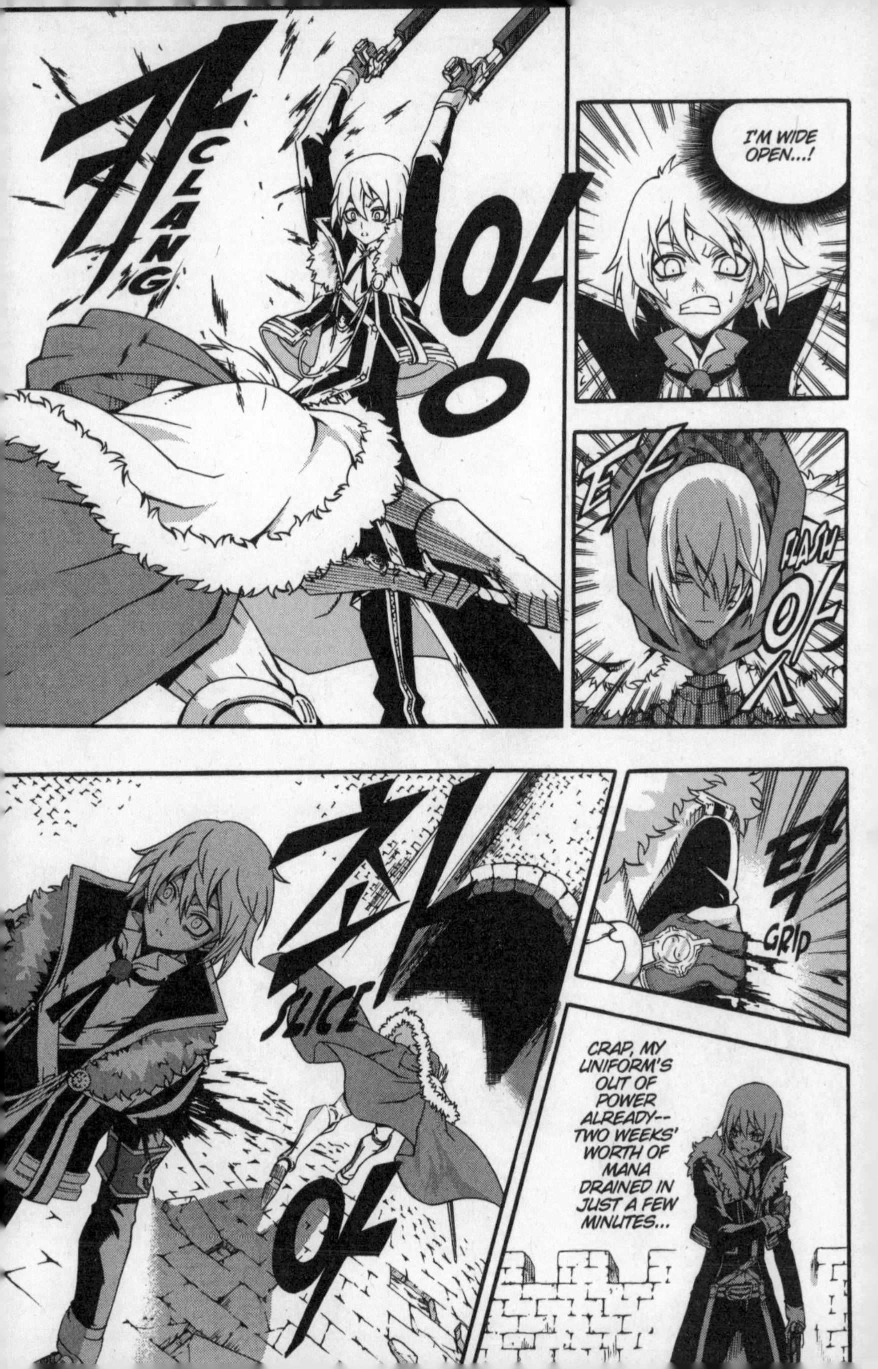
CLANG
I'M WIDE OPEN...!
SLASH
SLICE
GRIP
CRAP, MY UNIFORM'S OUT OF POWER ALREADY-- TWO WEEKS' WORTH OF MANA DRAINED IN JUST A FEW MINUTES...

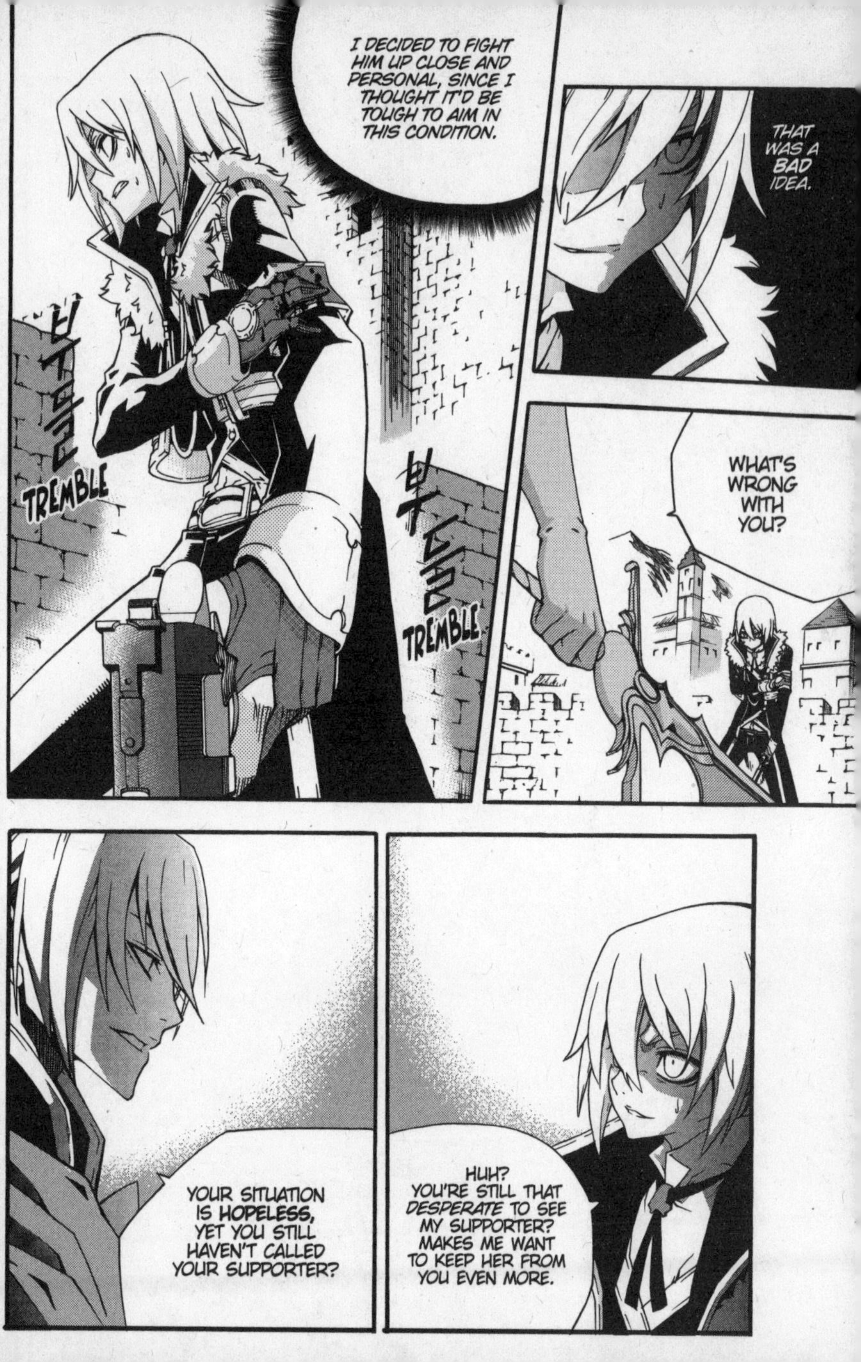
I DECIDED TO FIGHT HIM UP CLOSE AND PERSONAL, SINCE I THOUGHT IT'D BE TOUGH TO AIM IN THIS CONDITION.
TREMBLE
TREMBLE
THAT WAS A BAD IDEA.
WHAT'S WRONG WITH YOU?
YOUR SITUATION IS HOPELESS, YET YOU STILL HAVEN'T CALLED YOUR SUPPORTER?
HUH? YOU'RE STILL THAT DESPERATE TO SEE MY SUPPORTER? MAKES ME WANT TO KEEP HER FROM YOU EVEN MORE.

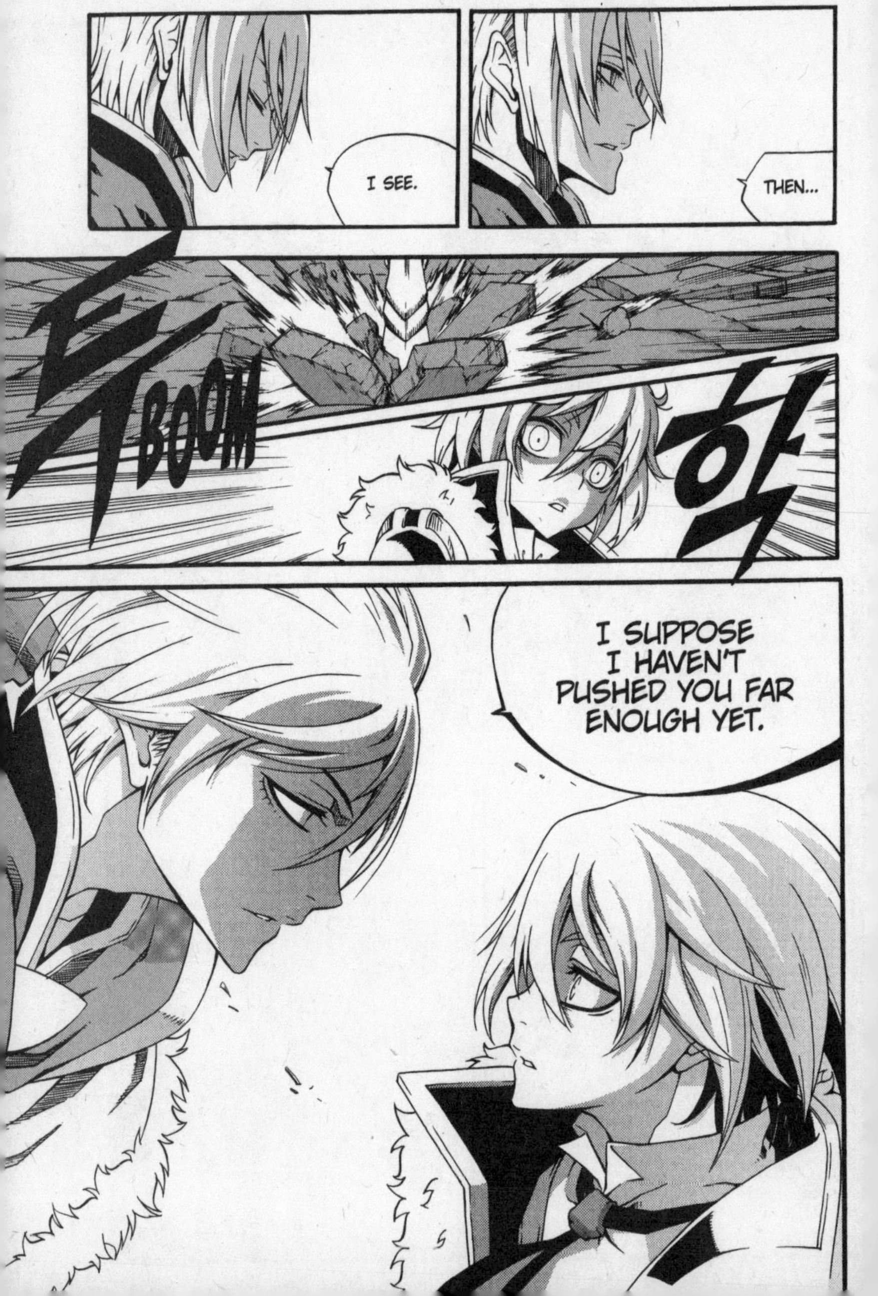
I SEE.
THEN...
BOOM
하
I SUPPOSE I HAVEN'T PUSHED YOU FAR ENOUGH YET.

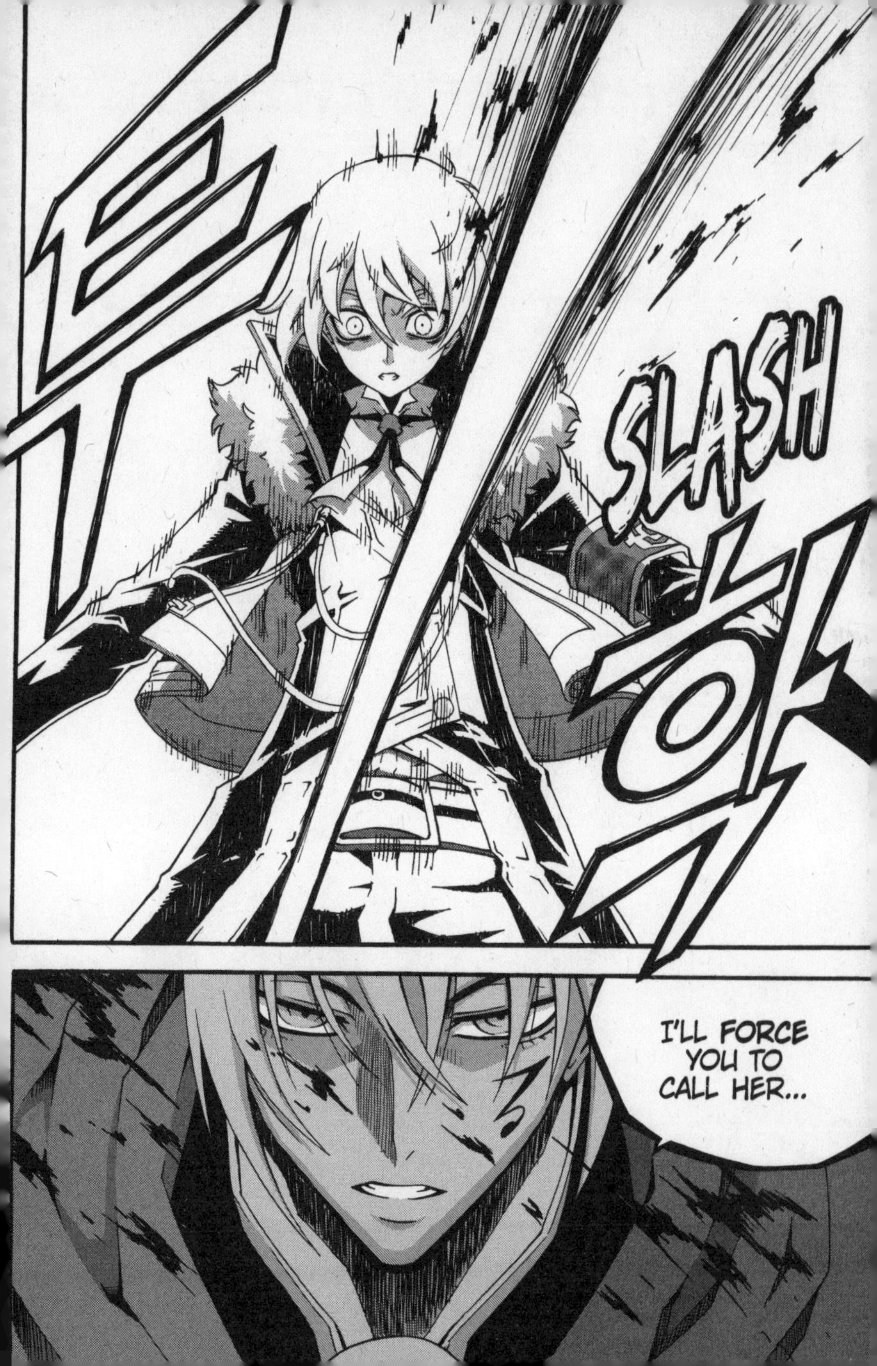
SLASH
I'LL FORCE YOU TO CALL HER...

40. The Difference in Power

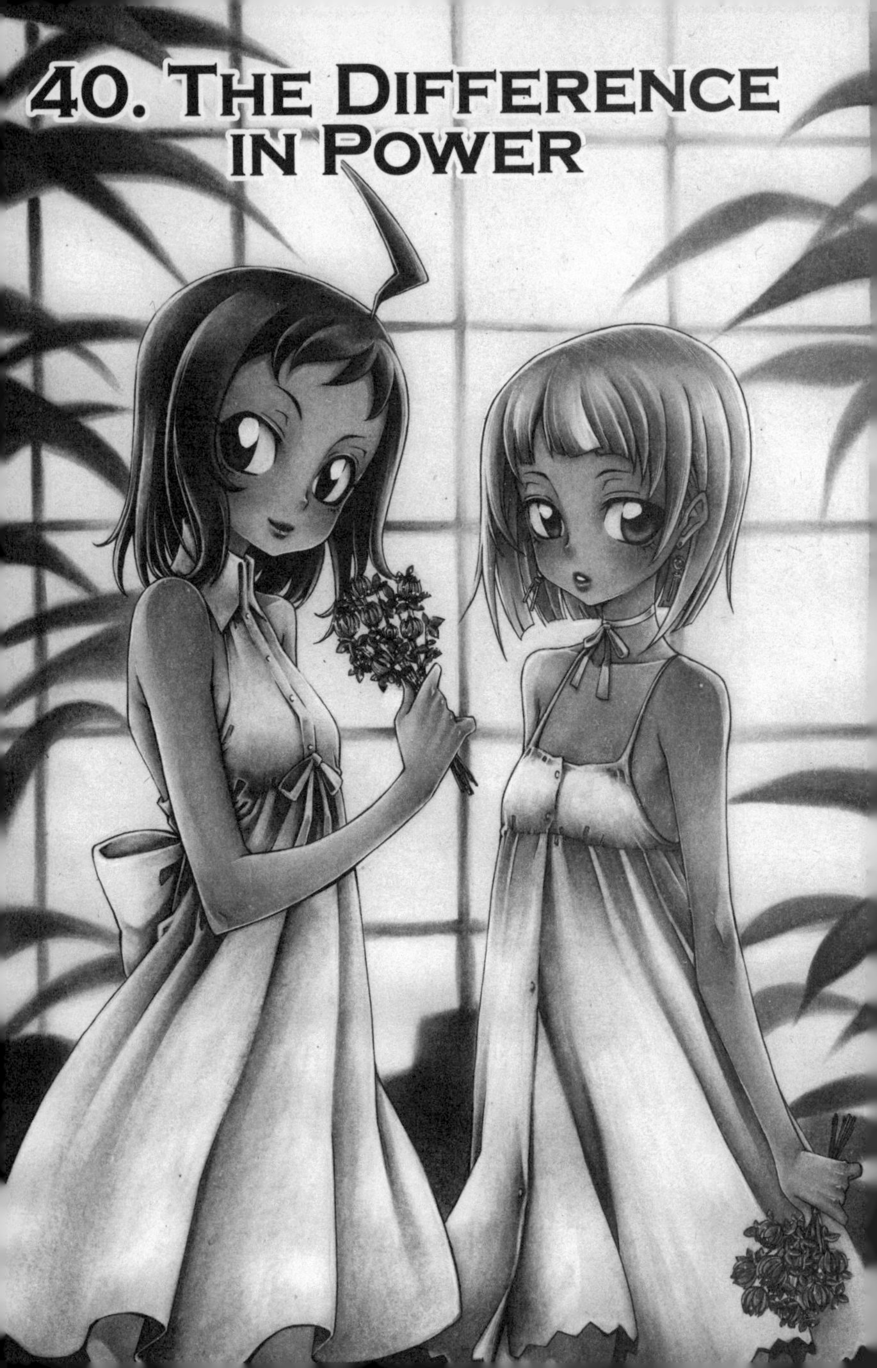

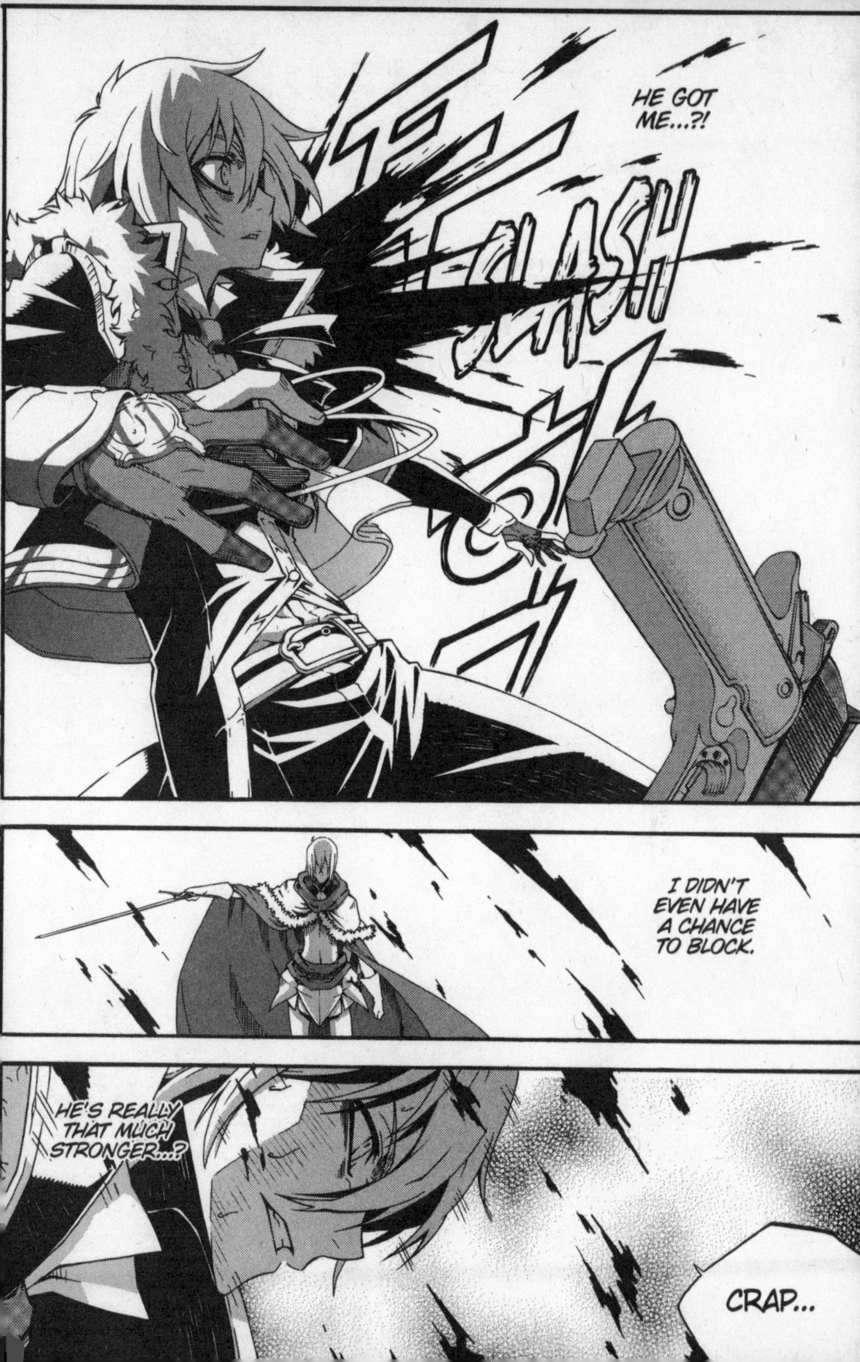
HE GOT ME...?!
SLASH
I DIDN'T EVEN HAVE A CHANCE TO BLOCK.
HE'S REALLY THAT MUCH STRONGER...?
CRAP...

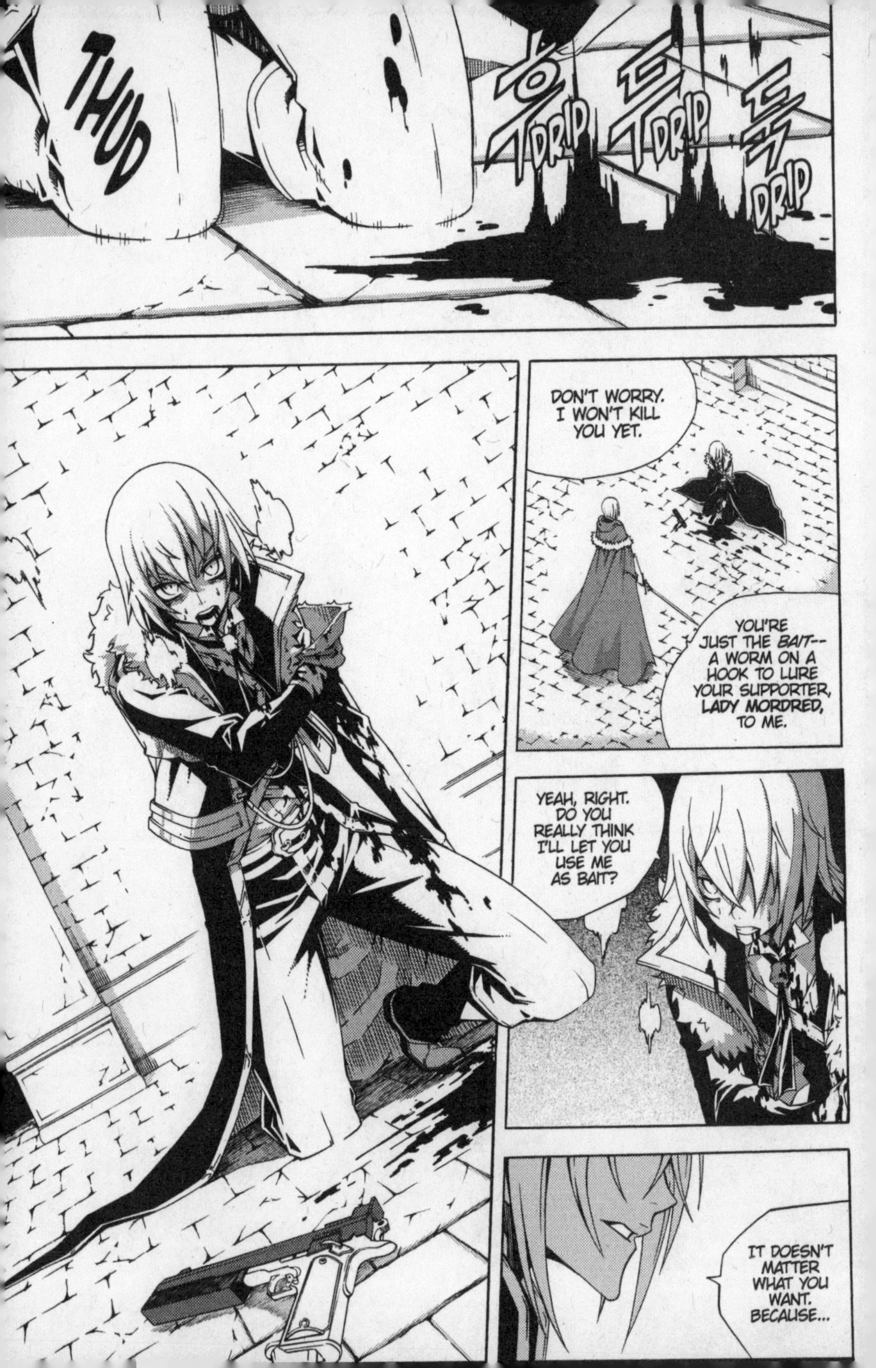
THUD
DRIP
DRIP
DRIP
DON'T WORRY. I WON'T KILL YOU YET.
YOU'RE JUST THE *BAIT*-- A WORM ON A HOOK TO LURE YOUR SUPPORTER, LADY MORDRED, TO ME.
YEAH, RIGHT. DO YOU REALLY THINK I'LL LET YOU USE ME AS BAIT?
IT DOESN'T MATTER WHAT YOU WANT. BECAUSE...

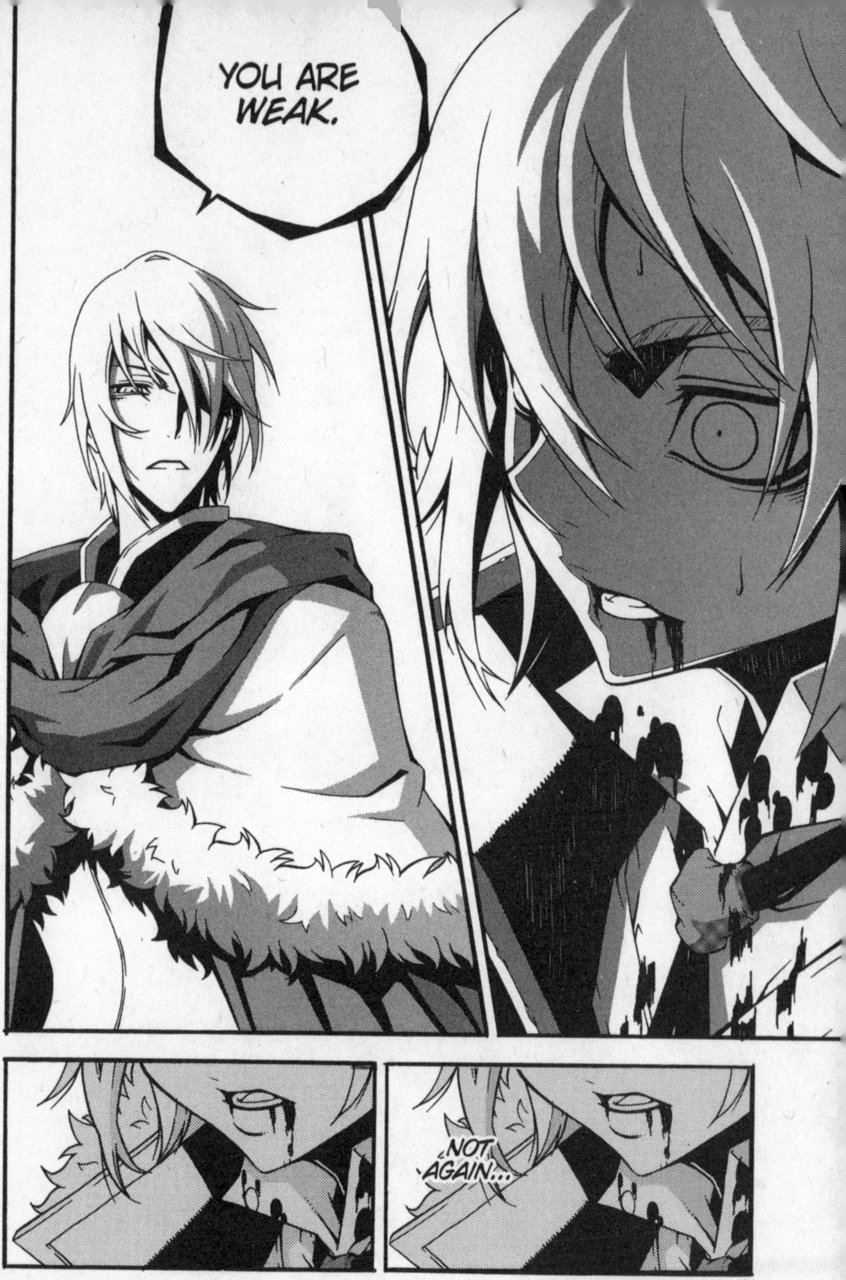
YOU ARE WEAK.
NOT AGAIN...

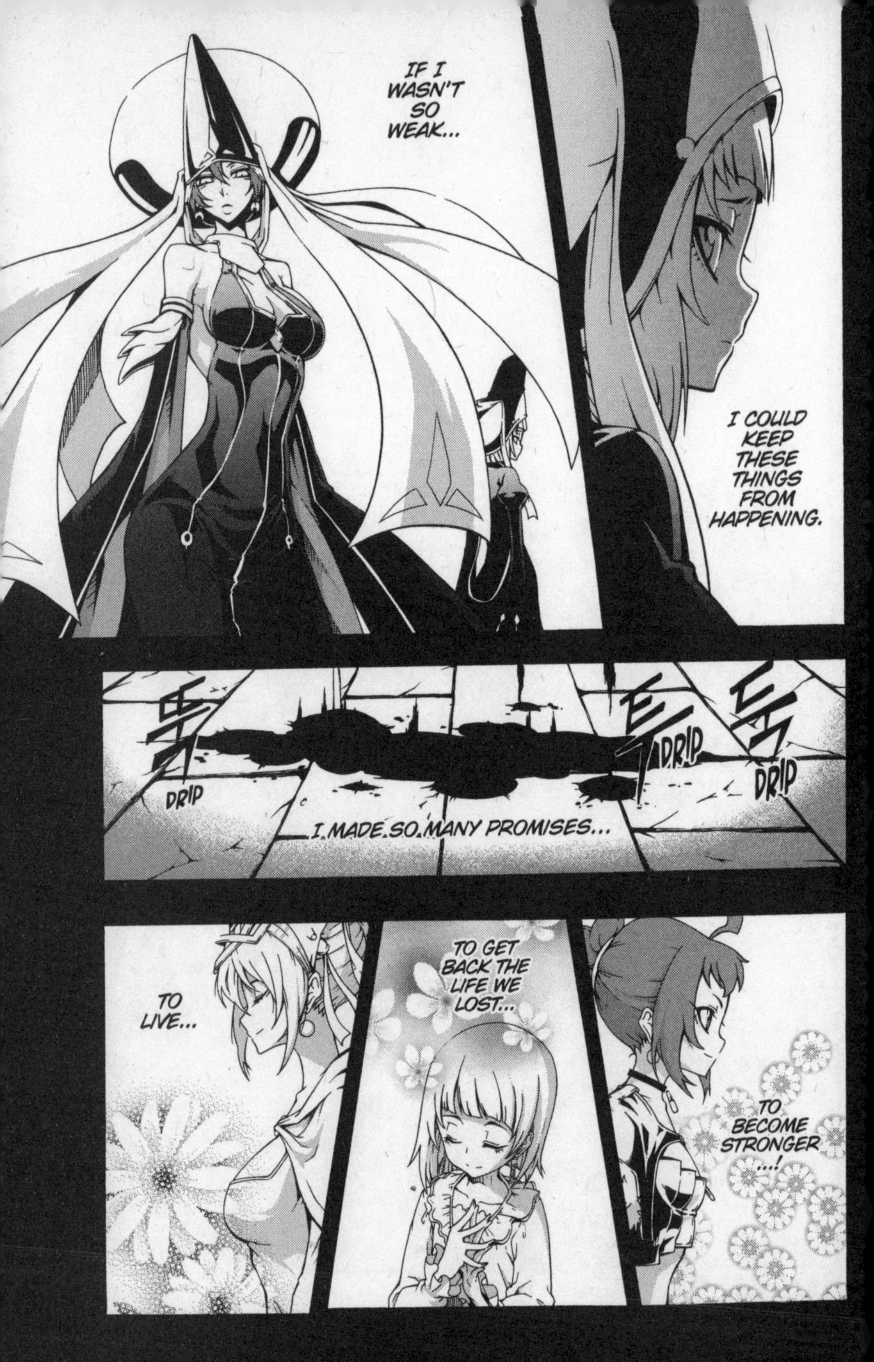
IF I WASN'T SO WEAK...
I COULD KEEP THESE THINGS FROM HAPPENING.
DRIP
I MADE SO MANY PROMISES...
DRIP
DRIP
TO LIVE...
TO GET BACK THE LIFE WE LOST...
TO BECOME STRONGER ...!

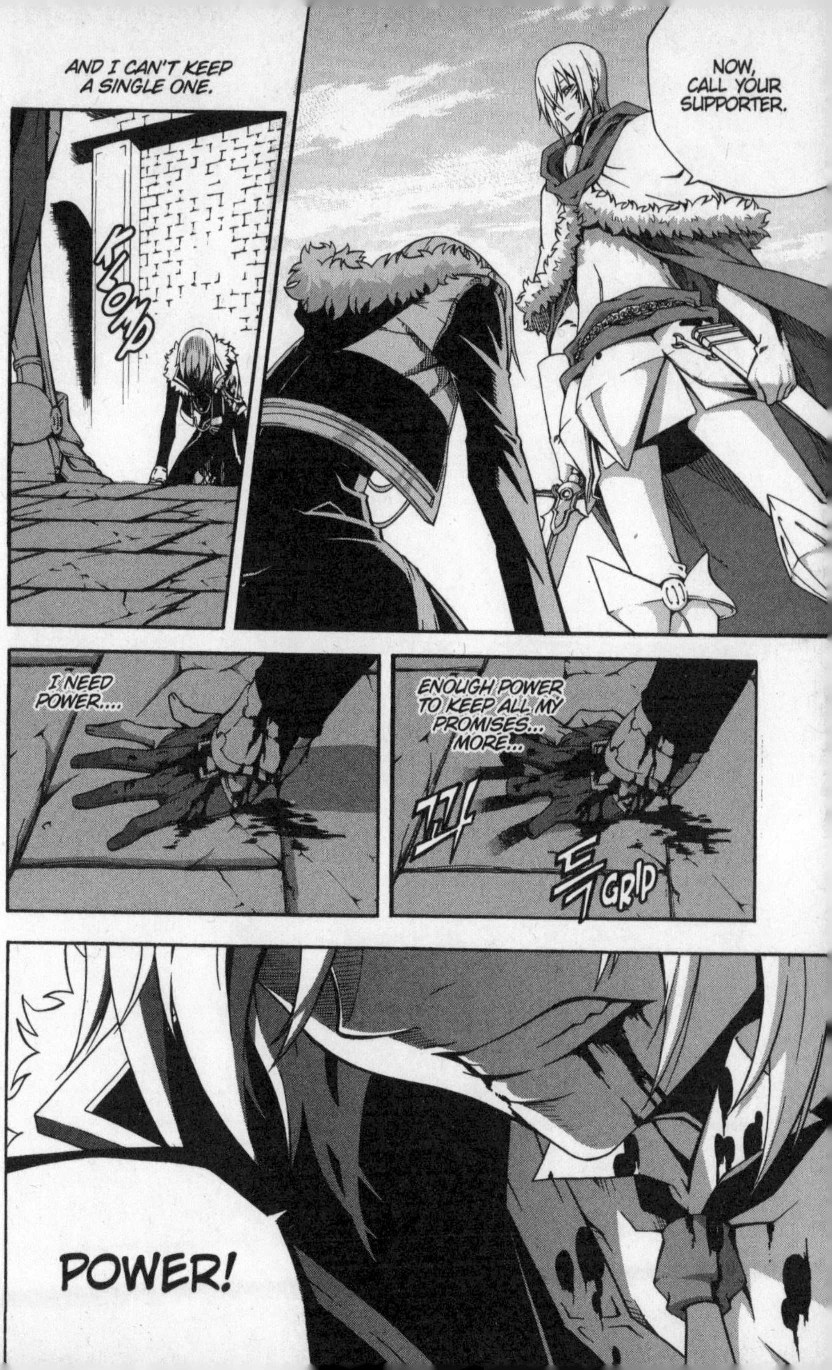
AND I CAN'T KEEP A SINGLE ONE.
KLOMP
NOW, CALL YOUR SUPPORTER.
I NEED POWER....
ENOUGH POWER TO KEEP ALL MY PROMISES... MORE...
GRIP
POWER!

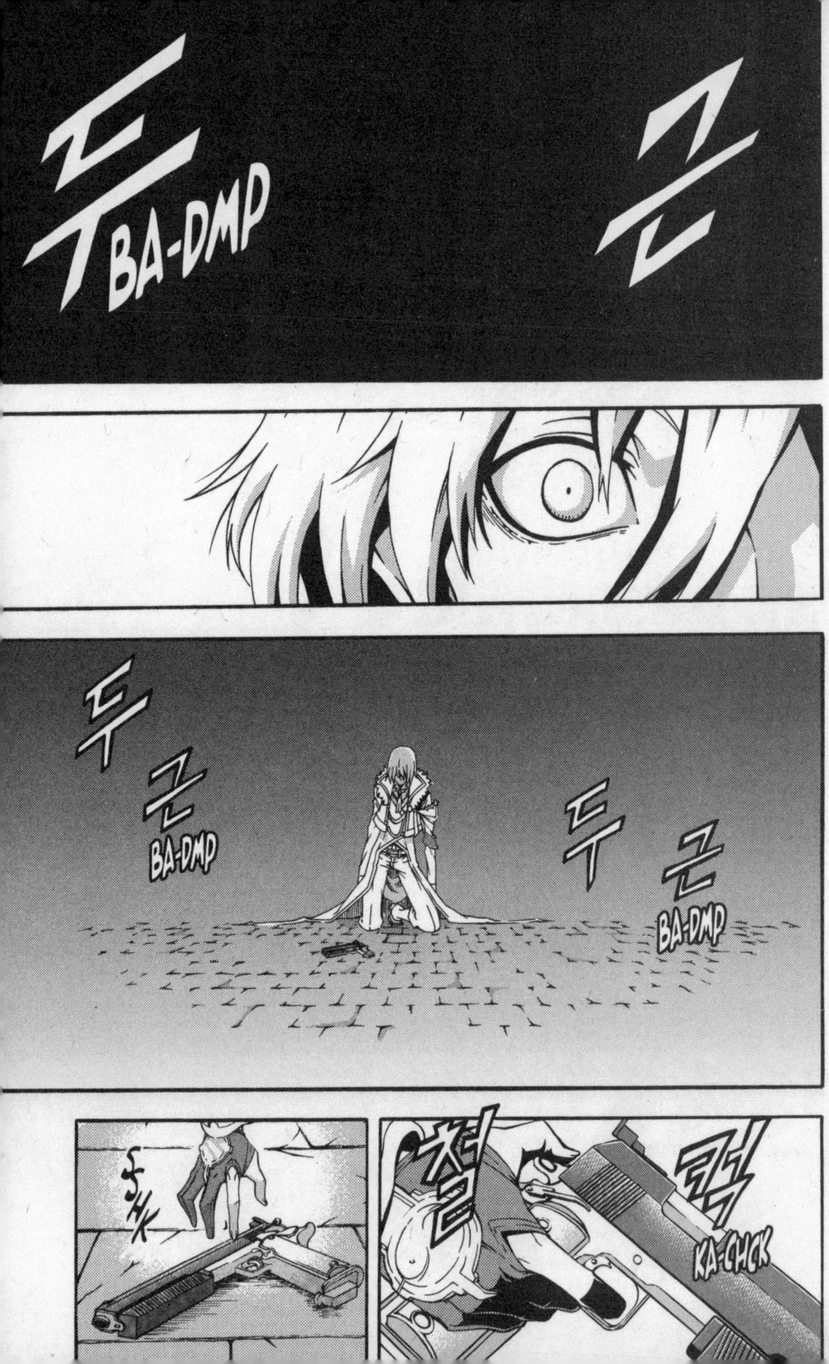

두
BA-DMP
근
두근
BA-DMP
두근
BA-DMP
SHK
철컥
KA-CHICK

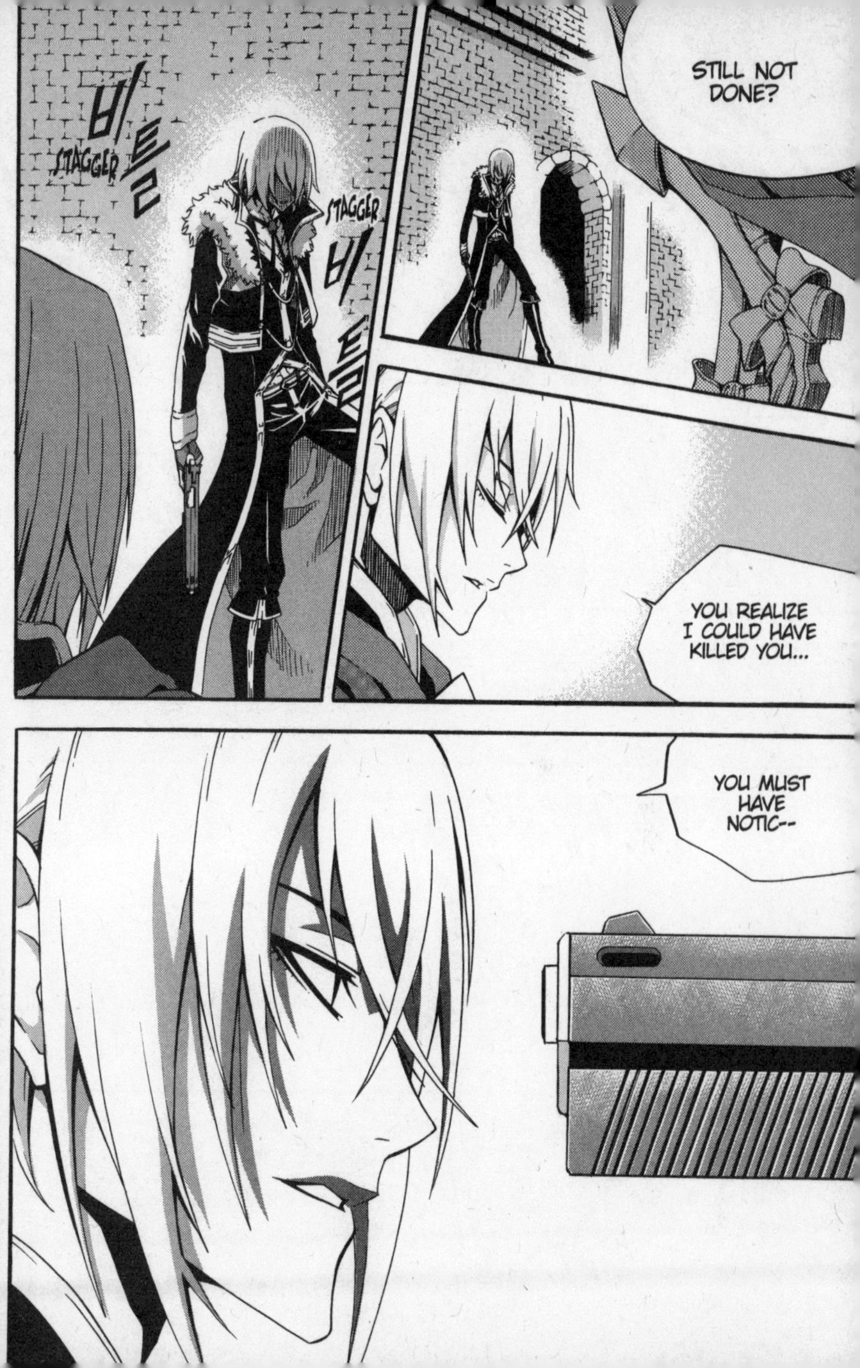
비틀
STAGGER
STAGGER
비틀
STILL NOT DONE?
YOU REALIZE I COULD HAVE KILLED YOU...
YOU MUST HAVE NOTIC--

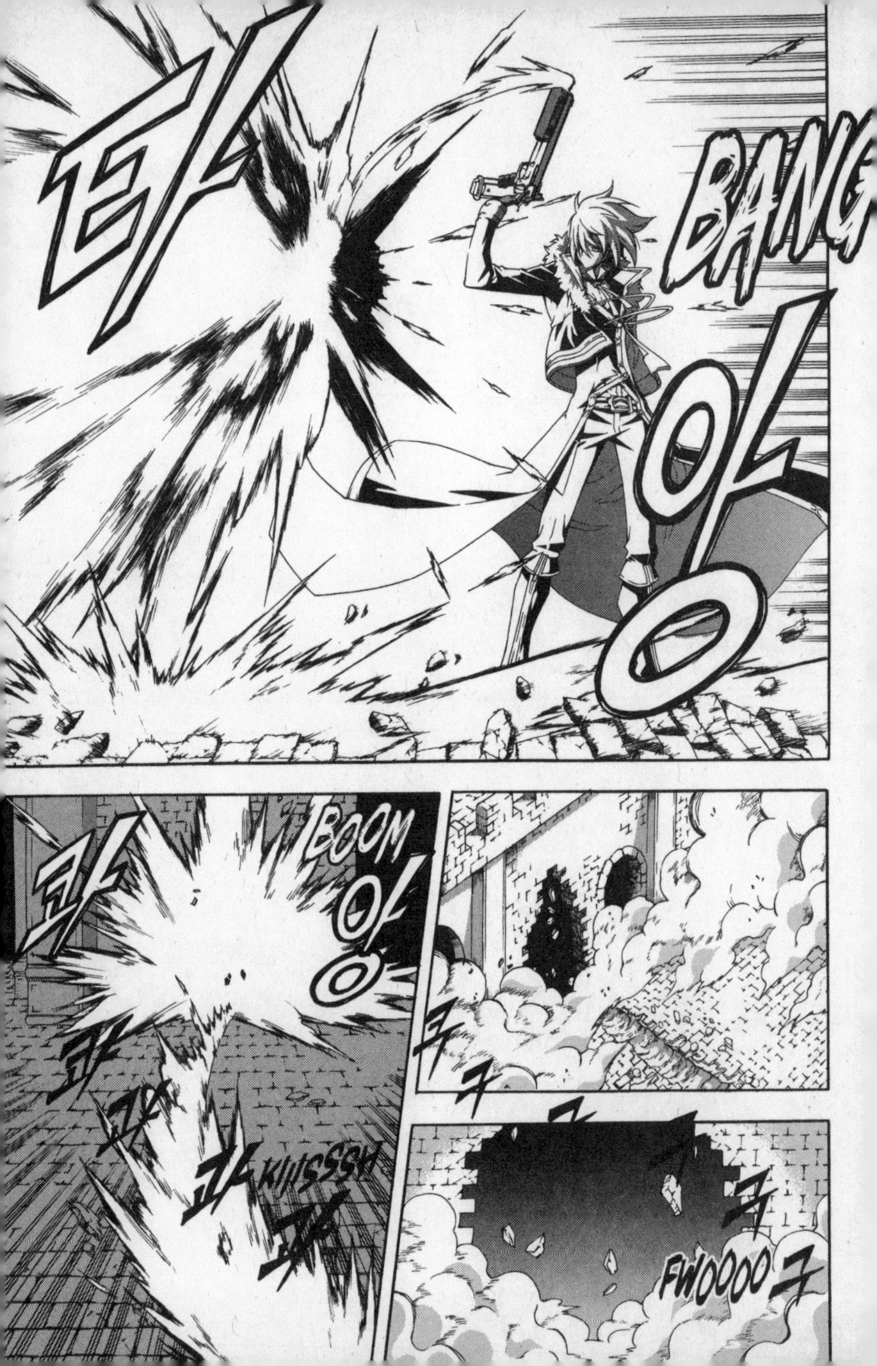
BANG
BOOM
FWOOOO

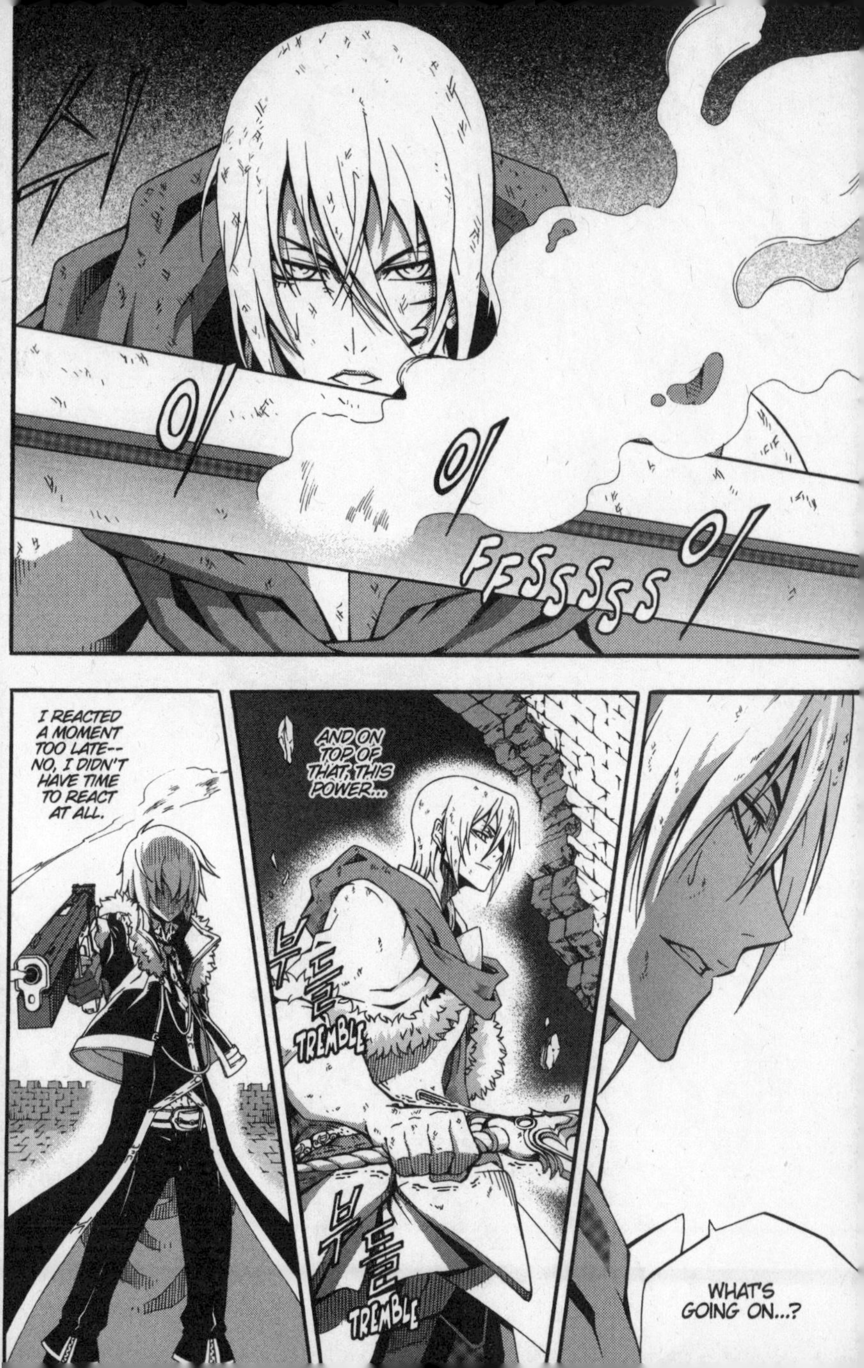
FSSSSS
I REACTED A MOMENT TOO LATE-- NO, I DIDN'T HAVE TIME TO REACT AT ALL.
AND ON TOP OF THAT, THIS POWER...
TREMBLE
TREMBLE
WHAT'S GOING ON...?

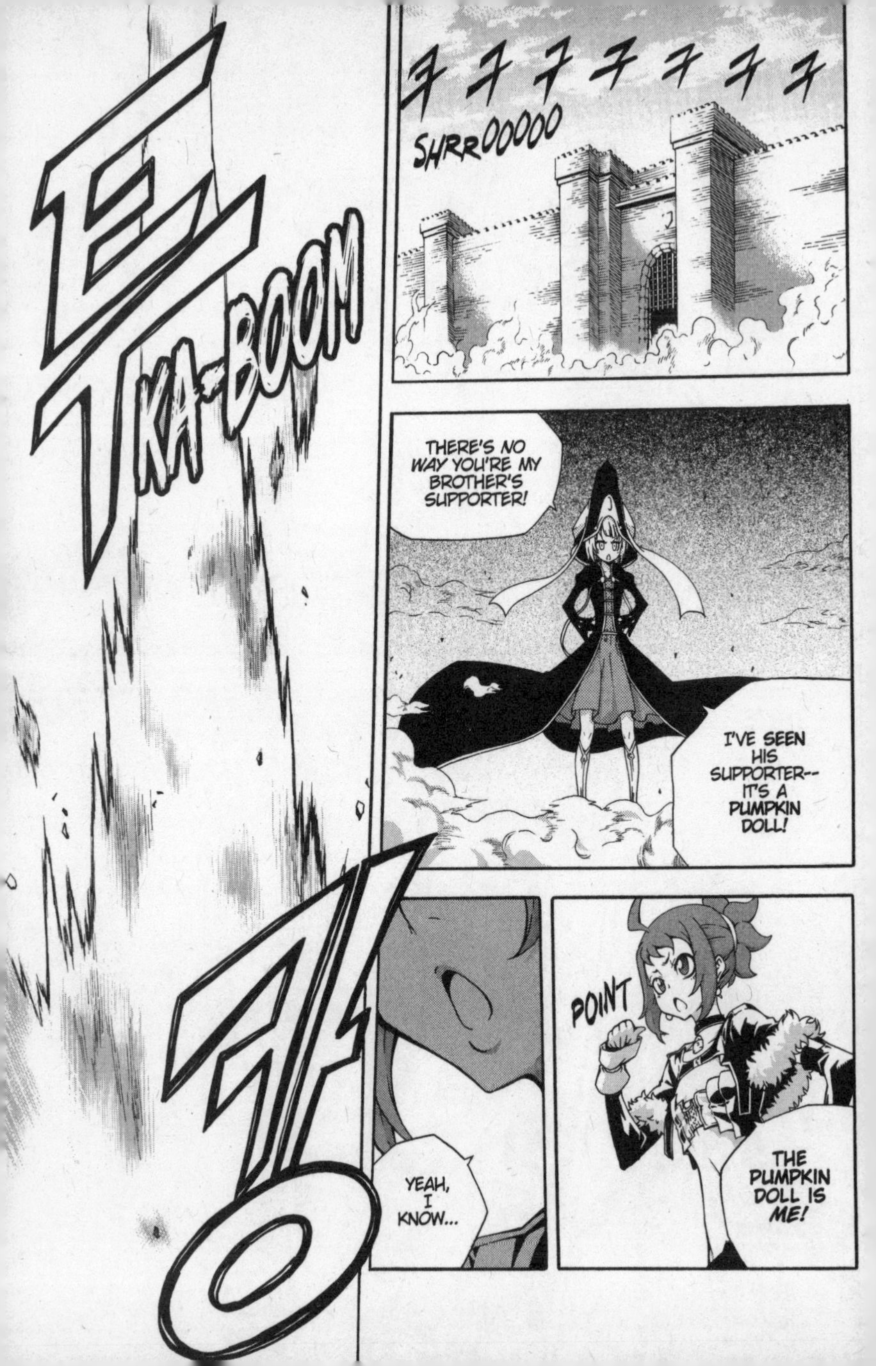
KA-BOOM
SHRROOOOO
THERE'S NO WAY YOU'RE MY BROTHER'S SUPPORTER!
I'VE SEEN HIS SUPPORTER-- IT'S A PUMPKIN DOLL!
YEAH, I KNOW...
POINT
THE PUMPKIN DOLL IS ME!

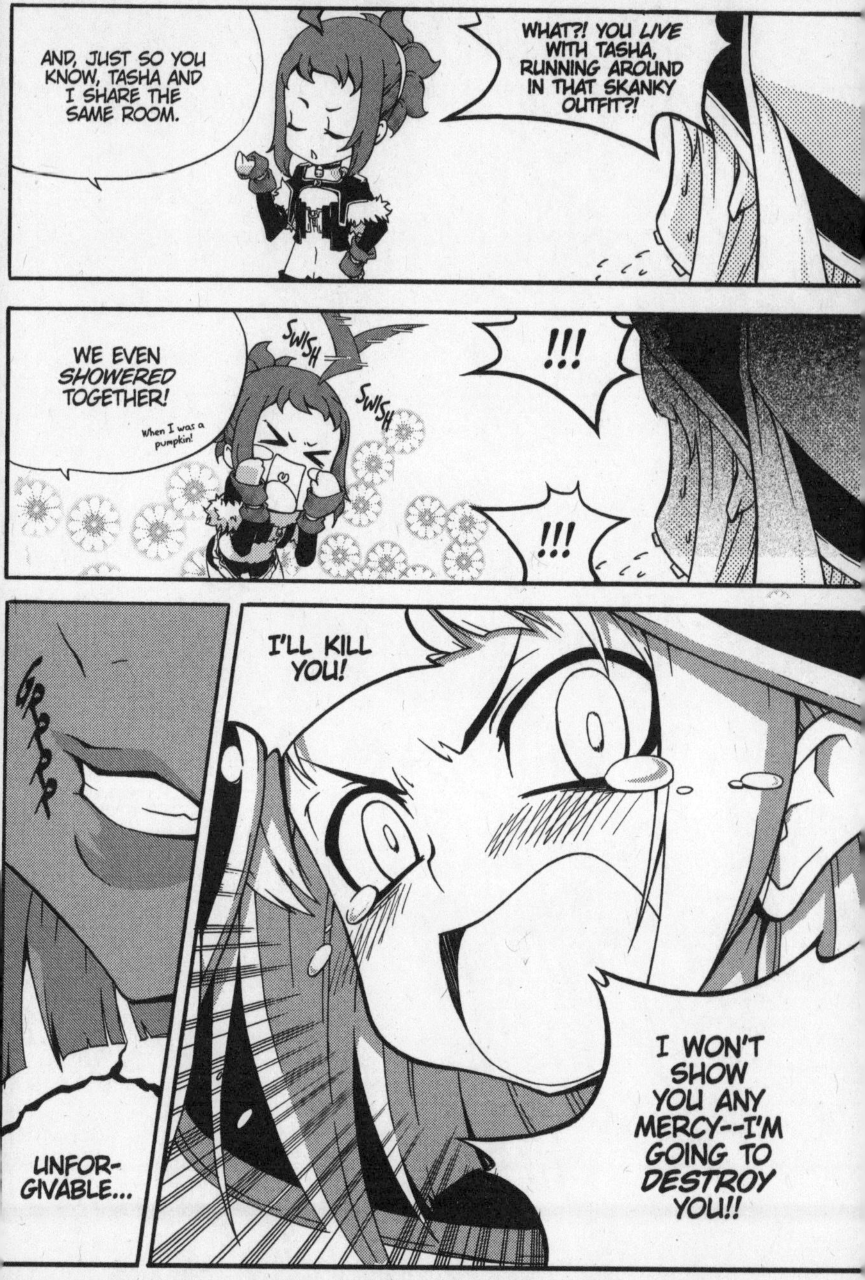
AND, JUST SO YOU KNOW, TASHA AND I SHARE THE SAME ROOM.
WHAT?! YOU LIVE WITH TASHA, RUNNING AROUND IN THAT SKANKY OUTFIT?!
WE EVEN SHOWERED TOGETHER!
When I was a pumpkin!
SWISH
SWISH
!!!
!!!
GRRRR
UNFOR-GIVABLE...
I'LL KILL YOU!
I WON'T SHOW YOU ANY MERCY--I'M GOING TO DESTROY YOU!!

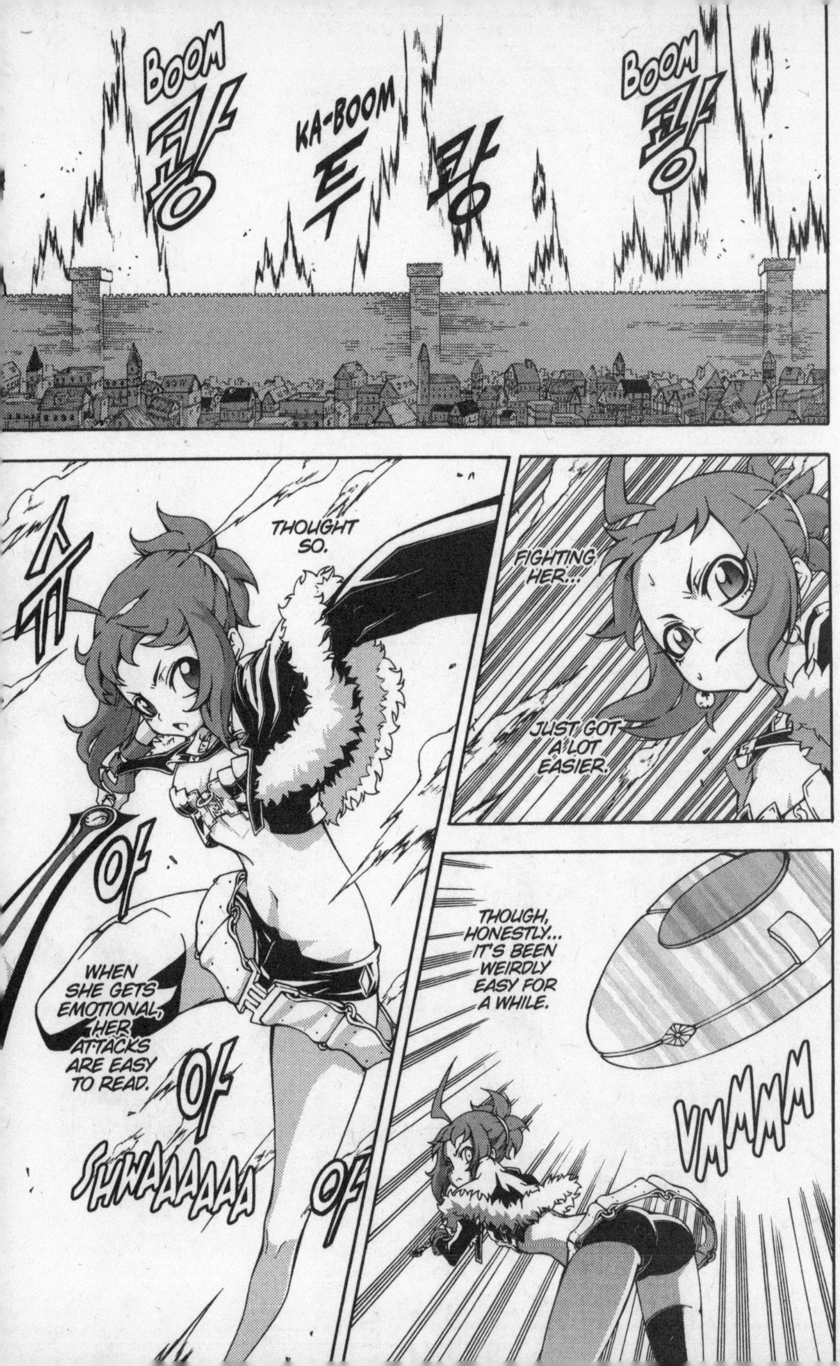
BOOM
KA-BOOM
BOOM
THOUGHT SO.
WHEN SHE GETS EMOTIONAL, HER ATTACKS ARE EASY TO READ.
SHWAAAAAA
FIGHTING HER...
JUST GOT A LOT EASIER.
THOUGH, HONESTLY... IT'S BEEN WEIRDLY EASY FOR A WHILE.
VMMMM

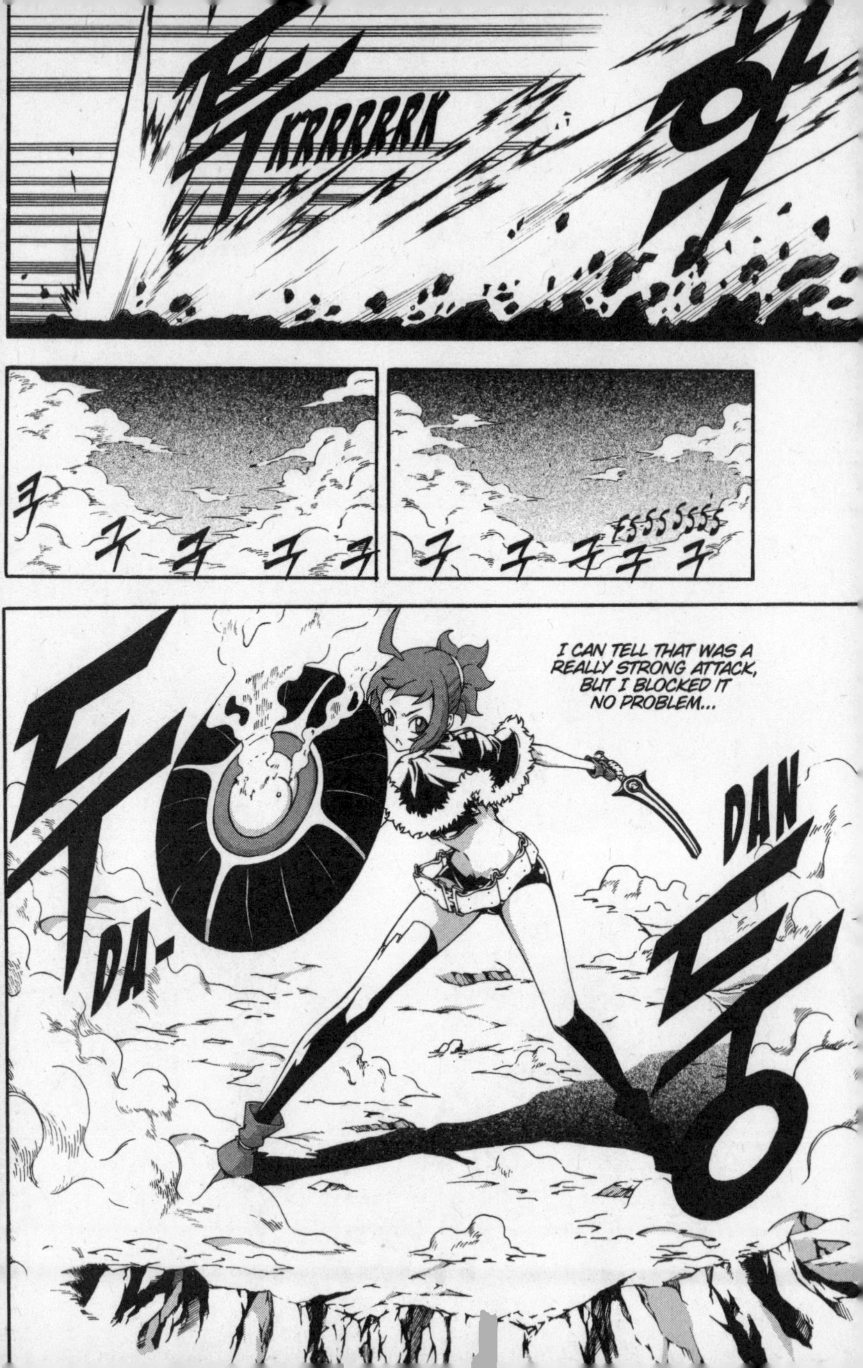
KRRRRRRK
FSSSSSSSS
I CAN TELL THAT WAS A REALLY STRONG ATTACK, BUT I BLOCKED IT NO PROBLEM...
DA-
DAN

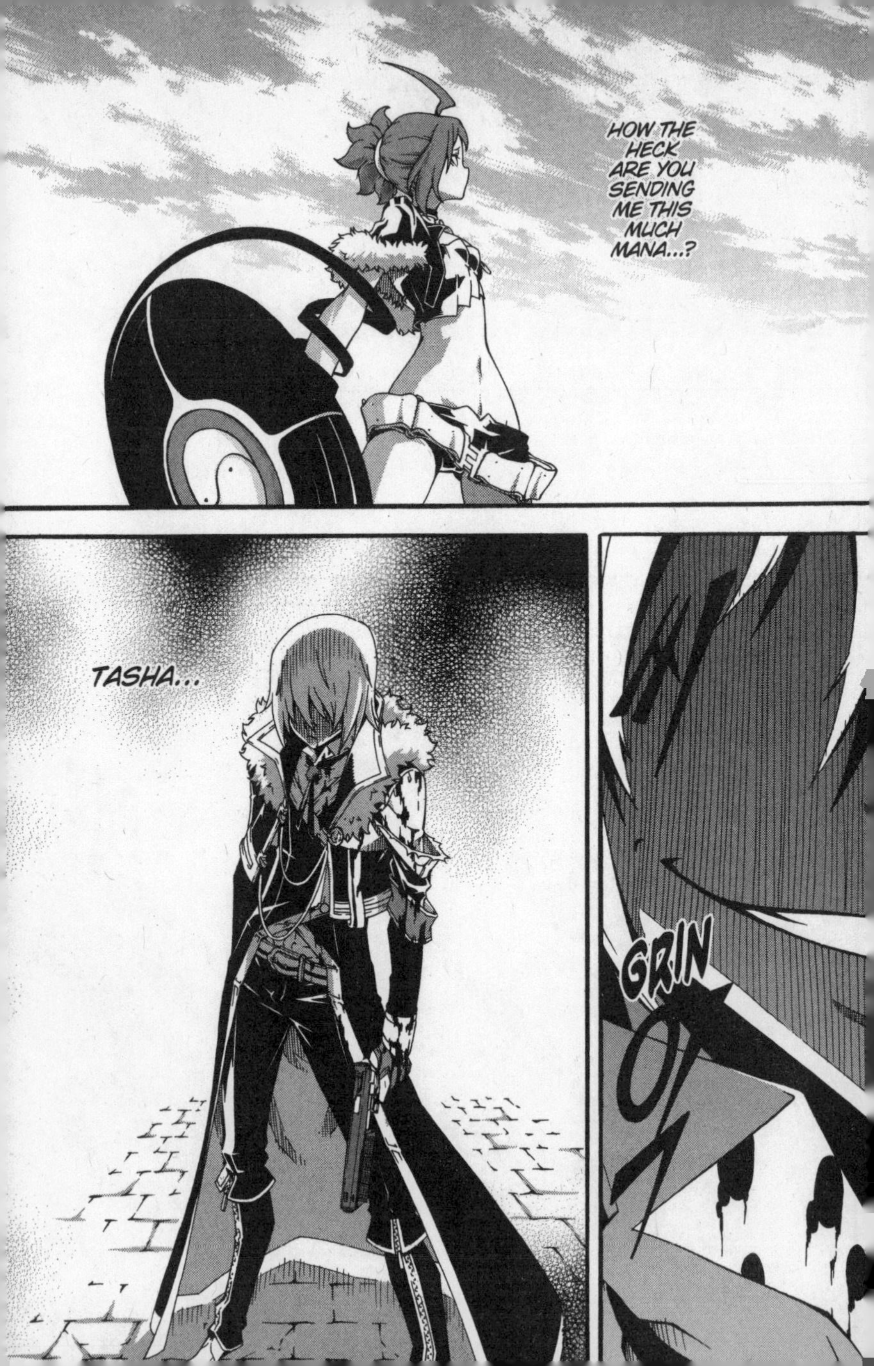
HOW THE HECK ARE YOU SENDING ME THIS MUCH MANA...?
TASHA...
GRIN

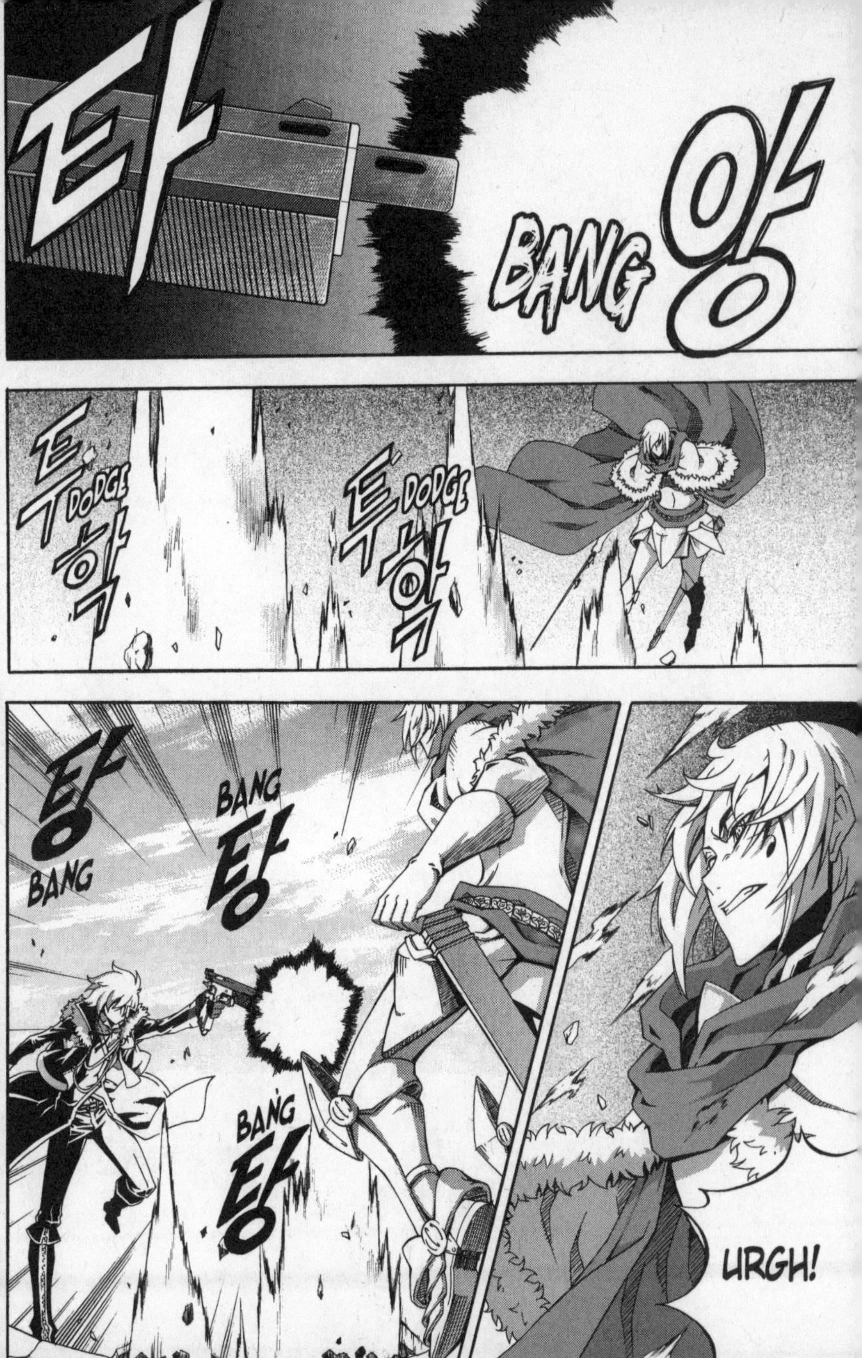

타앙
BANG
DODGE
DODGE
탕
BANG
BANG
탕
BANG
탕
URGH!

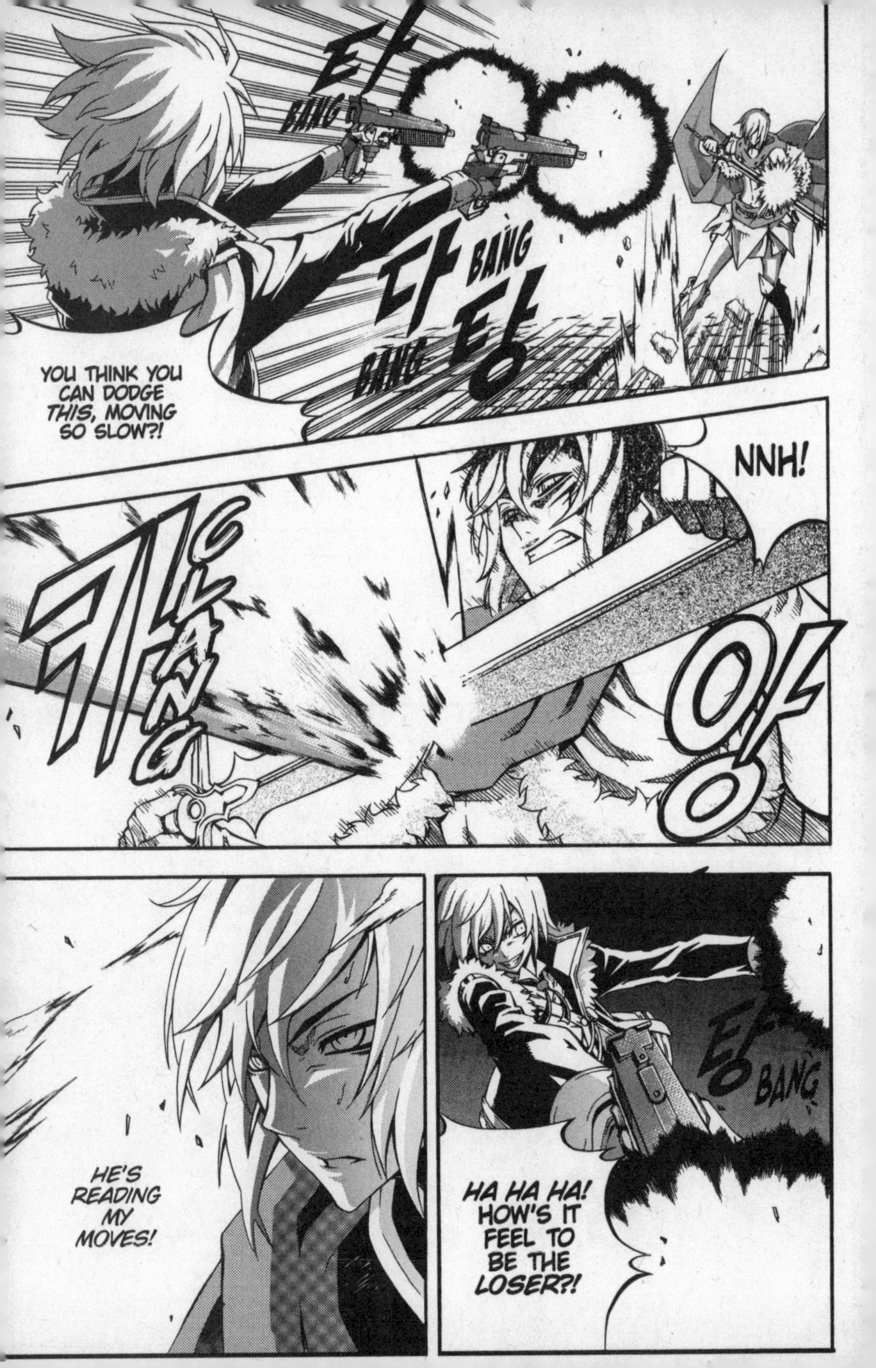

BANG
YOU THINK YOU CAN DODGE *THIS*, MOVING SO SLOW?!
BANG
BANG
NNH!
HE'S READING MY MOVES!
BANG
HA HA HA! HOW'S IT FEEL TO BE THE LOSER?!

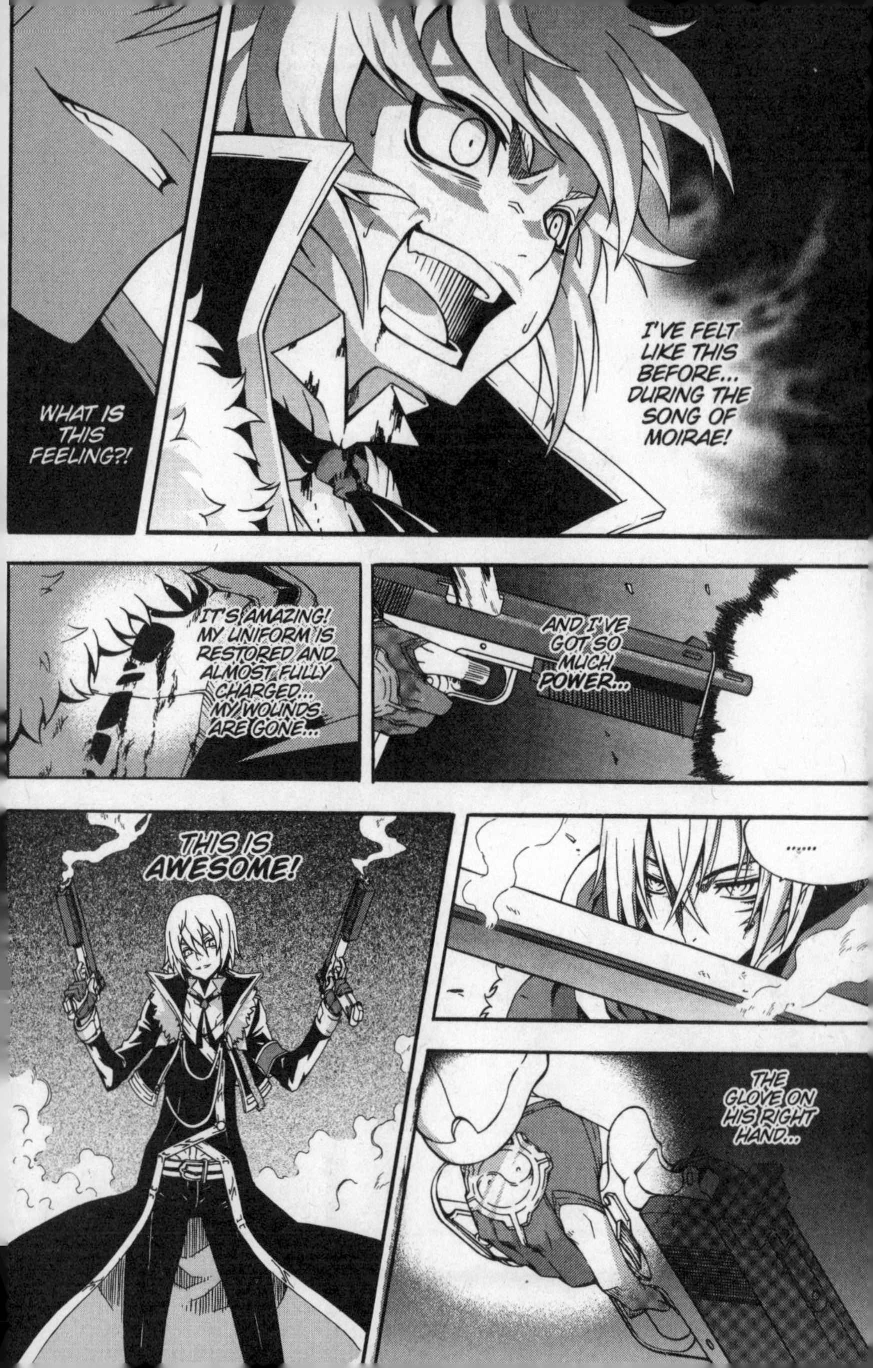
WHAT IS THIS FEELING?!
I'VE FELT LIKE THIS BEFORE... DURING THE SONG OF MOIRAE!
IT'S AMAZING! MY UNIFORM IS RESTORED AND ALMOST FULLY CHARGED... MY WOUNDS ARE GONE...
AND I'VE GOT SO MUCH POWER...
THIS IS AWESOME!
......
THE GLOVE ON HIS RIGHT HAND...

41. Mana Supply

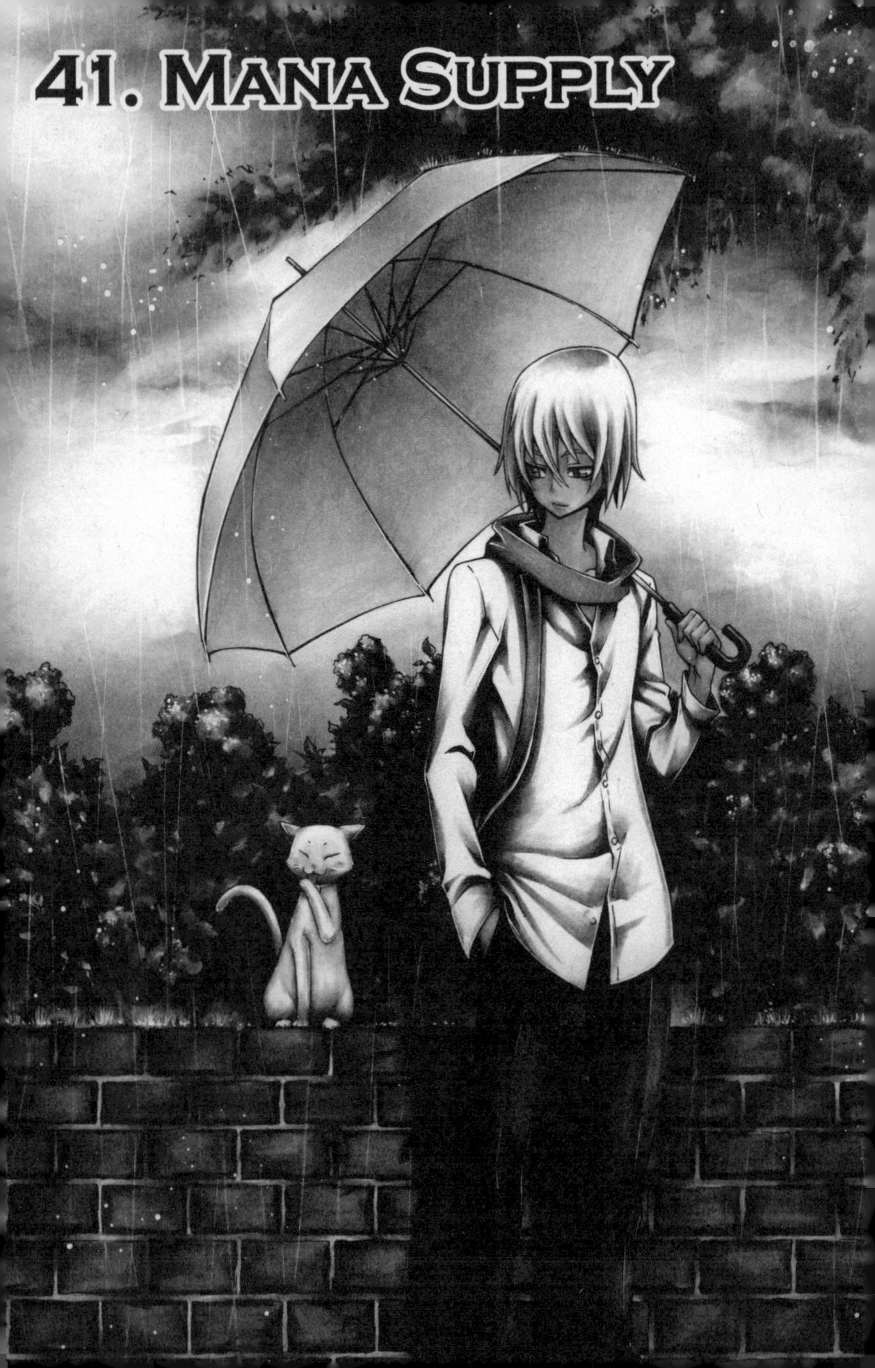

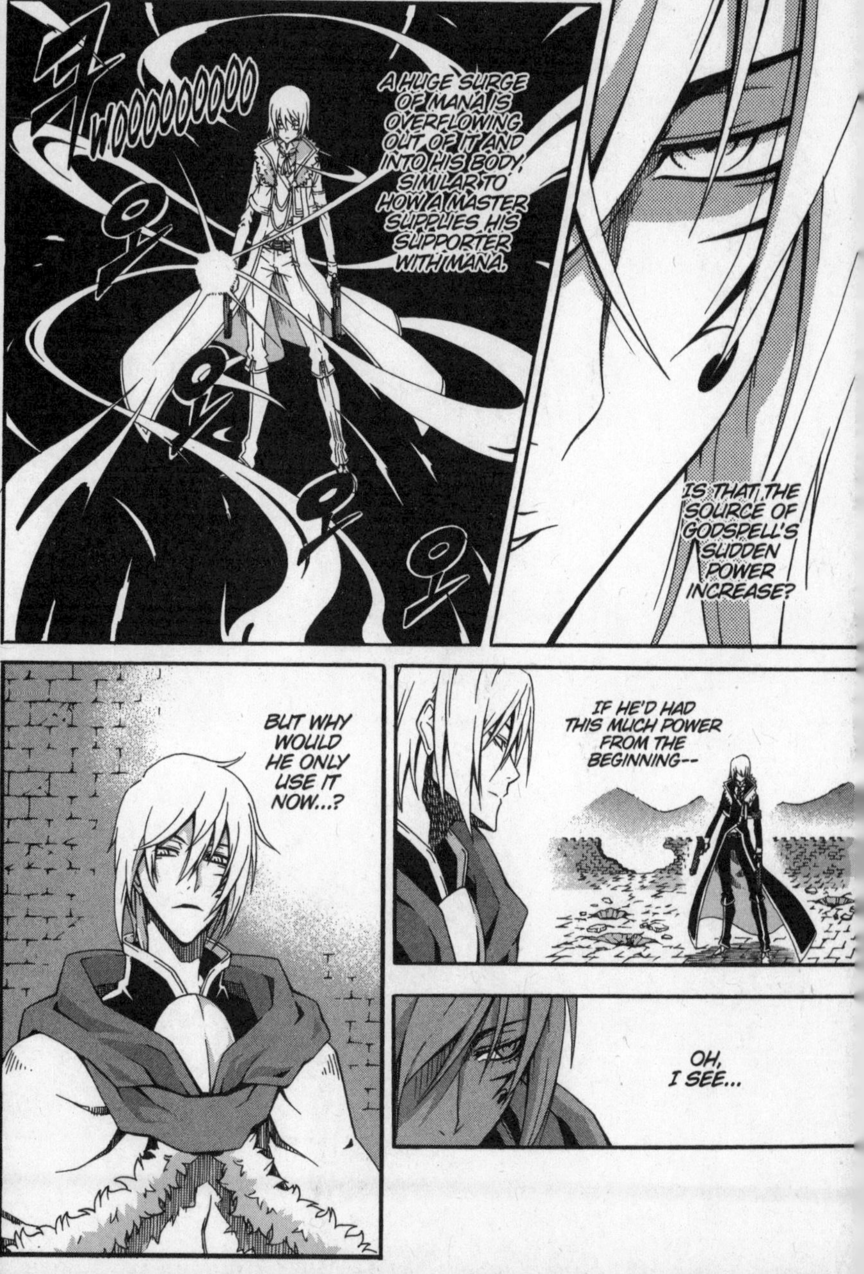
WOOOOOOOOOO
A HUGE SURGE OF MANA IS OVERFLOWING OUT OF IT AND INTO HIS BODY, SIMILAR TO HOW A MASTER SUPPLIES HIS SUPPORTER WITH MANA.
IS THAT THE SOURCE OF GODSPELL'S SUDDEN POWER INCREASE?
BUT WHY WOULD HE ONLY USE IT NOW...?
IF HE'D HAD THIS MUCH POWER FROM THE BEGINNING--
OH, I SEE...

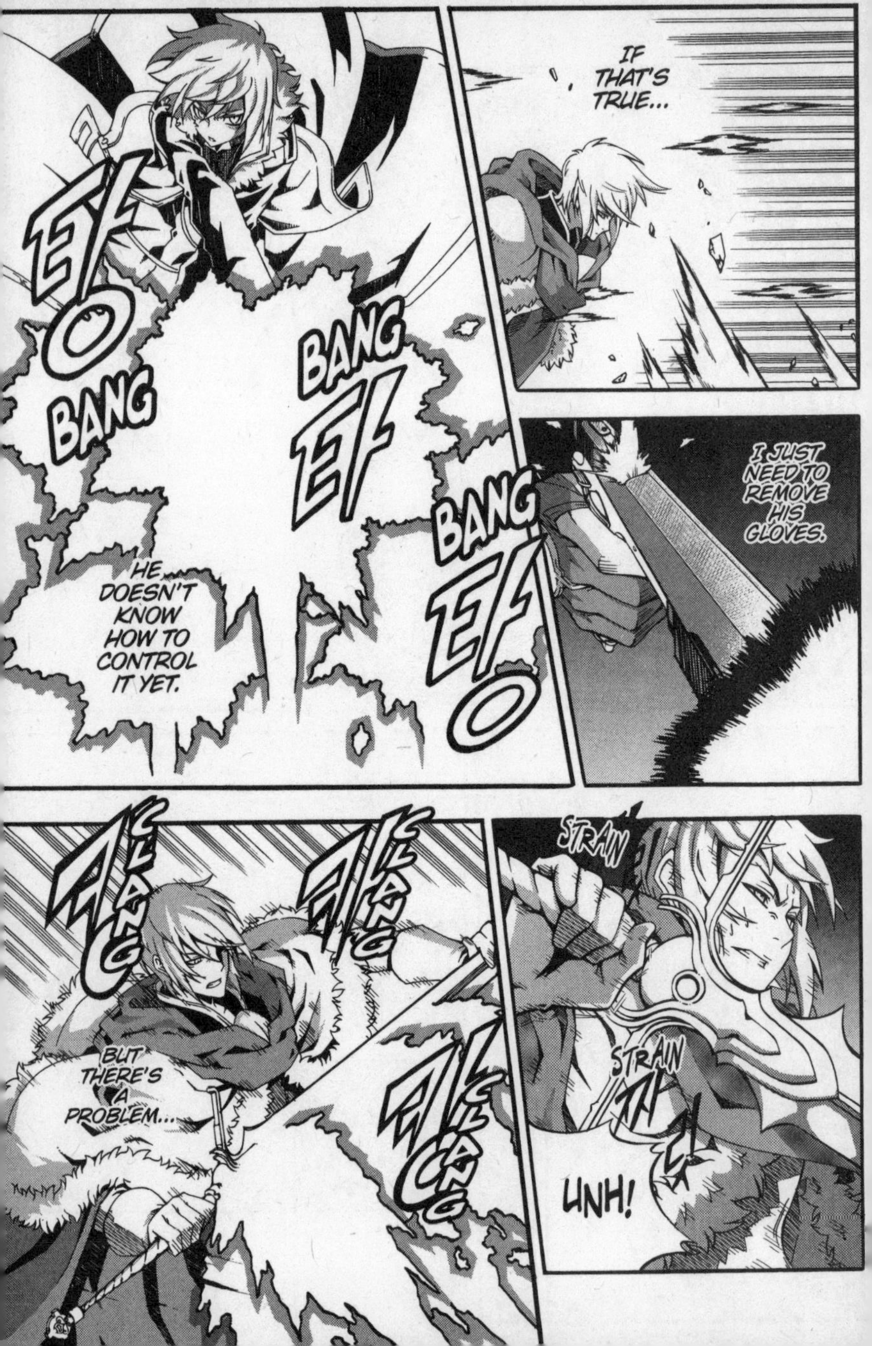
BANG
BANG
BANG
HE DOESN'T KNOW HOW TO CONTROL IT YET.
IF THAT'S TRUE...
I JUST NEED TO REMOVE HIS GLOVES.
CLANG
CLANG
BUT THERE'S A PROBLEM...
CLANG
STRAIN
STRAIN
UNH!

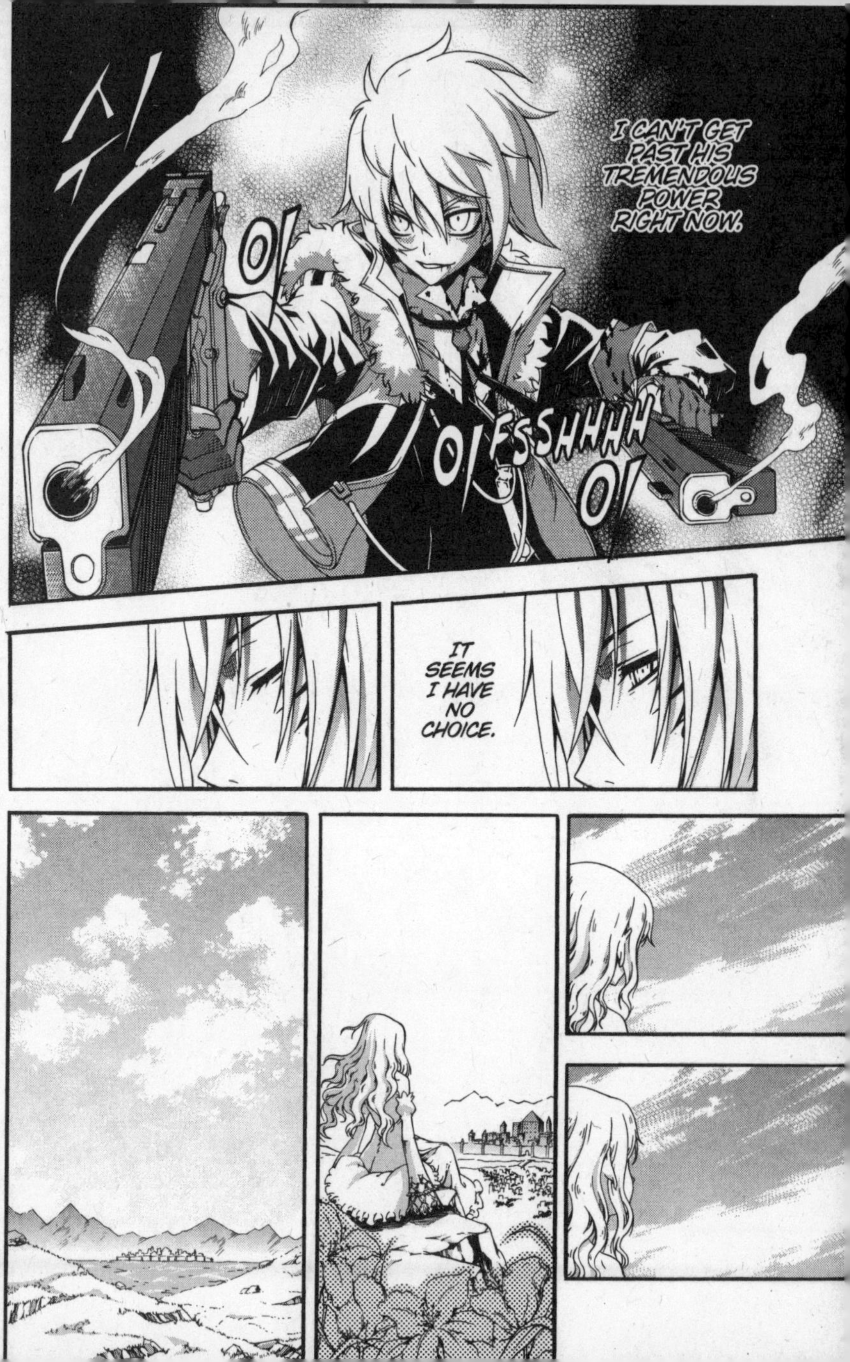
I CAN'T GET PAST HIS TREMENDOUS POWER RIGHT NOW.
FSSHHHH
IT SEEMS I HAVE NO CHOICE.

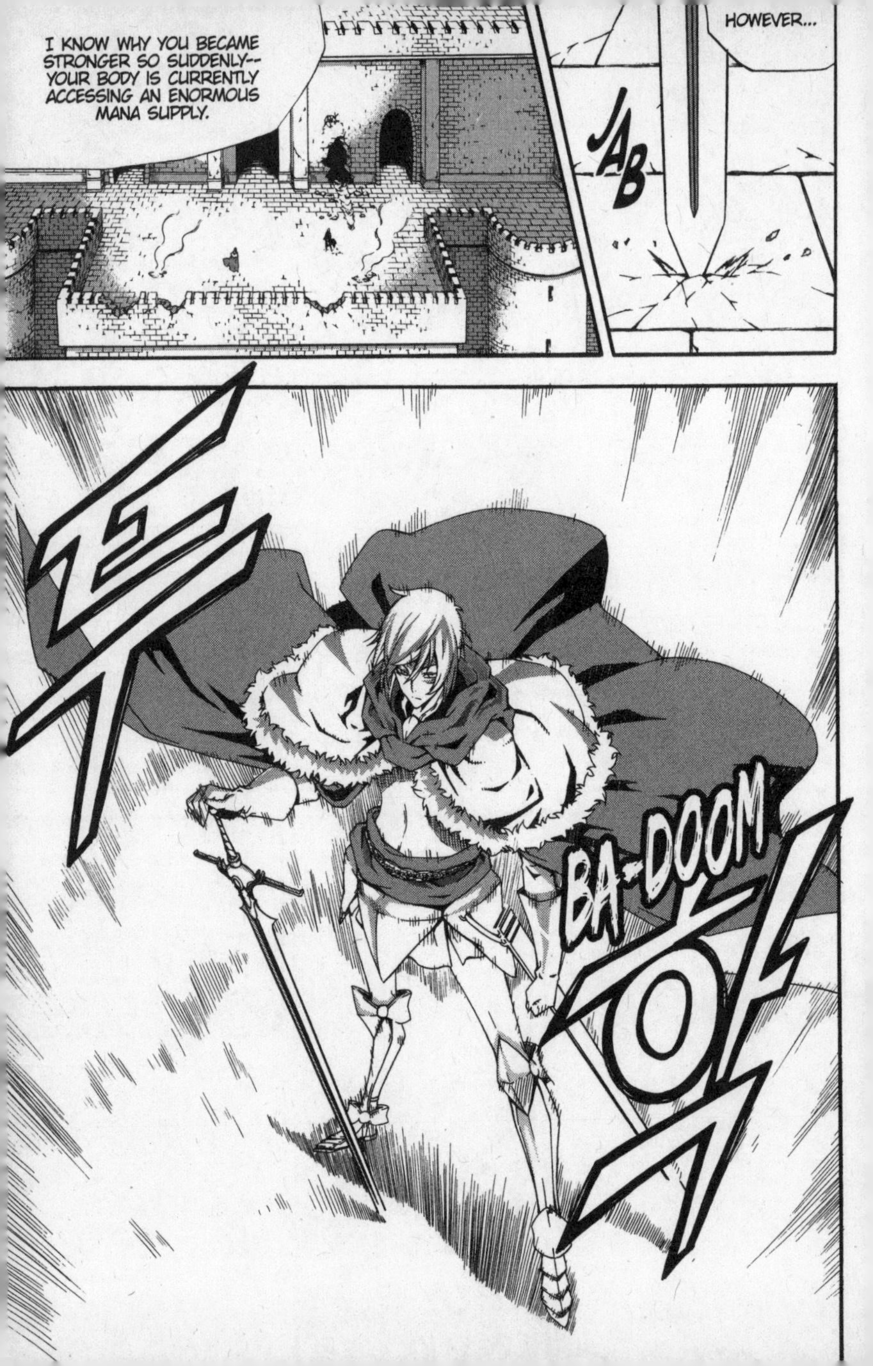
I KNOW WHY YOU BECAME STRONGER SO SUDDENLY--YOUR BODY IS CURRENTLY ACCESSING AN ENORMOUS MANA SUPPLY.
HOWEVER...
JAB
BA-DOOM

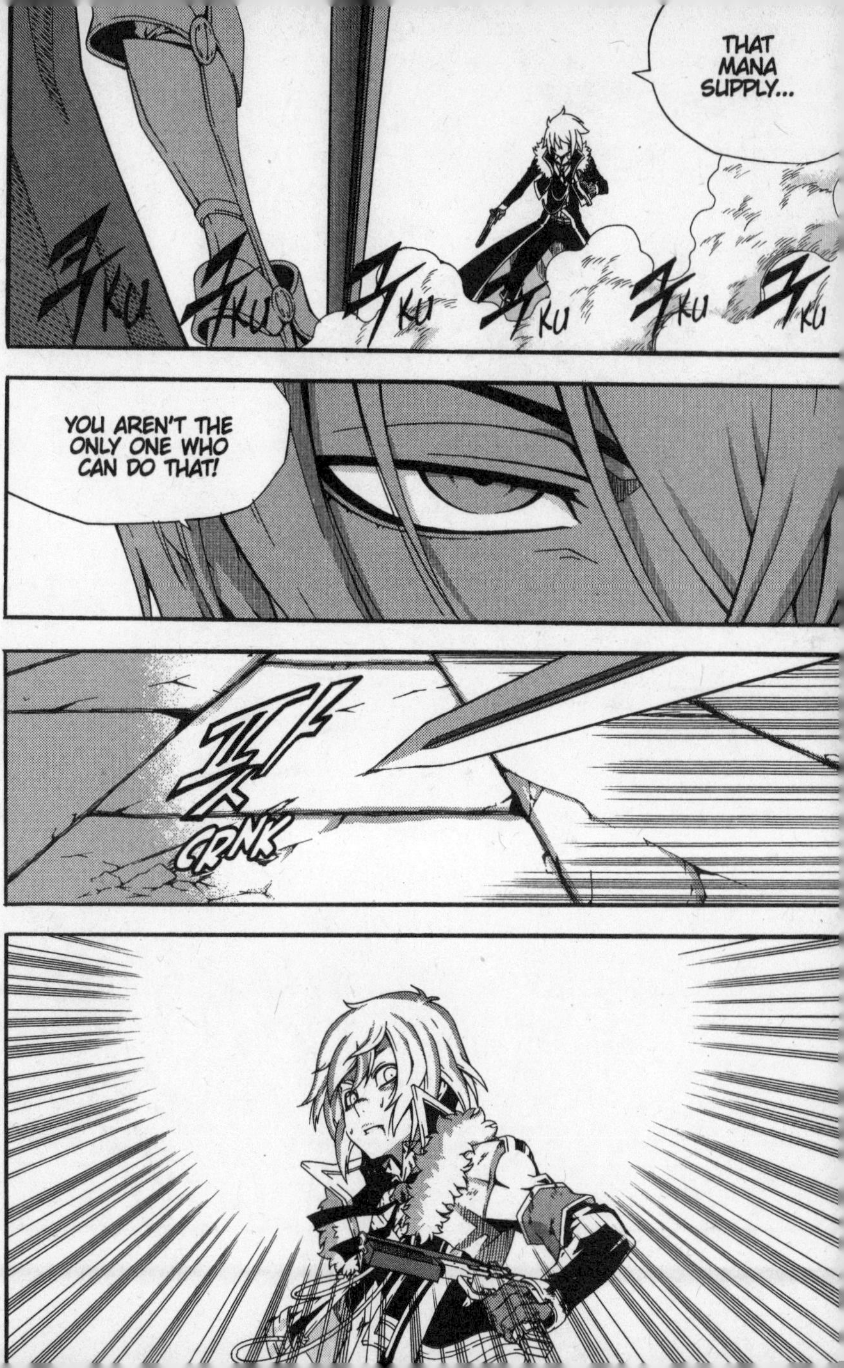
THAT MANA SUPPLY...
YOU AREN'T THE ONLY ONE WHO CAN DO THAT!
CRNK

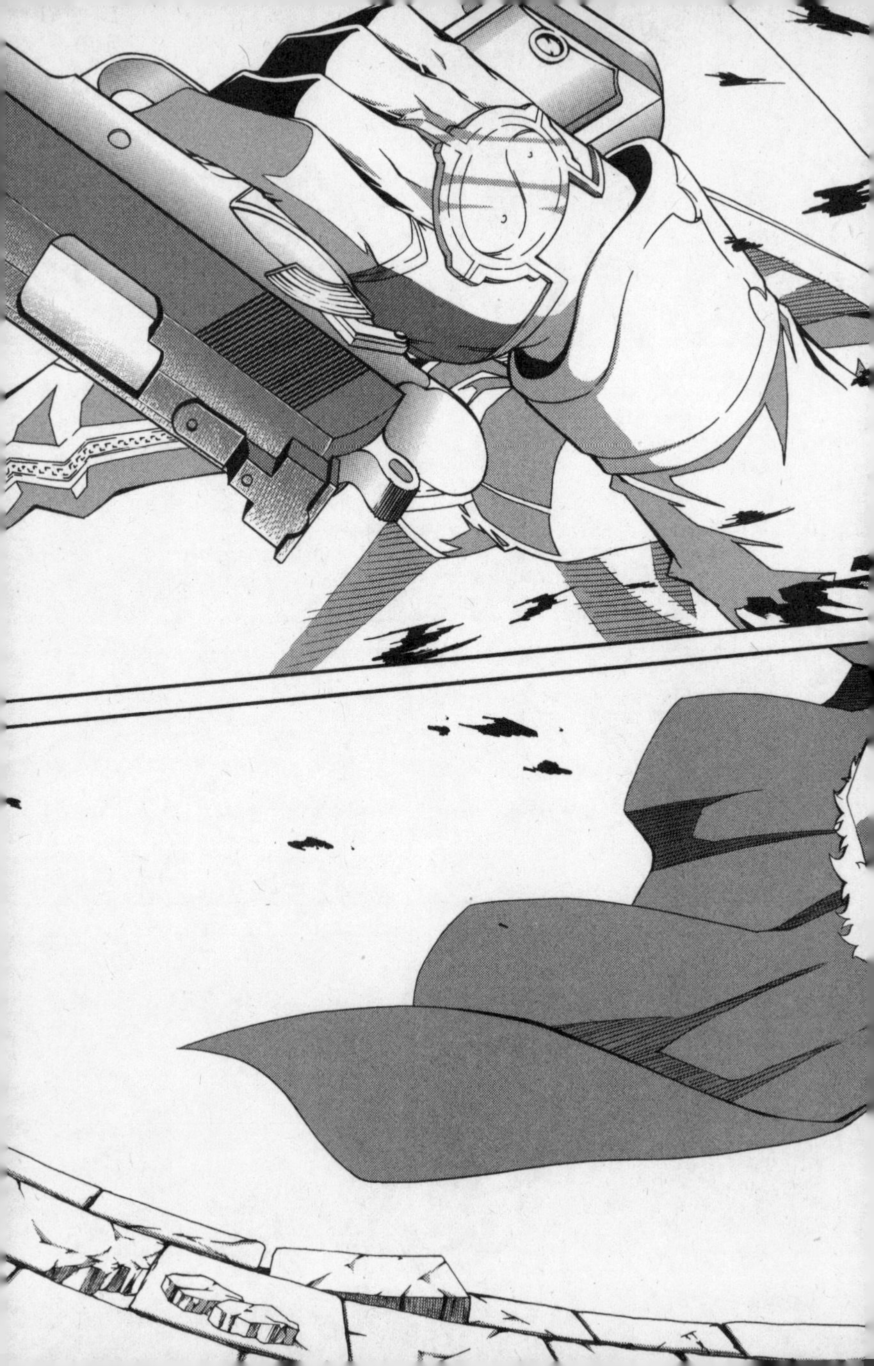

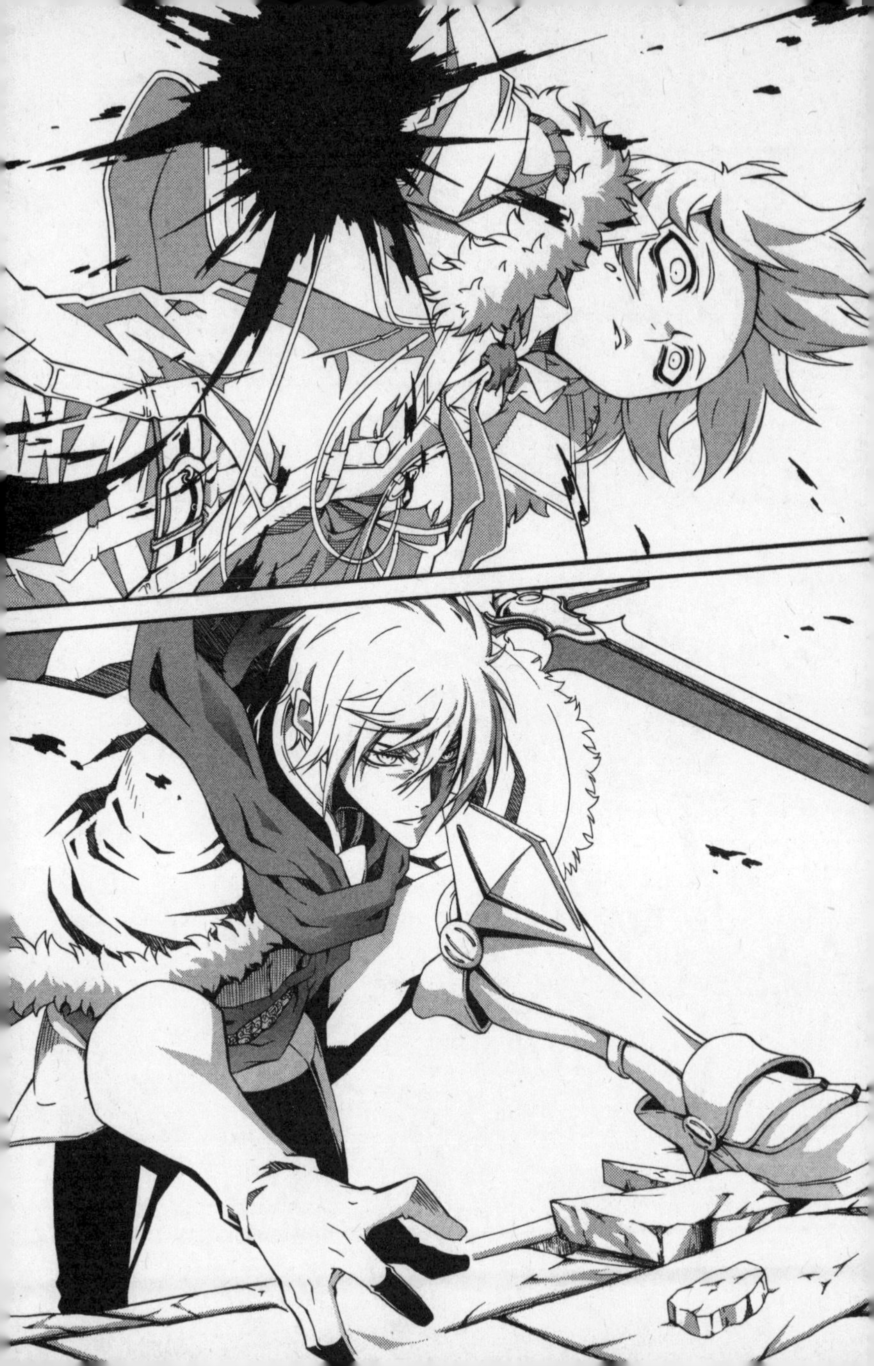

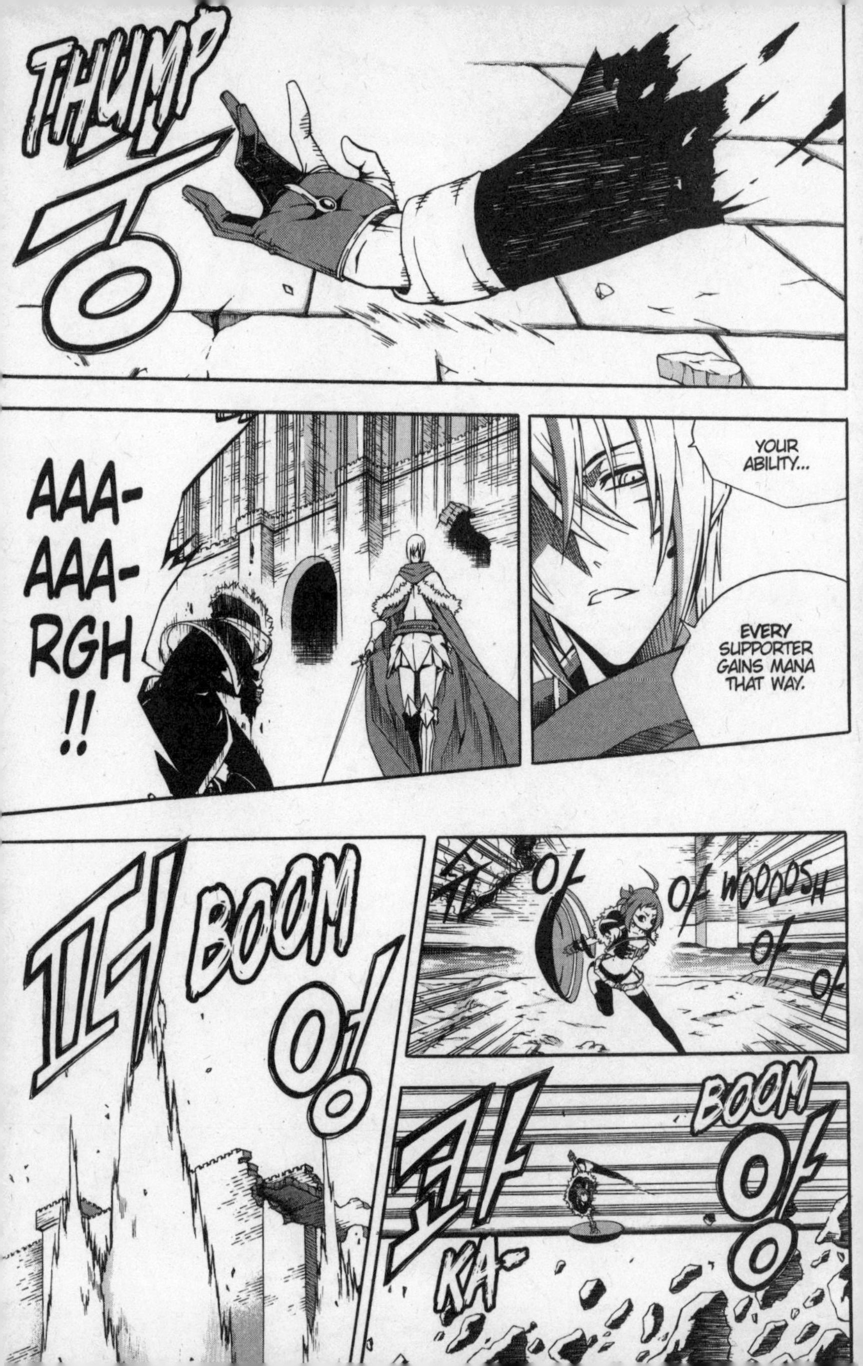
THUMP
AAA-AAA-ARGH!!
YOUR ABILITY...
EVERY SUPPORTER GAINS MANA THAT WAY.
BOOM
WOOOOSH
KA-
BOOM

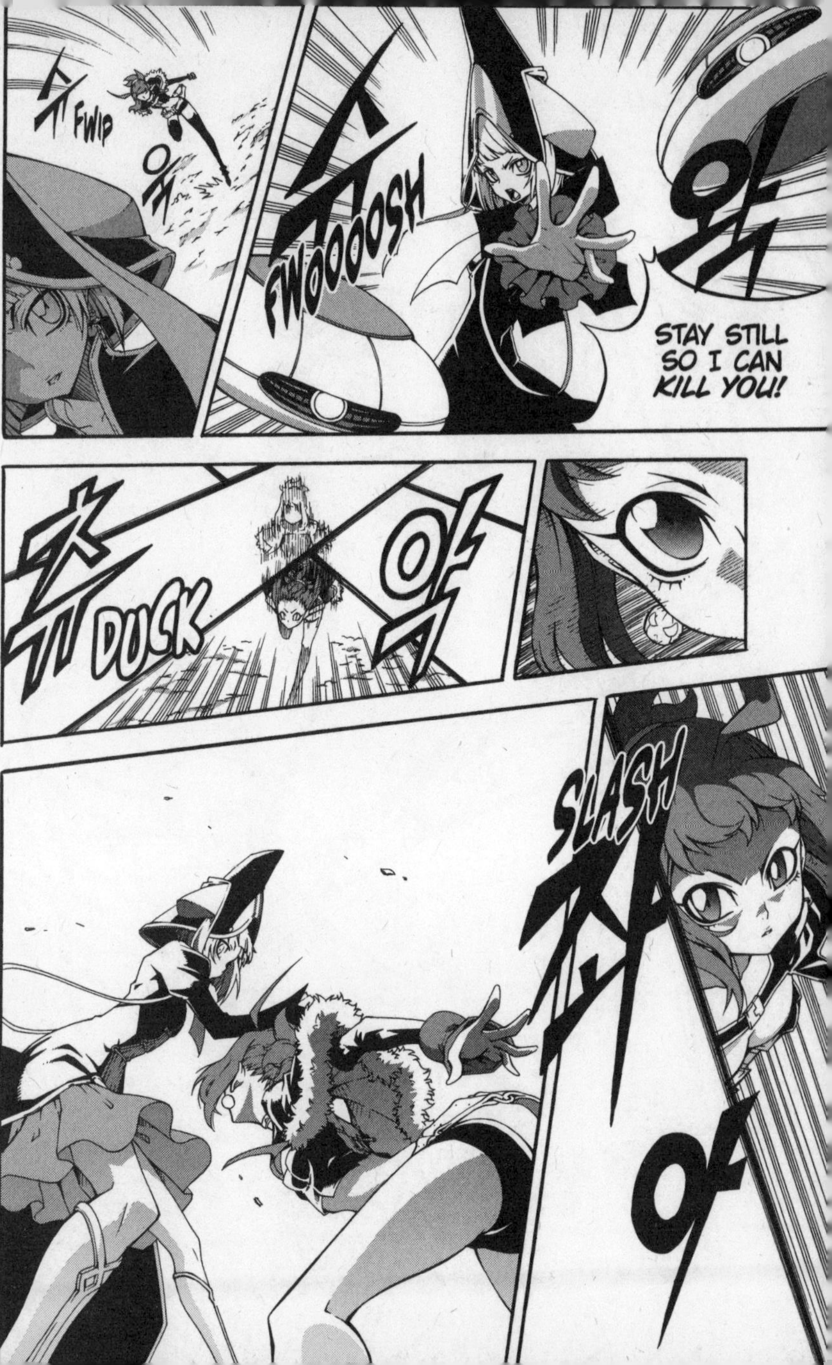
FWIP
FWOOOOSH
STAY STILL SO I CAN KILL YOU!
DUCK
SLASH

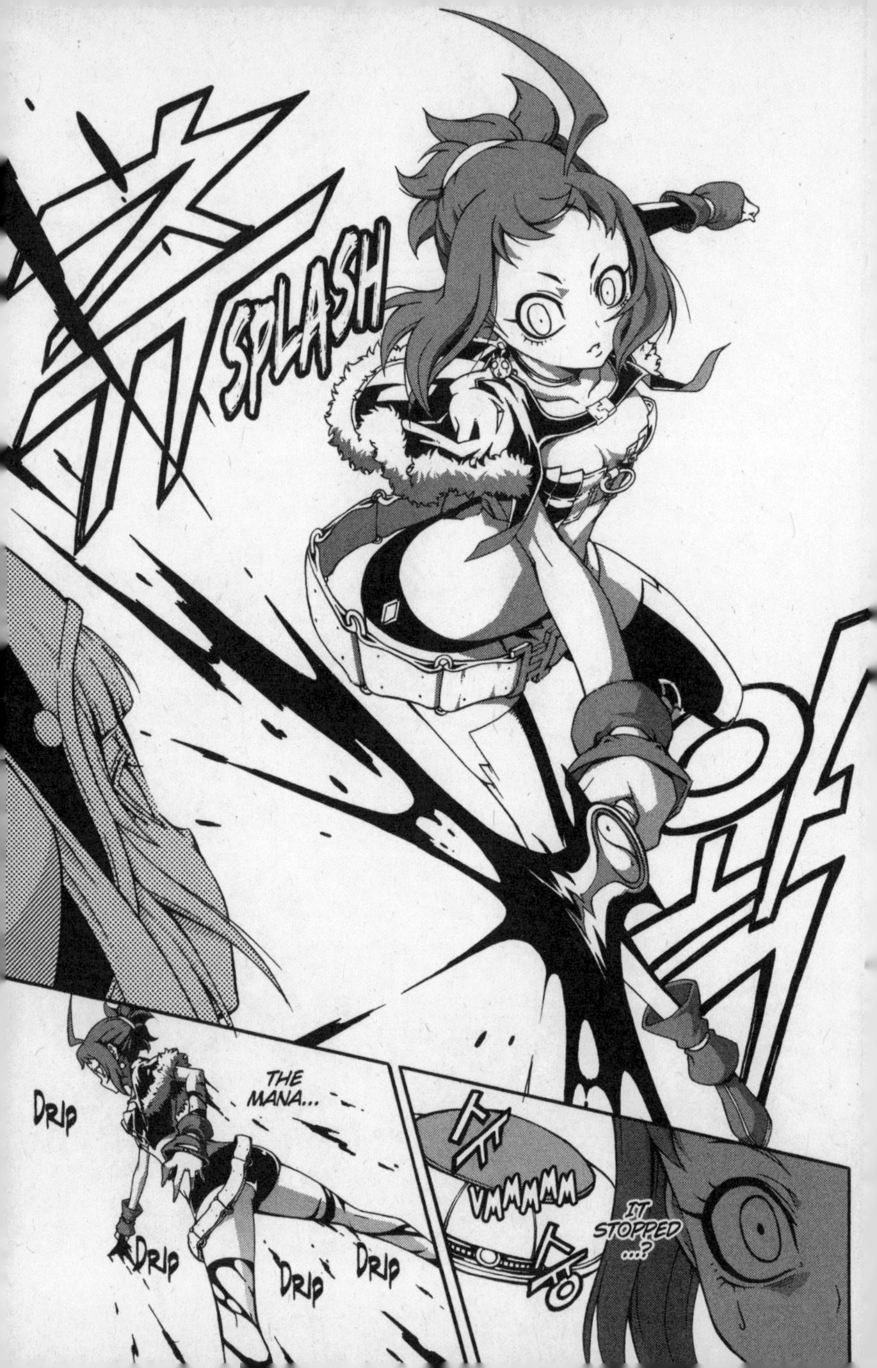
SPLASH
Drip
THE MANA...
Drip
Drip
Drip
VMMMMM
IT STOPPED ...?

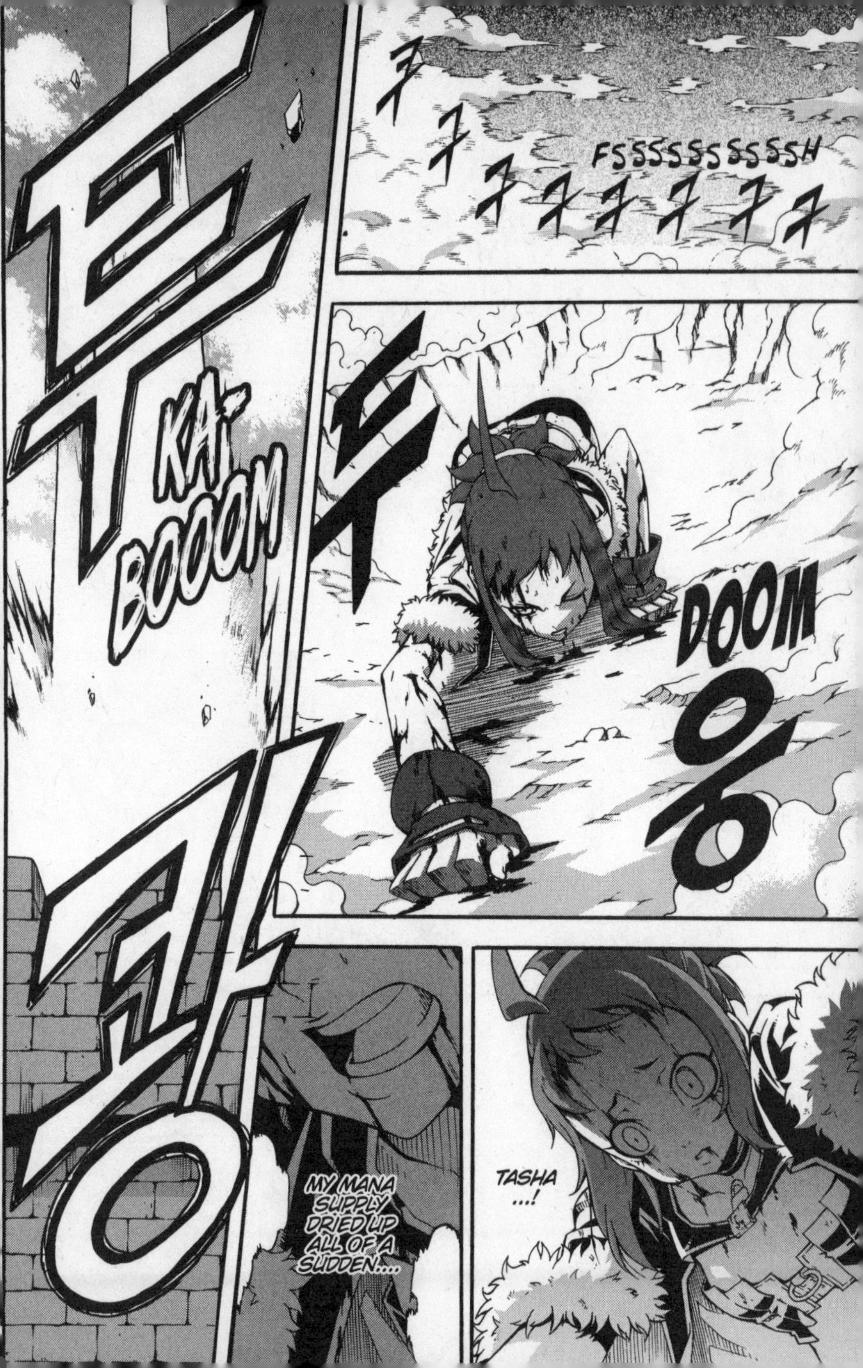
FSSSSSSSSSSH
KA-BOOOM
DOOM
MY MANA SUPPLY DRIED UP ALL OF A SUDDEN....
TASHA ...!

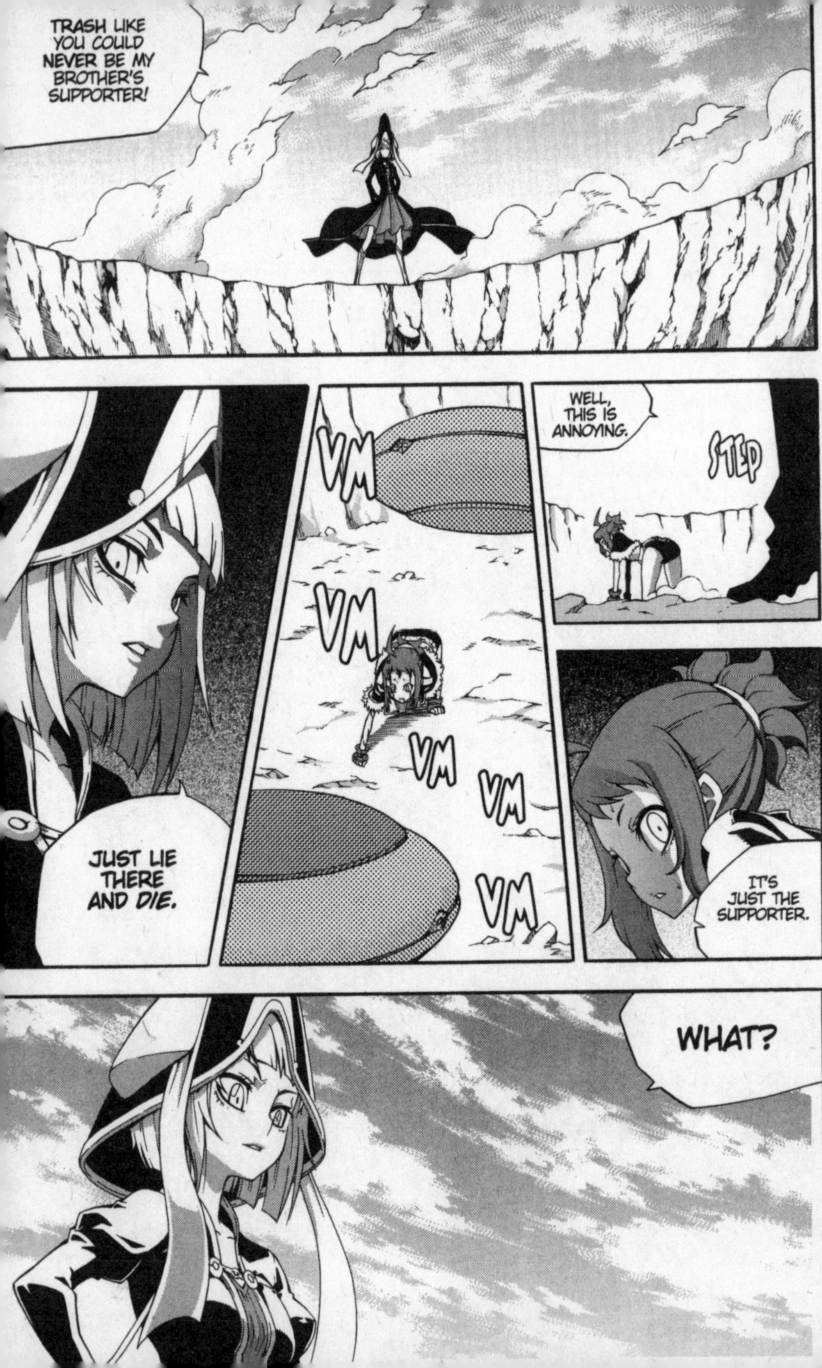
TRASH LIKE YOU COULD NEVER BE MY BROTHER'S SUPPORTER!
JUST LIE THERE AND *DIE*.
VM
VM
VM
VM
VM
WELL, THIS IS ANNOYING.
STEP
IT'S JUST THE SUPPORTER.
WHAT?

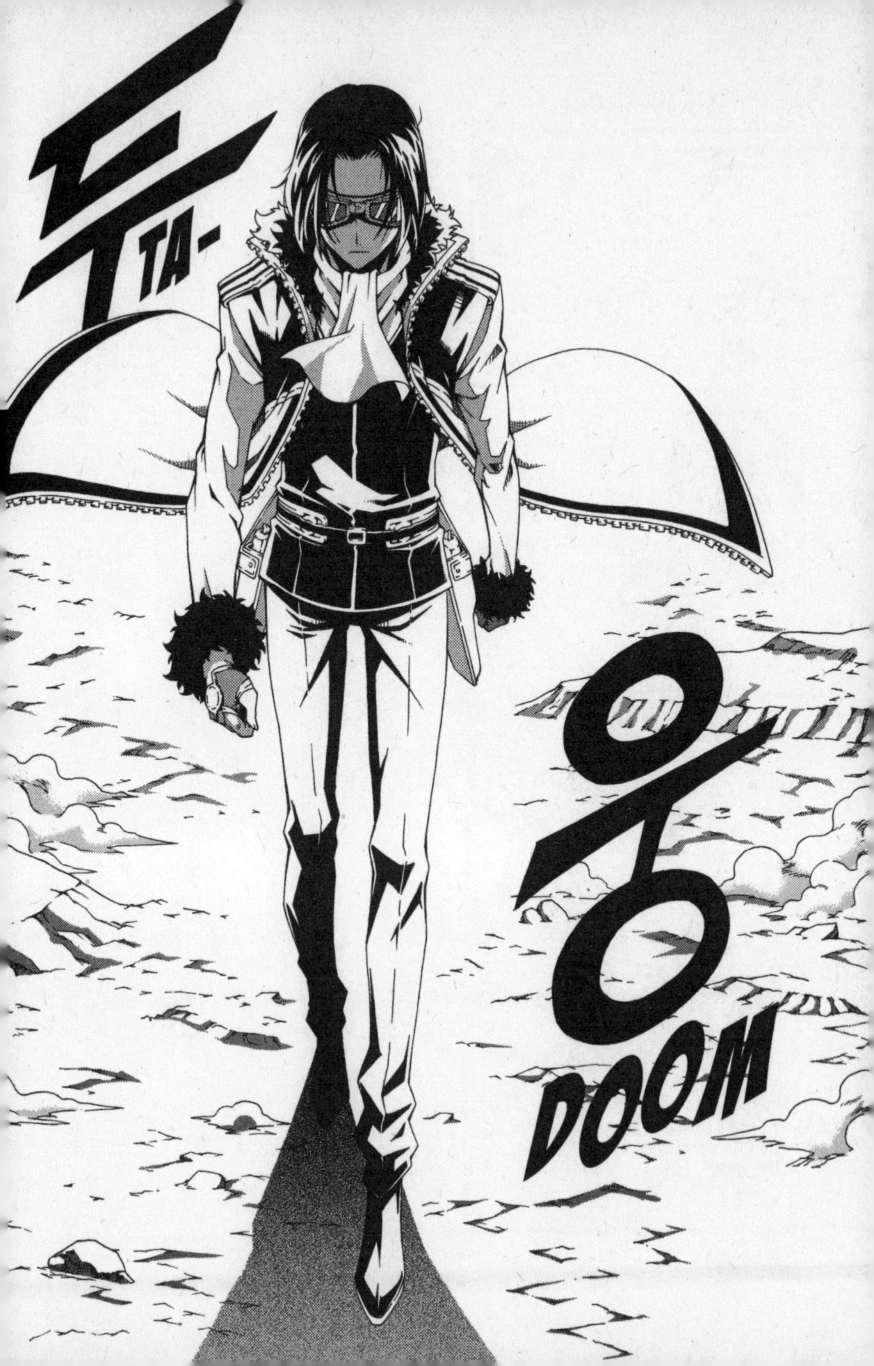
TA-
DOOM

OPTION (2)

I HAVEN'T BEEN BACK HERE IN SO LONG... IT'S SO DUSTY!
AEGIS.
FLASH
INITIATE VACUUM MODE!
VMM
VMM
VMM
VMM

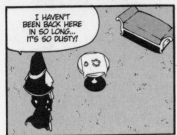

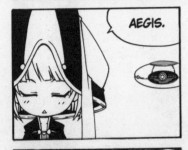

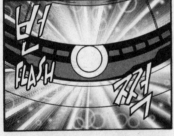

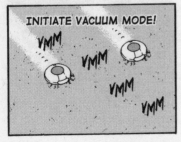

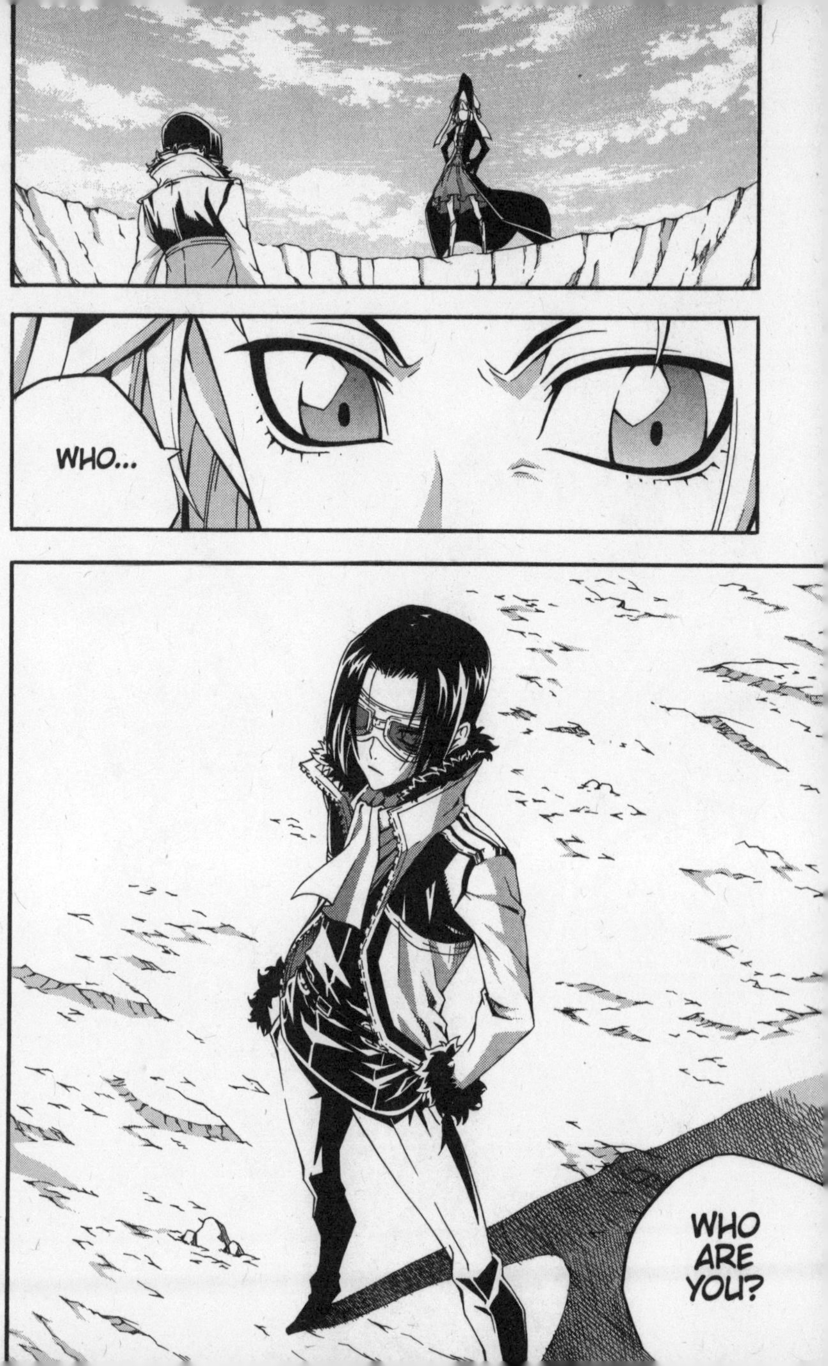
WHO...
WHO ARE YOU?

42. Precious Person

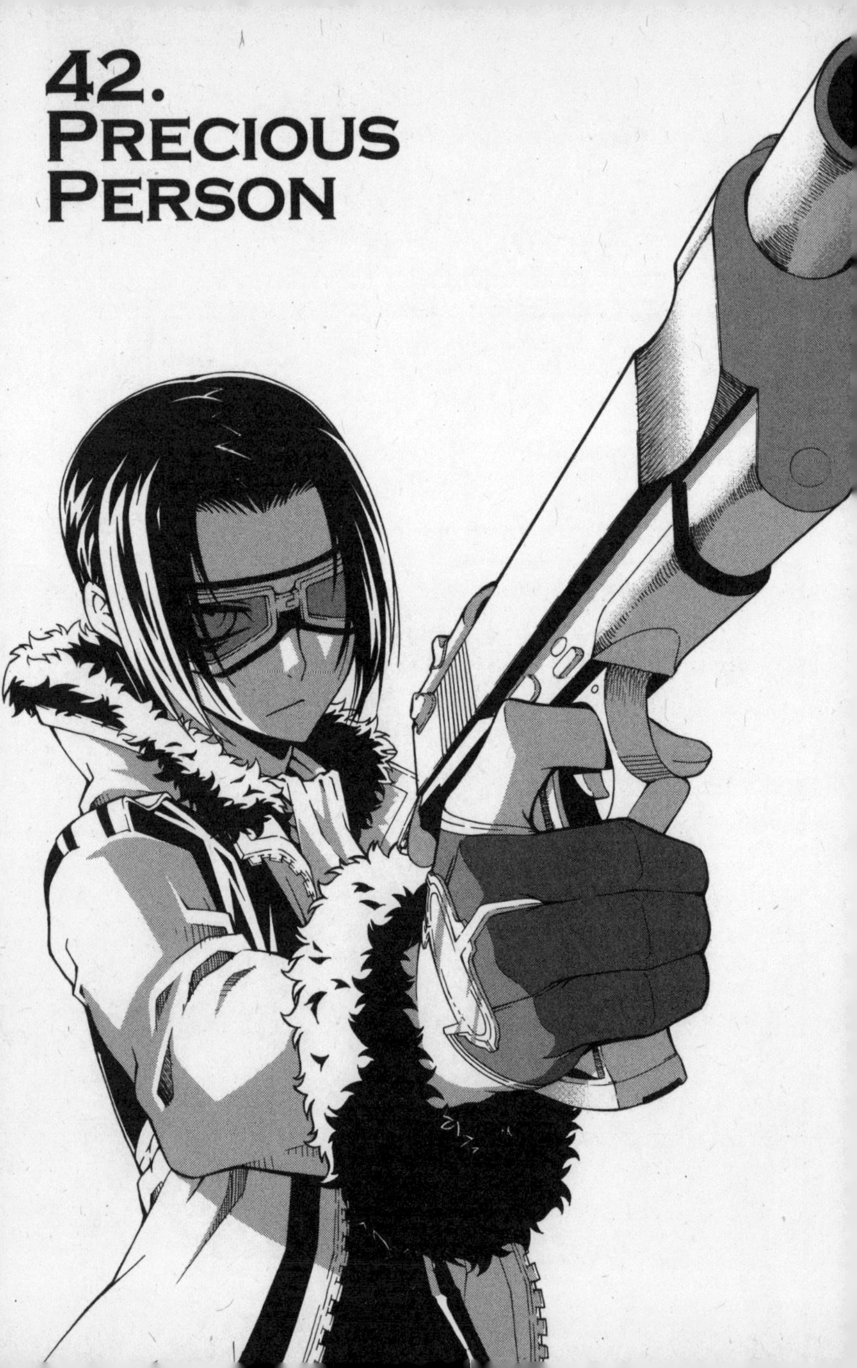

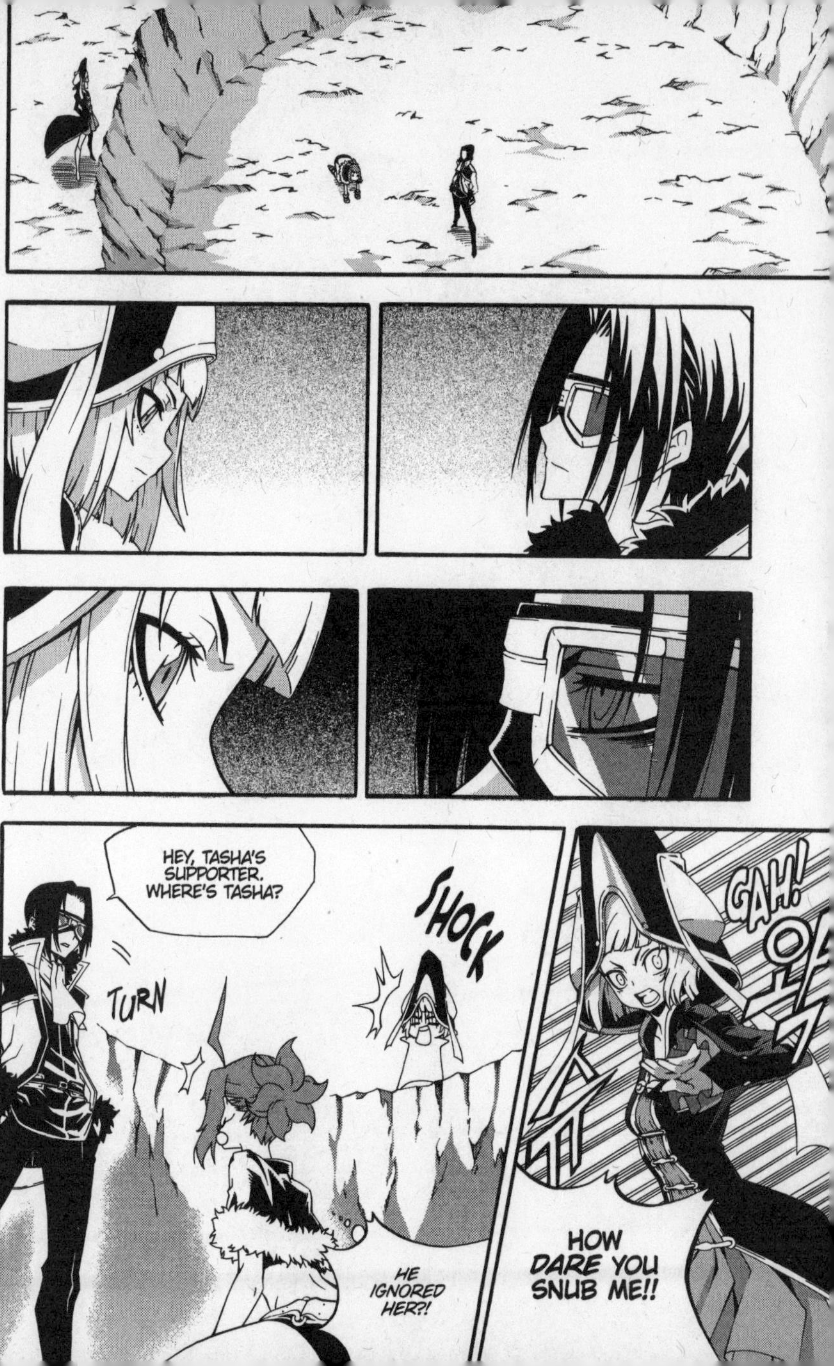

HEY, TASHA'S SUPPORTER. WHERE'S TASHA?
TURN
SHOCK
HE IGNORED HER?!
GAH!
HOW DARE YOU SNUB ME!!

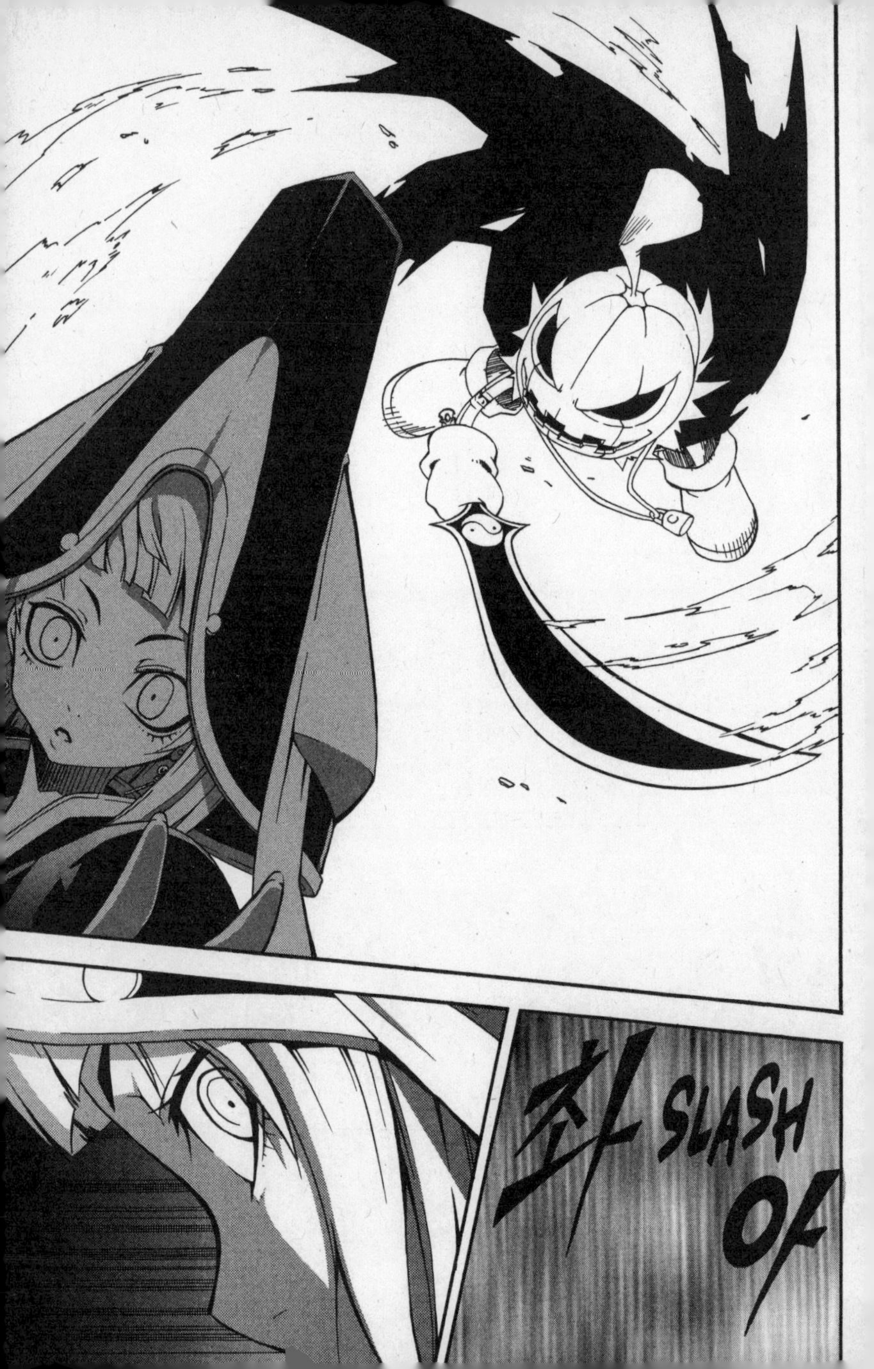
SLASH

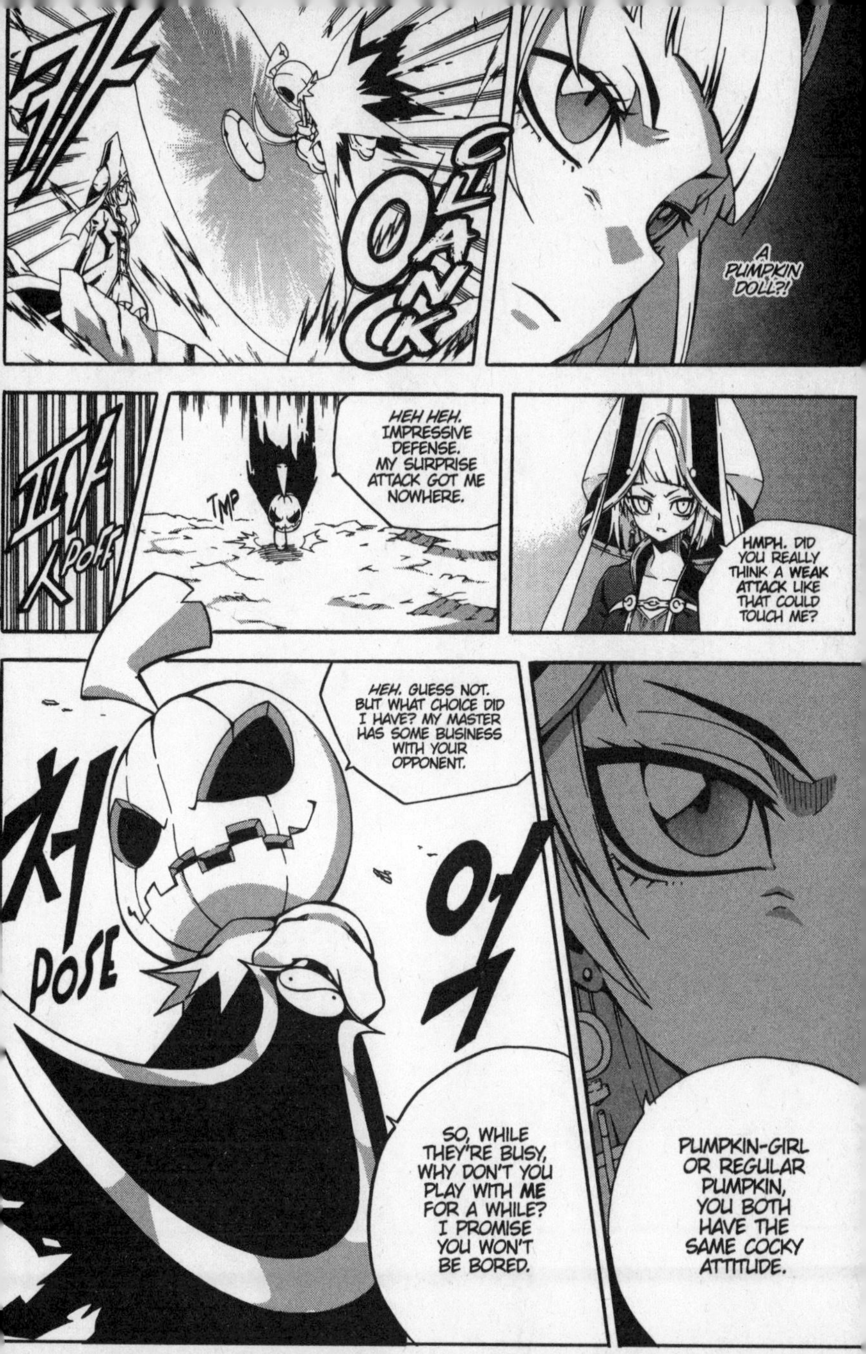
CLANCK
A PUMPKIN DOLL?!
TMP
POFF
HEH HEH. IMPRESSIVE DEFENSE. MY SURPRISE ATTACK GOT ME NOWHERE.
HMPH. DID YOU REALLY THINK A WEAK ATTACK LIKE THAT COULD TOUCH ME?
POSE
HEH. GUESS NOT. BUT WHAT CHOICE DID I HAVE? MY MASTER HAS SOME BUSINESS WITH YOUR OPPONENT.
SO, WHILE THEY'RE BUSY, WHY DON'T YOU PLAY WITH ME FOR A WHILE? I PROMISE YOU WON'T BE BORED.
PUMPKIN-GIRL OR REGULAR PUMPKIN, YOU BOTH HAVE THE SAME COCKY ATTITUDE.

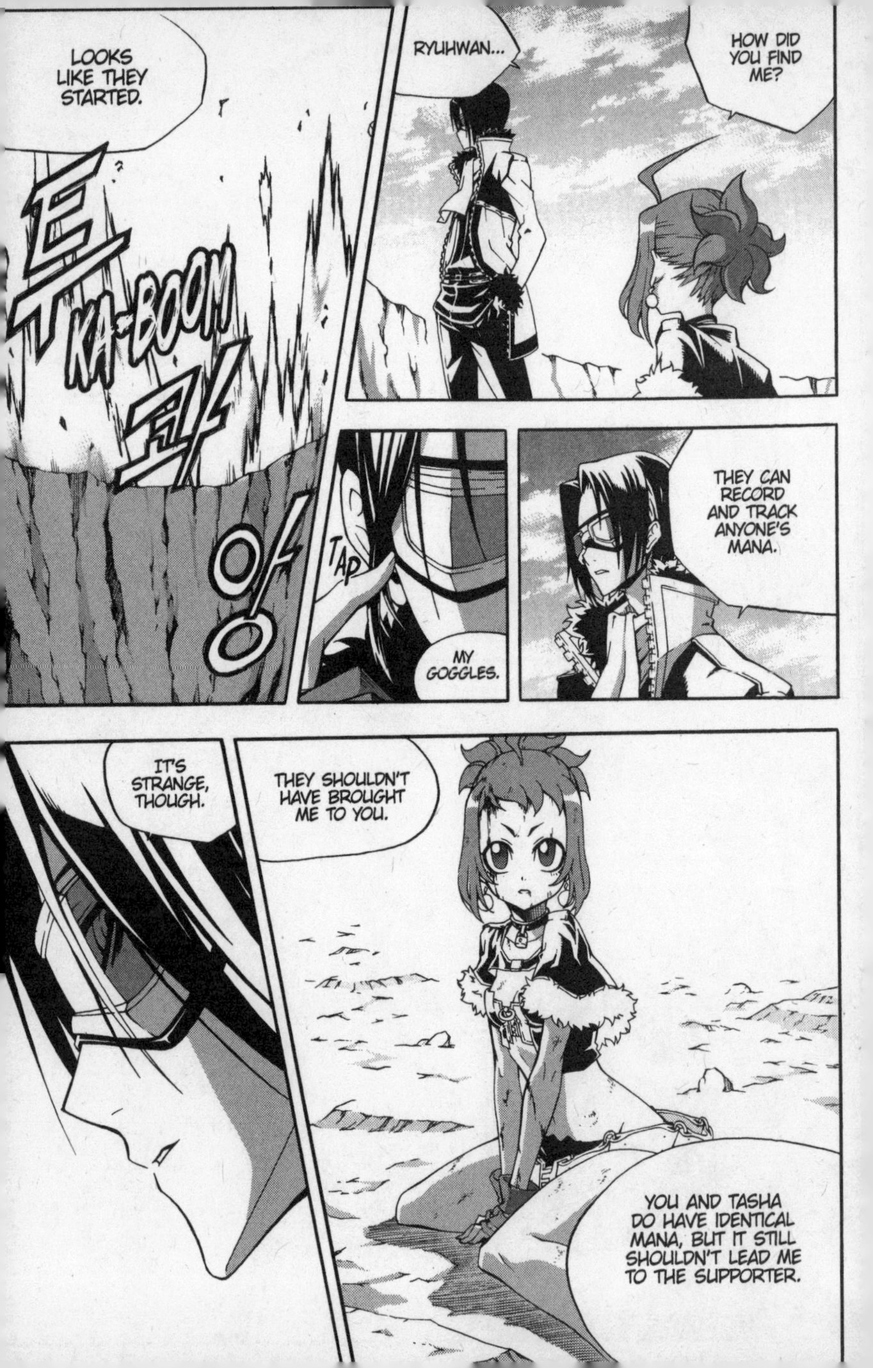
LOOKS LIKE THEY STARTED.
KA-BOOM
RYUHWAN...
HOW DID YOU FIND ME?
TAP
MY GOGGLES.
THEY CAN RECORD AND TRACK ANYONE'S MANA.
IT'S STRANGE, THOUGH.
THEY SHOULDN'T HAVE BROUGHT ME TO YOU.
YOU AND TASHA DO HAVE IDENTICAL MANA, BUT IT STILL SHOULDN'T LEAD ME TO THE SUPPORTER.

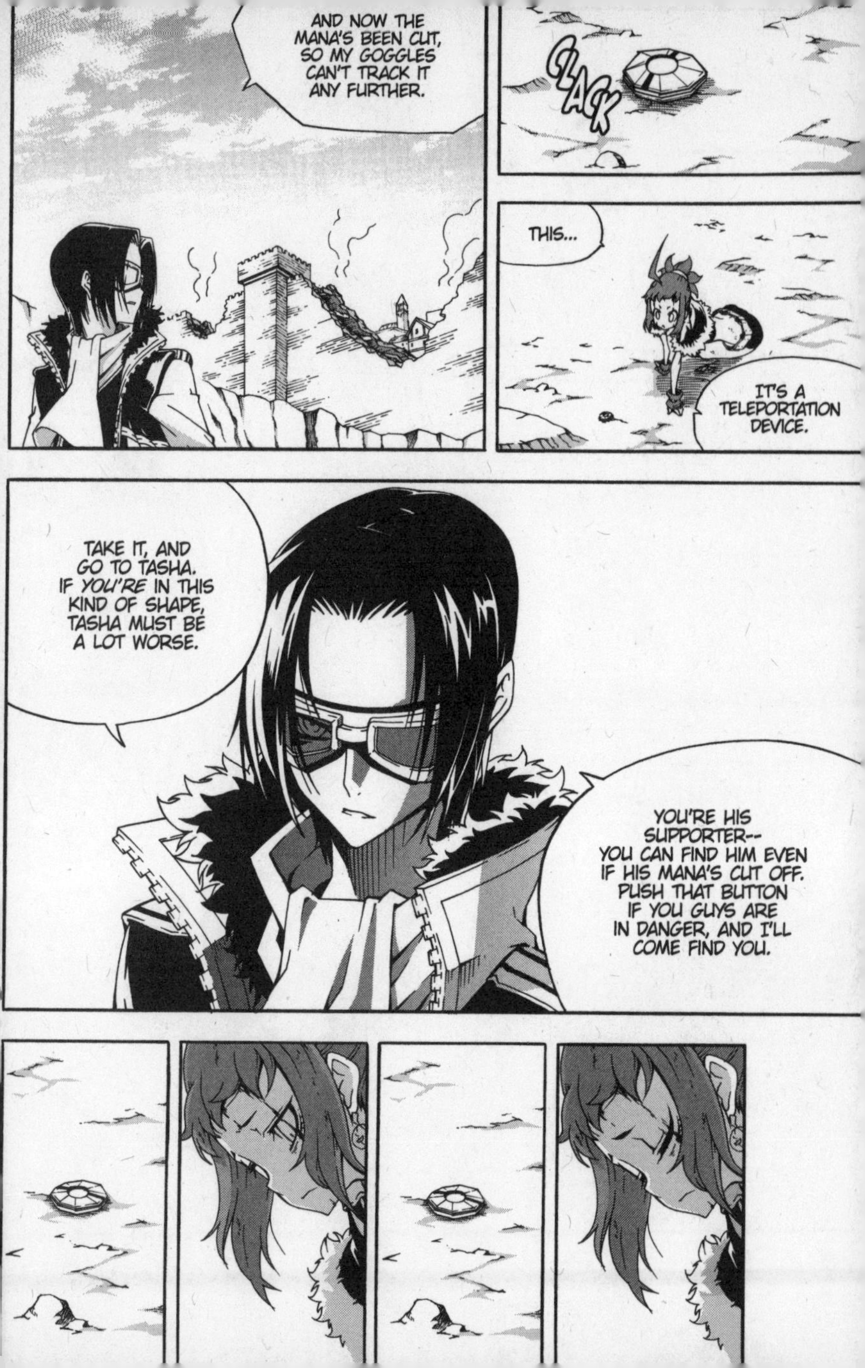
AND NOW THE MANA'S BEEN CUT, SO MY GOGGLES CAN'T TRACK IT ANY FURTHER.
CLACK
THIS...
IT'S A TELEPORTATION DEVICE.
TAKE IT, AND GO TO TASHA. IF *YOU'RE* IN THIS KIND OF SHAPE, TASHA MUST BE A LOT WORSE.
YOU'RE HIS SUPPORTER-- YOU CAN FIND HIM EVEN IF HIS MANA'S CUT OFF. PUSH THAT BUTTON IF YOU GUYS ARE IN DANGER, AND I'LL COME FIND YOU.

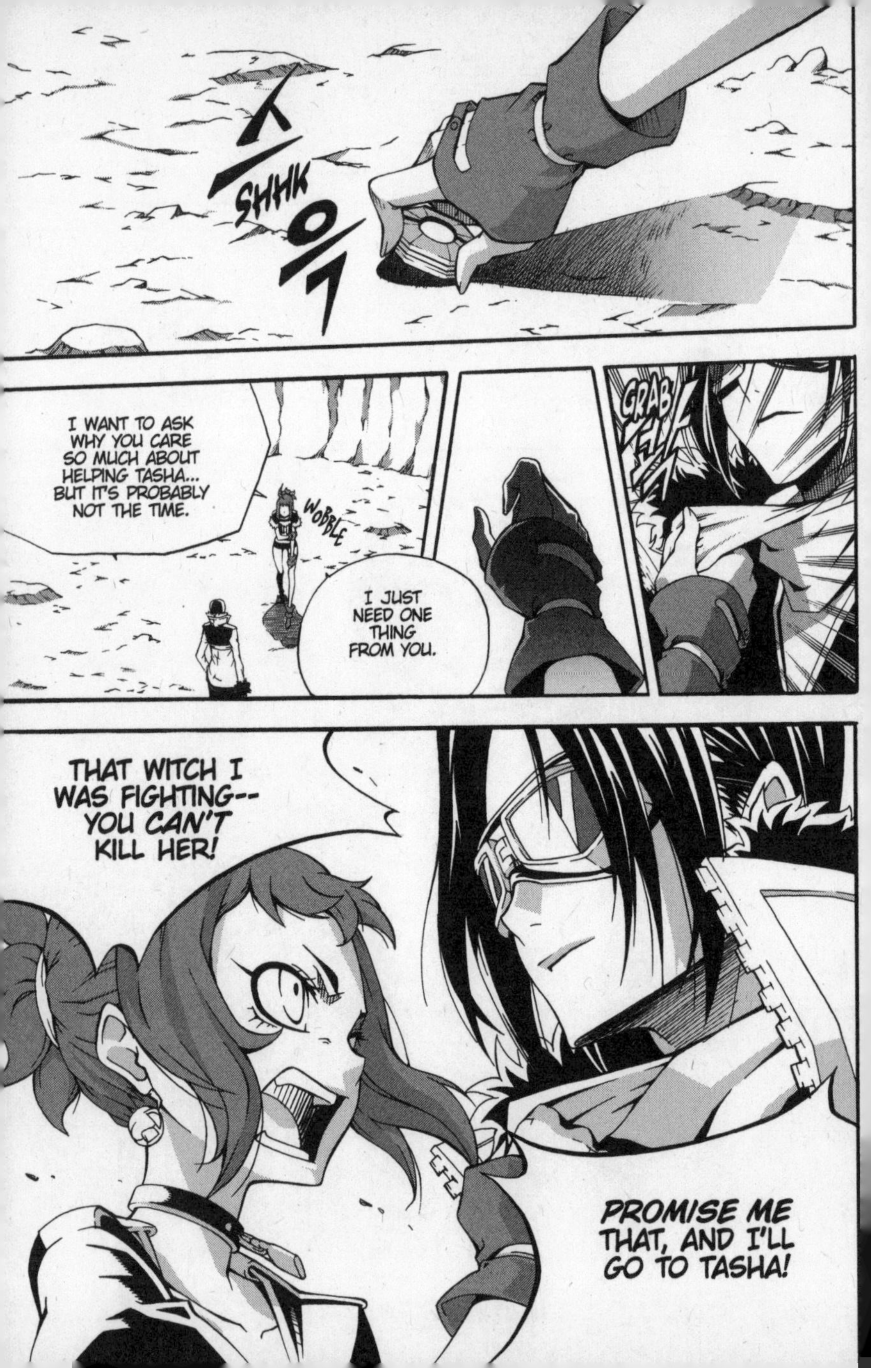
SHHK
I WANT TO ASK WHY YOU CARE SO MUCH ABOUT HELPING TASHA... BUT IT'S PROBABLY NOT THE TIME.
WOBBLE
I JUST NEED ONE THING FROM YOU.
GRAB
THAT WITCH I WAS FIGHTING-- YOU *CAN'T* KILL HER!
PROMISE ME THAT, AND I'LL GO TO TASHA!

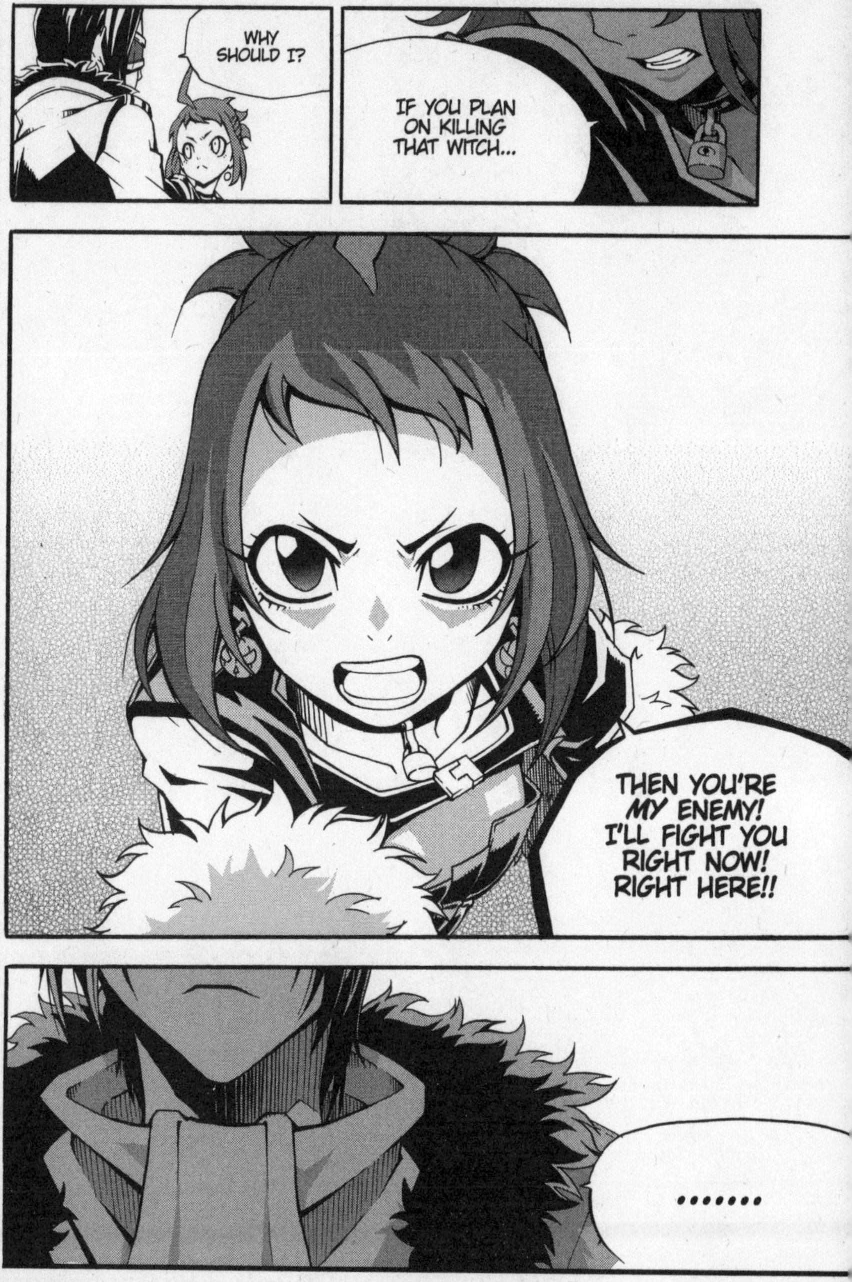
WHY SHOULD I?
IF YOU PLAN ON KILLING THAT WITCH...
THEN YOU'RE *MY* ENEMY! I'LL FIGHT YOU RIGHT NOW! RIGHT HERE!!
....

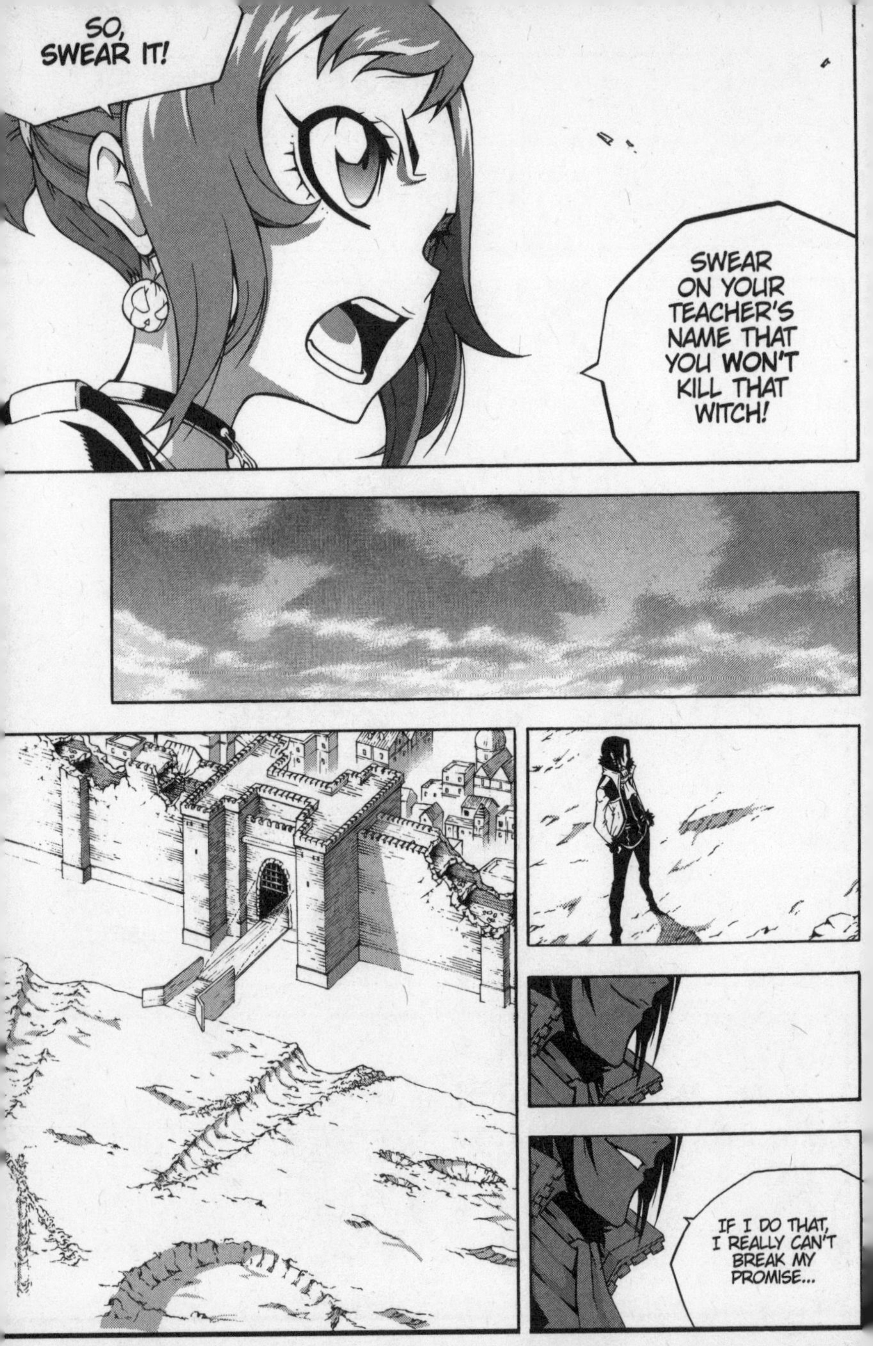
SO, SWEAR IT!
SWEAR ON YOUR TEACHER'S NAME THAT YOU WON'T KILL THAT WITCH!
IF I DO THAT, I REALLY CAN'T BREAK MY PROMISE...

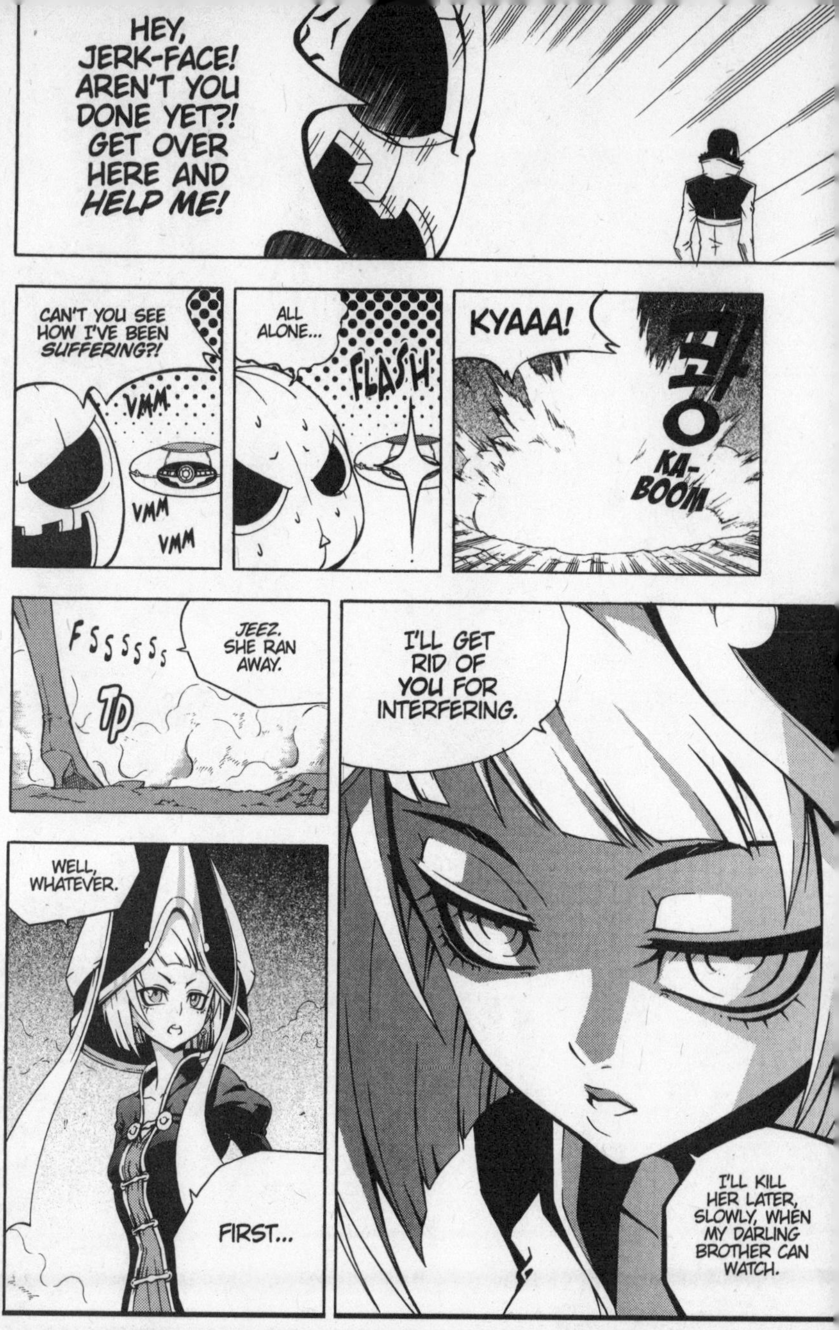
HEY, JERK-FACE! AREN'T YOU DONE YET?! GET OVER HERE AND *HELP ME!*
CAN'T YOU SEE HOW I'VE BEEN *SUFFERING?!*
VMM
VMM
VMM
ALL ALONE...
FLASH
KYAAA!
쾅
KA-BOOM
FSSSSSS
TP
JEEZ. SHE RAN AWAY.
WELL, WHATEVER.
FIRST...
I'LL GET RID OF YOU FOR INTERFERING.
I'LL KILL HER LATER, SLOWLY, WHEN MY DARLING BROTHER CAN WATCH.

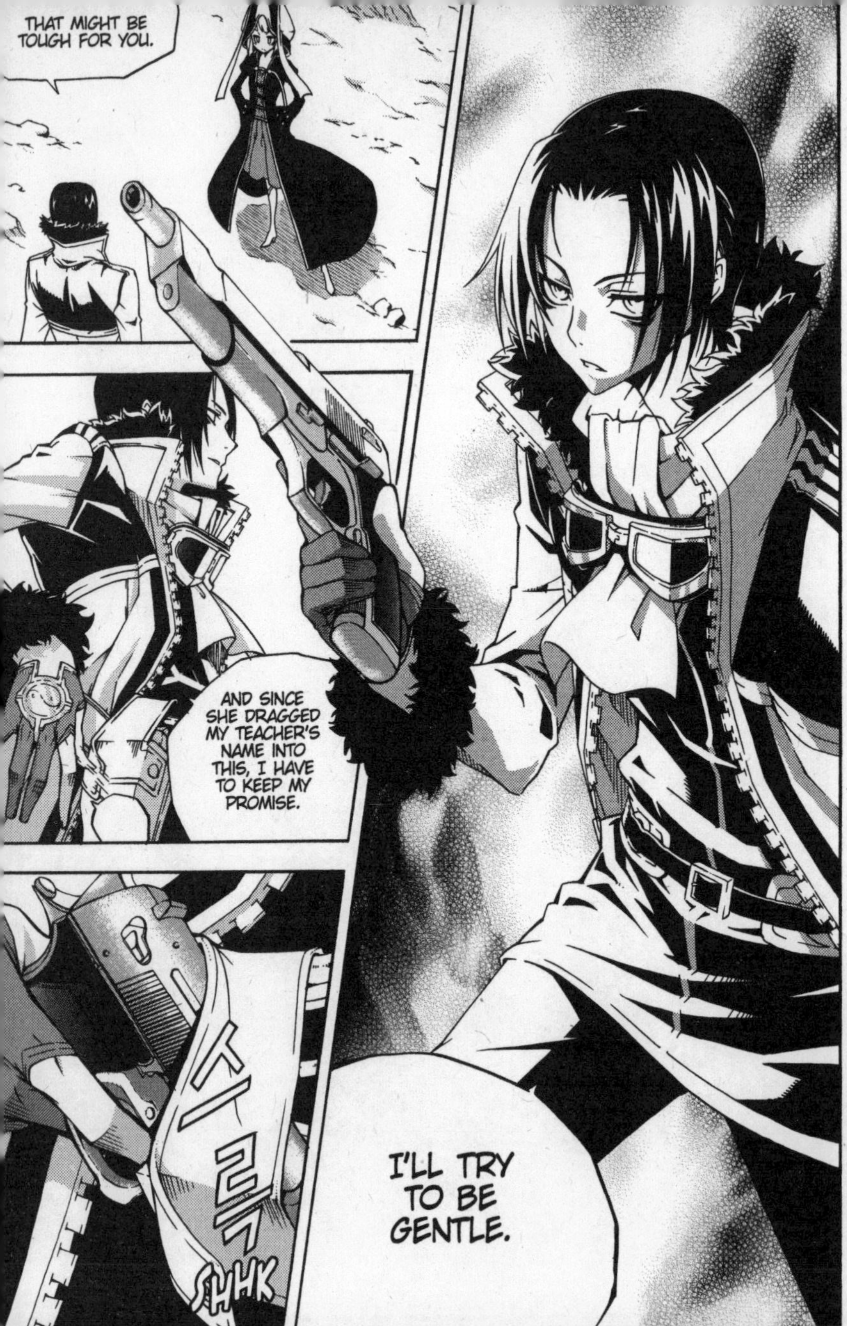
THAT MIGHT BE TOUGH FOR YOU.
AND SINCE SHE DRAGGED MY TEACHER'S NAME INTO THIS, I HAVE TO KEEP MY PROMISE.
SHHK
I'LL TRY TO BE GENTLE.

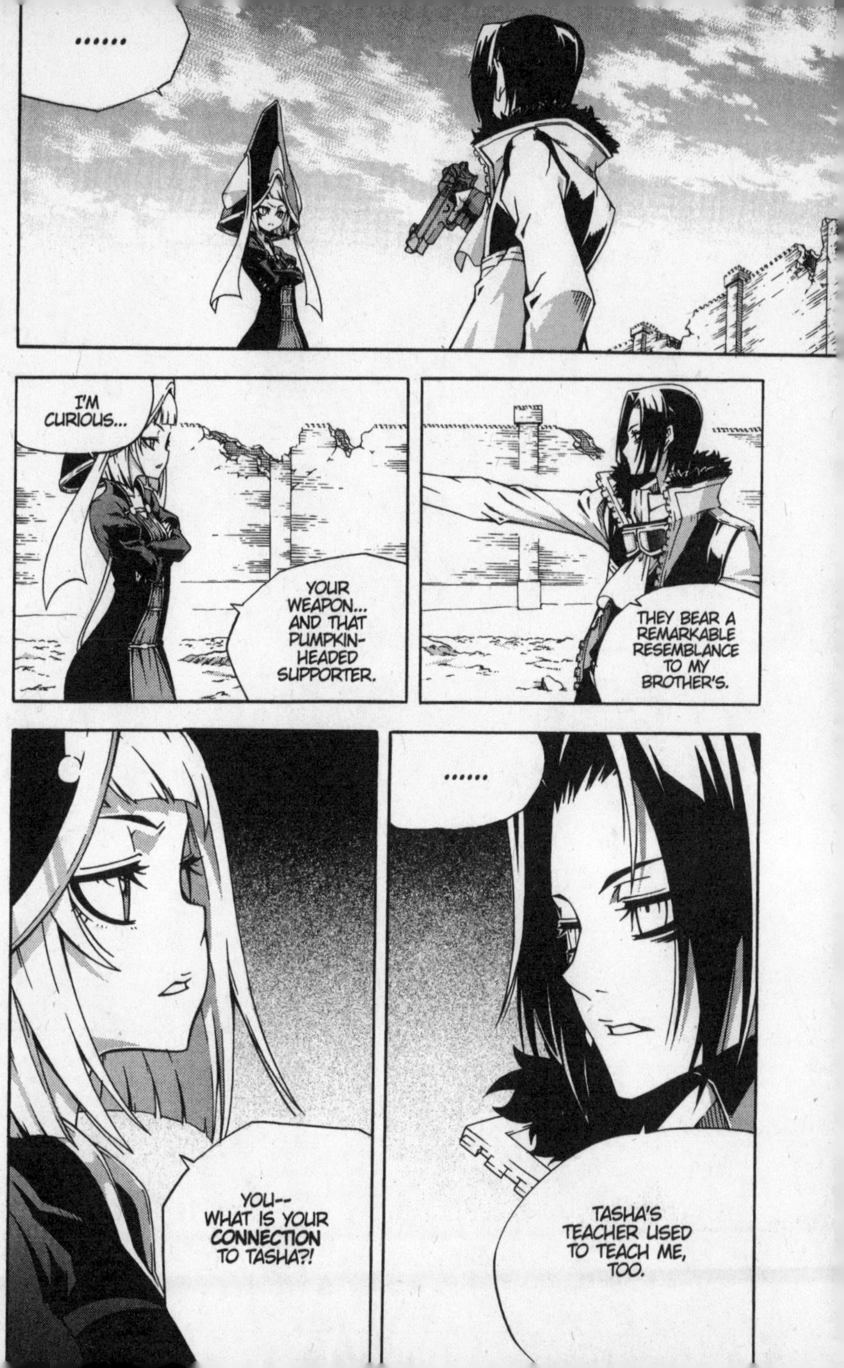
......
I'M CURIOUS...
YOUR WEAPON... AND THAT PUMPKIN-HEADED SUPPORTER.
THEY BEAR A REMARKABLE RESEMBLANCE TO MY BROTHER'S.
YOU-- WHAT IS YOUR CONNECTION TO TASHA?!
......
TASHA'S TEACHER USED TO TEACH ME, TOO.

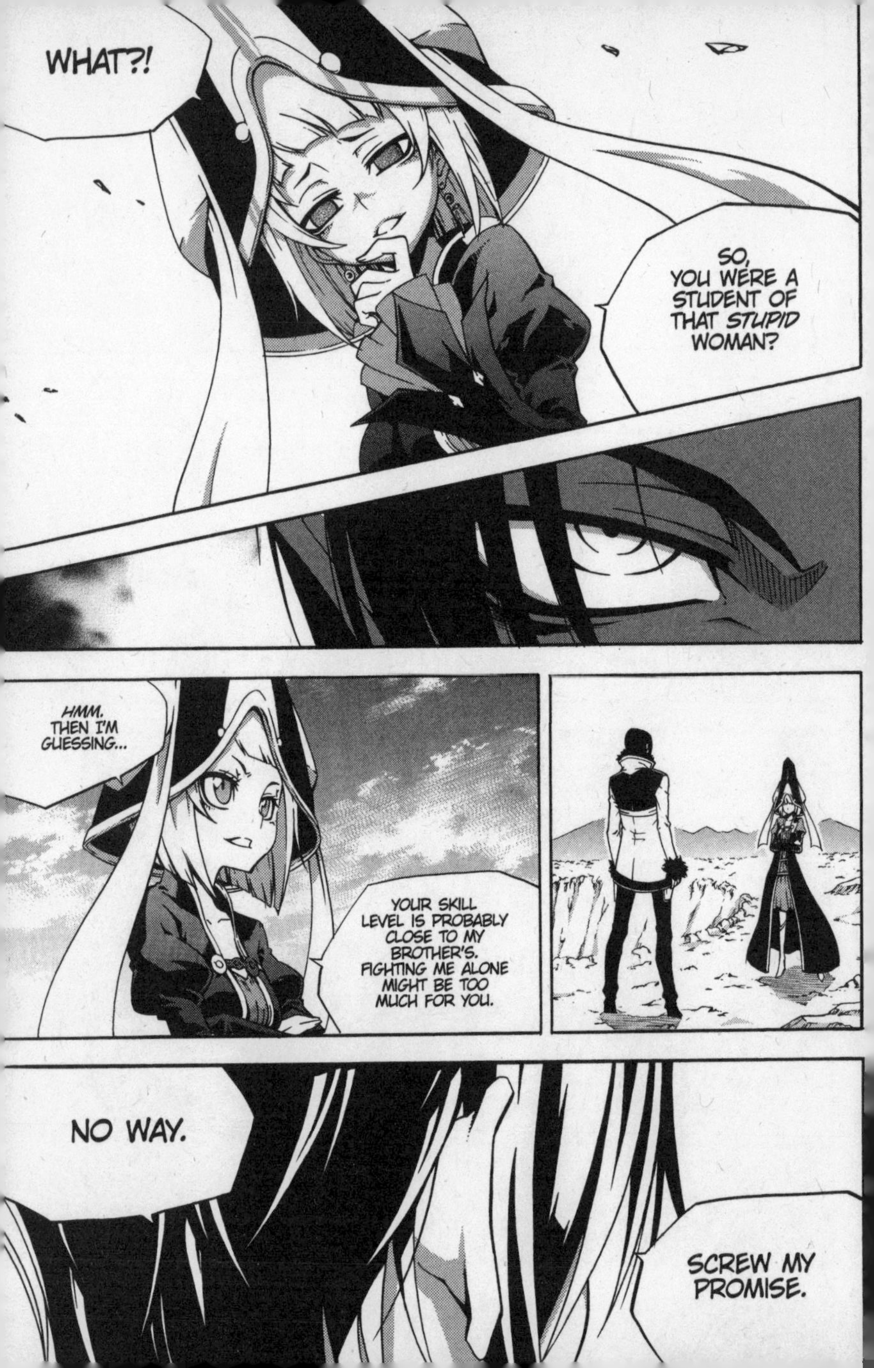
WHAT?!
SO, YOU WERE A STUDENT OF THAT *STUPID* WOMAN?
HMM. THEN I'M GUESSING...
YOUR SKILL LEVEL IS PROBABLY CLOSE TO MY BROTHER'S. FIGHTING ME ALONE MIGHT BE TOO MUCH FOR YOU.
NO WAY.
SCREW MY PROMISE.

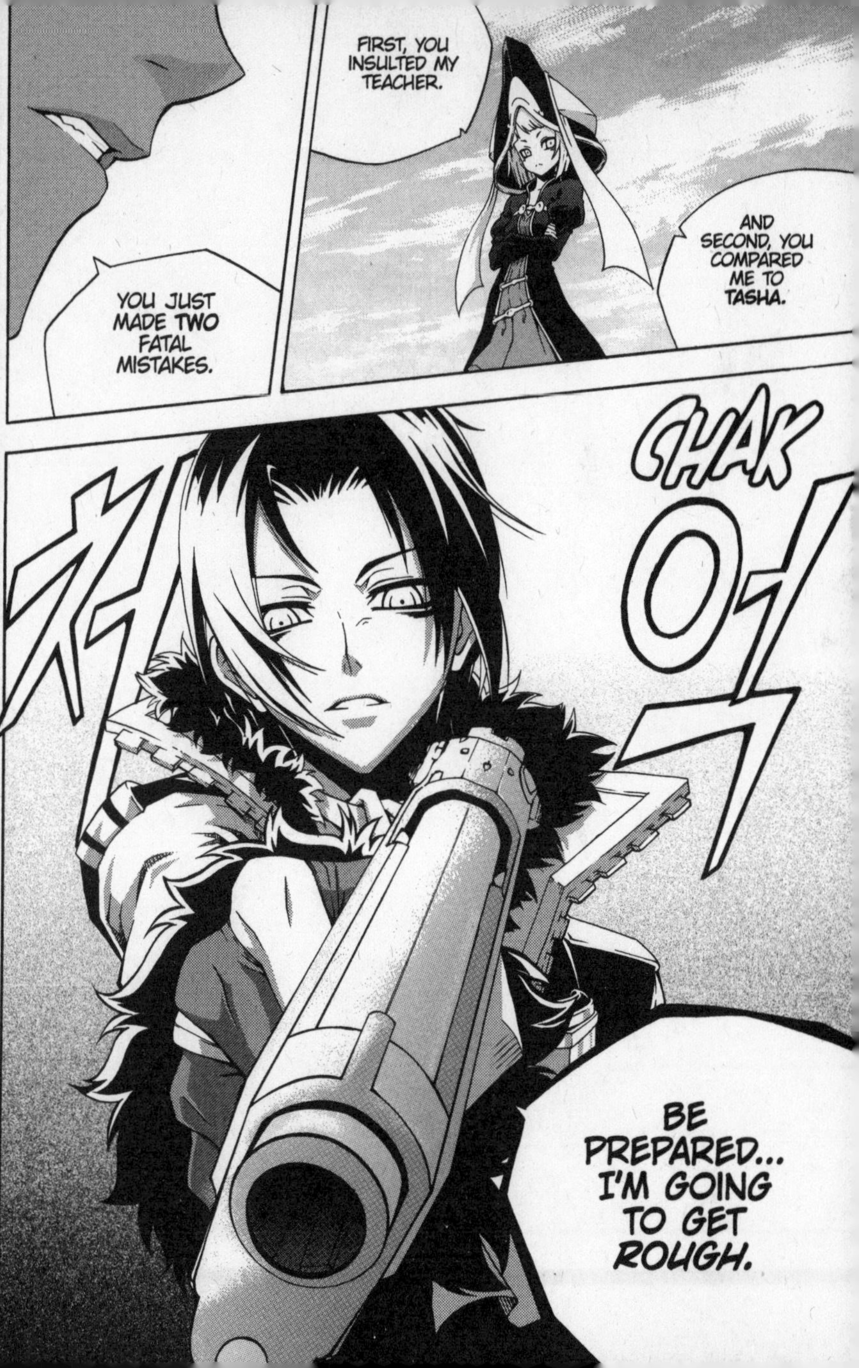

YOU JUST MADE TWO FATAL MISTAKES.
FIRST, YOU INSULTED MY TEACHER.
AND SECOND, YOU COMPARED ME TO TASHA.
CHAK
BE PREPARED... I'M GOING TO GET *ROUGH.*

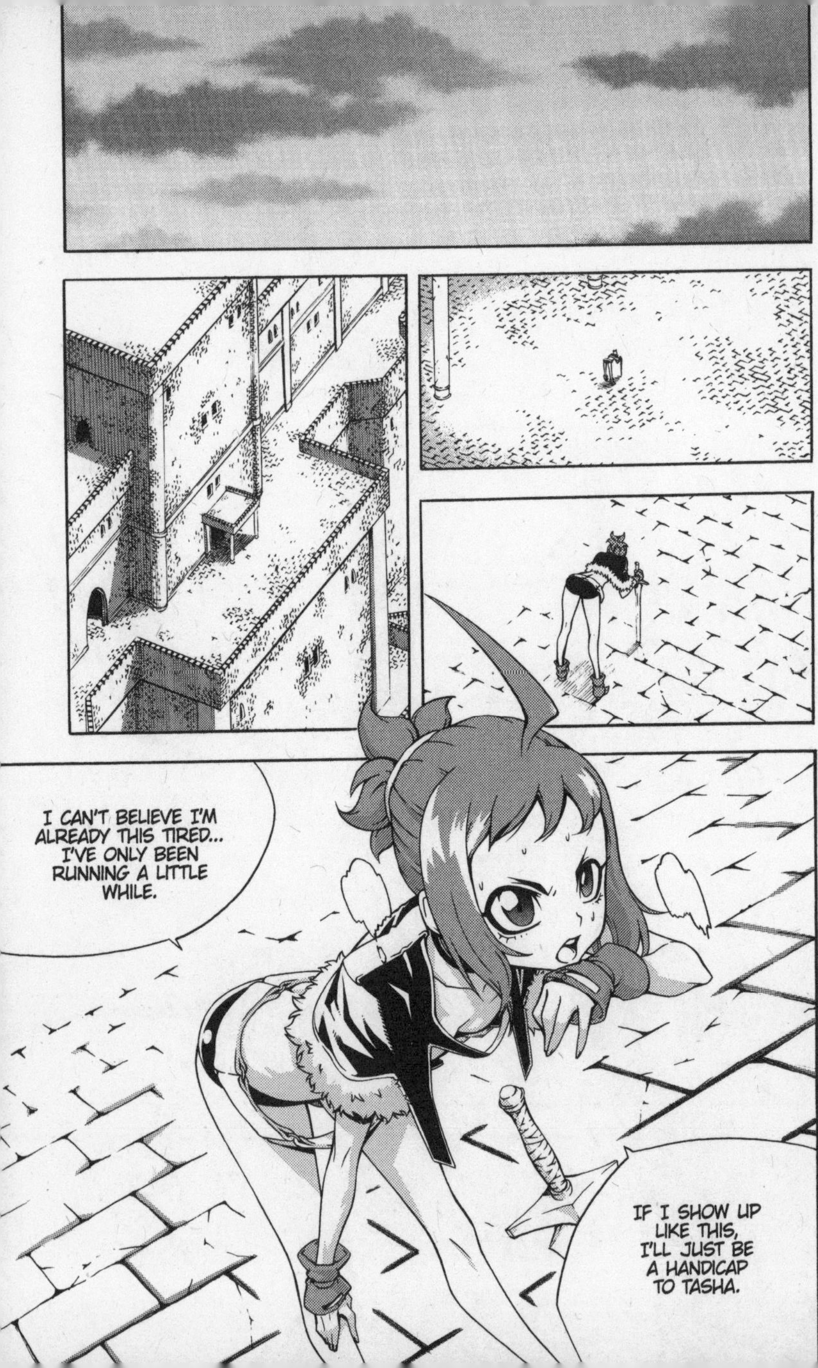

I CAN'T BELIEVE I'M ALREADY THIS TIRED... I'VE ONLY BEEN RUNNING A LITTLE WHILE.
IF I SHOW UP LIKE THIS, I'LL JUST BE A HANDICAP TO TASHA.

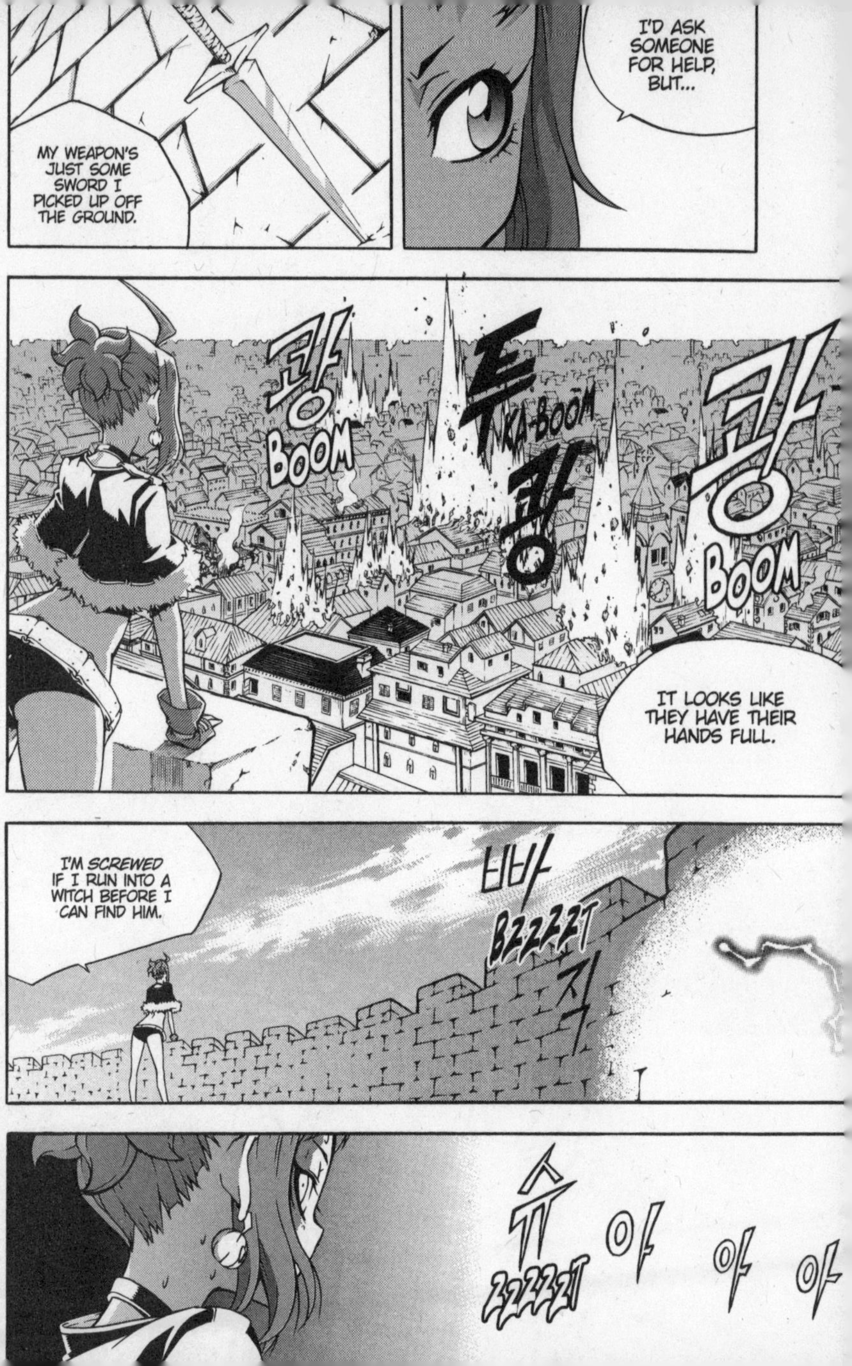
MY WEAPON'S JUST SOME SWORD I PICKED UP OFF THE GROUND.
I'D ASK SOMEONE FOR HELP, BUT...
쾅
BOOM
KA-BOOM
쾅
BOOM
IT LOOKS LIKE THEY HAVE THEIR HANDS FULL.
I'M *SCREWED* IF I RUN INTO A WITCH BEFORE I CAN FIND HIM.
BZZZZT
슈 아 아 아
ZZZZZT

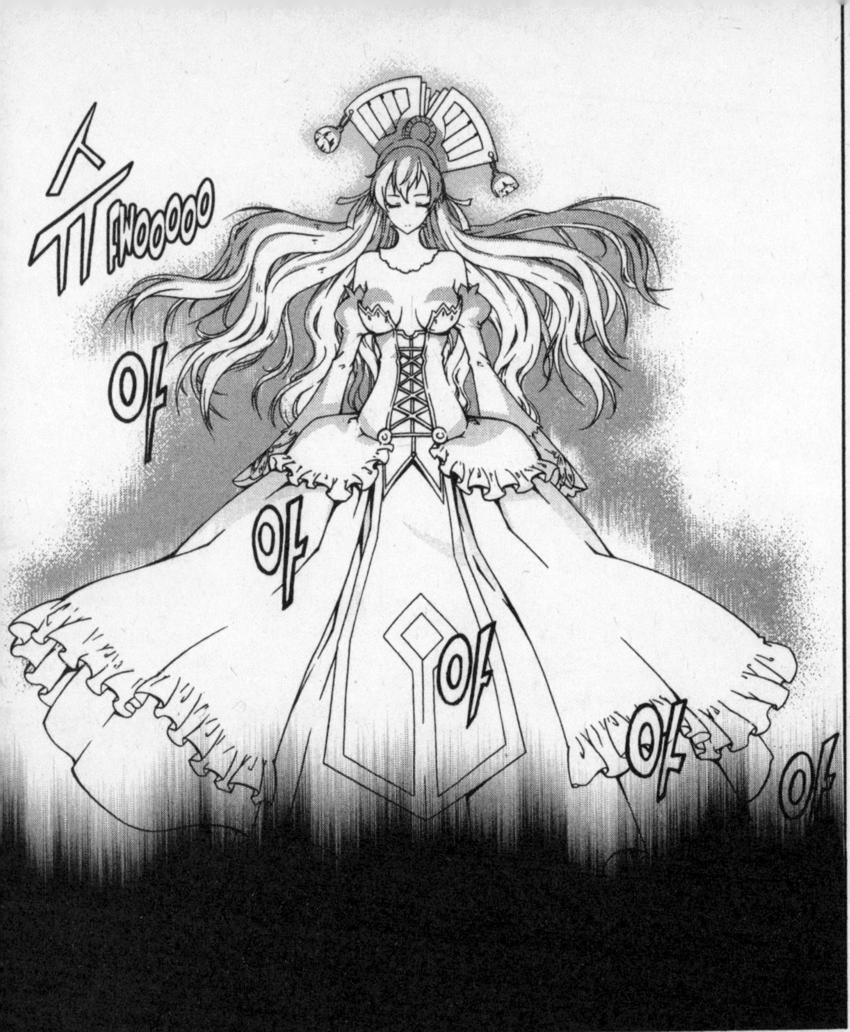
FWOOOOO
아
아
아
아
아
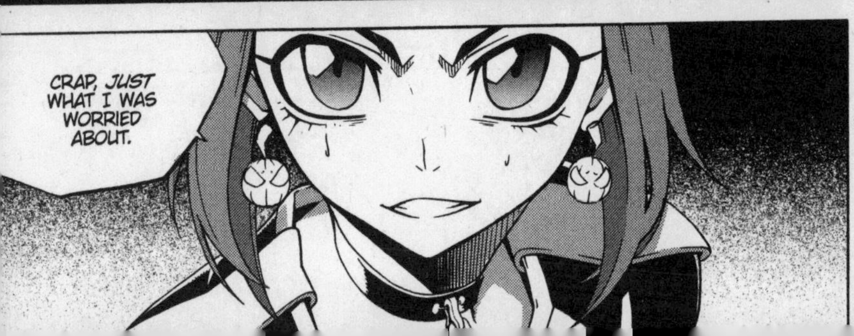
CRAP, JUST WHAT I WAS WORRIED ABOUT.

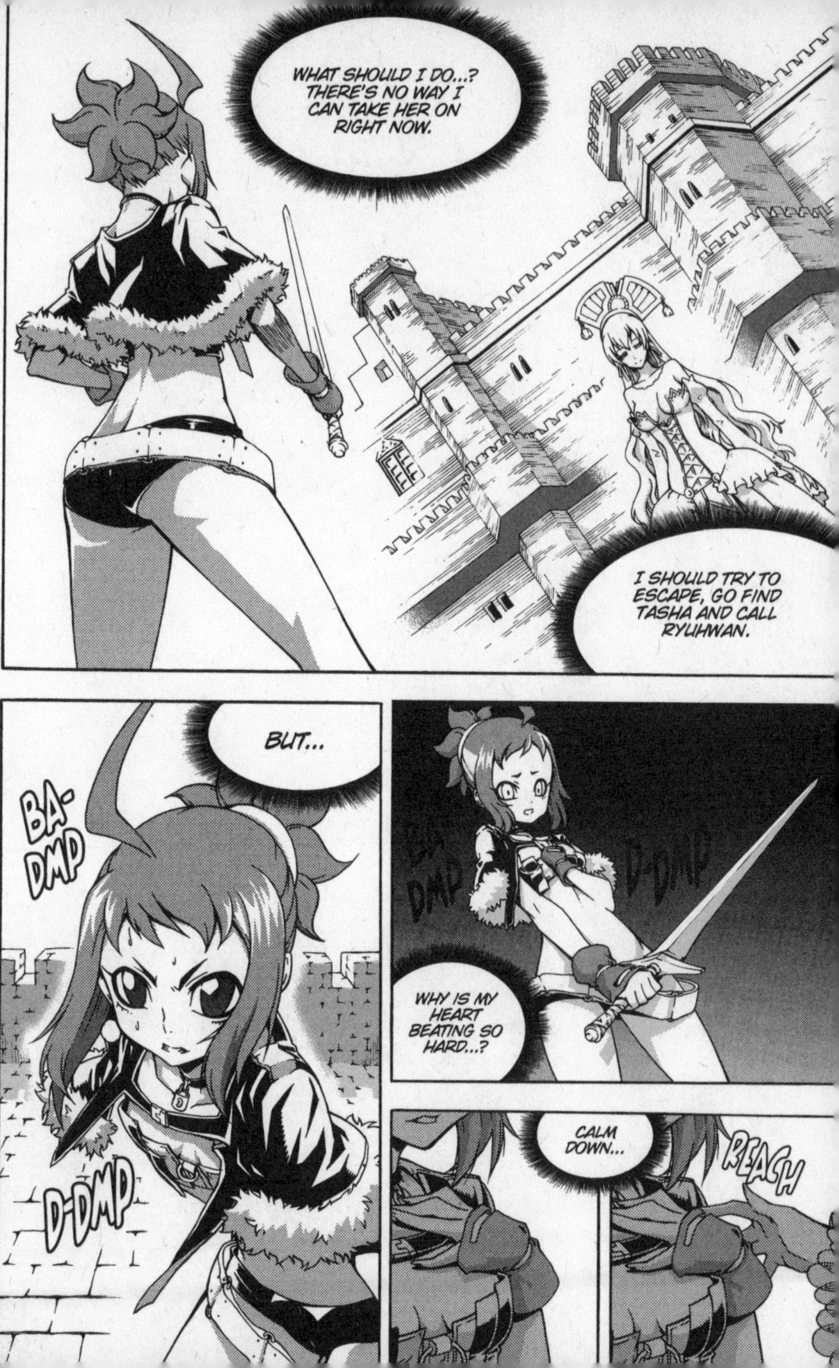
WHAT SHOULD I DO...? THERE'S NO WAY I CAN TAKE HER ON RIGHT NOW.
I SHOULD TRY TO ESCAPE, GO FIND TASHA AND CALL RYUHWAN.
BUT...
BA-DMP
D-DMP
BA-DMP
D-DMP
WHY IS MY HEART BEATING SO HARD...?
CALM DOWN...
REACH

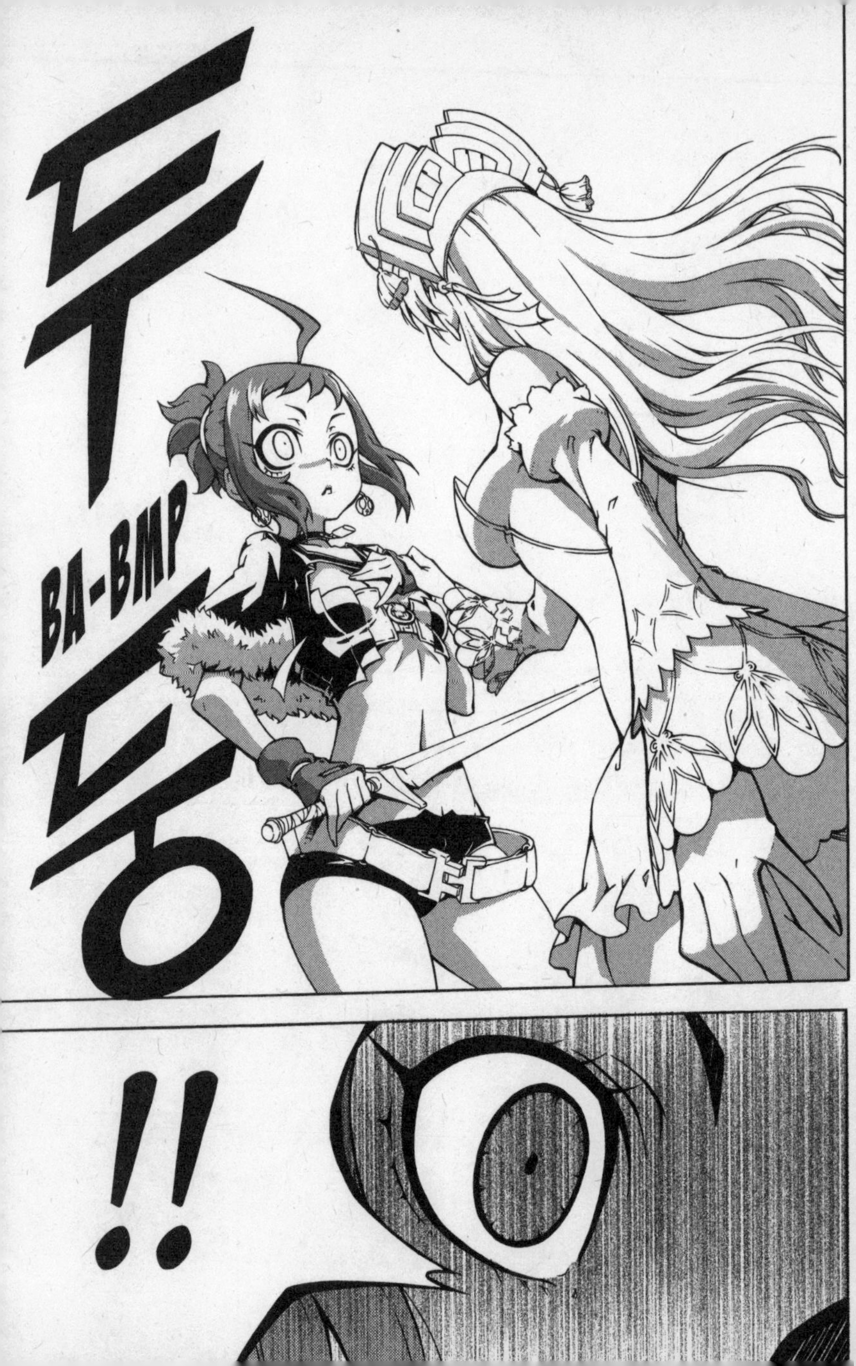
BA-BMP
!!

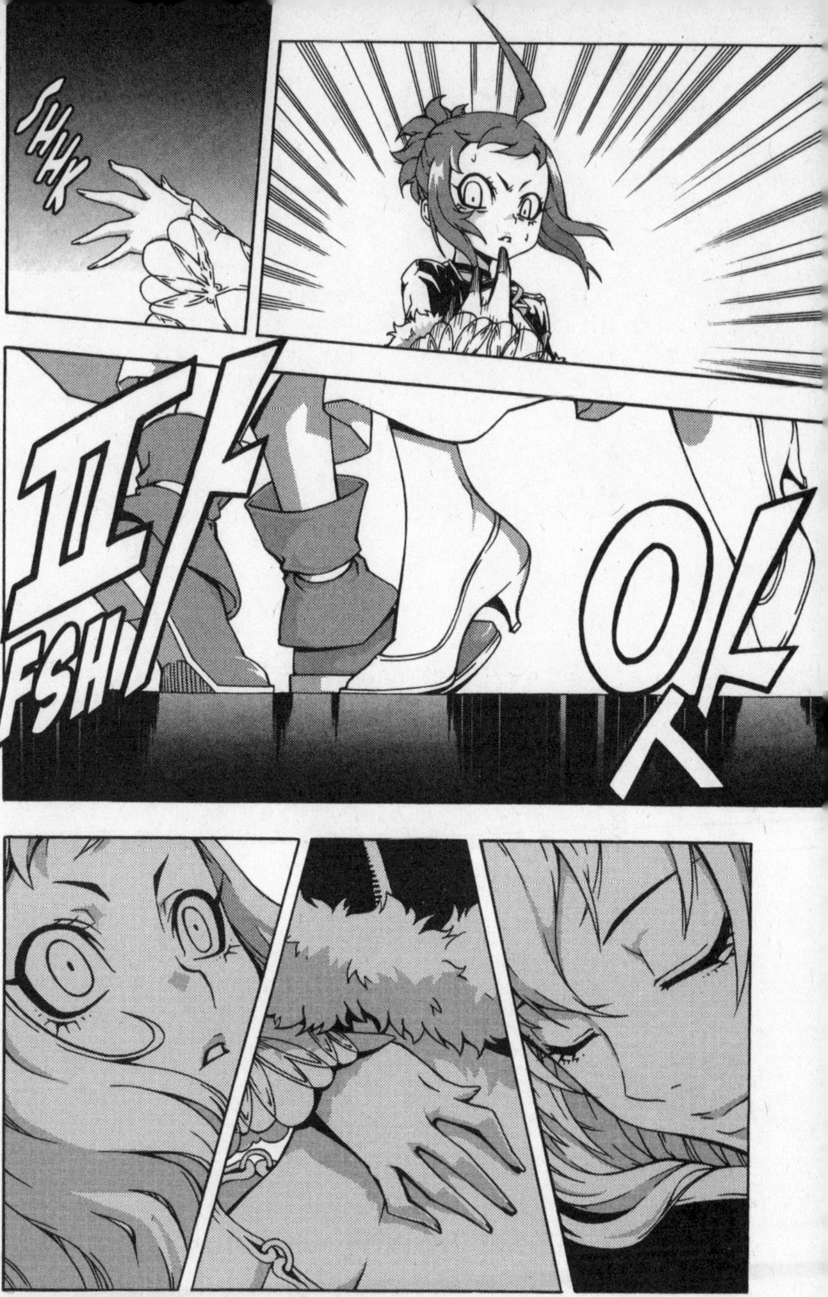
SHHK
피
FSH
잇

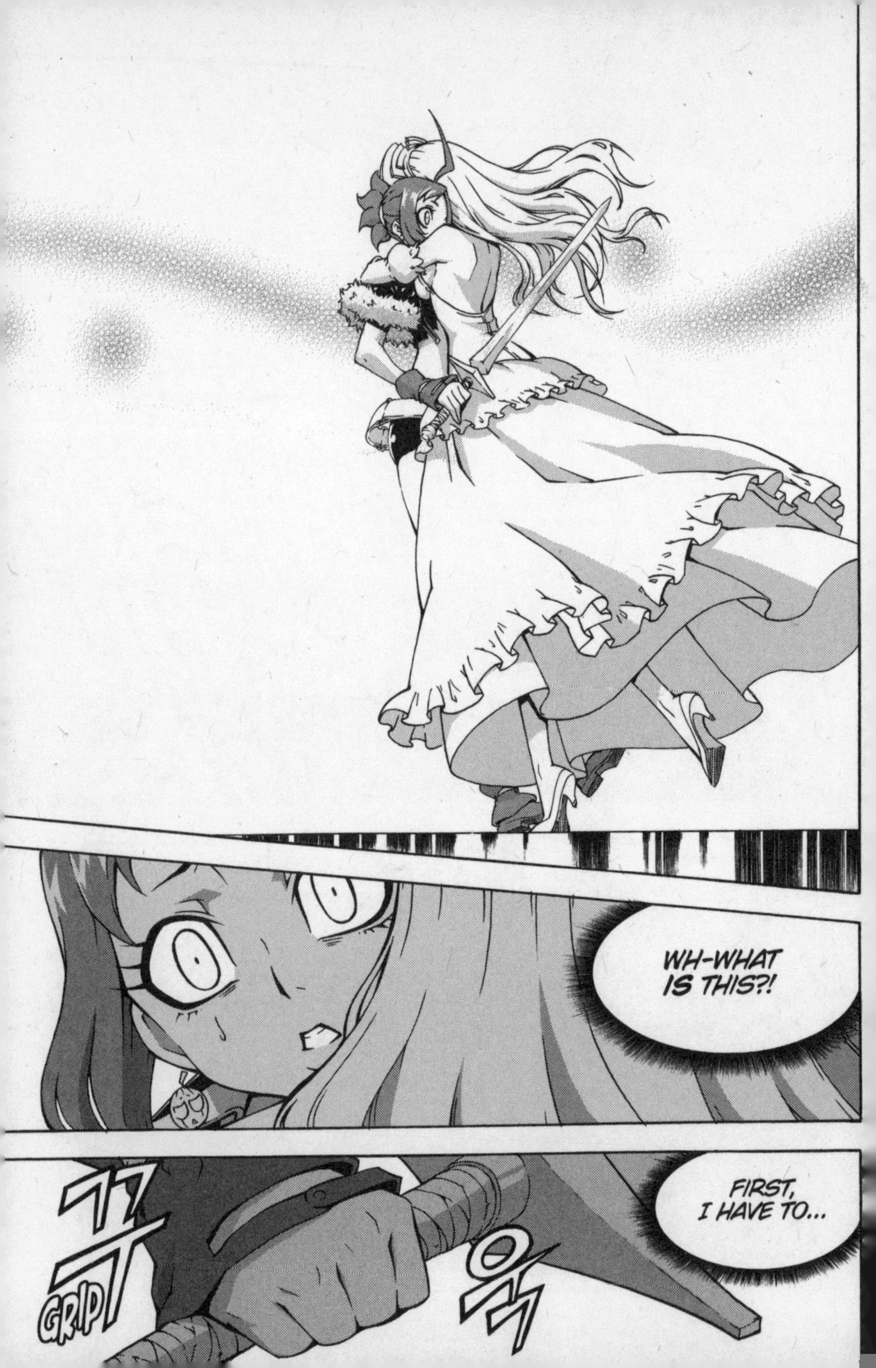
WH-WHAT IS THIS?!
GRIP
FIRST, I HAVE TO...

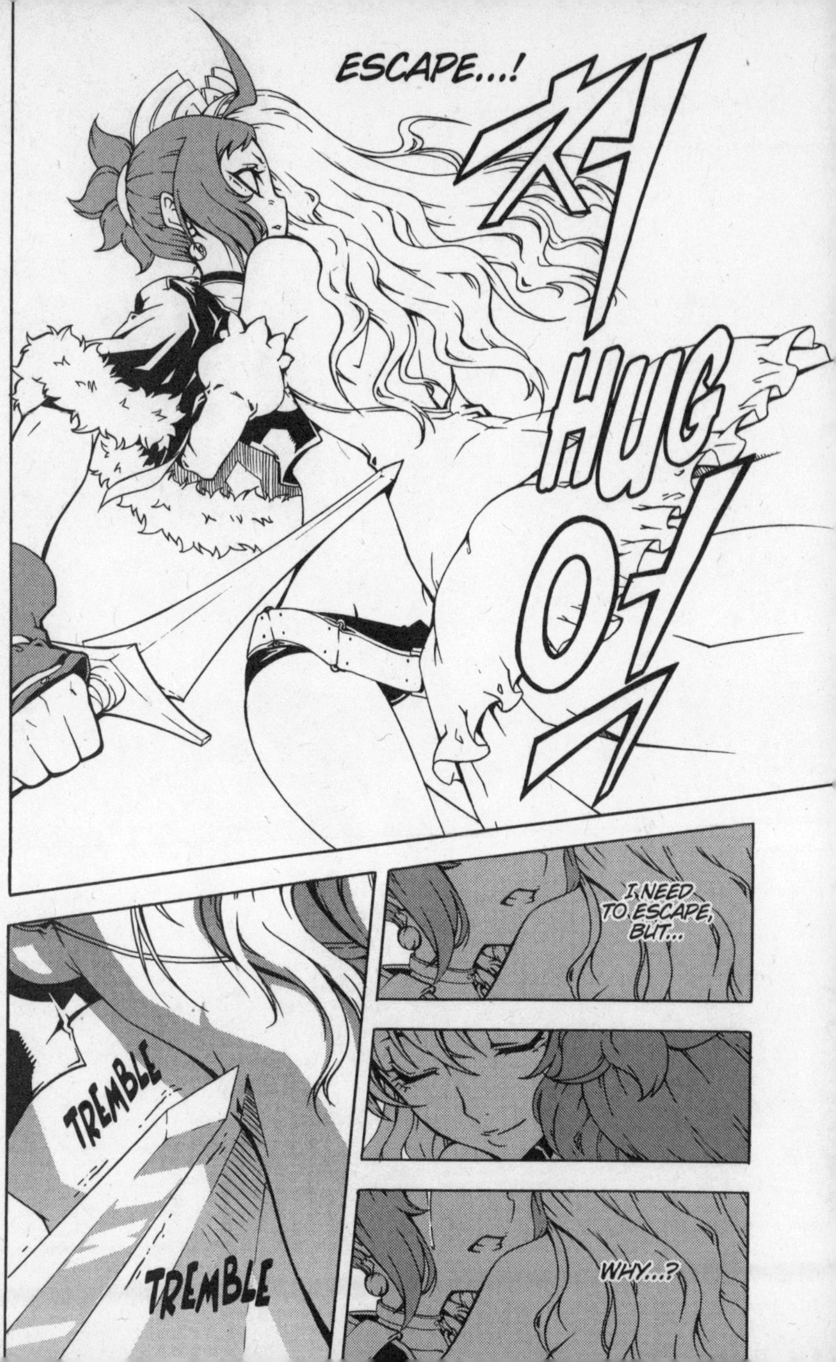
ESCAPE...!
HUG
TREMBLE
TREMBLE
I NEED TO ESCAPE, BUT...
WHY...?

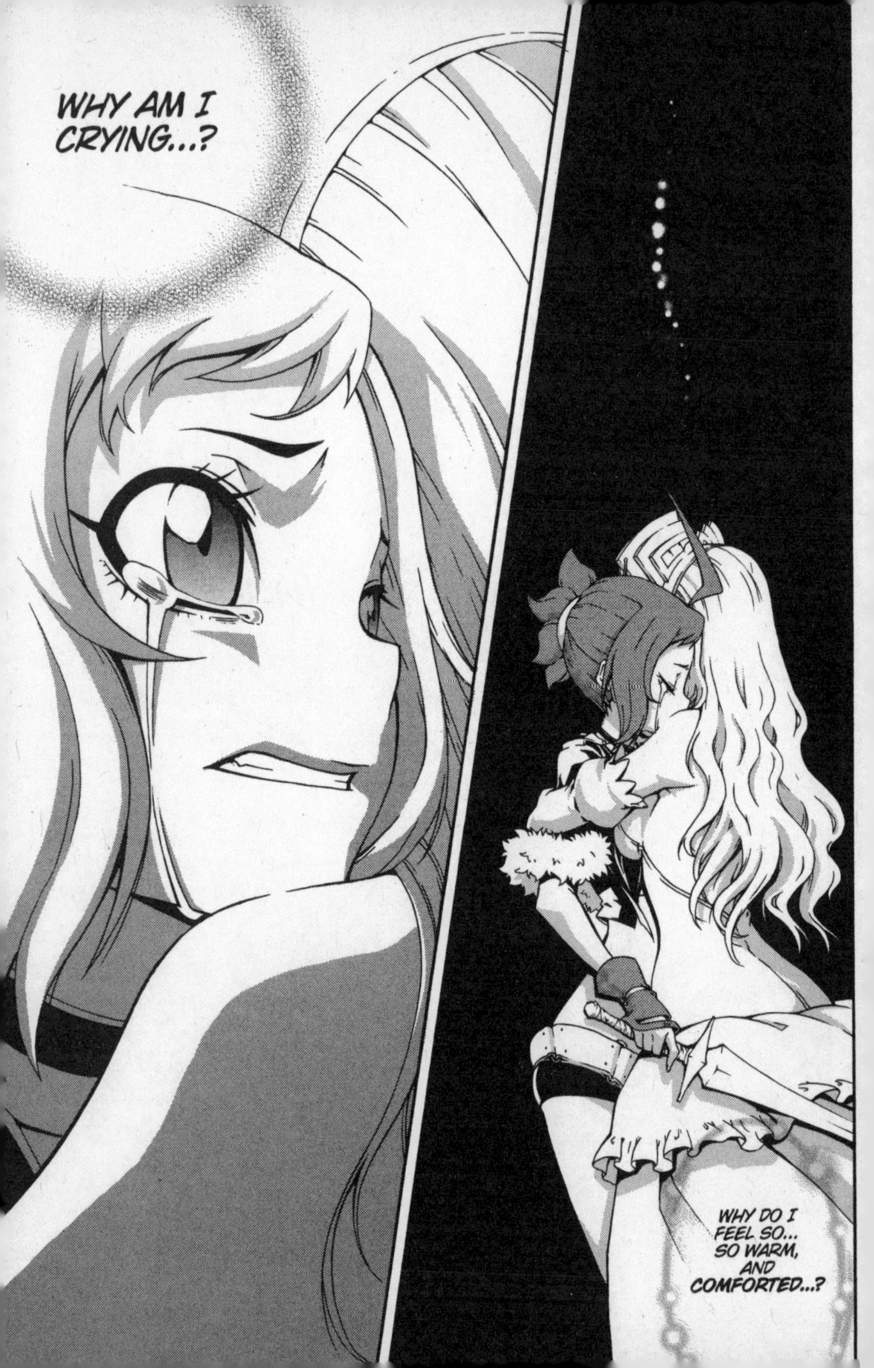
WHY DO I FEEL SO... SO WARM, AND COMFORTED...?
WHY AM I CRYING...?

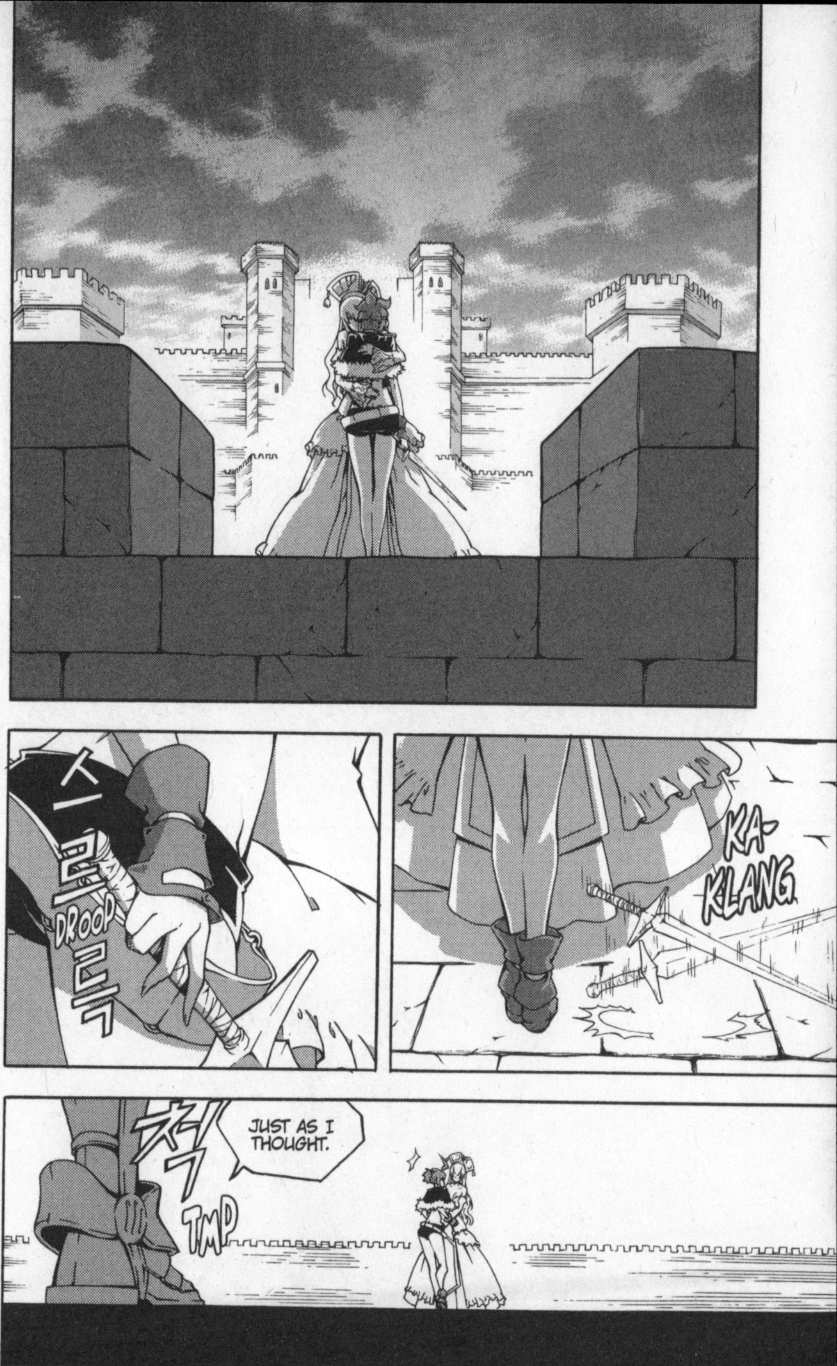
DROOP
KA-
KLANG
JUST AS I
THOUGHT.
TMP

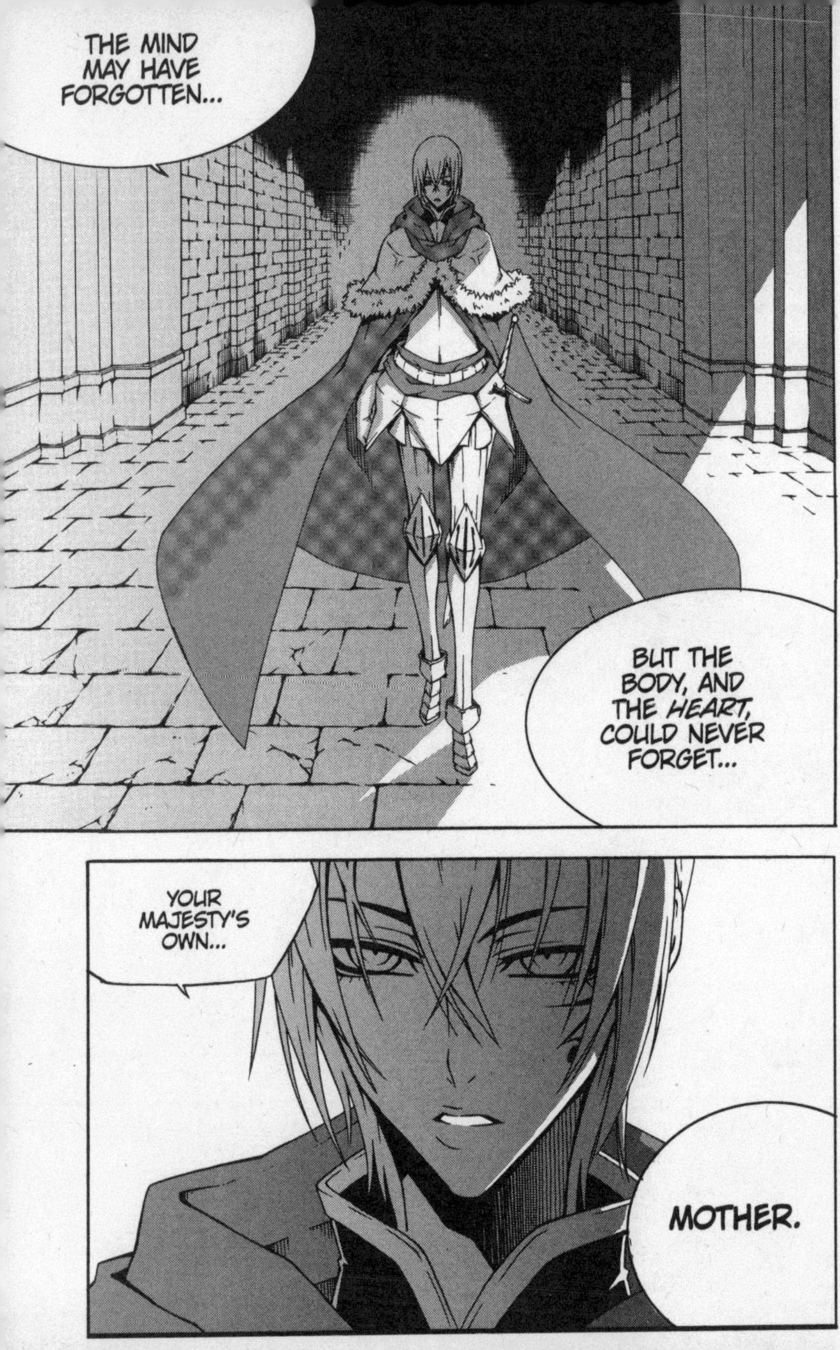
THE MIND MAY HAVE FORGOTTEN...
BUT THE BODY, AND THE *HEART*, COULD NEVER FORGET...
YOUR MAJESTY'S OWN...
MOTHER.

WITCH BUSTER

CHIN UP, NEPTIS! (3)

TINY BOOBS CLUB PRESIDENT NEPTIS
MS. PRESIDENT, I HAVE SOMETHING TO TELL YOU.
WHAT IS IT, MEMBER 1 (A.K.A. HALLOWEEN)?
I'M...THINKING OF LEAVING THE TINY BOOBS CLUB.
WHAT? WHY?! YOU MEET ALL OUR QUALIFICATIONS PERFECTLY-- WHY WOULD YOU LEAVE?!
LET ME INTRODUCE YOU...TO MY MOTHER.
BOING!
BOING!
SO...AS YOU CAN SEE, I HAVE HOPE FOR THE FUTURE NOW.
UH...

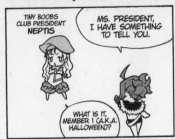

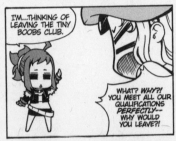

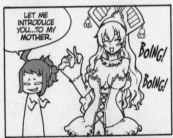

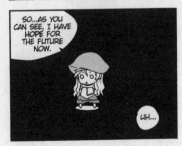

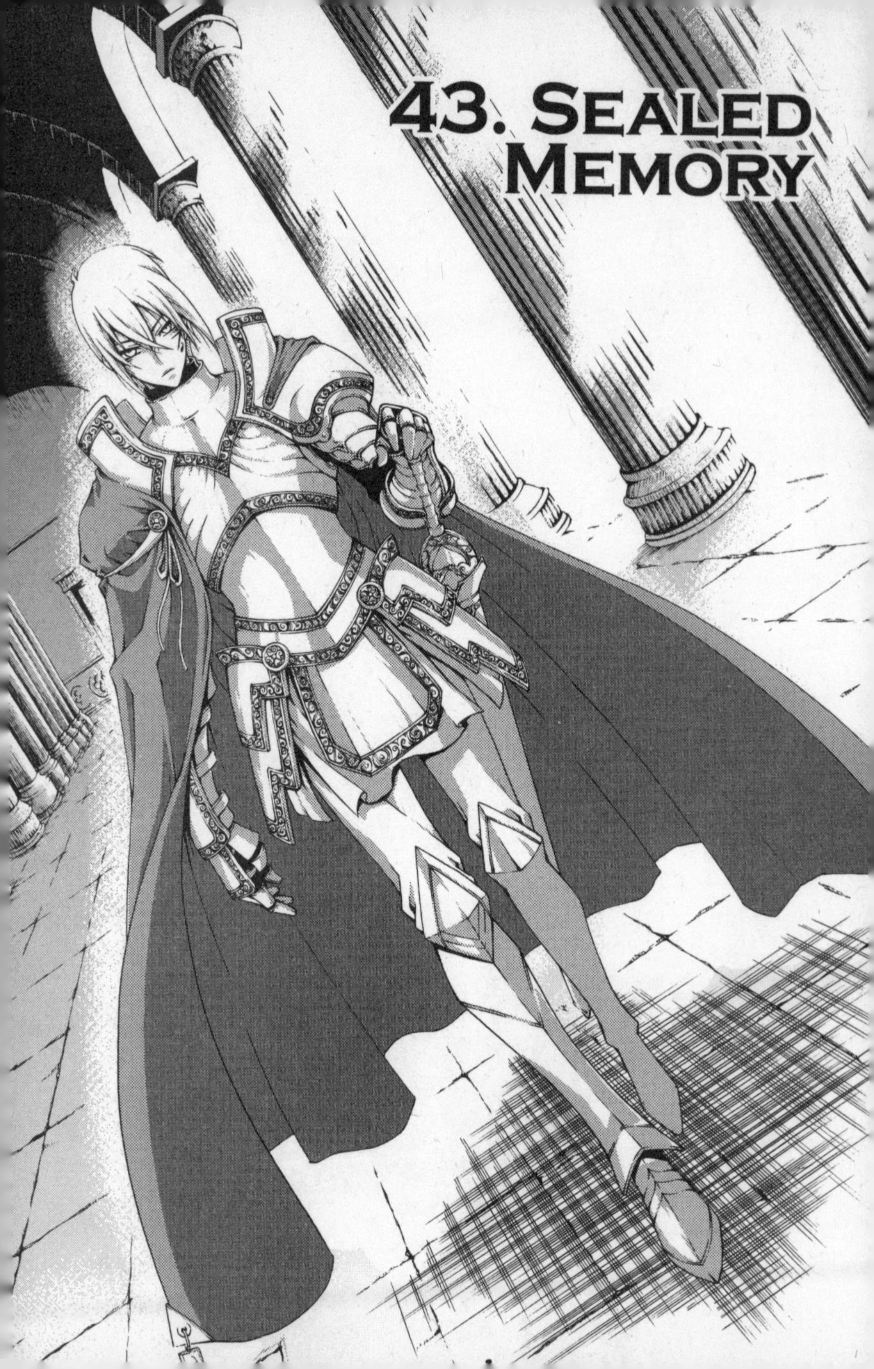
43. Sealed Memory

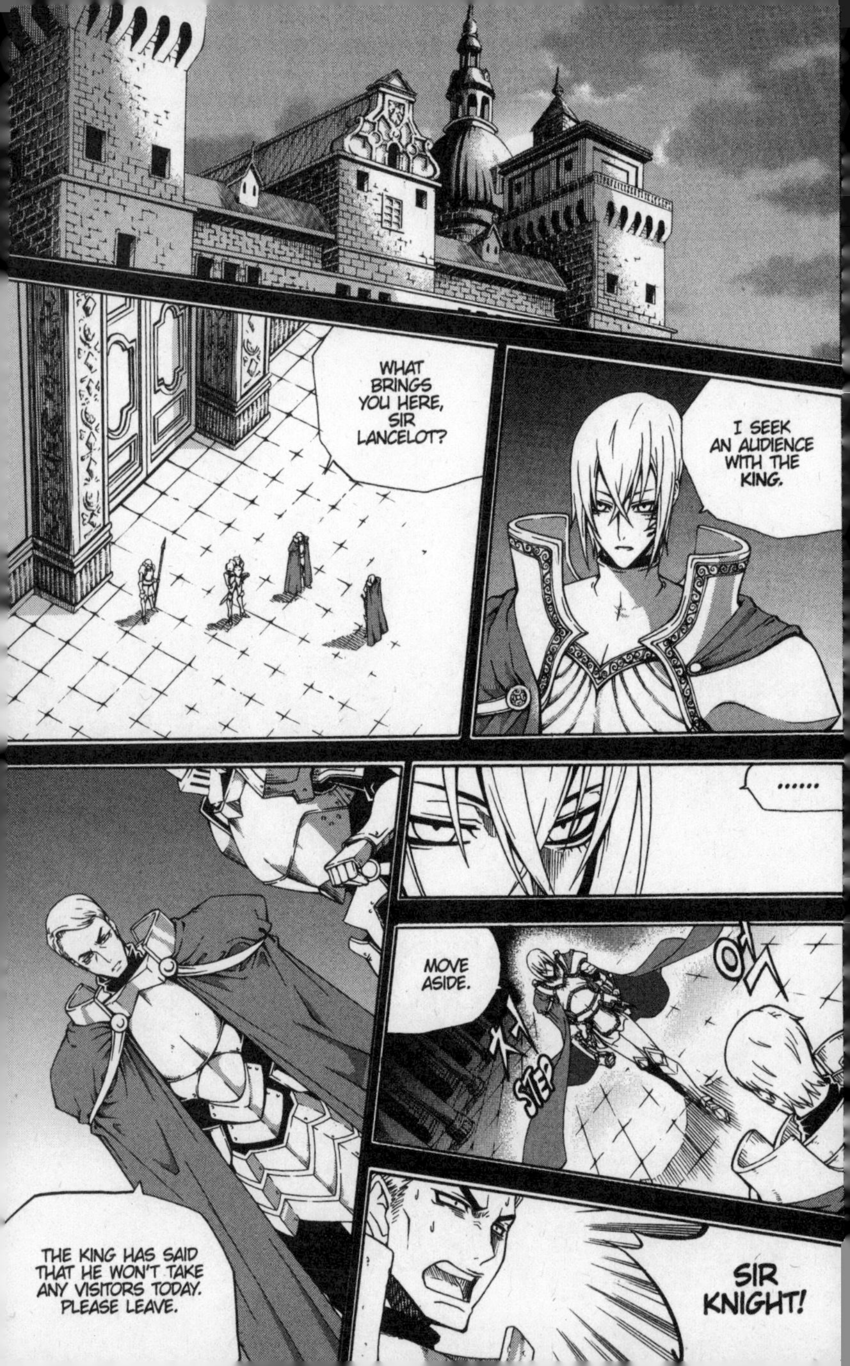
WHAT BRINGS YOU HERE, SIR LANCELOT?
I SEEK AN AUDIENCE WITH THE KING.
......
MOVE ASIDE.
STEP
THE KING HAS SAID THAT HE WON'T TAKE ANY VISITORS TODAY. PLEASE LEAVE.
SIR KNIGHT!

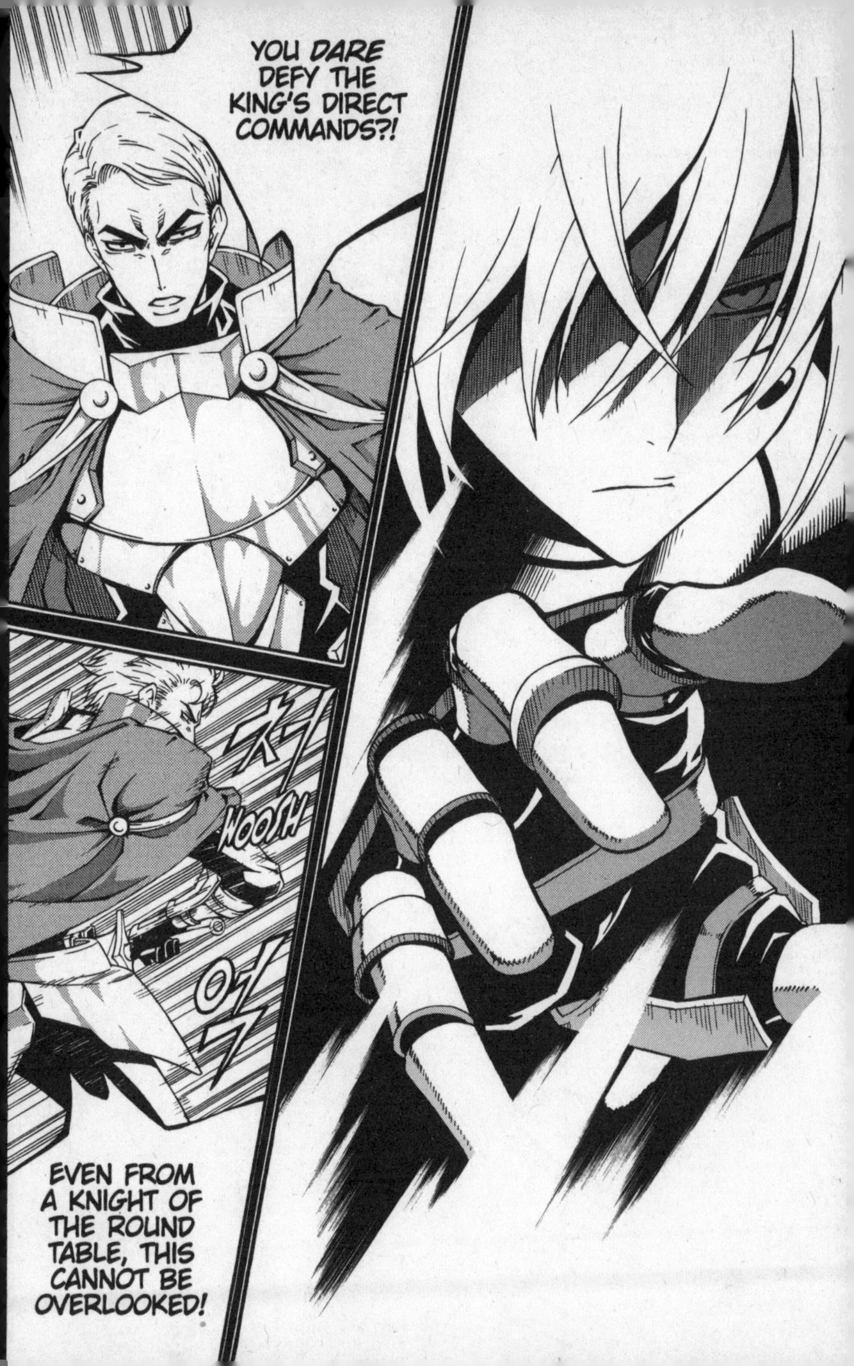
YOU DARE DEFY THE KING'S DIRECT COMMANDS?!
WOOSH
EVEN FROM A KNIGHT OF THE ROUND TABLE, THIS CANNOT BE OVERLOOKED!

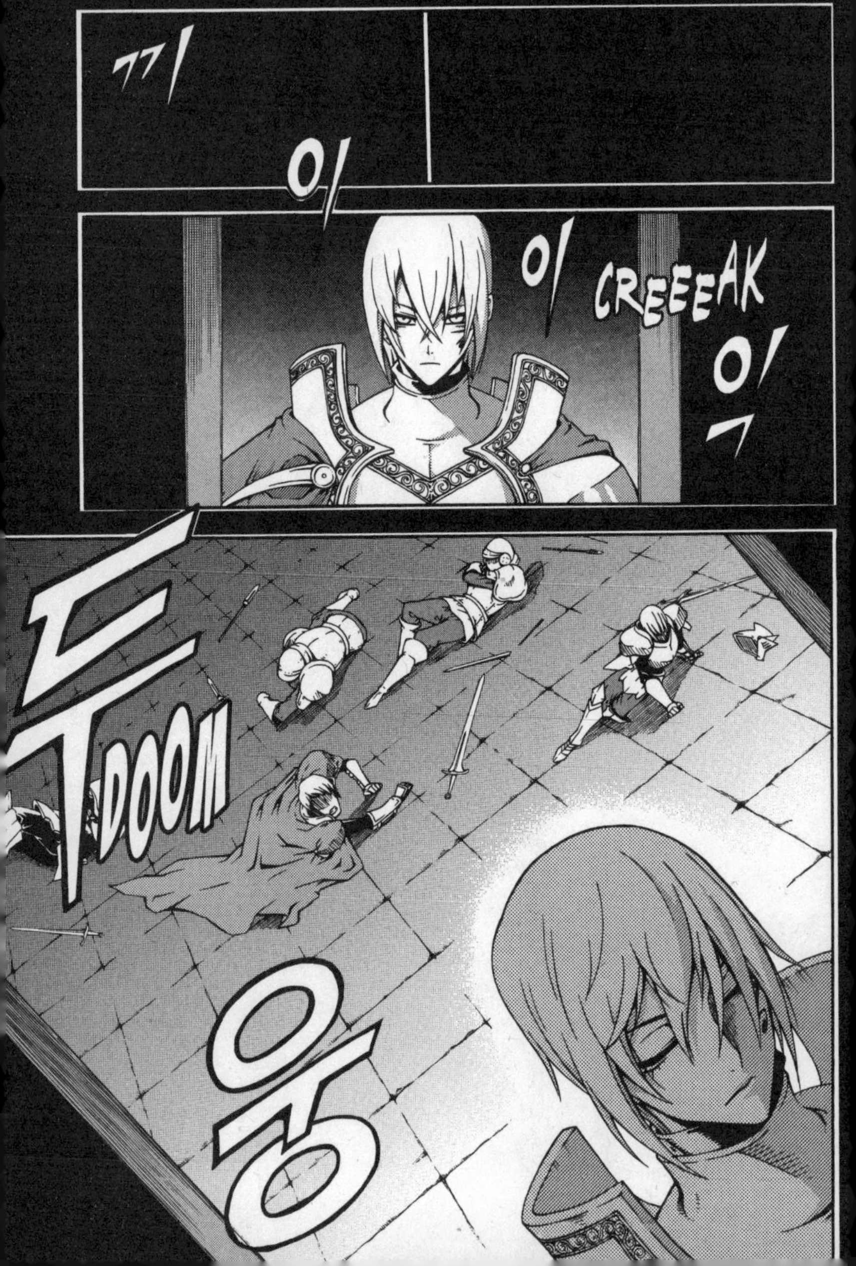
CREEEAK
DOOM

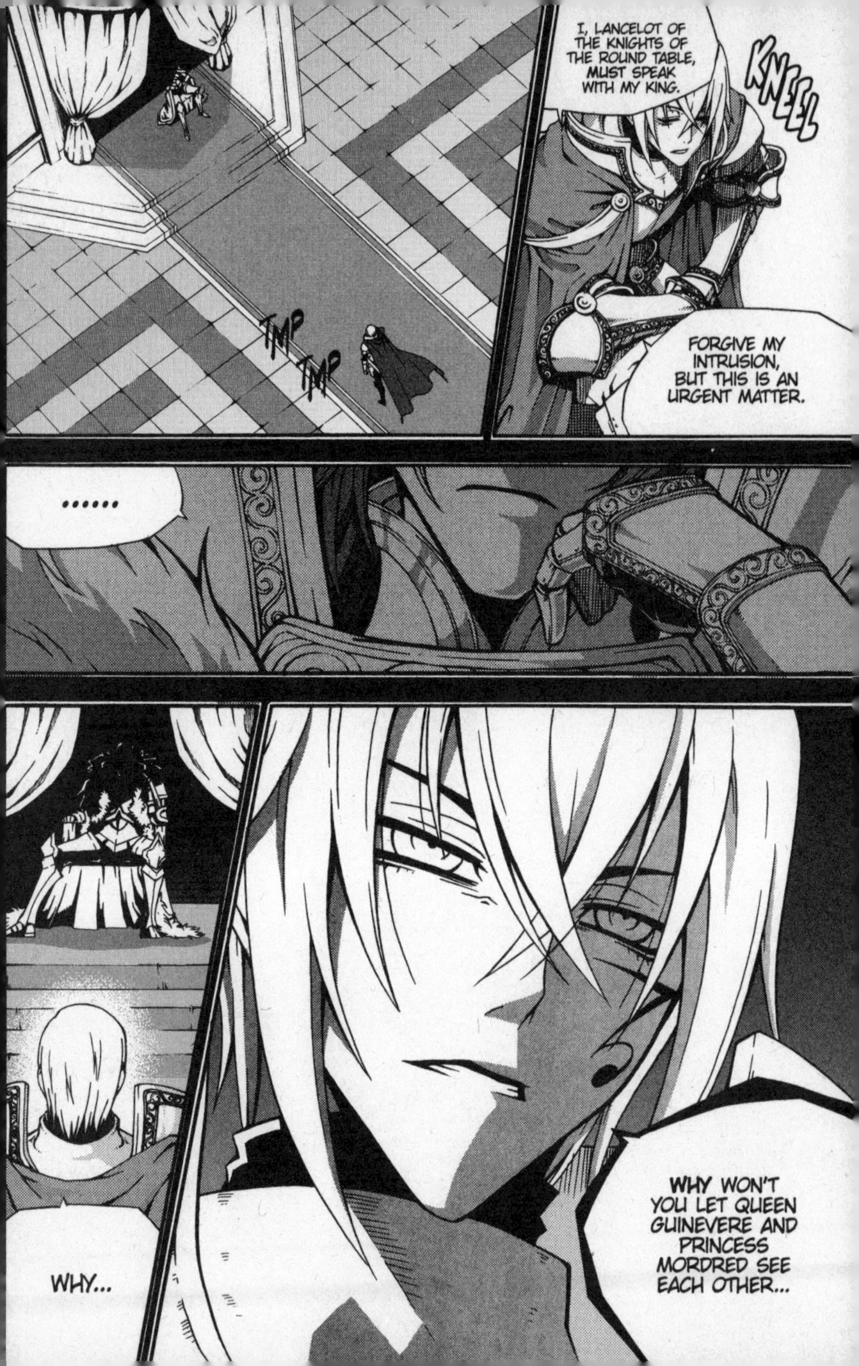
TMP TMP
I, LANCELOT OF THE KNIGHTS OF THE ROUND TABLE, MUST SPEAK WITH MY KING.
KNEEL
FORGIVE MY INTRUSION, BUT THIS IS AN URGENT MATTER.
......
WHY...
WHY WON'T YOU LET QUEEN GUINEVERE AND PRINCESS MORDRED SEE EACH OTHER...

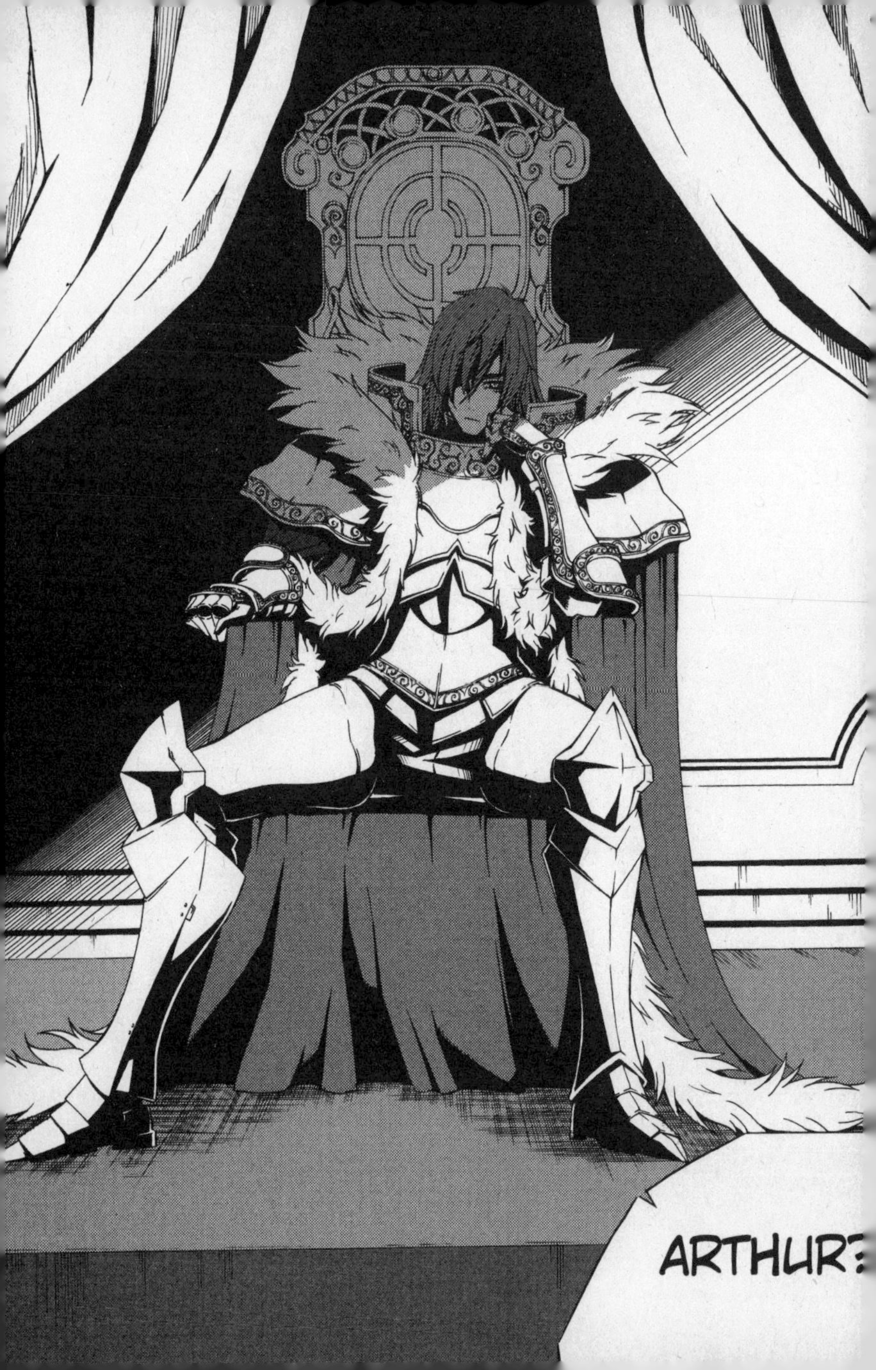
ARTHUR?

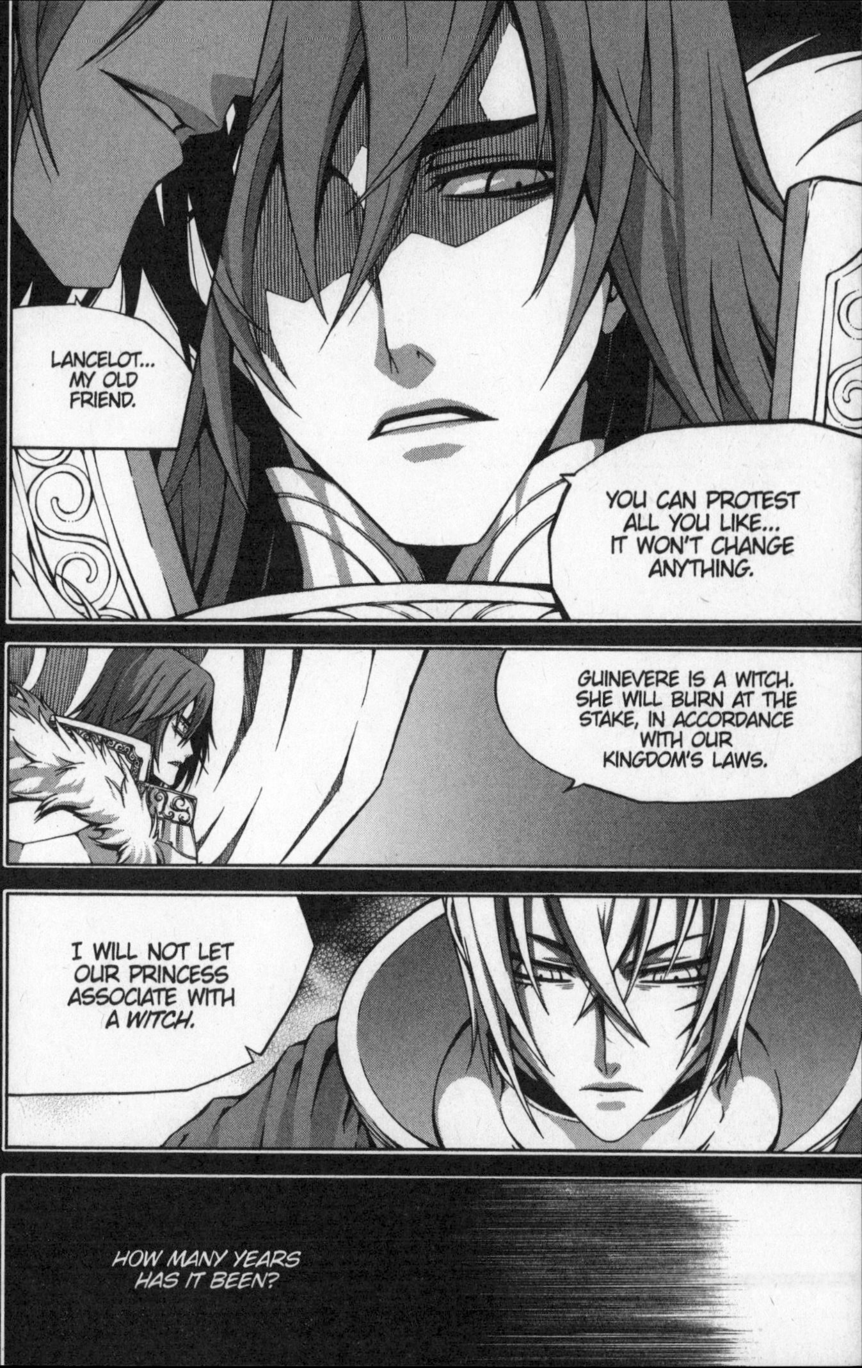
LANCELOT... MY OLD FRIEND.
YOU CAN PROTEST ALL YOU LIKE... IT WON'T CHANGE ANYTHING.
GUINEVERE IS A WITCH. SHE WILL BURN AT THE STAKE, IN ACCORDANCE WITH OUR KINGDOM'S LAWS.
I WILL NOT LET OUR PRINCESS ASSOCIATE WITH A *WITCH*.
HOW MANY YEARS HAS IT BEEN?

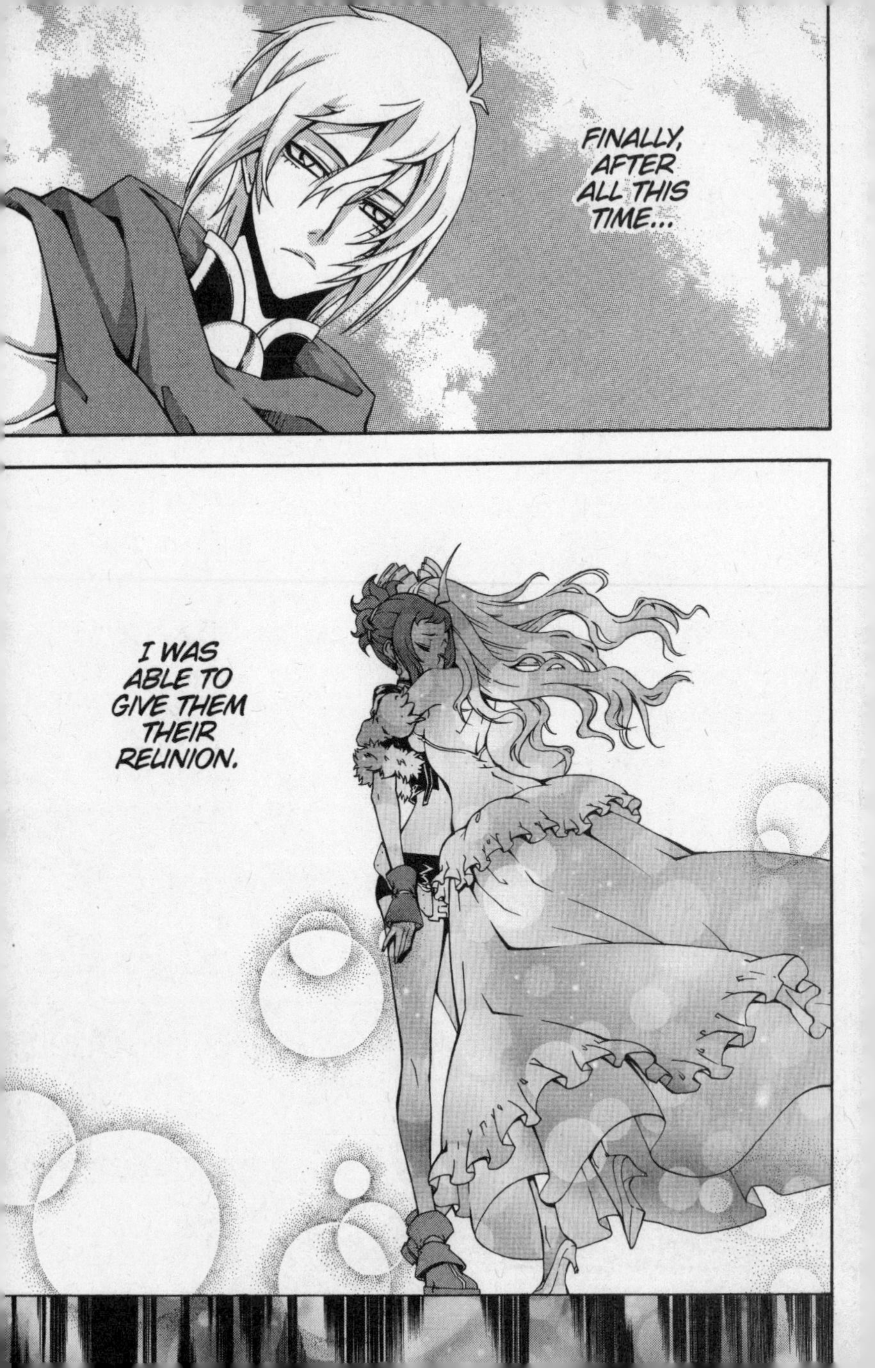
FINALLY, AFTER ALL THIS TIME...
I WAS ABLE TO GIVE THEM THEIR REUNION.

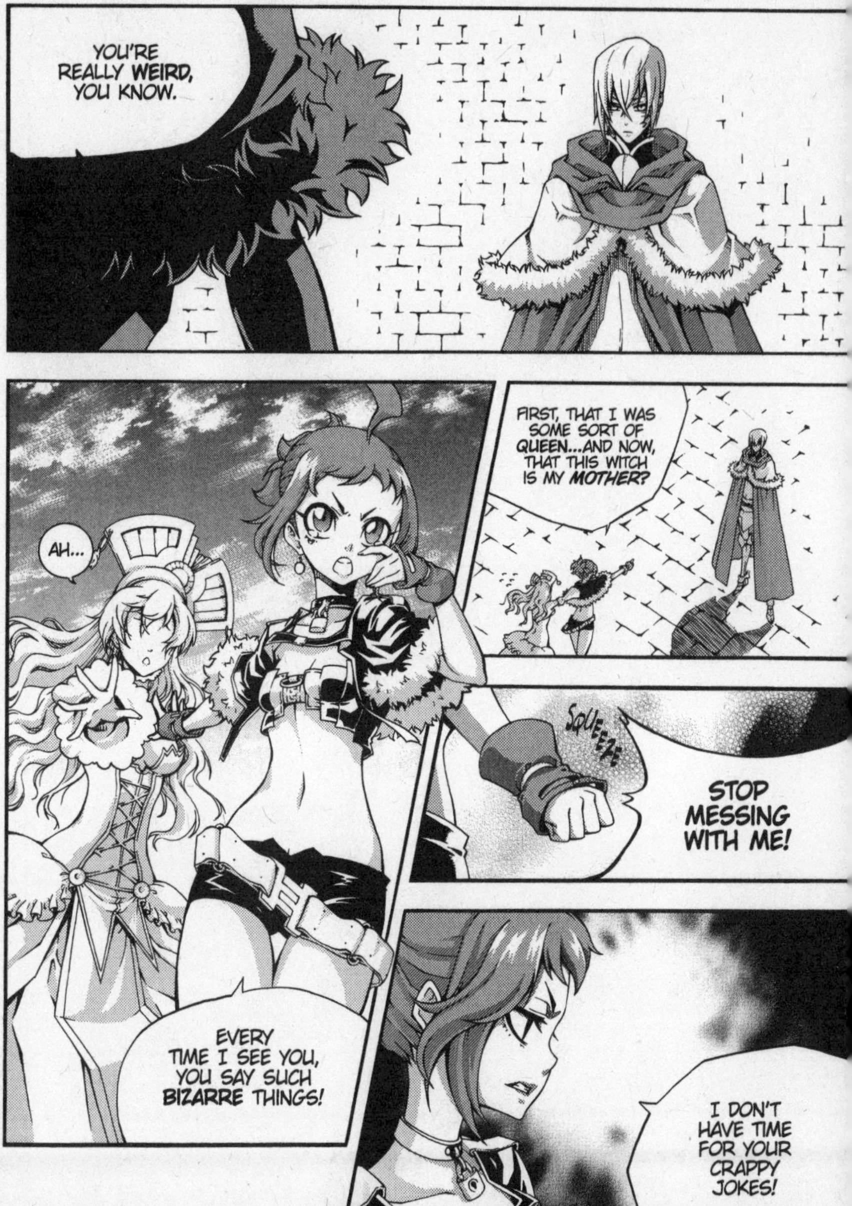
YOU'RE REALLY WEIRD, YOU KNOW.
AH...
EVERY TIME I SEE YOU, YOU SAY SUCH BIZARRE THINGS!
FIRST, THAT I WAS SOME SORT OF QUEEN...AND NOW, THAT THIS WITCH IS MY MOTHER?
SQUEEEZE
STOP MESSING WITH ME!
I DON'T HAVE TIME FOR YOUR CRAPPY JOKES!

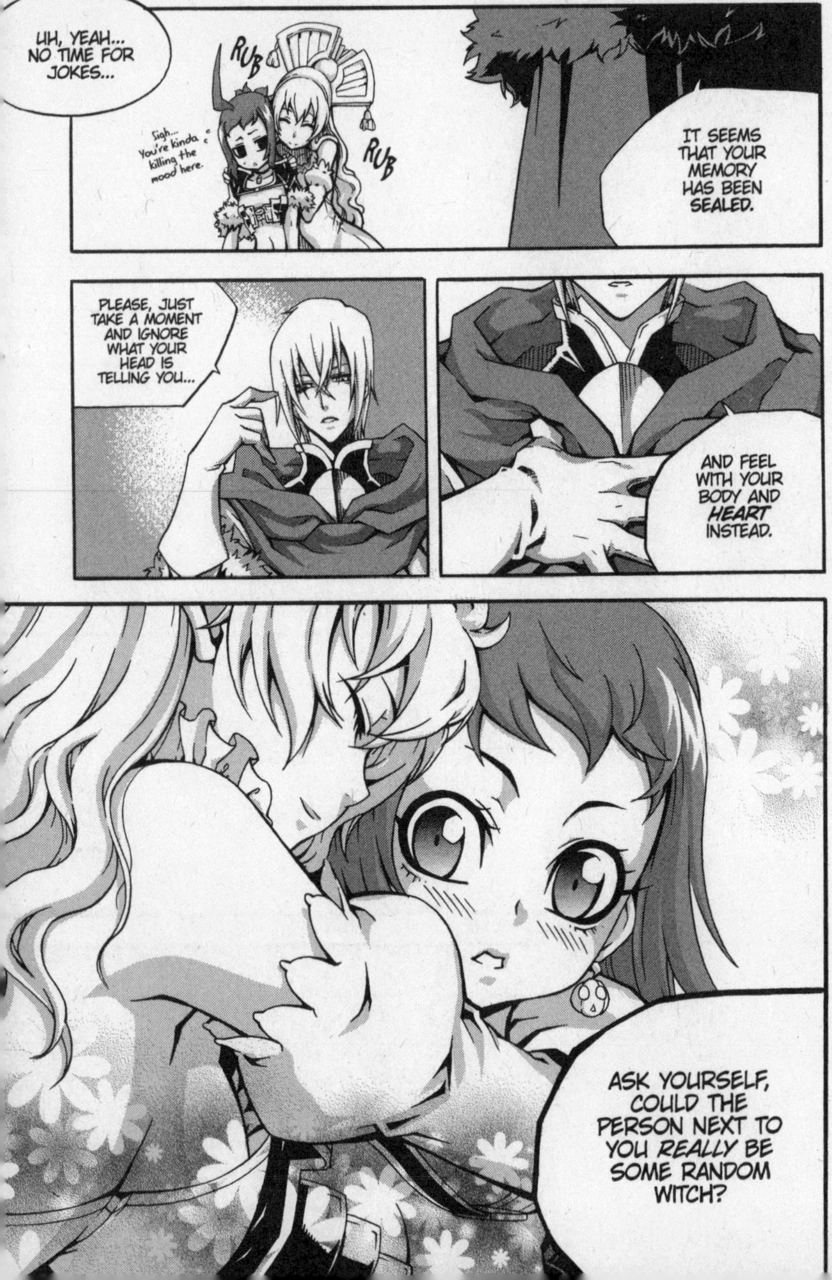
UH, YEAH... NO TIME FOR JOKES...
RUB
Sigh... You're kinda killing the mood here.
RUB
IT SEEMS THAT YOUR MEMORY HAS BEEN SEALED.
PLEASE, JUST TAKE A MOMENT AND IGNORE WHAT YOUR HEAD IS TELLING YOU...
AND FEEL WITH YOUR BODY AND *HEART* INSTEAD.
ASK YOURSELF, COULD THE PERSON NEXT TO YOU *REALLY* BE SOME RANDOM WITCH?

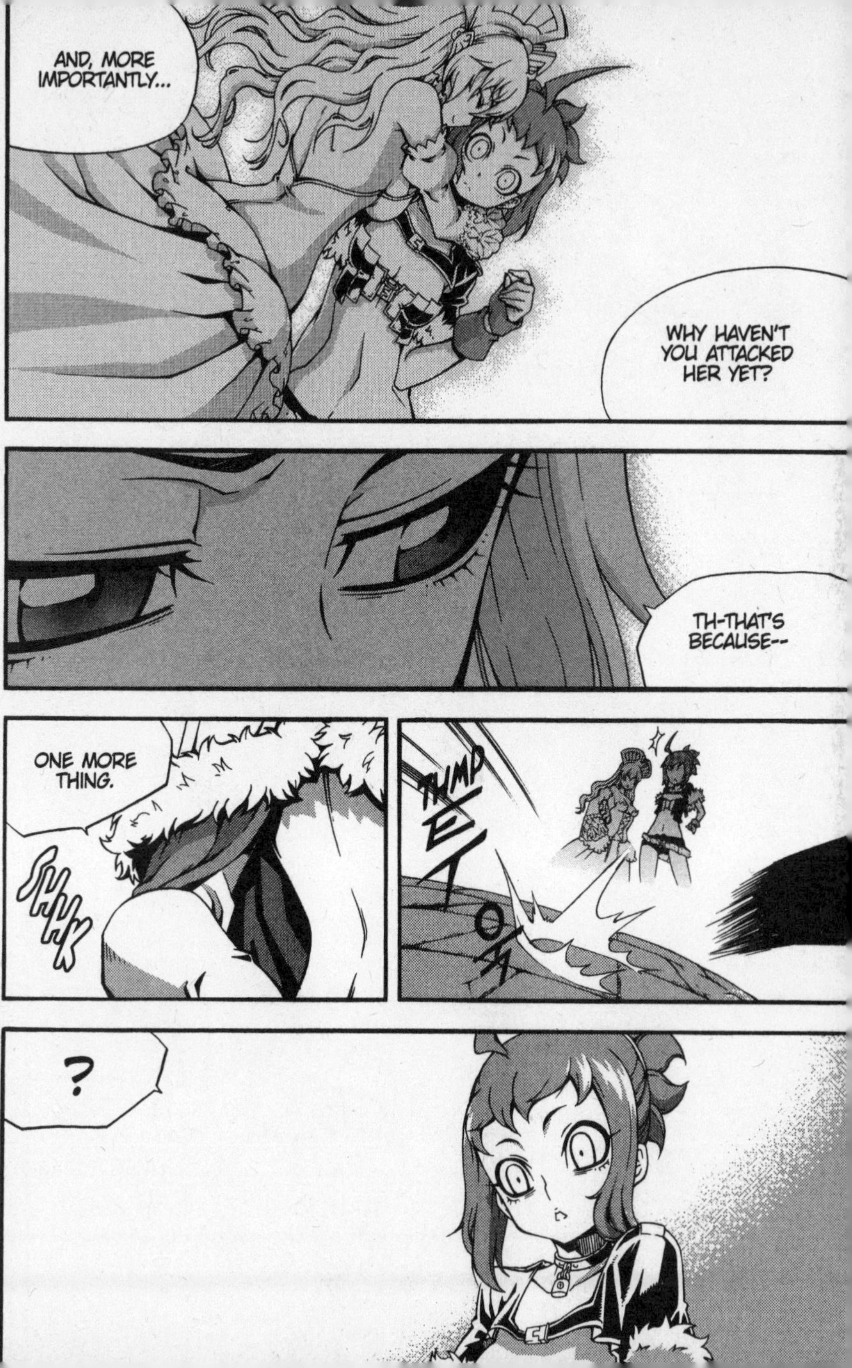
AND, MORE IMPORTANTLY...
WHY HAVEN'T YOU ATTACKED HER YET?
TH-THAT'S BECAUSE--
ONE MORE THING.
?

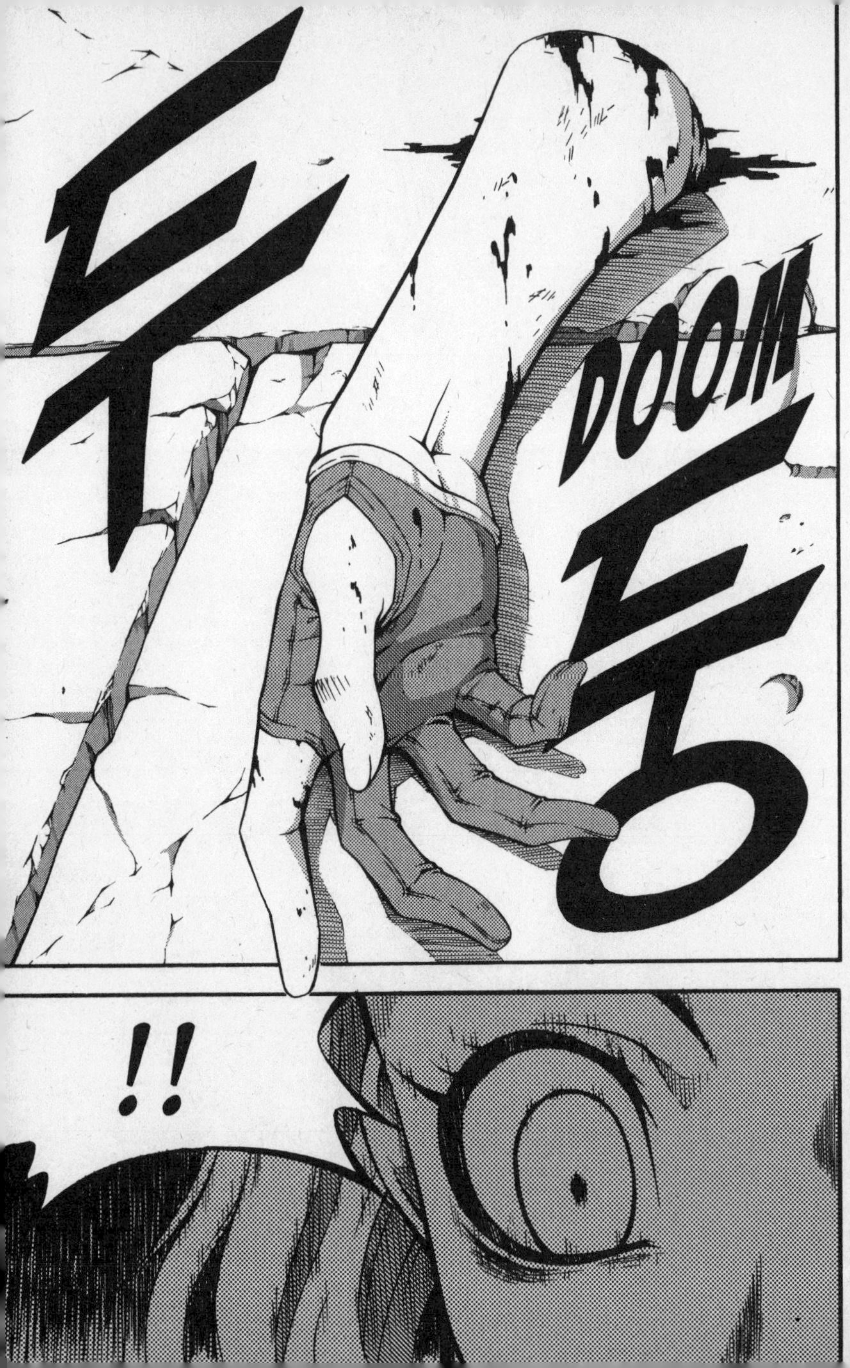
DOOM
!!

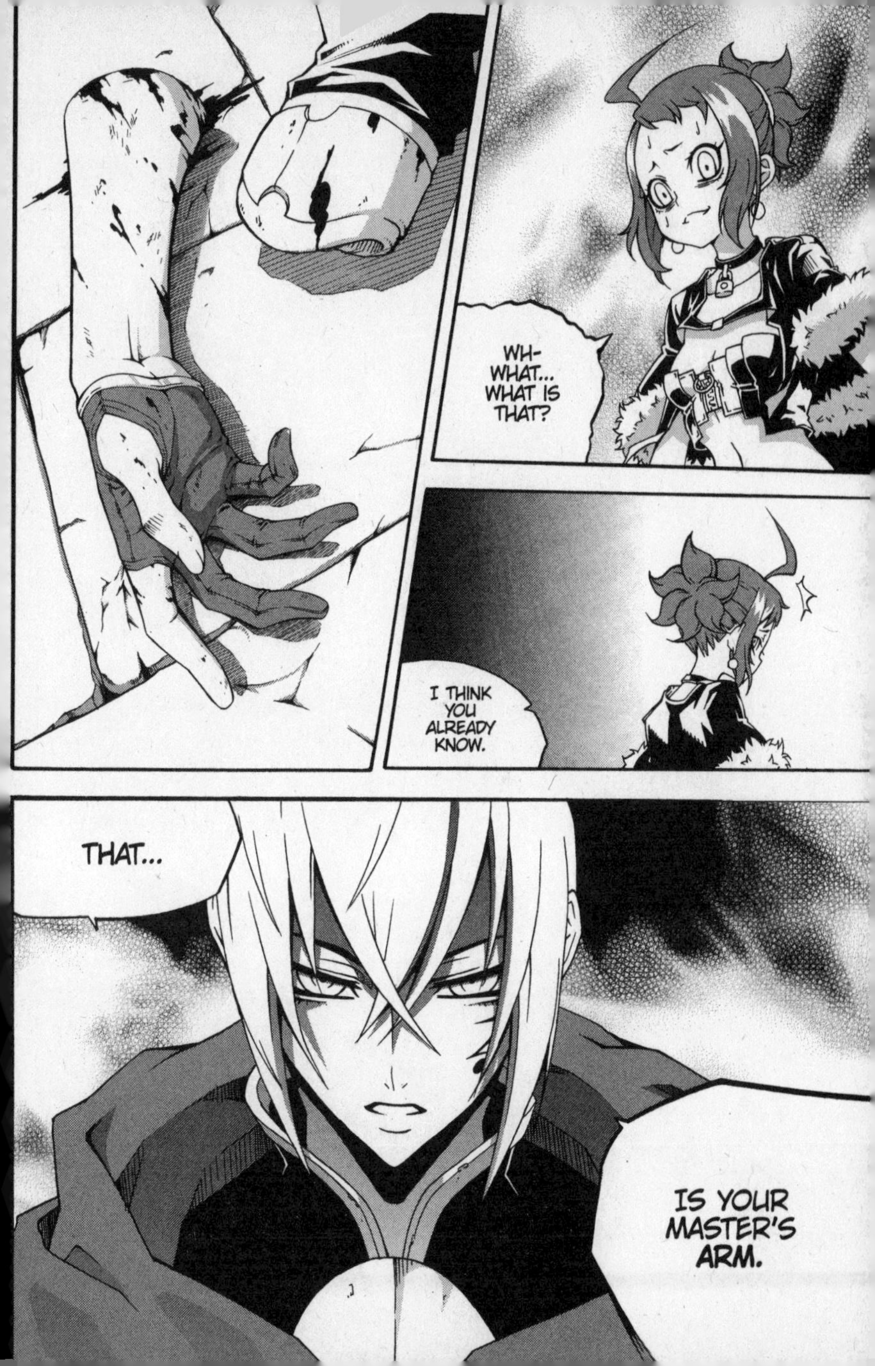
WH-
WHAT...
WHAT IS
THAT?
I THINK
YOU
ALREADY
KNOW.
THAT...
IS YOUR
MASTER'S
ARM.

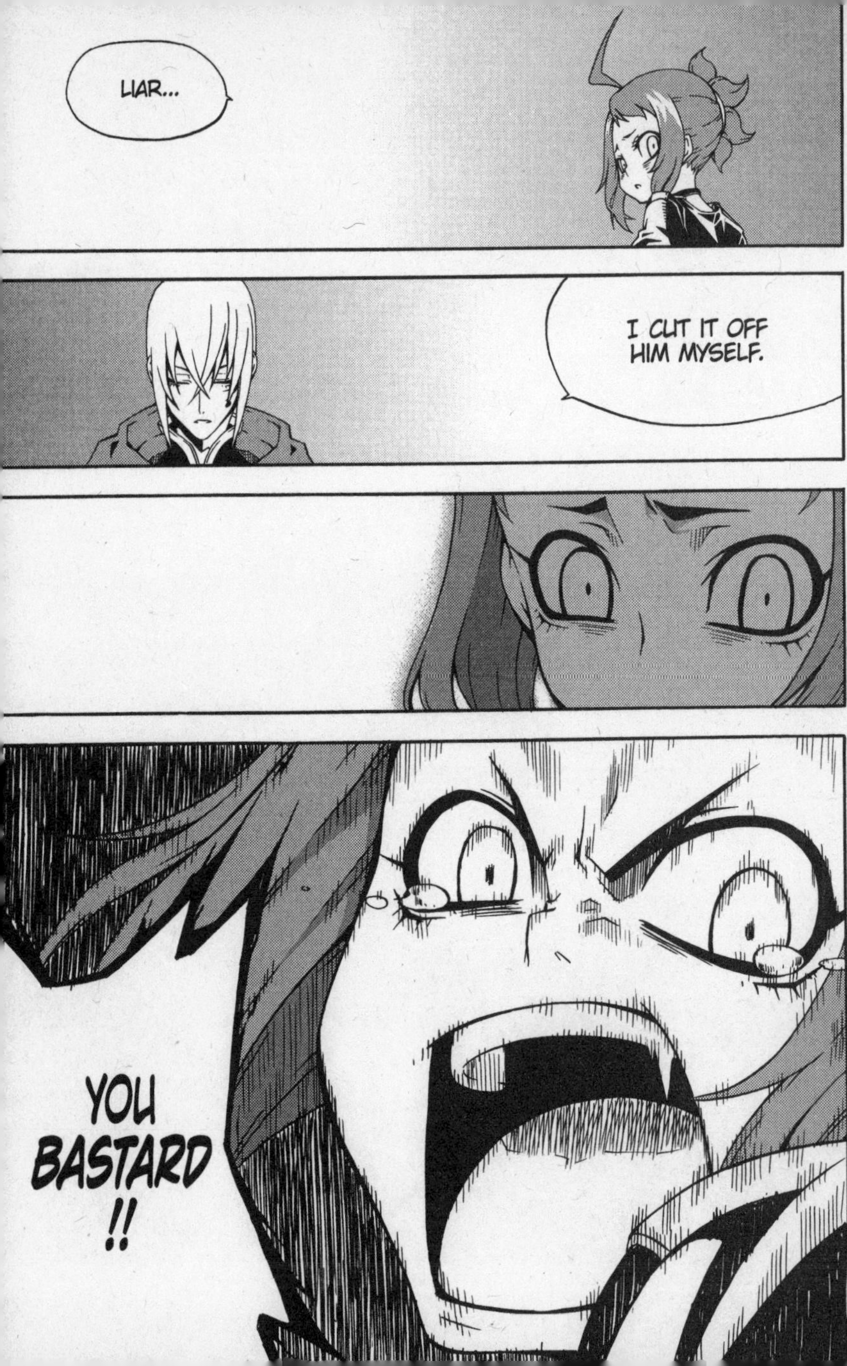
LIAR...
I CUT IT OFF HIM MYSELF.
YOU BASTARD !!

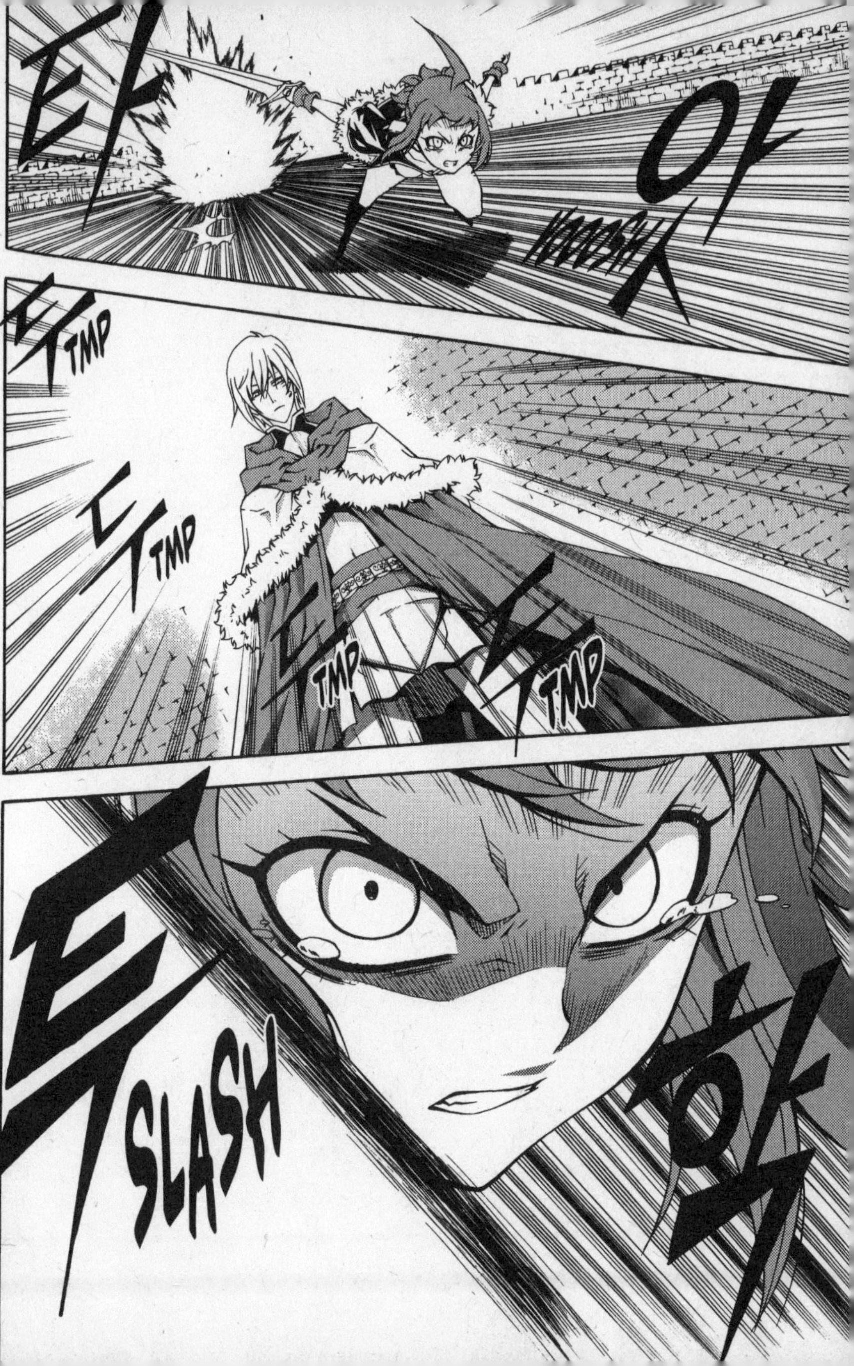
WHOOSH
TMP
TMP
TMP
TMP
SLASH

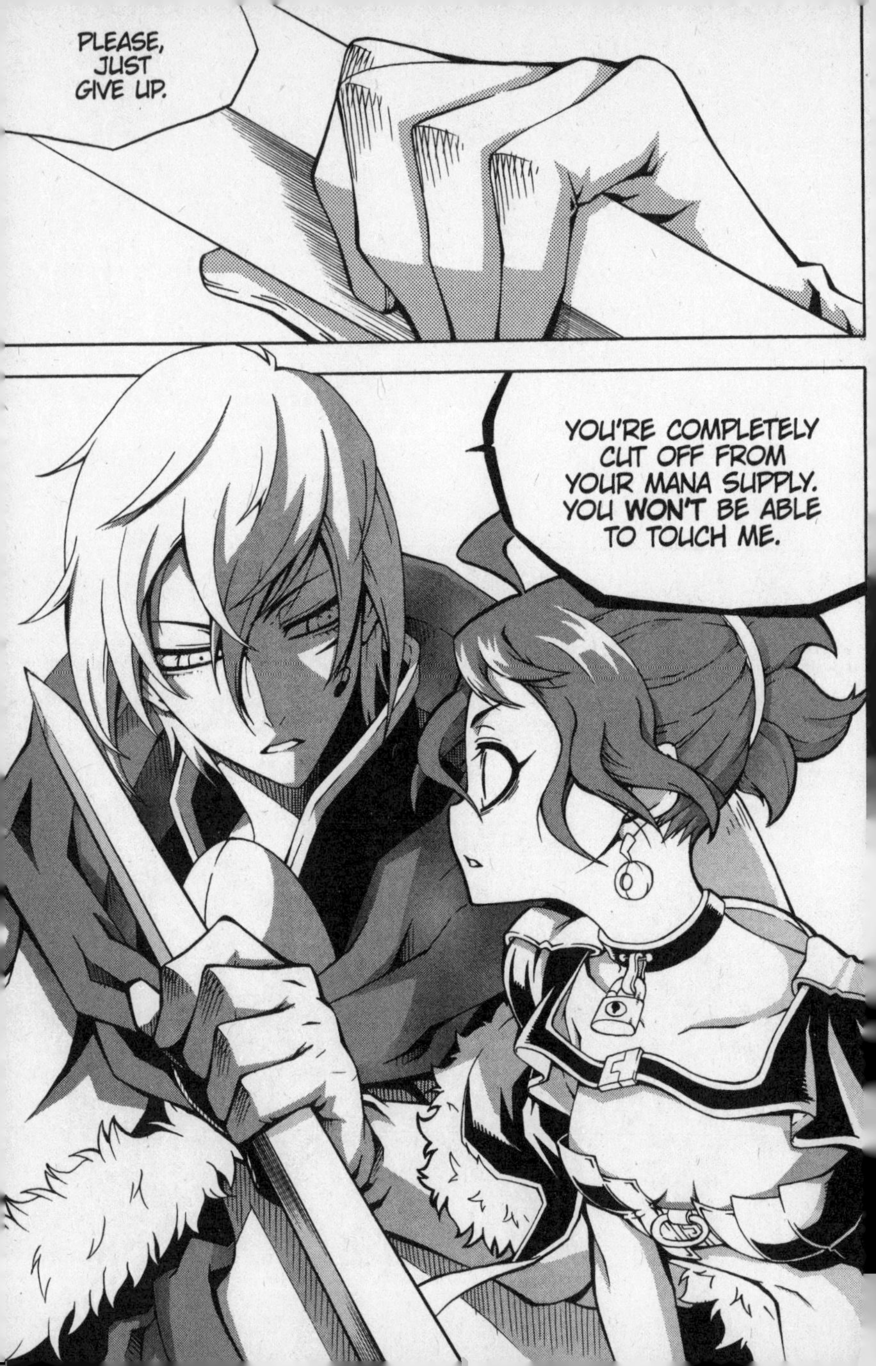
PLEASE, JUST GIVE UP.
YOU'RE COMPLETELY CUT OFF FROM YOUR MANA SUPPLY. YOU WON'T BE ABLE TO TOUCH ME.

WITCH BUSTER

REASON

AH...
RUB
Sigh... You're kinda killing the mood here.
RUB
HEY, WHY DOES YOUR MASTER ACT LIKE A LITTLE KID, ONLY SAYING "AH"?
THE REASON IS...
FOR HER, THAT'S NORMAL.
AH.
OH...

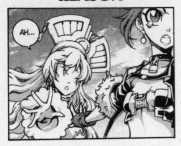

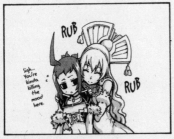

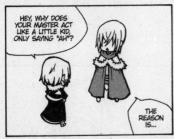

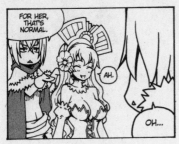

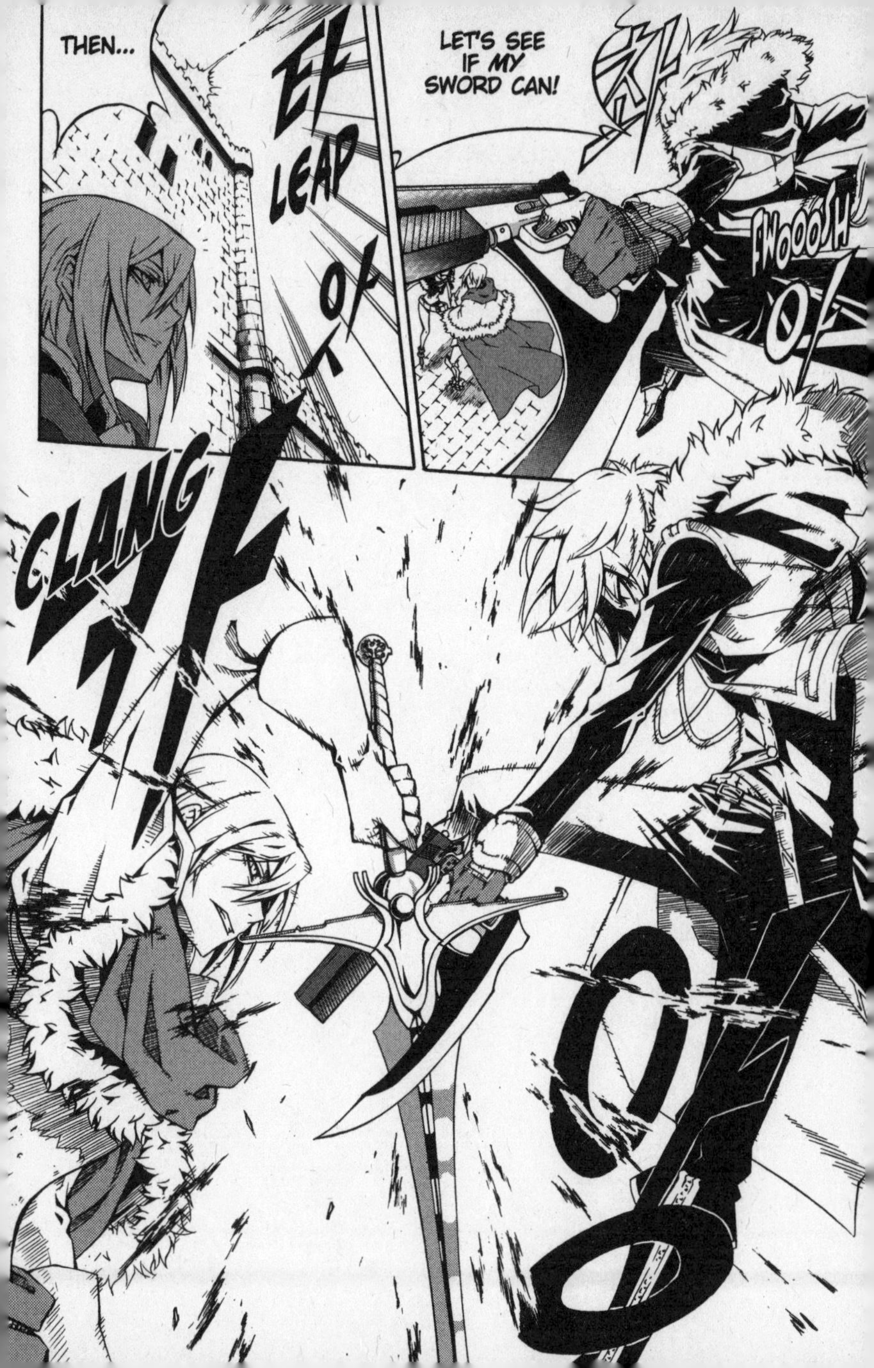
THEN...
LEAP
LET'S SEE IF MY SWORD CAN!
FWOOOSH
CLANG

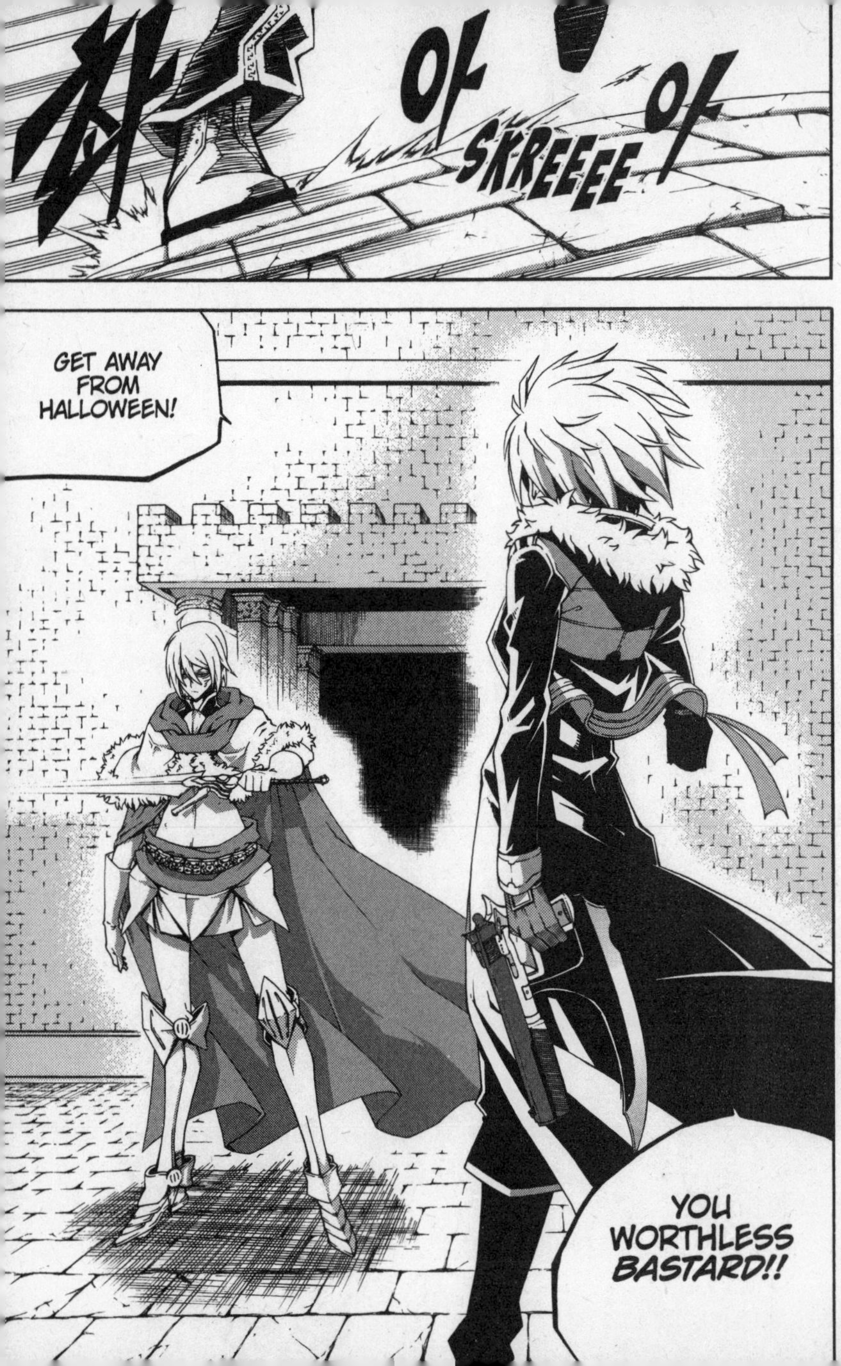
GET AWAY FROM HALLOWEEN!
YOU WORTHLESS BASTARD!!

44. Choice/ Decision

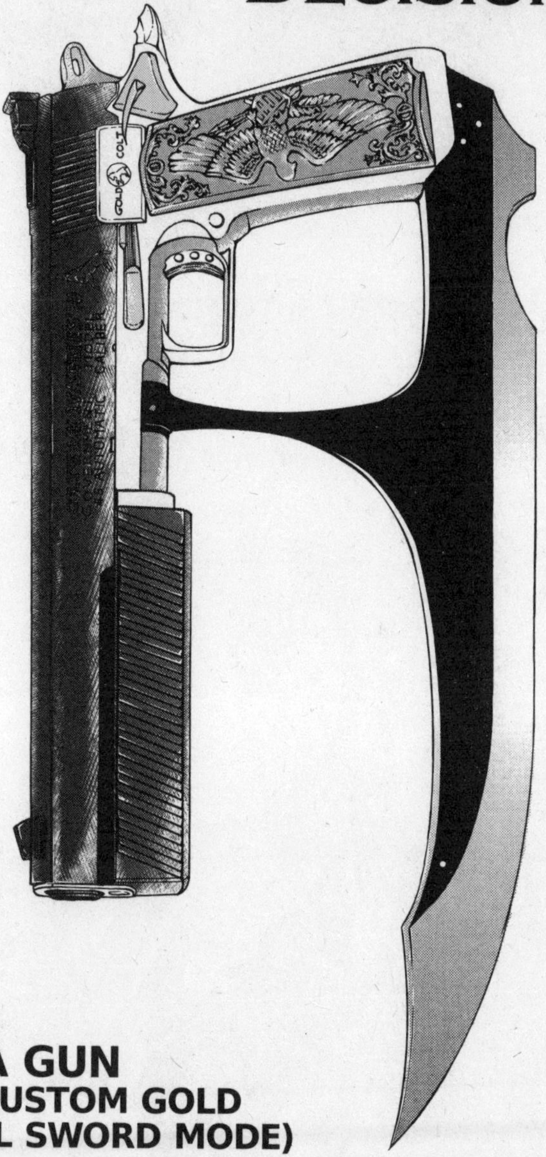
GOLD COLT

MANA GUN
COLT CUSTOM GOLD
(PISTOL SWORD MODE)

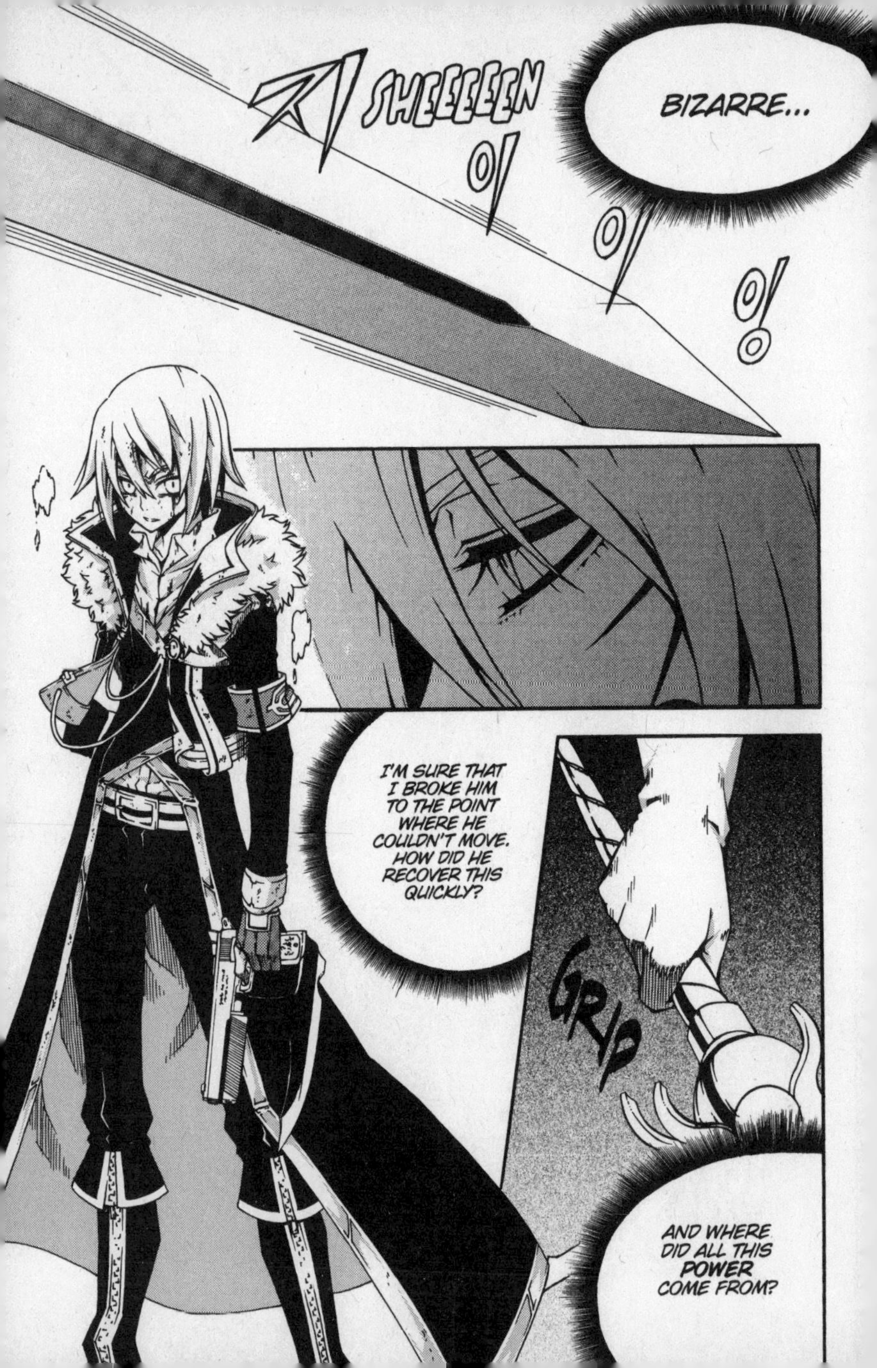
SHEEEEEN
BIZARRE...
I'M SURE THAT I BROKE HIM TO THE POINT WHERE HE COULDN'T MOVE. HOW DID HE RECOVER THIS QUICKLY?
GRIP
AND WHERE DID ALL THIS POWER COME FROM?

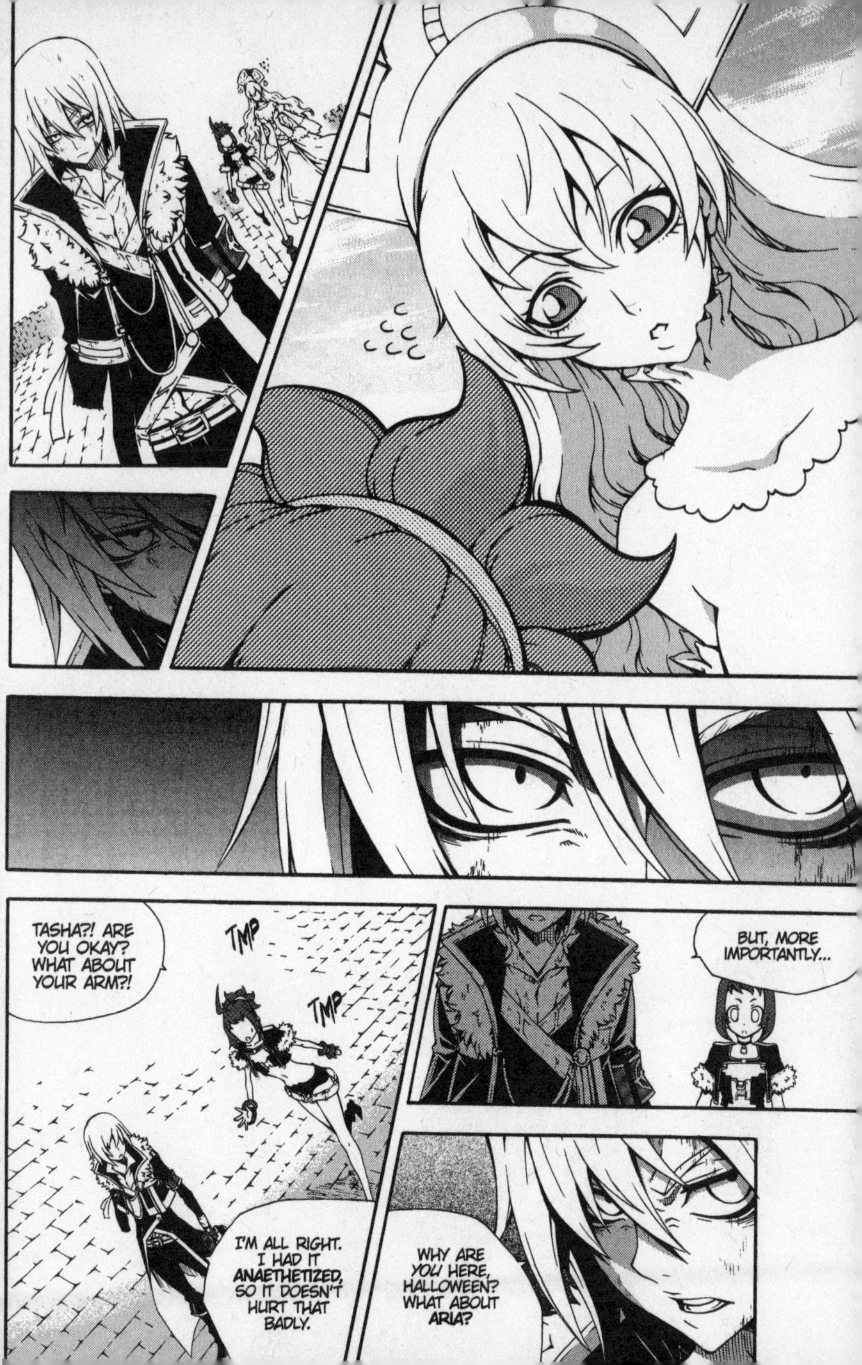
TASHA?! ARE YOU OKAY? WHAT ABOUT YOUR ARM?!
TMP
TMP
BUT, MORE IMPORTANTLY...
I'M ALL RIGHT. I HAD IT ANAETHETIZED, SO IT DOESN'T HURT THAT BADLY.
WHY ARE YOU HERE, HALLOWEEN? WHAT ABOUT ARIA?

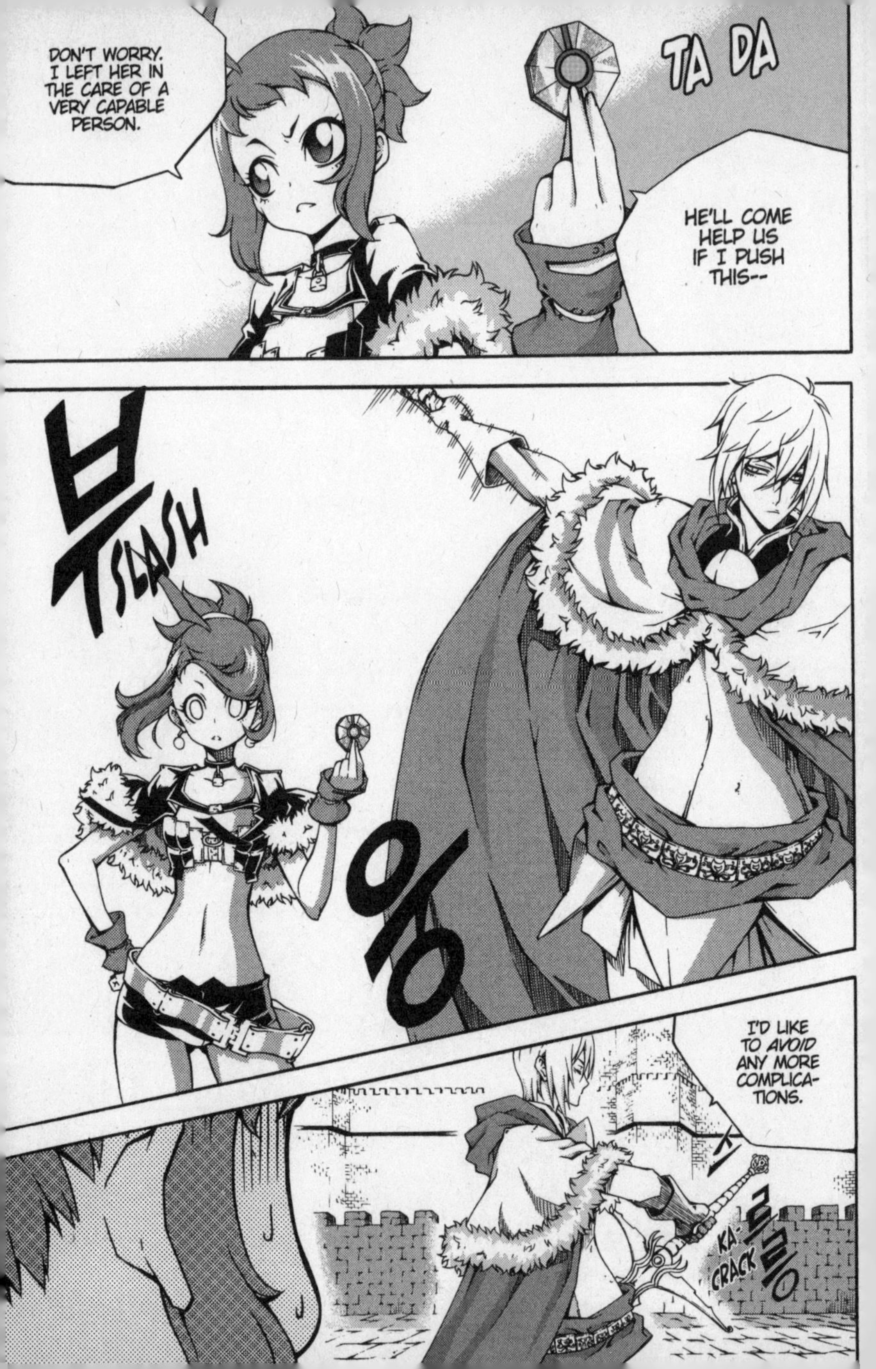
DON'T WORRY. I LEFT HER IN THE CARE OF A VERY CAPABLE PERSON.
TA DA
HE'LL COME HELP US IF I PUSH THIS--
SLASH
I'D LIKE TO AVOID ANY MORE COMPLICATIONS.
KA-CRACK

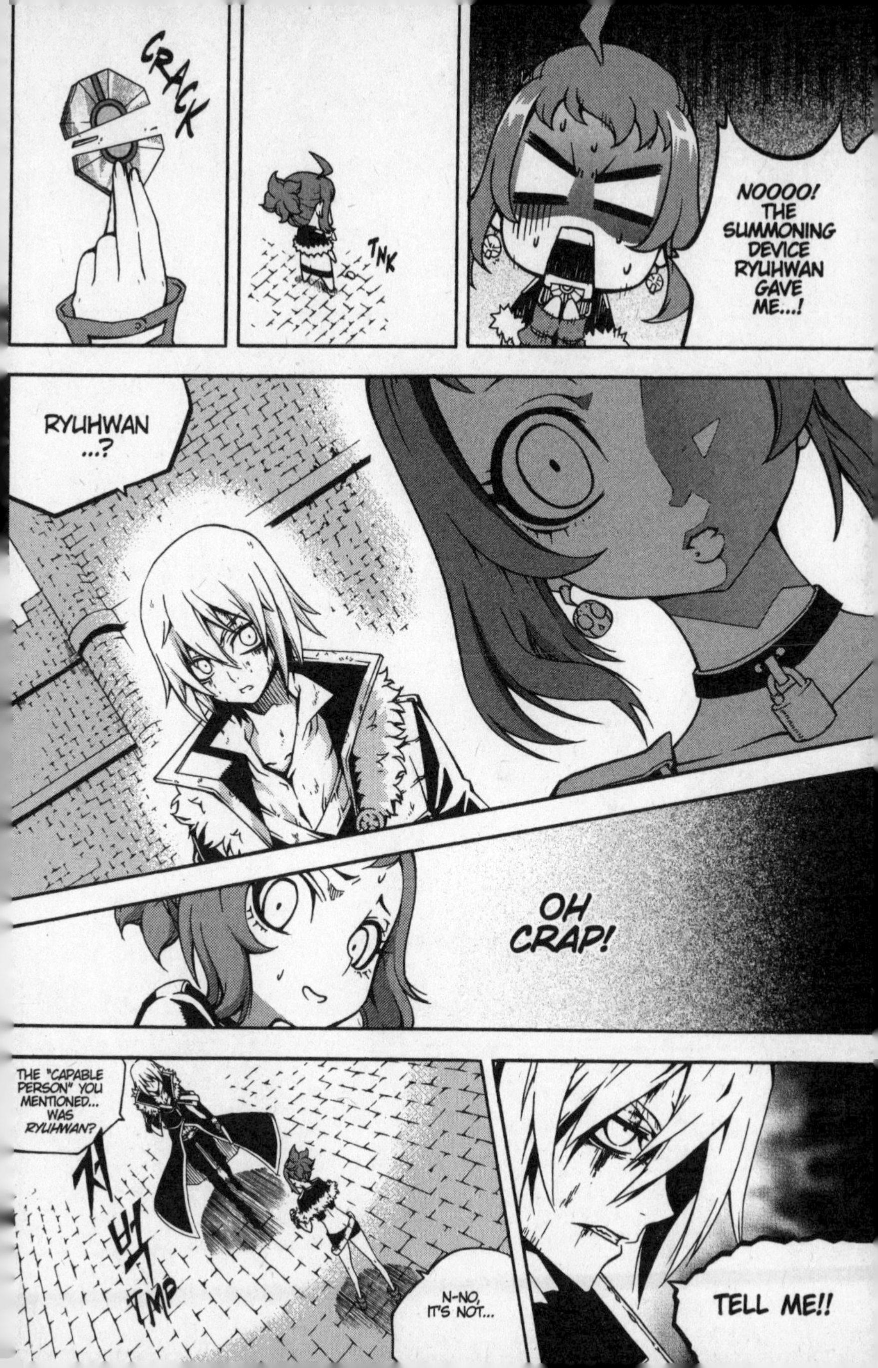
CRACK
TNK
NOOOO! THE SUMMONING DEVICE RYUHWAN GAVE ME...!
RYUHWAN ...?
OH CRAP!
THE "CAPABLE PERSON" YOU MENTIONED... WAS RYUHWAN?
저벅
TMP
N-NO, IT'S NOT...
TELL ME!!

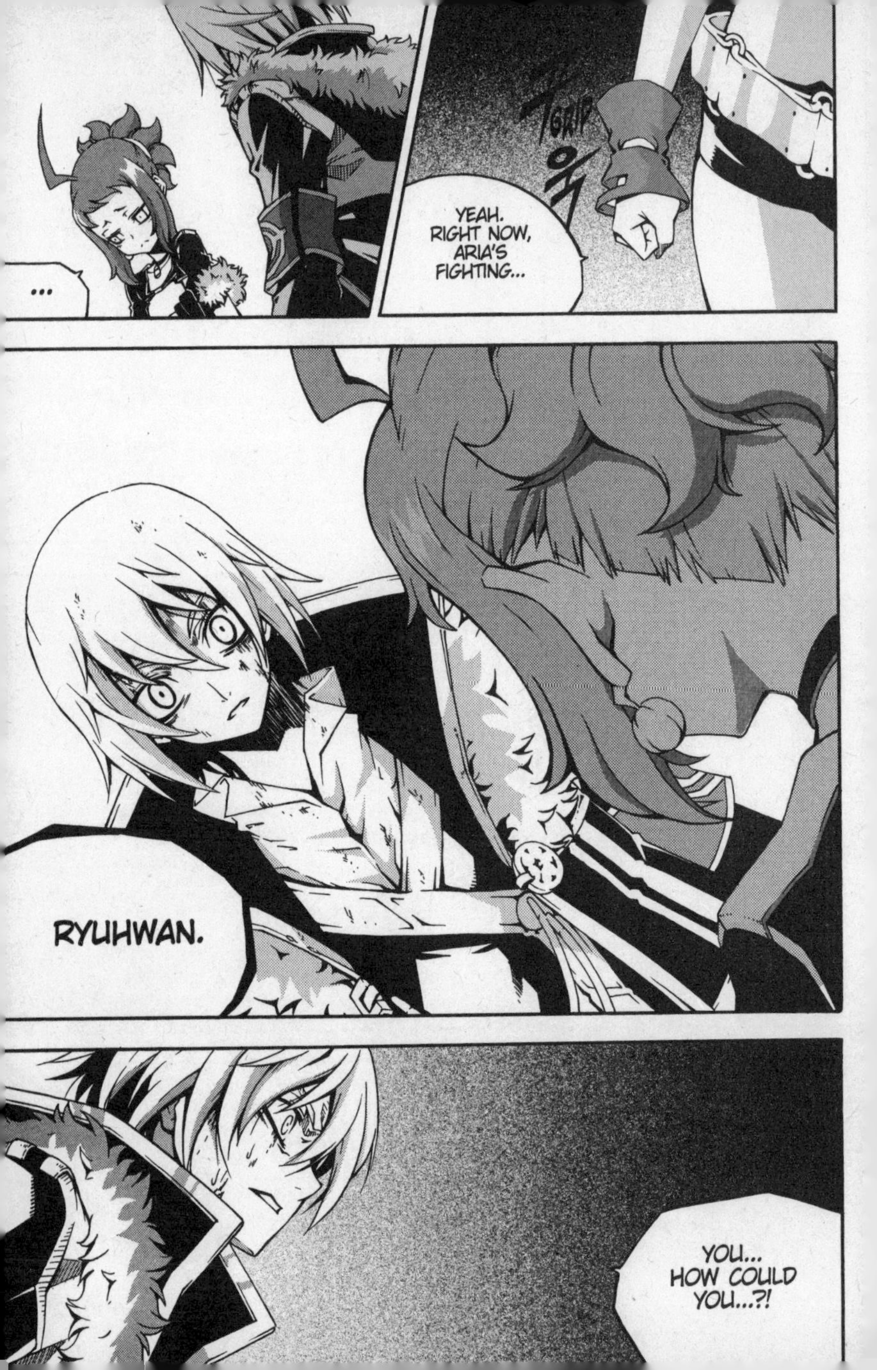
...
GRIP
YEAH. RIGHT NOW, ARIA'S FIGHTING...
RYUHWAN.
YOU... HOW COULD YOU...?!

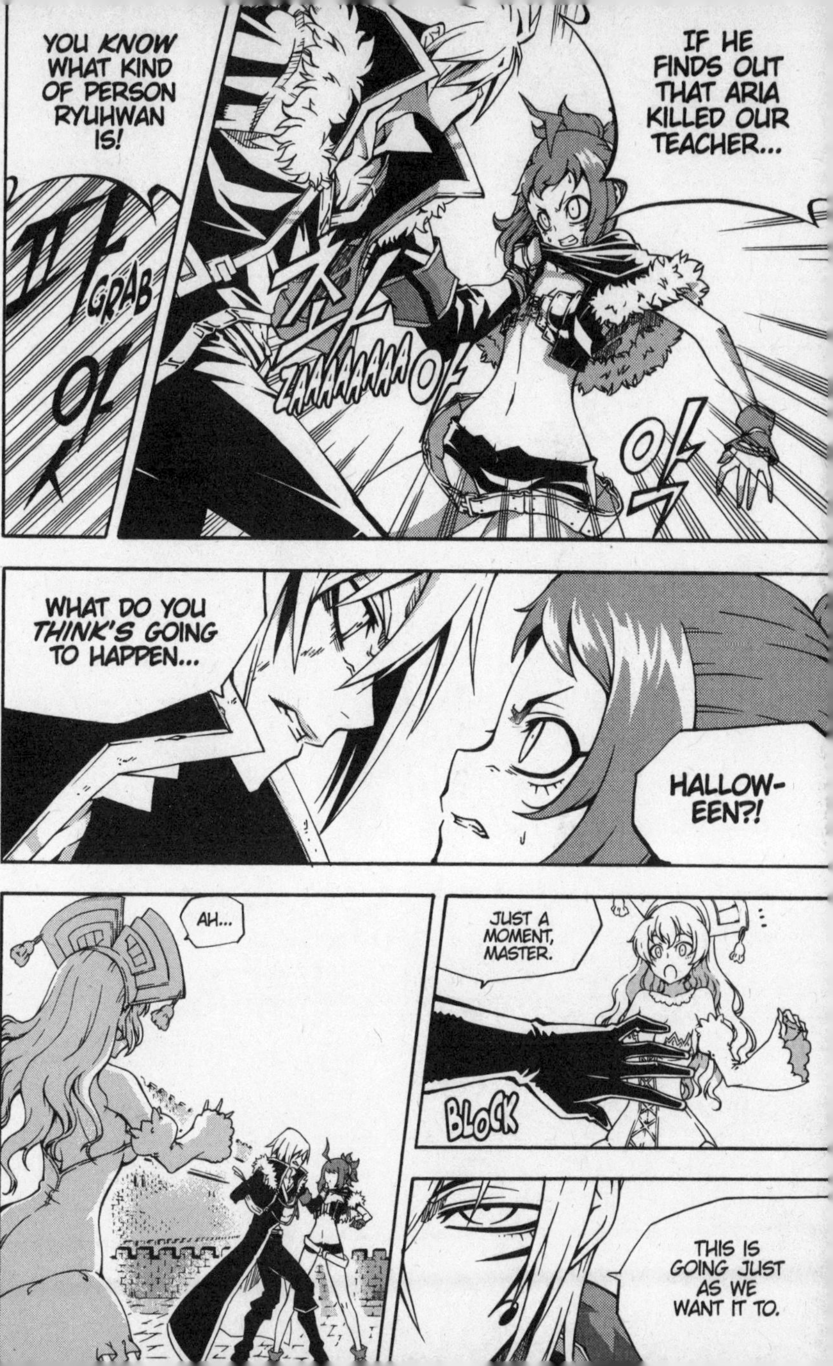
YOU *KNOW* WHAT KIND OF PERSON RYUHWAN IS!
GRAB
ZAAAAAAAA
IF HE FINDS OUT THAT ARIA KILLED OUR TEACHER...
WHAT DO YOU *THINK'S* GOING TO HAPPEN...
HALLOW-EEN?!
AH...
JUST A MOMENT, MASTER.
BLOCK
THIS IS GOING JUST AS WE WANT IT TO.

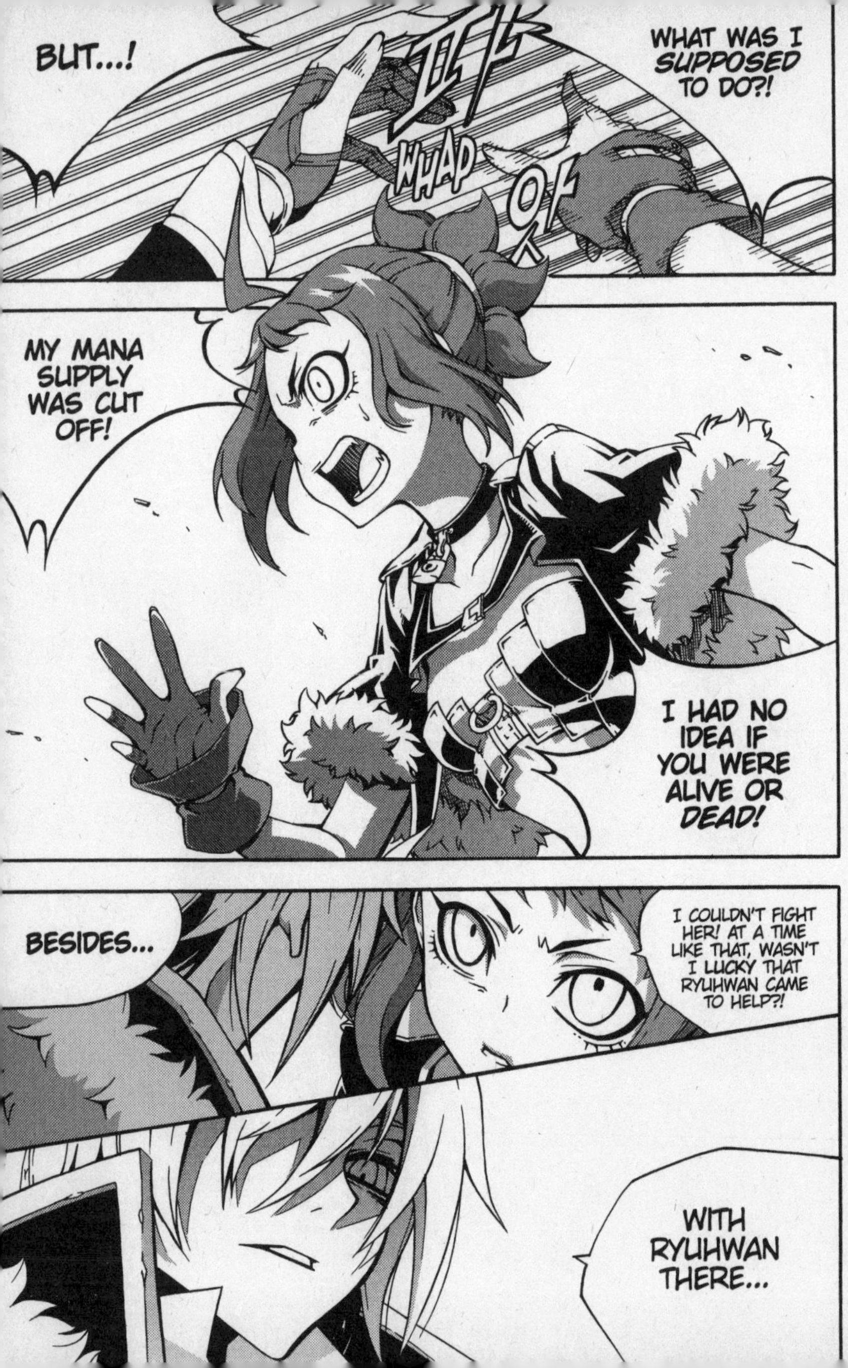
BUT...!
WHAP
WHAT WAS I SUPPOSED TO DO?!
MY MANA SUPPLY WAS CUT OFF!
I HAD NO IDEA IF YOU WERE ALIVE OR DEAD!
BESIDES...
I COULDN'T FIGHT HER! AT A TIME LIKE THAT, WASN'T I LUCKY THAT RYUHWAN CAME TO HELP?!
WITH RYUHWAN THERE...

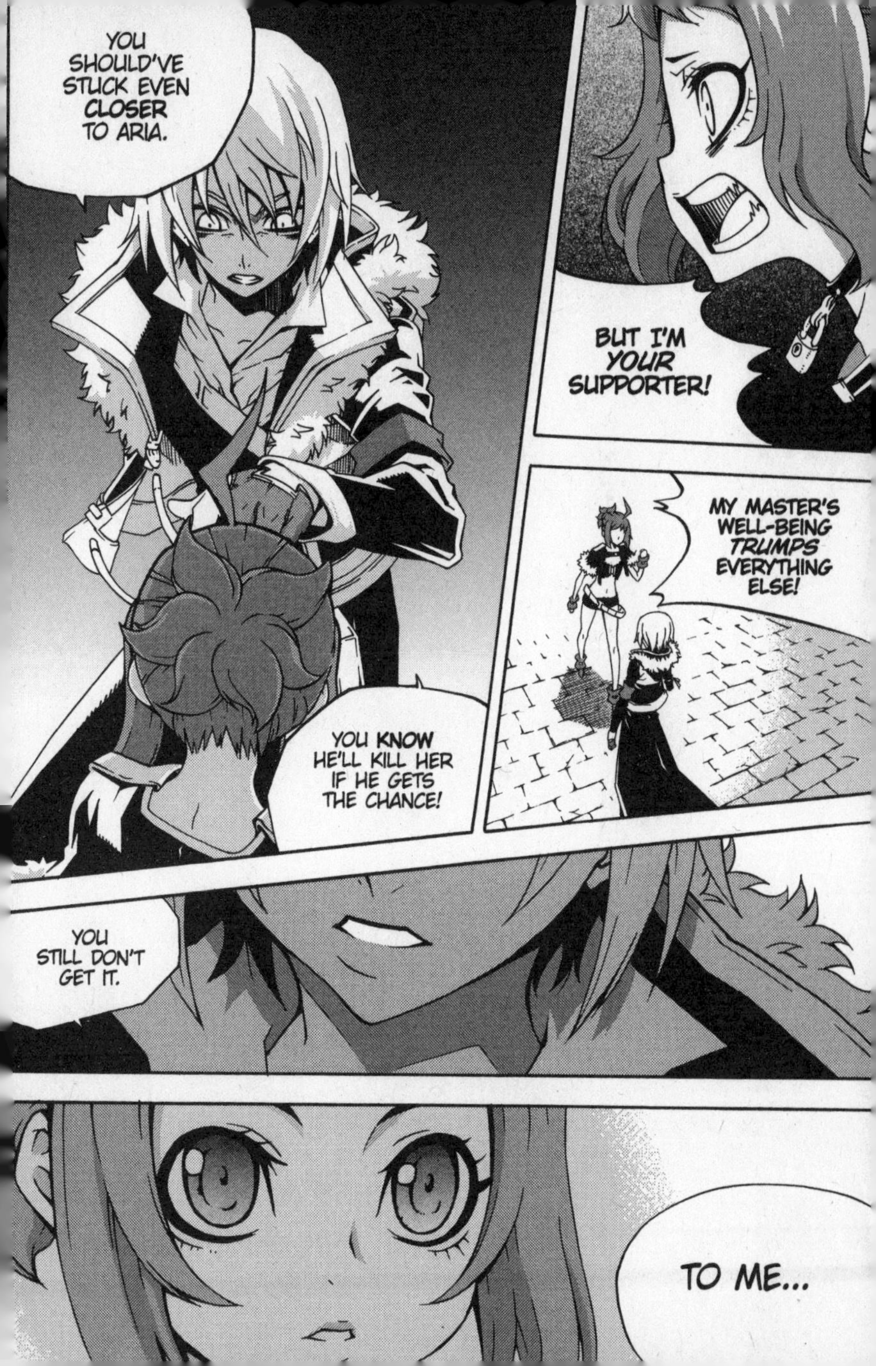
YOU SHOULD'VE STUCK EVEN CLOSER TO ARIA.
YOU KNOW HE'LL KILL HER IF HE GETS THE CHANCE!
BUT I'M *YOUR* SUPPORTER!
MY MASTER'S WELL-BEING *TRUMPS* EVERYTHING ELSE!
YOU STILL DON'T GET IT.
TO ME...

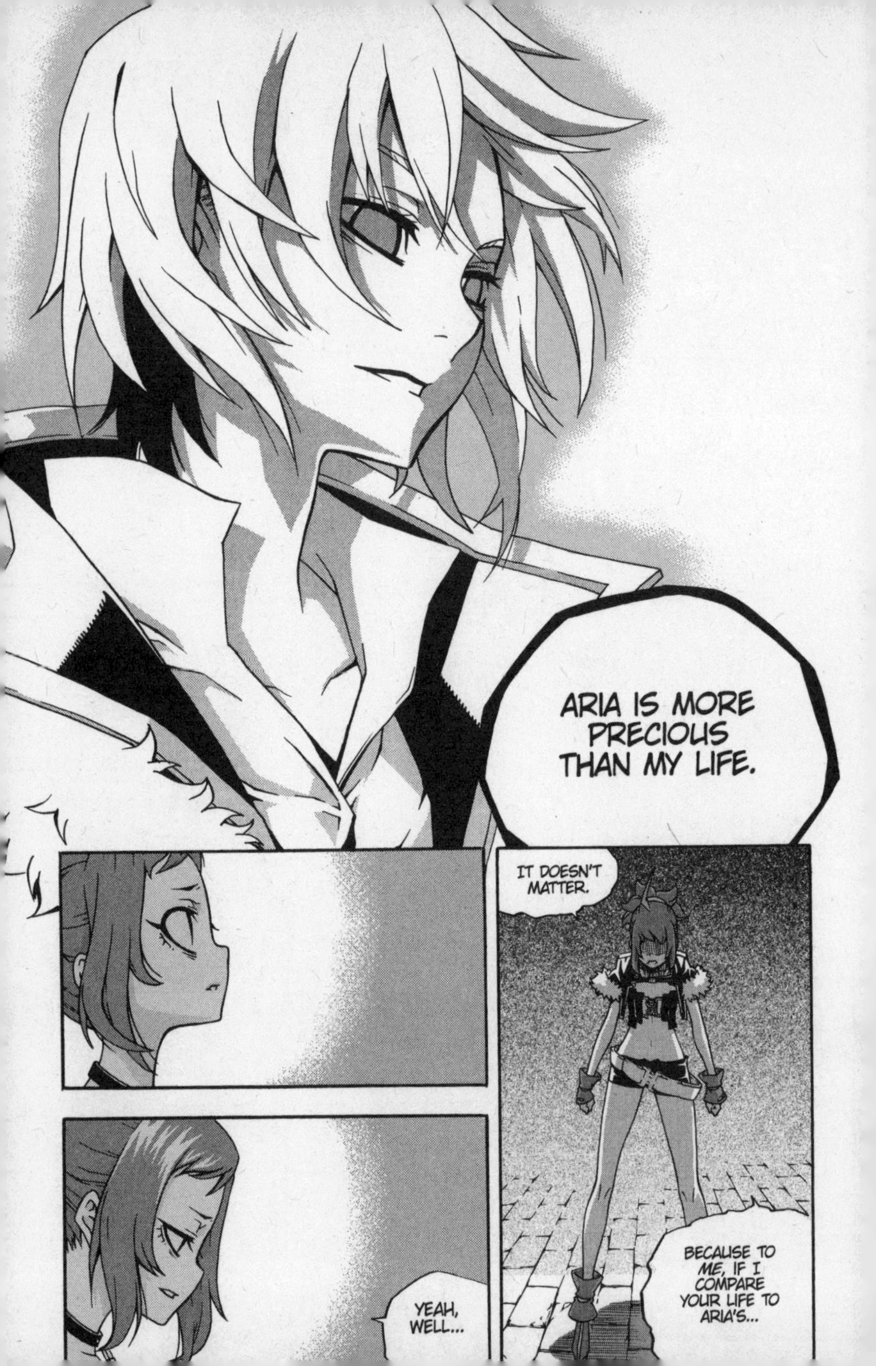
ARIA IS MORE PRECIOUS THAN MY LIFE.
IT DOESN'T MATTER.
YEAH, WELL...
BECAUSE TO *ME*, IF I COMPARE YOUR LIFE TO ARIA'S...

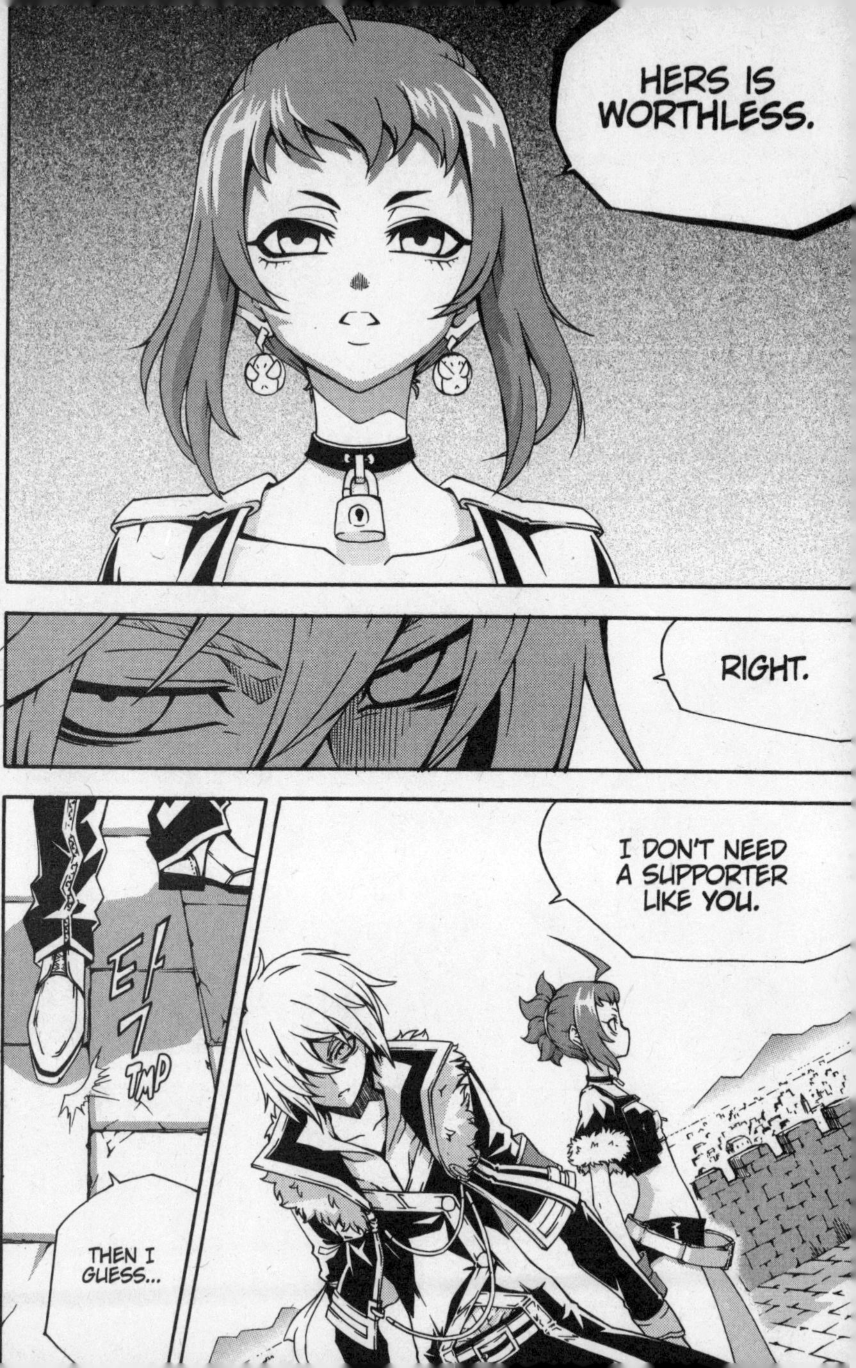
HERS IS WORTHLESS.
RIGHT.
TMP
I DON'T NEED A SUPPORTER LIKE YOU.
THEN I GUESS...

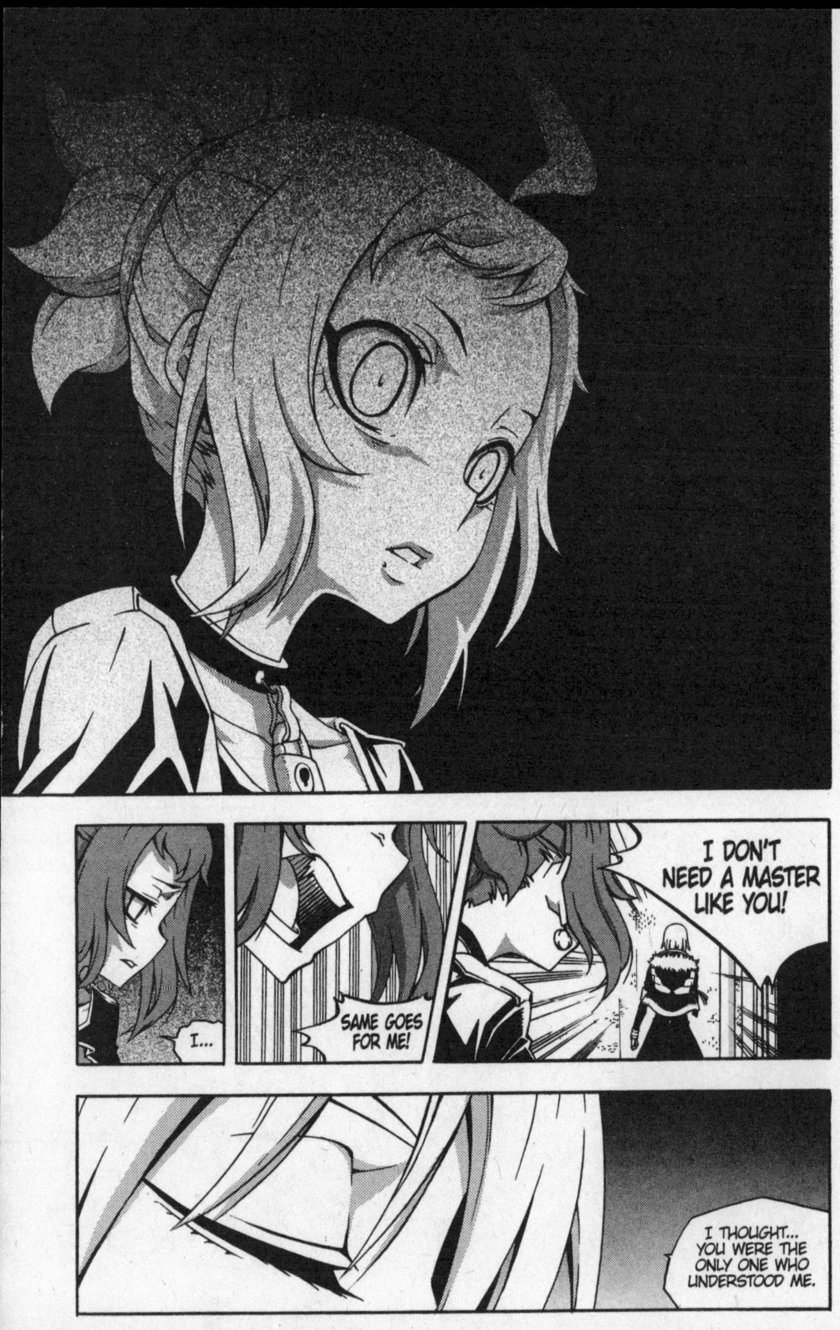
I...
SAME GOES FOR ME!
I DON'T NEED A MASTER LIKE YOU!
I THOUGHT... YOU WERE THE ONLY ONE WHO UNDERSTOOD ME.

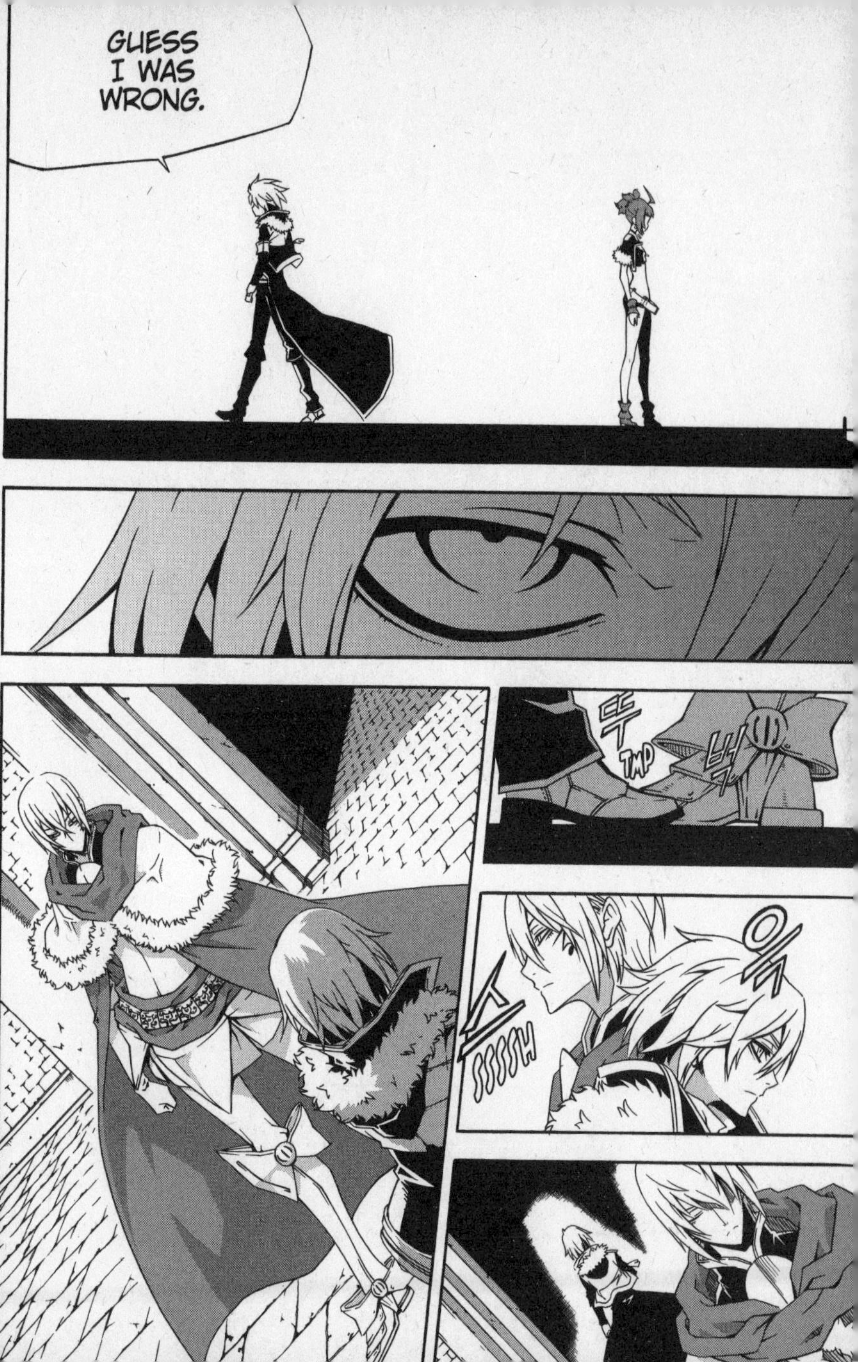
GUESS I WAS WRONG.
뚜
TMP
벅
스
SSSSH
윽

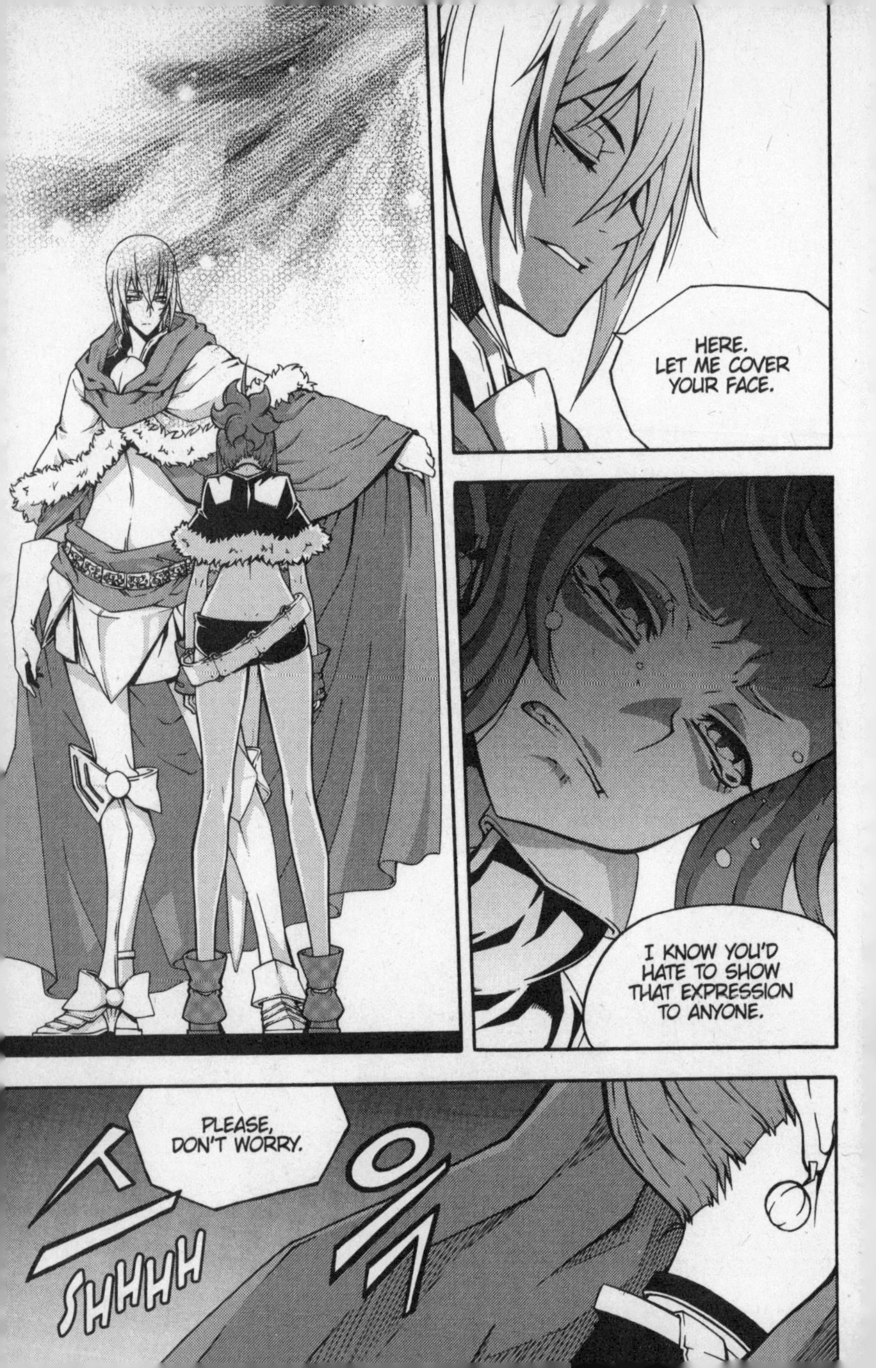
HERE.
LET ME COVER YOUR FACE.
I KNOW YOU'D HATE TO SHOW THAT EXPRESSION TO ANYONE.
PLEASE, DON'T WORRY.
SHHHH

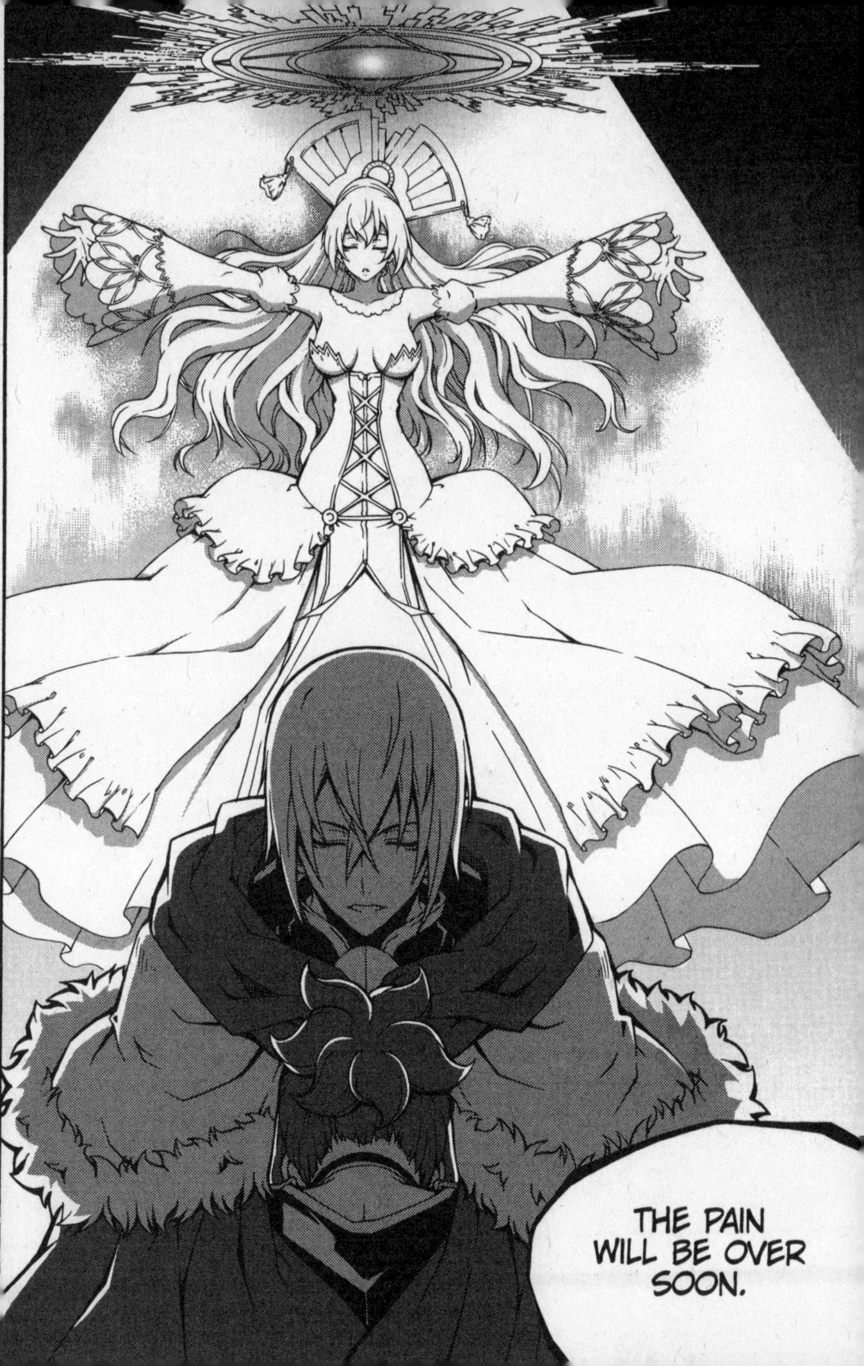
THE PAIN WILL BE OVER SOON.

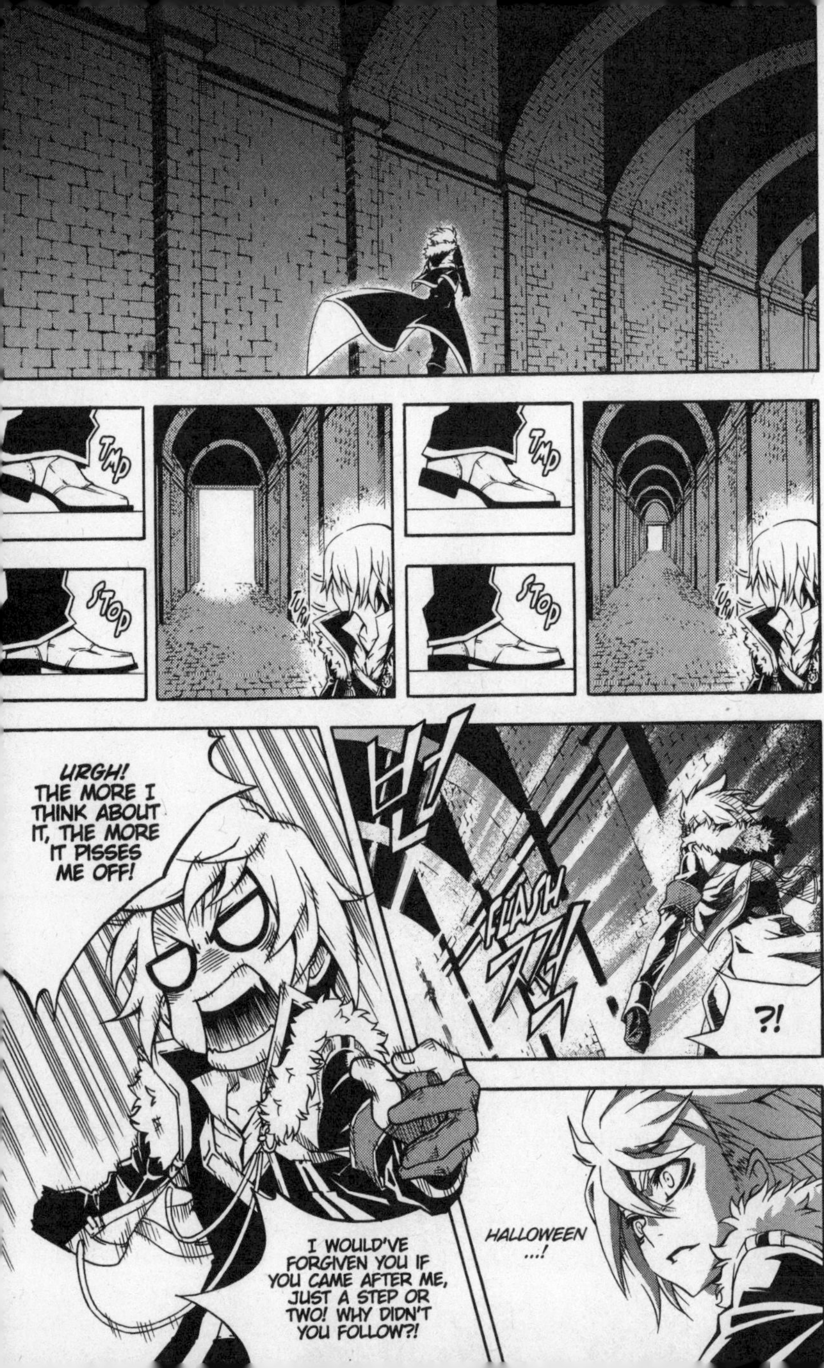
TMP
STOP
TURN
TMP
STOP
TURN
URGH! THE MORE I THINK ABOUT IT, THE MORE IT PISSES ME OFF!
I WOULD'VE FORGIVEN YOU IF YOU CAME AFTER ME, JUST A STEP OR TWO! WHY DIDN'T YOU FOLLOW?!
FLASH
?!
HALLOWEEN ...!

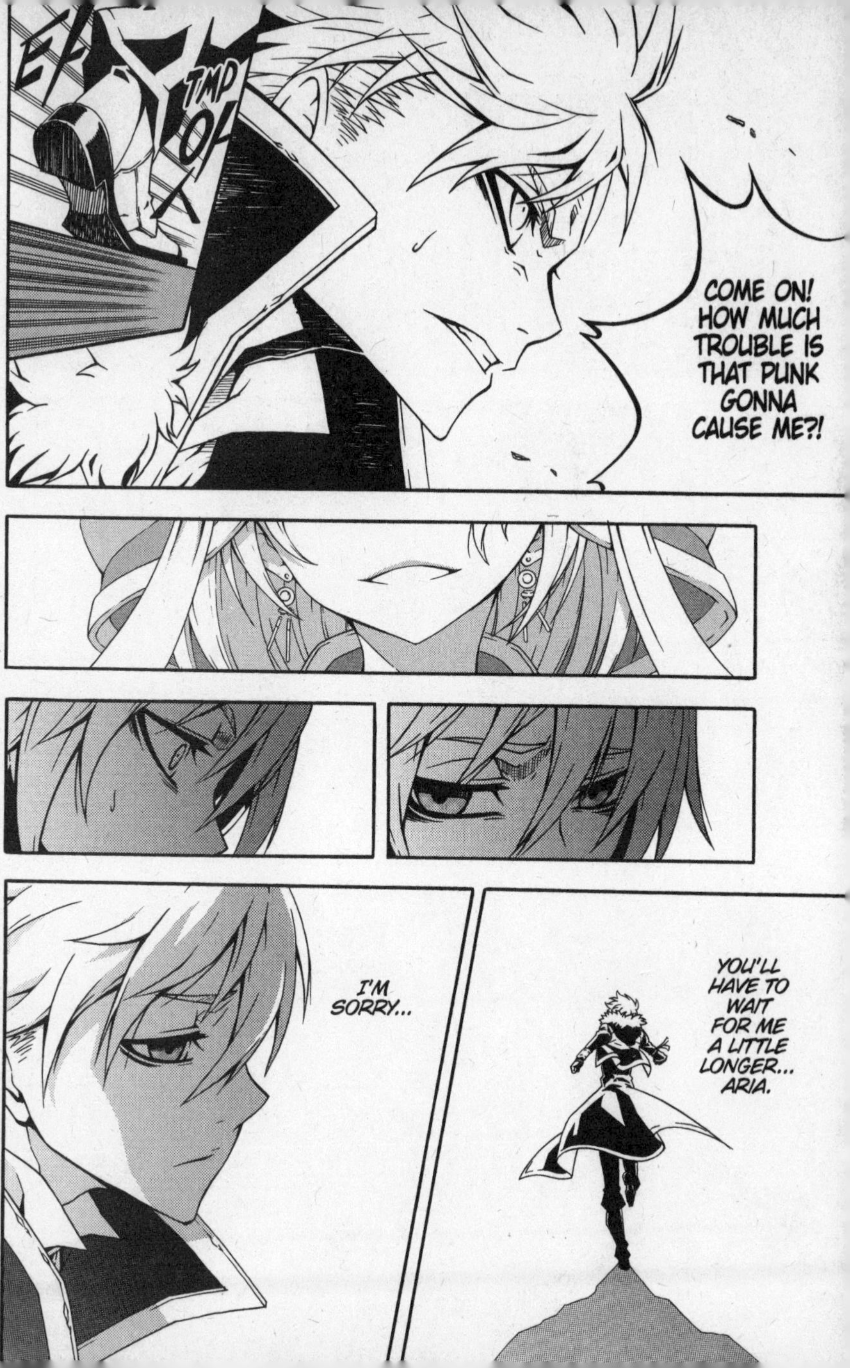
TMP
COME ON! HOW MUCH TROUBLE IS THAT PUNK GONNA CAUSE ME?!
I'M SORRY...
YOU'LL HAVE TO WAIT FOR ME A LITTLE LONGER... ARIA.

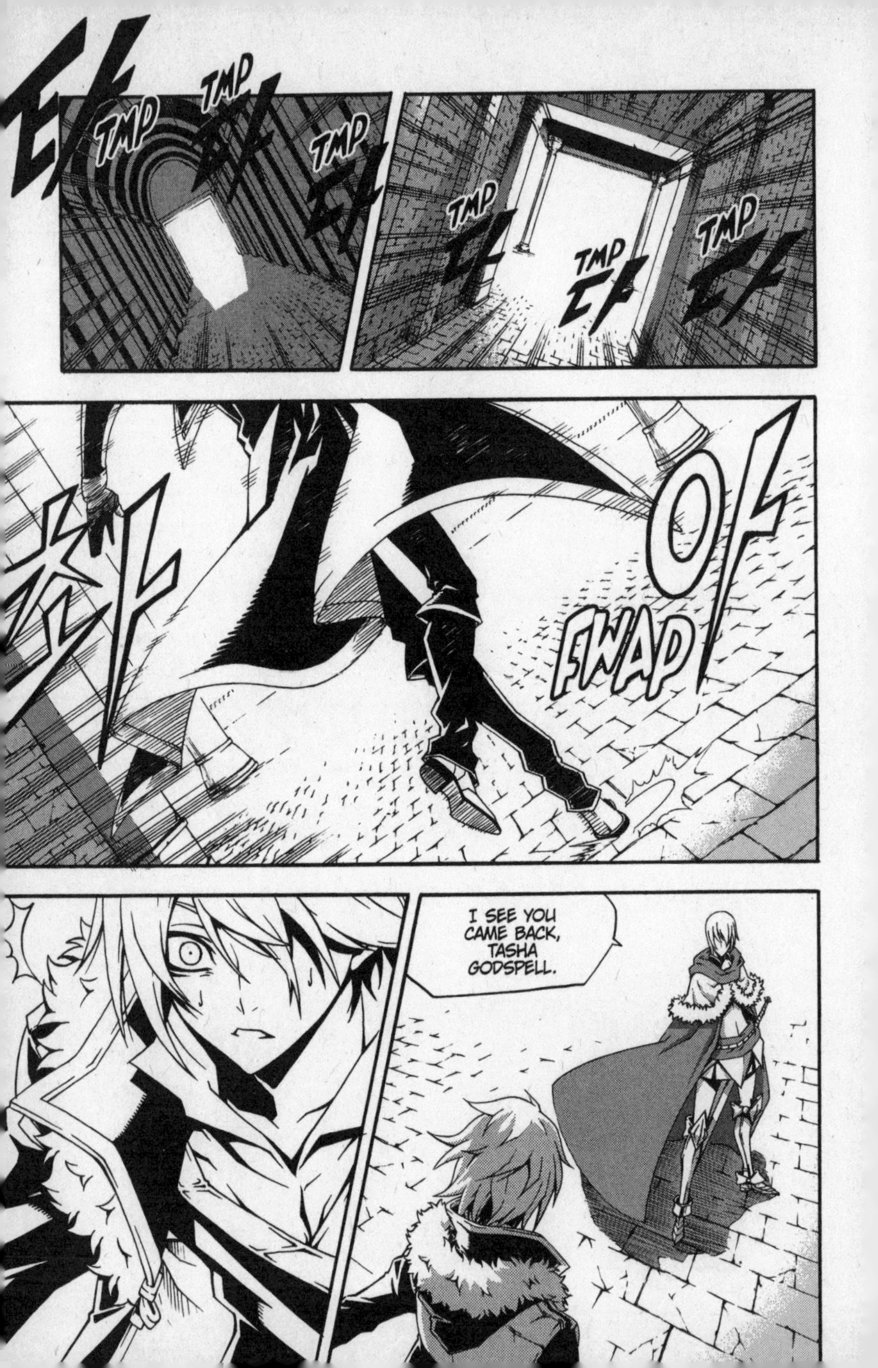

TMP
TMP
TMP
TMP
TMP
TMP
FWAP
I SEE YOU CAME BACK, TASHA GODSPELL.

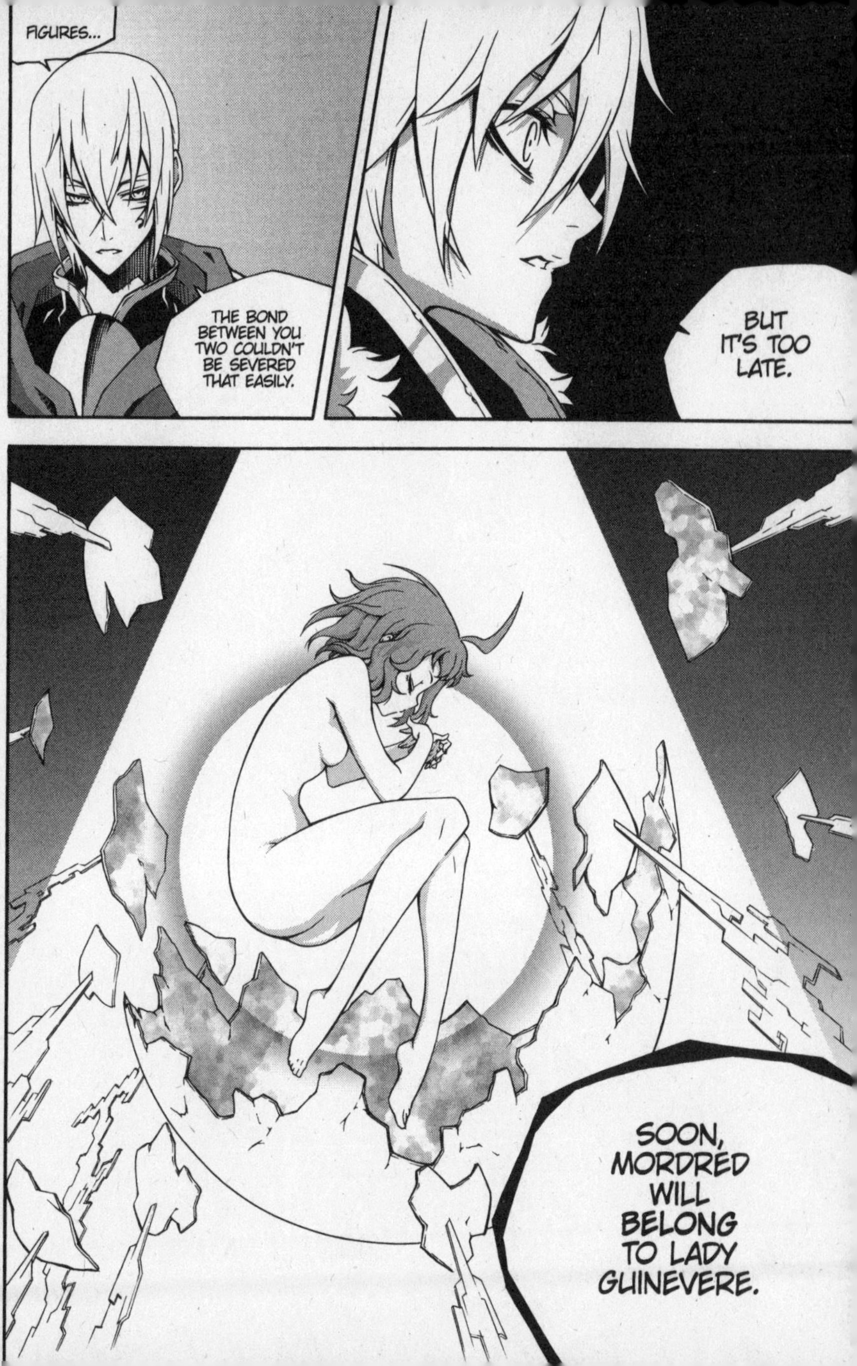
FIGURES...
THE BOND BETWEEN YOU TWO COULDN'T BE SEVERED THAT EASILY.
BUT IT'S TOO LATE.
SOON, MORDRED WILL BELONG TO LADY GUINEVERE.

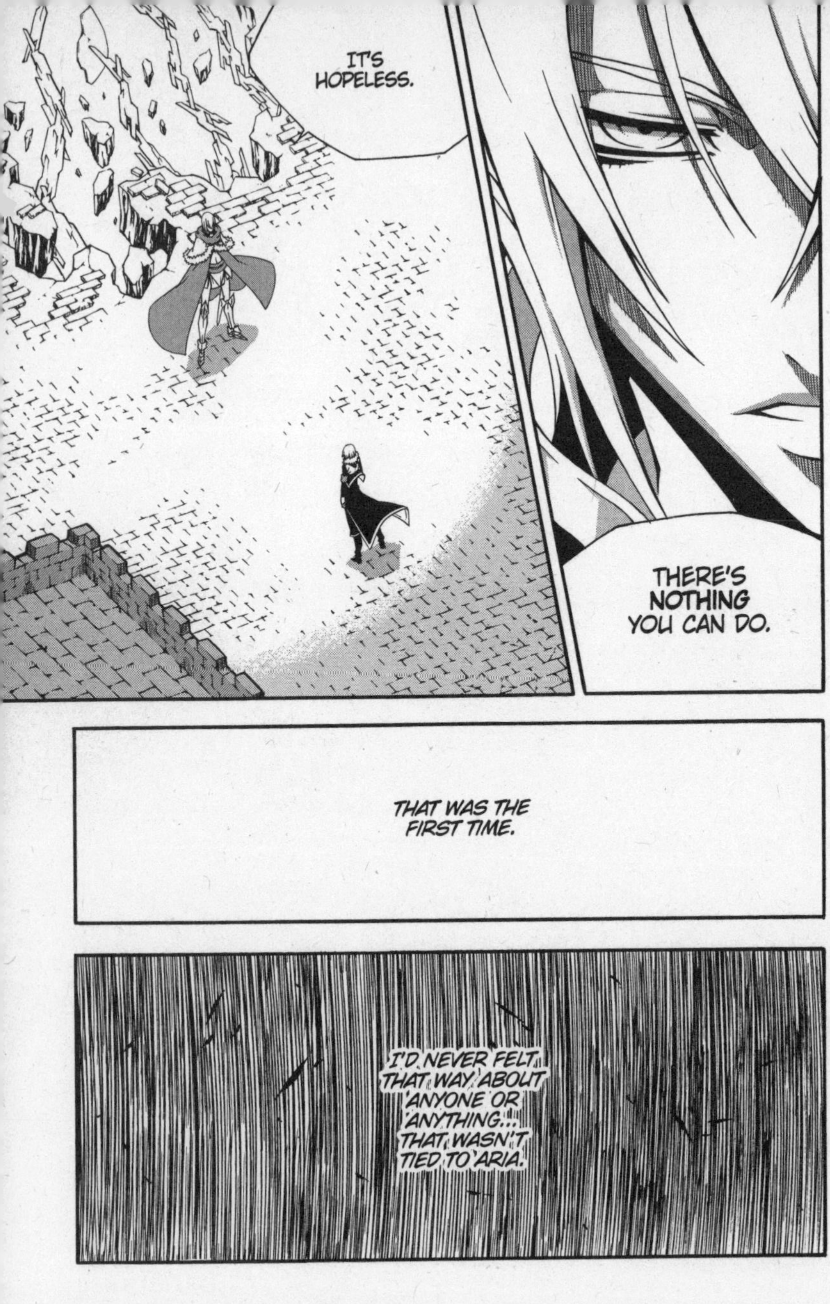
IT'S HOPELESS.
THERE'S NOTHING YOU CAN DO.
THAT WAS THE FIRST TIME.
I'D NEVER FELT THAT WAY ABOUT ANYONE OR ANYTHING... THAT WASN'T TIED TO ARIA.

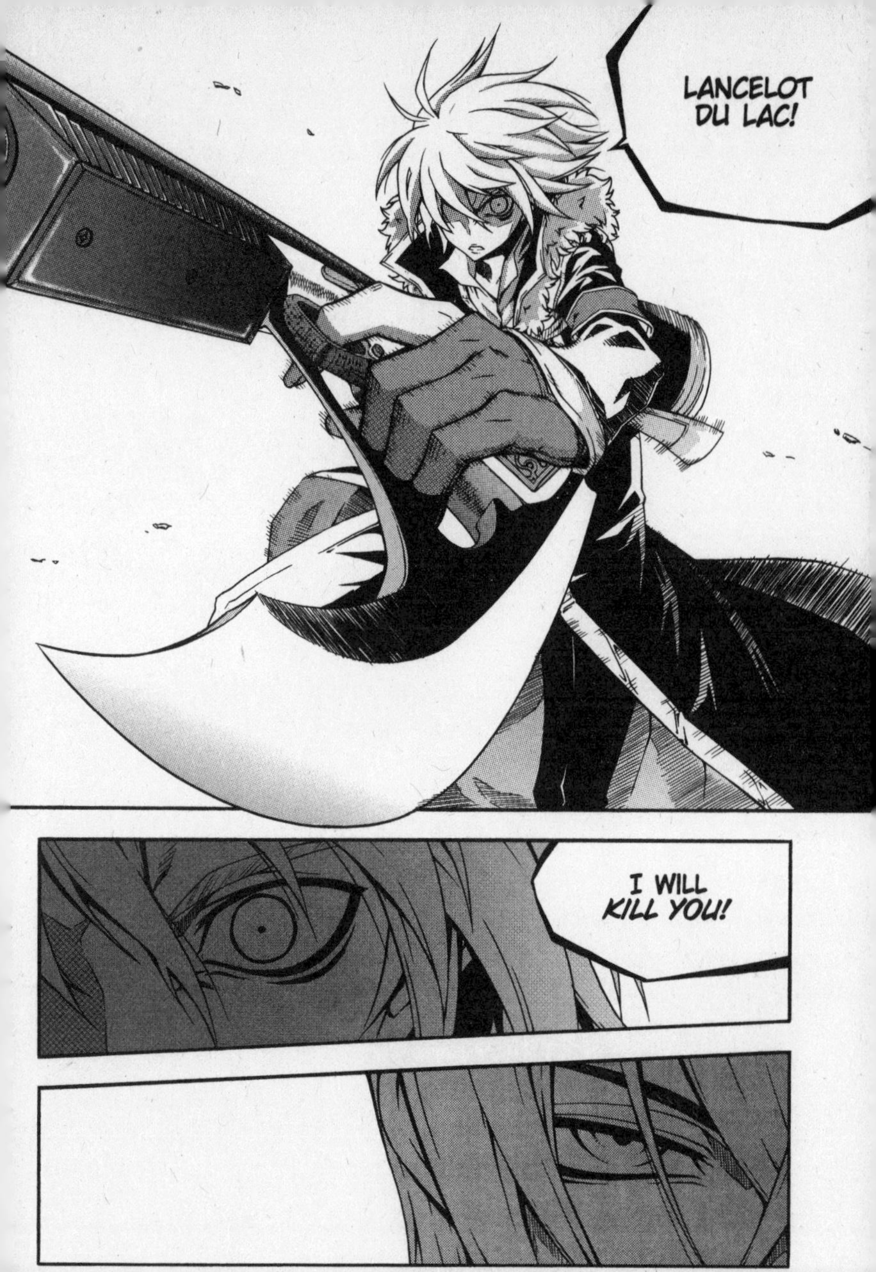
LANCELOT DU LAC!
I WILL KILL YOU!

LANCELOT'S POPULARITY DECLINES

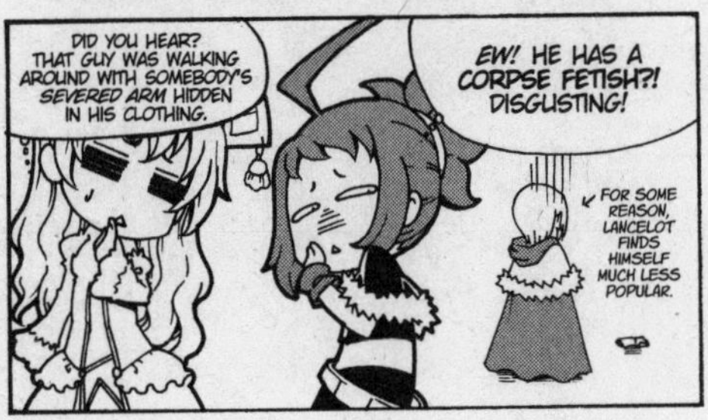
DID YOU HEAR? THAT GUY WAS WALKING AROUND WITH SOMEBODY'S SEVERED ARM HIDDEN IN HIS CLOTHING.
EW! HE HAS A CORPSE FETISH?! DISGUSTING!
FOR SOME REASON, LANCELOT FINDS HIMSELF MUCH LESS POPULAR.

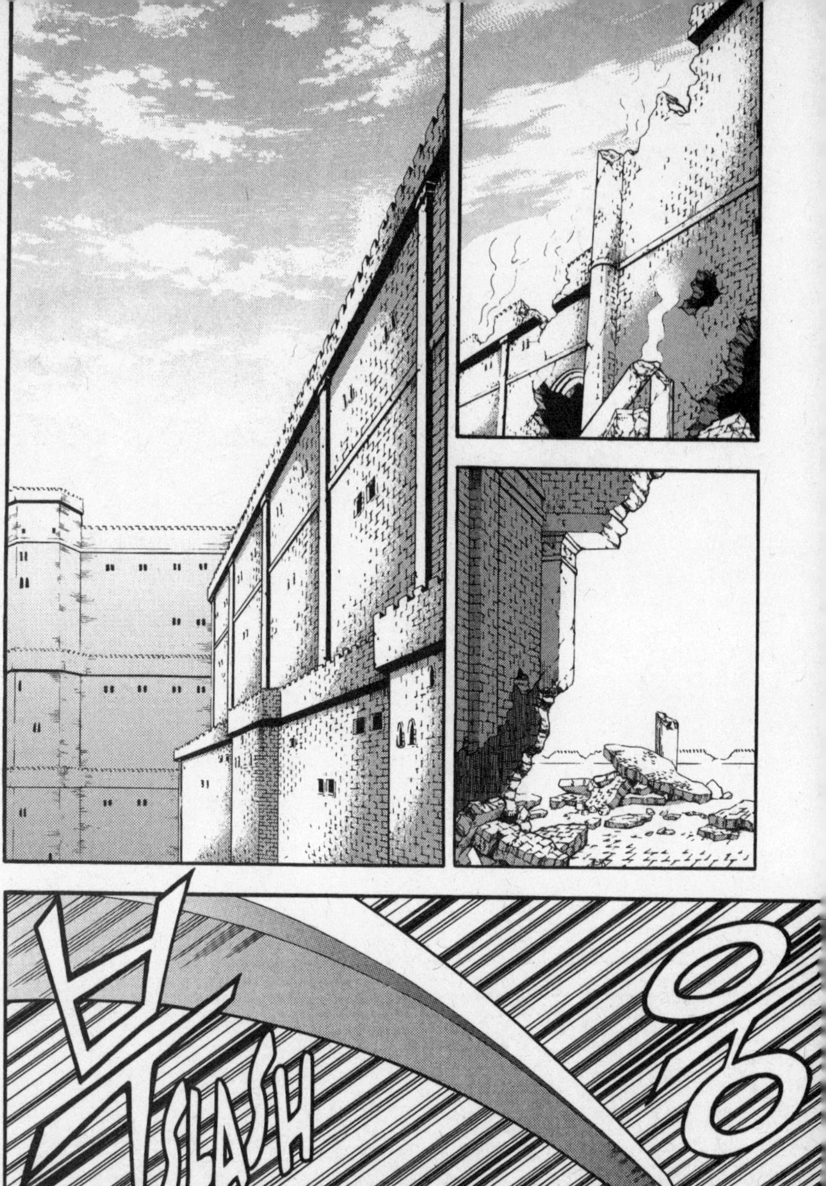
SLASH

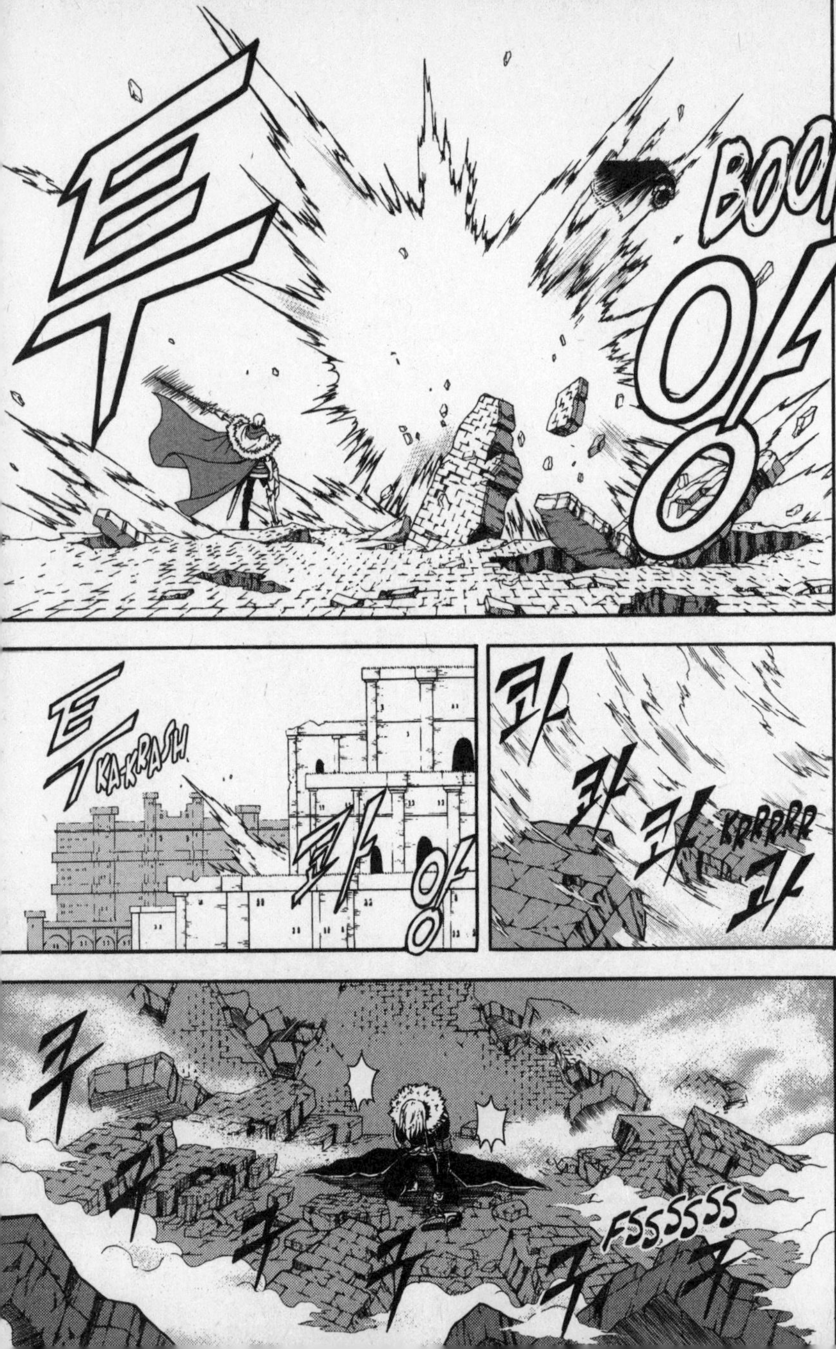
BOOM
KA-KRASH
KRRRRR
FSSSSSS

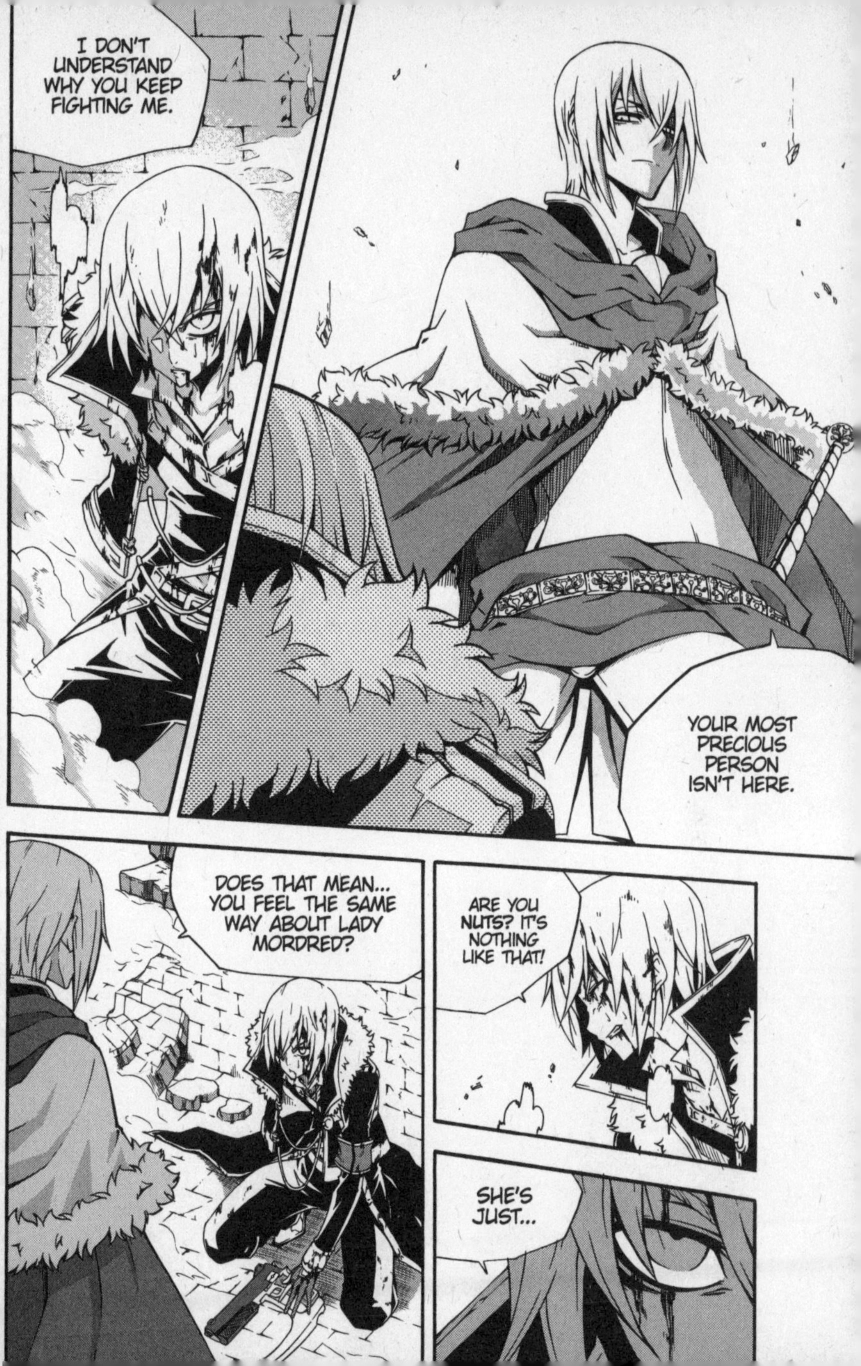
I DON'T UNDERSTAND WHY YOU KEEP FIGHTING ME.
YOUR MOST PRECIOUS PERSON ISN'T HERE.
DOES THAT MEAN... YOU FEEL THE SAME WAY ABOUT LADY MORDRED?
ARE YOU NUTS? IT'S NOTHING LIKE THAT!
SHE'S JUST...

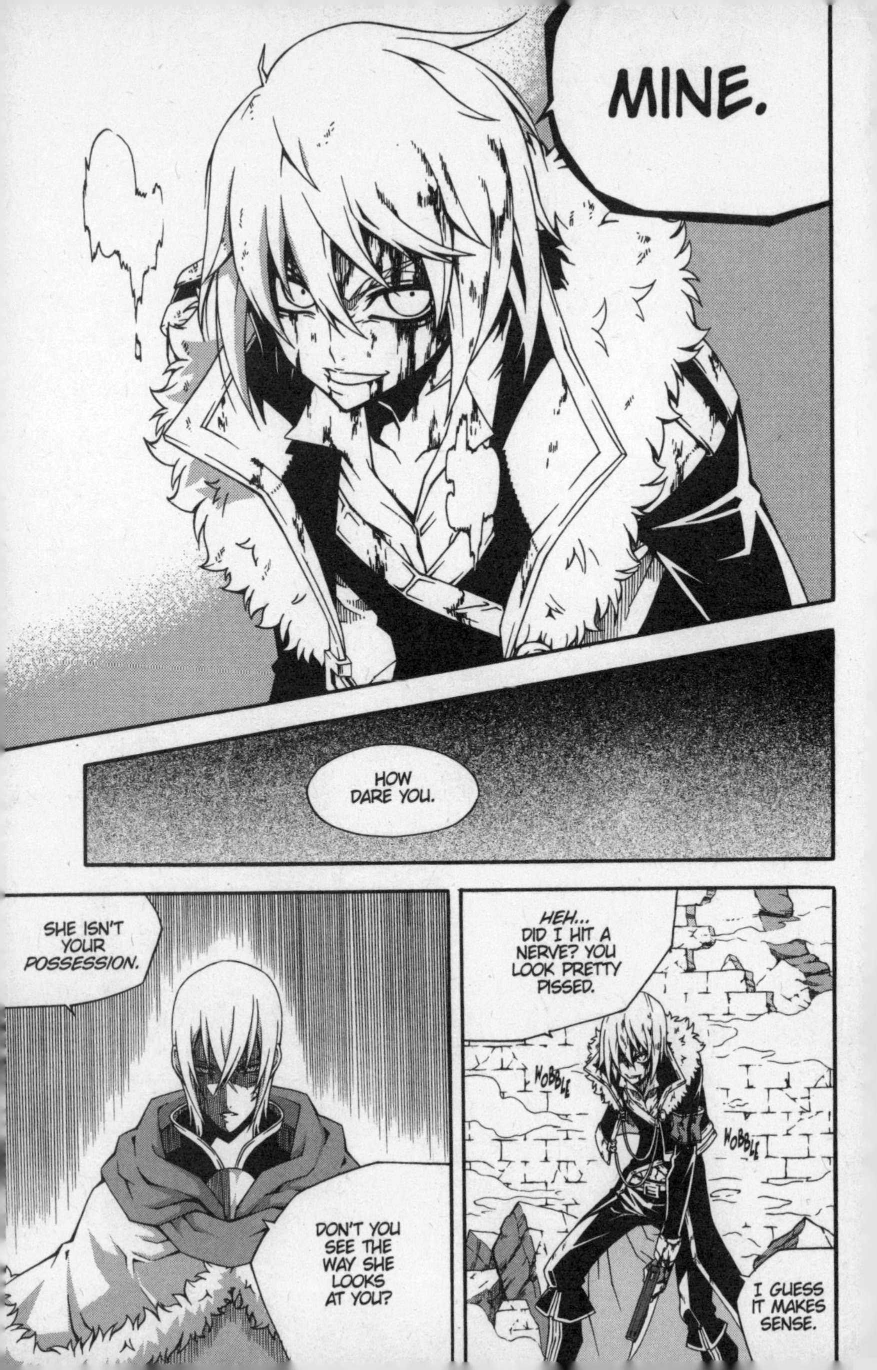
MINE.
HOW DARE YOU.
SHE ISN'T YOUR POSSESSION.
DON'T YOU SEE THE WAY SHE LOOKS AT YOU?
HEH... DID I HIT A NERVE? YOU LOOK PRETTY PISSED.
WOBBLE
WOBBLE
I GUESS IT MAKES SENSE.

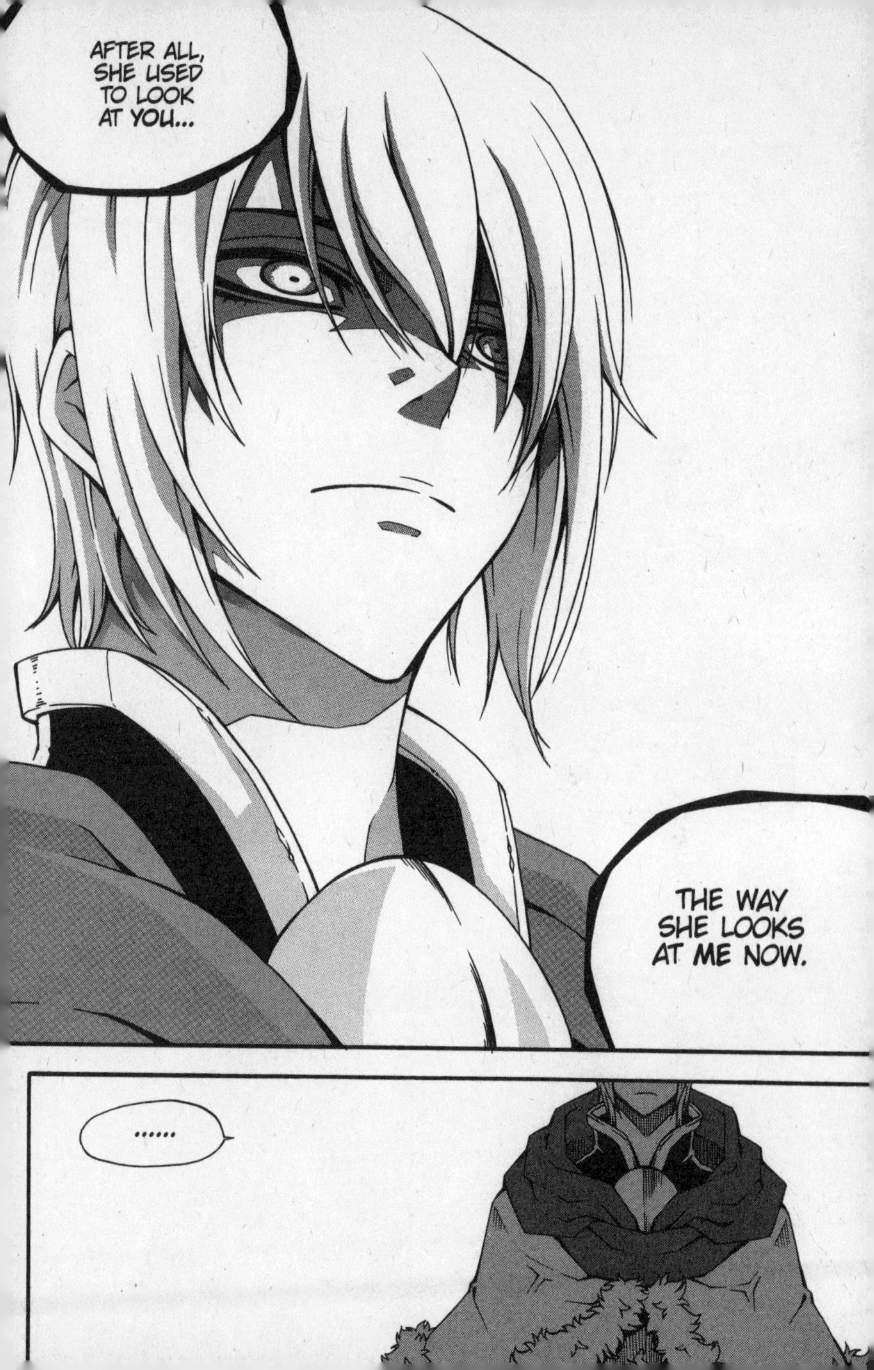
AFTER ALL, SHE USED TO LOOK AT YOU...
THE WAY SHE LOOKS AT ME NOW.
......

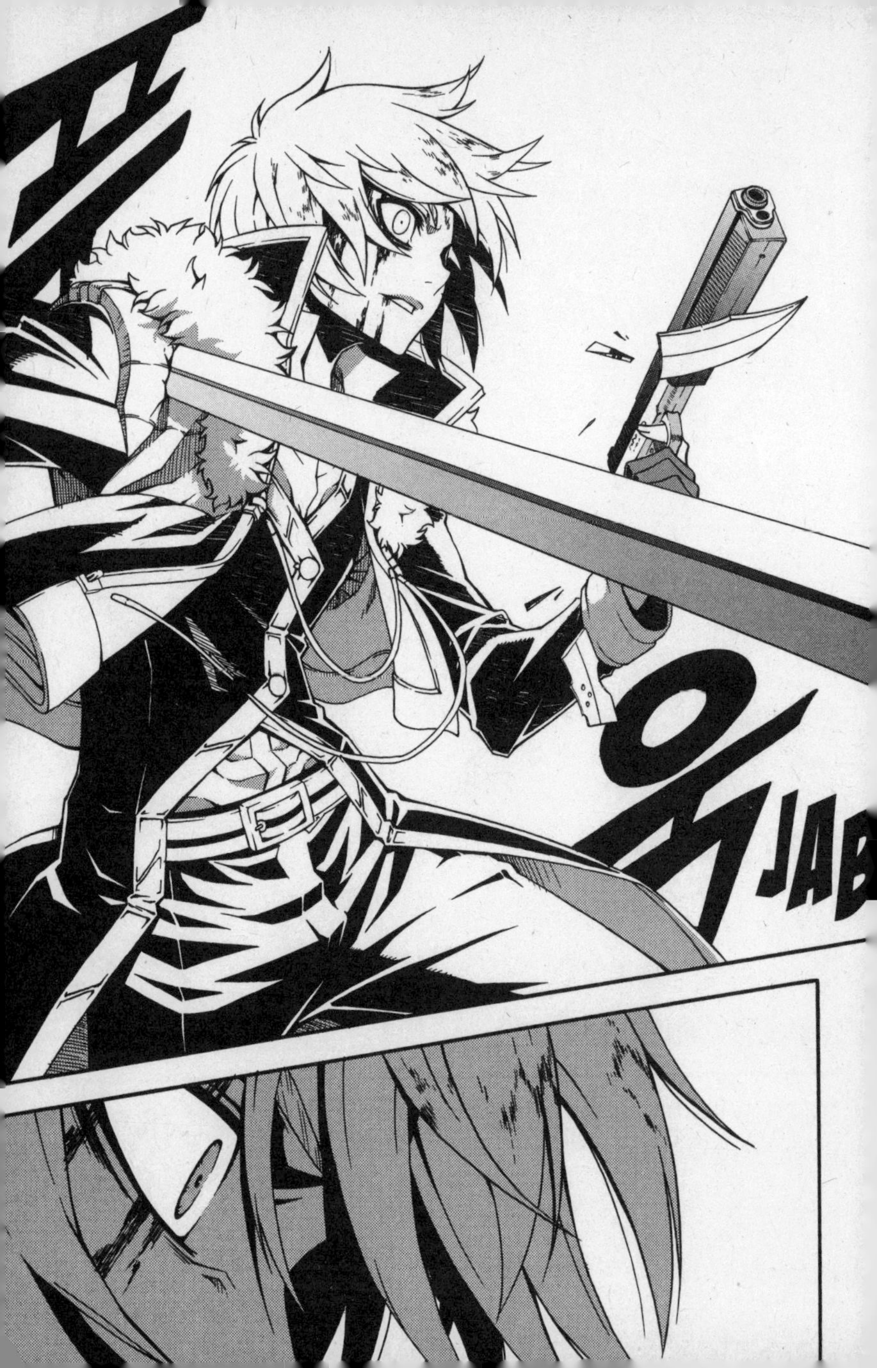
JAB

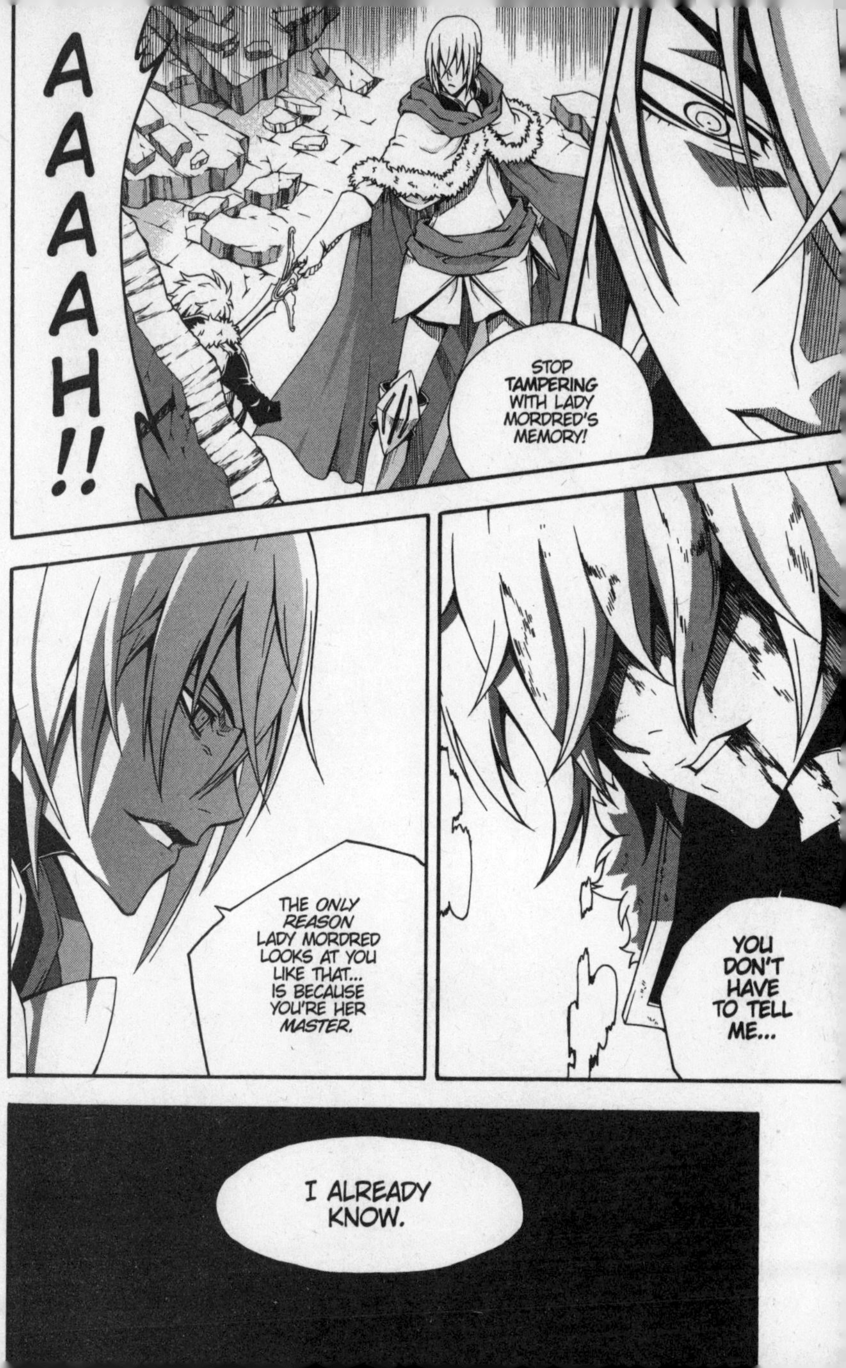
AAAAAH!!
STOP TAMPERING WITH LADY MORDRED'S MEMORY!
THE ONLY REASON LADY MORDRED LOOKS AT YOU LIKE THAT... IS BECAUSE YOU'RE HER MASTER.
YOU DON'T HAVE TO TELL ME...
I ALREADY KNOW.

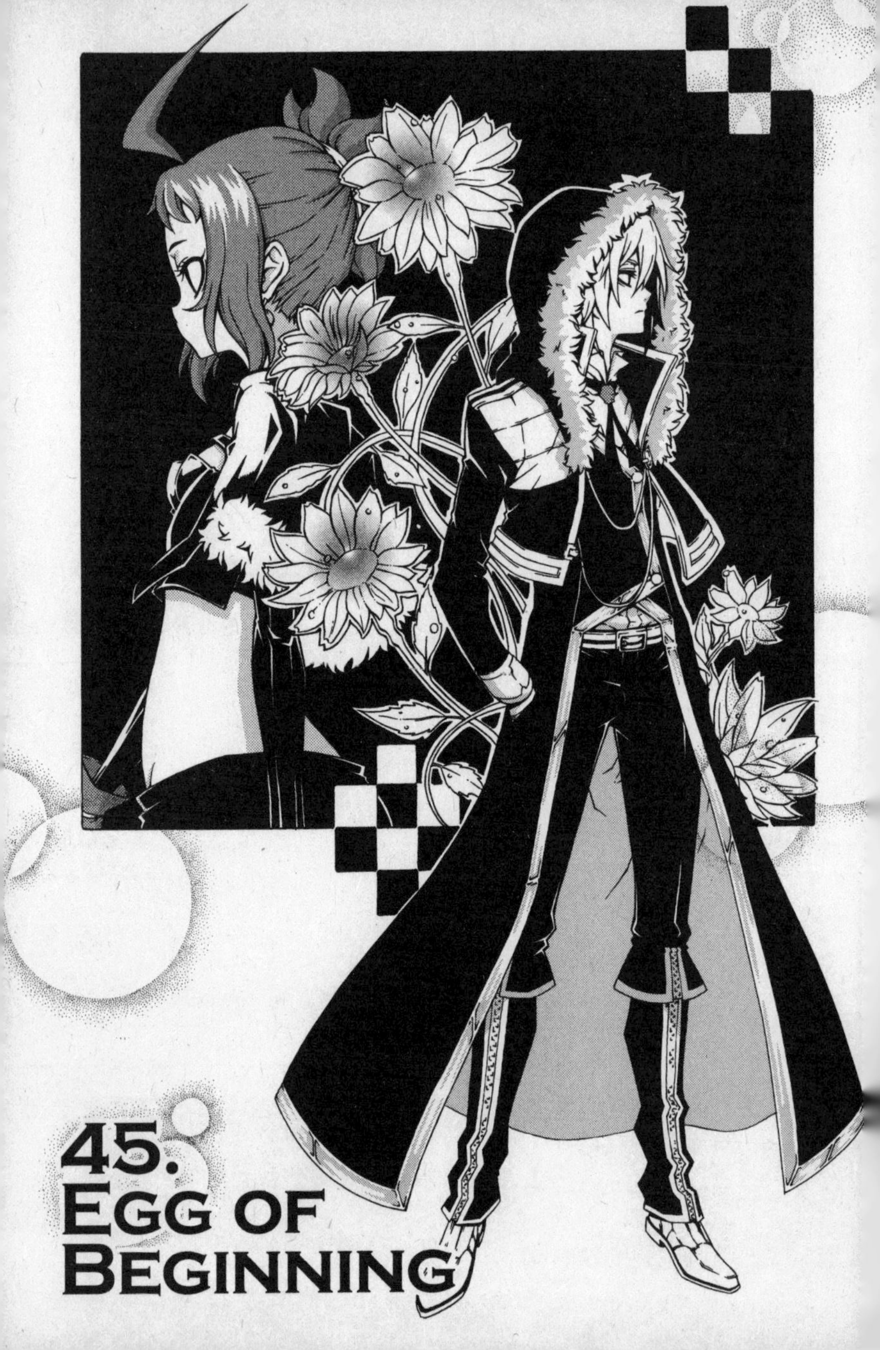

45. Egg of Beginning

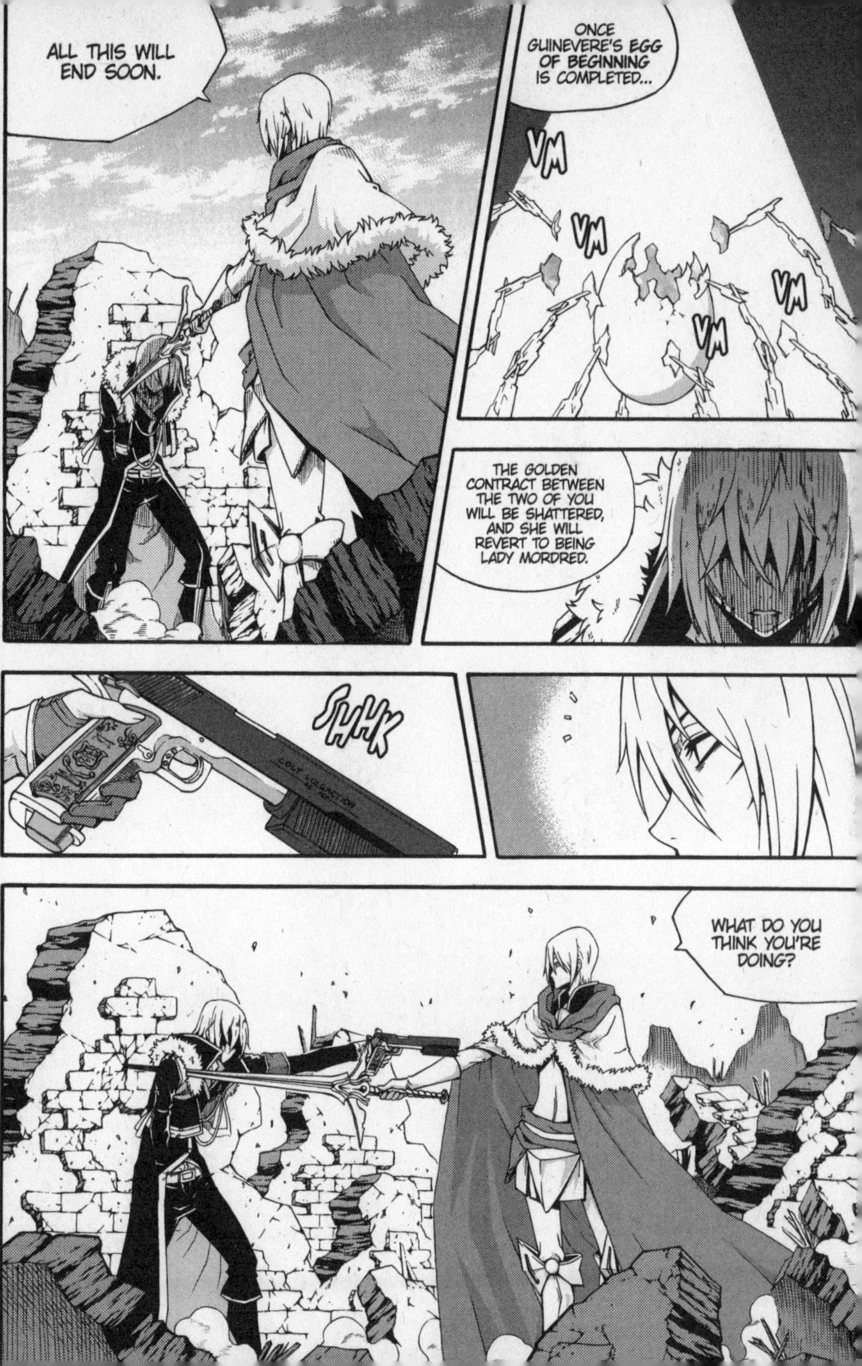
ALL THIS WILL END SOON.
ONCE GUINEVERE'S EGG OF BEGINNING IS COMPLETED...
VM
VM
VM
VM
THE GOLDEN CONTRACT BETWEEN THE TWO OF YOU WILL BE SHATTERED, AND SHE WILL REVERT TO BEING LADY MORDRED.
SHHK
WHAT DO YOU THINK YOU'RE DOING?

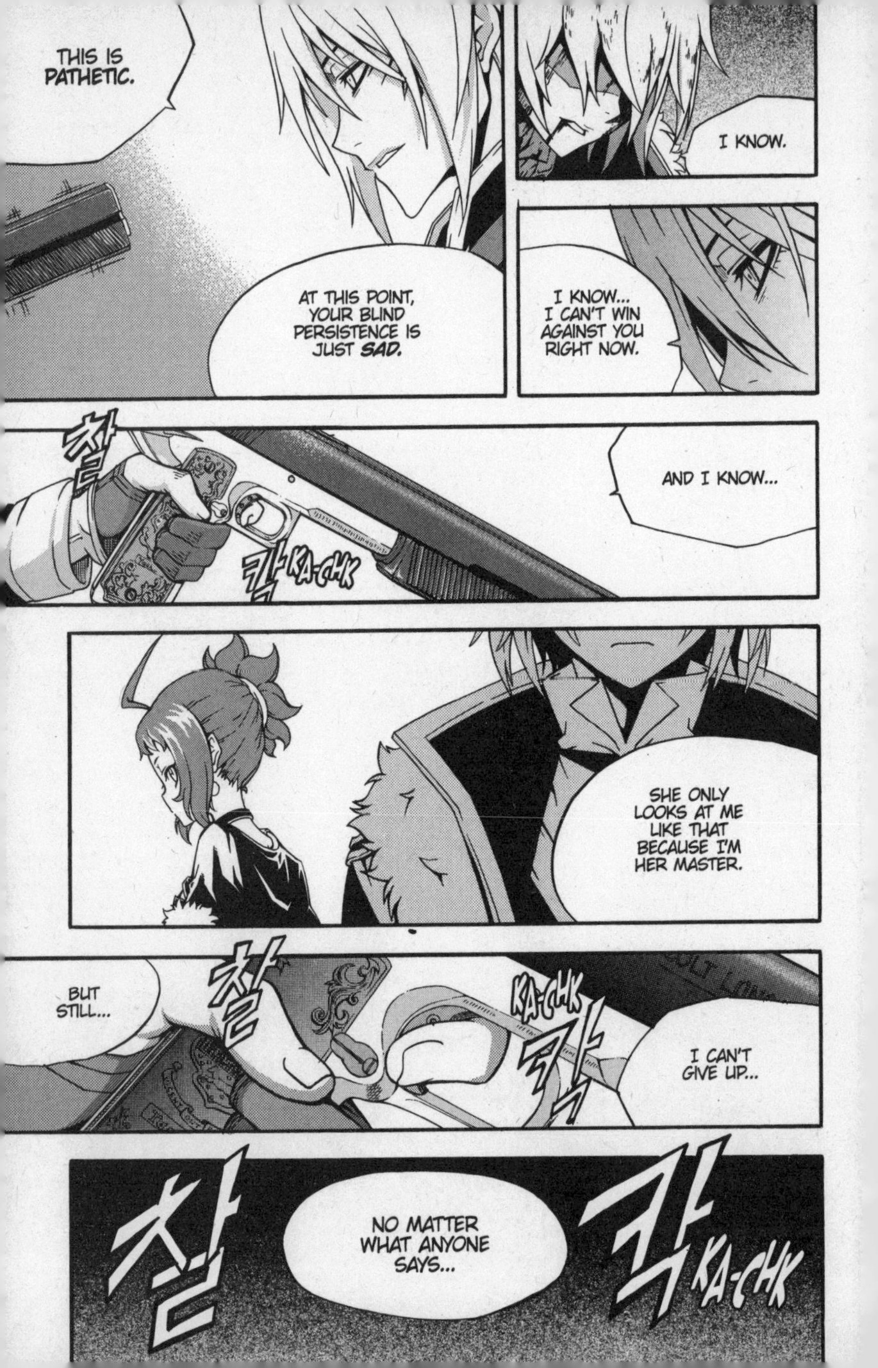
THIS IS PATHETIC.
AT THIS POINT, YOUR BLIND PERSISTENCE IS JUST *SAD.*
I KNOW.
I KNOW... I CAN'T WIN AGAINST YOU RIGHT NOW.
찰칵 KA-CHK
AND I KNOW...
SHE ONLY LOOKS AT ME LIKE THAT BECAUSE I'M HER MASTER.
BUT STILL...
찰칵 KA-CHK
I CAN'T GIVE UP...
찰칵 KA-CHK
NO MATTER WHAT ANYONE SAYS...

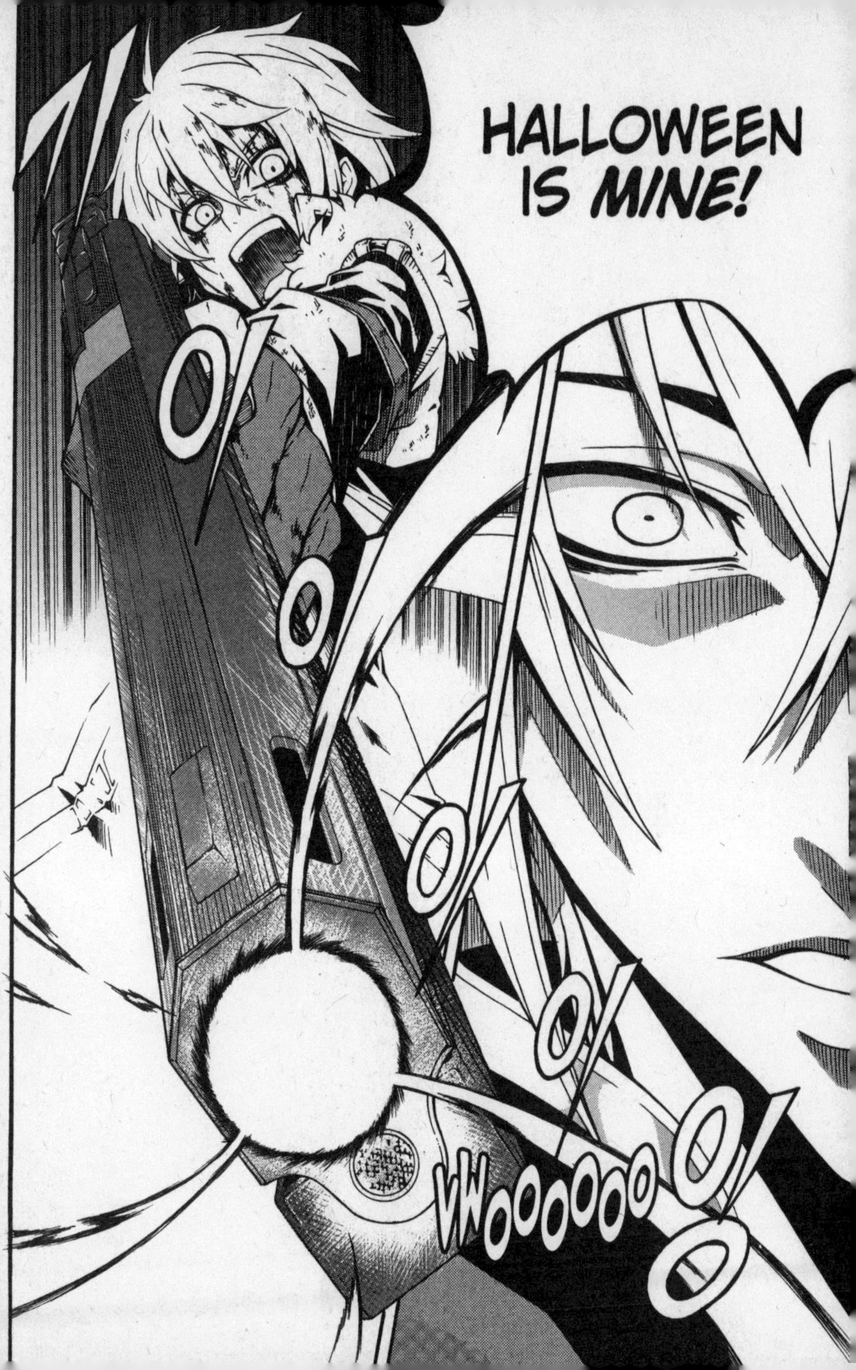
HALLOWEEN IS MINE!
VWOOOOOOO

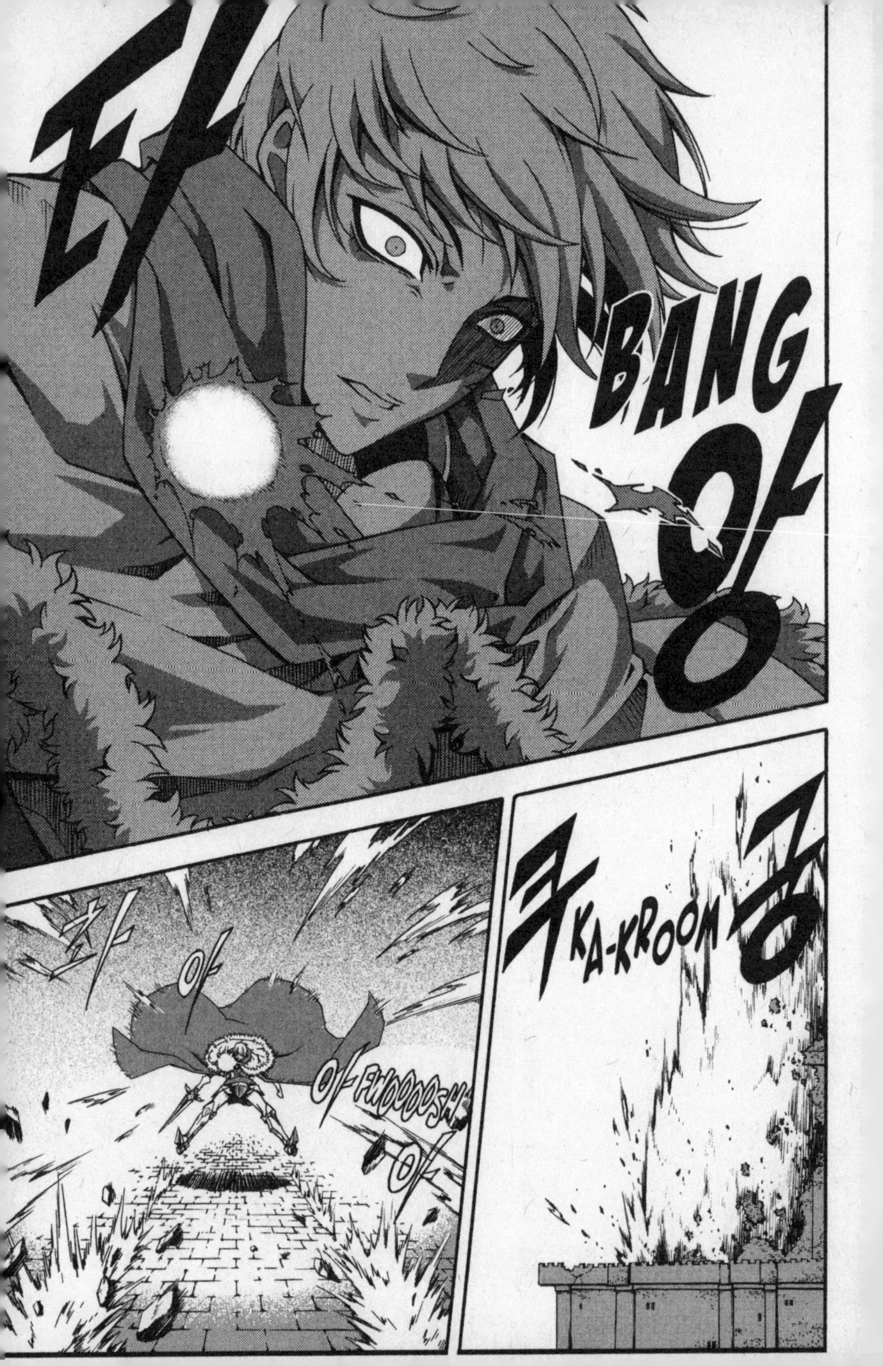
BANG
FWOOOOSH
KA-KROOM

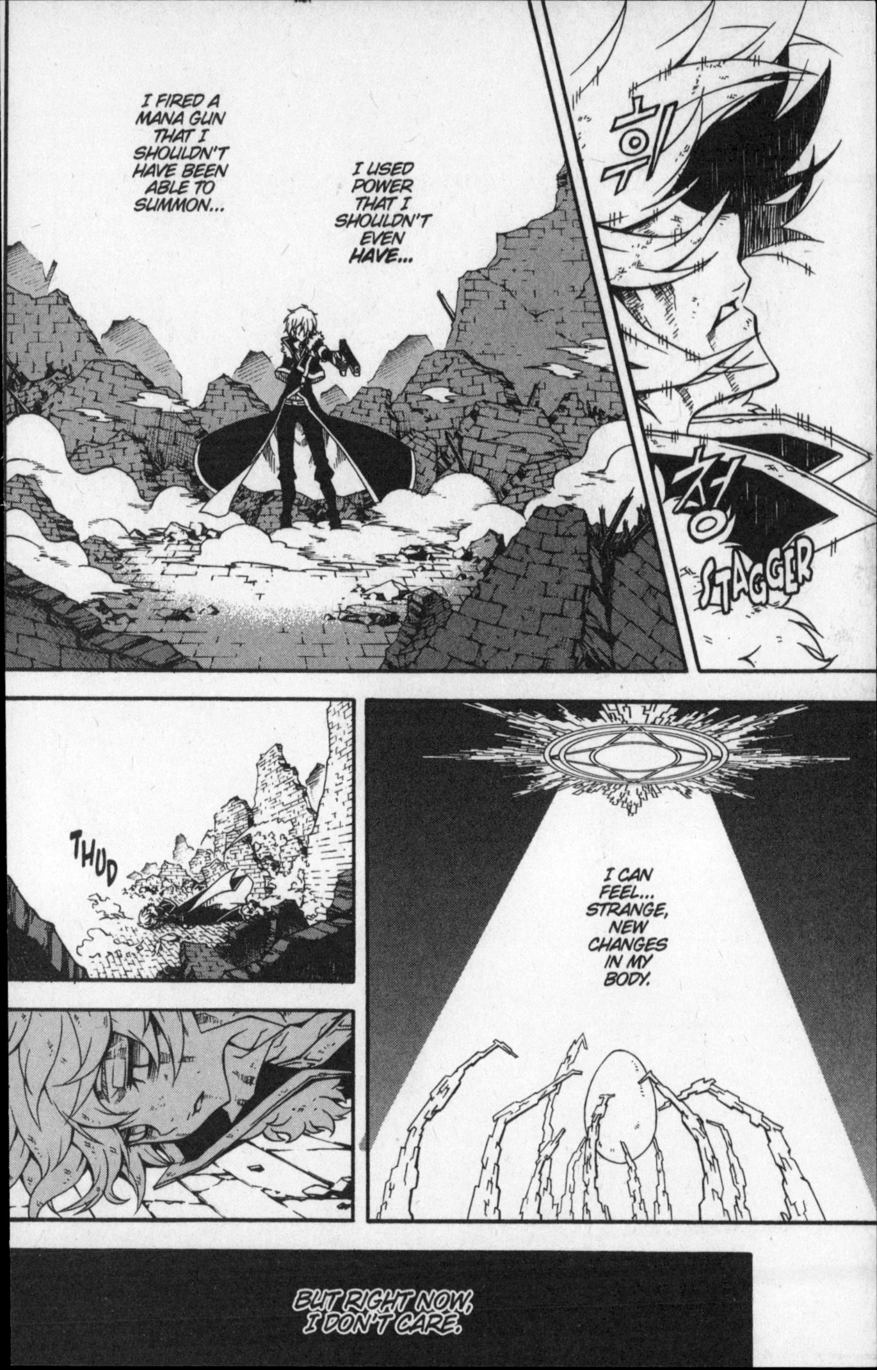
I FIRED A MANA GUN THAT I SHOULDN'T HAVE BEEN ABLE TO SUMMON...
I USED POWER THAT I SHOULDN'T EVEN HAVE...
STAGGER
THUD
I CAN FEEL... STRANGE, NEW CHANGES IN MY BODY.
BUT RIGHT NOW, I DON'T CARE.

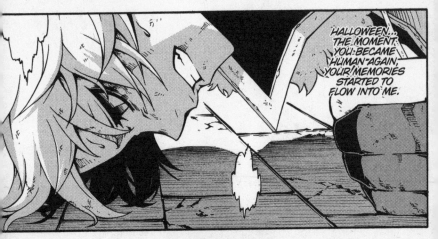

HALLOWEEN... THE MOMENT YOU BECAME HUMAN AGAIN, YOUR MEMORIES STARTED TO FLOW INTO ME.

SO...I KNOW YOU'D BE A LOT HAPPIER WITH THEM.

WITH ME, YOU'RE ALWAYS FIGHTING, ALWAYS INJURED, ALWAYS IN DANGER. I CAN'T GIVE YOU A LIFE OF COMFORT AND LUXURY LIKE THEY COULD.

DRIP

DRIP

DRIP

MAYBE YOU'LL NEVER BE HAPPY IF YOU STAY WITH ME. BUT...

I...

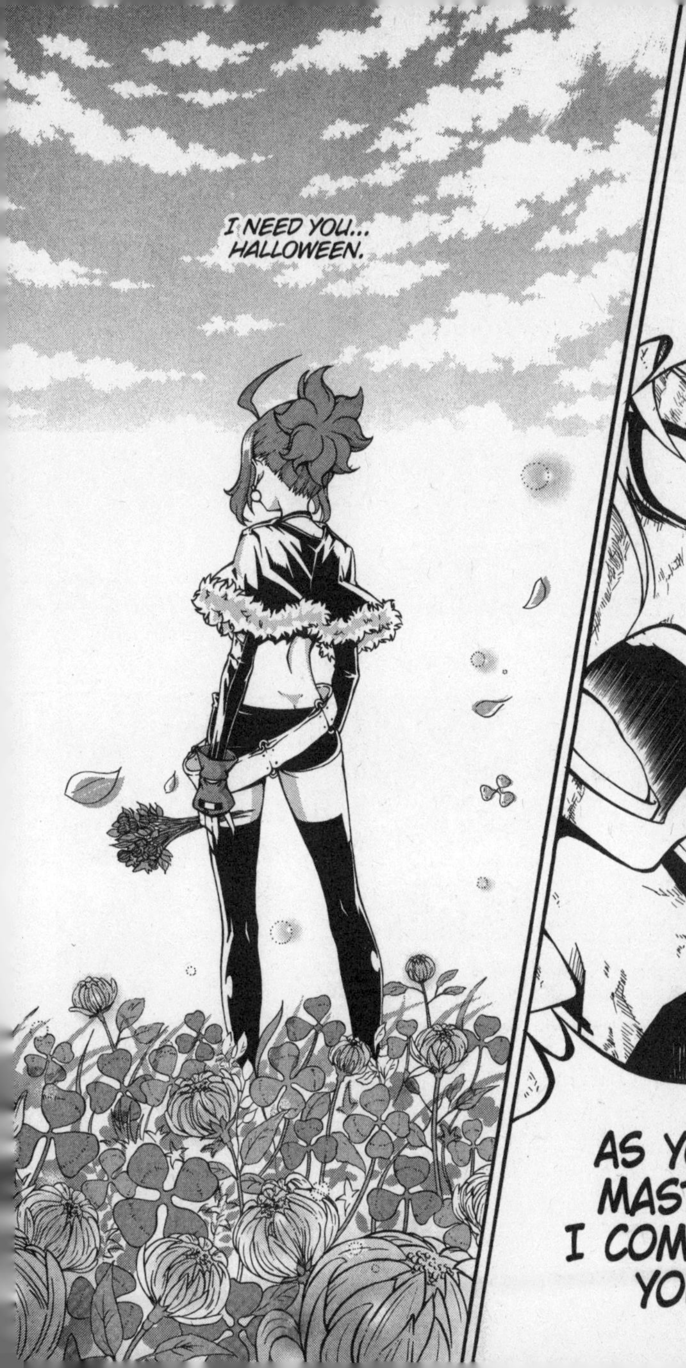
I NEED YOU... HALLOWEEN.
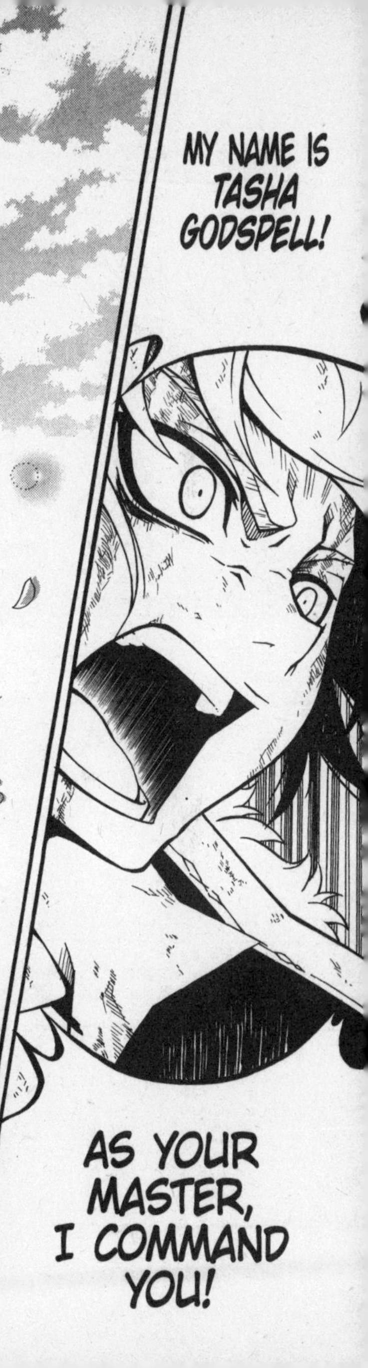
MY NAME IS TASHA GODSPELL!
AS YOUR MASTER, I COMMAND YOU!

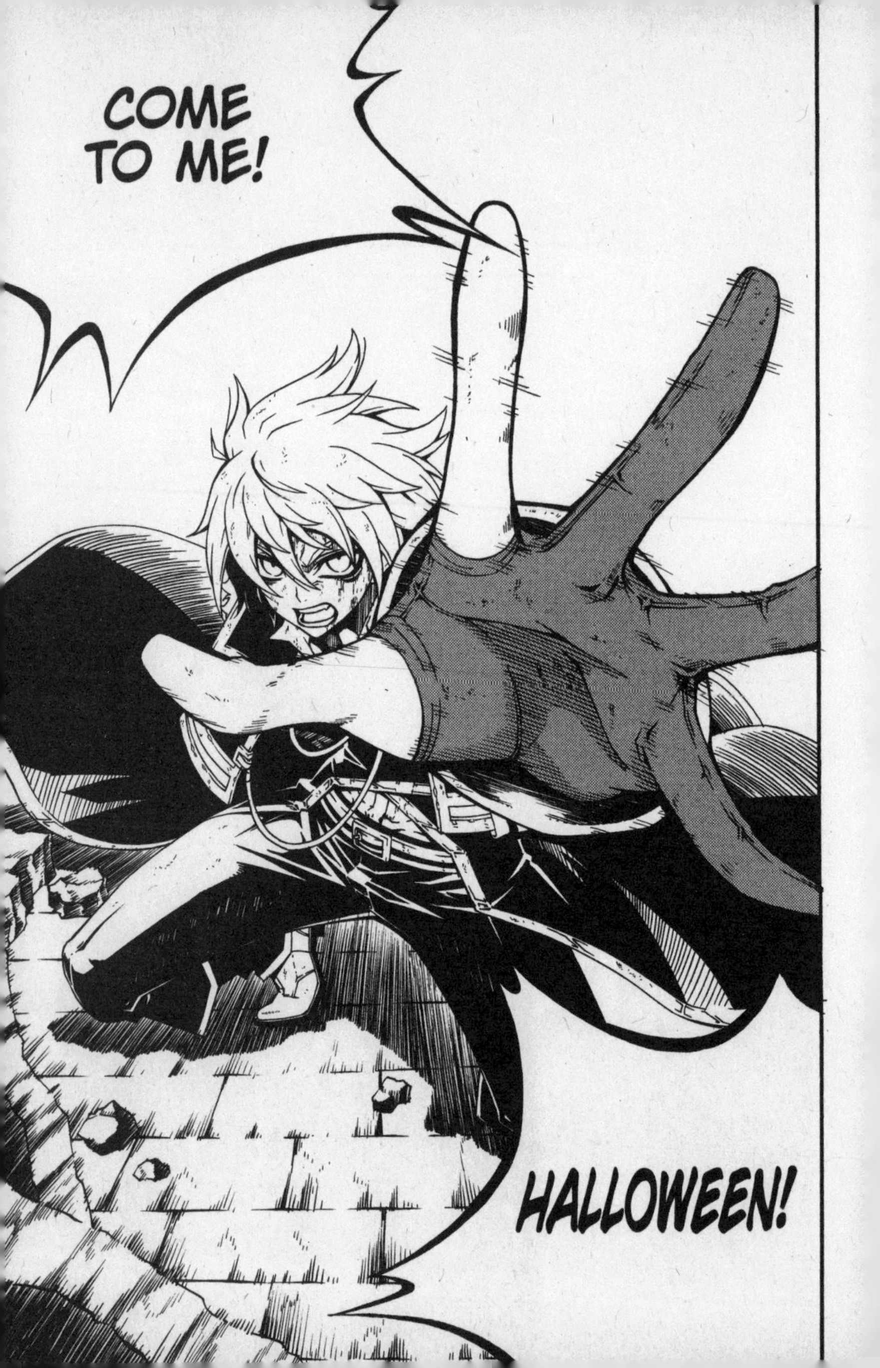
COME TO ME!
HALLOWEEN!

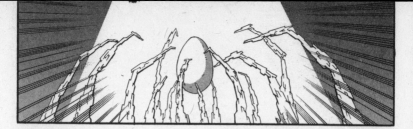

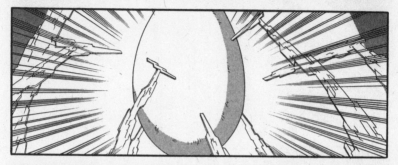

BA-BMP

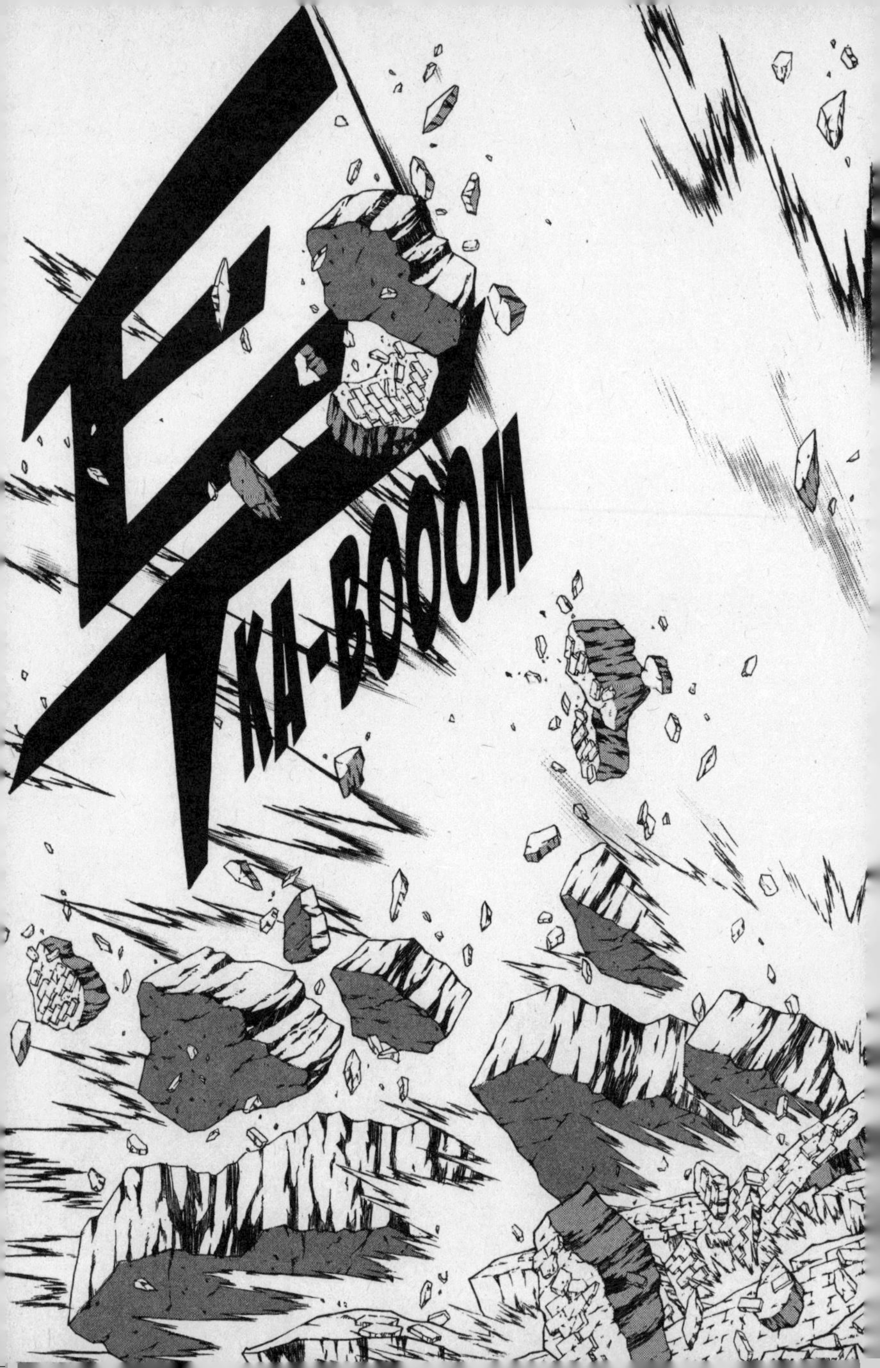
KA-BOOOM

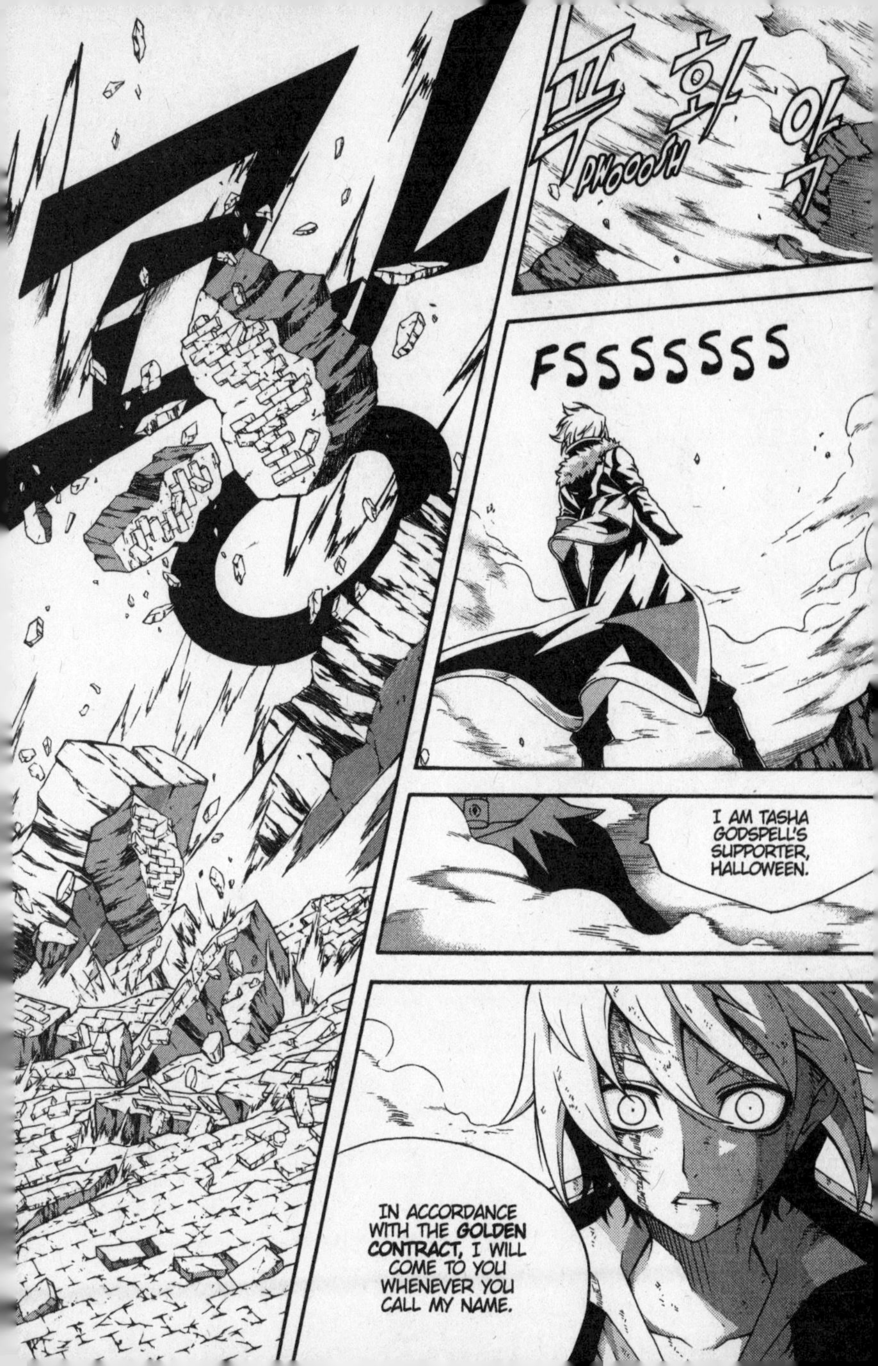
푸화악
PWOOOSH
FSSSSSSS
I AM TASHA GODSPELL'S SUPPORTER, HALLOWEEN.
IN ACCORDANCE WITH THE GOLDEN CONTRACT, I WILL COME TO YOU WHENEVER YOU CALL MY NAME.

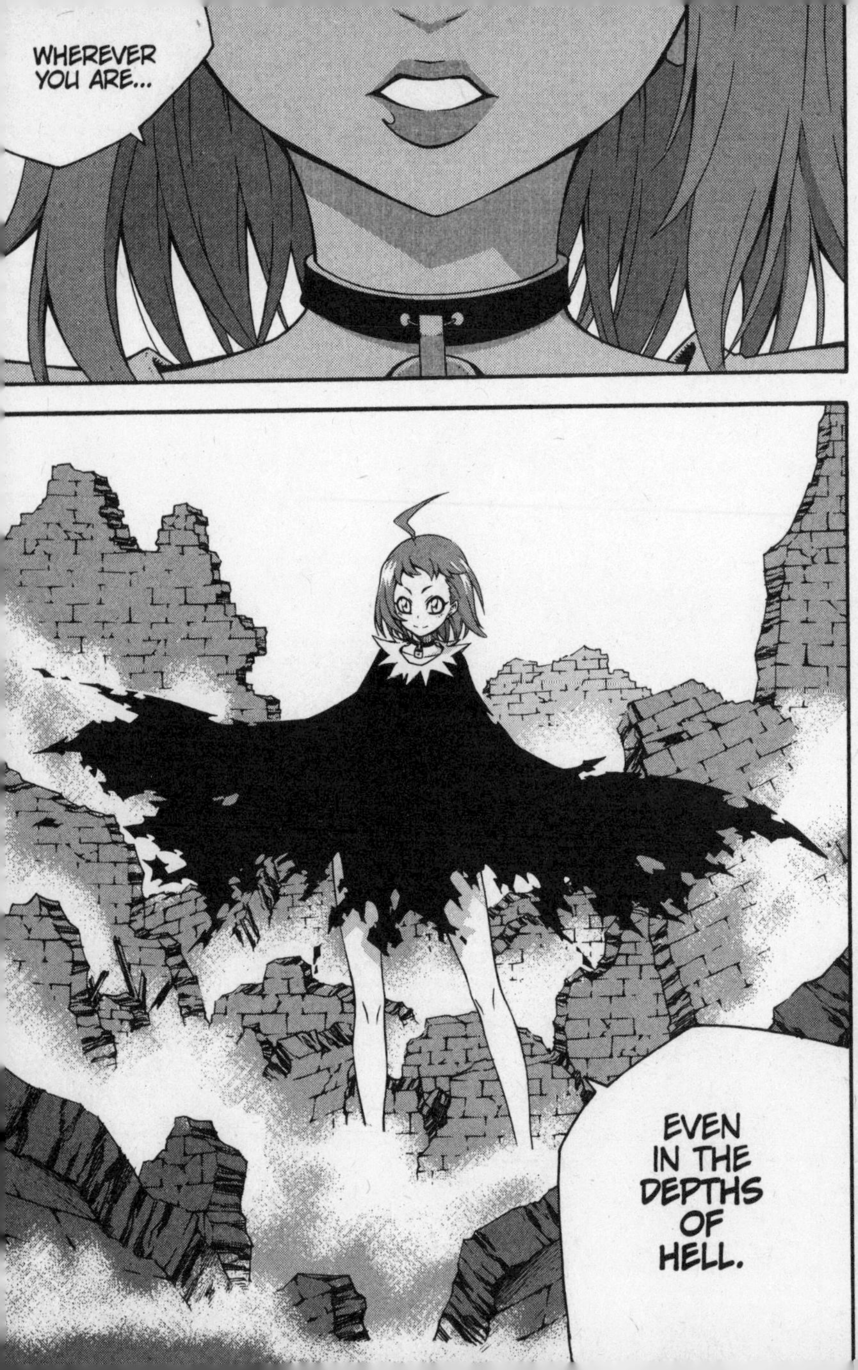
WHEREVER YOU ARE...
EVEN IN THE DEPTHS OF HELL.

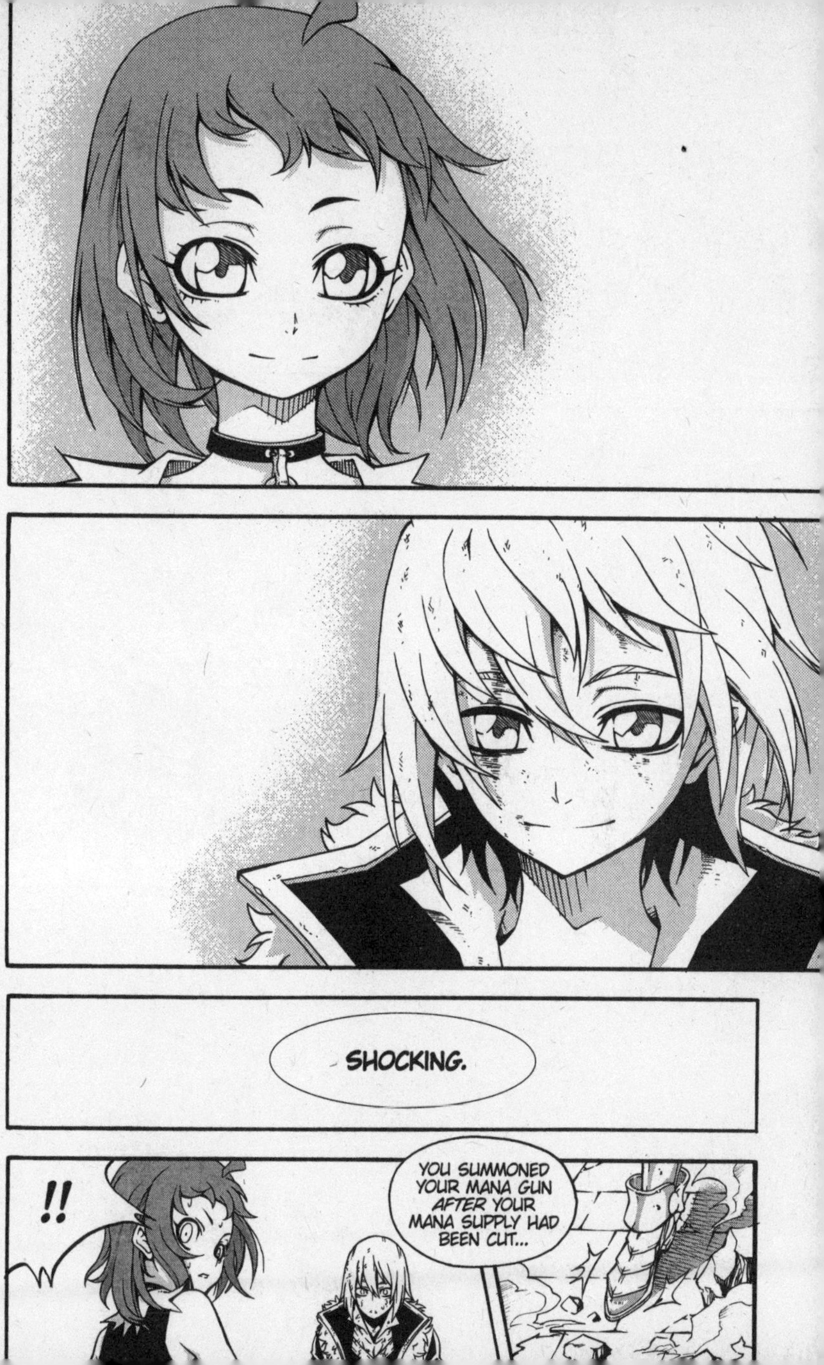
SHOCKING.
!!
YOU SUMMONED YOUR MANA GUN *AFTER* YOUR MANA SUPPLY HAD BEEN CUT...

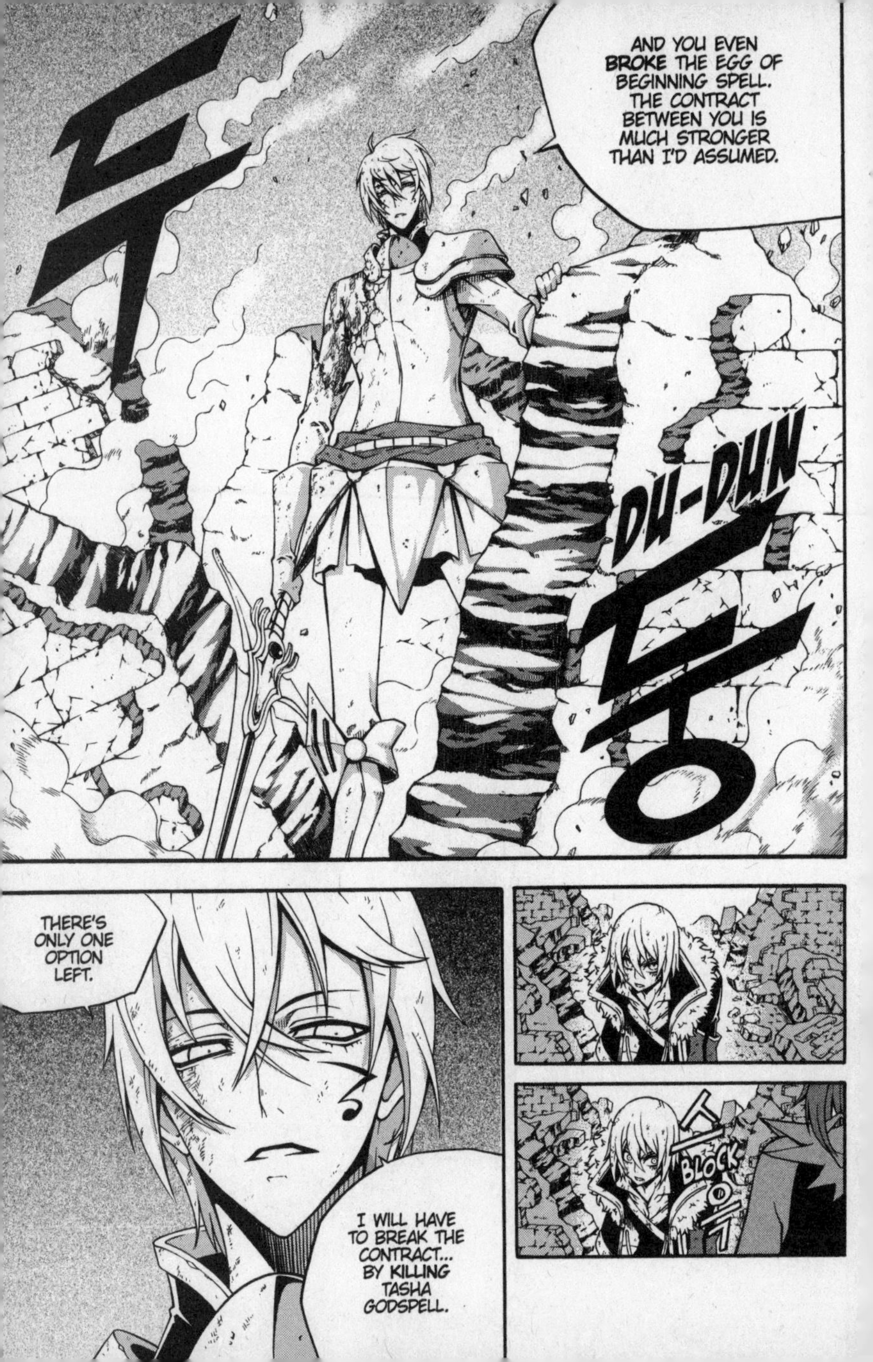
AND YOU EVEN BROKE THE EGG OF BEGINNING SPELL. THE CONTRACT BETWEEN YOU IS MUCH STRONGER THAN I'D ASSUMED.
DU-DUN
THERE'S ONLY ONE OPTION LEFT.
I WILL HAVE TO BREAK THE CONTRACT... BY KILLING TASHA GODSPELL.
BLOCK

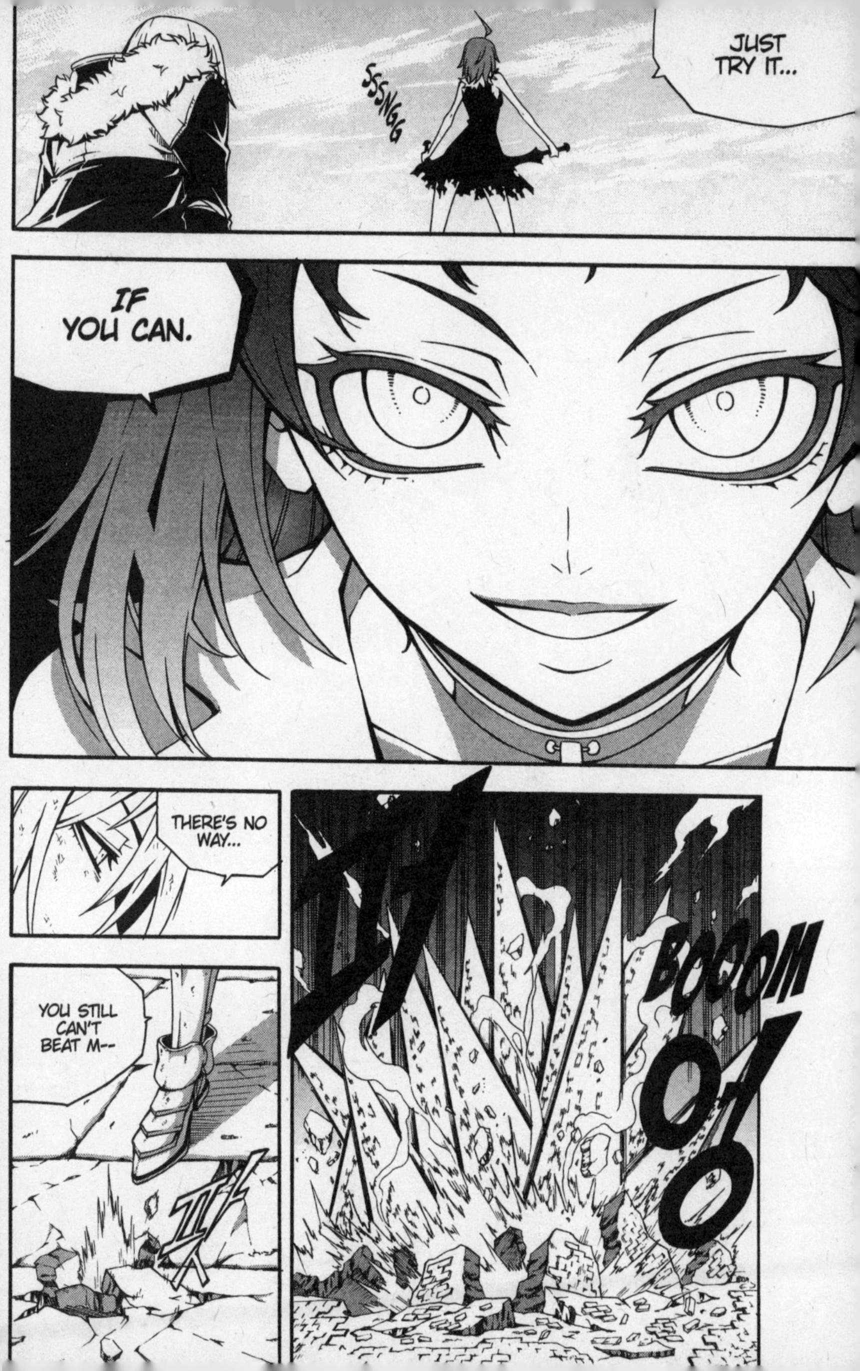
SSSNGG
JUST TRY IT...
IF YOU CAN.
THERE'S NO WAY...
YOU STILL CAN'T BEAT M--
BOOOM

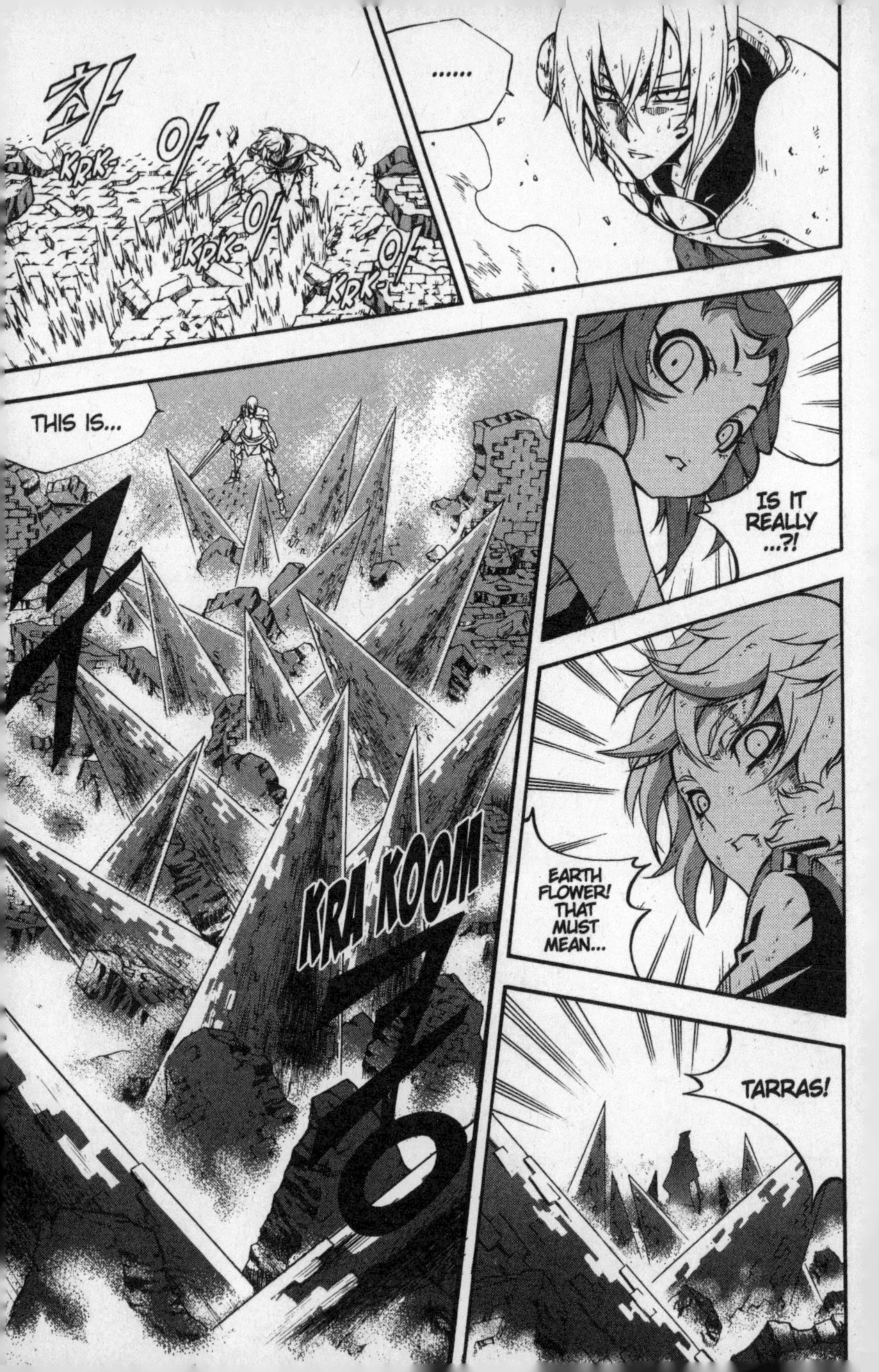
KRK-
KRK-
KRK-
......
THIS IS...
KRA KOOM
IS IT REALLY ...?!
EARTH FLOWER! THAT MUST MEAN...
TARRAS!

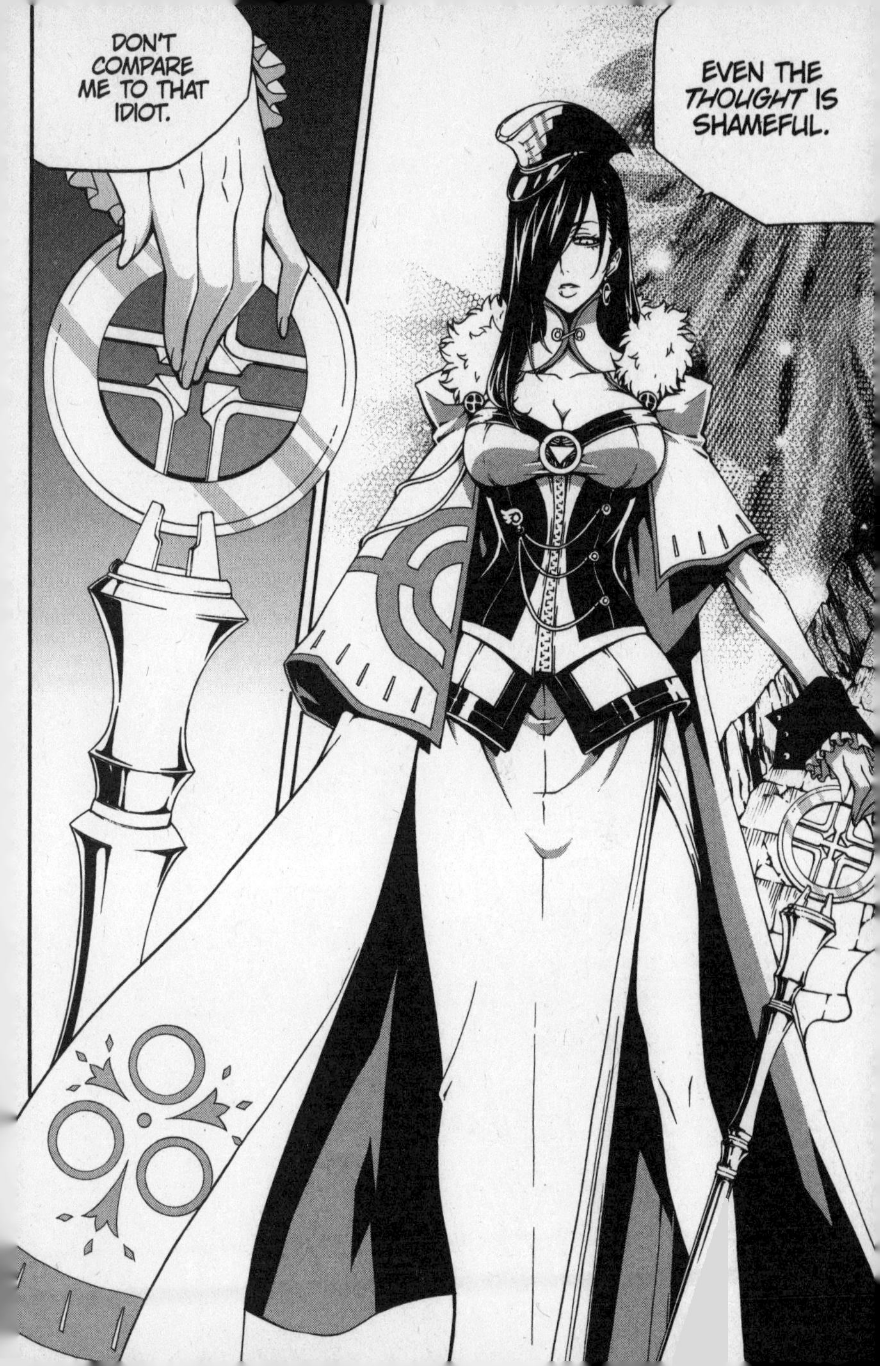
DON'T COMPARE ME TO THAT IDIOT.
EVEN THE *THOUGHT* IS SHAMEFUL.

WITCH BUSTER

THE SYMBOL OF PRITHVI, A SYMBOL OF GREAT POWER, THAT REPRESENTS THE PRITHVI SPIRIT. IT IS ALSO THE CREST OF THE DOBERG FAMILY.

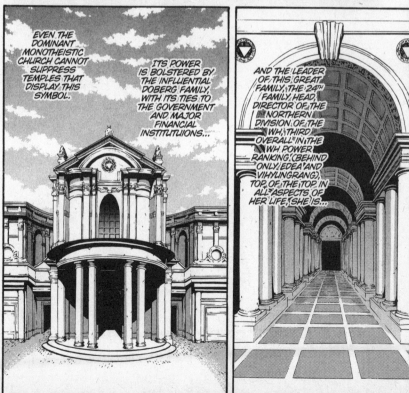

EVEN THE DOMINANT MONOTHEISTIC CHURCH CANNOT SUPPRESS TEMPLES THAT DISPLAY THIS SYMBOL.

ITS POWER IS BOLSTERED BY THE INFLUENTIAL DOBERG FAMILY, WITH ITS TIES TO THE GOVERNMENT AND MAJOR FINANCIAL INSTITUTIONS...

AND THE LEADER OF THIS GREAT FAMILY, THE 24TH FAMILY HEAD, DIRECTOR OF THE NORTHERN DIVISION OF THE WH, THIRD OVERALL IN THE WH POWER RANKING (BEHIND ONLY EDEA AND VIHYUNGRANG), TOP OF THE TOP IN ALL ASPECTS OF HER LIFE, SHE IS...

46. Tania Doberg

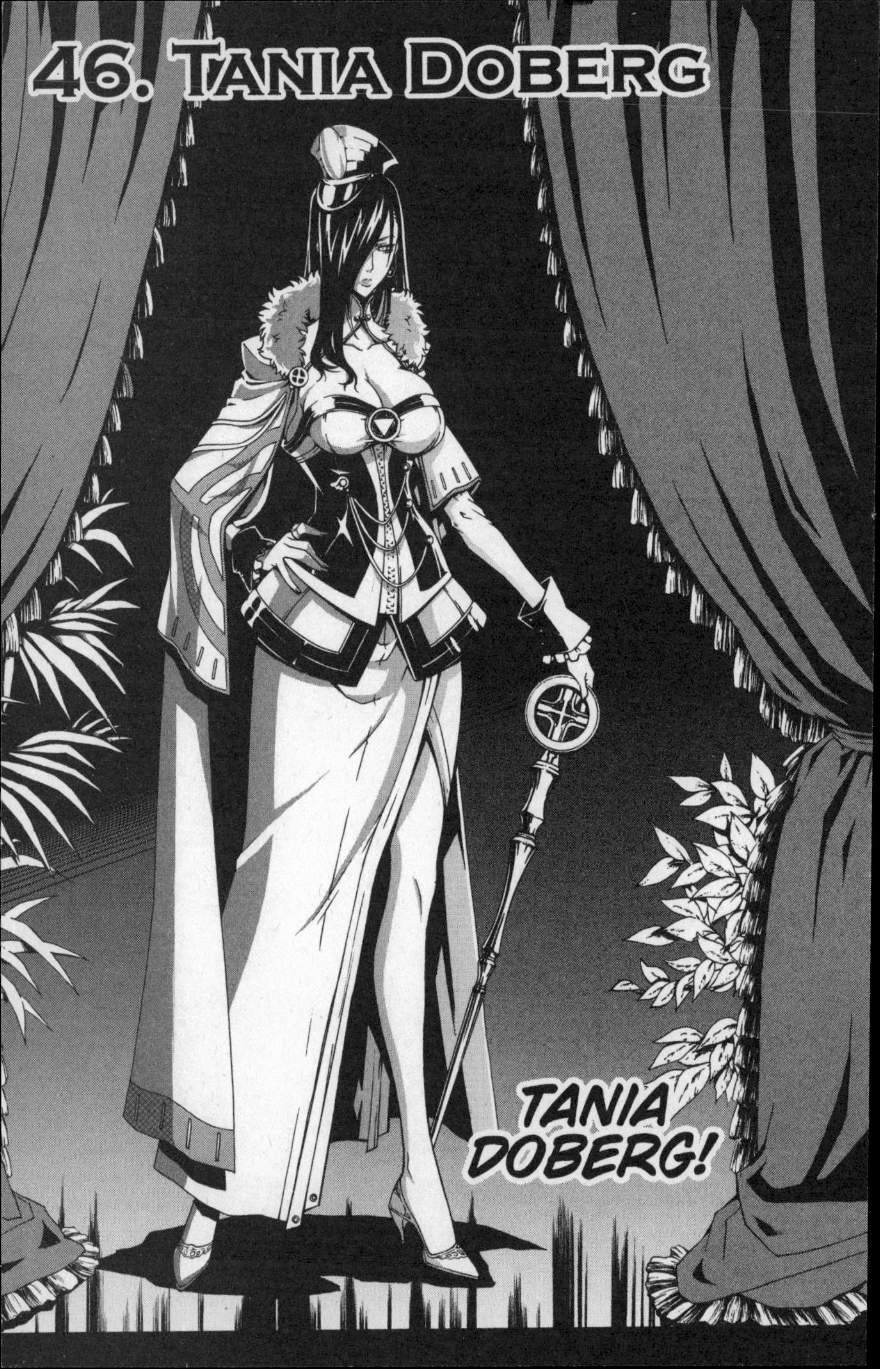
TANIA DOBERG!

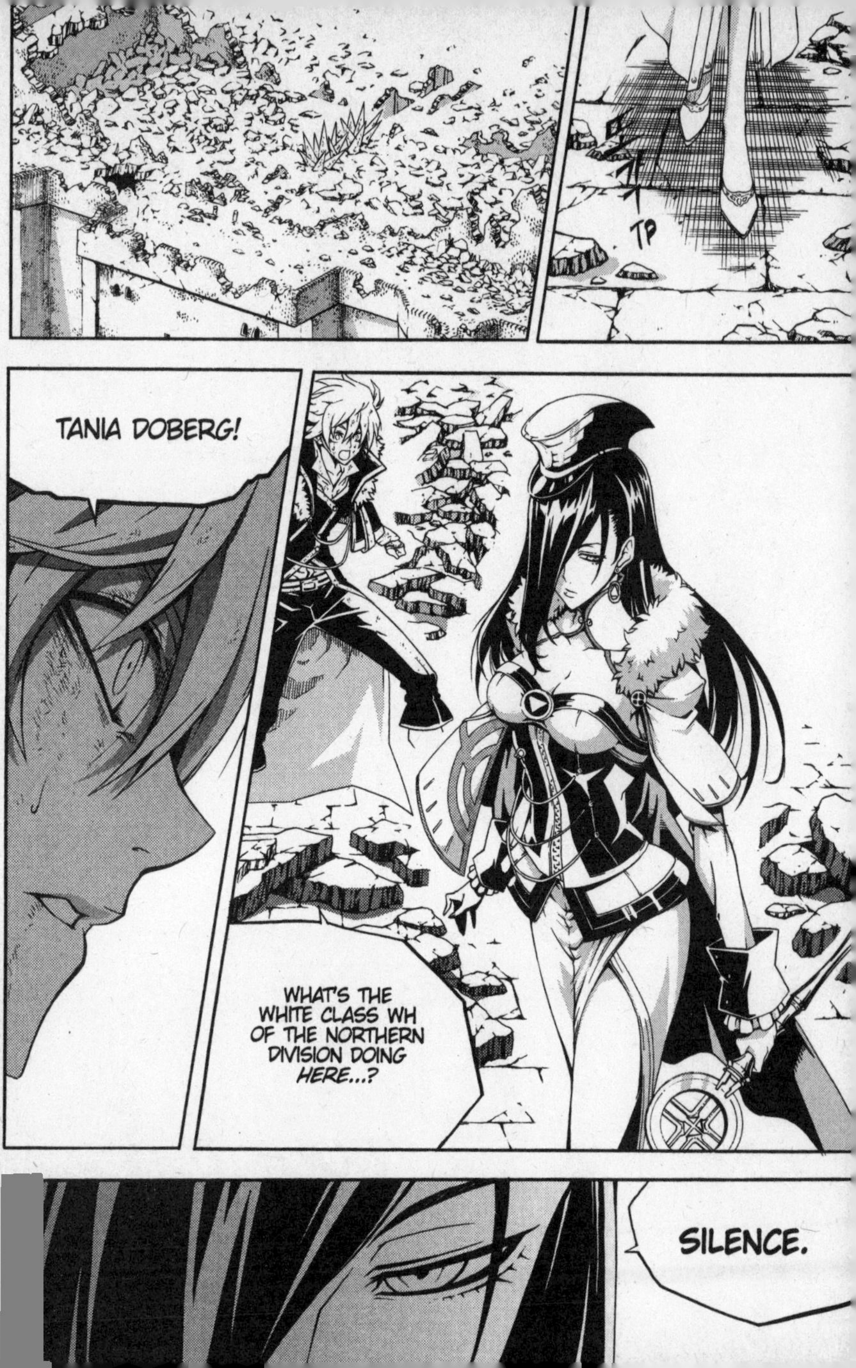
TP
TANIA DOBERG!
WHAT'S THE WHITE CLASS WH OF THE NORTHERN DIVISION DOING HERE...?
SILENCE.

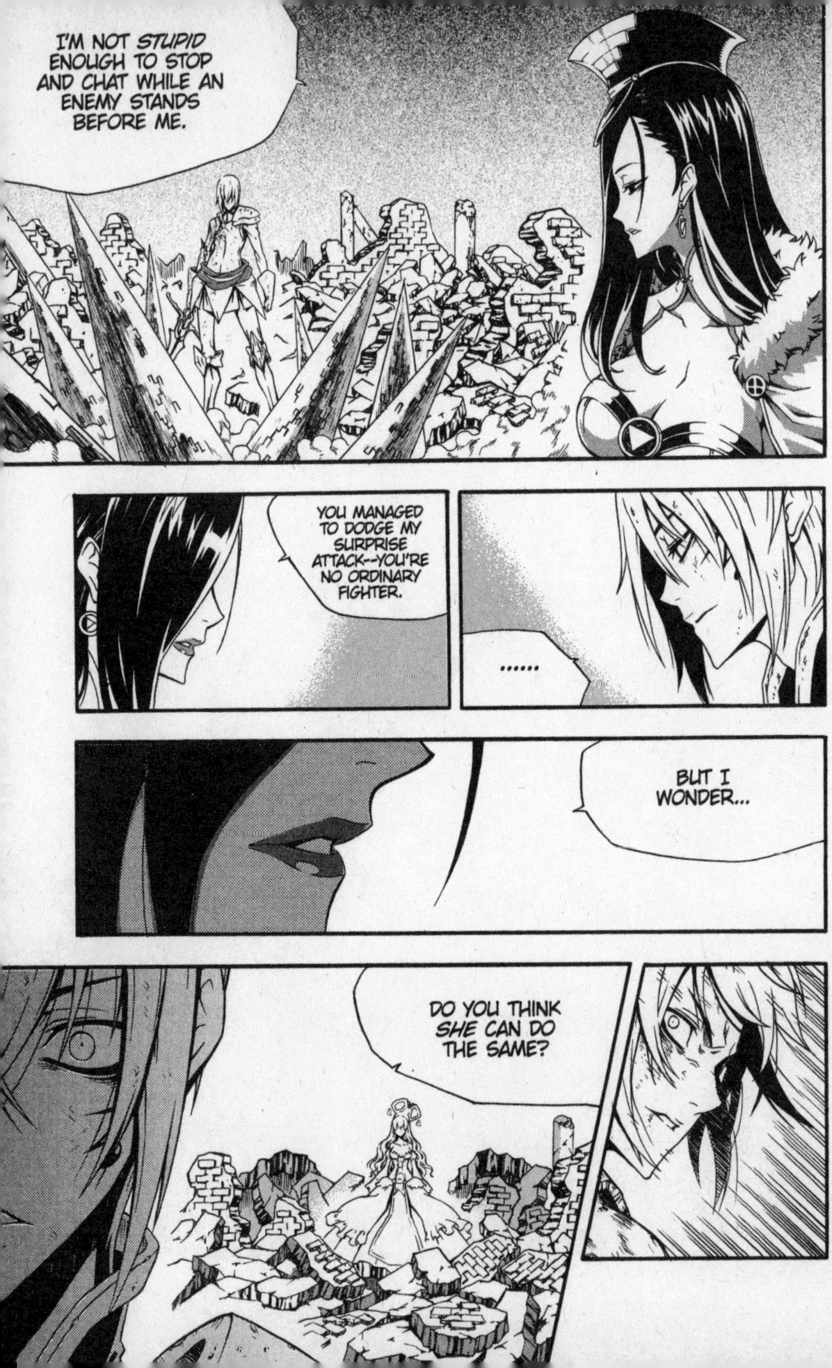

I'M NOT *STUPID* ENOUGH TO STOP AND CHAT WHILE AN ENEMY STANDS BEFORE ME.
YOU MANAGED TO DODGE MY SURPRISE ATTACK--YOU'RE NO ORDINARY FIGHTER.
......
BUT I WONDER...
DO YOU THINK *SHE* CAN DO THE SAME?

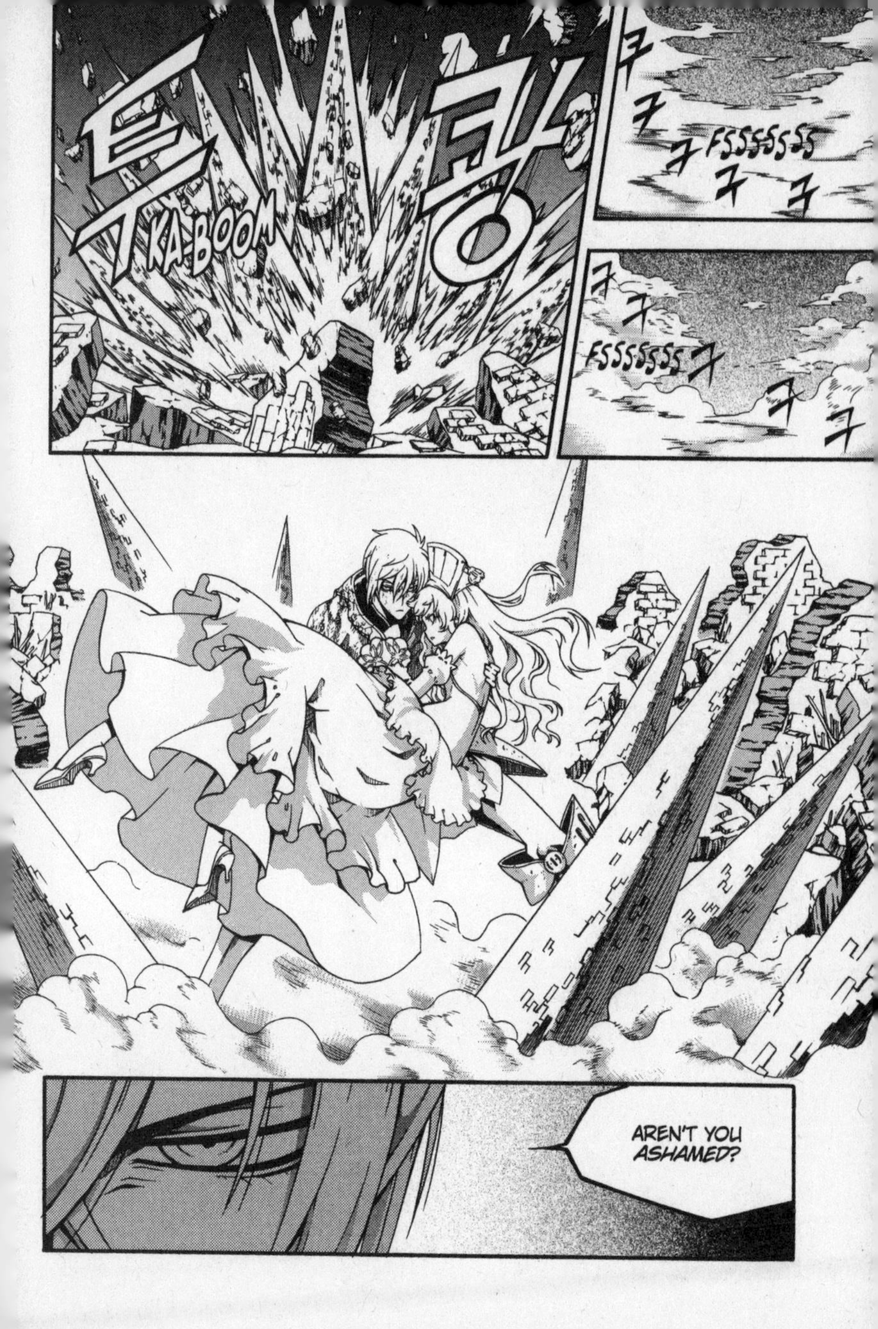
KA-BOOM
FSSSSSSS
FSSSSSSS
AREN'T YOU ASHAMED?

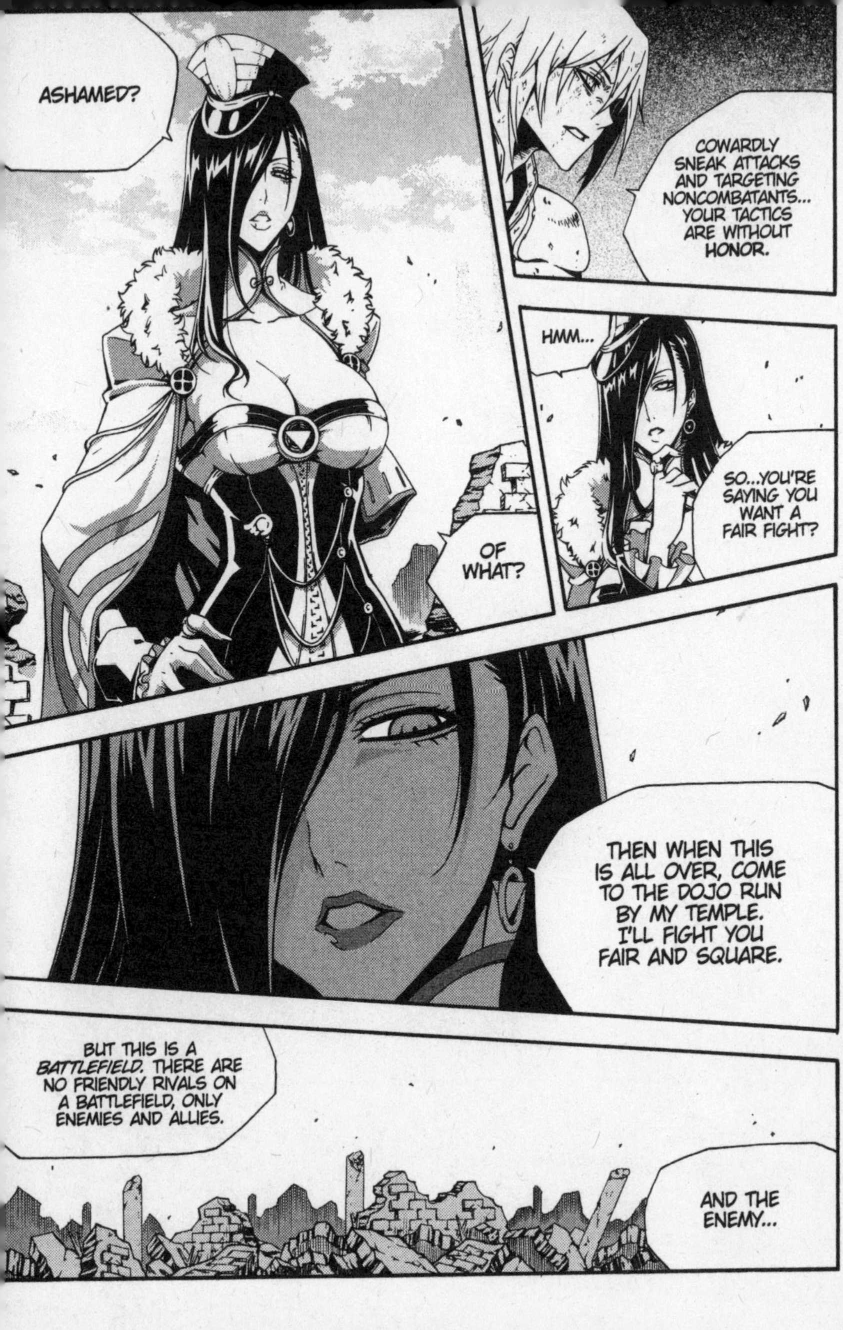
ASHAMED?
OF WHAT?
COWARDLY SNEAK ATTACKS AND TARGETING NONCOMBATANTS... YOUR TACTICS ARE WITHOUT HONOR.
HMM...
SO...YOU'RE SAYING YOU WANT A FAIR FIGHT?
THEN WHEN THIS IS ALL OVER, COME TO THE DOJO RUN BY MY TEMPLE. I'LL FIGHT YOU FAIR AND SQUARE.
BUT THIS IS A *BATTLEFIELD*. THERE ARE NO FRIENDLY RIVALS ON A BATTLEFIELD, ONLY ENEMIES AND ALLIES.
AND THE ENEMY...

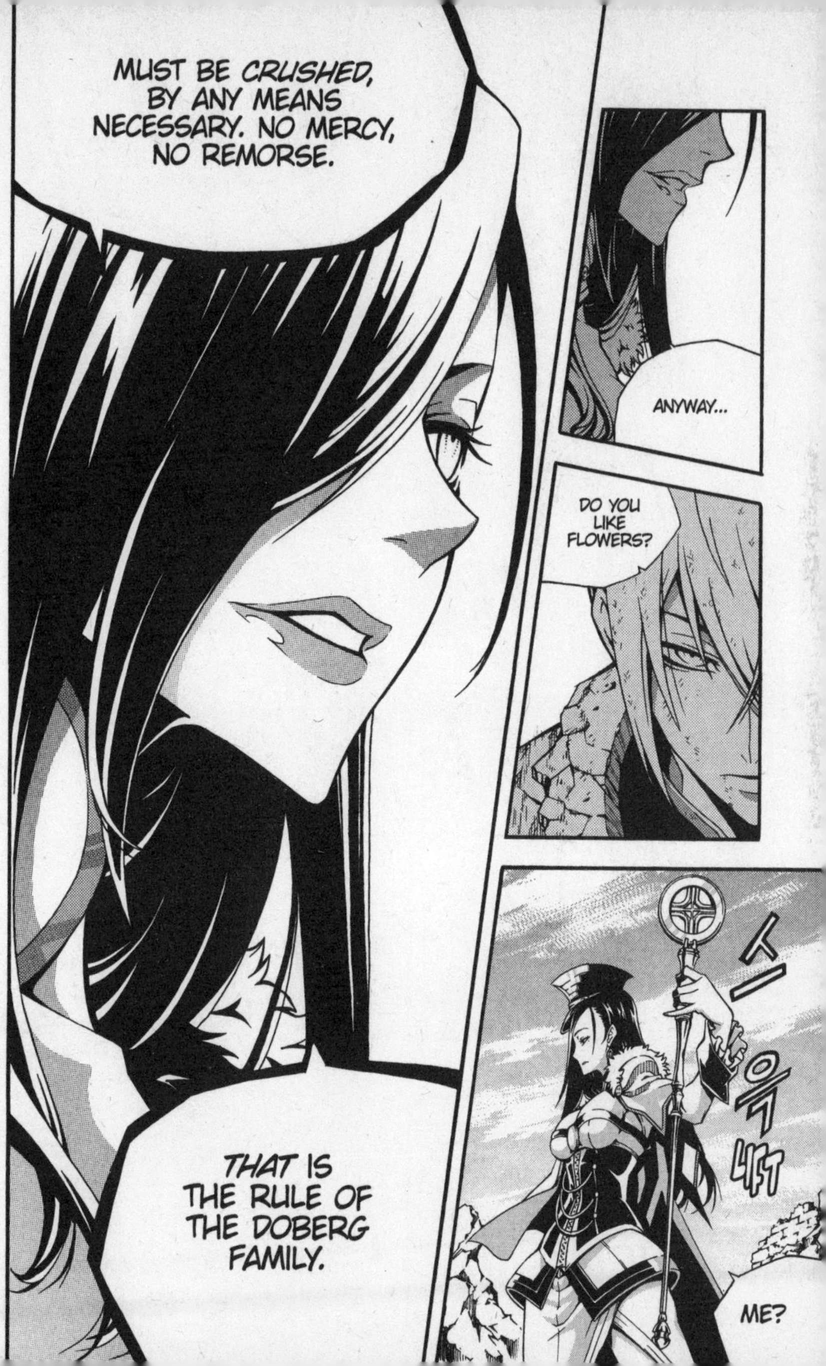
MUST BE *CRUSHED*, BY ANY MEANS NECESSARY. NO MERCY, NO REMORSE.
THAT IS THE RULE OF THE DOBERG FAMILY.
ANYWAY...
DO YOU LIKE FLOWERS?
LIFT
ME?

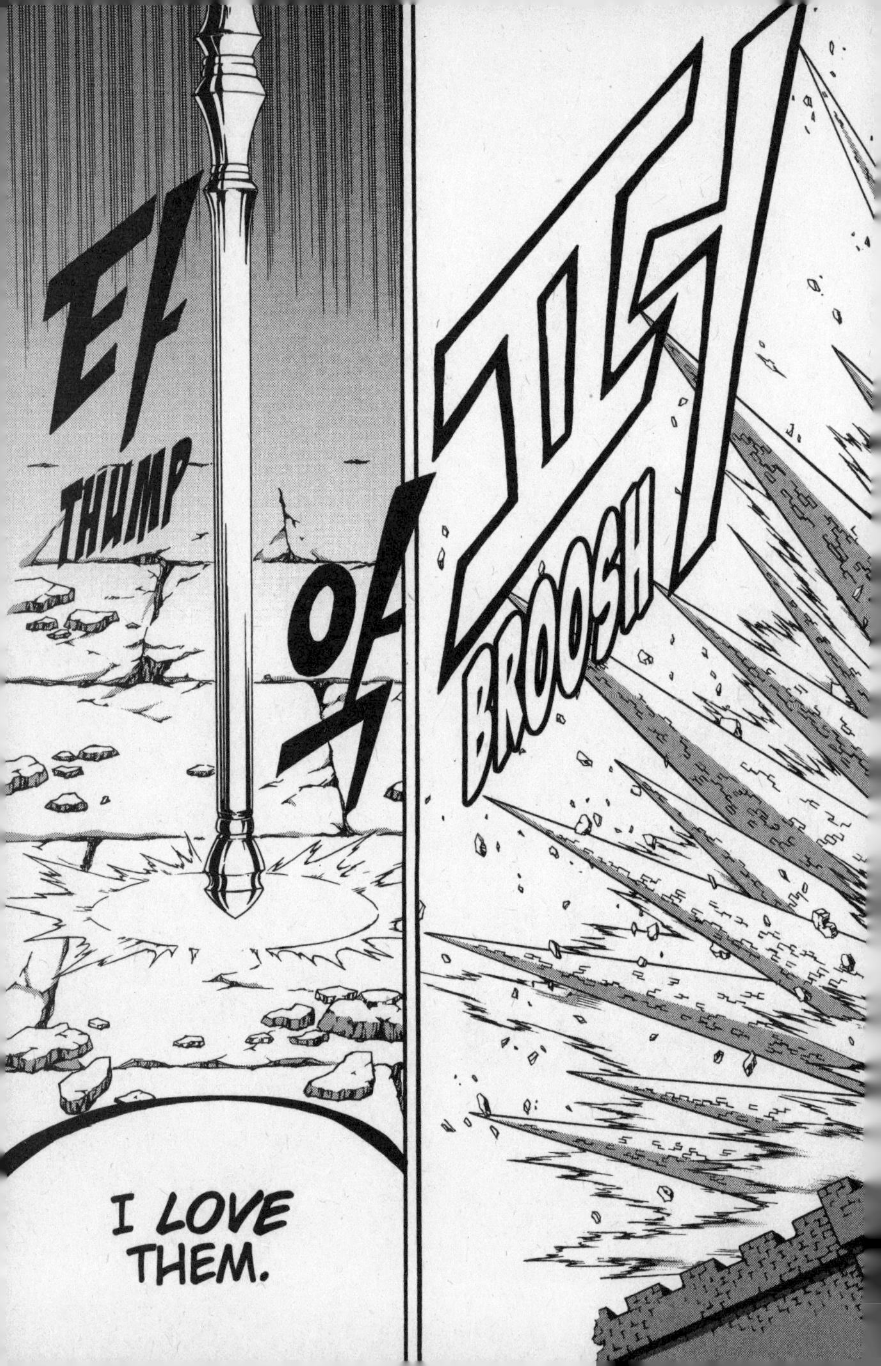
THUMP
I LOVE THEM.
BROOSH

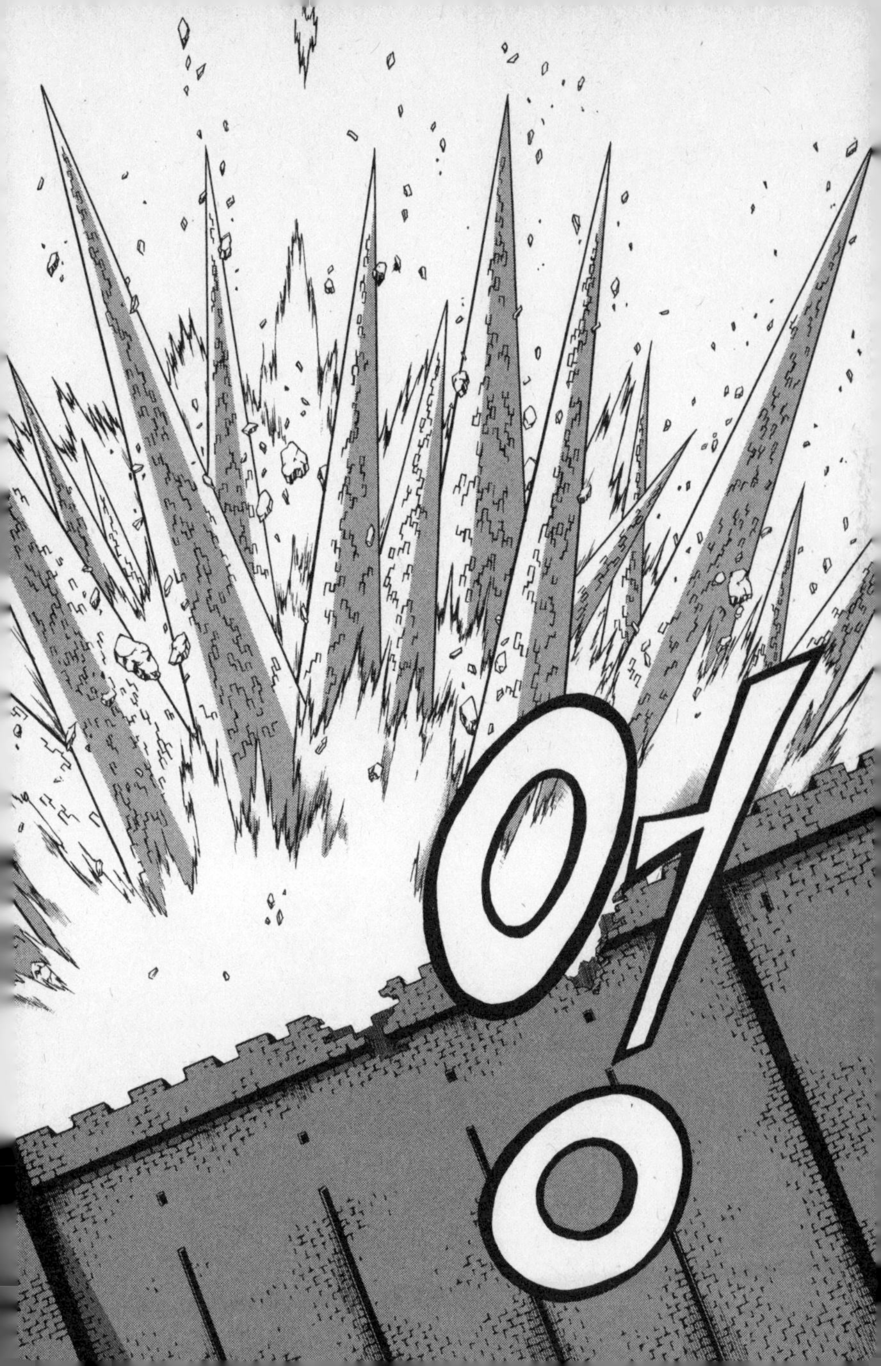

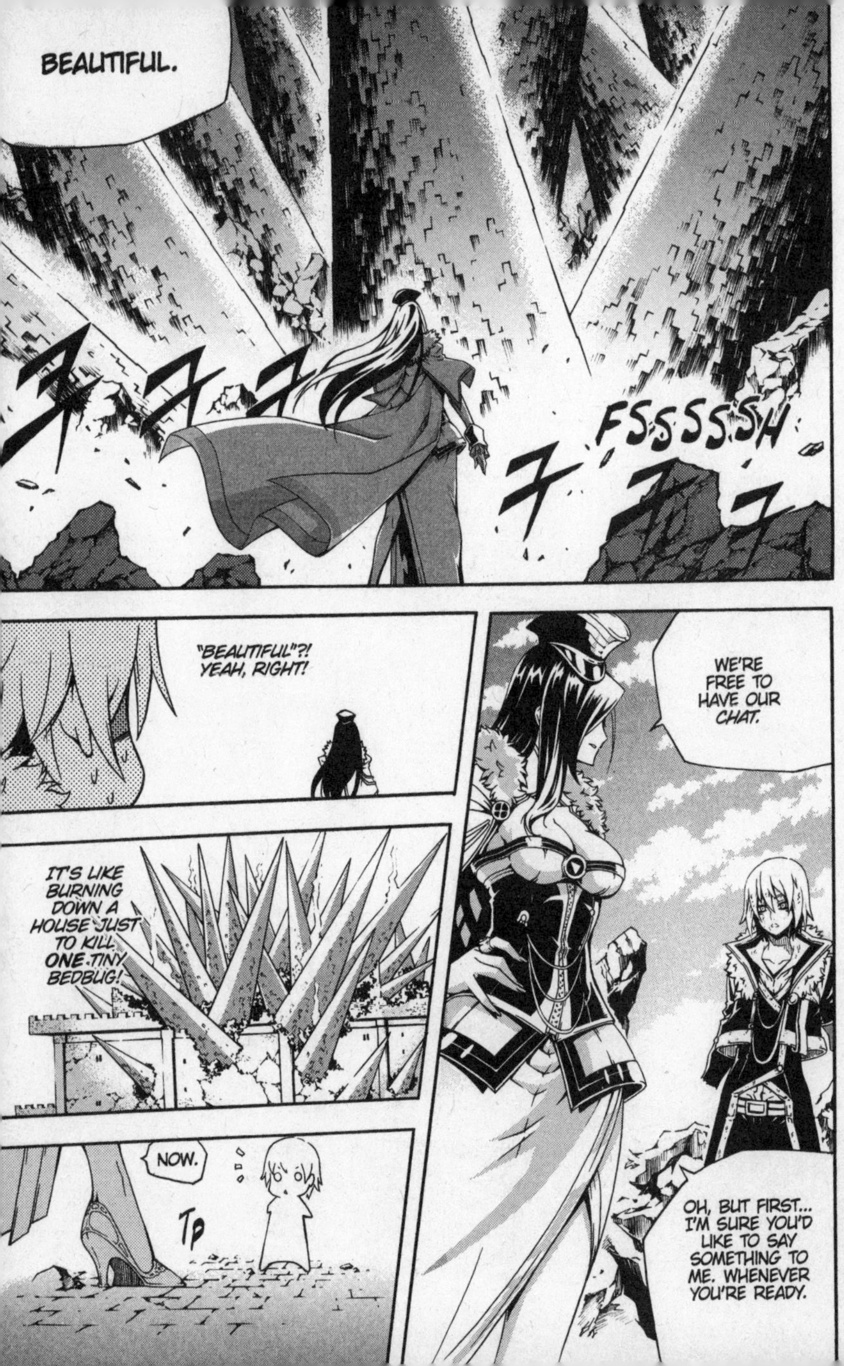
BEAUTIFUL.
FSSSSSH
"BEAUTIFUL"?! YEAH, RIGHT!
IT'S LIKE BURNING DOWN A HOUSE JUST TO KILL ONE TINY BEDBUG!
NOW.
Tp
WE'RE FREE TO HAVE OUR CHAT.
OH, BUT FIRST... I'M SURE YOU'D LIKE TO SAY SOMETHING TO ME. WHENEVER YOU'RE READY.

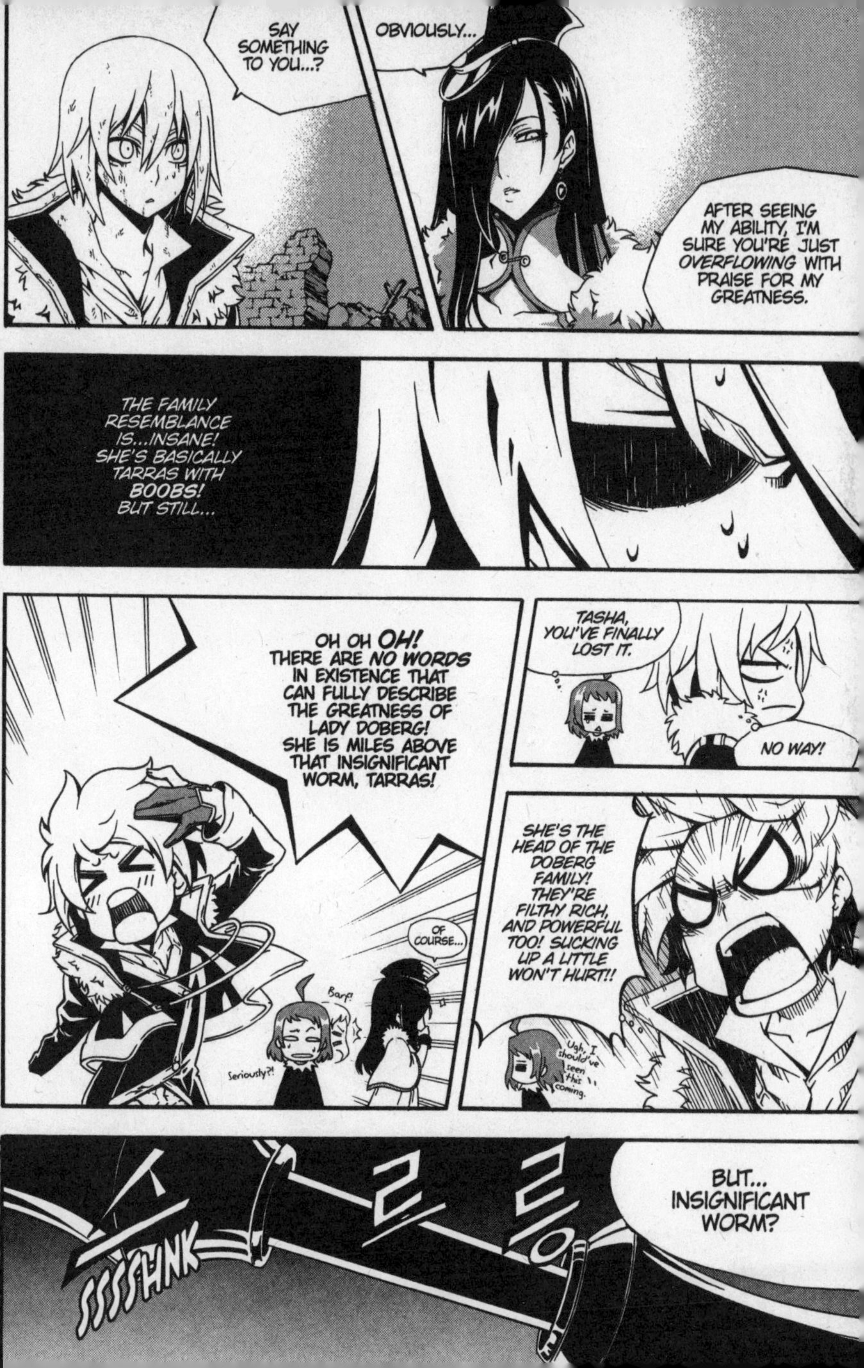
SAY SOMETHING TO YOU...?
OBVIOUSLY...
AFTER SEEING MY ABILITY, I'M SURE YOU'RE JUST *OVERFLOWING* WITH PRAISE FOR MY GREATNESS.
*THE FAMILY RESEMBLANCE IS...INSANE! SHE'S BASICALLY TARRAS WITH **BOOBS!** BUT STILL...*
OH OH ***OH!*** THERE ARE *NO WORDS* IN EXISTENCE THAT CAN FULLY DESCRIBE THE GREATNESS OF LADY DOBERG! SHE IS MILES ABOVE THAT INSIGNIFICANT WORM, TARRAS!
OF COURSE...
Barf!
Seriously?!
TASHA, YOU'VE FINALLY LOST IT.
NO WAY!
SHE'S THE HEAD OF THE DOBERG FAMILY! THEY'RE FILTHY RICH, AND POWERFUL TOO! SUCKING UP A LITTLE WON'T HURT!!
Ugh, I should've seen this coming.
SSSSHNK
BUT... INSIGNIFICANT WORM?

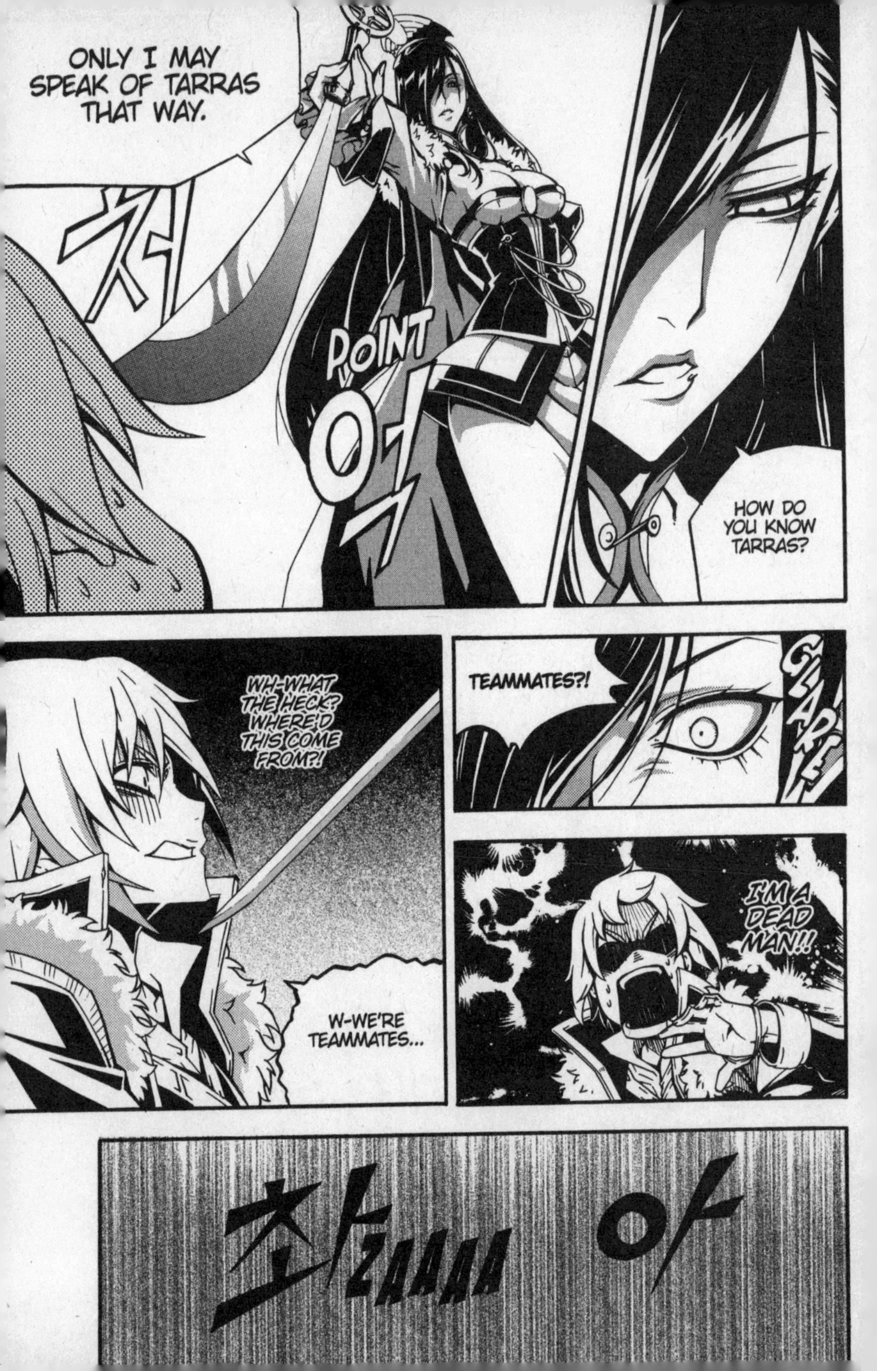

ONLY I MAY SPEAK OF TARRAS THAT WAY.
POINT
HOW DO YOU KNOW TARRAS?
WH-WHAT THE HECK? WHERE'D THIS COME FROM?!
W-WE'RE TEAMMATES...
TEAMMATES?!
GLARE
I'M A DEAD MAN!!
ZAAAA

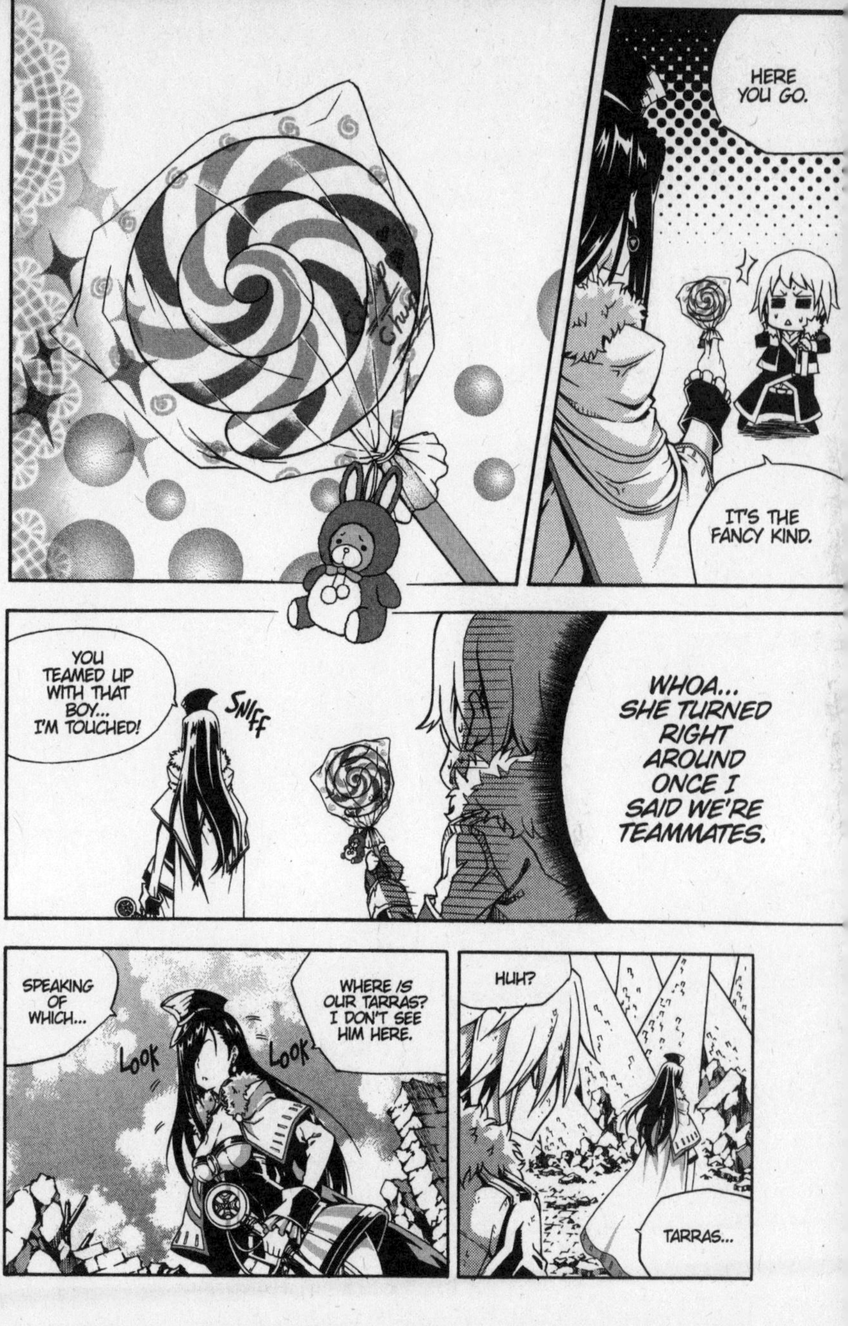

HERE YOU GO.
IT'S THE FANCY KIND.
YOU TEAMED UP WITH THAT BOY... I'M TOUCHED!
SNIFF
WHOA... SHE TURNED RIGHT AROUND ONCE I SAID WE'RE TEAMMATES.
SPEAKING OF WHICH...
LOOK
LOOK
WHERE IS OUR TARRAS? I DON'T SEE HIM HERE.
HUH?
TARRAS...

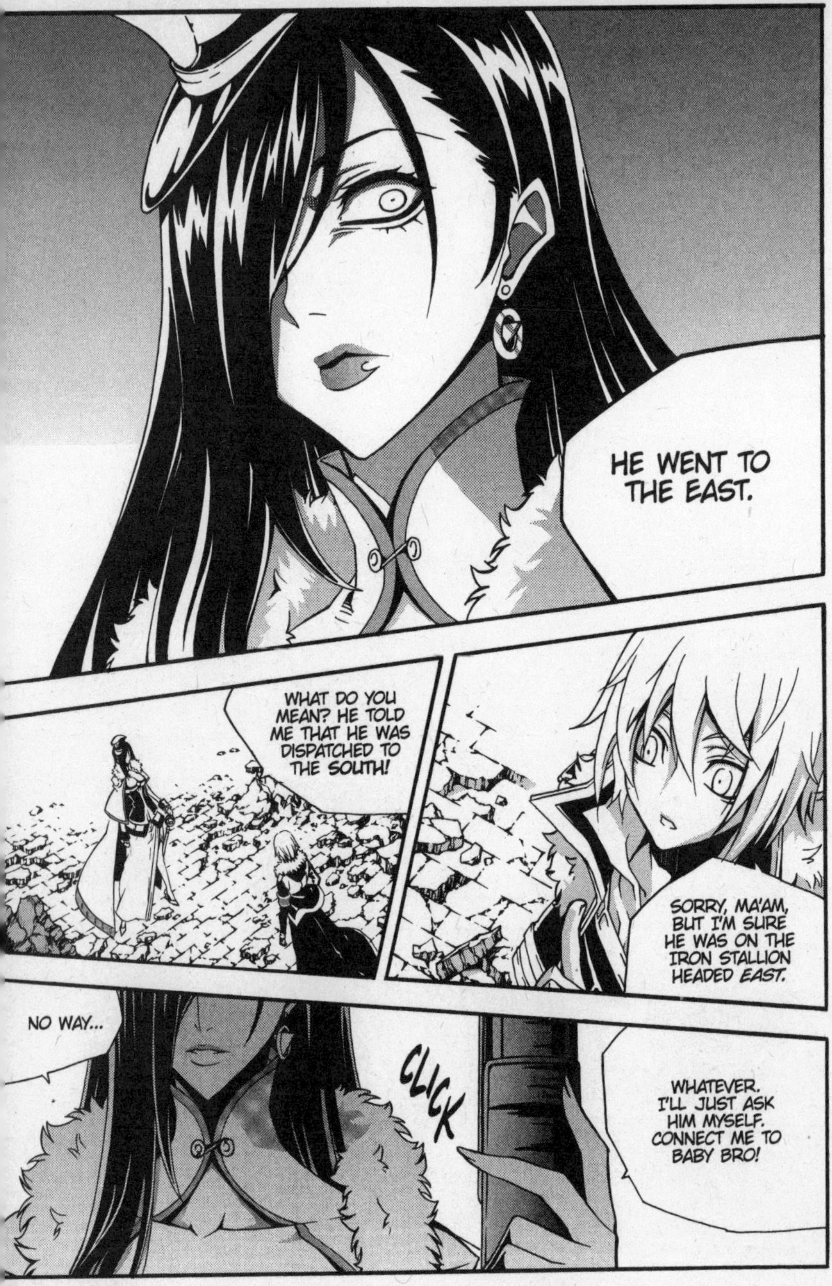
HE WENT TO THE EAST.
WHAT DO YOU MEAN? HE TOLD ME THAT HE WAS DISPATCHED TO THE SOUTH!
SORRY, MA'AM, BUT I'M SURE HE WAS ON THE IRON STALLION HEADED EAST.
NO WAY...
CLICK
WHATEVER. I'LL JUST ASK HIM MYSELF. CONNECT ME TO BABY BRO!

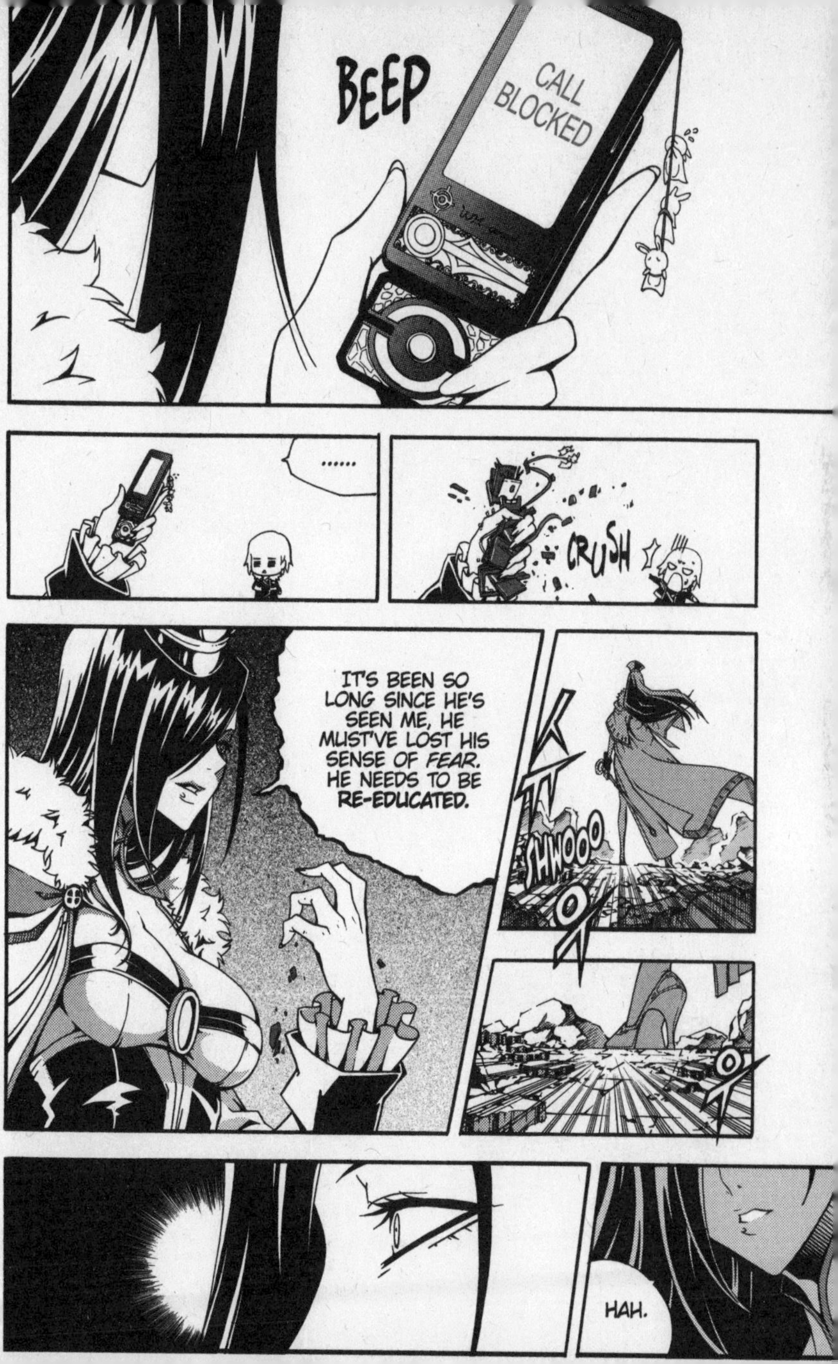
BEEP
CALL BLOCKED
......
CRUSH
IT'S BEEN SO LONG SINCE HE'S SEEN ME, HE MUST'VE LOST HIS SENSE OF *FEAR*. HE NEEDS TO BE **RE-EDUCATED.**
SHWOOO
HAH.

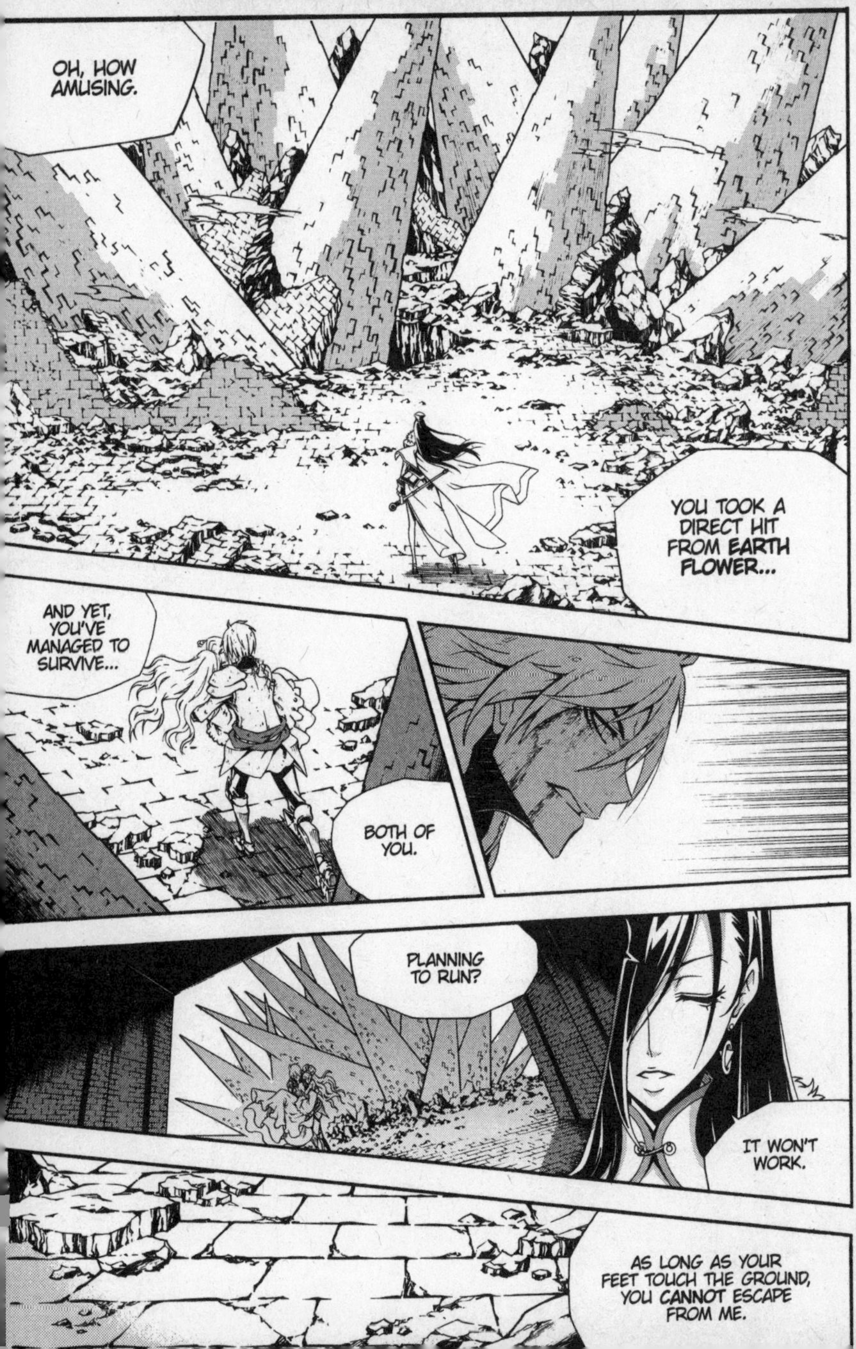
OH, HOW AMUSING.
YOU TOOK A DIRECT HIT FROM EARTH FLOWER...
AND YET, YOU'VE MANAGED TO SURVIVE...
BOTH OF YOU.
PLANNING TO RUN?
IT WON'T WORK.
AS LONG AS YOUR FEET TOUCH THE GROUND, YOU CANNOT ESCAPE FROM ME.

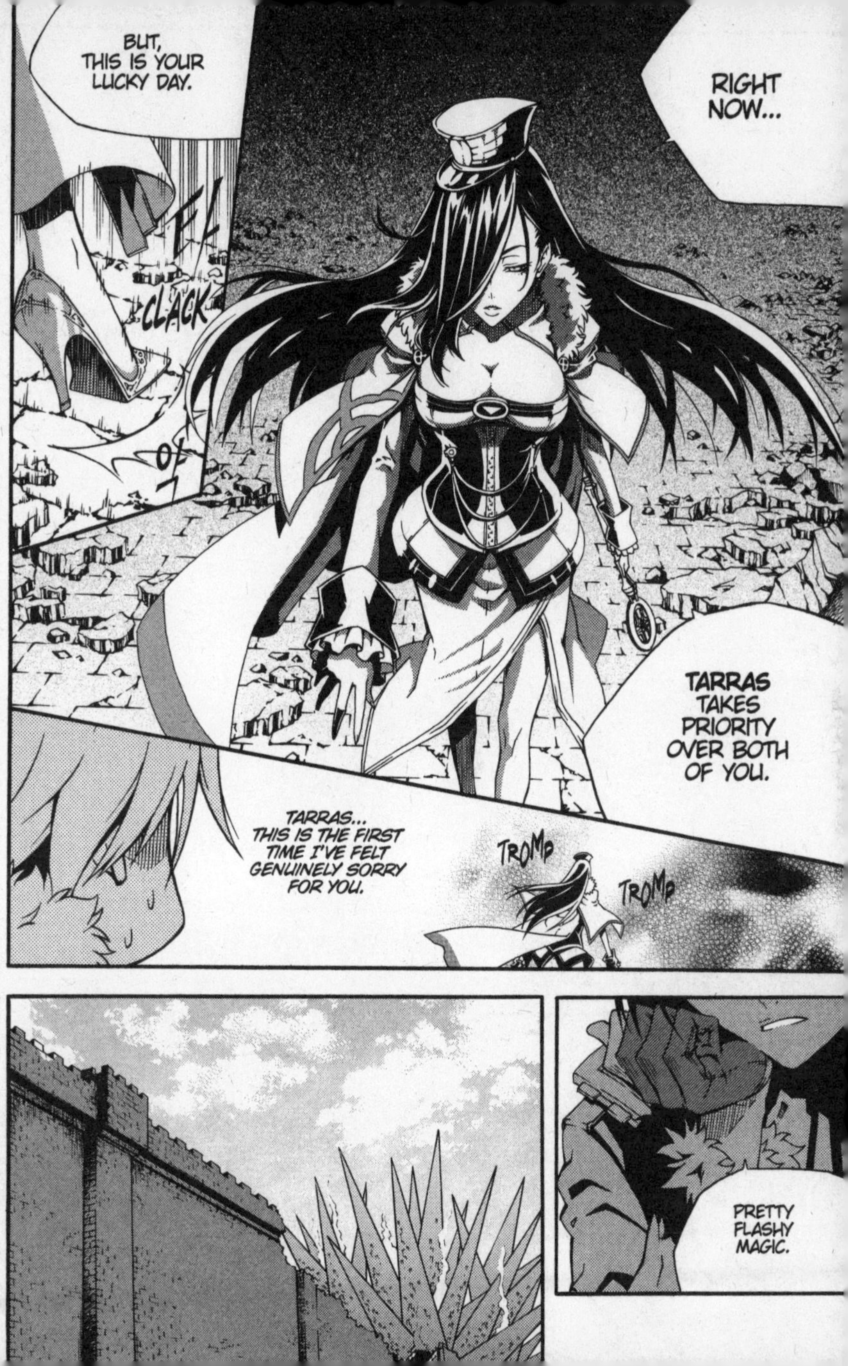
BUT, THIS IS YOUR LUCKY DAY.
CLACK
RIGHT NOW...
TARRAS TAKES PRIORITY OVER BOTH OF YOU.
TARRAS... THIS IS THE FIRST TIME I'VE FELT GENUINELY SORRY FOR YOU.
TROMP
TROMP
PRETTY FLASHY MAGIC.

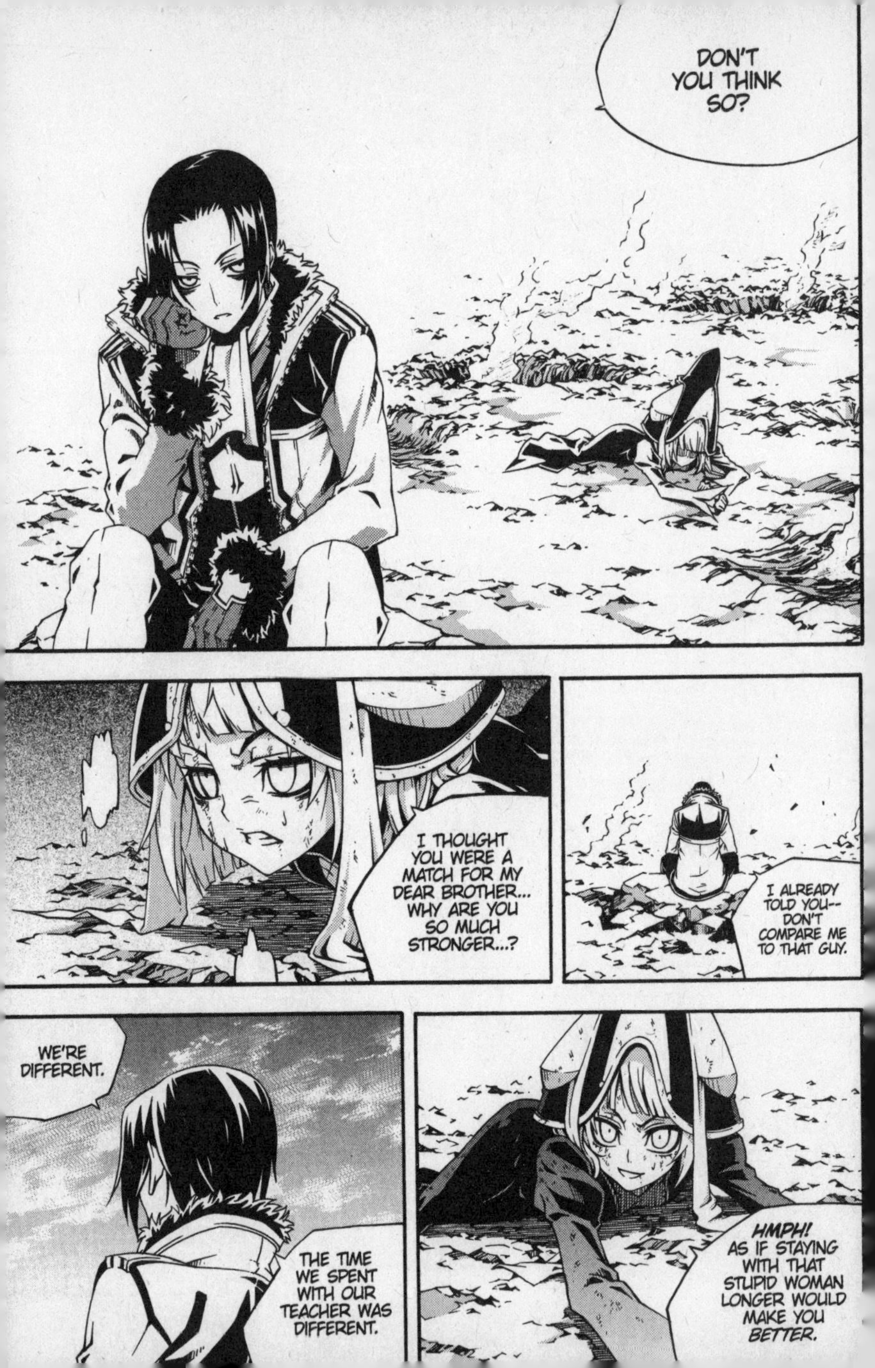
DON'T YOU THINK SO?
I THOUGHT YOU WERE A MATCH FOR MY DEAR BROTHER... WHY ARE YOU SO MUCH STRONGER...?
I ALREADY TOLD YOU-- DON'T COMPARE ME TO THAT GUY.
WE'RE DIFFERENT.
THE TIME WE SPENT WITH OUR TEACHER WAS DIFFERENT.
HMPH! AS IF STAYING WITH THAT STUPID WOMAN LONGER WOULD MAKE YOU BETTER.

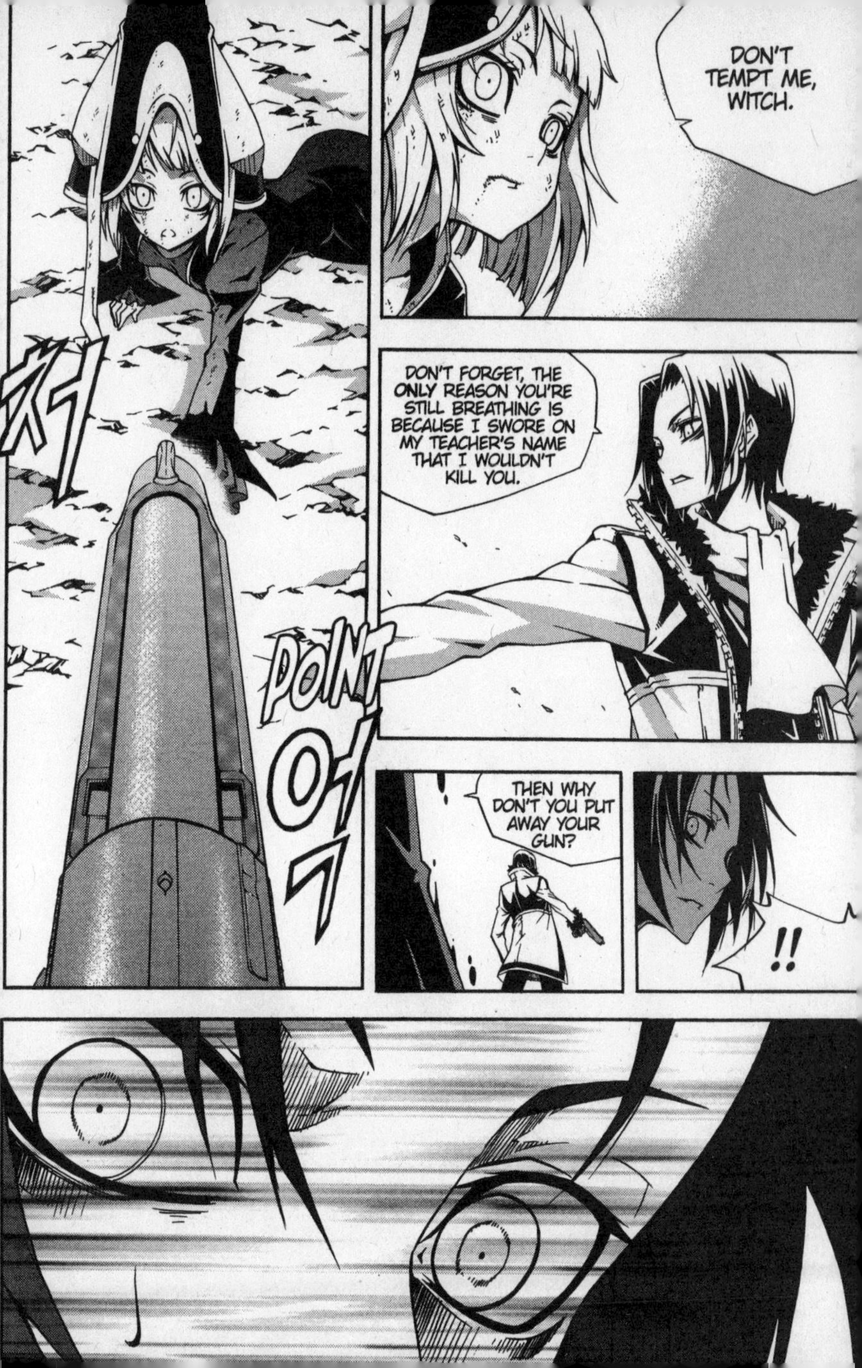
POINT
DON'T TEMPT ME, WITCH.
DON'T FORGET, THE ONLY REASON YOU'RE STILL BREATHING IS BECAUSE I SWORE ON MY TEACHER'S NAME THAT I WOULDN'T KILL YOU.
THEN WHY DON'T YOU PUT AWAY YOUR GUN?
!!

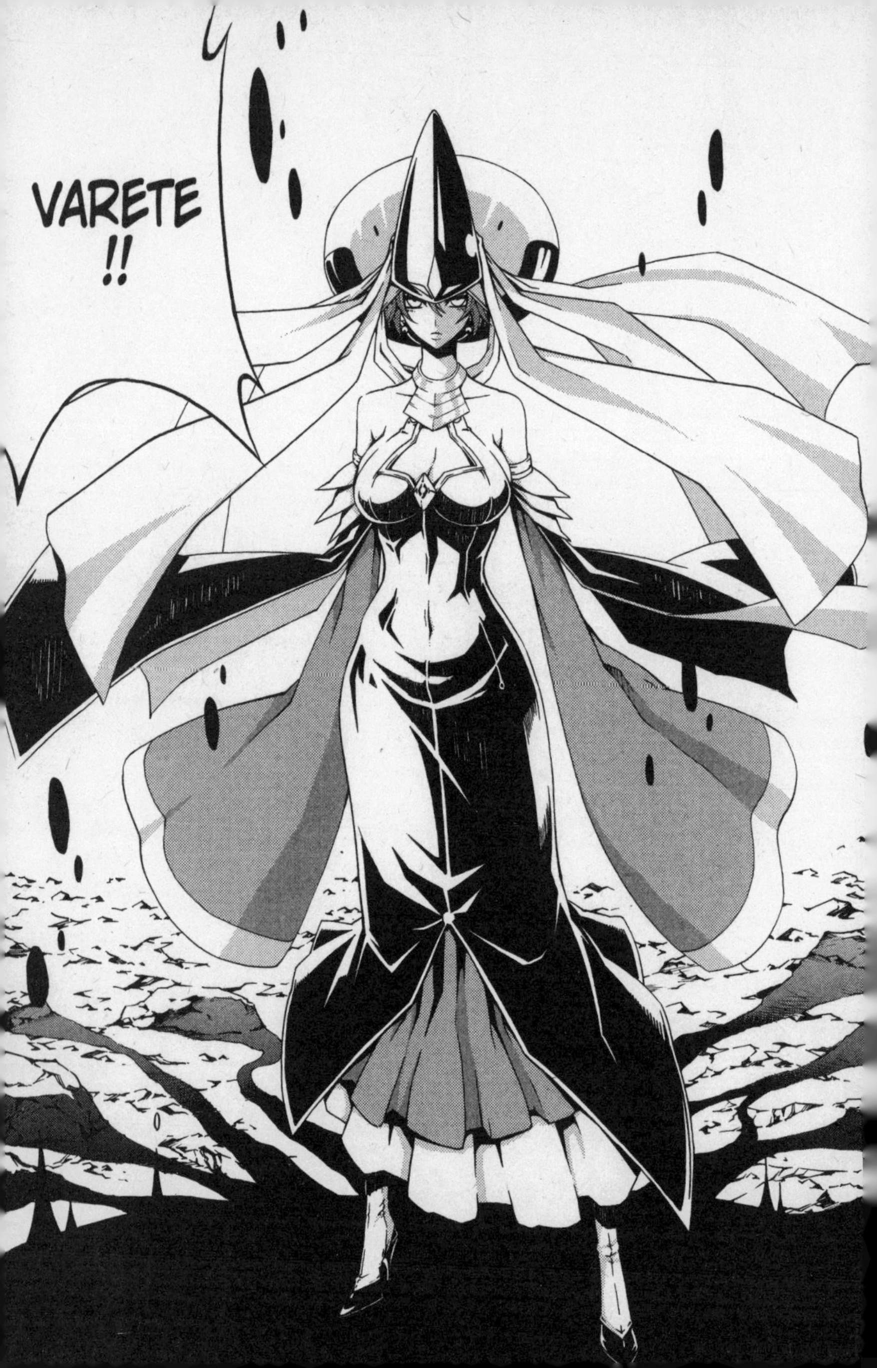
VARETE
!!

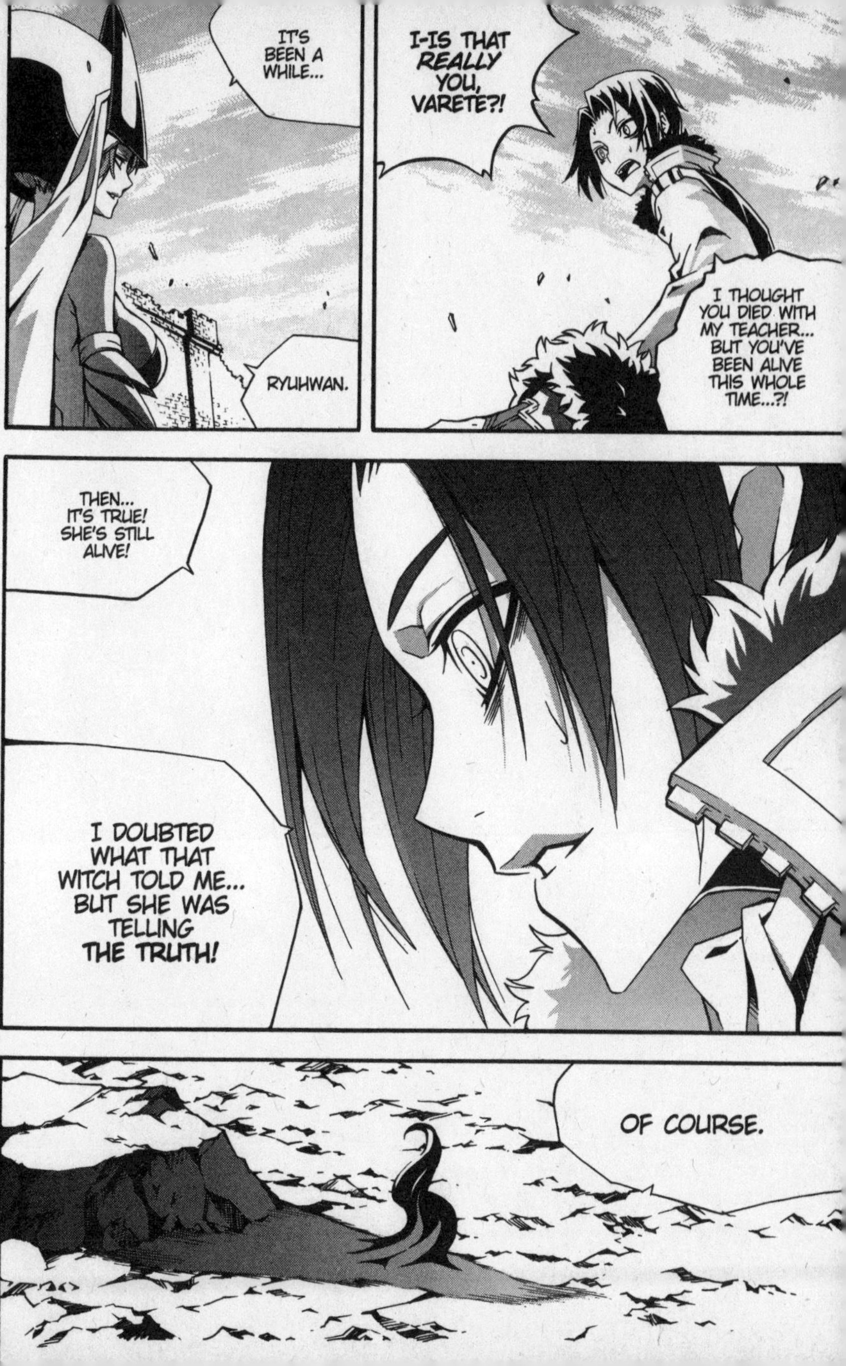
IT'S BEEN A WHILE...
RYUHWAN.
I-IS THAT REALLY YOU, VARETE?!
I THOUGHT YOU DIED WITH MY TEACHER... BUT YOU'VE BEEN ALIVE THIS WHOLE TIME...?!
THEN... IT'S TRUE! SHE'S STILL ALIVE!
I DOUBTED WHAT THAT WITCH TOLD ME... BUT SHE WAS TELLING THE TRUTH!
OF COURSE.

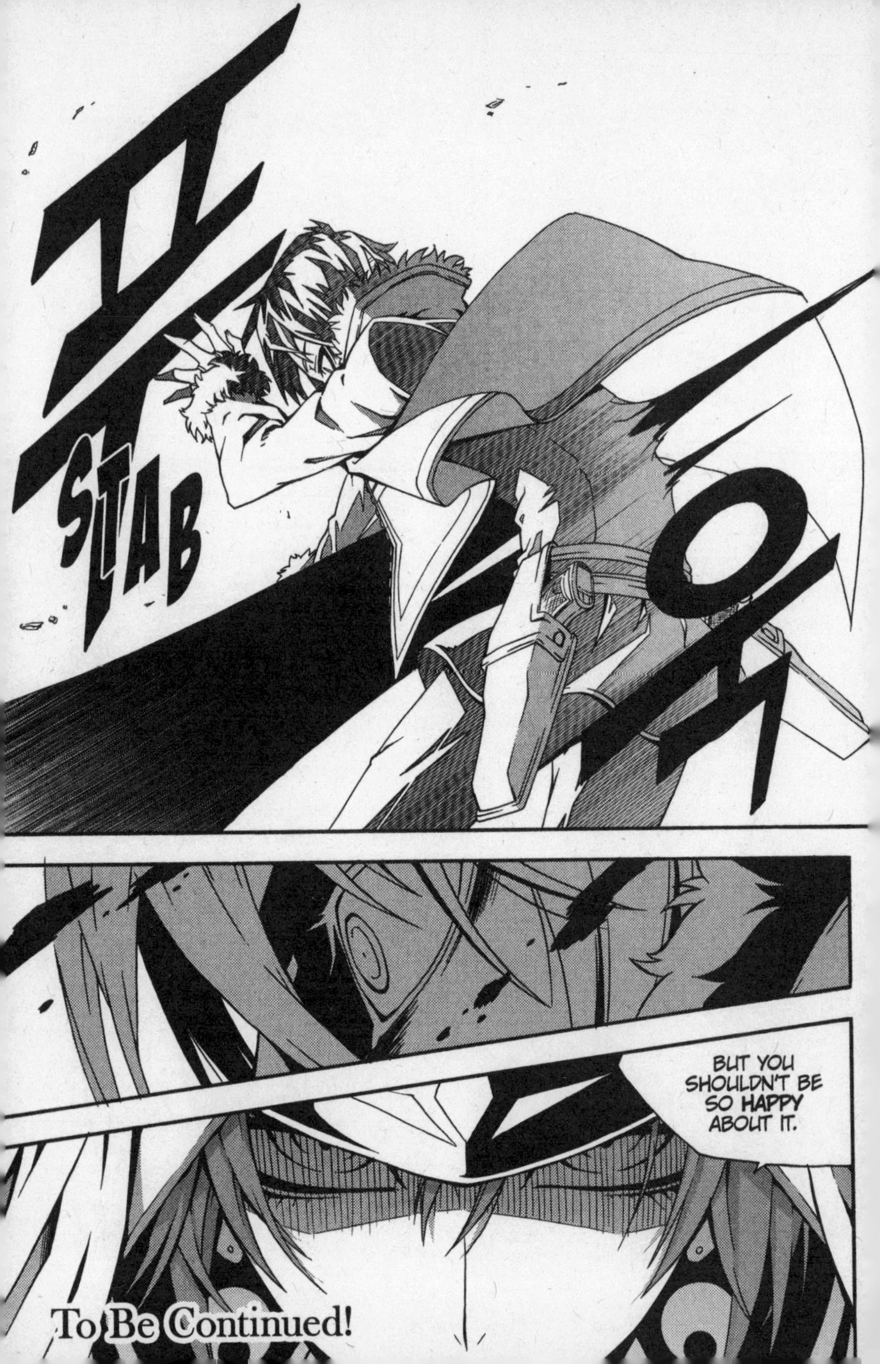
STAB
BUT YOU SHOULDN'T BE SO HAPPY ABOUT IT.
To Be Continued!

BECAUSE IT'S NICE

LIFT
TUCK
Why just that ...?

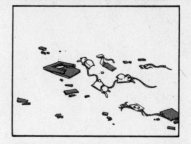

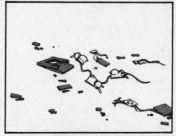

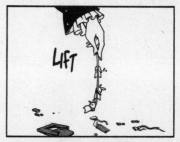

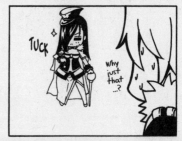

WITCH BUSTER

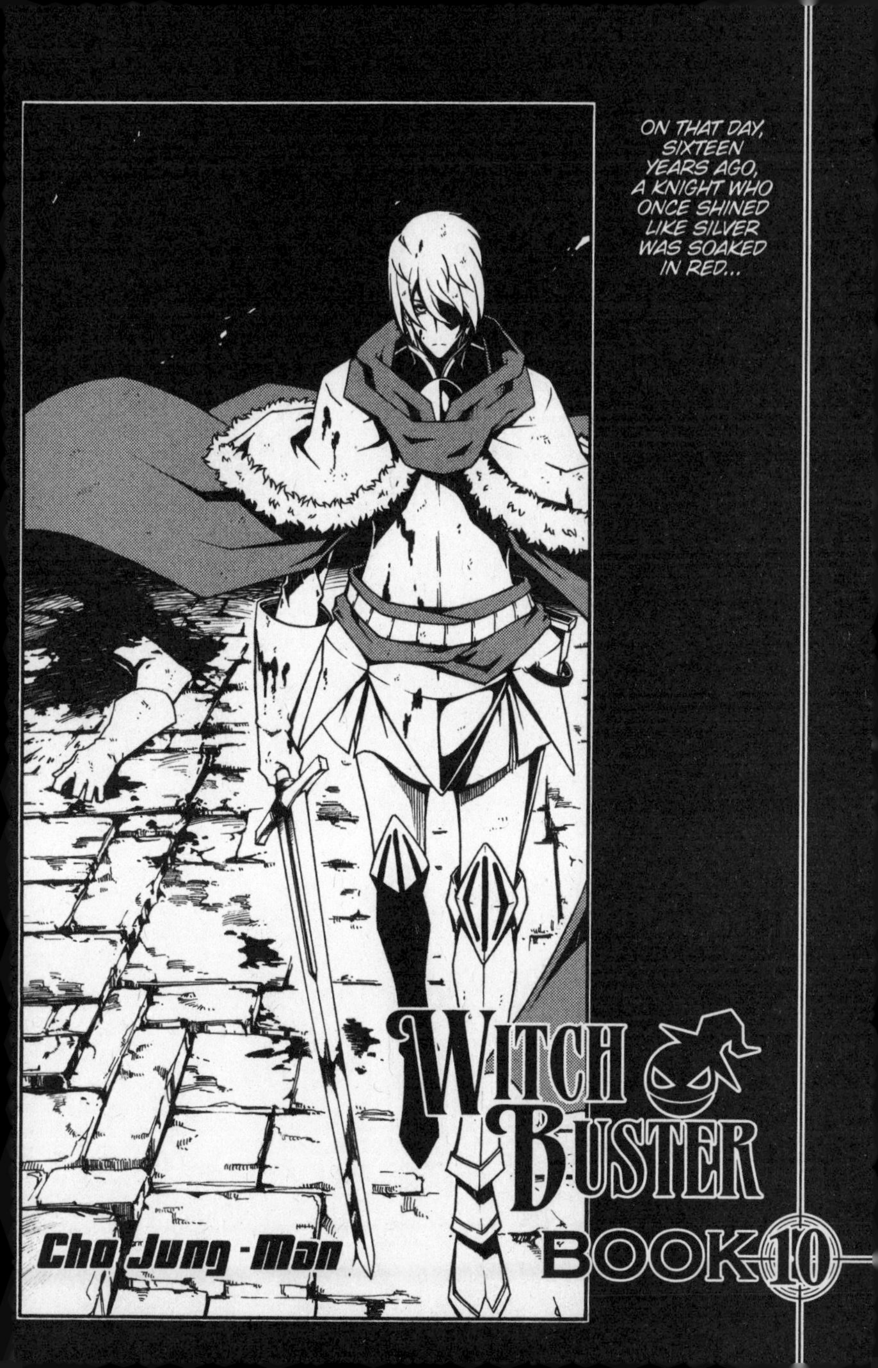

ON THAT DAY, SIXTEEN YEARS AGO, A KNIGHT WHO ONCE SHINED LIKE SILVER WAS SOAKED IN RED...
WITCH BUSTER
Cho Jung-Man
BOOK 10

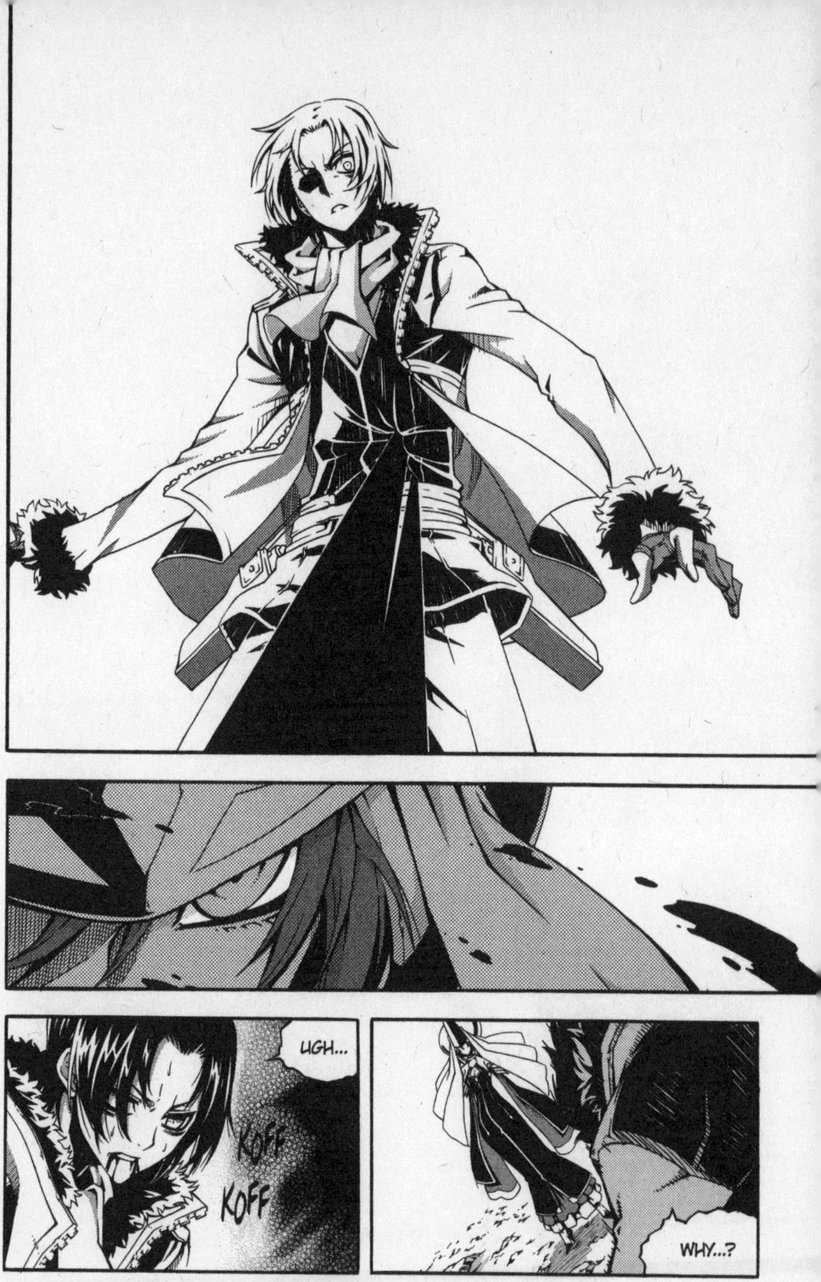
UGH...
KOFF
KOFF
WHY...?

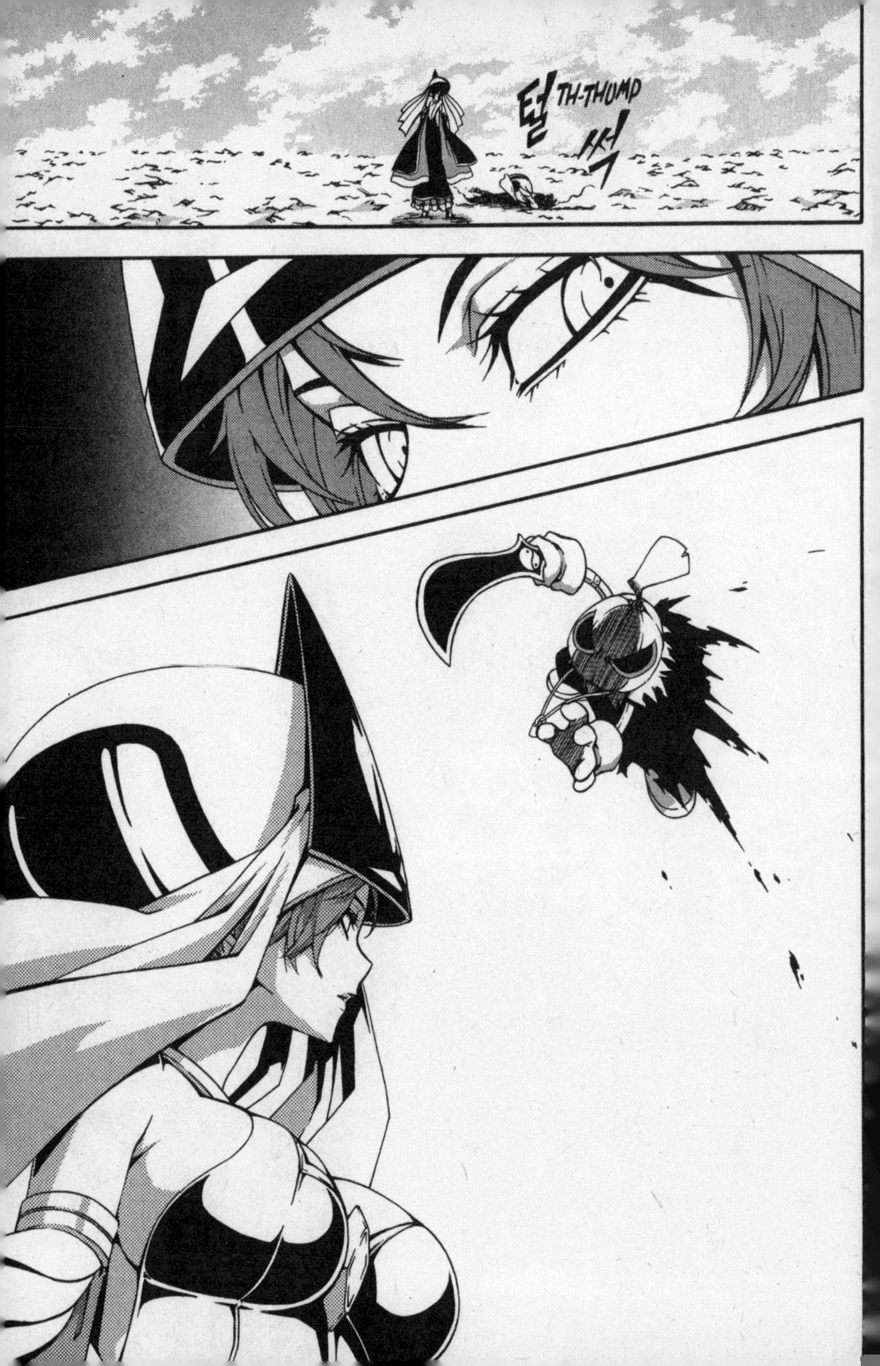
털썩 TH-THUMP

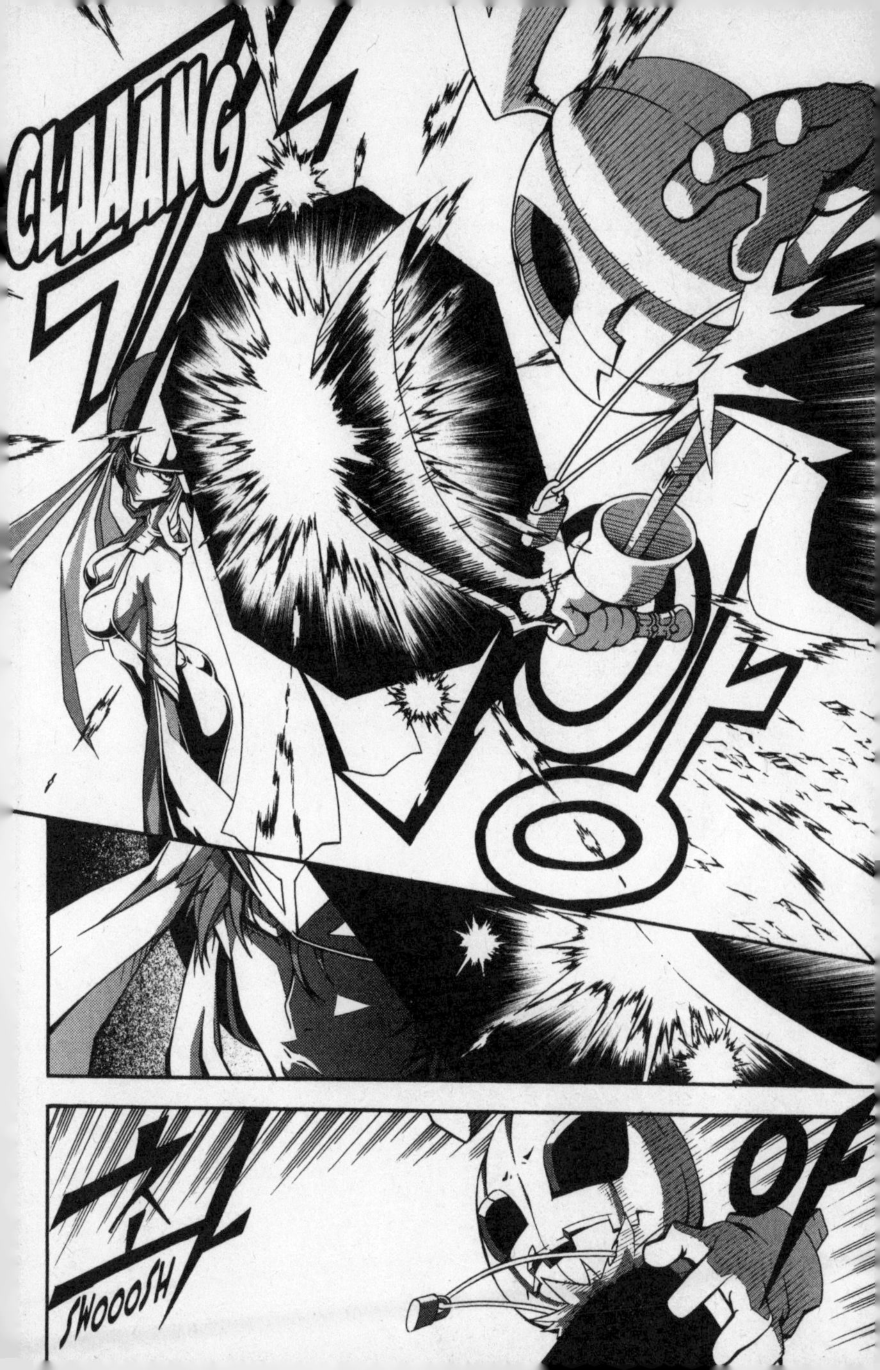
CLAAANG
SWOOOSH

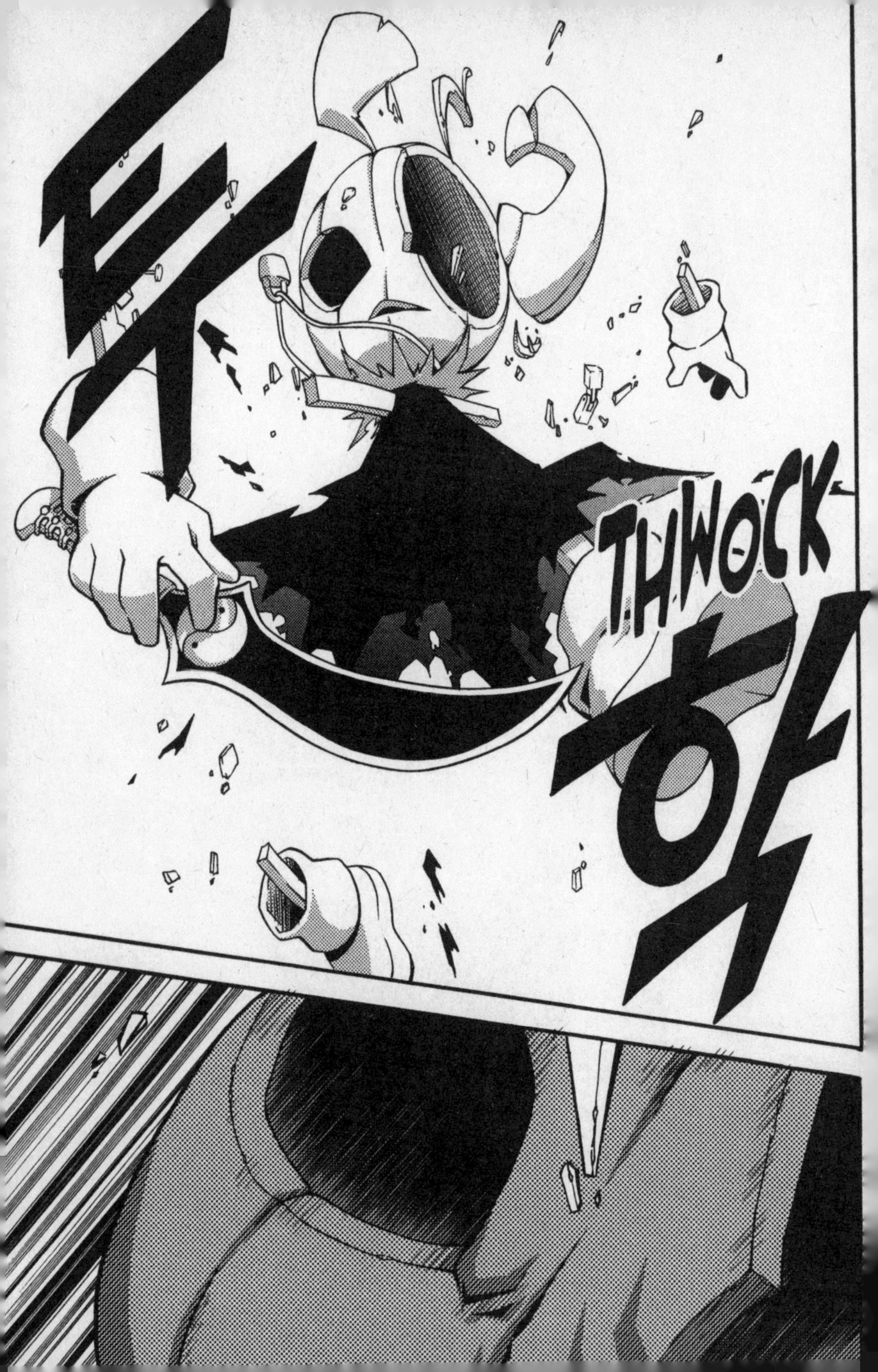
THWOCK

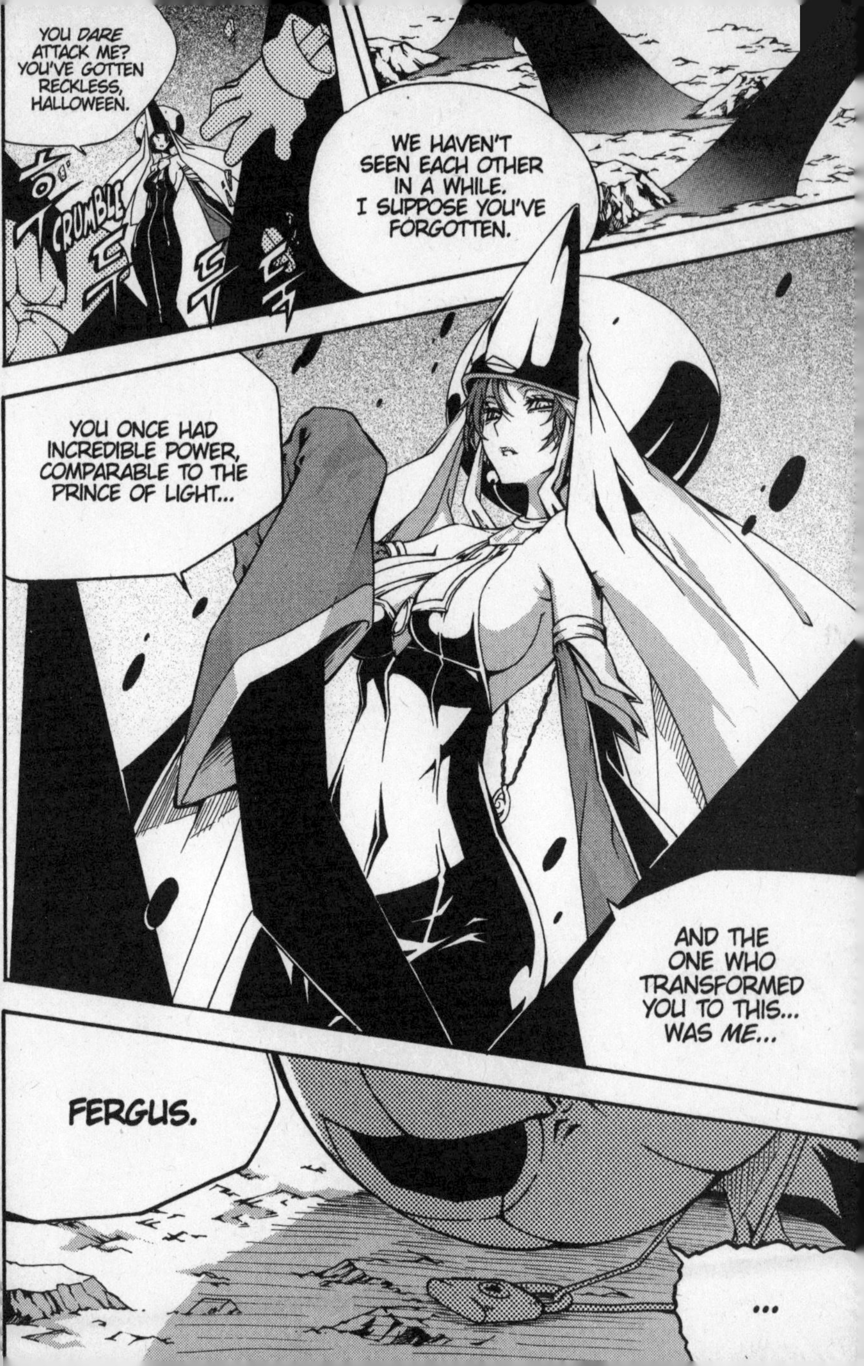
YOU DARE ATTACK ME? YOU'VE GOTTEN RECKLESS, HALLOWEEN.
CRUMBLE
WE HAVEN'T SEEN EACH OTHER IN A WHILE. I SUPPOSE YOU'VE FORGOTTEN.
YOU ONCE HAD INCREDIBLE POWER, COMPARABLE TO THE PRINCE OF LIGHT...
AND THE ONE WHO TRANSFORMED YOU TO THIS... WAS ME...
FERGUS.
...

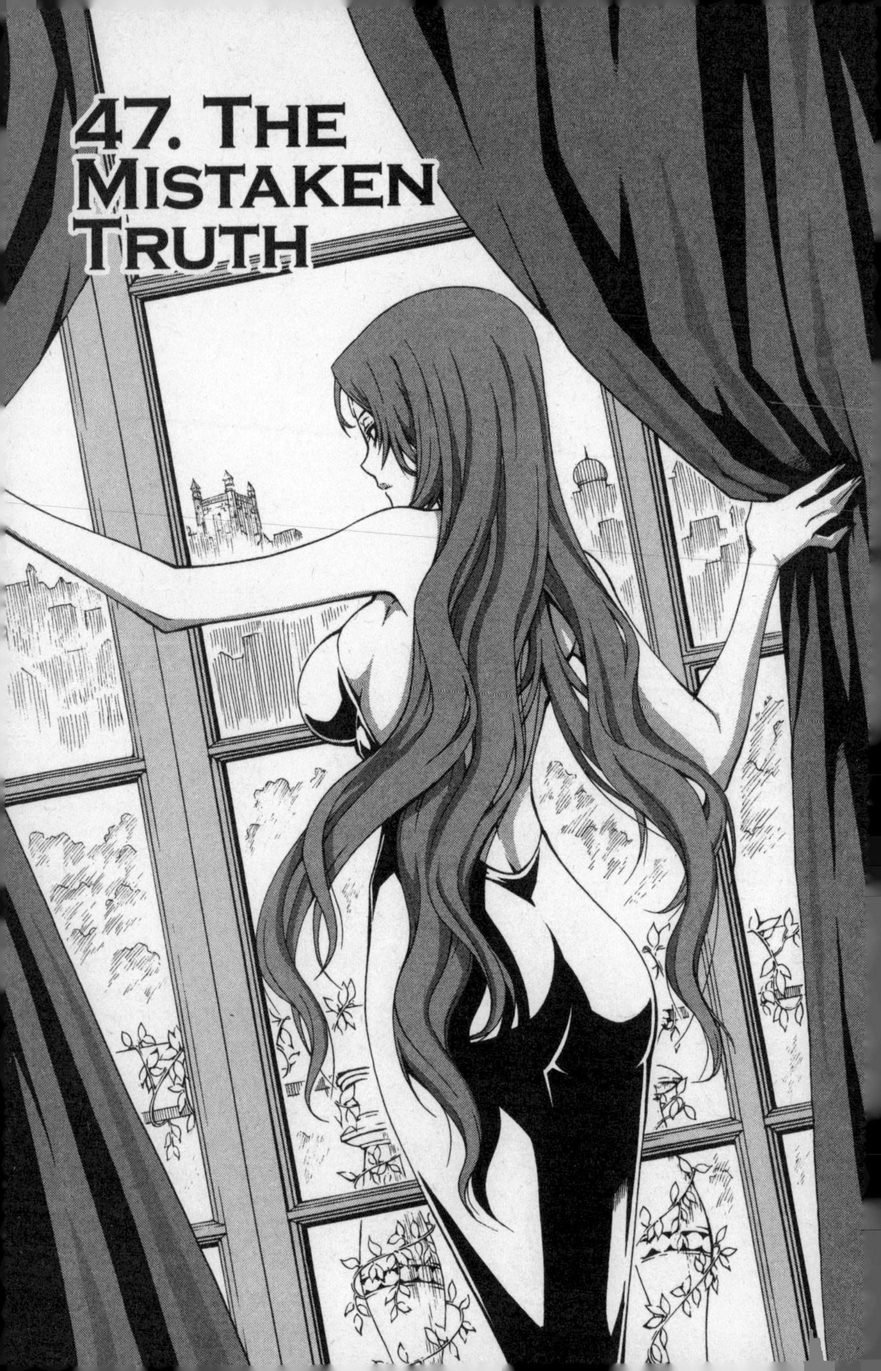
47. The Mistaken Truth

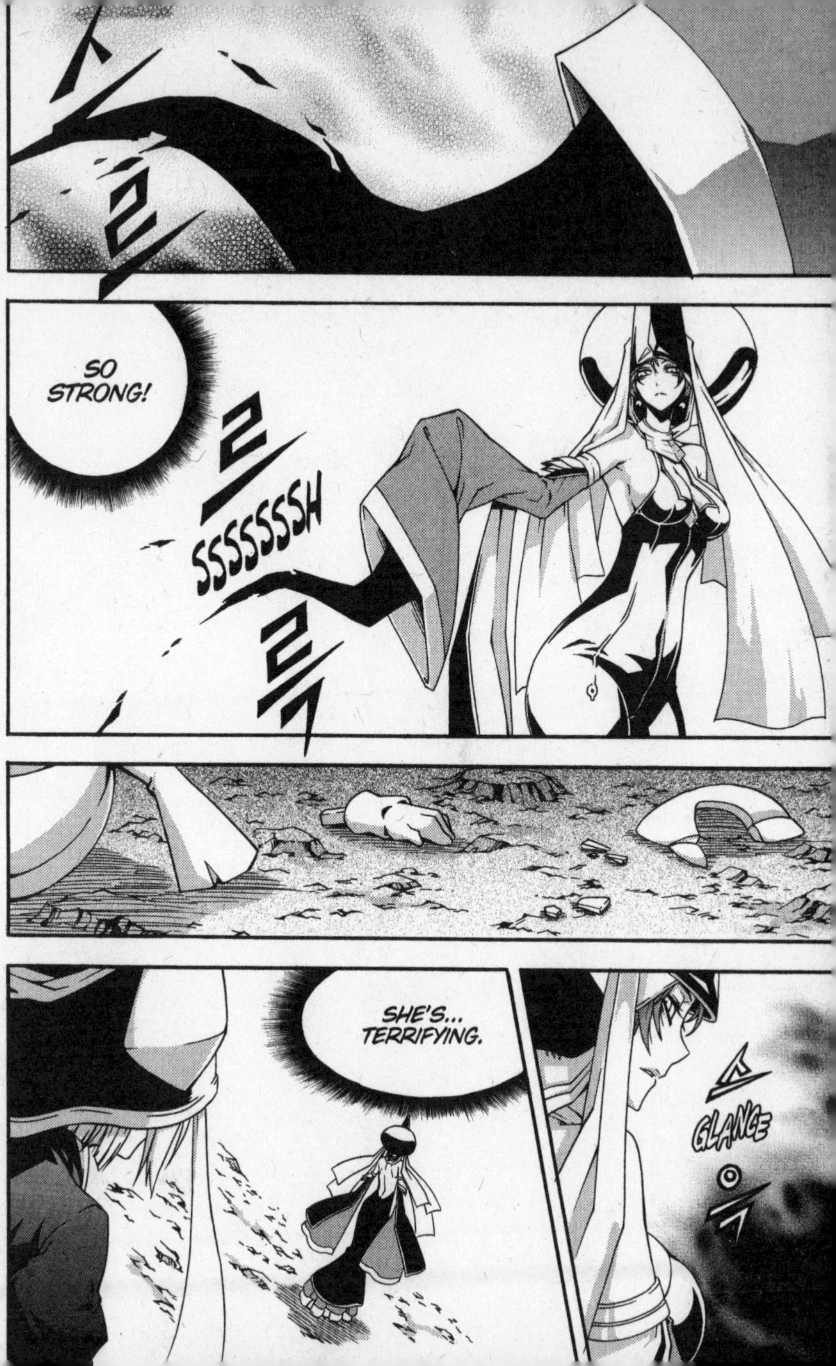
SO STRONG!
SSSSSSSSH
SHE'S... TERRIFYING.
GLANCE

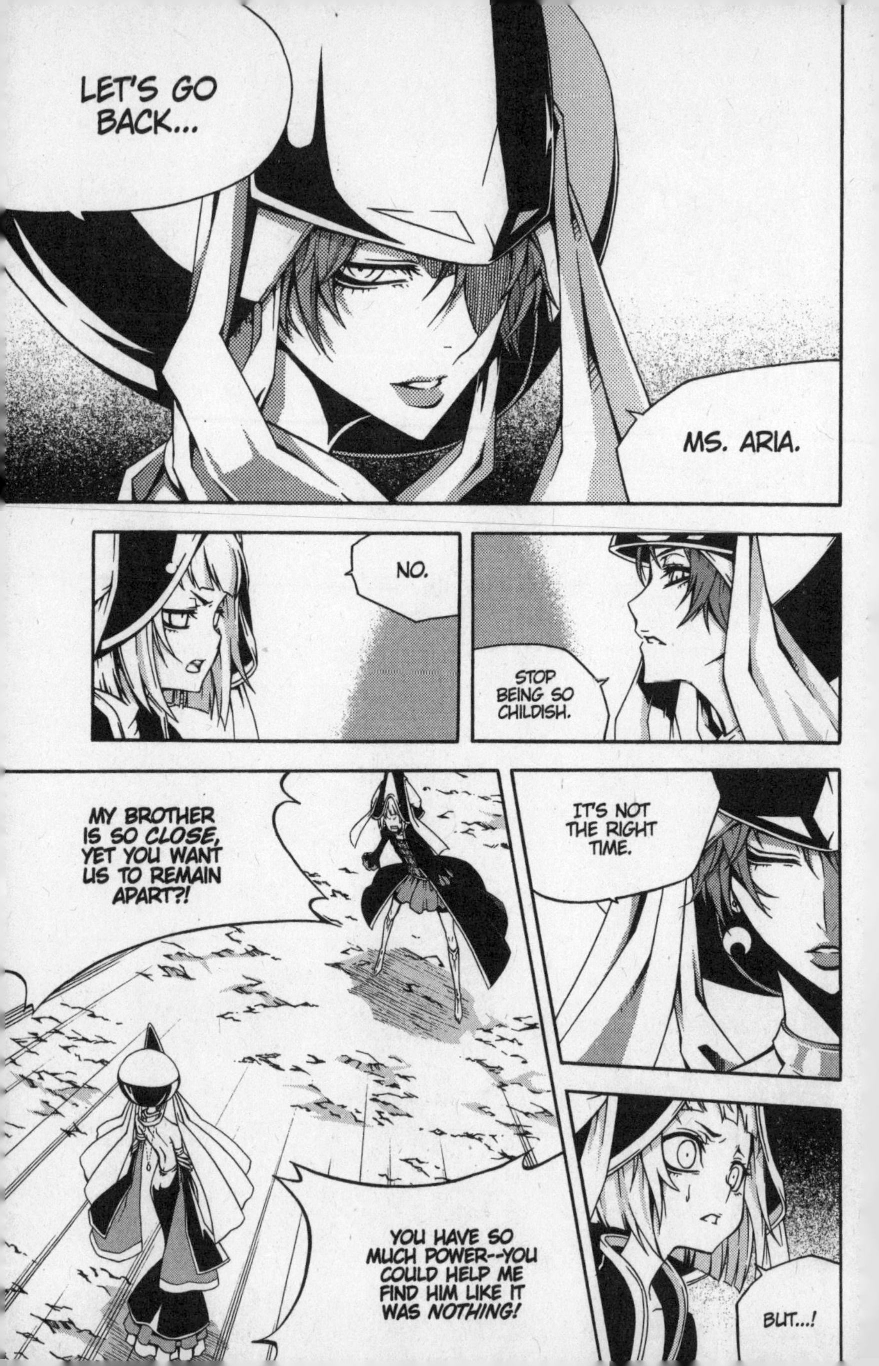
LET'S GO BACK...
MS. ARIA.
NO.
STOP BEING SO CHILDISH.
MY BROTHER IS SO *CLOSE*, YET YOU WANT US TO REMAIN APART?!
YOU HAVE SO MUCH POWER--YOU COULD HELP ME FIND HIM LIKE IT WAS *NOTHING*!
IT'S NOT THE RIGHT TIME.
BUT...!

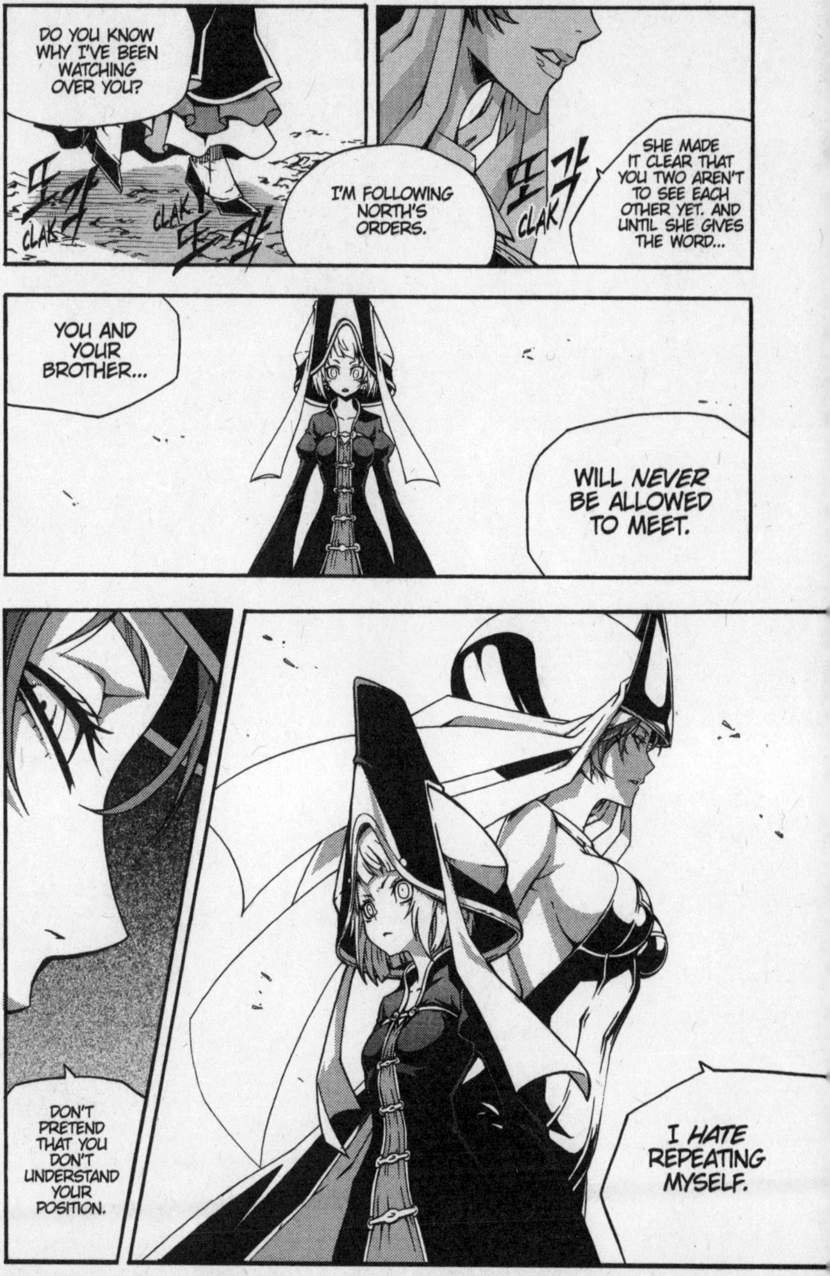
DO YOU KNOW WHY I'VE BEEN WATCHING OVER YOU?
또각
CLAK
CLAK
또각
I'M FOLLOWING NORTH'S ORDERS.
또각
CLAK
SHE MADE IT CLEAR THAT YOU TWO AREN'T TO SEE EACH OTHER YET. AND UNTIL SHE GIVES THE WORD...
YOU AND YOUR BROTHER...
WILL *NEVER* BE ALLOWED TO MEET.
DON'T PRETEND THAT YOU DON'T UNDERSTAND YOUR POSITION.
I *HATE* REPEATING MYSELF.

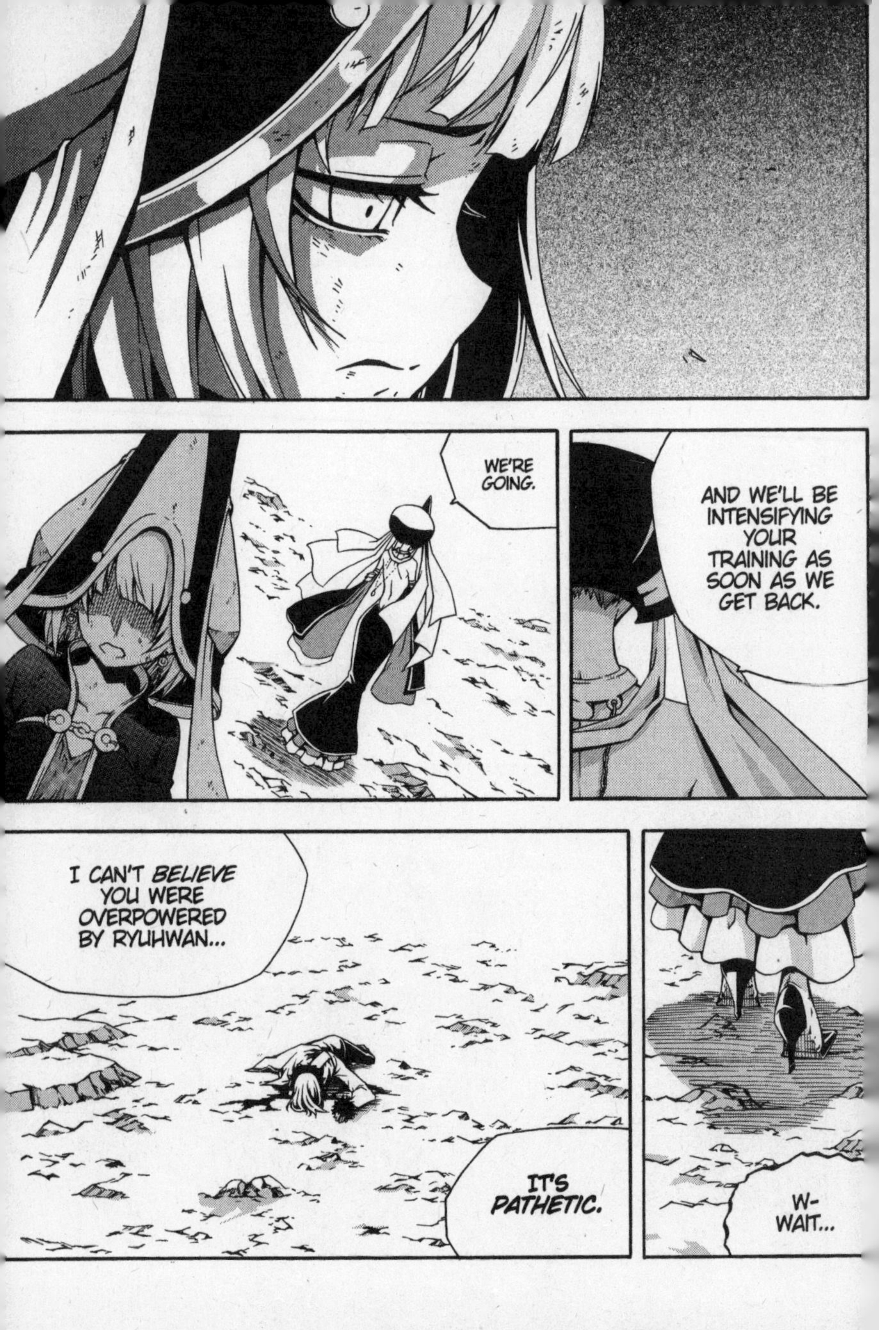
WE'RE GOING.
AND WE'LL BE INTENSIFYING YOUR TRAINING AS SOON AS WE GET BACK.
I CAN'T *BELIEVE* YOU WERE OVERPOWERED BY RYUHWAN...
IT'S *PATHETIC.*
W- WAIT...

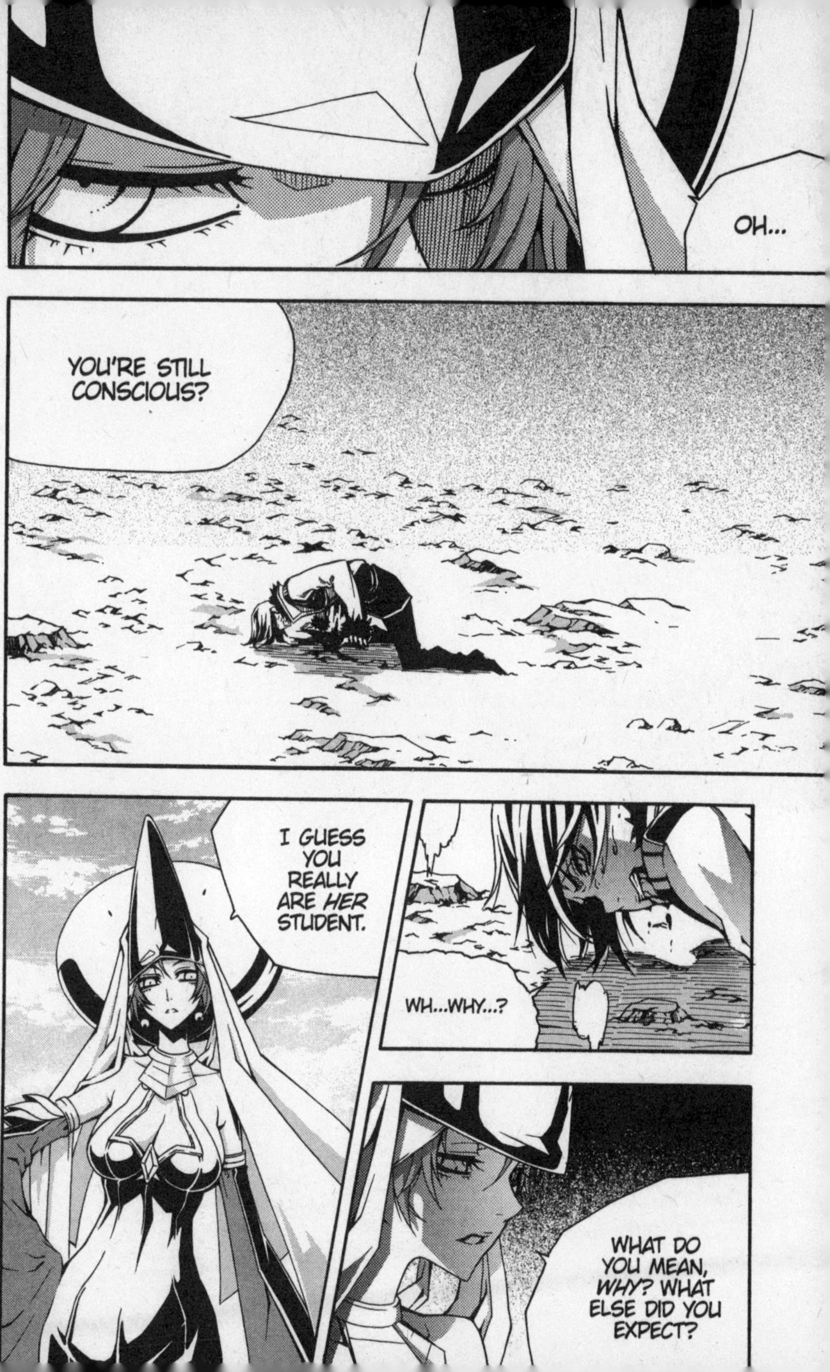
OH...
YOU'RE STILL CONSCIOUS?
I GUESS YOU REALLY ARE *HER* STUDENT.
WH...WHY...?
WHAT DO YOU MEAN, *WHY?* WHAT ELSE DID YOU EXPECT?

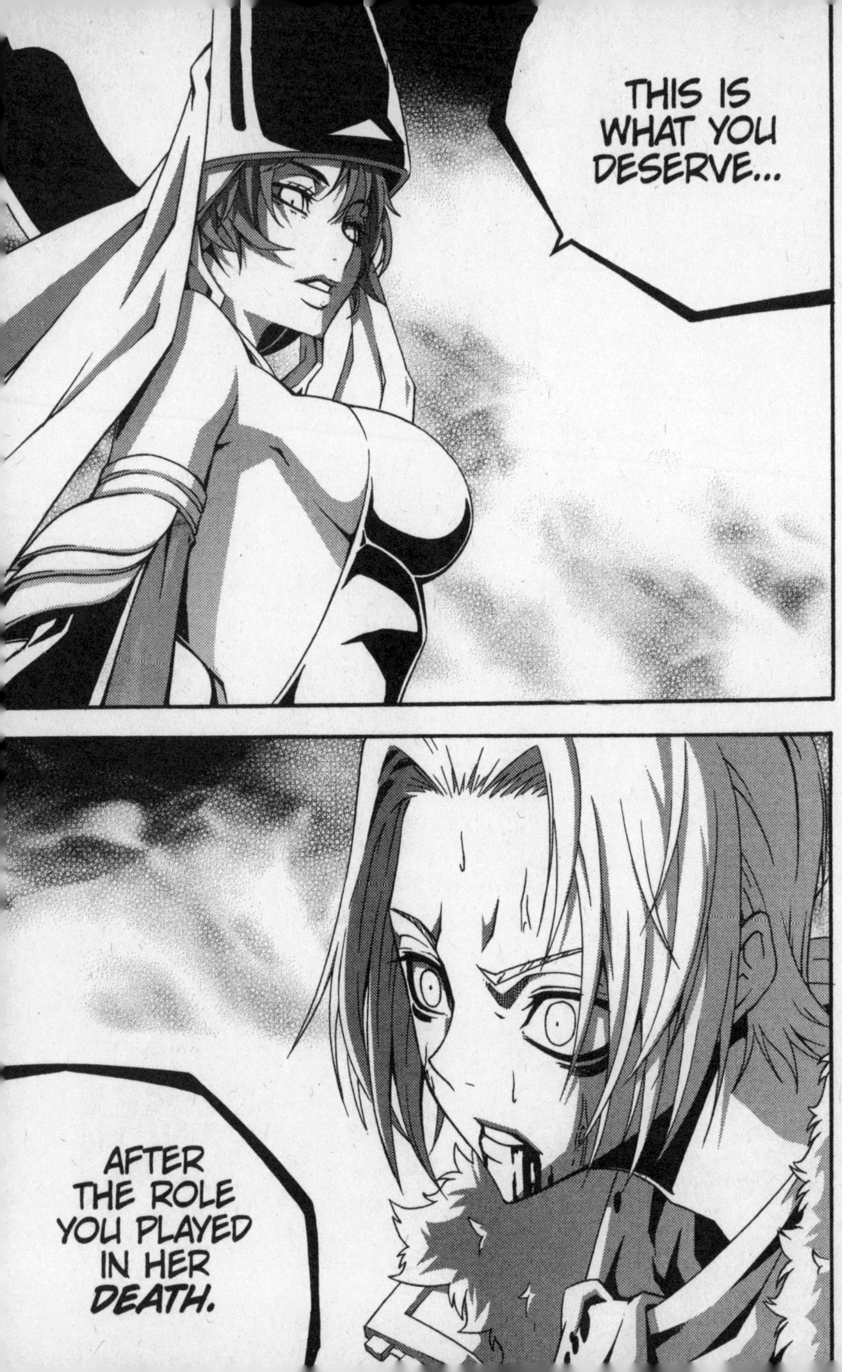
THIS IS WHAT YOU DESERVE...
AFTER THE ROLE YOU PLAYED IN HER *DEATH.*

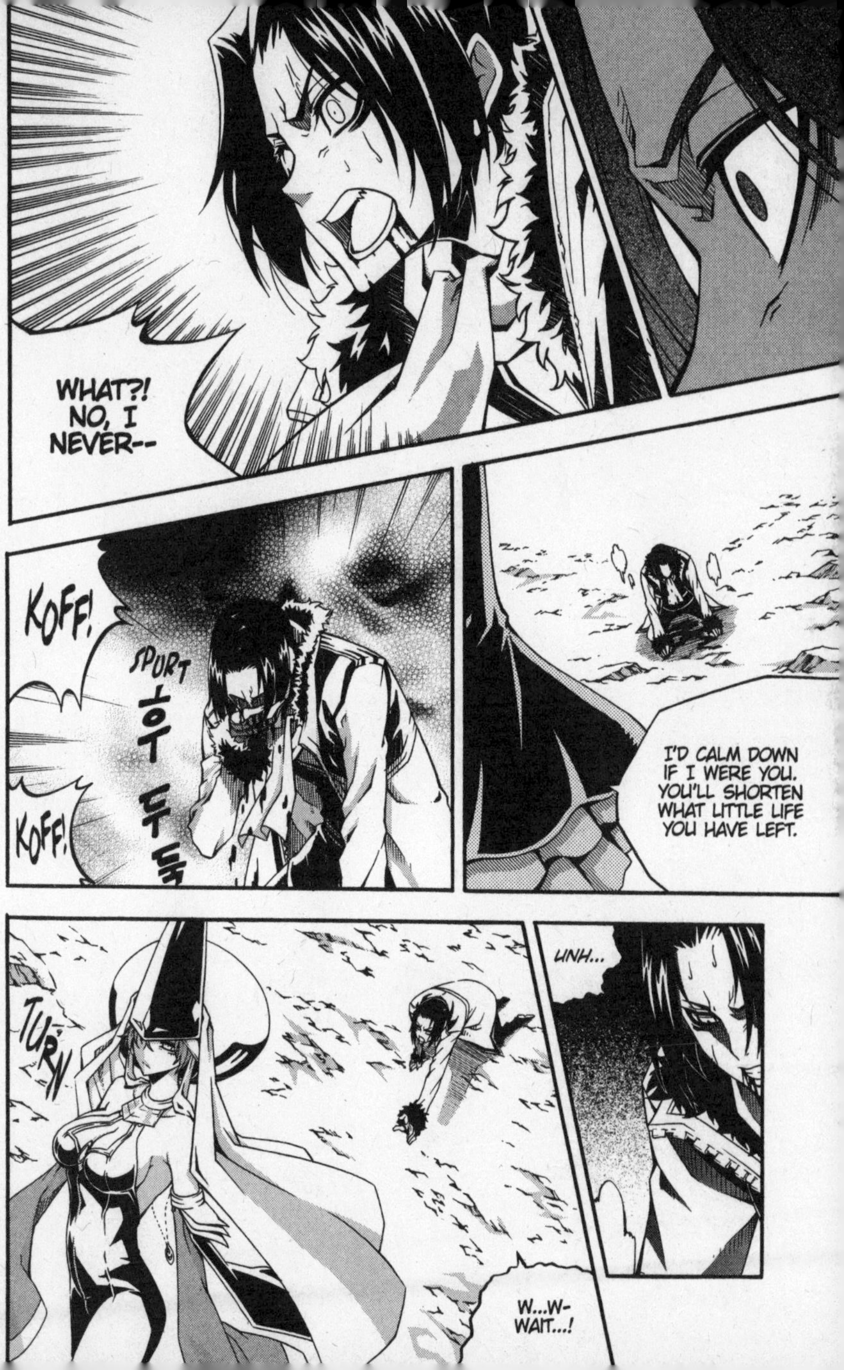
WHAT?! NO, I NEVER--
KOFF!
SPURT
후두둑
KOFF!
I'D CALM DOWN IF I WERE YOU. YOU'LL SHORTEN WHAT LITTLE LIFE YOU HAVE LEFT.
TURN
UNH...
W...W-WAIT...!

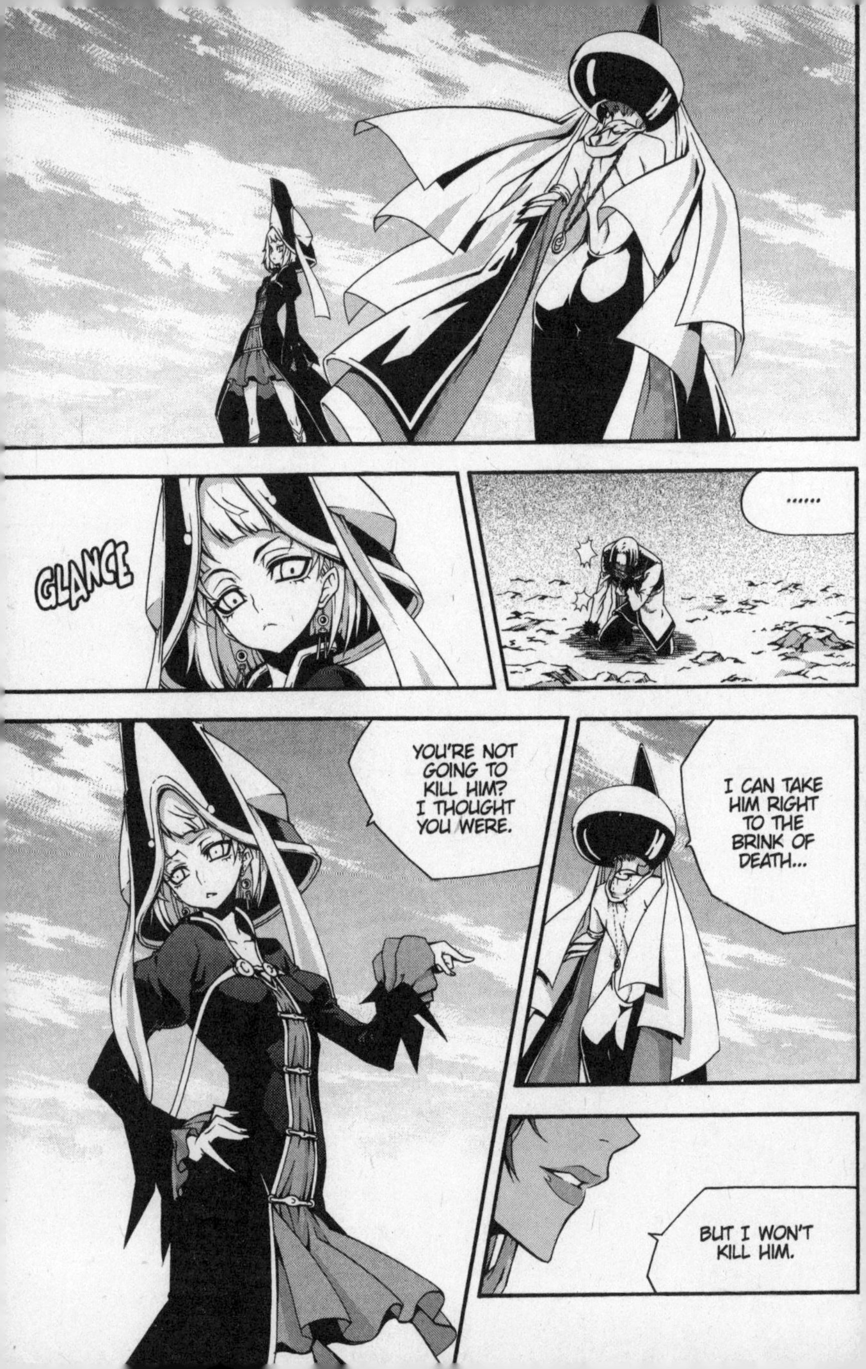
GLANCE
......
YOU'RE NOT GOING TO KILL HIM? I THOUGHT YOU WERE.
I CAN TAKE HIM RIGHT TO THE BRINK OF DEATH...
BUT I WON'T KILL HIM.

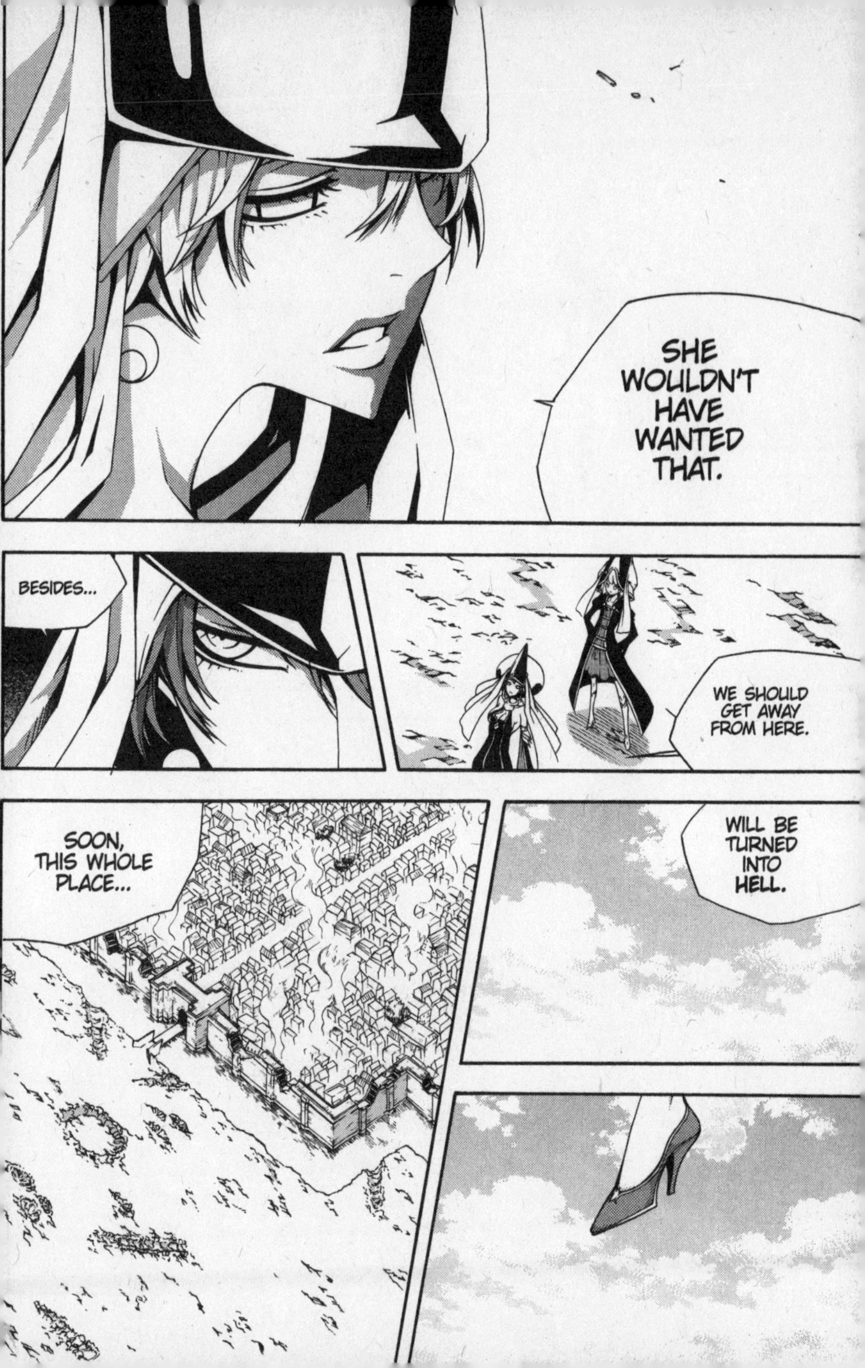
SHE WOULDN'T HAVE WANTED THAT.
BESIDES...
WE SHOULD GET AWAY FROM HERE.
SOON, THIS WHOLE PLACE...
WILL BE TURNED INTO HELL.

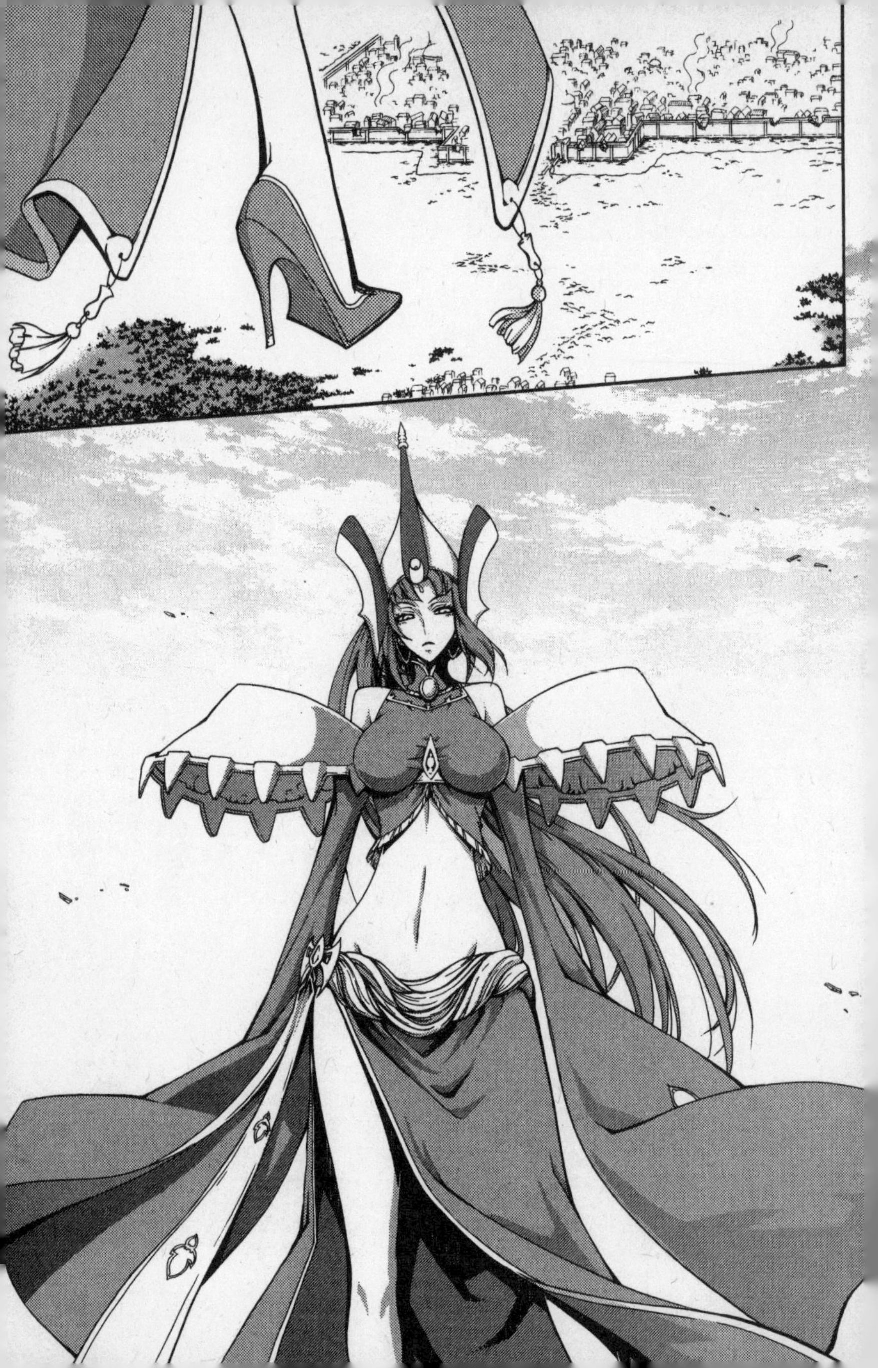

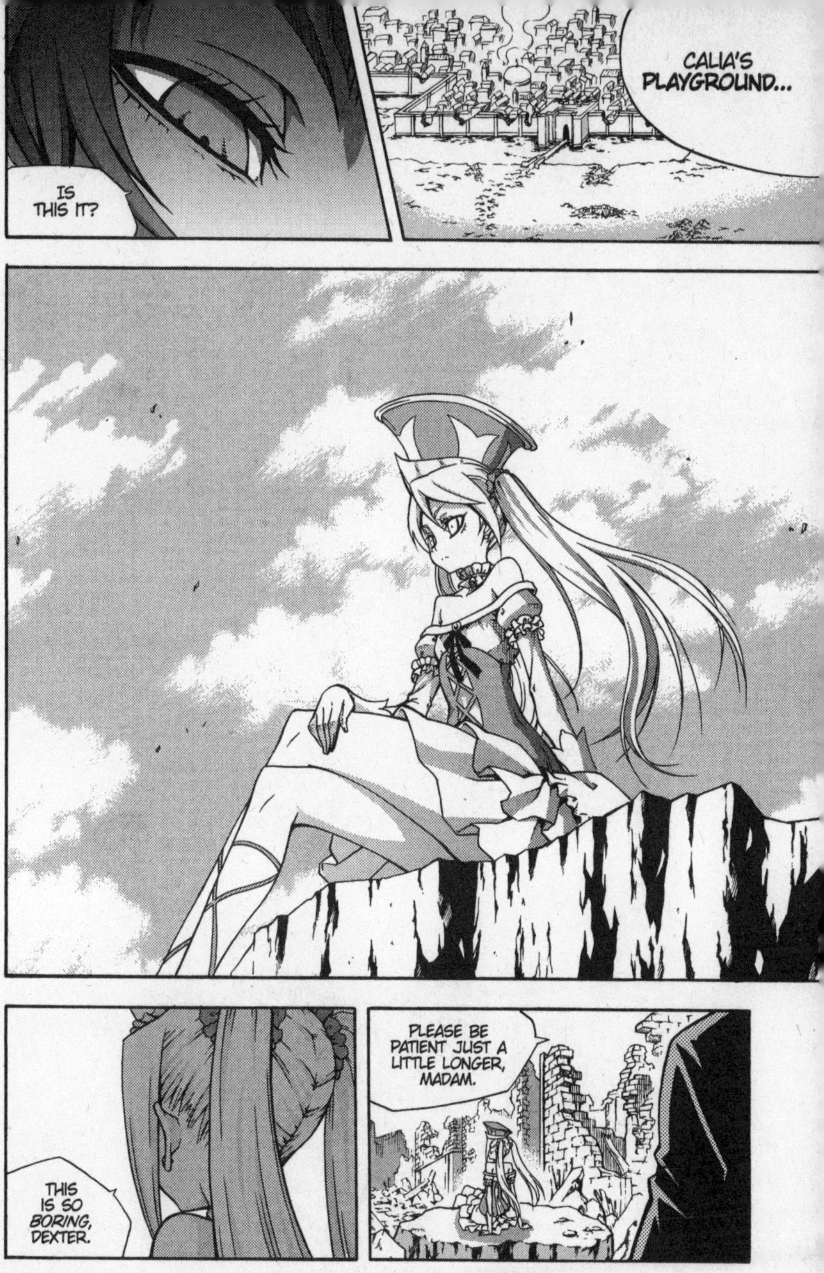
IS THIS IT?
CALIA'S PLAYGROUND...
THIS IS SO BORING, DEXTER.
PLEASE BE PATIENT JUST A LITTLE LONGER, MADAM.

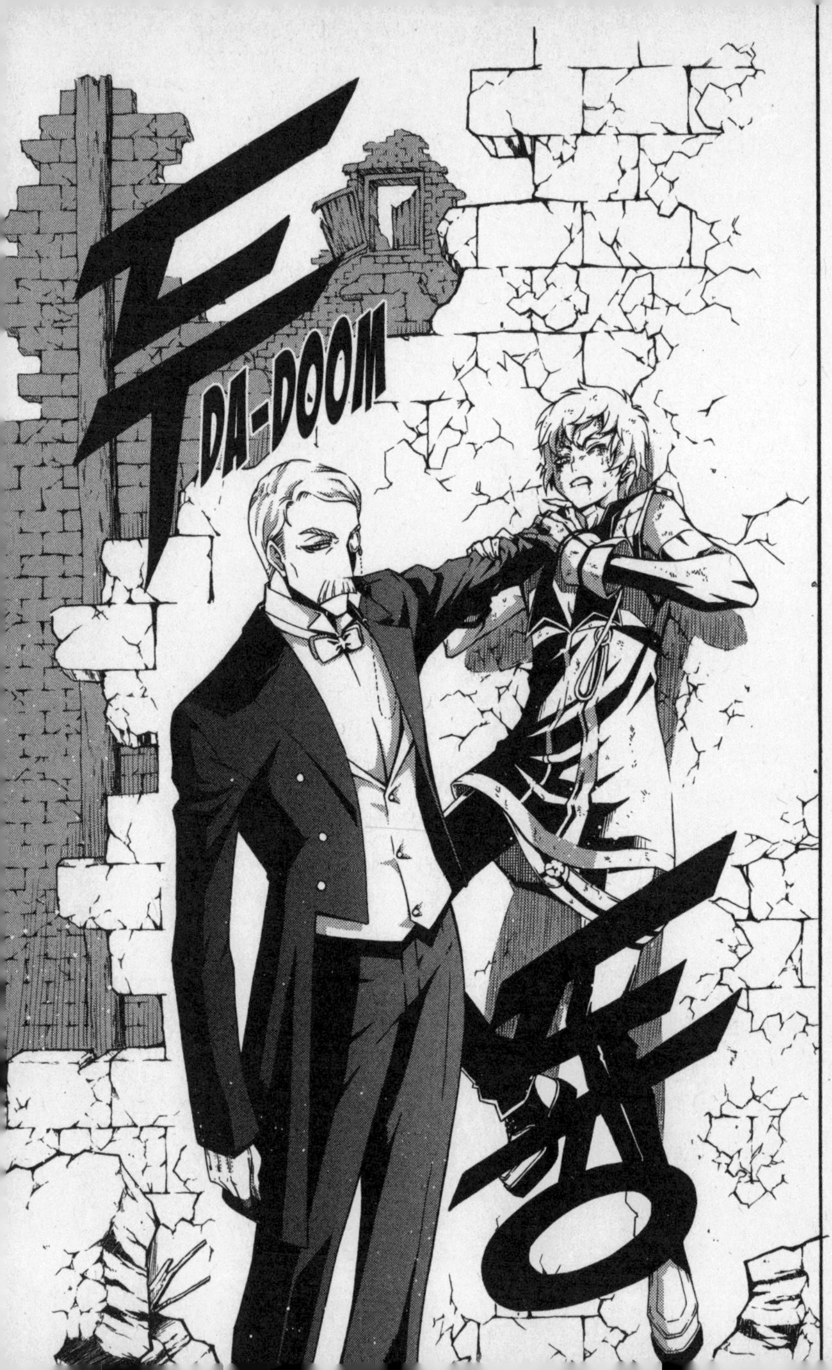
DA-DOOM

48. Complete Dominance

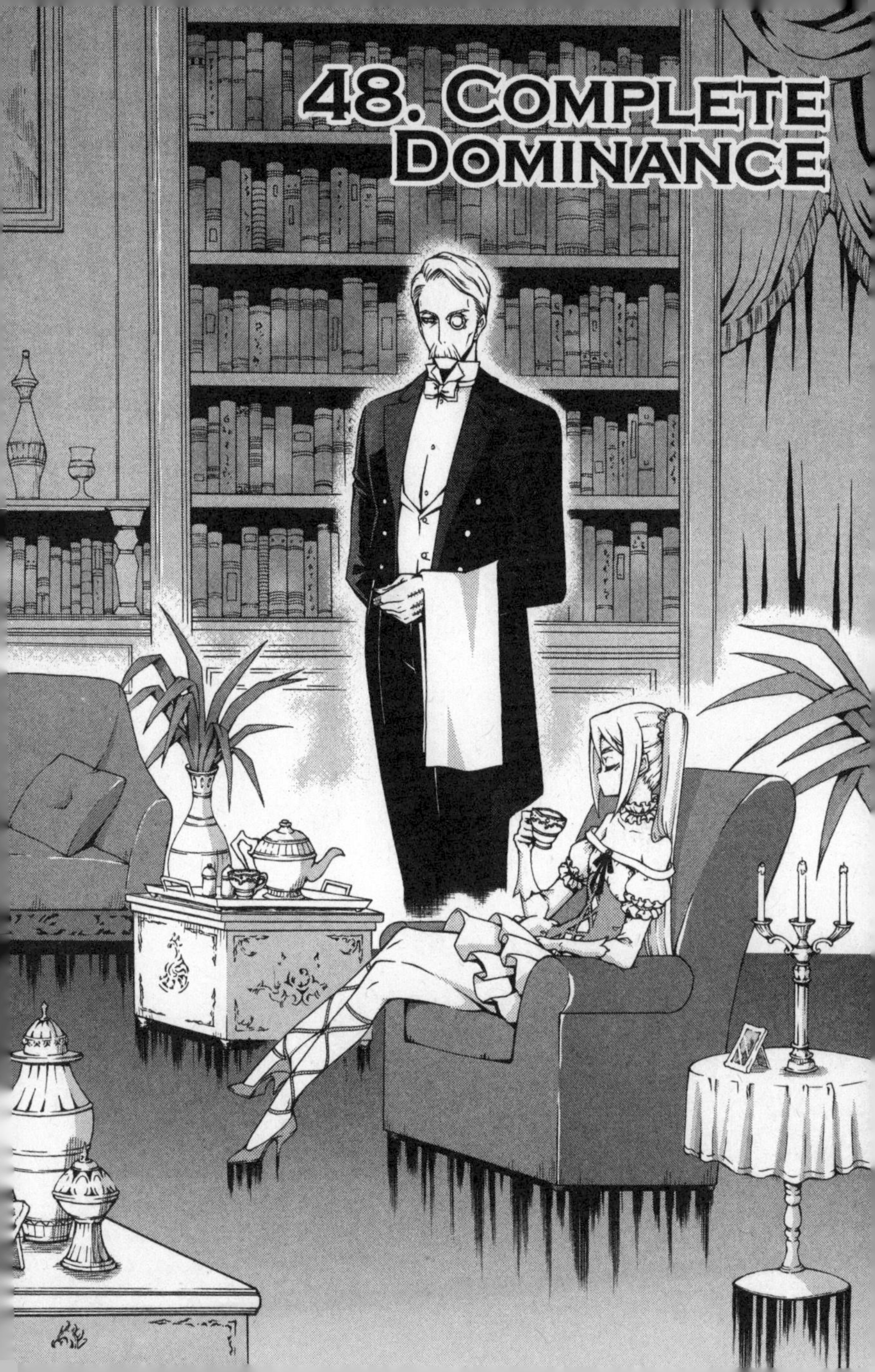

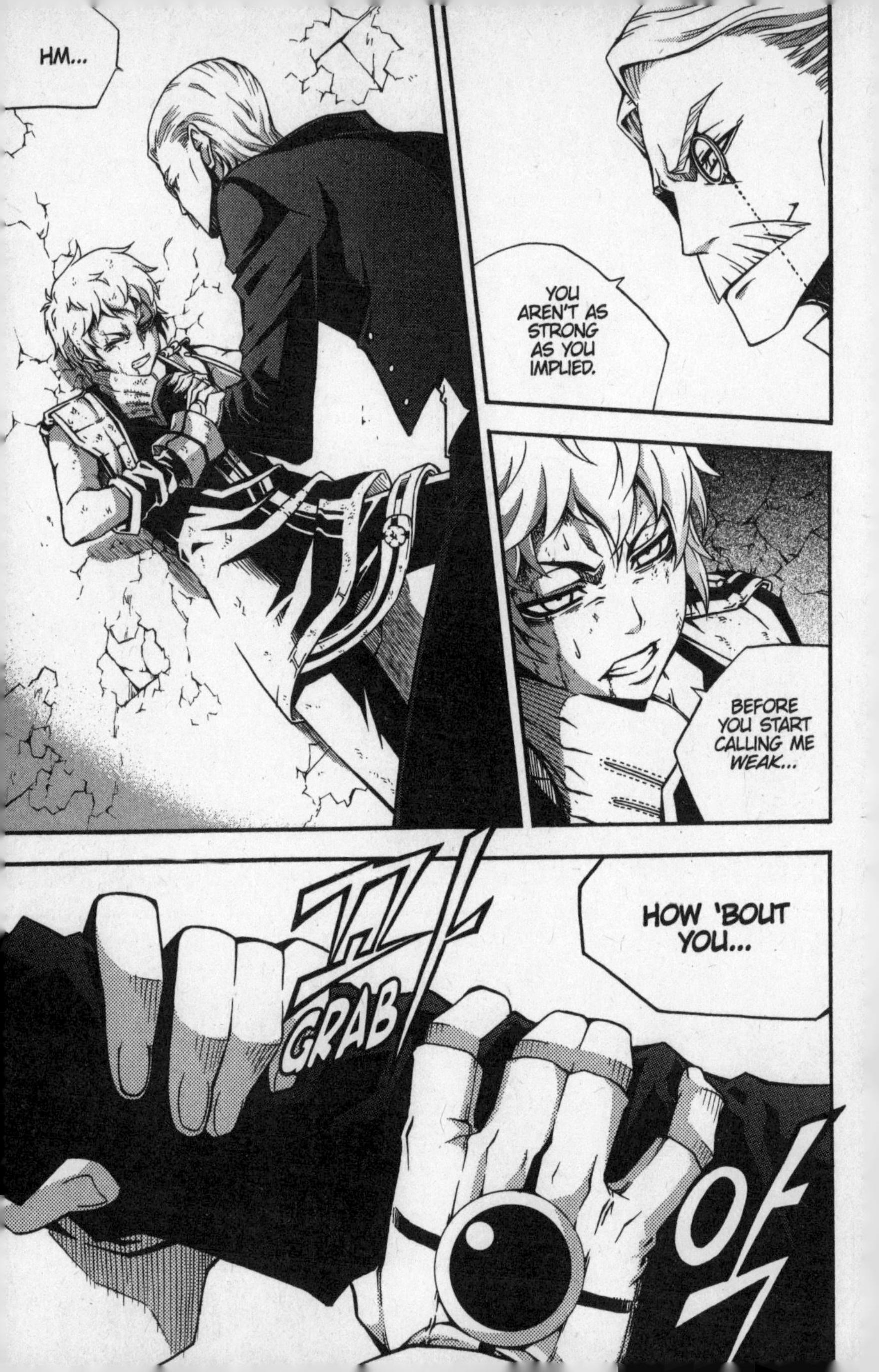
HM...
YOU AREN'T AS STRONG AS YOU IMPLIED.
BEFORE YOU START CALLING ME WEAK...
HOW 'BOUT YOU...
GRAB

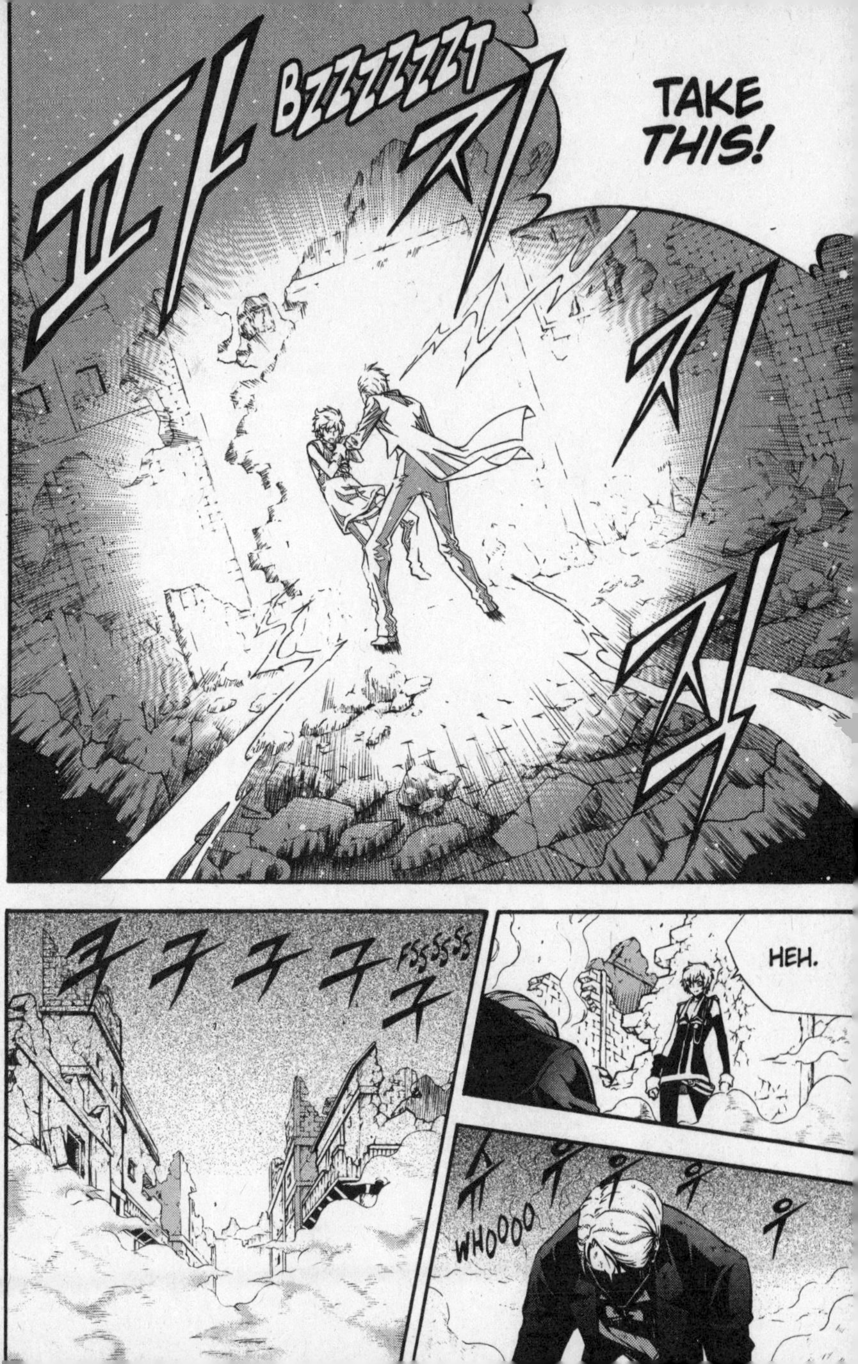
BZZZZZZZT
TAKE THIS!
FSSSSSS
HEH.
WHOOOO

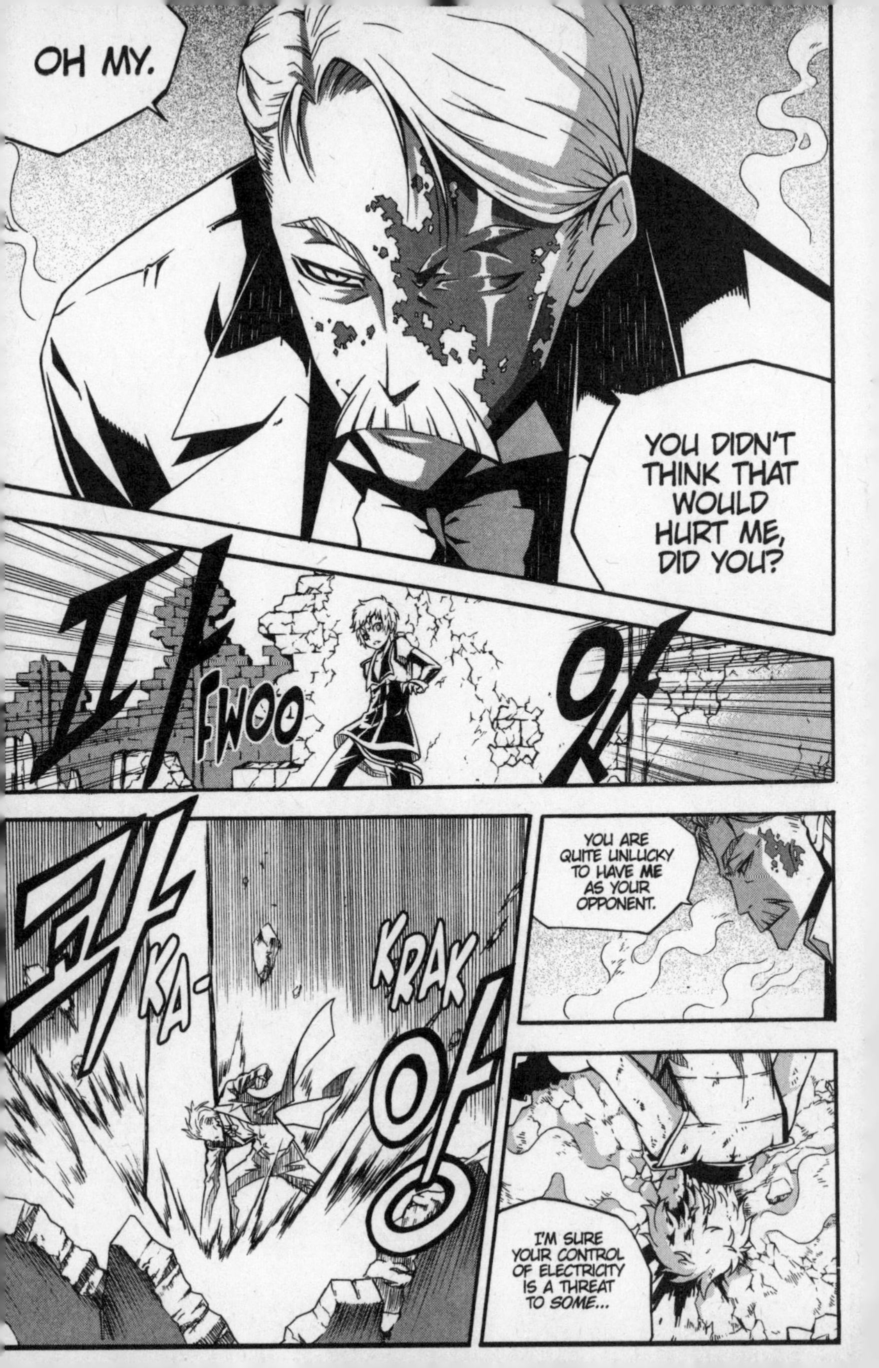
OH MY.
YOU DIDN'T THINK THAT WOULD HURT ME, DID YOU?
FWOO
KA-
KRAK
YOU ARE QUITE UNLUCKY TO HAVE ME AS YOUR OPPONENT.
I'M SURE YOUR CONTROL OF ELECTRICITY IS A THREAT TO SOME...

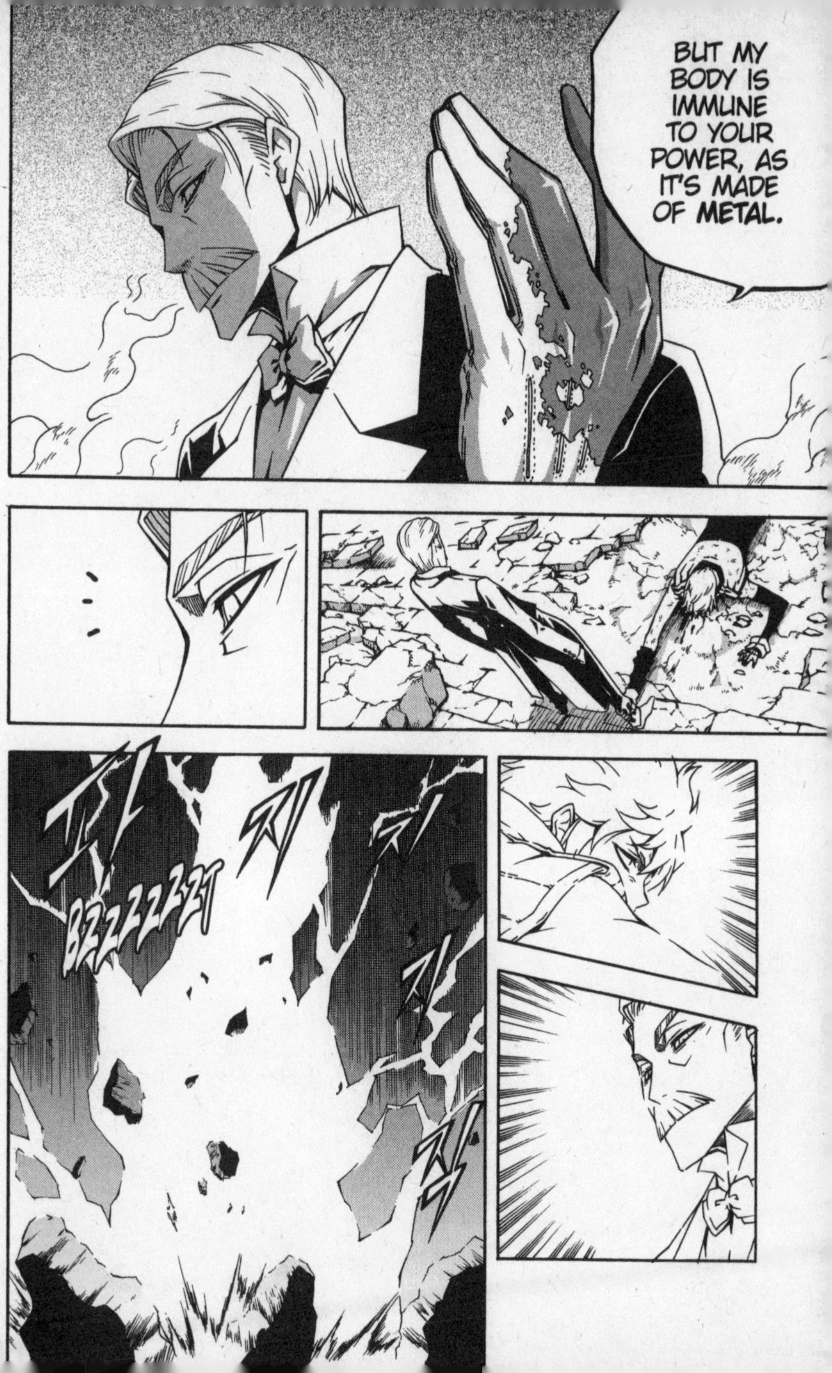
BUT MY BODY IS IMMUNE TO YOUR POWER, AS IT'S MADE OF METAL.
...
BZZZZZZZT

I ALREADY TOLD YOU, THAT WON'T WORK.

PAT PAT

YOUR ELECTRICITY FLOWS STRAIGHT THROUGH MY BODY WITHOUT HARMING IT.

MAYBE MY ATTACKS DIDN'T HARM YOU DIRECTLY, BUT I WOULDN'T CALL THEM USELESS.

MY SPECIALTY IS CONTROLLING ELECTRIC CURRENTS. ALL MY ATTACKS HIT YOU, RIGHT?

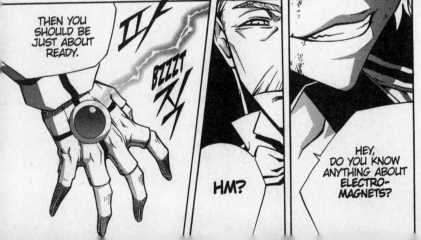

THEN YOU SHOULD BE JUST ABOUT READY.

IIZ

BZZZT

HM?

HEY, DO YOU KNOW ANYTHING ABOUT ELECTRO-MAGNETS?

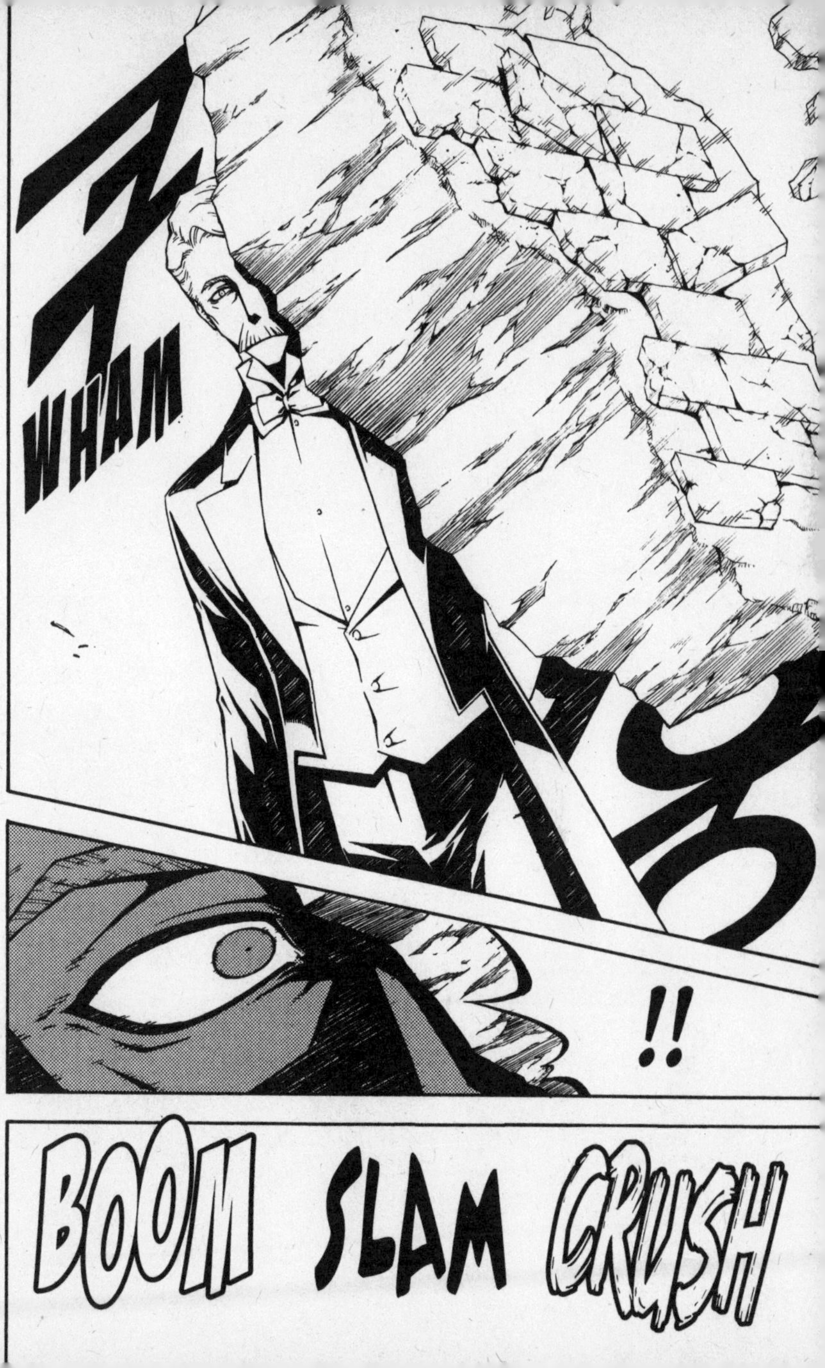
WHAM
!!
BOOM
SLAM
CRUSH

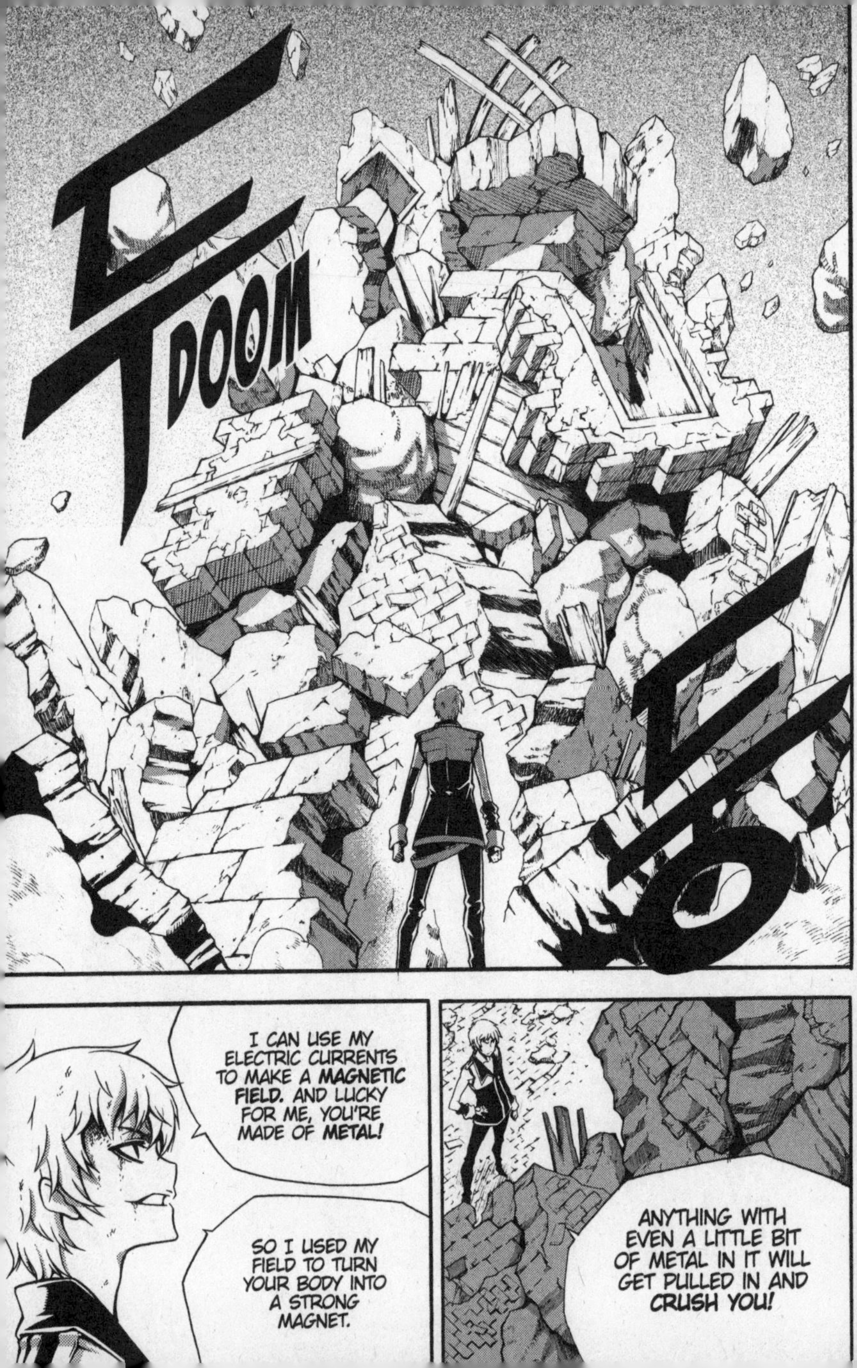
DOOM
I CAN USE MY ELECTRIC CURRENTS TO MAKE A MAGNETIC FIELD. AND LUCKY FOR ME, YOU'RE MADE OF METAL!
SO I USED MY FIELD TO TURN YOUR BODY INTO A STRONG MAGNET.
ANYTHING WITH EVEN A LITTLE BIT OF METAL IN IT WILL GET PULLED IN AND CRUSH YOU!

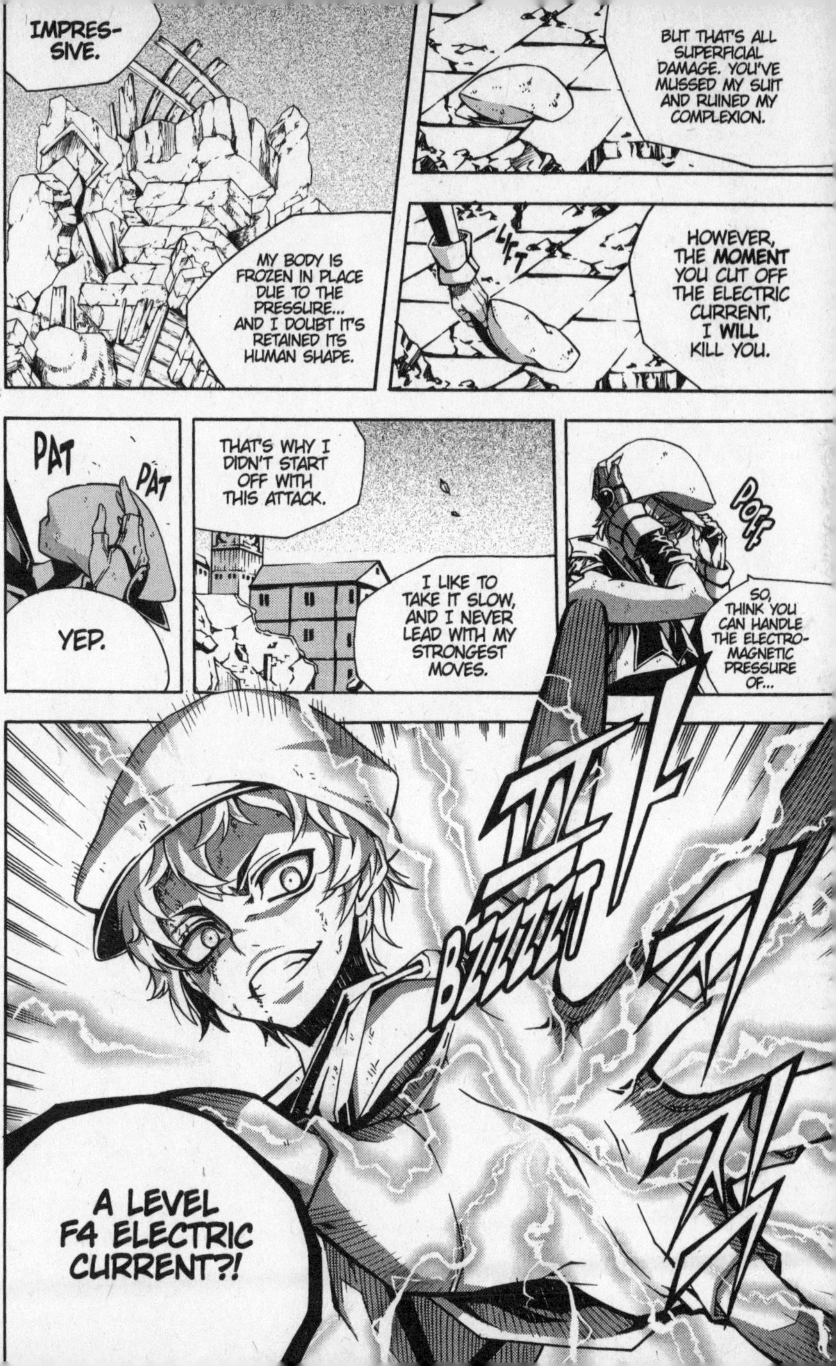
IMPRES-SIVE.
MY BODY IS FROZEN IN PLACE DUE TO THE PRESSURE... AND I DOUBT IT'S RETAINED ITS HUMAN SHAPE.
BUT THAT'S ALL SUPERFICIAL DAMAGE. YOU'VE MUSSED MY SUIT AND RUINED MY COMPLEXION.
LIFT
HOWEVER, THE **MOMENT** YOU CUT OFF THE ELECTRIC CURRENT, I **WILL** KILL YOU.
PAT
PAT
YEP.
THAT'S WHY I DIDN'T START OFF WITH THIS ATTACK.
I LIKE TO TAKE IT SLOW, AND I NEVER LEAD WITH MY STRONGEST MOVES.
POFF
SO, THINK YOU CAN HANDLE THE ELECTRO-MAGNETIC PRESSURE OF...
BZZZZT
A LEVEL F4 ELECTRIC CURRENT?!

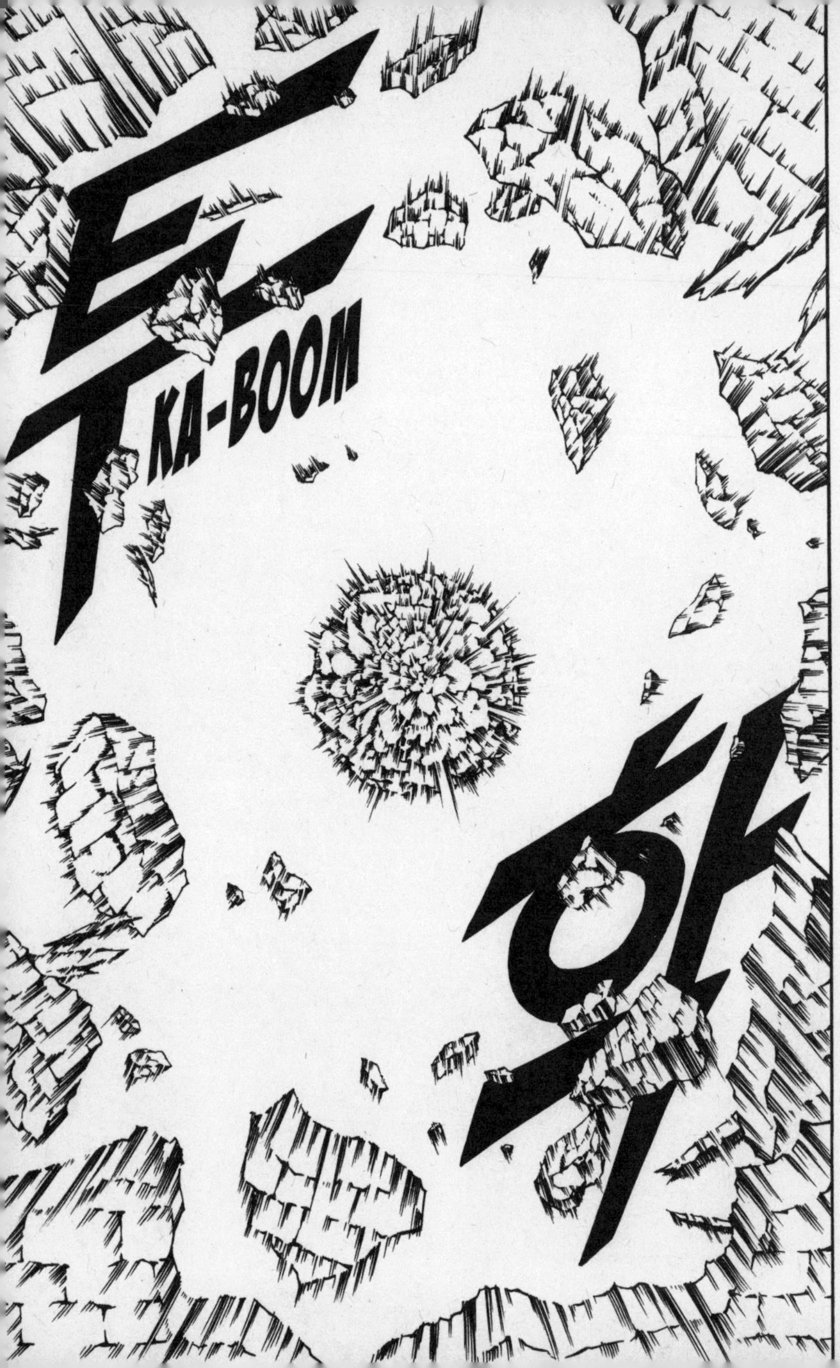
KA-BOOM

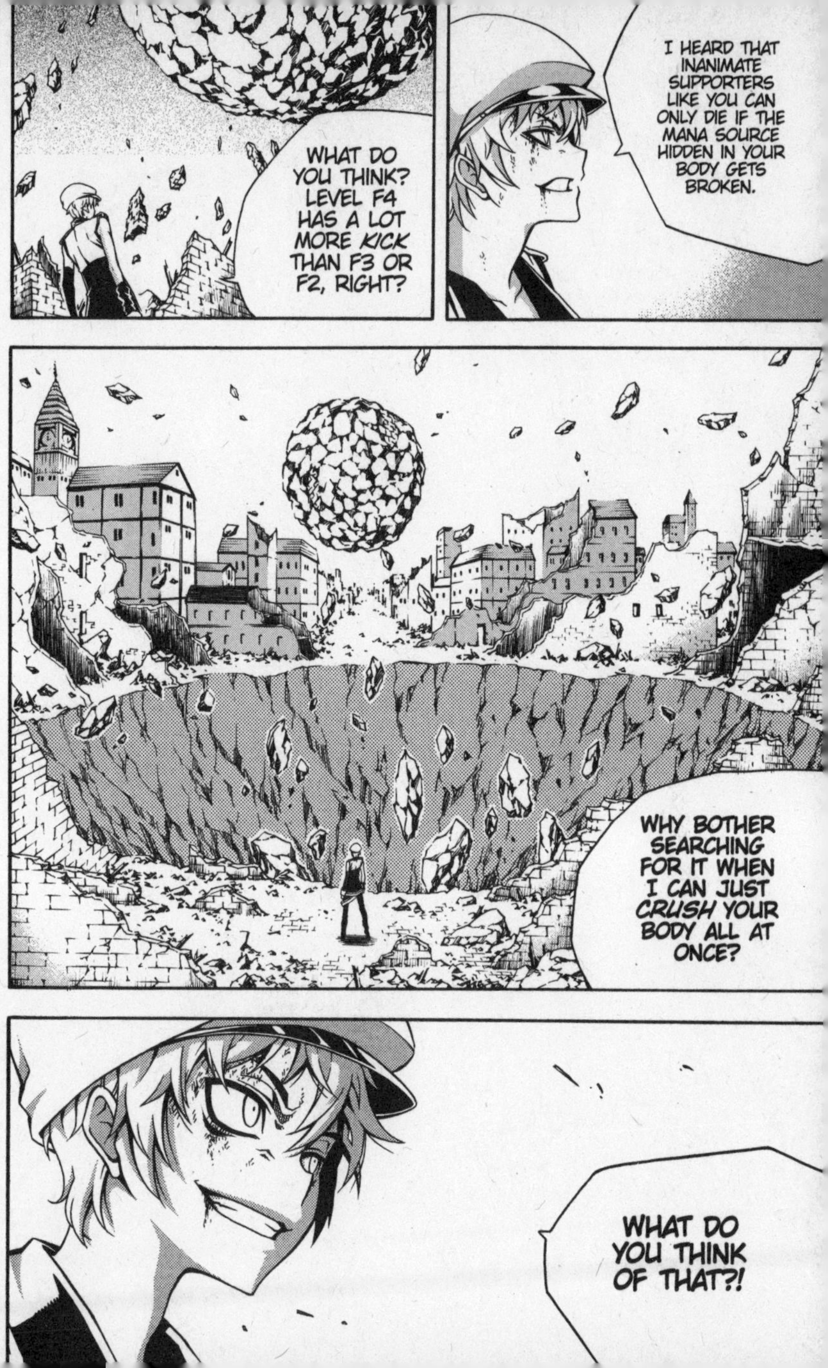
WHAT DO YOU THINK? LEVEL F4 HAS A LOT MORE *KICK* THAN F3 OR F2, RIGHT?
I HEARD THAT INANIMATE SUPPORTERS LIKE YOU CAN ONLY DIE IF THE MANA SOURCE HIDDEN IN YOUR BODY GETS BROKEN.
WHY BOTHER SEARCHING FOR IT WHEN I CAN JUST *CRUSH* YOUR BODY ALL AT ONCE?
WHAT DO YOU THINK OF THAT?!

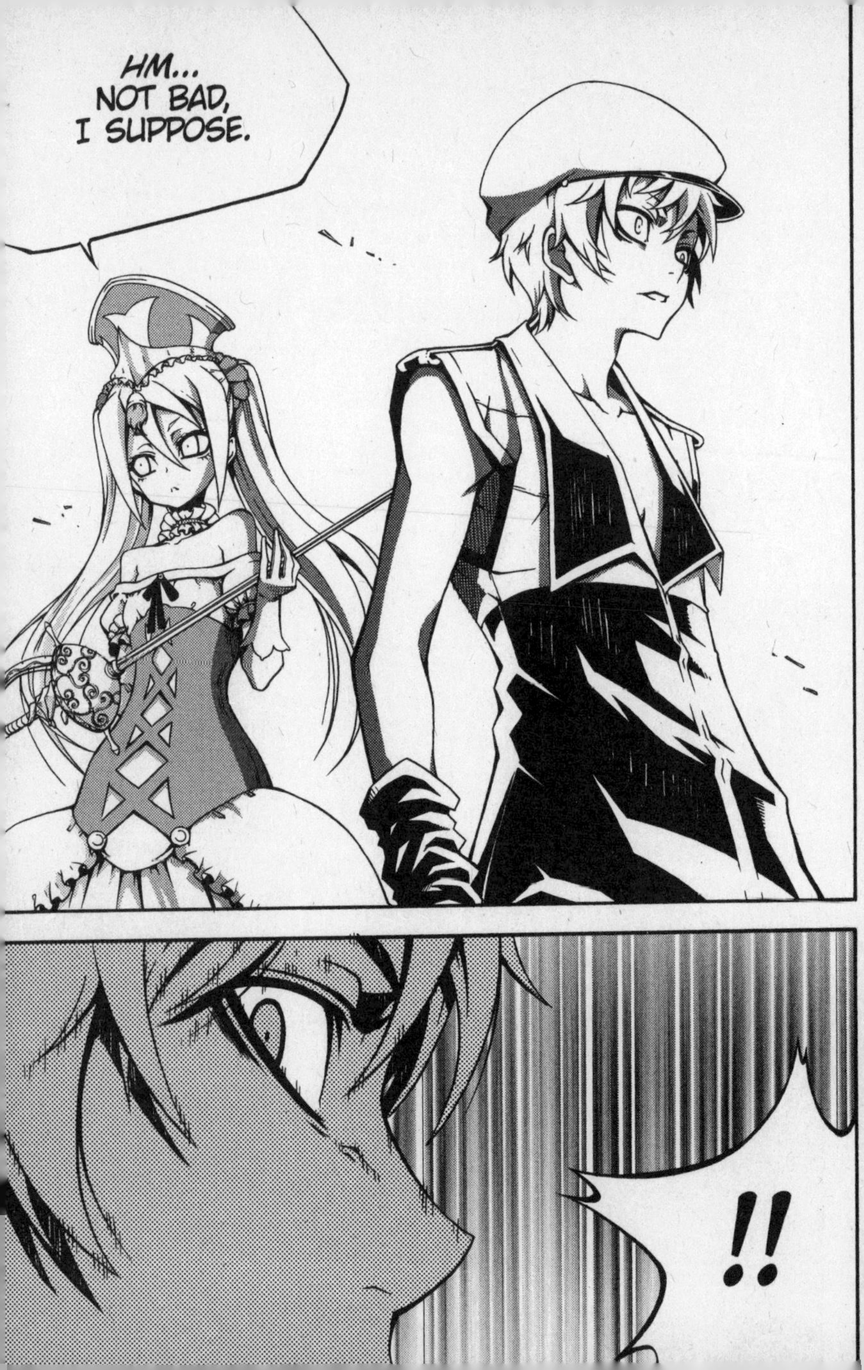
HM... NOT BAD, I SUPPOSE.
!!

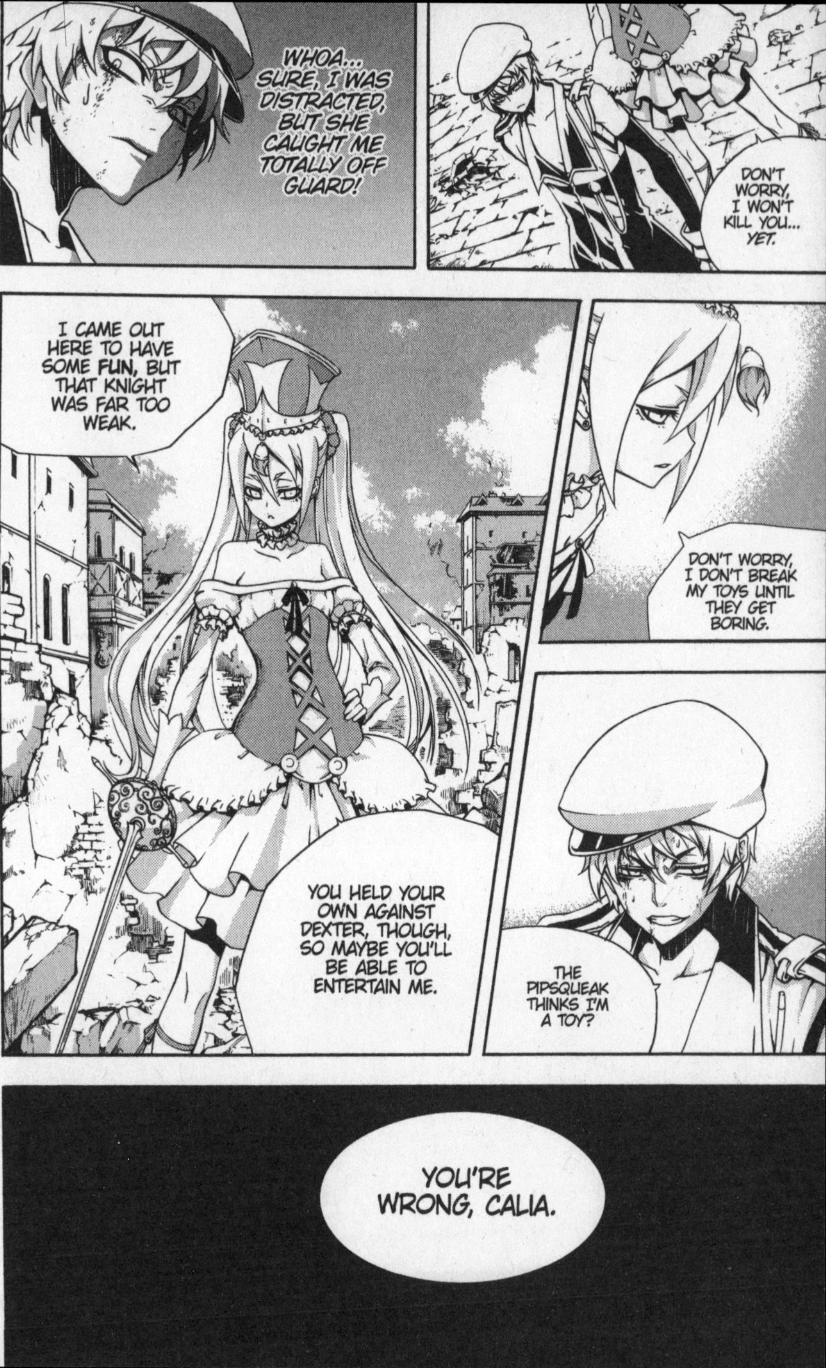
WHOA... SURE, I WAS DISTRACTED, BUT SHE CAUGHT ME TOTALLY OFF GUARD!
DON'T WORRY, I WON'T KILL YOU... YET.
I CAME OUT HERE TO HAVE SOME FUN, BUT THAT KNIGHT WAS FAR TOO WEAK.
YOU HELD YOUR OWN AGAINST DEXTER, THOUGH, SO MAYBE YOU'LL BE ABLE TO ENTERTAIN ME.
DON'T WORRY, I DON'T BREAK MY TOYS UNTIL THEY GET BORING.
THE PIPSQUEAK THINKS I'M A TOY?
YOU'RE WRONG, CALIA.

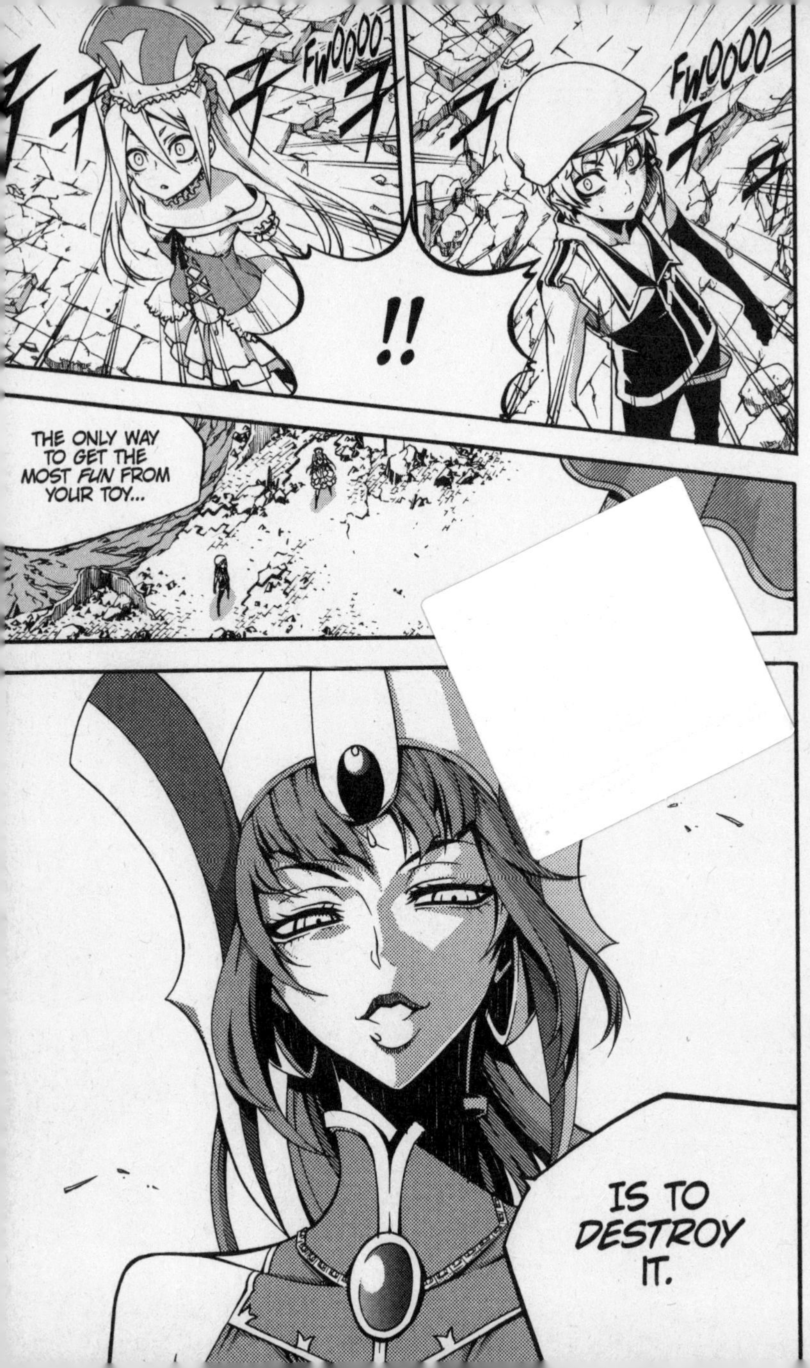
FWOOO
FWOOO
!!
THE ONLY WAY TO GET THE MOST *FUN* FROM YOUR TOY...
IS TO DESTROY IT.

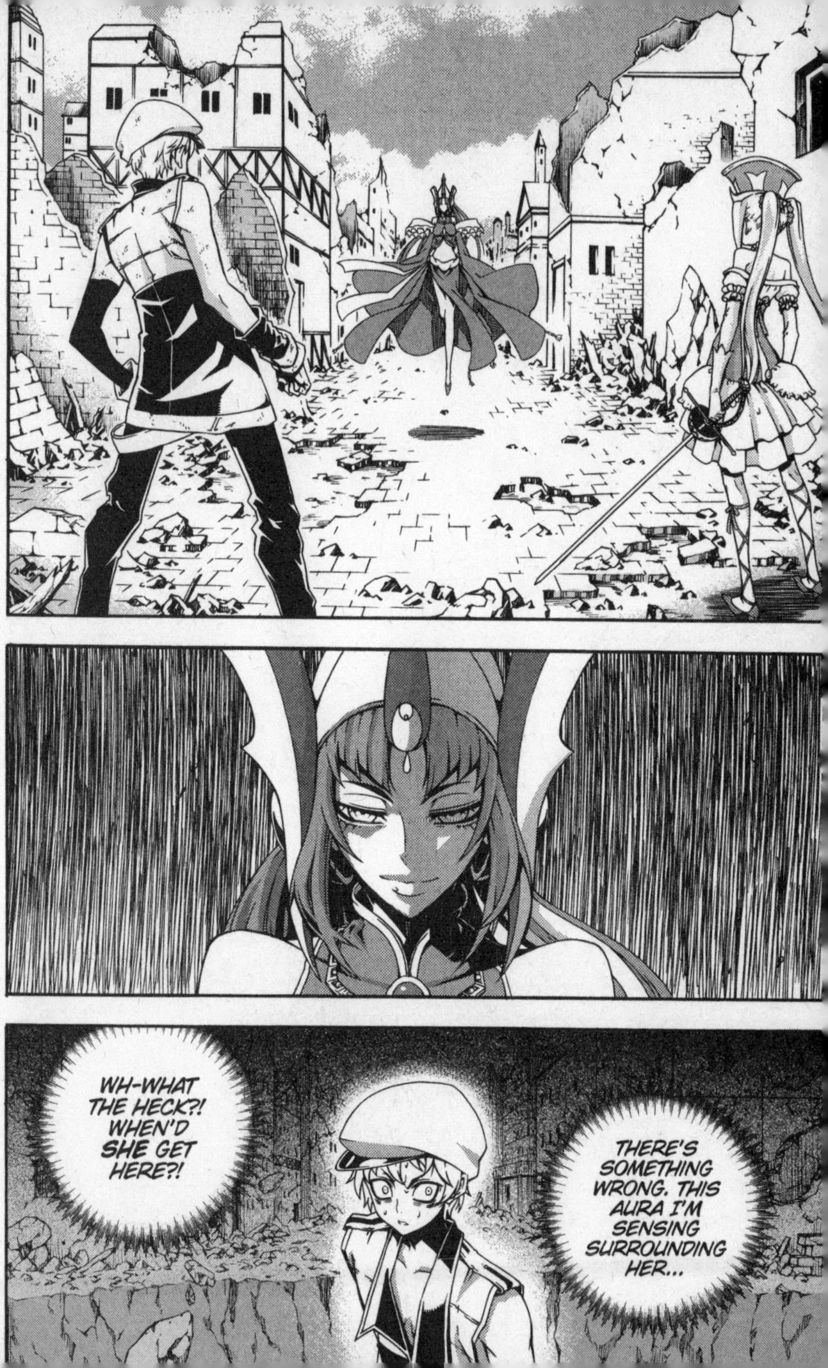
WH-WHAT THE HECK?! WHEN'D SHE GET HERE?!
THERE'S SOMETHING WRONG. THIS AURA I'M SENSING SURROUNDING HER...

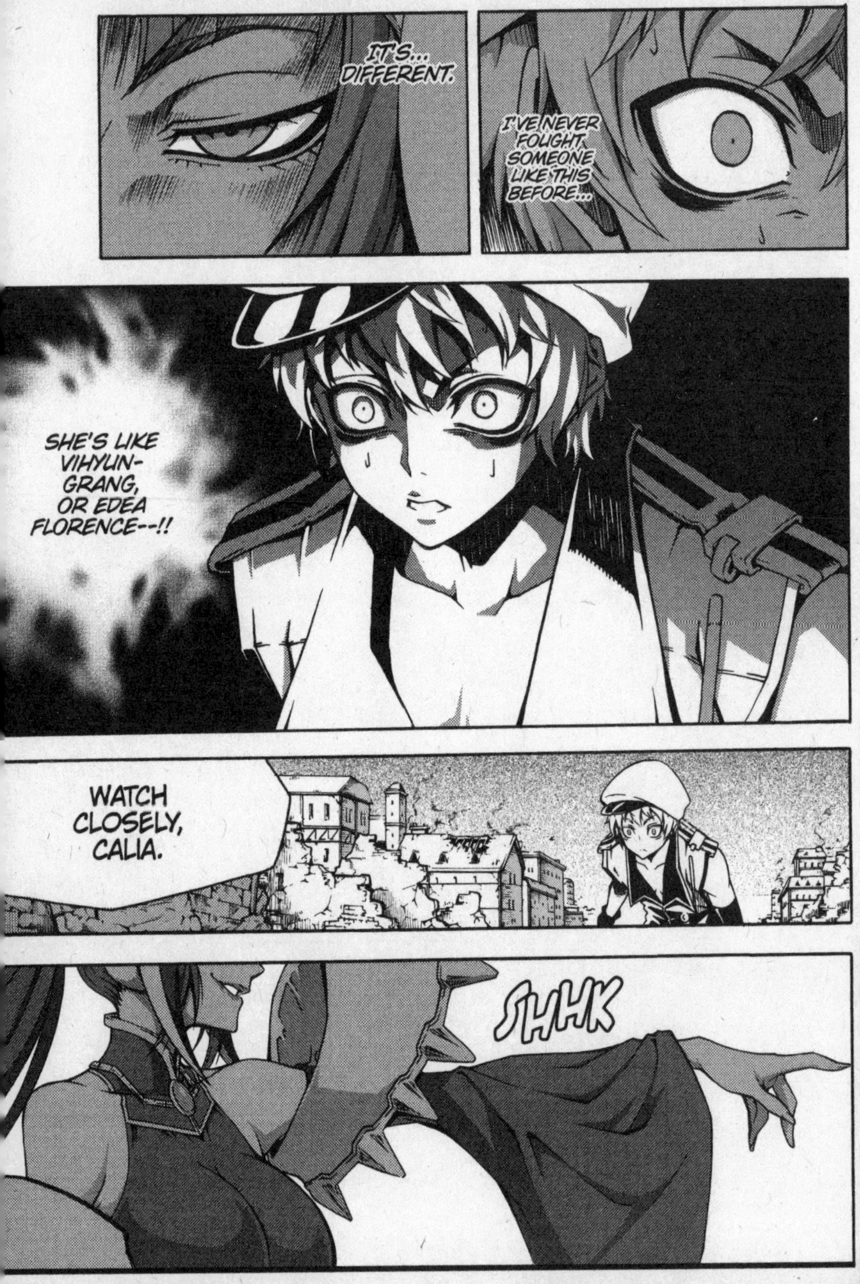

IT'S... DIFFERENT.
I'VE NEVER FOUGHT SOMEONE LIKE THIS BEFORE...
SHE'S LIKE VIHYUN-GRANG, OR EDEA FLORENCE--!!
WATCH CLOSELY, CALIA.
SHHK

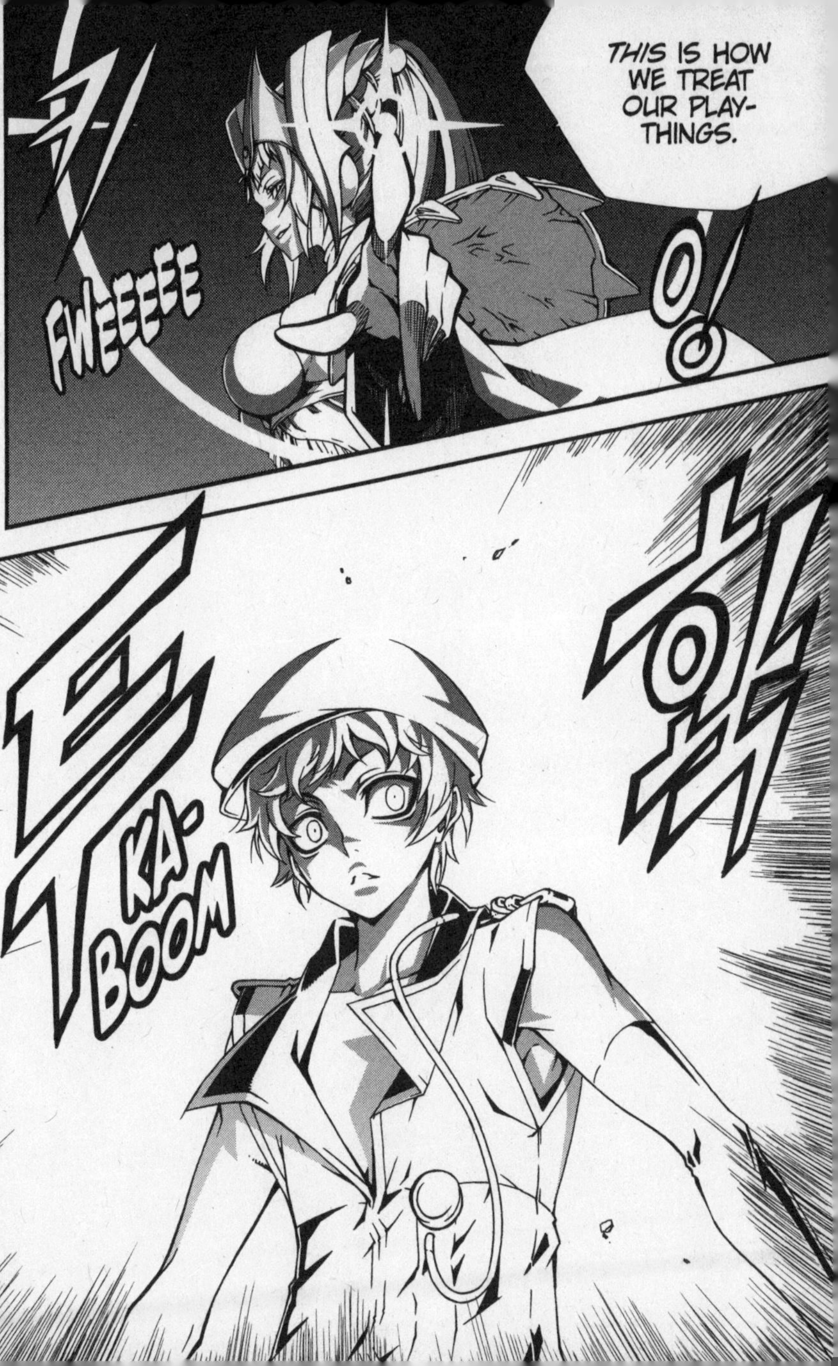
THIS IS HOW WE TREAT OUR PLAY-THINGS.
FWEEEEE
KA-BOOM

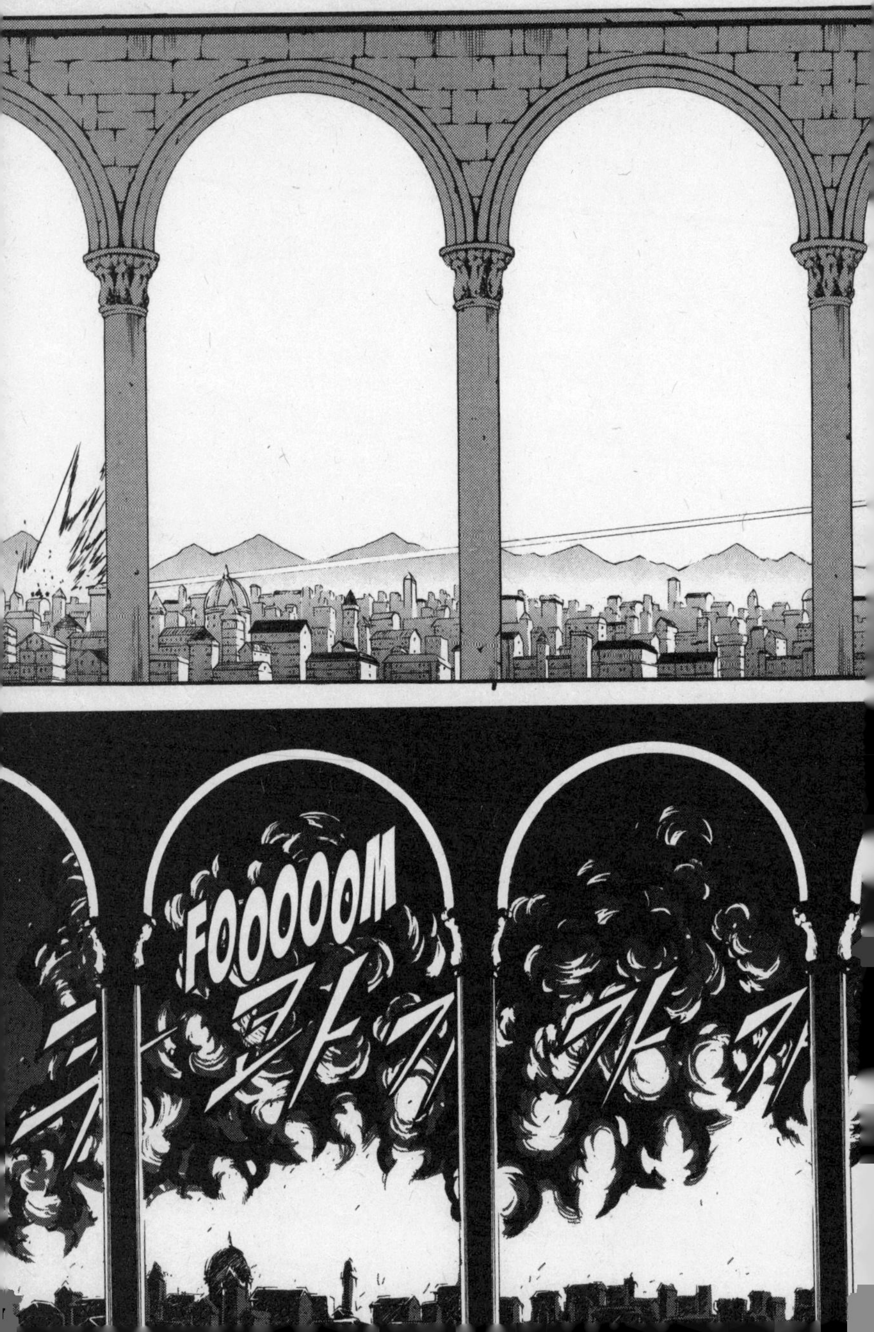
FOOOOOM

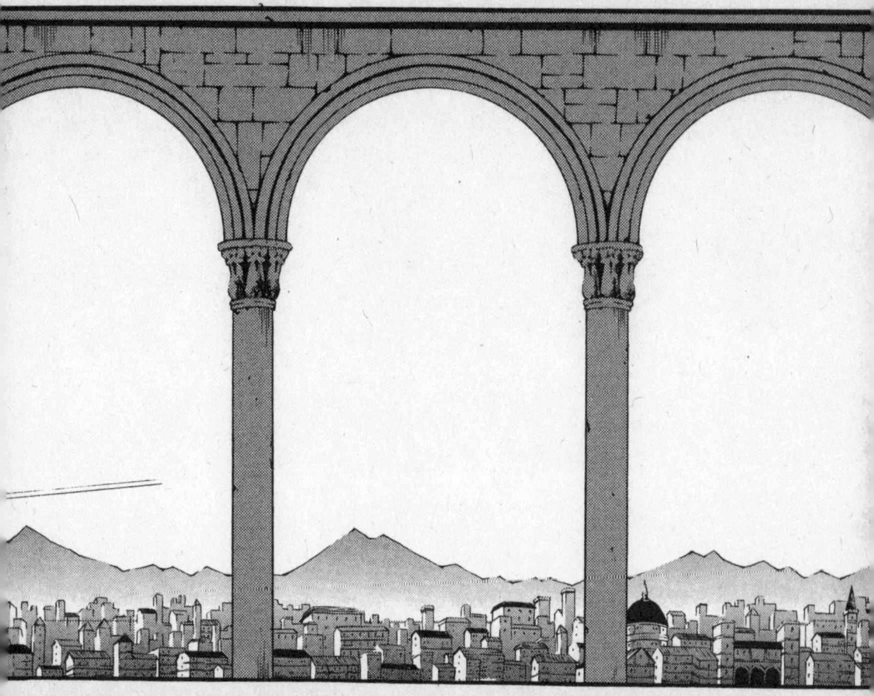

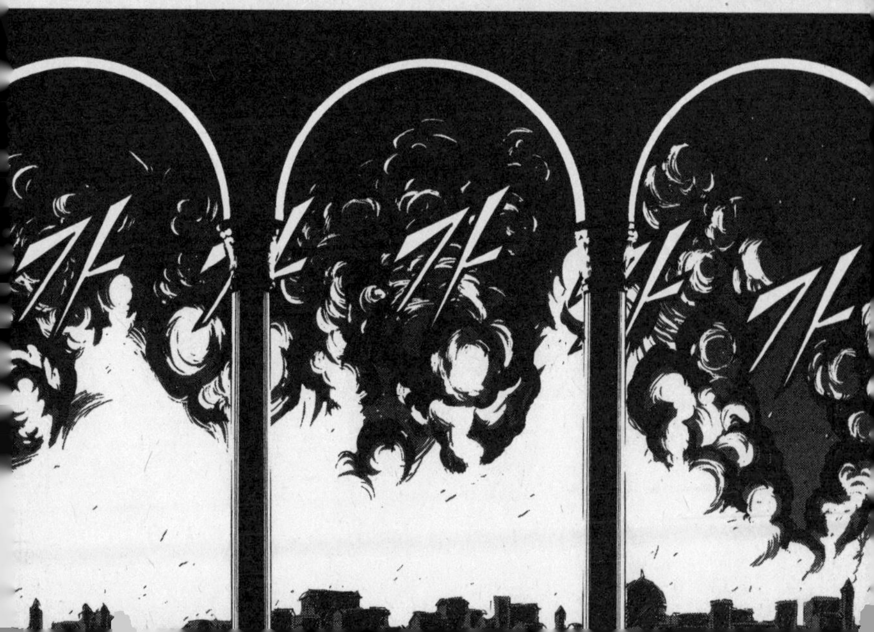

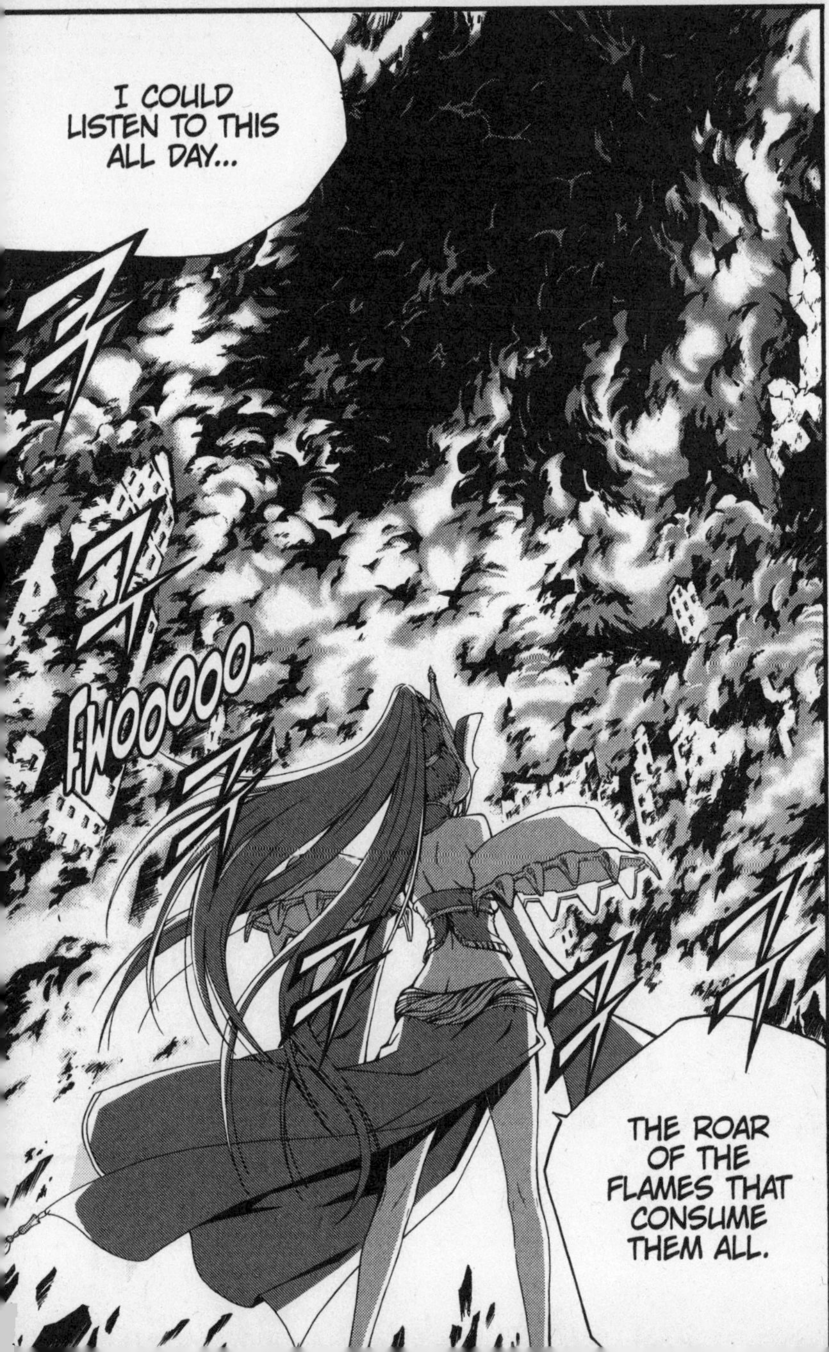

I COULD LISTEN TO THIS ALL DAY...
FWOOOOO
THE ROAR OF THE FLAMES THAT CONSUME THEM ALL.

WITCH BUSTER

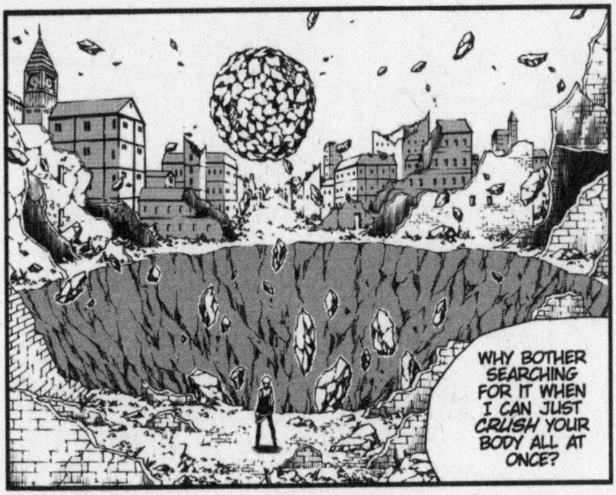
WHY BOTHER SEARCHING FOR IT WHEN I CAN JUST CRUSH YOUR BODY ALL AT ONCE?

COOGA...
YOU'VE FORGOTTEN ONE
IMPORTANT DETAIL.

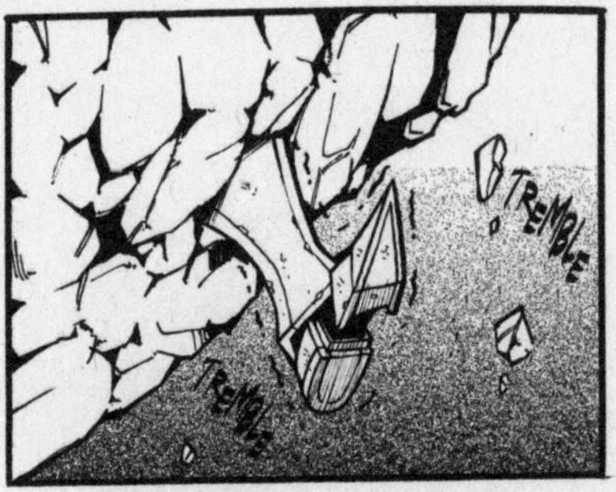
TREMBLE
TREMBLE

THE KNIGHTS' ARMOR IS
ALSO MADE OF METAL.

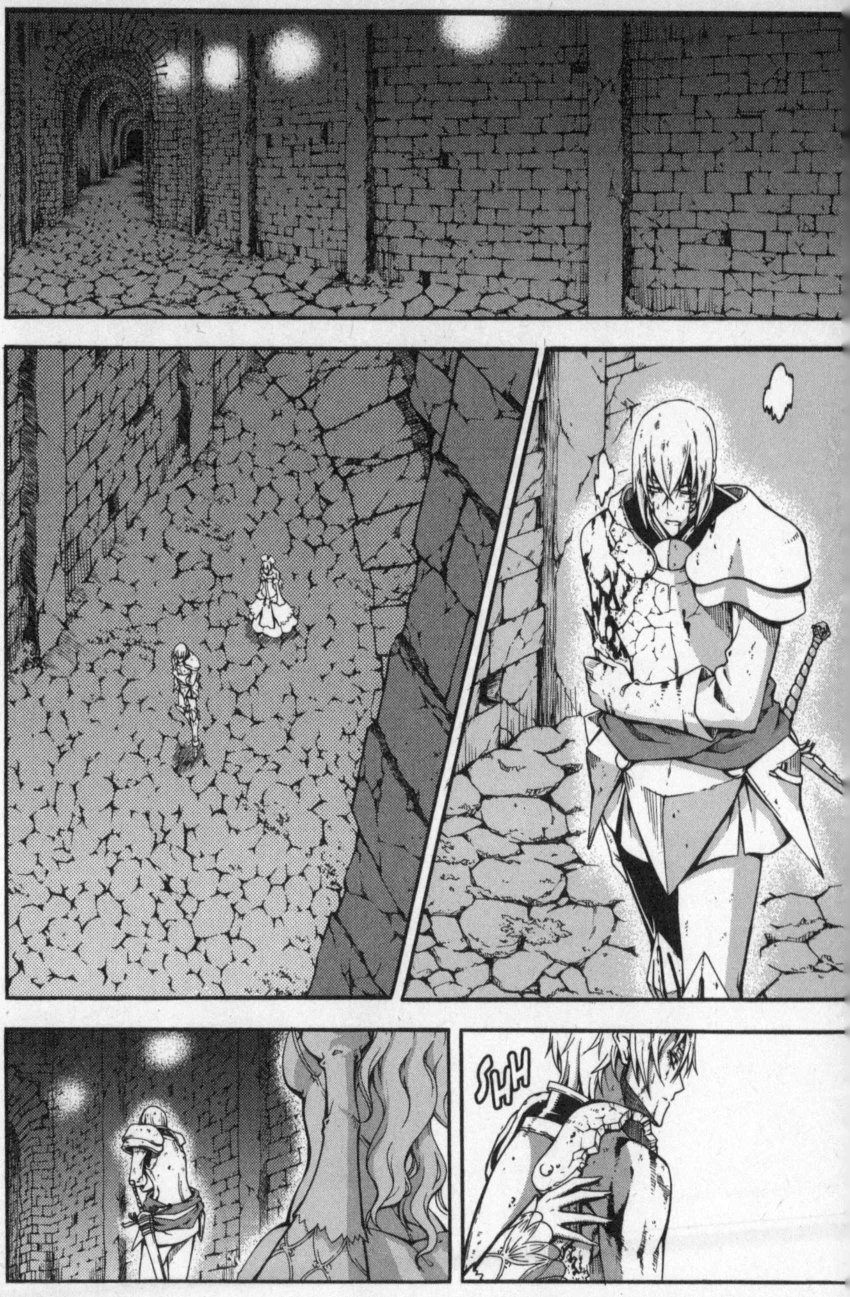
SHH

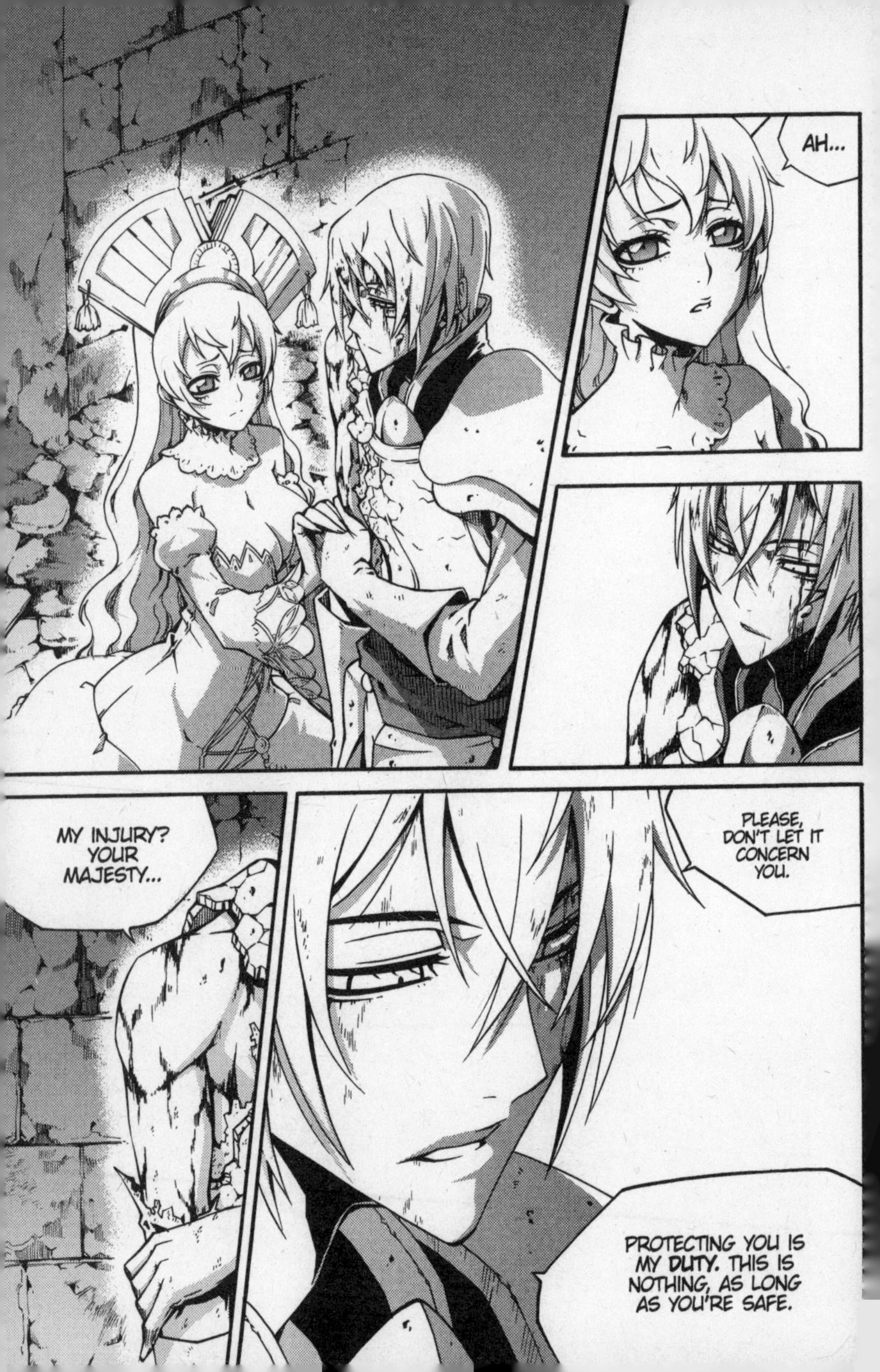
AH...
MY INJURY? YOUR MAJESTY...
PLEASE, DON'T LET IT CONCERN YOU.
PROTECTING YOU IS MY DUTY. THIS IS NOTHING, AS LONG AS YOU'RE SAFE.

I SWEAR, I **WILL** PROTECT YOU.

I'LL GIVE MY LIFE **GLADLY**, IF I HAVE TO.

THAT WAS...

THE LAST PROMISE I MADE TO ARTHUR.

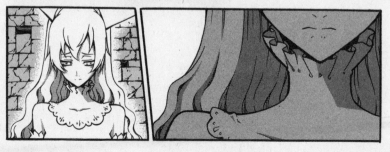

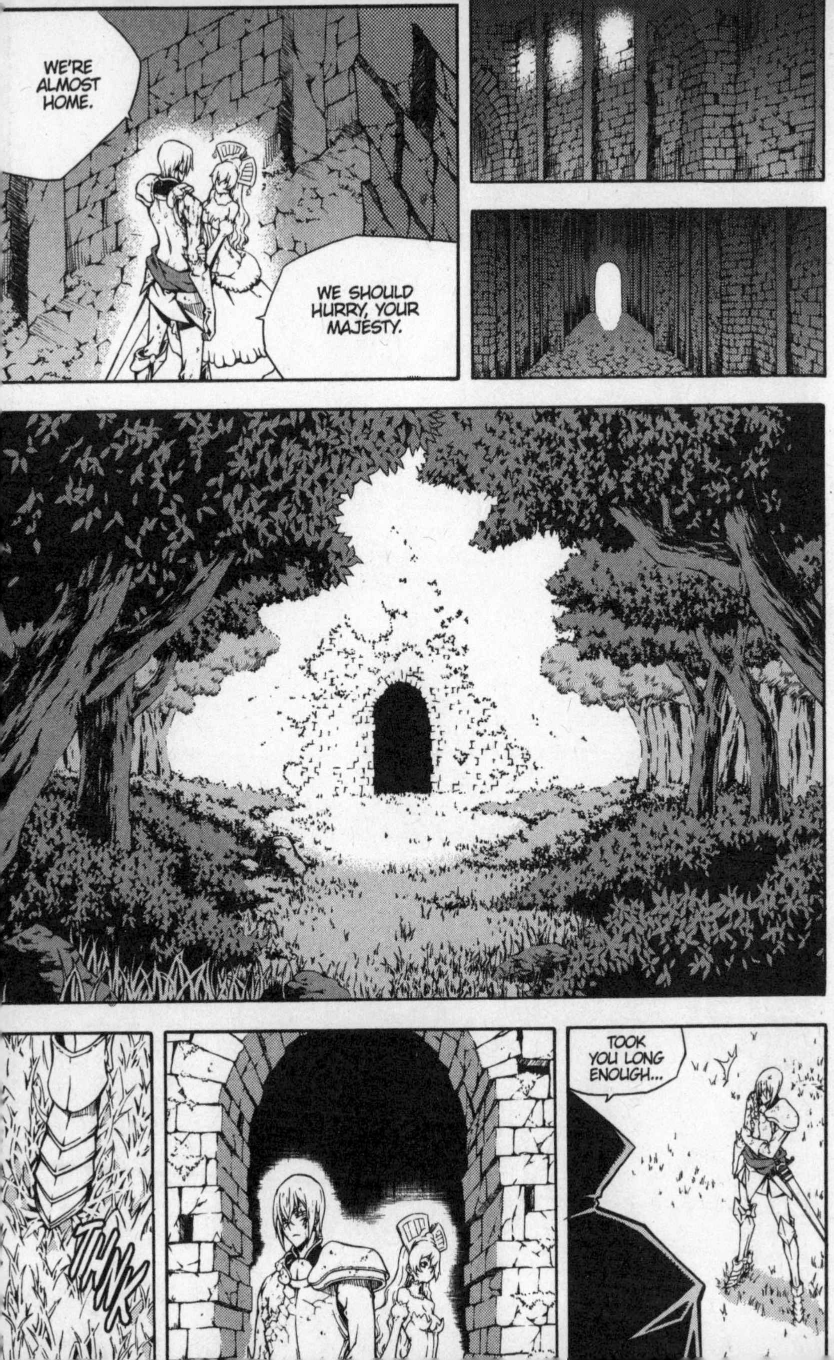
WE'RE ALMOST HOME.
WE SHOULD HURRY, YOUR MAJESTY.
THNK
TOOK YOU LONG ENOUGH...

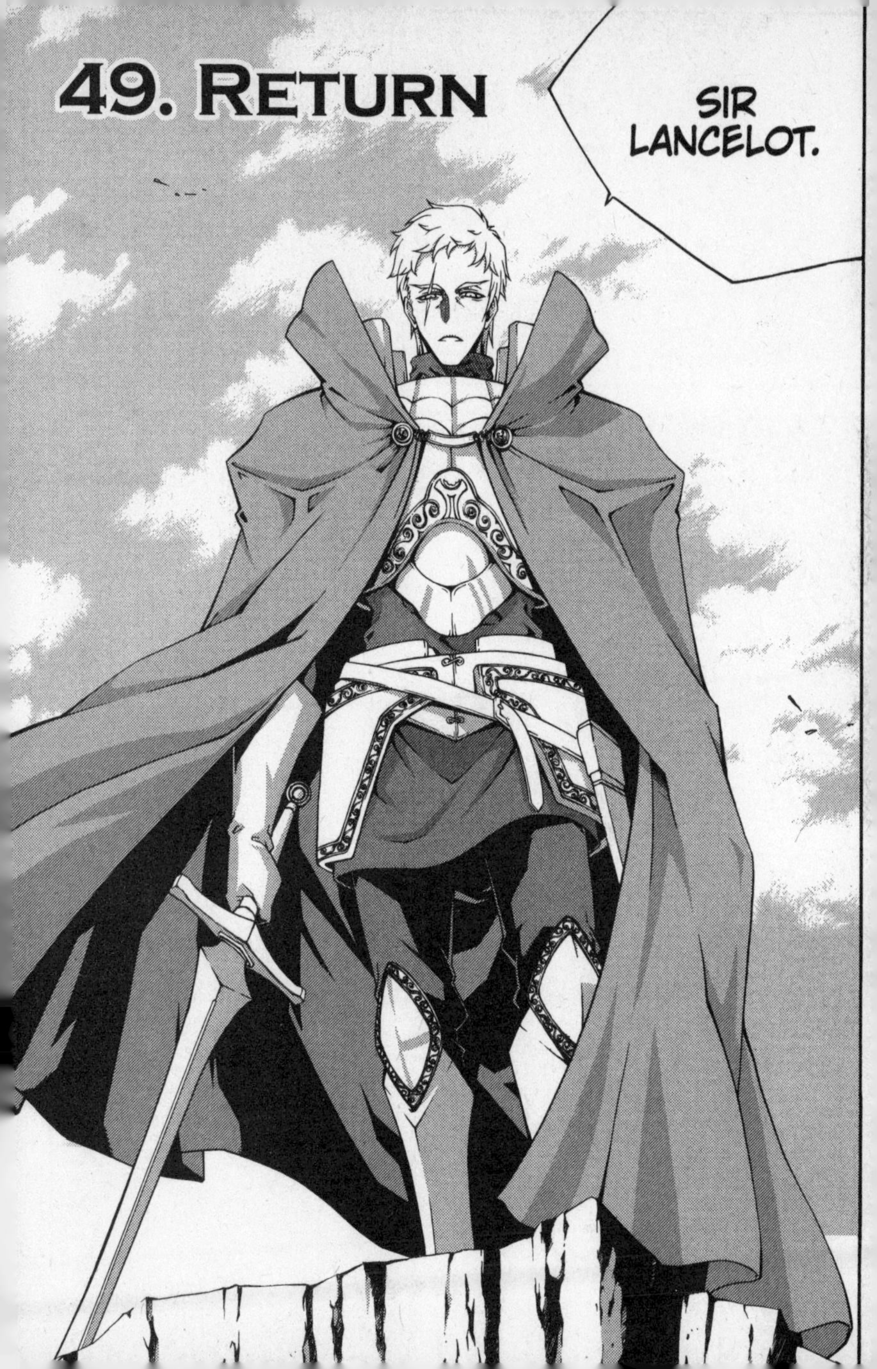
49. RETURN
SIR LANCELOT.

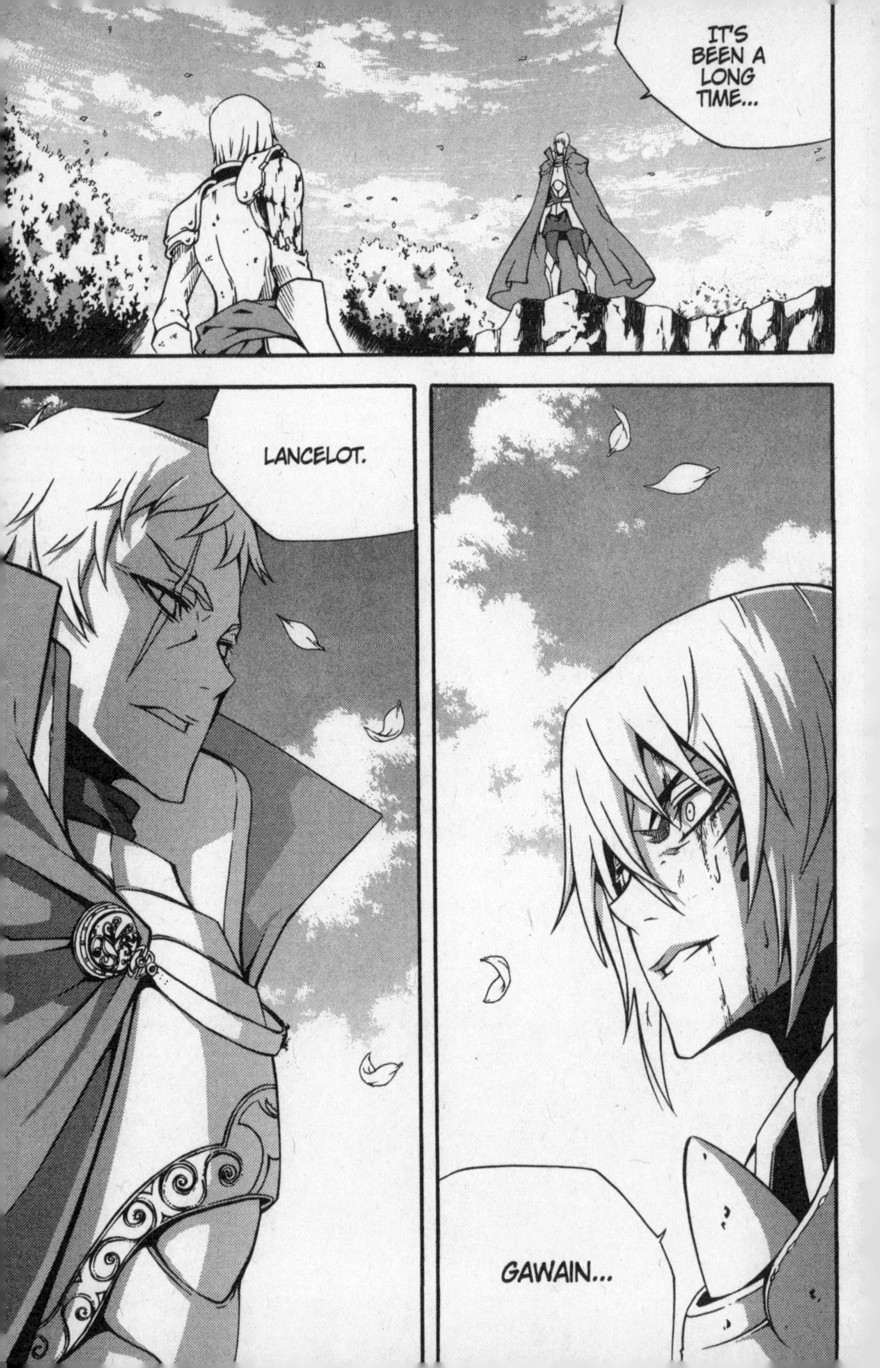
IT'S BEEN A LONG TIME...
LANCELOT.
GAWAIN...

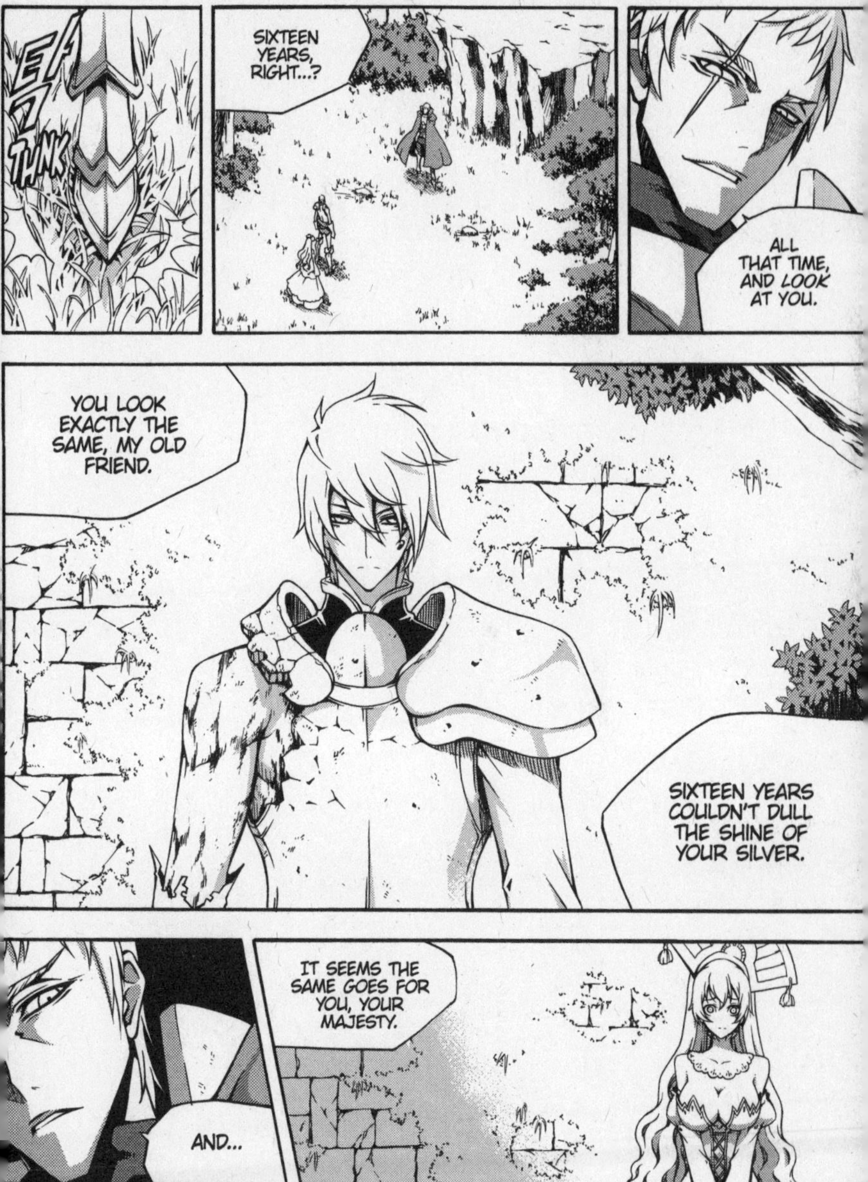
THNK
SIXTEEN YEARS, RIGHT...?
ALL THAT TIME, AND LOOK AT YOU.
YOU LOOK EXACTLY THE SAME, MY OLD FRIEND.
SIXTEEN YEARS COULDN'T DULL THE SHINE OF YOUR SILVER.
AND...
IT SEEMS THE SAME GOES FOR YOU, YOUR MAJESTY.

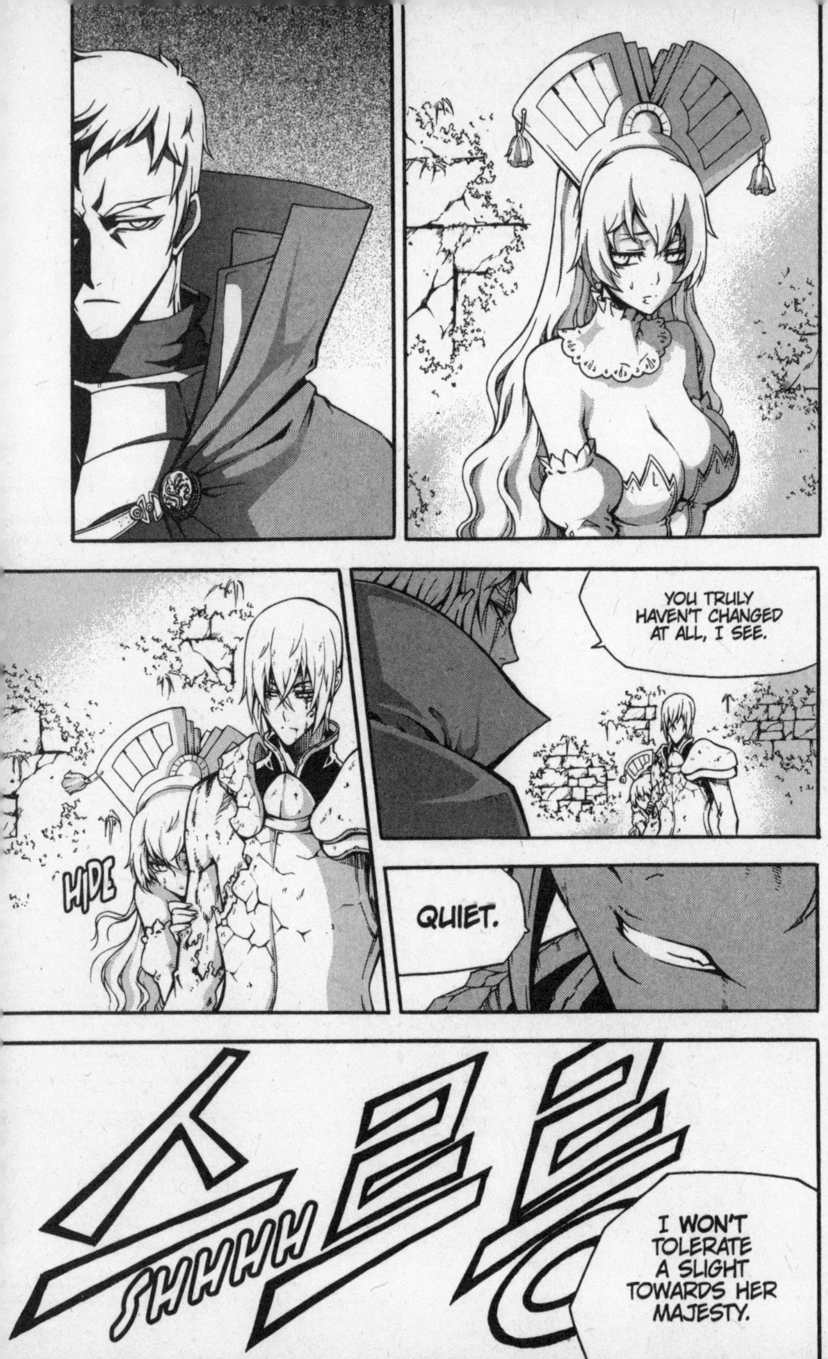
HIDE
YOU TRULY HAVEN'T CHANGED AT ALL, I SEE.
QUIET.
SHHHH
I WON'T TOLERATE A SLIGHT TOWARDS HER MAJESTY.

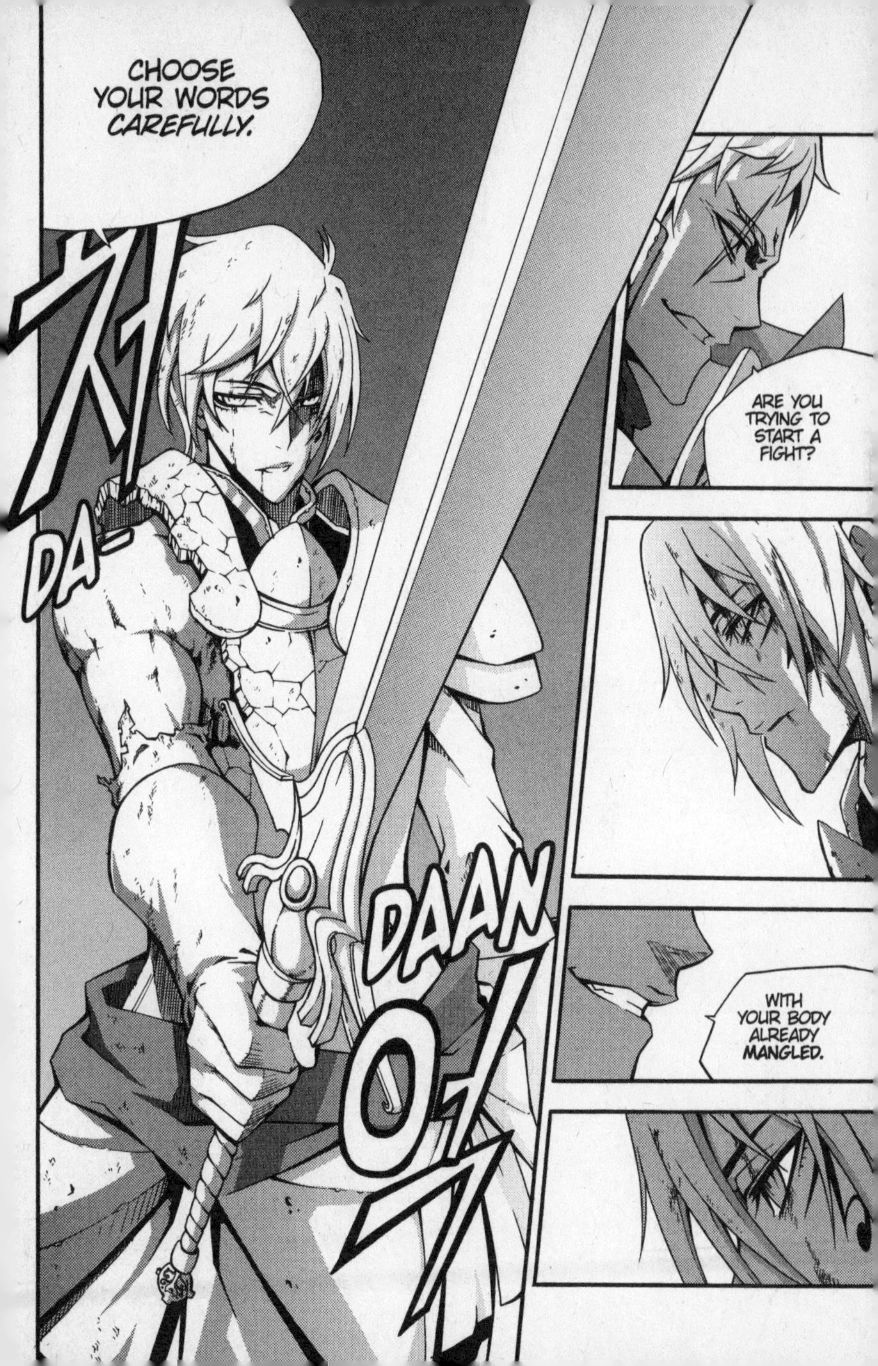
CHOOSE YOUR WORDS CAREFULLY.
DA-
DAAN
ARE YOU TRYING TO START A FIGHT?
WITH YOUR BODY ALREADY MANGLED.

YOU REALLY HAVEN'T CHANGED.

PUT AWAY YOUR SWORD, SIR LANCELOT.

STILL HOTHEADED, AND JUST AS QUICK TO JUMP TO THE QUEEN'S DEFENSE.

IF I REALLY INTENDED TO FIGHT YOU...

I WOULD HAVE KILLED YOU BEFORE YOU LEFT THE CASTLE.

I'M ALSO STILL THE MAN YOU KNEW.

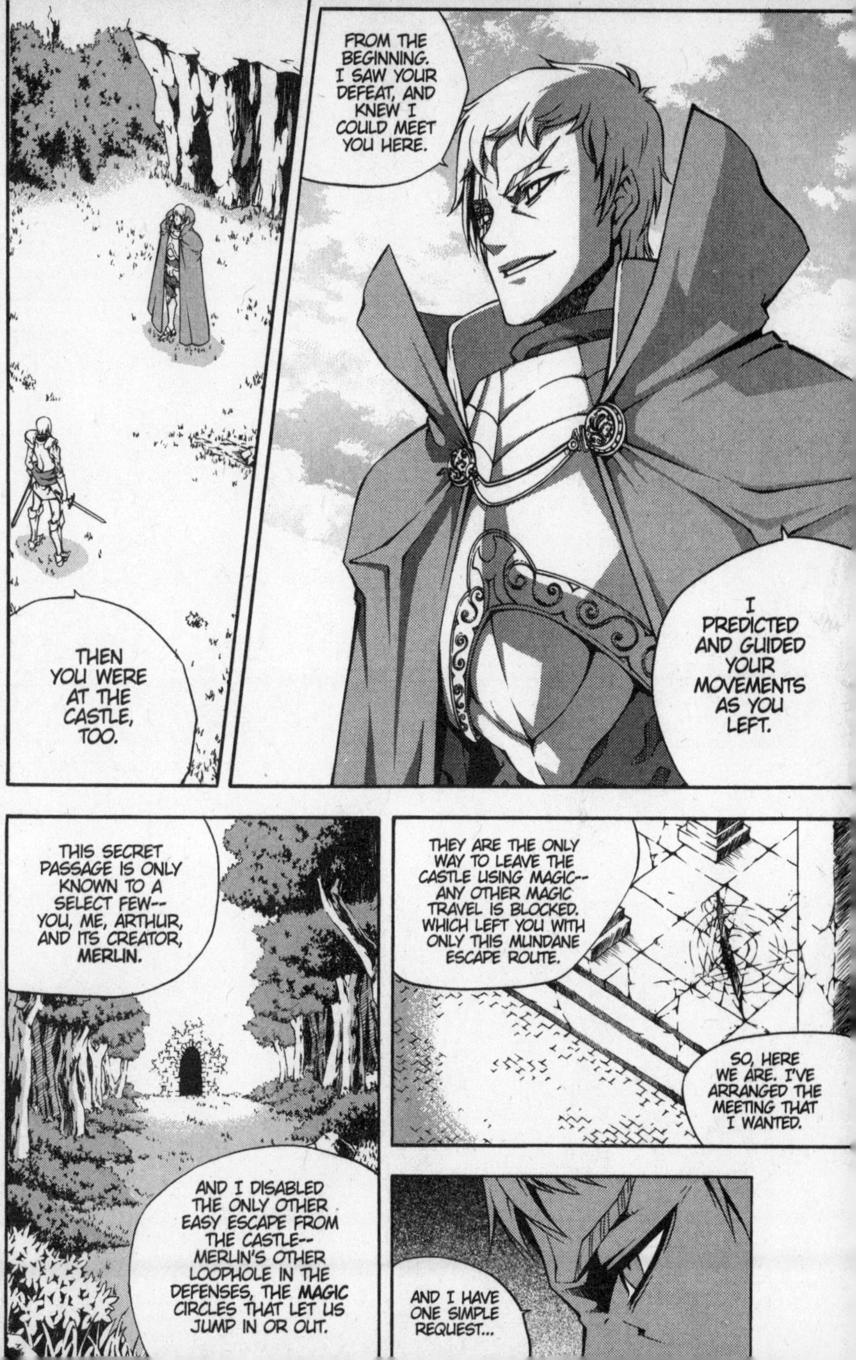
THEN YOU WERE AT THE CASTLE, TOO.
FROM THE BEGINNING. I SAW YOUR DEFEAT, AND KNEW I COULD MEET YOU HERE.
I PREDICTED AND GUIDED YOUR MOVEMENTS AS YOU LEFT.
THIS SECRET PASSAGE IS ONLY KNOWN TO A SELECT FEW-- YOU, ME, ARTHUR, AND ITS CREATOR, MERLIN.
AND I DISABLED THE ONLY OTHER EASY ESCAPE FROM THE CASTLE-- MERLIN'S OTHER LOOPHOLE IN THE DEFENSES, THE MAGIC CIRCLES THAT LET US JUMP IN OR OUT.
THEY ARE THE ONLY WAY TO LEAVE THE CASTLE USING MAGIC-- ANY OTHER MAGIC TRAVEL IS BLOCKED. WHICH LEFT YOU WITH ONLY THIS MUNDANE ESCAPE ROUTE.
SO, HERE WE ARE. I'VE ARRANGED THE MEETING THAT I WANTED.
AND I HAVE ONE SIMPLE REQUEST...

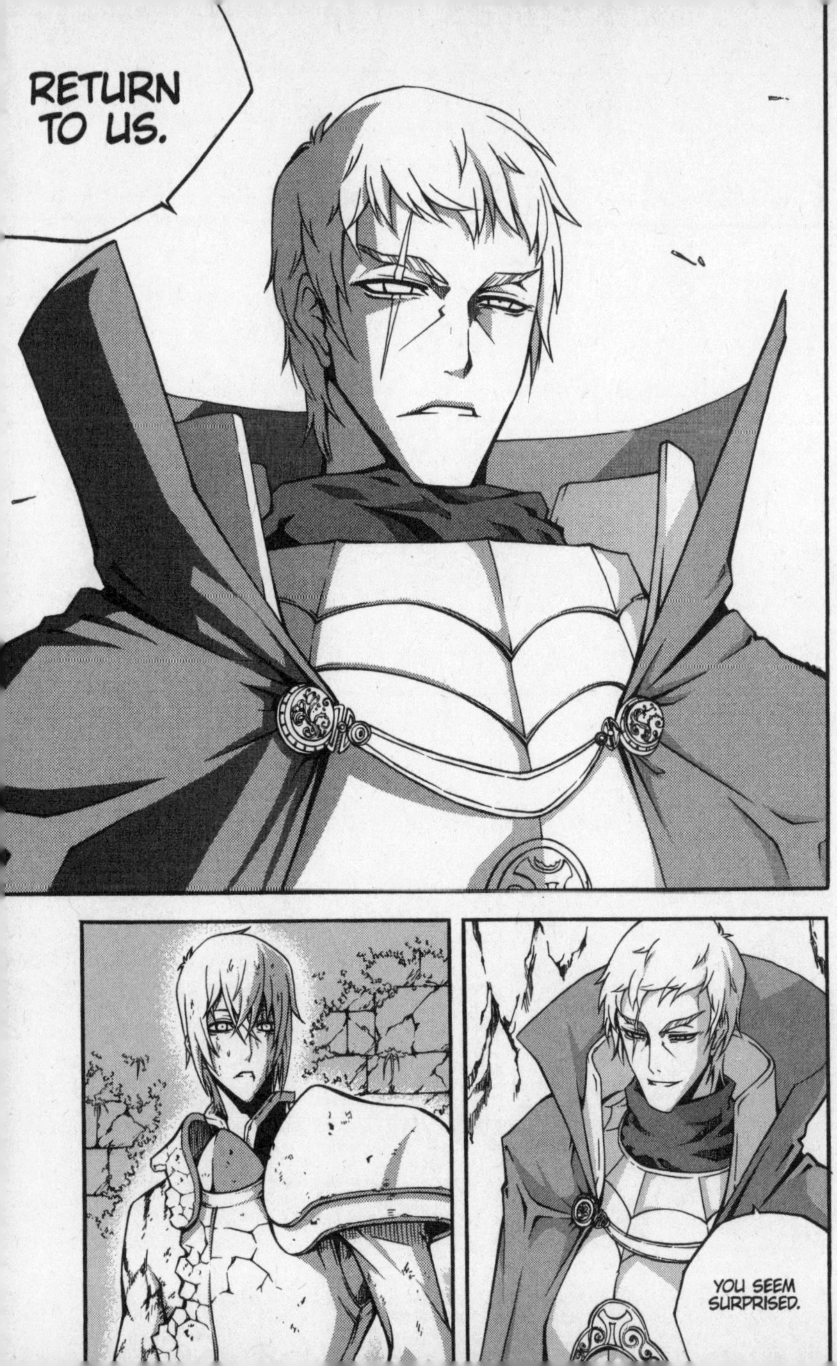
RETURN TO US.
YOU SEEM SURPRISED.

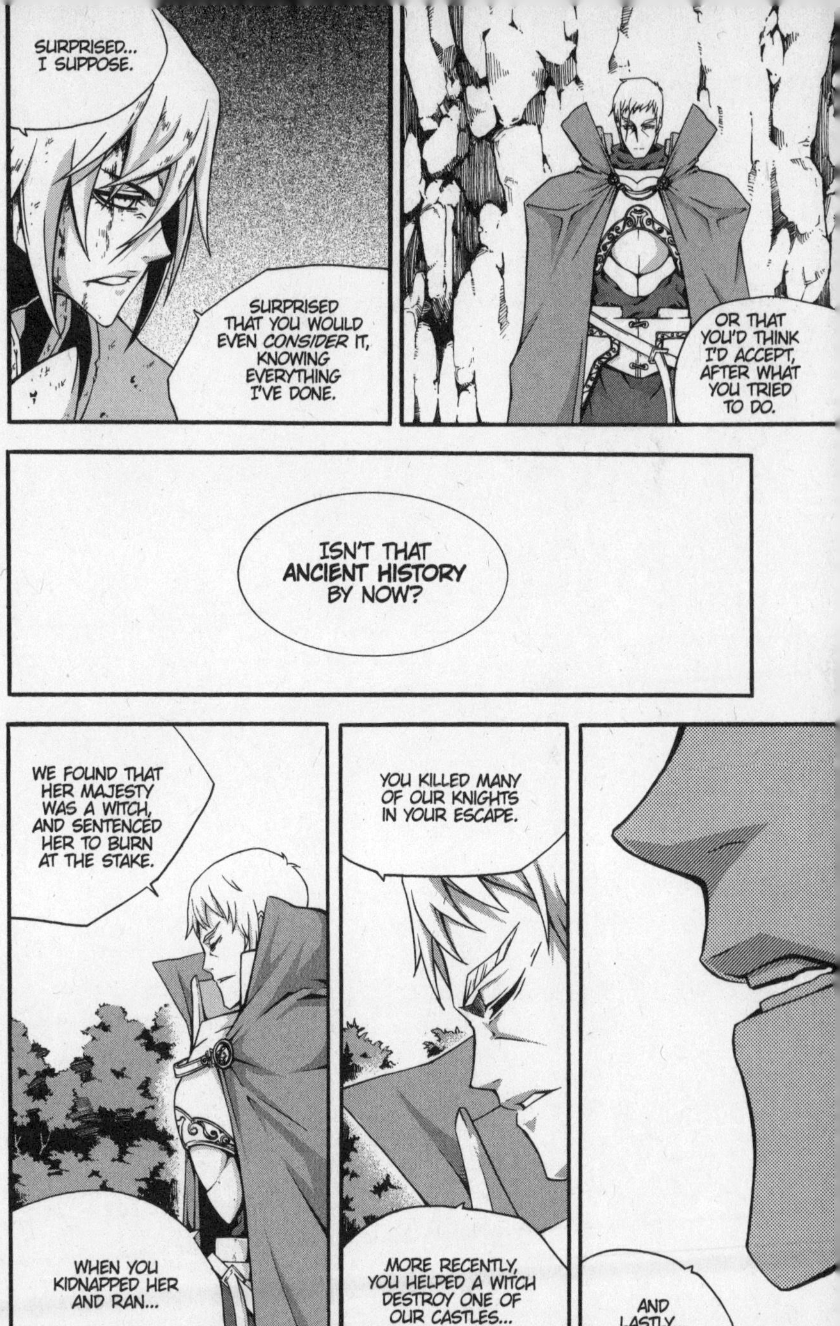
SURPRISED... I SUPPOSE.
SURPRISED THAT YOU WOULD EVEN *CONSIDER* IT, KNOWING EVERYTHING I'VE DONE.
OR THAT YOU'D THINK I'D ACCEPT, AFTER WHAT YOU TRIED TO DO.
ISN'T THAT **ANCIENT HISTORY** BY NOW?
WE FOUND THAT HER MAJESTY WAS A WITCH, AND SENTENCED HER TO BURN AT THE STAKE.
WHEN YOU KIDNAPPED HER AND RAN...
YOU KILLED MANY OF OUR KNIGHTS IN YOUR ESCAPE.
MORE RECENTLY, YOU HELPED A WITCH DESTROY ONE OF OUR CASTLES...
AND LASTLY...

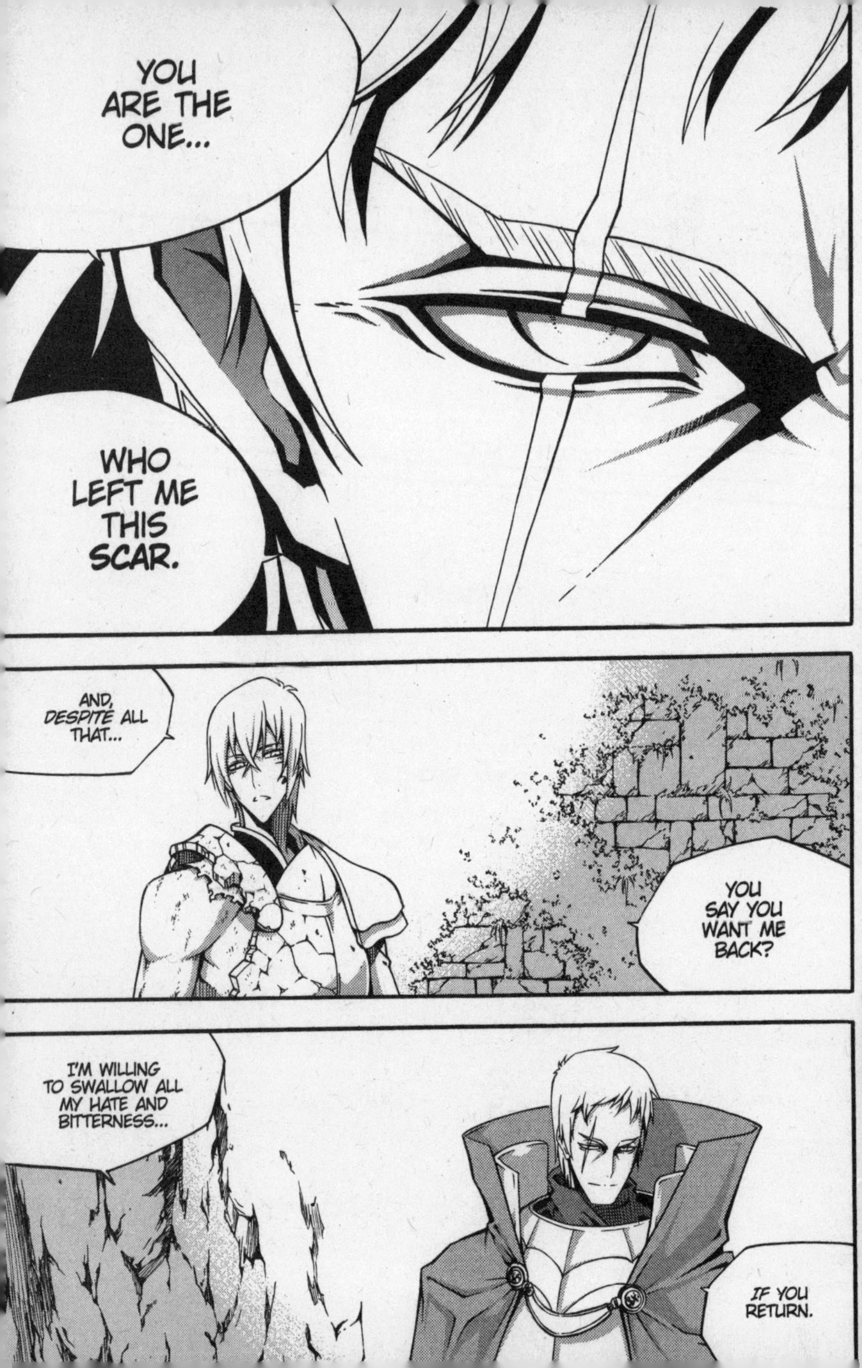
YOU ARE THE ONE...
WHO LEFT ME THIS SCAR.
AND, DESPITE ALL THAT...
YOU SAY YOU WANT ME BACK?
I'M WILLING TO SWALLOW ALL MY HATE AND BITTERNESS...
IF YOU RETURN.

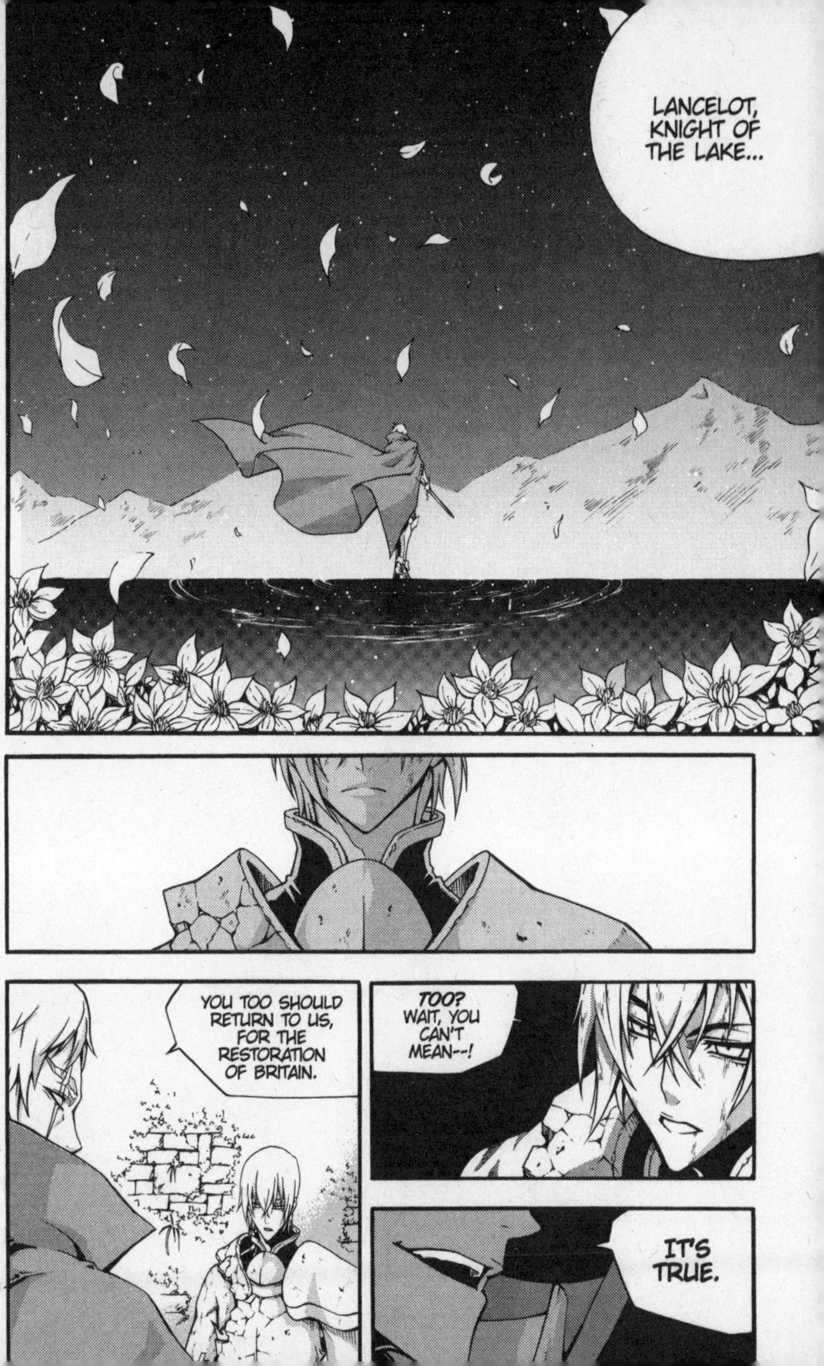
LANCELOT, KNIGHT OF THE LAKE...
YOU TOO SHOULD RETURN TO US, FOR THE RESTORATION OF BRITAIN.
TOO? WAIT, YOU CAN'T MEAN--!
IT'S TRUE.

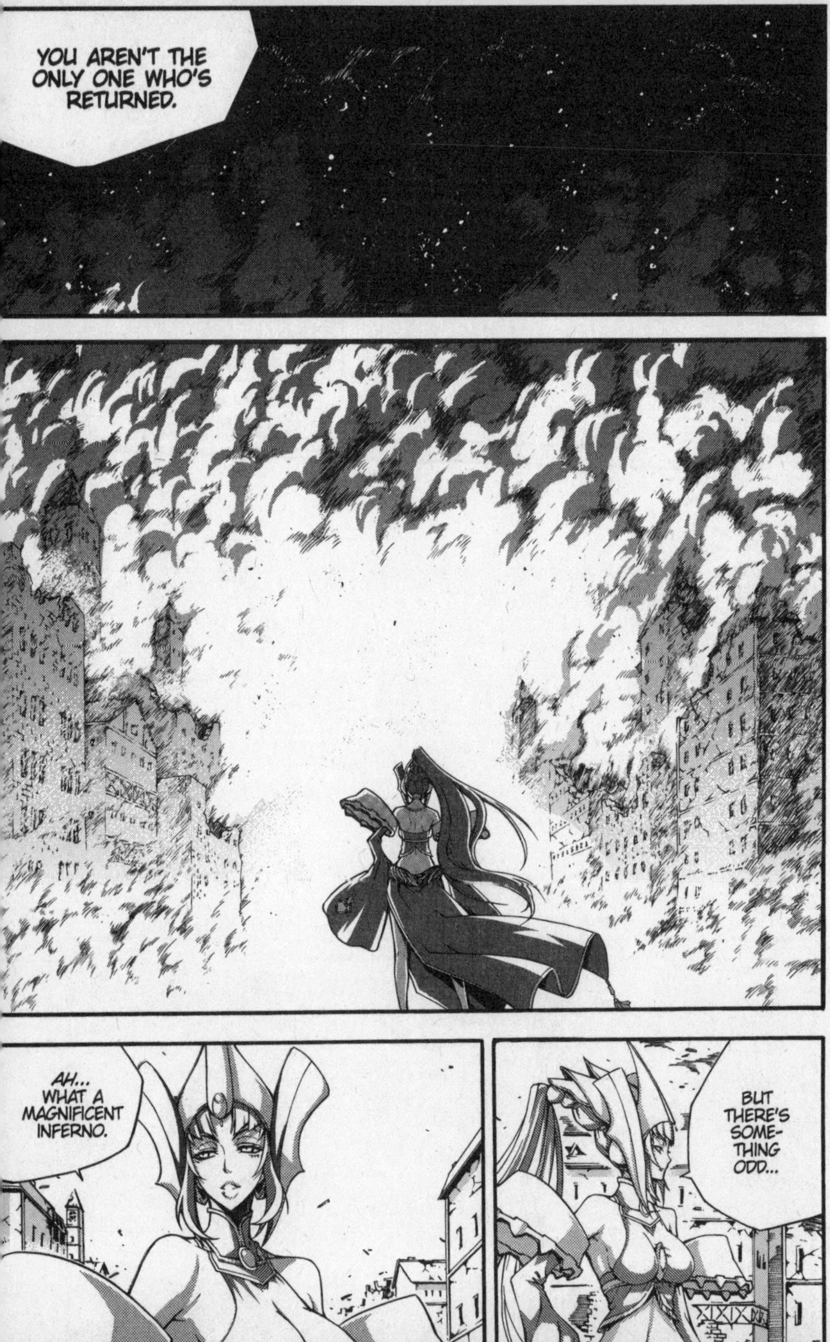
YOU AREN'T THE ONLY ONE WHO'S RETURNED.
AH... WHAT A MAGNIFICENT INFERNO.
BUT THERE'S SOME-THING ODD...

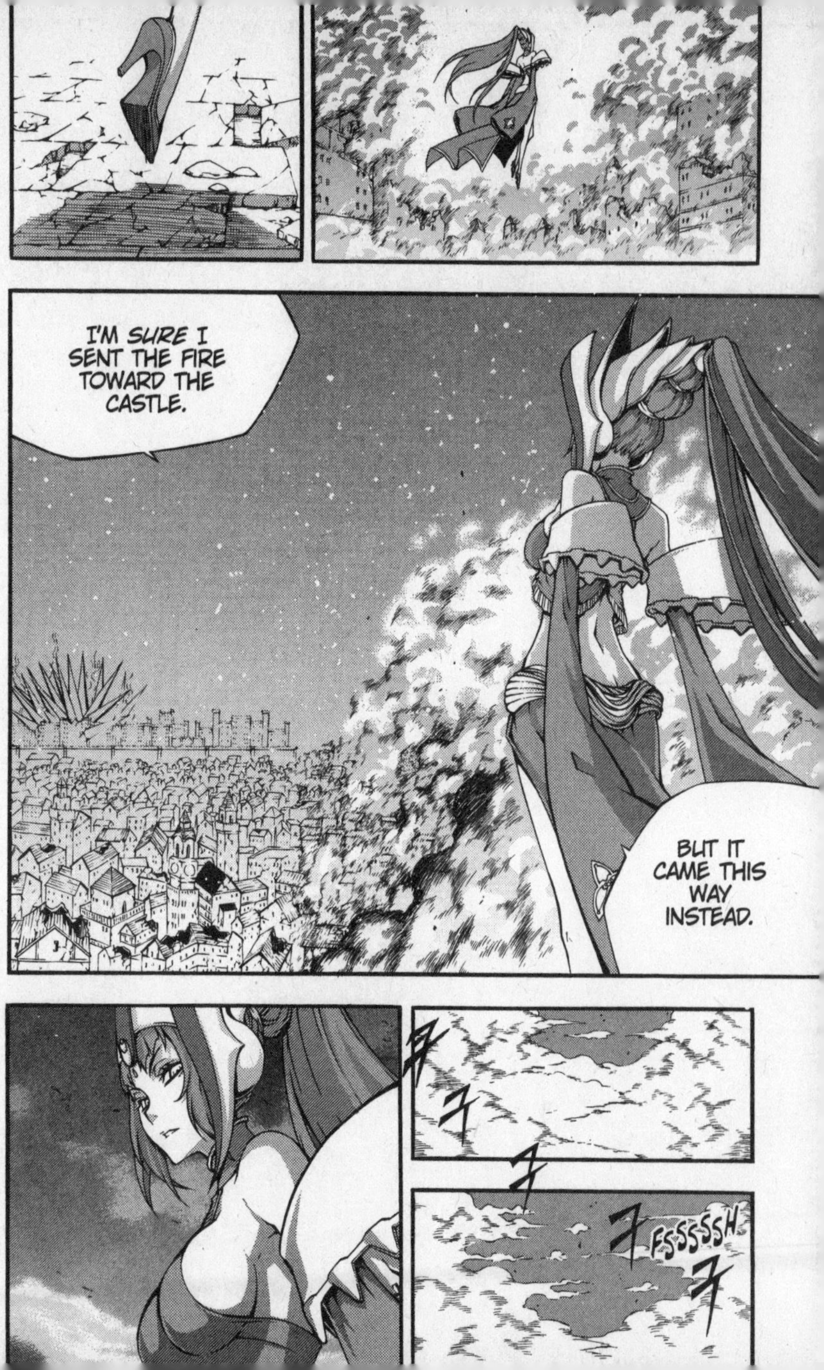
I'M SURE I SENT THE FIRE TOWARD THE CASTLE.
BUT IT CAME THIS WAY INSTEAD.
FSSSSSH

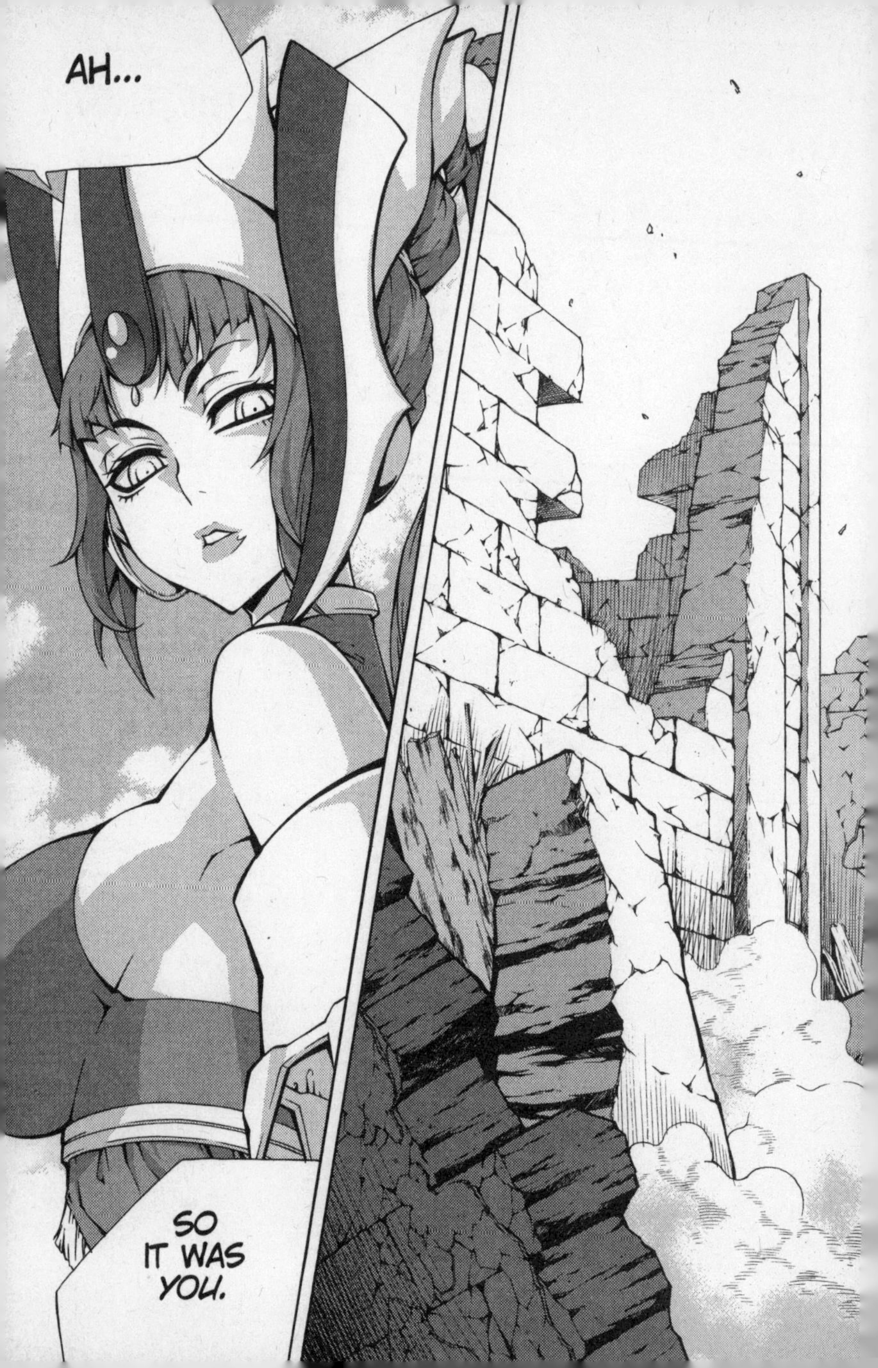
AH...
SO IT WAS YOU.

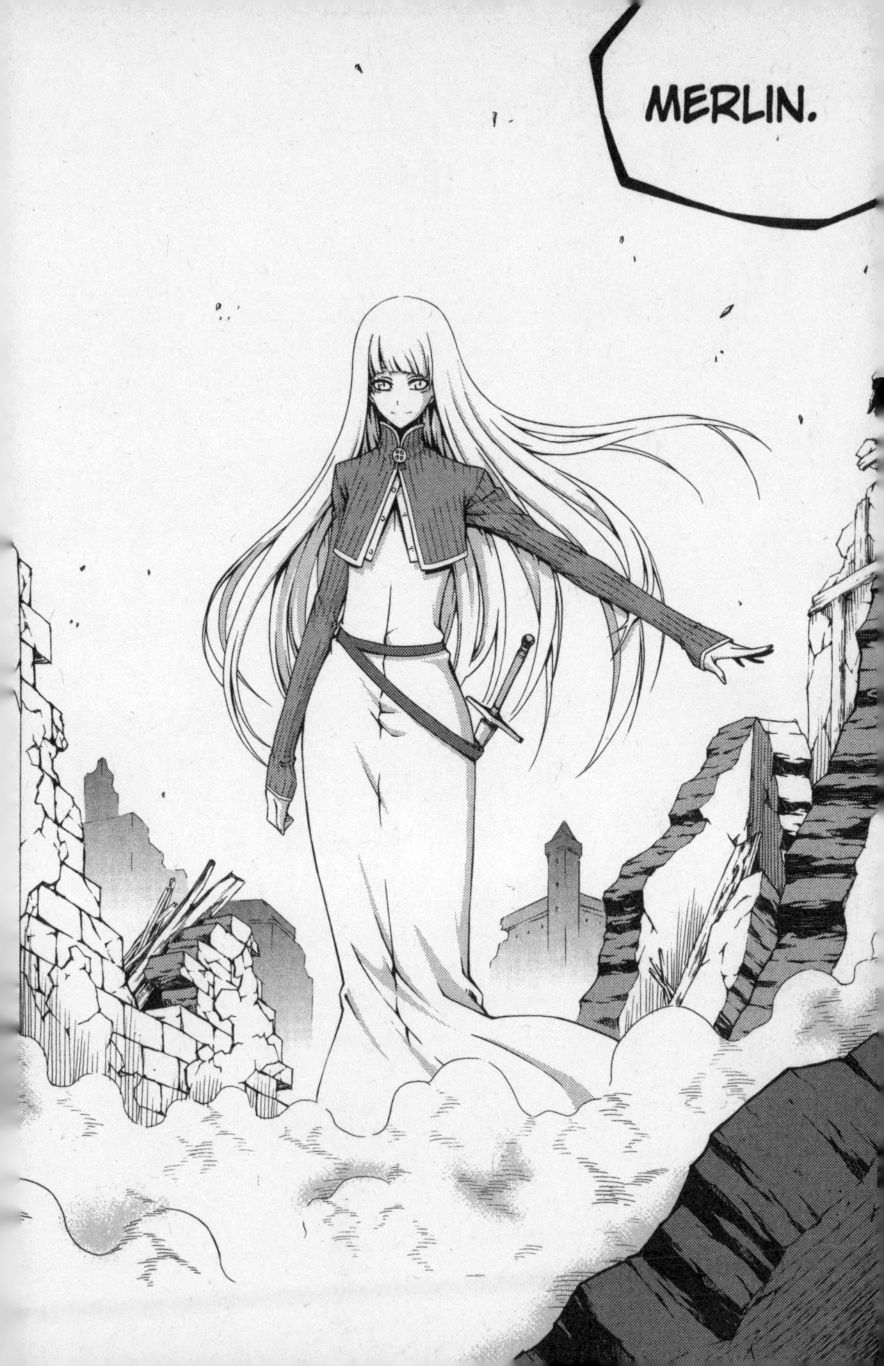
MERLIN.

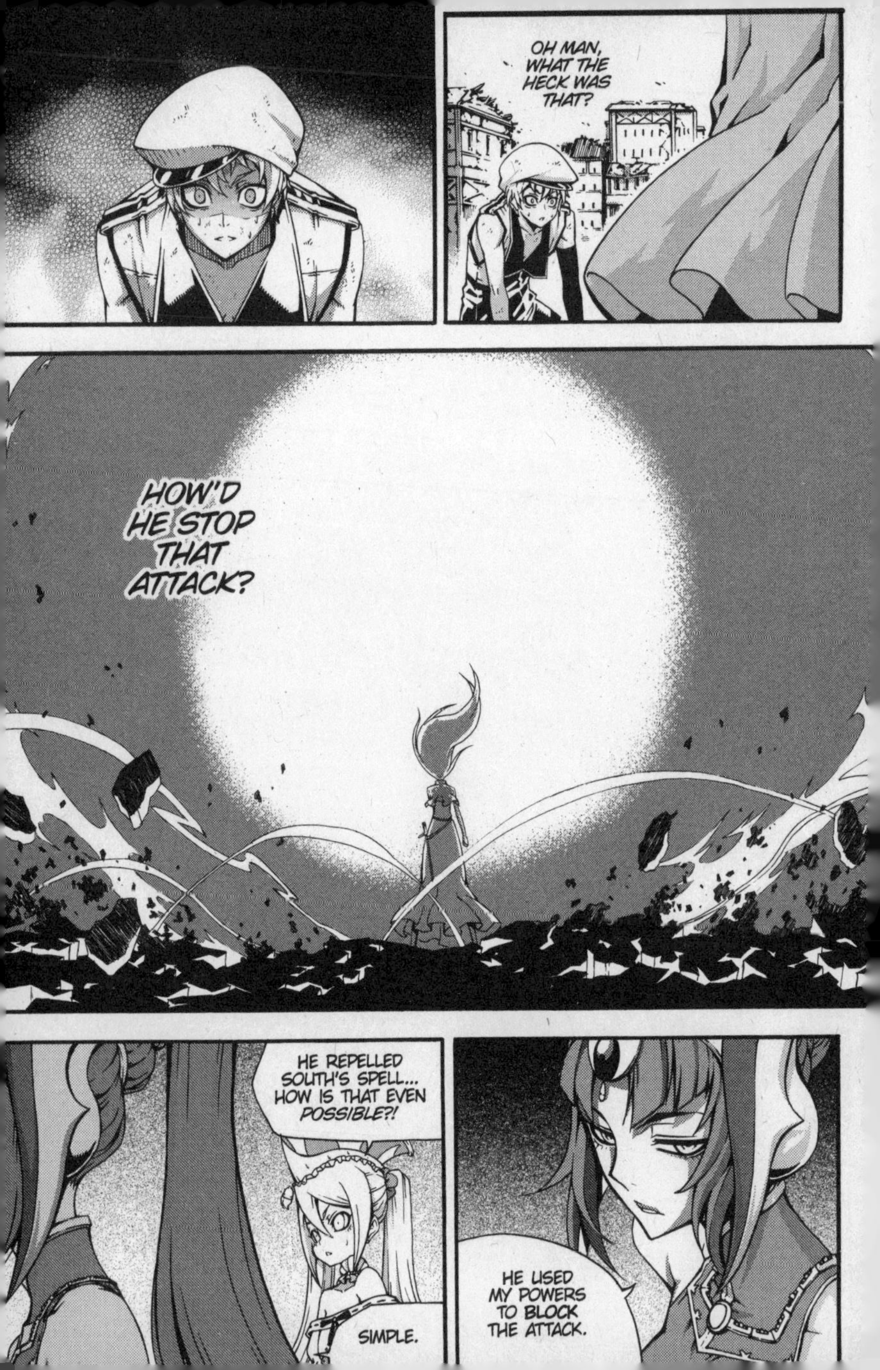
OH MAN, WHAT THE HECK WAS THAT?
HOW'D HE STOP THAT ATTACK?
HE REPELLED SOUTH'S SPELL... HOW IS THAT EVEN POSSIBLE?!
SIMPLE.
HE USED MY POWERS TO BLOCK THE ATTACK.

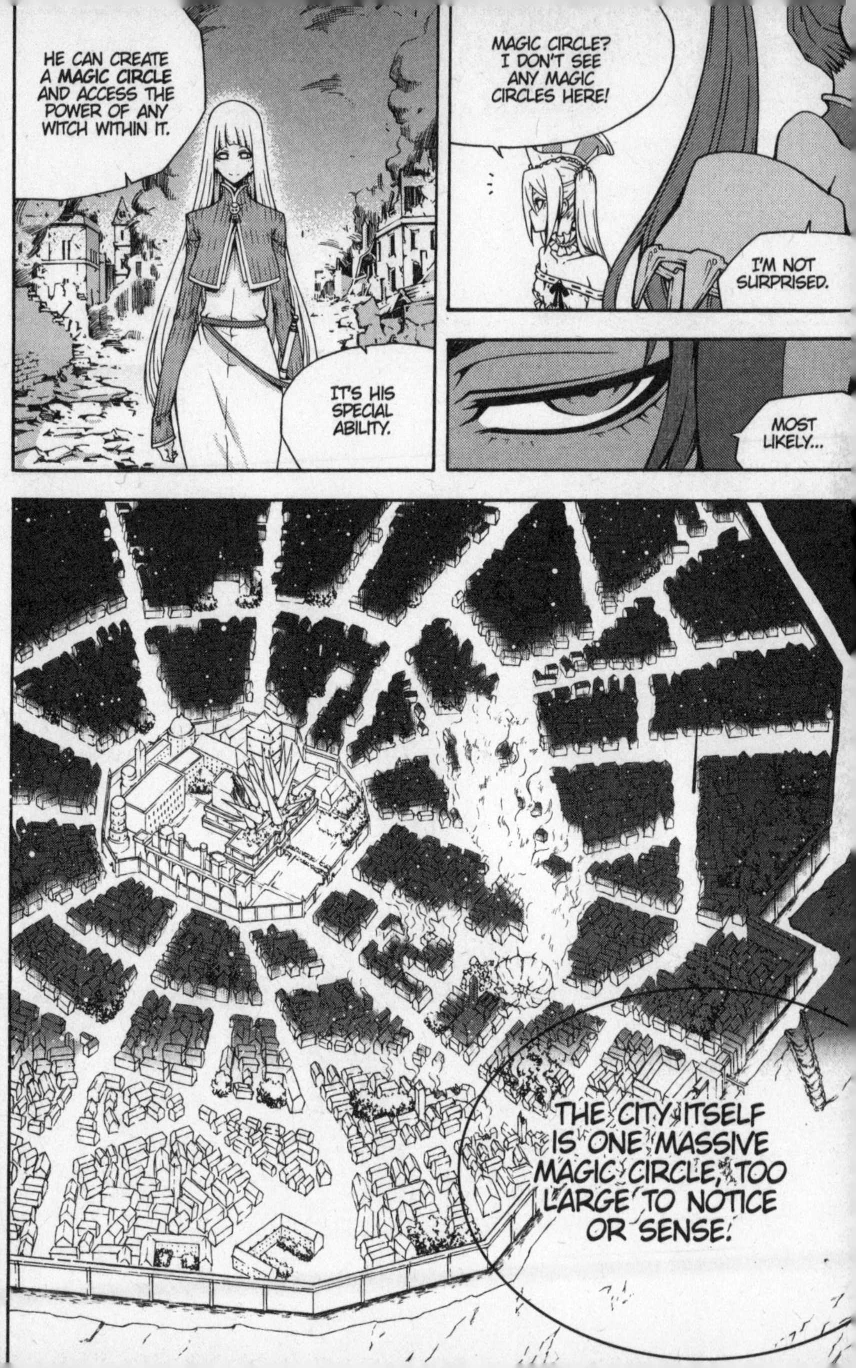
HE CAN CREATE A MAGIC CIRCLE AND ACCESS THE POWER OF ANY WITCH WITHIN IT.
IT'S HIS SPECIAL ABILITY.
MAGIC CIRCLE? I DON'T SEE ANY MAGIC CIRCLES HERE!
I'M NOT SURPRISED.
MOST LIKELY...
THE CITY ITSELF IS ONE MASSIVE MAGIC CIRCLE, TOO LARGE TO NOTICE OR SENSE.

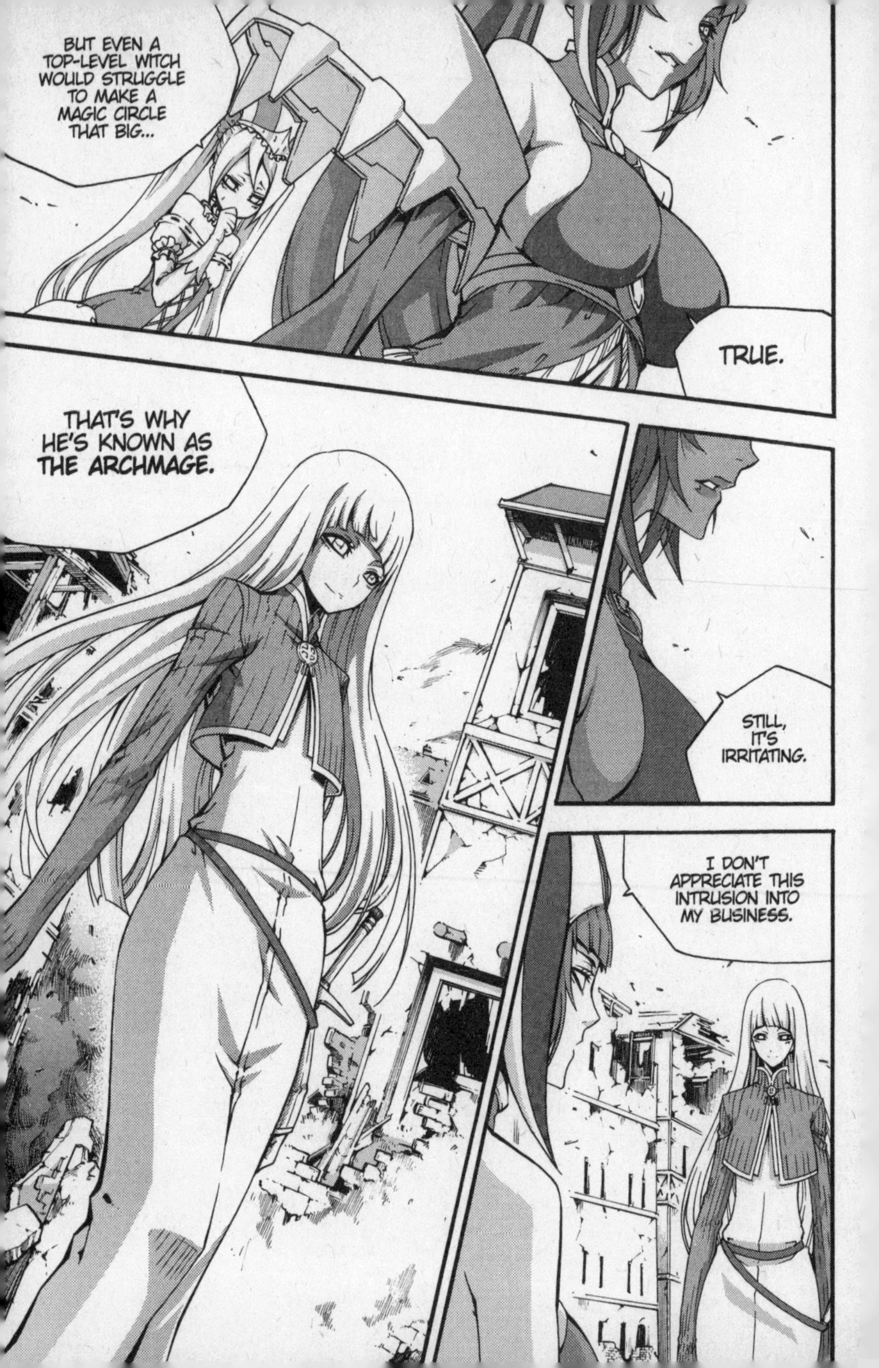
BUT EVEN A TOP-LEVEL WITCH WOULD STRUGGLE TO MAKE A MAGIC CIRCLE THAT BIG...
TRUE.
THAT'S WHY HE'S KNOWN AS THE ARCHMAGE.
STILL, IT'S IRRITATING.
I DON'T APPRECIATE THIS INTRUSION INTO MY BUSINESS.

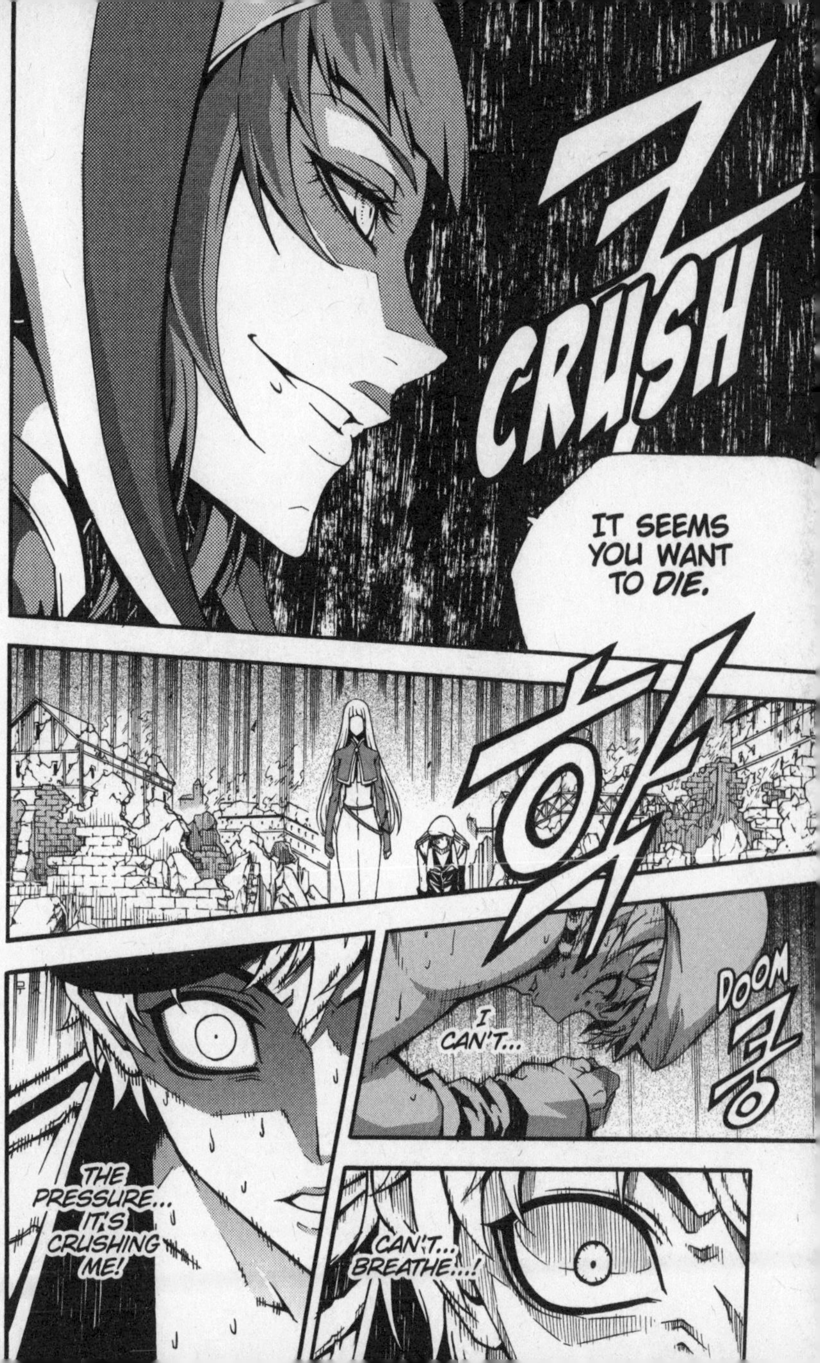
CRUSH
IT SEEMS YOU WANT TO DIE.
THE PRESSURE... IT'S CRUSHING ME!
I CAN'T...
DOOM
CAN'T... BREATHE...!

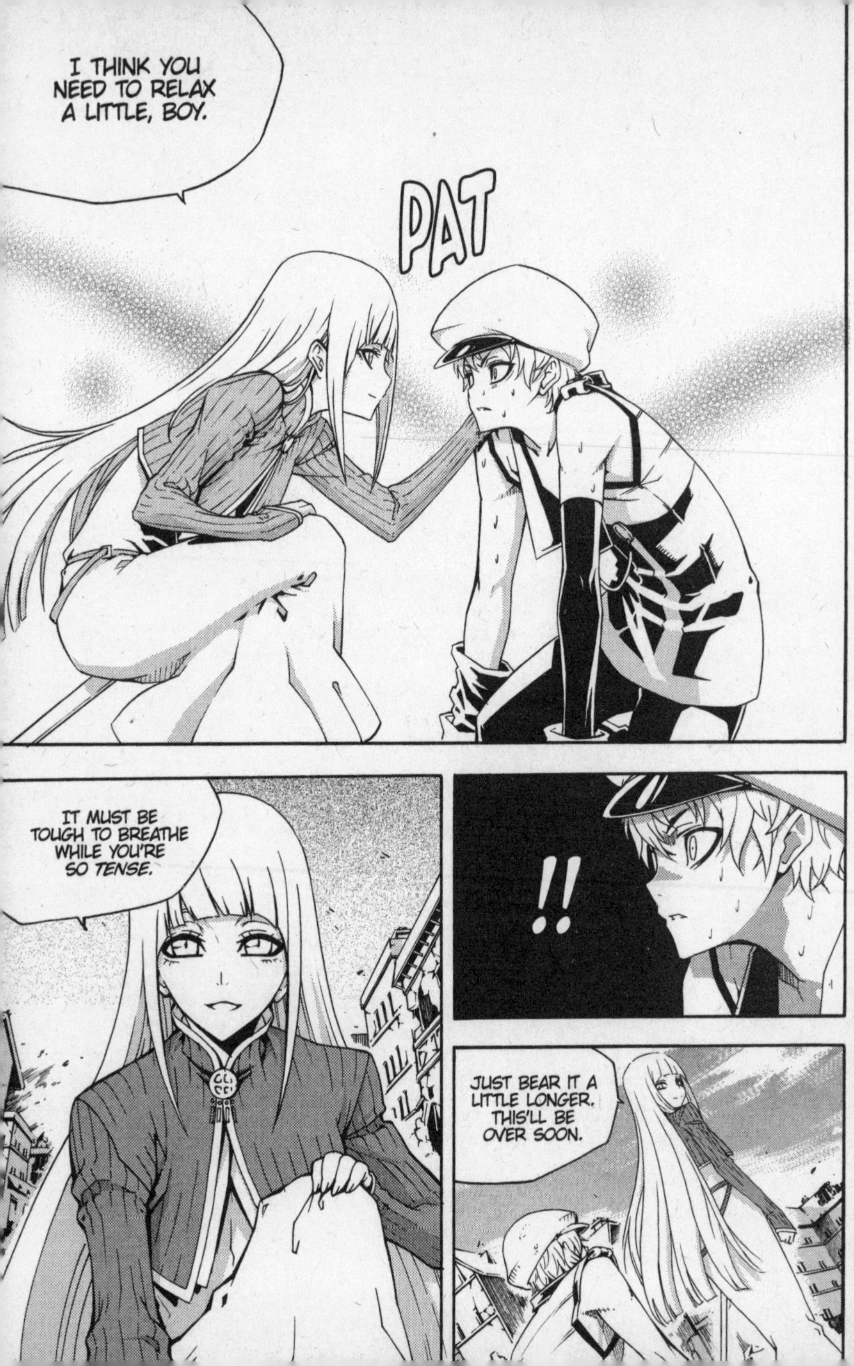
I THINK YOU NEED TO RELAX A LITTLE, BOY.
PAT
IT MUST BE TOUGH TO BREATHE WHILE YOU'RE SO *TENSE.*
!!
JUST BEAR IT A LITTLE LONGER. THIS'LL BE OVER SOON.

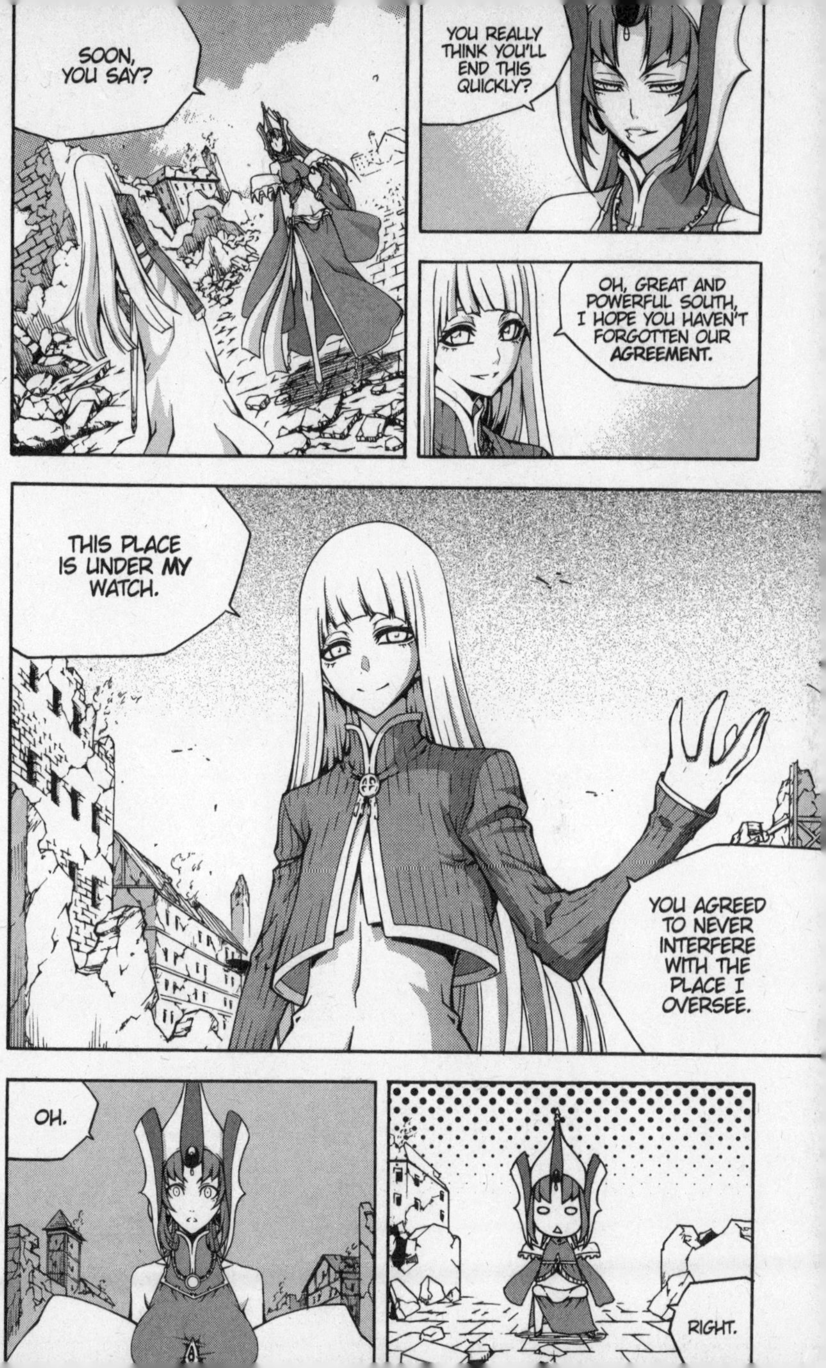
SOON, YOU SAY?
YOU REALLY THINK YOU'LL END THIS QUICKLY?
OH, GREAT AND POWERFUL SOUTH, I HOPE YOU HAVEN'T FORGOTTEN OUR AGREEMENT.
THIS PLACE IS UNDER MY WATCH.
YOU AGREED TO NEVER INTERFERE WITH THE PLACE I OVERSEE.
OH.
RIGHT.

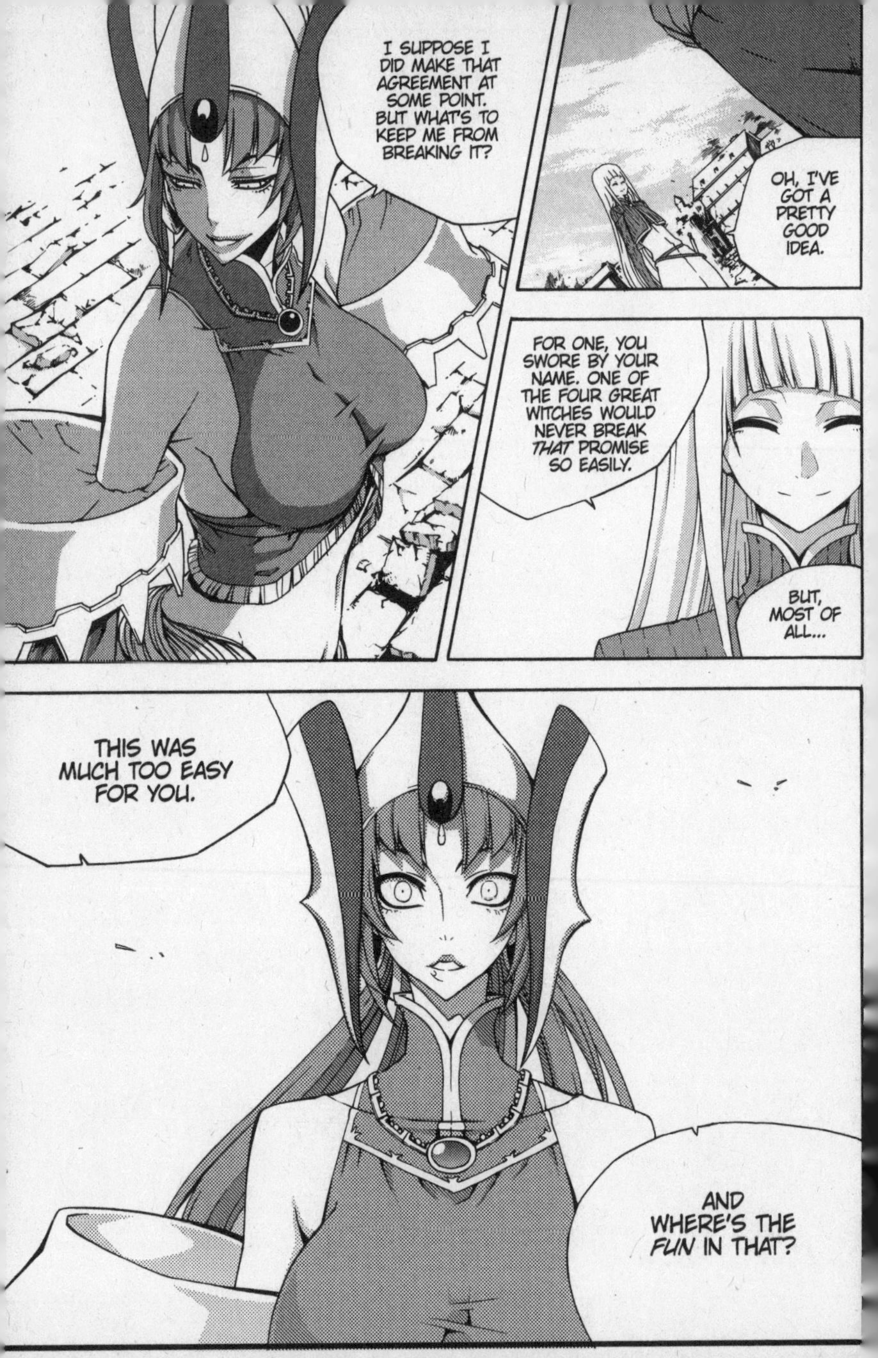
I SUPPOSE I DID MAKE THAT AGREEMENT AT SOME POINT. BUT WHAT'S TO KEEP ME FROM BREAKING IT?
OH, I'VE GOT A PRETTY GOOD IDEA.
FOR ONE, YOU SWORE BY YOUR NAME. ONE OF THE FOUR GREAT WITCHES WOULD NEVER BREAK *THAT* PROMISE SO EASILY.
BUT, MOST OF ALL...
THIS WAS MUCH TOO EASY FOR YOU.
AND WHERE'S THE *FUN* IN THAT?

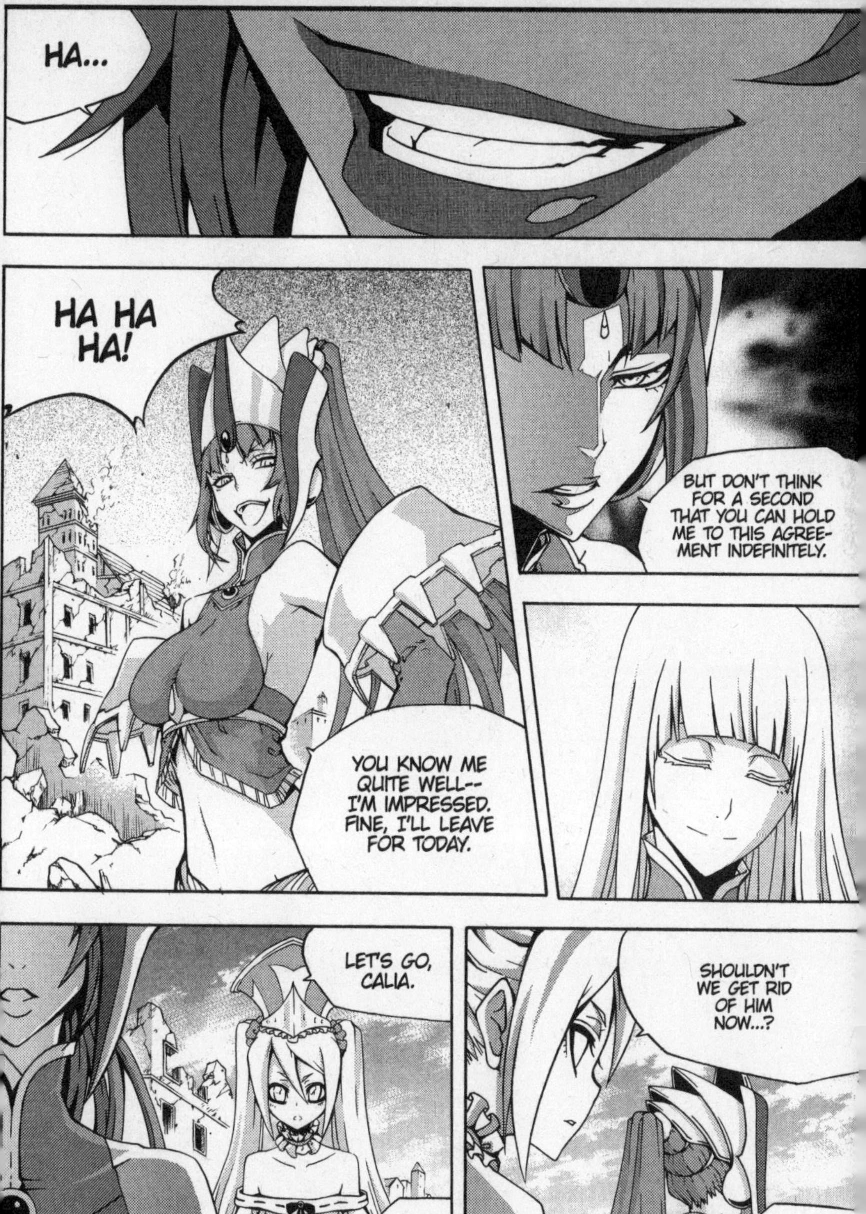
HA...
HA HA HA!
YOU KNOW ME QUITE WELL--I'M IMPRESSED. FINE, I'LL LEAVE FOR TODAY.
BUT DON'T THINK FOR A SECOND THAT YOU CAN HOLD ME TO THIS AGREE-MENT INDEFINITELY.
LET'S GO, CALIA.
LADY SOUTH...
SHOULDN'T WE GET RID OF HIM NOW...?
CALIA.

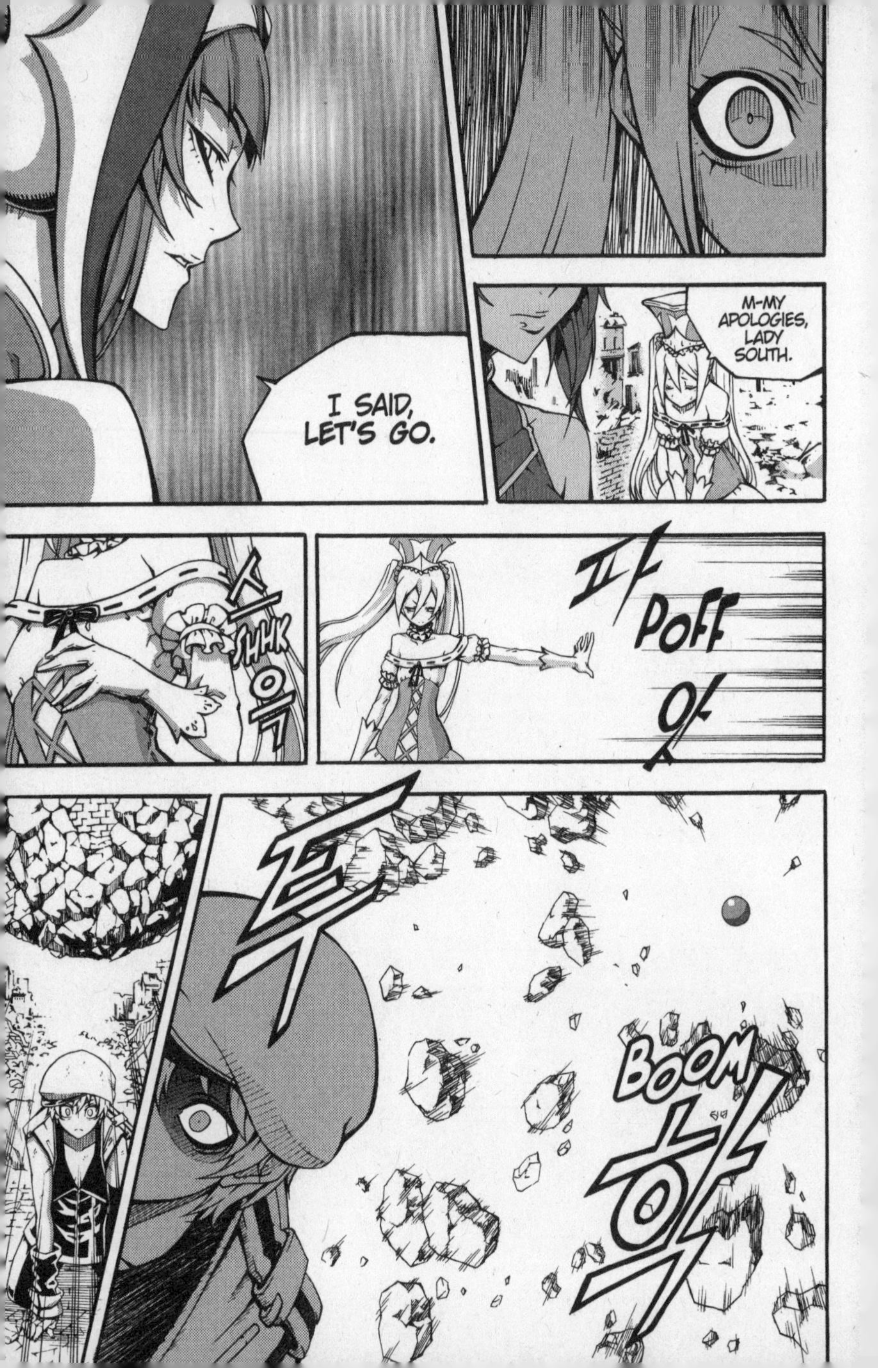

I SAID, LET'S GO.
M-MY APOLOGIES, LADY SOUTH.
SHHK
POFF
BOOM

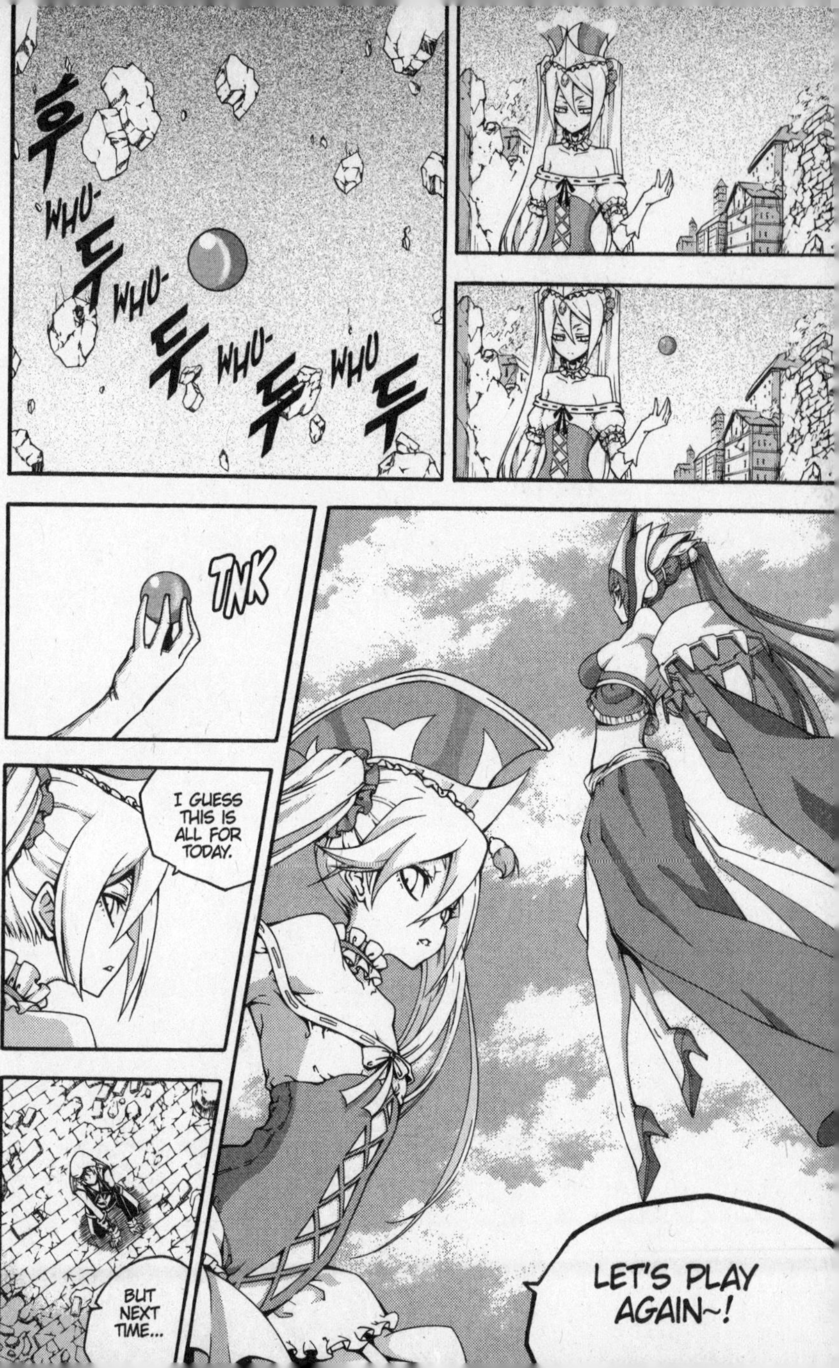

후
WHU-
두
WHU-
두
WHU-
두
WHU
두
TNK
I GUESS THIS IS ALL FOR TODAY.
BUT NEXT TIME...
LET'S PLAY AGAIN~!

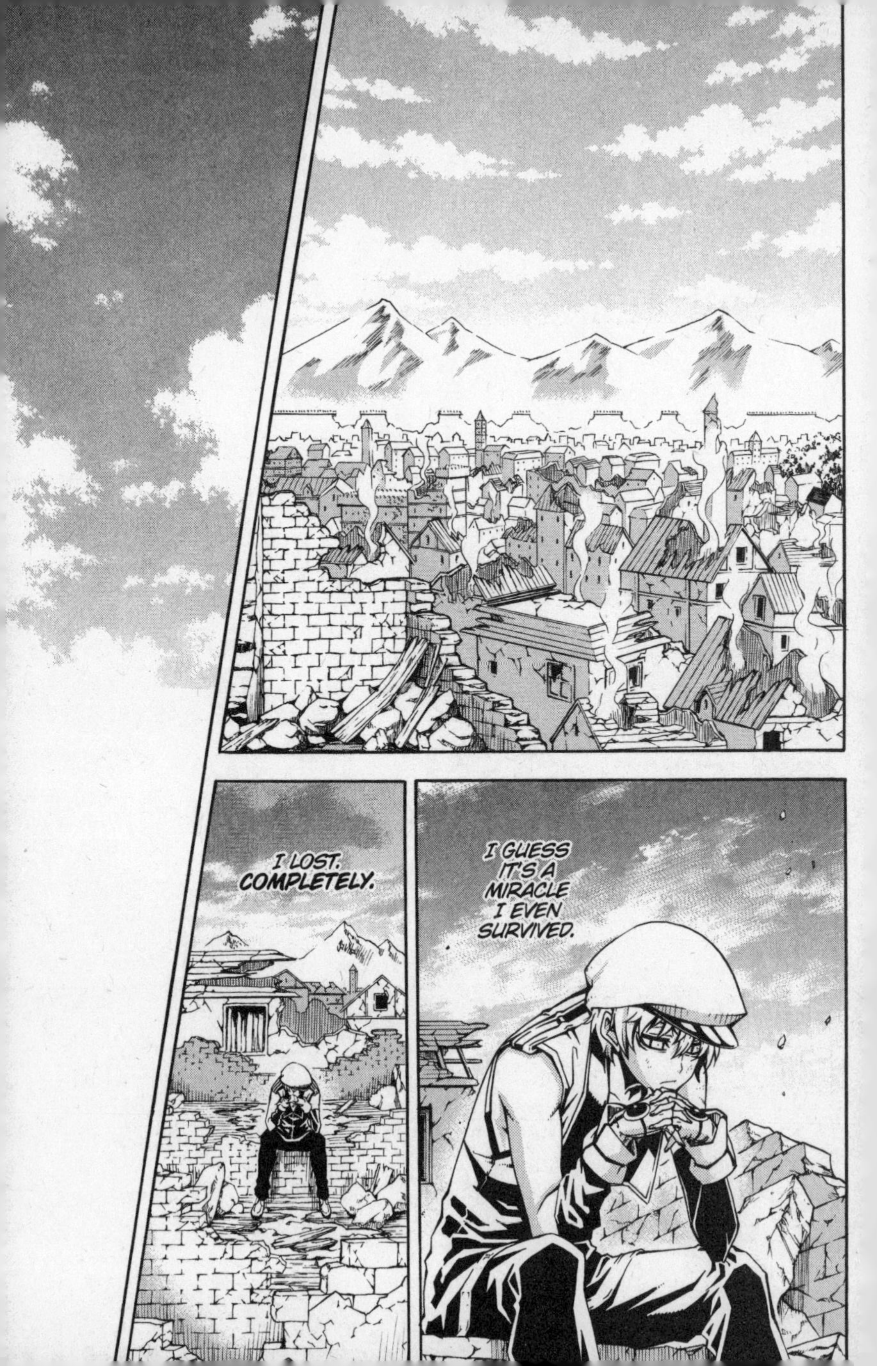
I LOST. COMPLETELY.
I GUESS IT'S A MIRACLE I EVEN SURVIVED.

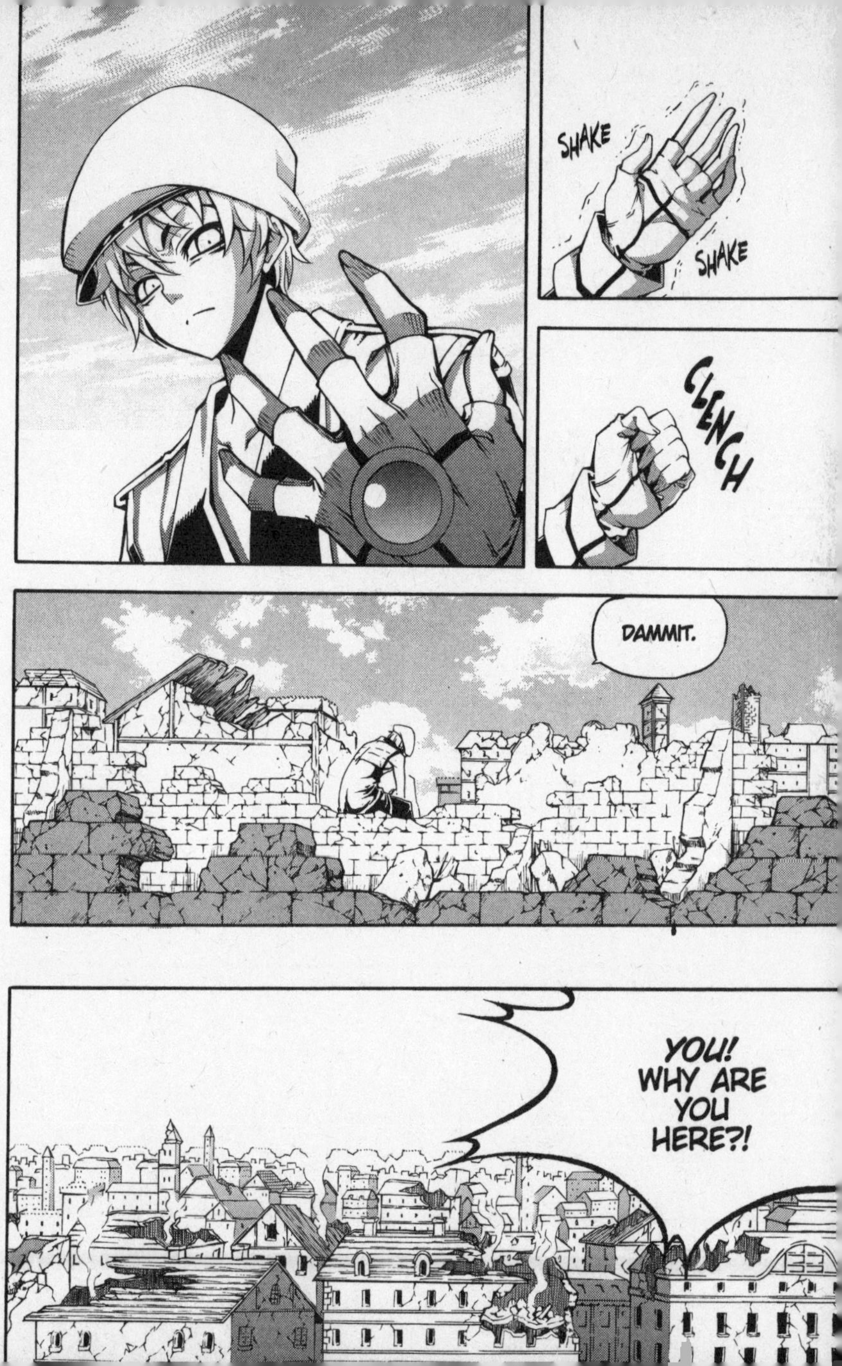
SHAKE
SHAKE
CLENCH
DAMMIT.
YOU! WHY ARE YOU HERE?!

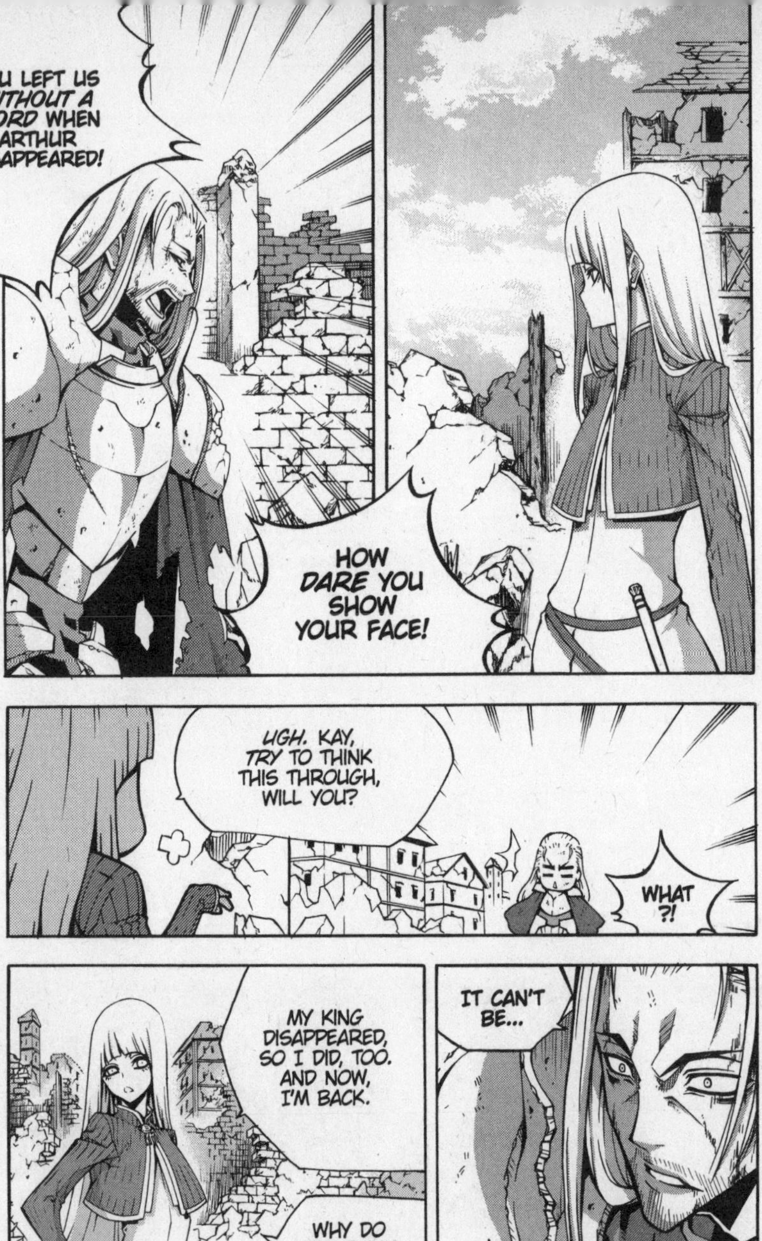
YOU LEFT US WITHOUT A WORD WHEN ARTHUR DISAPPEARED!
HOW DARE YOU SHOW YOUR FACE!
UGH. KAY, TRY TO THINK THIS THROUGH, WILL YOU?
WHAT ?!
MY KING DISAPPEARED, SO I DID, TOO. AND NOW, I'M BACK.
WHY DO YOU THINK THAT IS?
IT CAN'T BE...

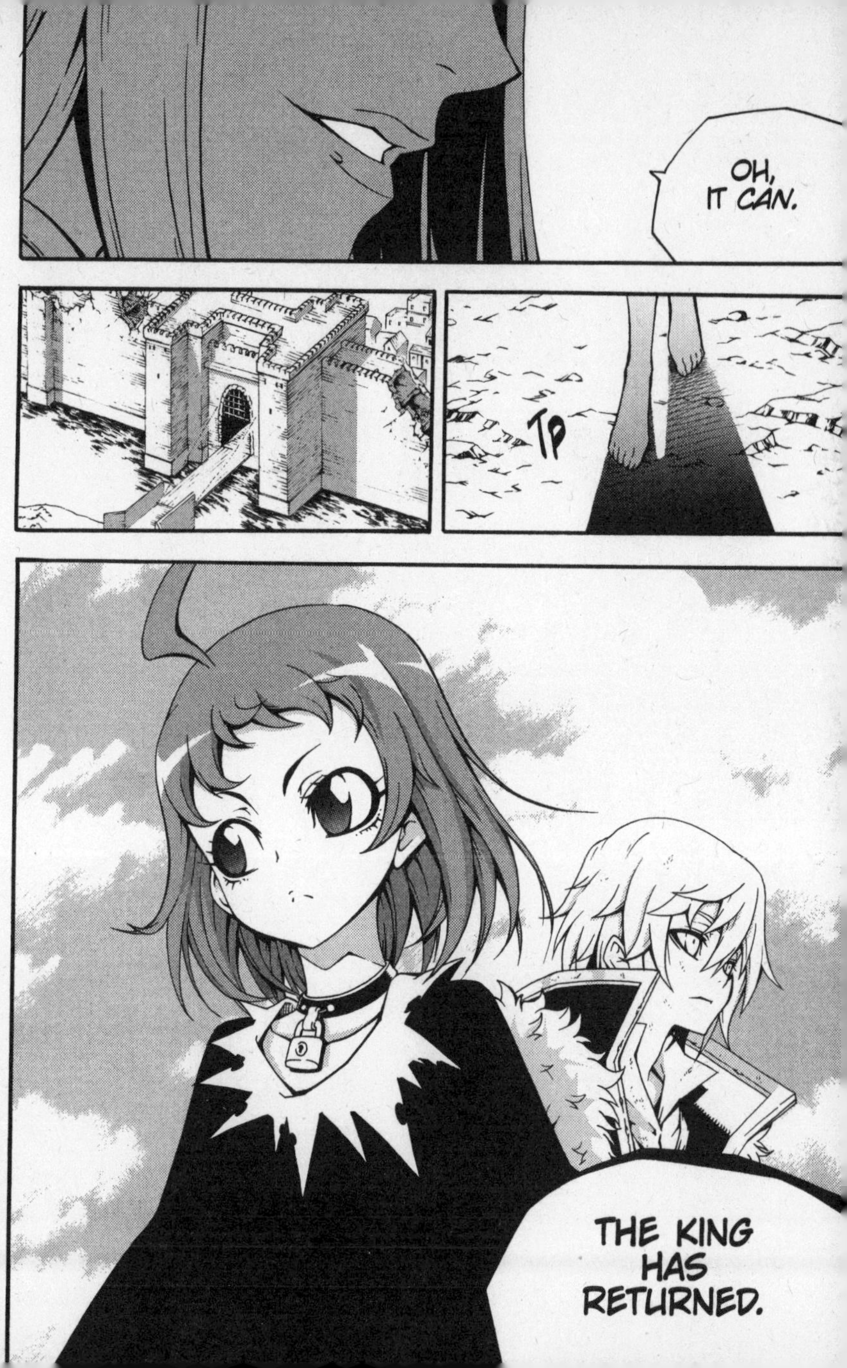
OH, IT CAN.
TP
THE KING HAS RETURNED.

THE WRATH OF MS. L!

UGH! EVERY TIME I SEE THIS GUY, I GET PISSED OFF!

READING WITCH BUSTER VOLUME 9.

HUH? WHO?

MS. L
THIS GUY.

ARTHUR
OH, YOU MEAN ARTHUR. BUT... WHY? HE HASN'T BEEN IN THE BOOKS MUCH, PLUS HE LOOKS COOL.

COOL?! SITTING THERE, LEGS WIDE OPEN, WITH ALL THAT ATTITUDE? IT MAKES ME *MAD!*

UM...?

50. Desire

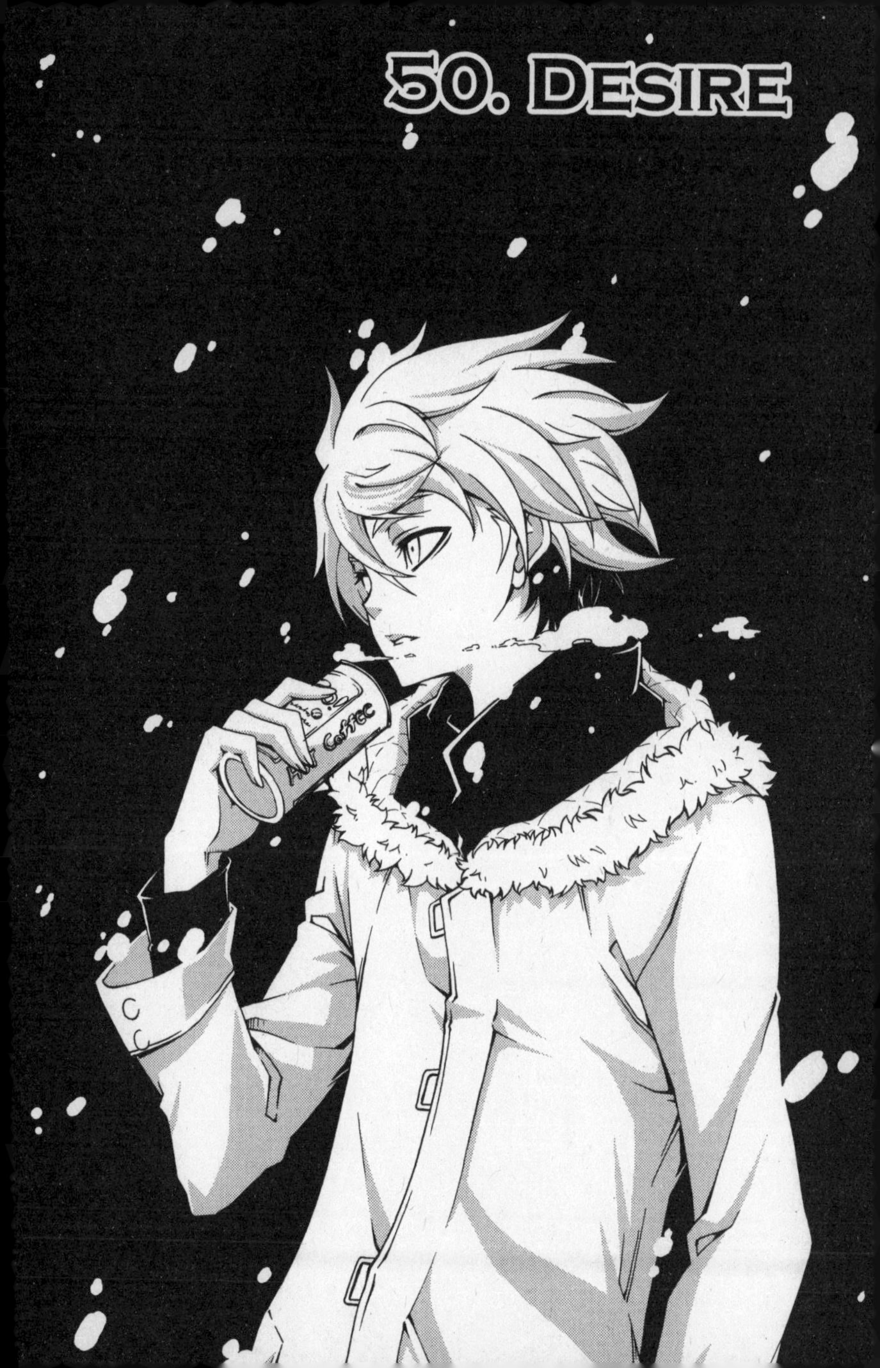

WEIRD...

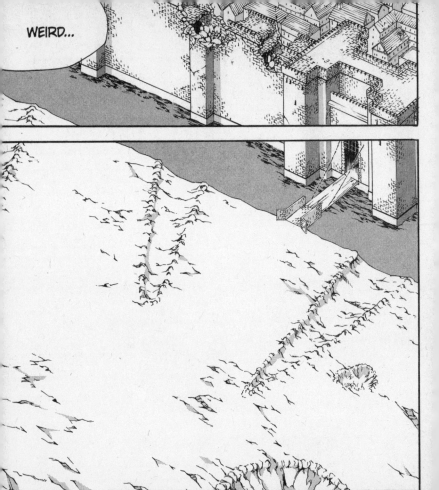

I WAS *SURE*
THEY'D STILL
BE HERE.

GLANCE

GLANCE

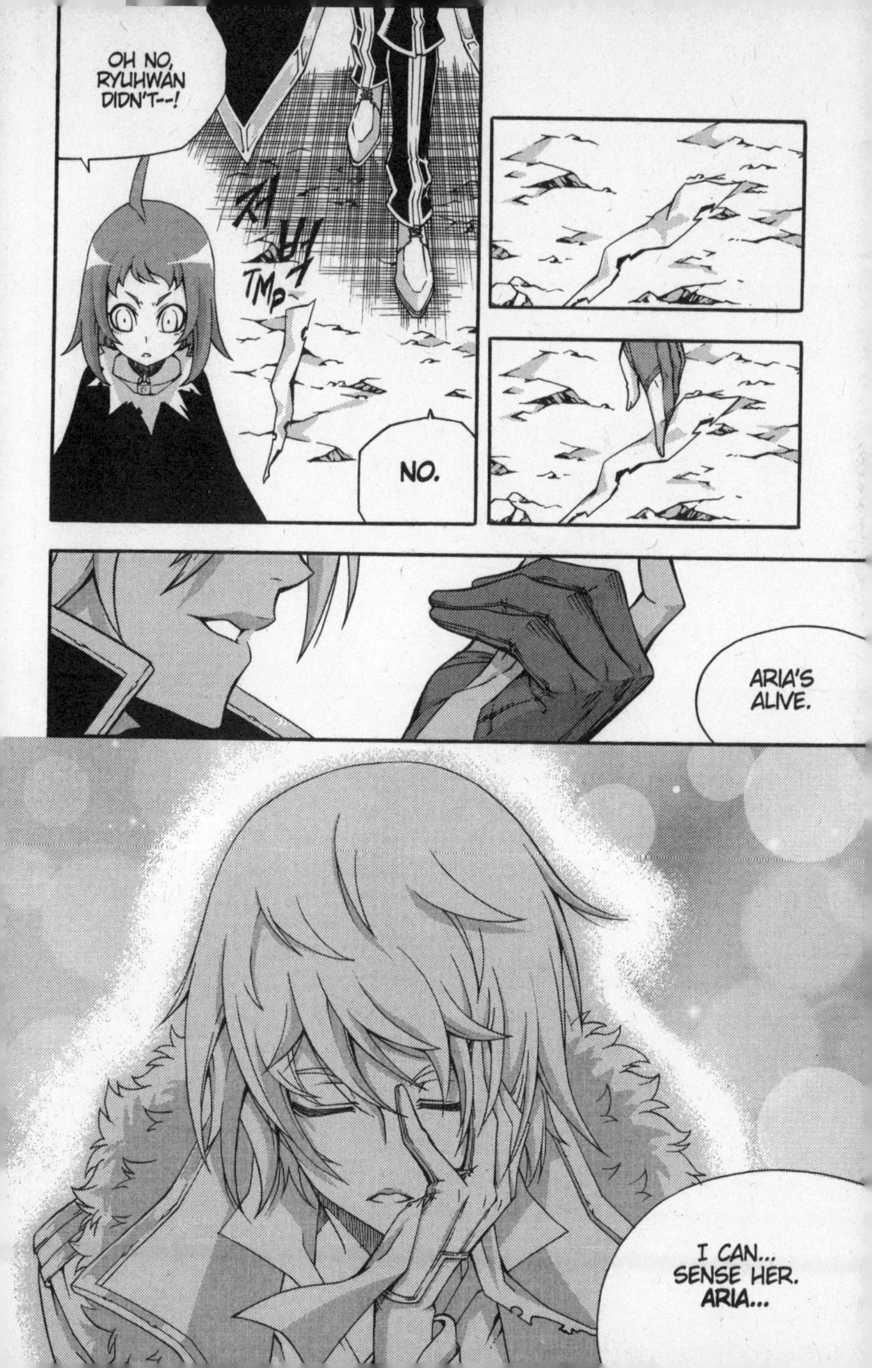
OH NO, RYUHWAN DIDN'T--!
TMP
NO.
ARIA'S ALIVE.
I CAN... SENSE HER. ARIA...

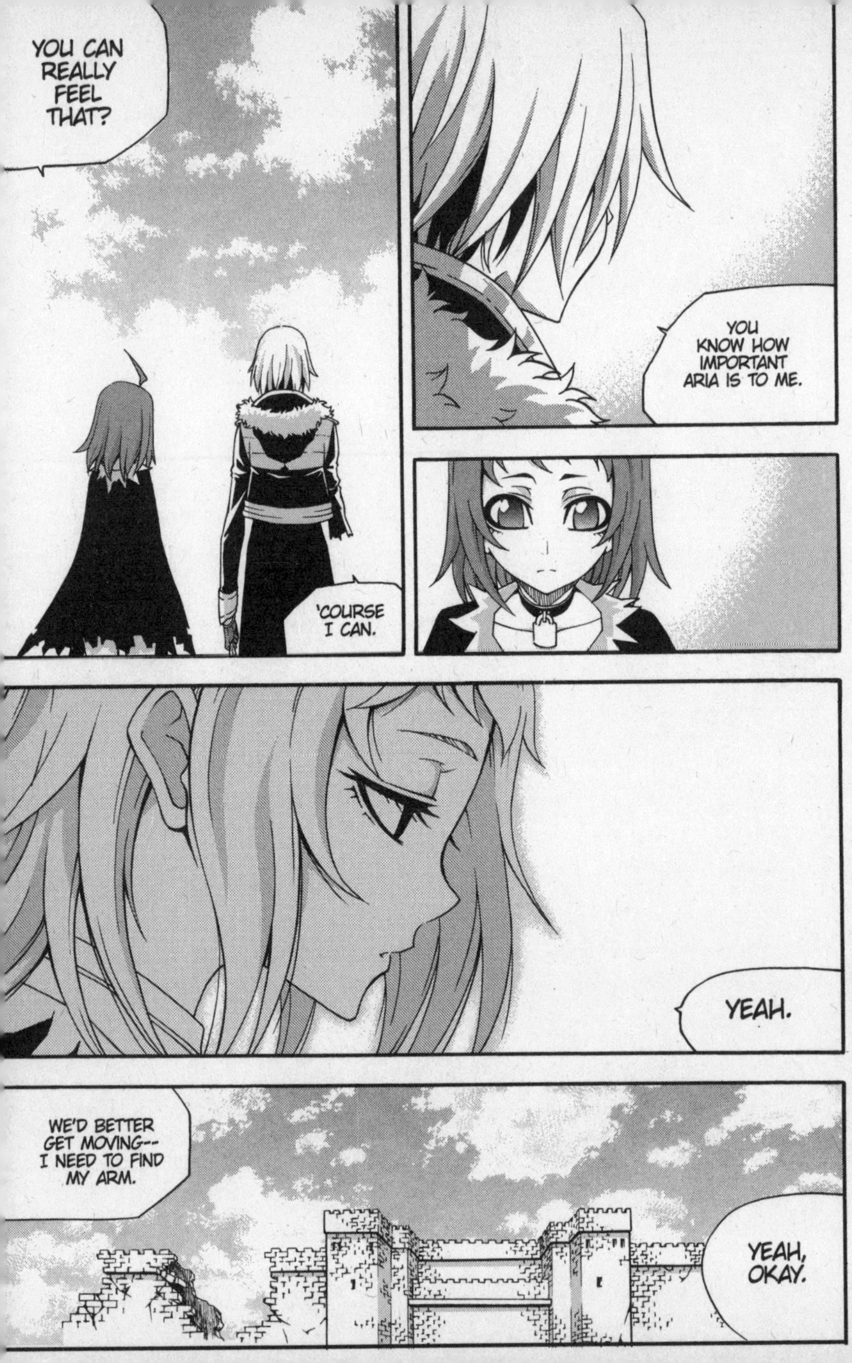
YOU CAN REALLY FEEL THAT?
'COURSE I CAN.
YOU KNOW HOW IMPORTANT ARIA IS TO ME.
YEAH.
WE'D BETTER GET MOVING-- I NEED TO FIND MY ARM.
YEAH, OKAY.

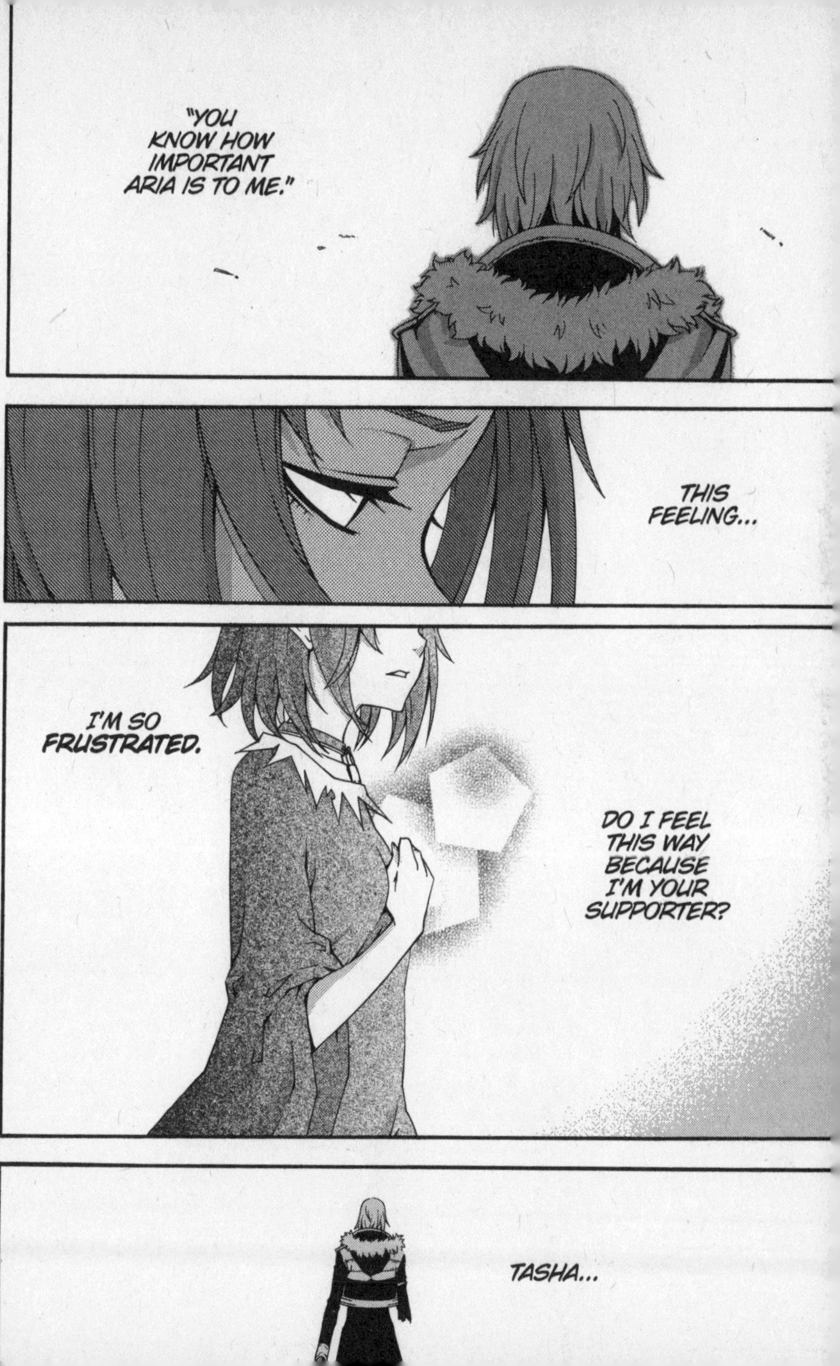
"YOU KNOW HOW IMPORTANT ARIA IS TO ME."
THIS FEELING...
I'M SO FRUSTRATED.
DO I FEEL THIS WAY BECAUSE I'M YOUR SUPPORTER?
TASHA...

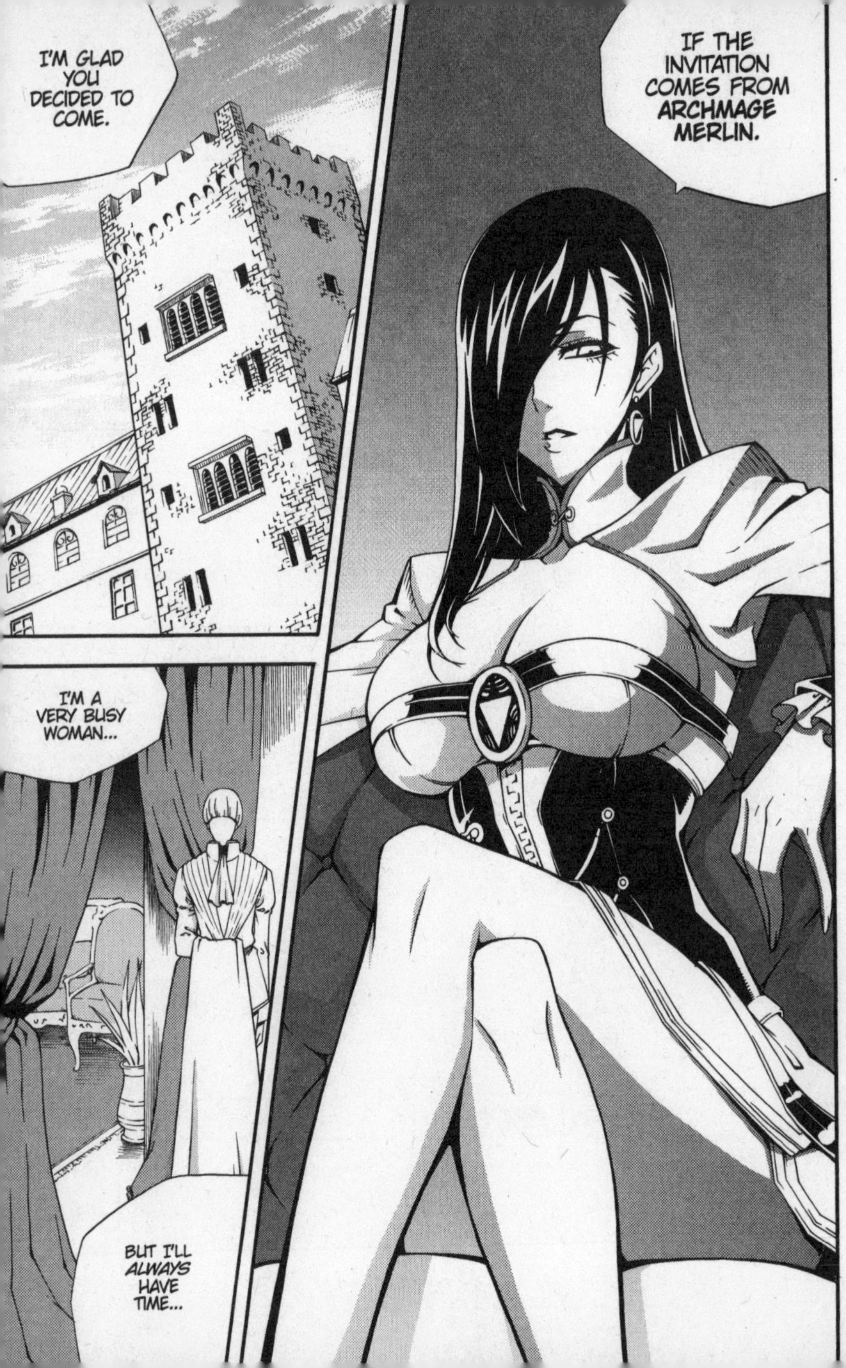
I'M GLAD YOU DECIDED TO COME.
I'M A VERY BUSY WOMAN...
BUT I'LL *ALWAYS* HAVE TIME...
IF THE INVITATION COMES FROM ARCHMAGE MERLIN.

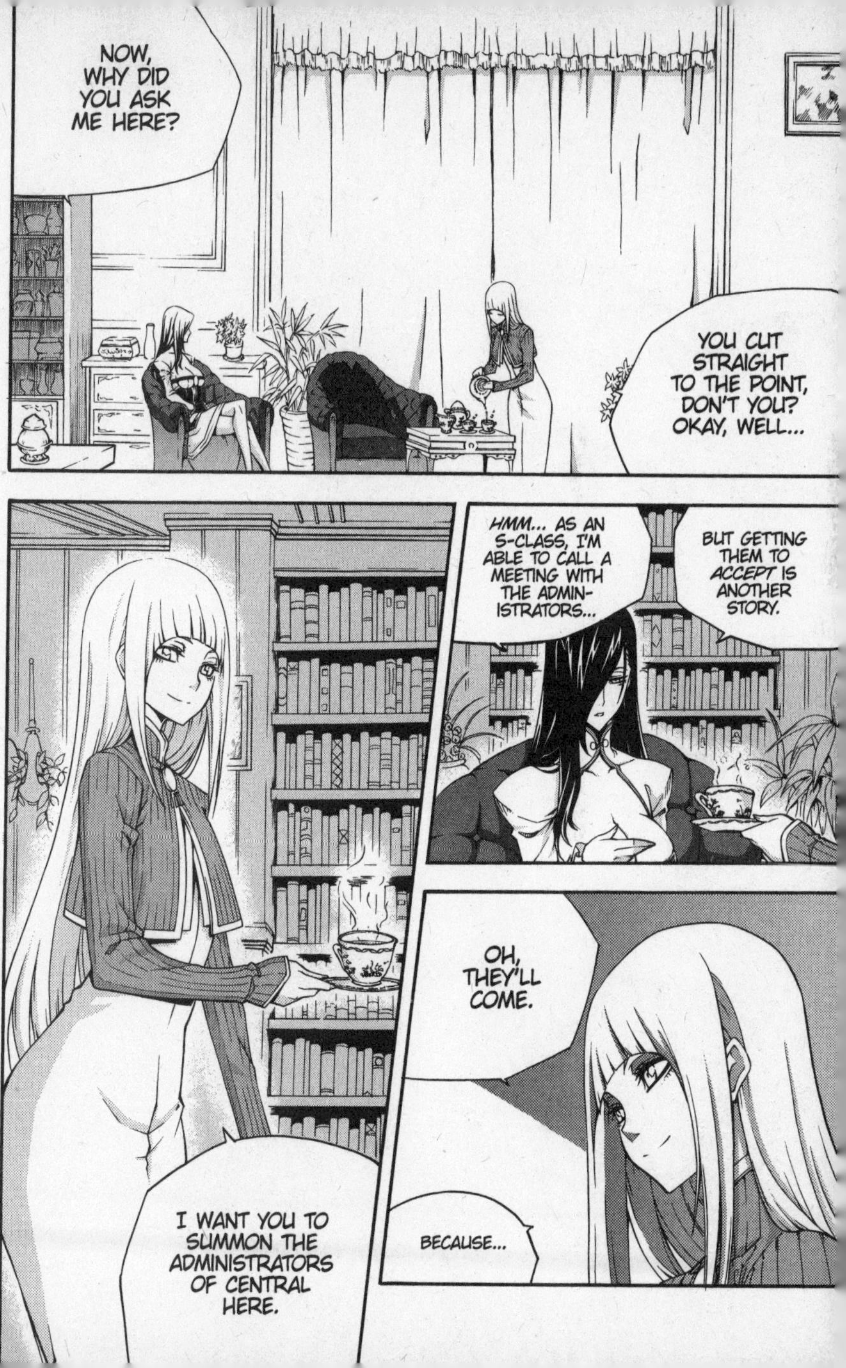
NOW, WHY DID YOU ASK ME HERE?
YOU CUT STRAIGHT TO THE POINT, DON'T YOU? OKAY, WELL...
I WANT YOU TO SUMMON THE ADMINISTRATORS OF CENTRAL HERE.
HMM... AS AN S-CLASS, I'M ABLE TO CALL A MEETING WITH THE ADMINISTRATORS...
BUT GETTING THEM TO ACCEPT IS ANOTHER STORY.
OH, THEY'LL COME.
BECAUSE...

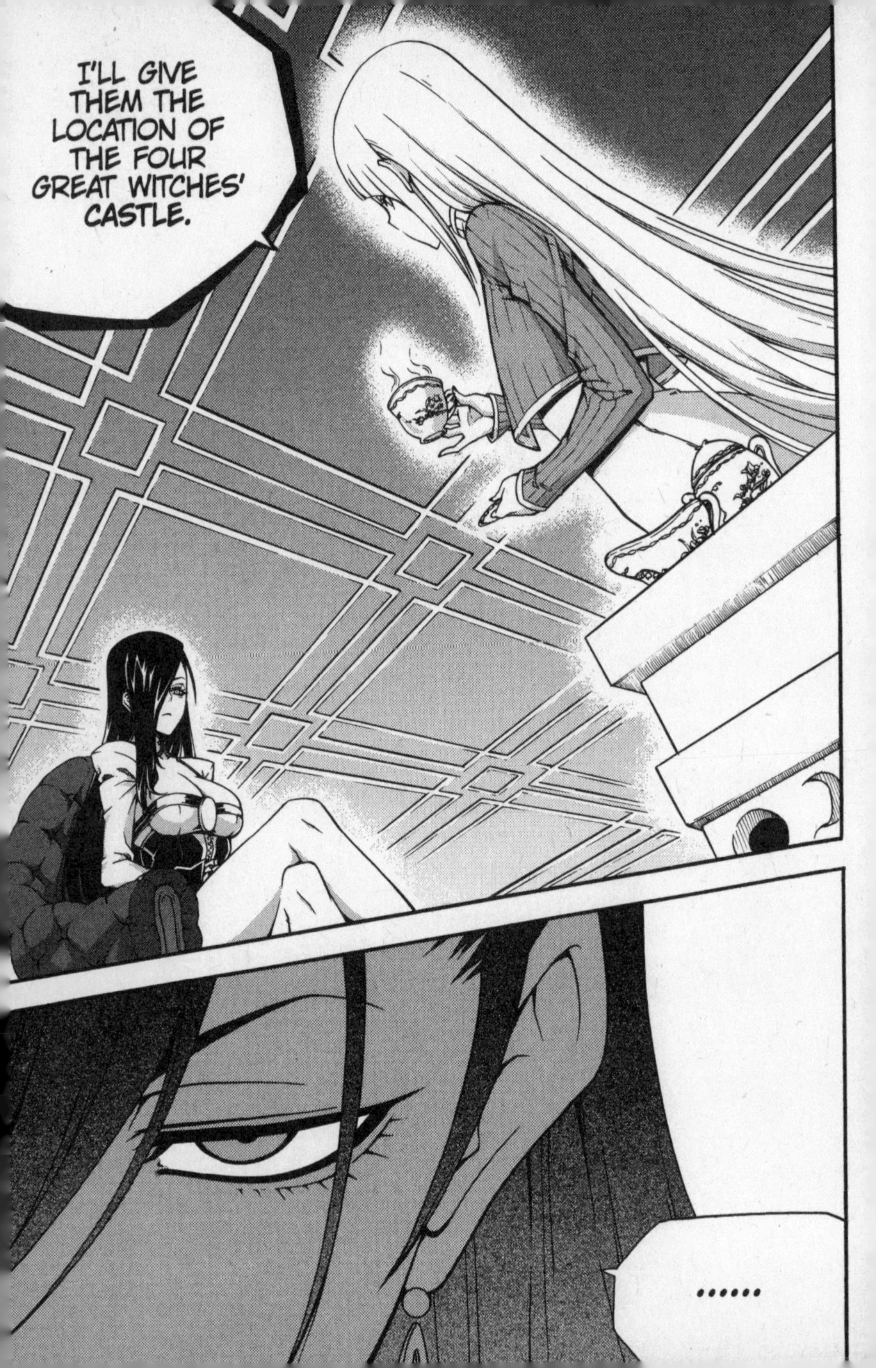
I'LL GIVE THEM THE LOCATION OF THE FOUR GREAT WITCHES' CASTLE.
......

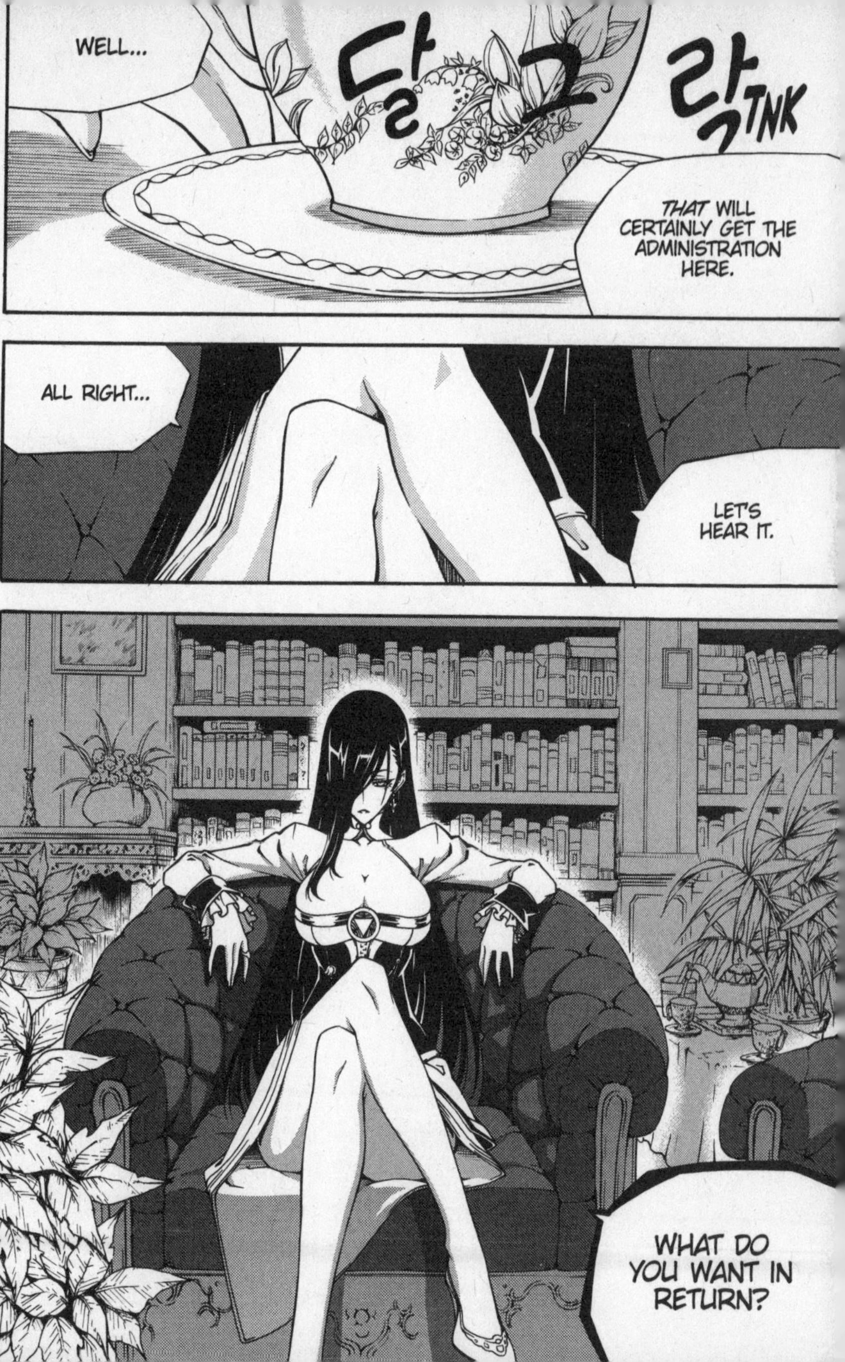

WELL...
달그락
TNK
THAT WILL CERTAINLY GET THE ADMINISTRATION HERE.
ALL RIGHT...
LET'S HEAR IT.
WHAT DO YOU WANT IN RETURN?

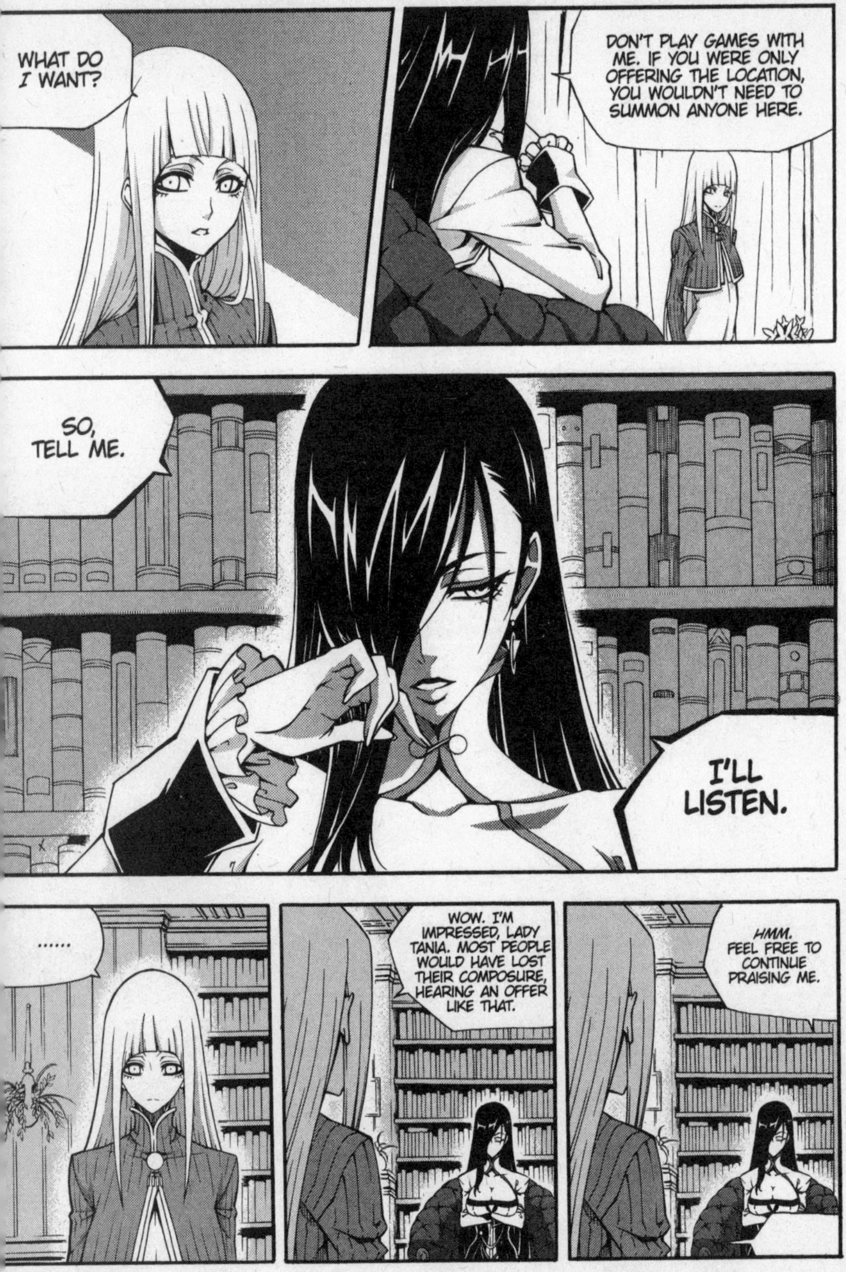
WHAT DO I WANT?
DON'T PLAY GAMES WITH ME. IF YOU WERE ONLY OFFERING THE LOCATION, YOU WOULDN'T NEED TO SUMMON ANYONE HERE.
SO, TELL ME.
I'LL LISTEN.
......
WOW. I'M IMPRESSED, LADY TANIA. MOST PEOPLE WOULD HAVE LOST THEIR COMPOSURE, HEARING AN OFFER LIKE THAT.
HMM. FEEL FREE TO CONTINUE PRAISING ME.

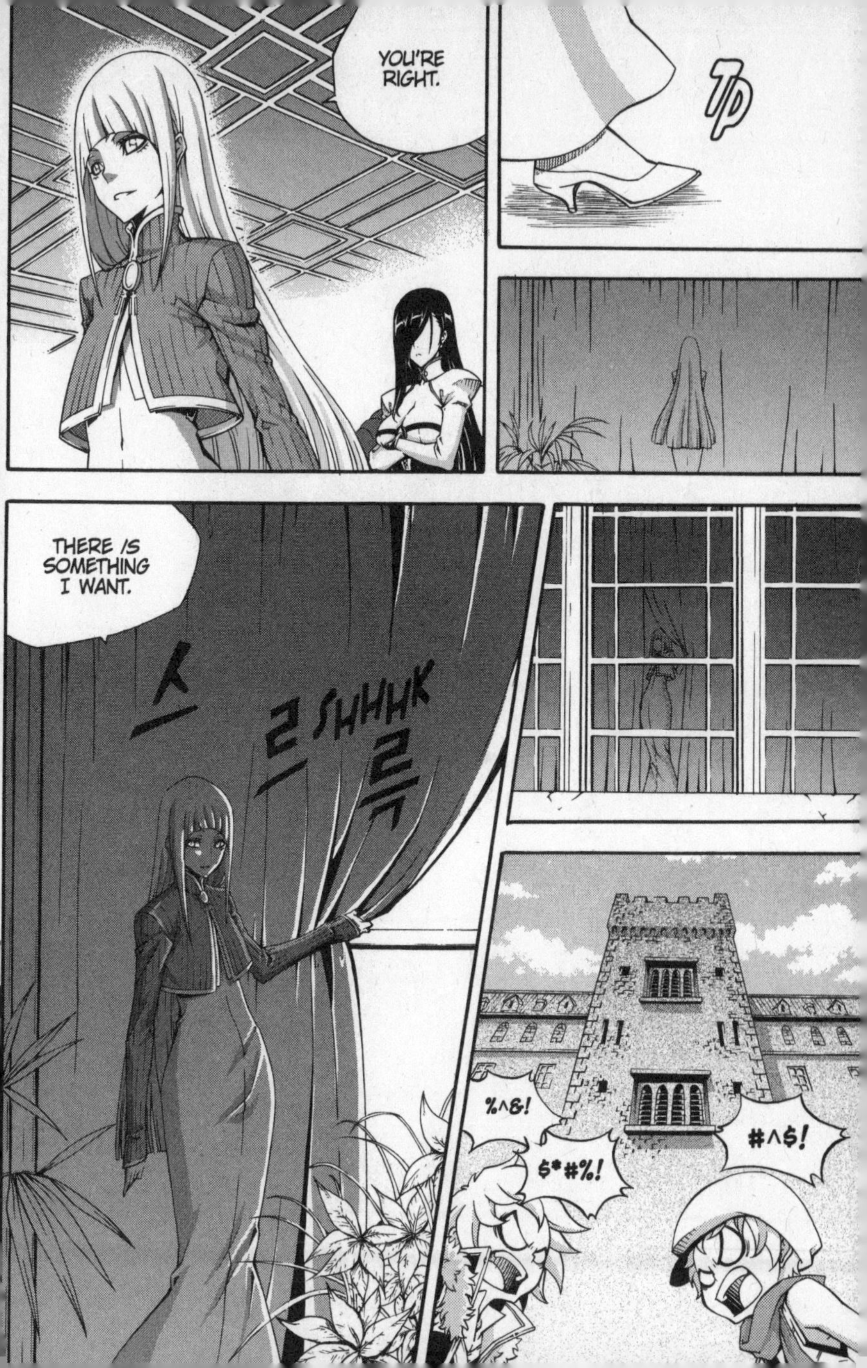
YOU'RE RIGHT.
Tp
THERE IS SOMETHING I WANT.
스르륵
SHHHK
%^&!
$*#%!
#^$!

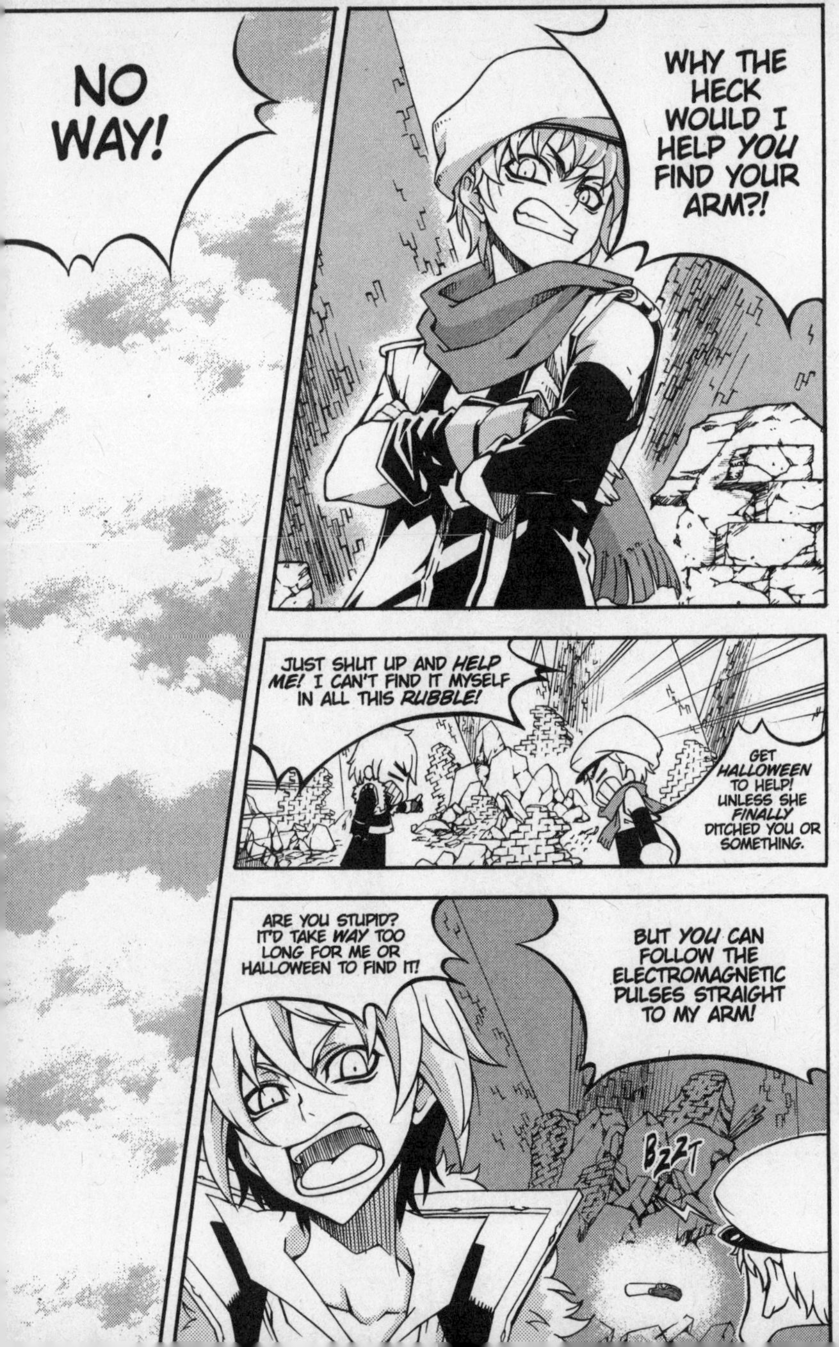
NO WAY!
WHY THE HECK WOULD I HELP *YOU* FIND YOUR ARM?!
JUST SHUT UP AND *HELP ME!* I CAN'T FIND IT MYSELF IN ALL THIS *RUBBLE!*
GET *HALLOWEEN* TO HELP! UNLESS SHE *FINALLY* DITCHED YOU OR SOMETHING.
ARE YOU STUPID? IT'D TAKE *WAY* TOO LONG FOR ME OR HALLOWEEN TO FIND IT!
BUT *YOU* CAN FOLLOW THE ELECTROMAGNETIC PULSES STRAIGHT TO MY ARM!
BZZT

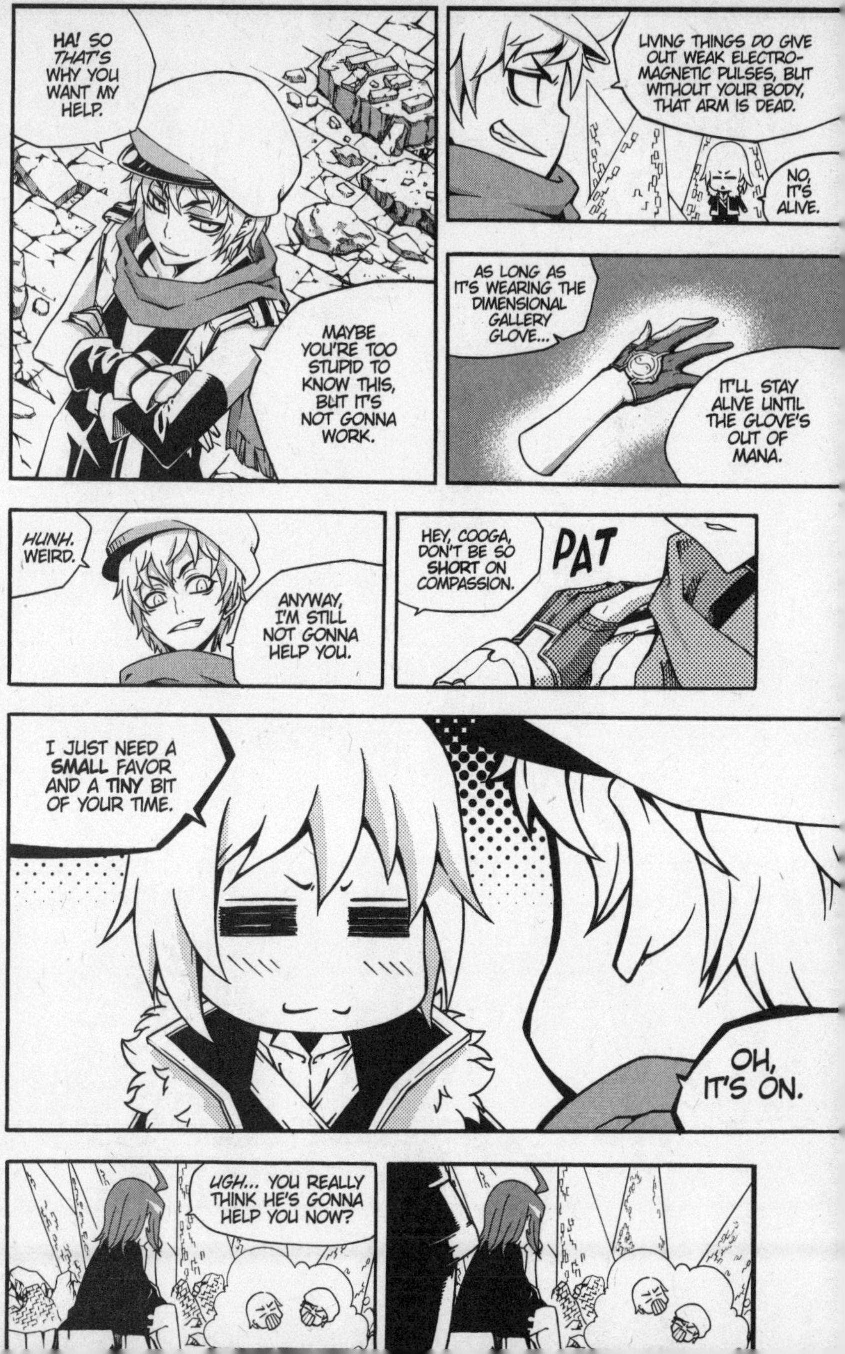
HA! SO *THAT'S* WHY YOU WANT MY HELP.
MAYBE YOU'RE TOO STUPID TO KNOW THIS, BUT IT'S NOT GONNA WORK.
LIVING THINGS *DO* GIVE OUT WEAK ELECTRO-MAGNETIC PULSES, BUT WITHOUT YOUR BODY, THAT ARM IS DEAD.
NO, IT'S ALIVE.
AS LONG AS IT'S WEARING THE DIMENSIONAL GALLERY GLOVE...
IT'LL STAY ALIVE UNTIL THE GLOVE'S OUT OF MANA.
HUNH. WEIRD.
ANYWAY, I'M STILL NOT GONNA HELP YOU.
HEY, COOGA, DON'T BE SO **SHORT** ON COMPASSION.
PAT
I JUST NEED A **SMALL** FAVOR AND A **TINY** BIT OF YOUR TIME.
OH, IT'S ON.
UGH... YOU REALLY THINK HE'S GONNA HELP YOU NOW?

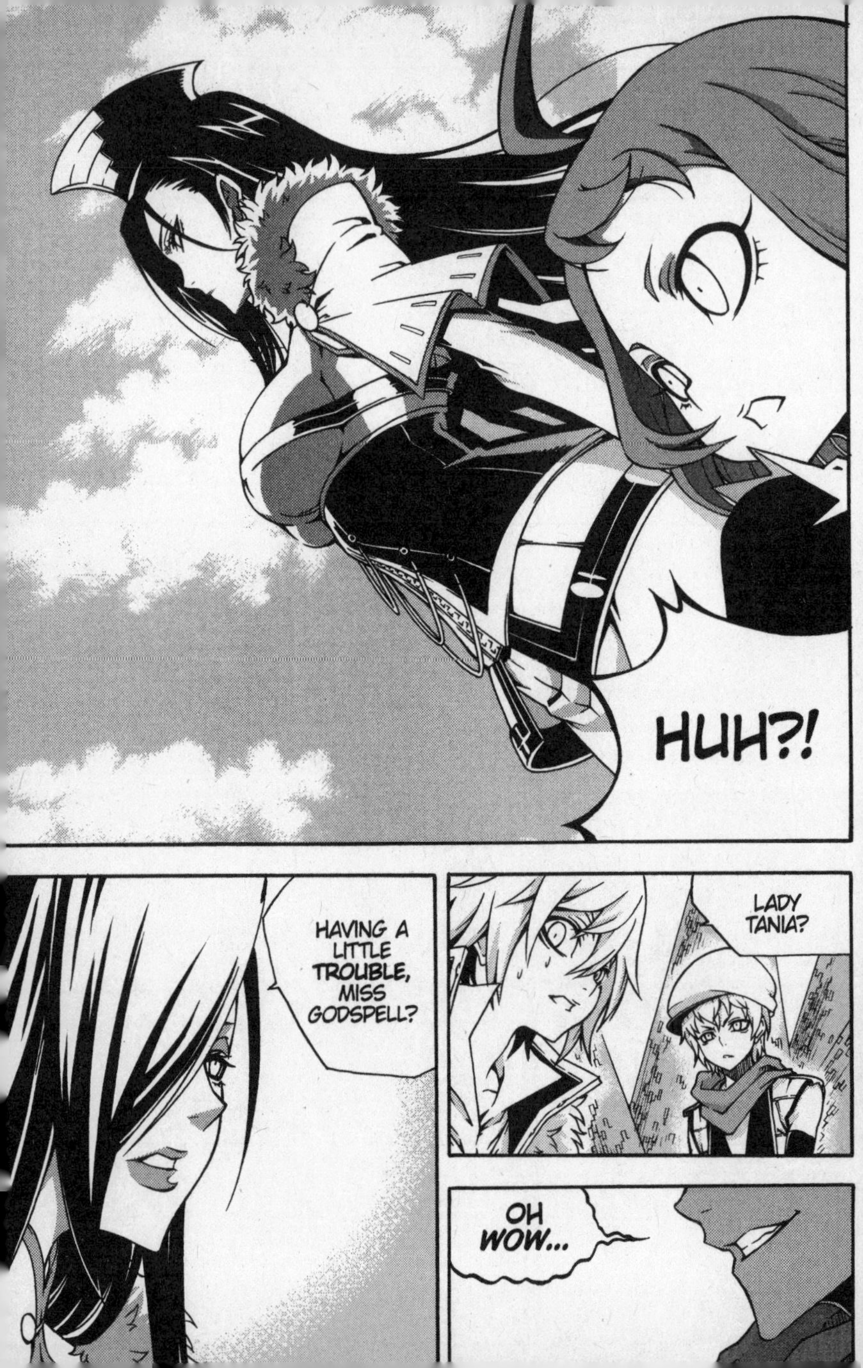
HUH?!
HAVING A LITTLE TROUBLE, MISS GODSPELL?
LADY TANIA?
OH WOW...

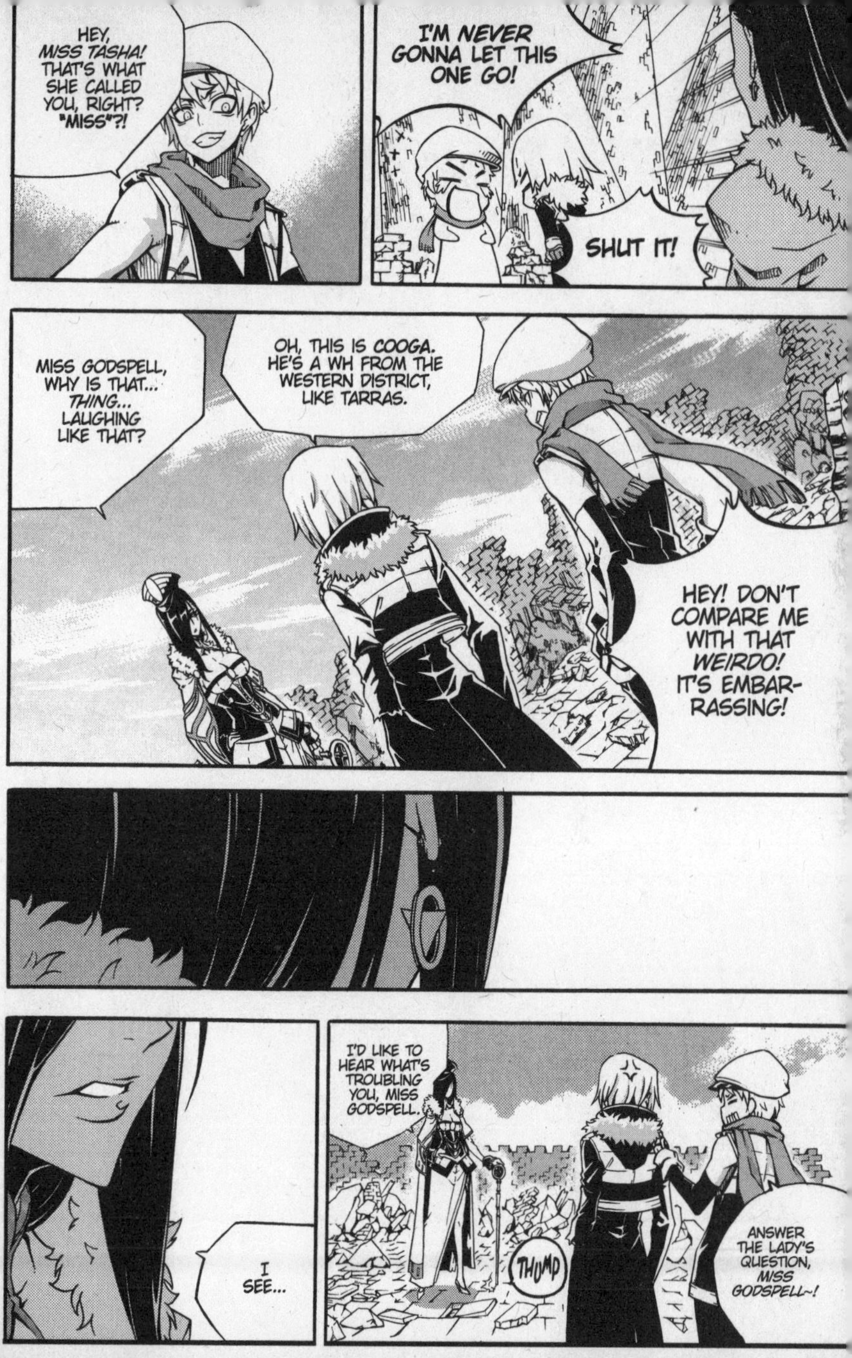
HEY, MISS TASHA! THAT'S WHAT SHE CALLED YOU, RIGHT? "MISS"?!
I'M NEVER GONNA LET THIS ONE GO!
SHUT IT!
MISS GODSPELL, WHY IS THAT... THING... LAUGHING LIKE THAT?
OH, THIS IS COOGA. HE'S A WH FROM THE WESTERN DISTRICT, LIKE TARRAS.
HEY! DON'T COMPARE ME WITH THAT WEIRDO! IT'S EMBARRASSING!
I SEE...
I'D LIKE TO HEAR WHAT'S TROUBLING YOU, MISS GODSPELL.
THUMP
ANSWER THE LADY'S QUESTION, MISS GODSPELL~!

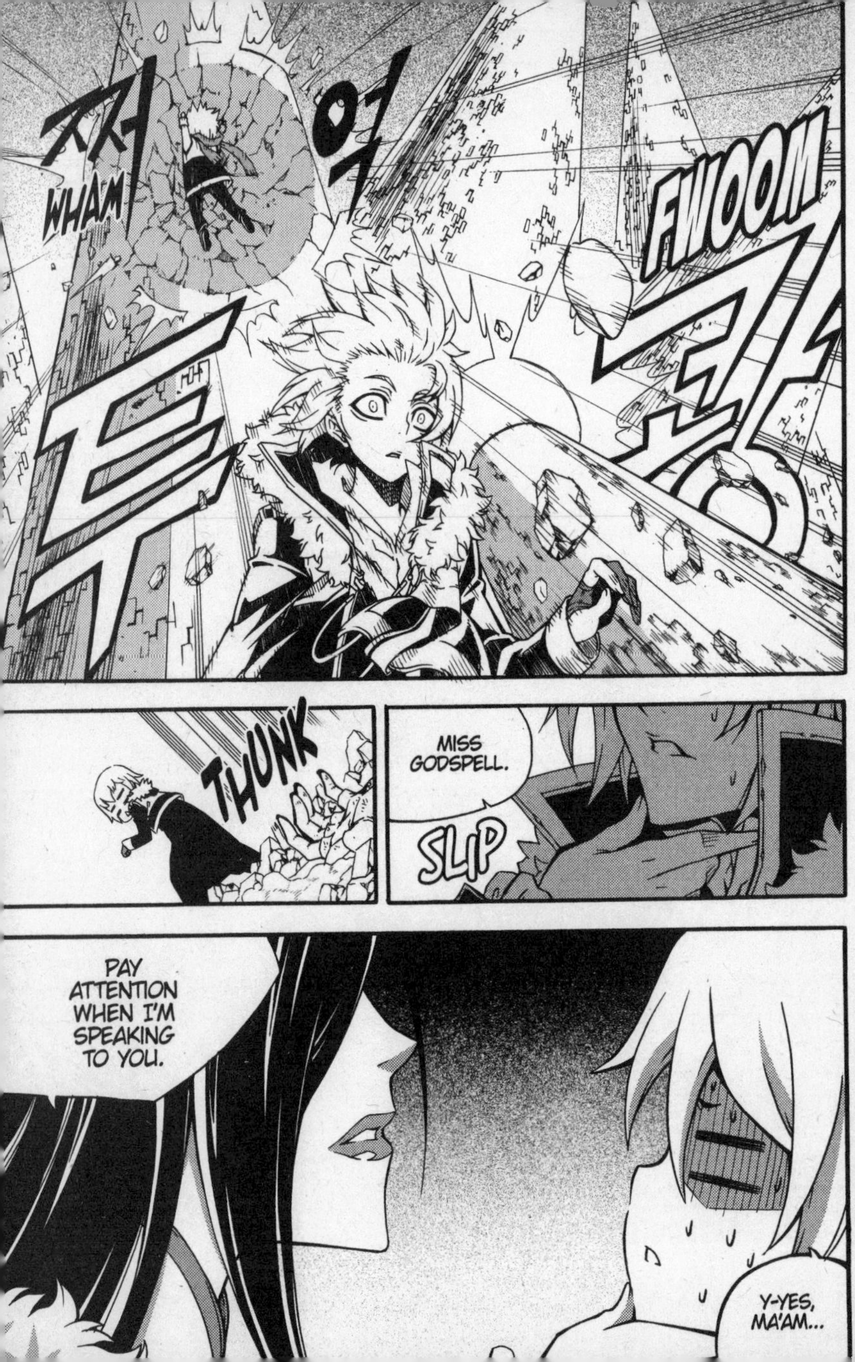
WHAM
FWOOM
THUNK
MISS GODSPELL.
SLIP
PAY ATTENTION WHEN I'M SPEAKING TO YOU.
Y-YES, MA'AM...

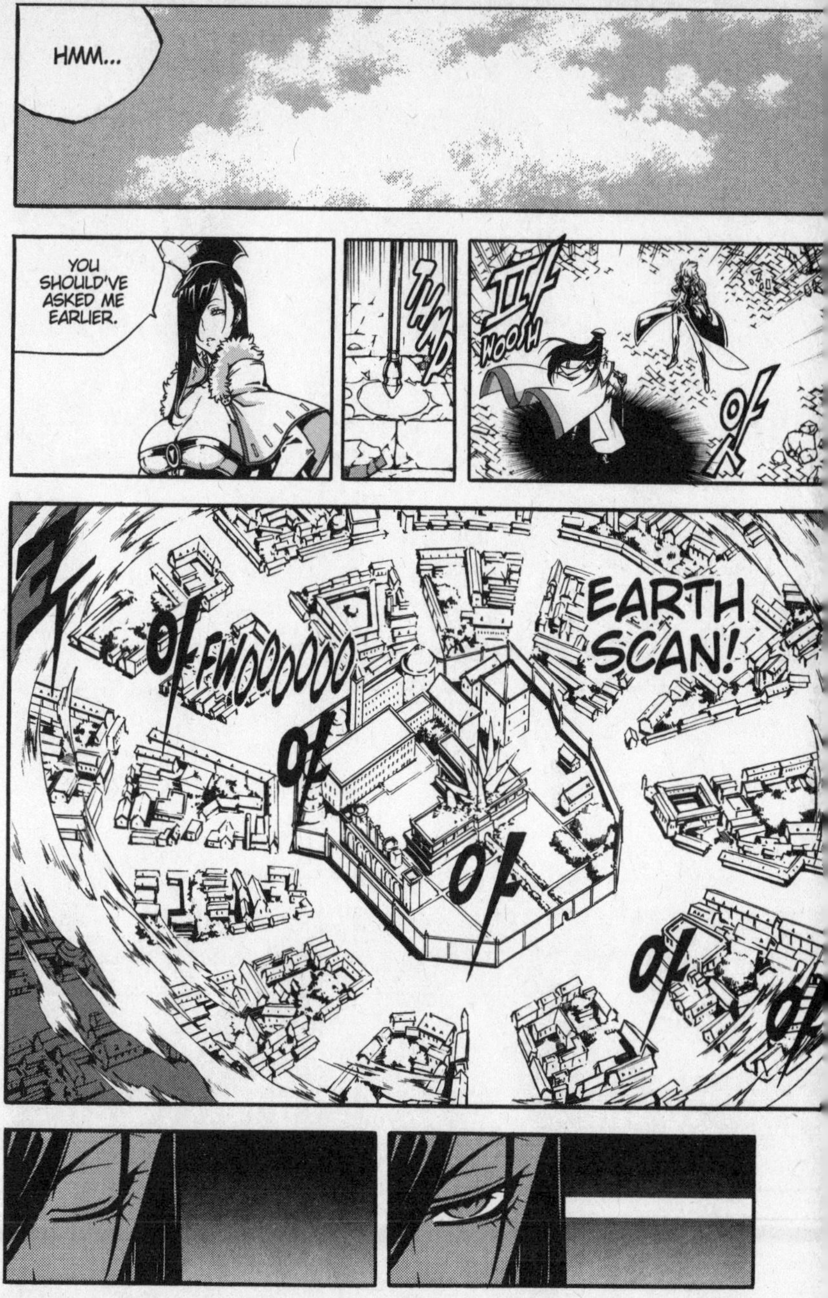
HMM...
YOU SHOULD'VE ASKED ME EARLIER.
THUMP
WOOSH
FWOOOOOO
EARTH SCAN!

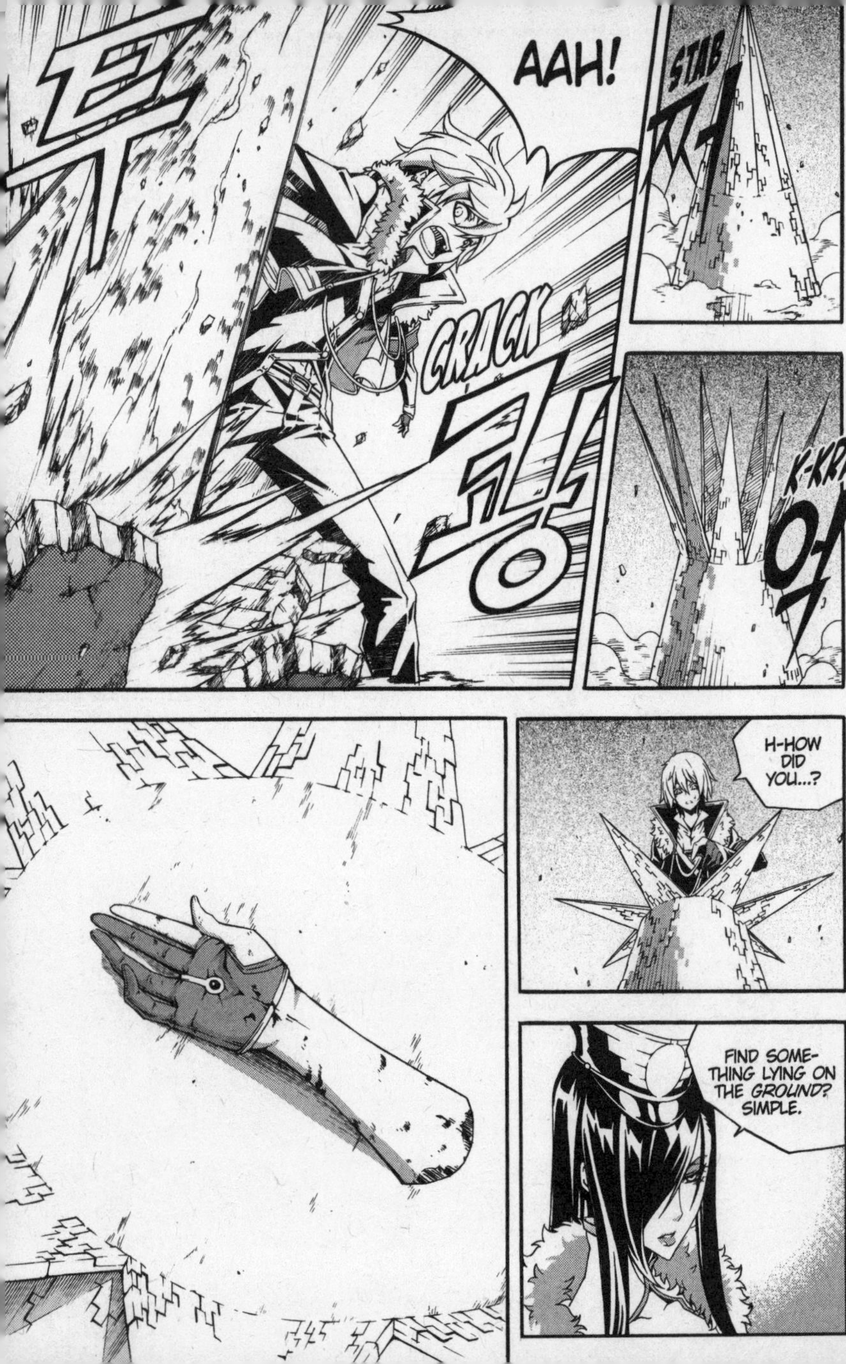
AAH!
CRACK
STAB
K-KRAK
H-HOW DID YOU...?
FIND SOME-THING LYING ON THE GROUND? SIMPLE.

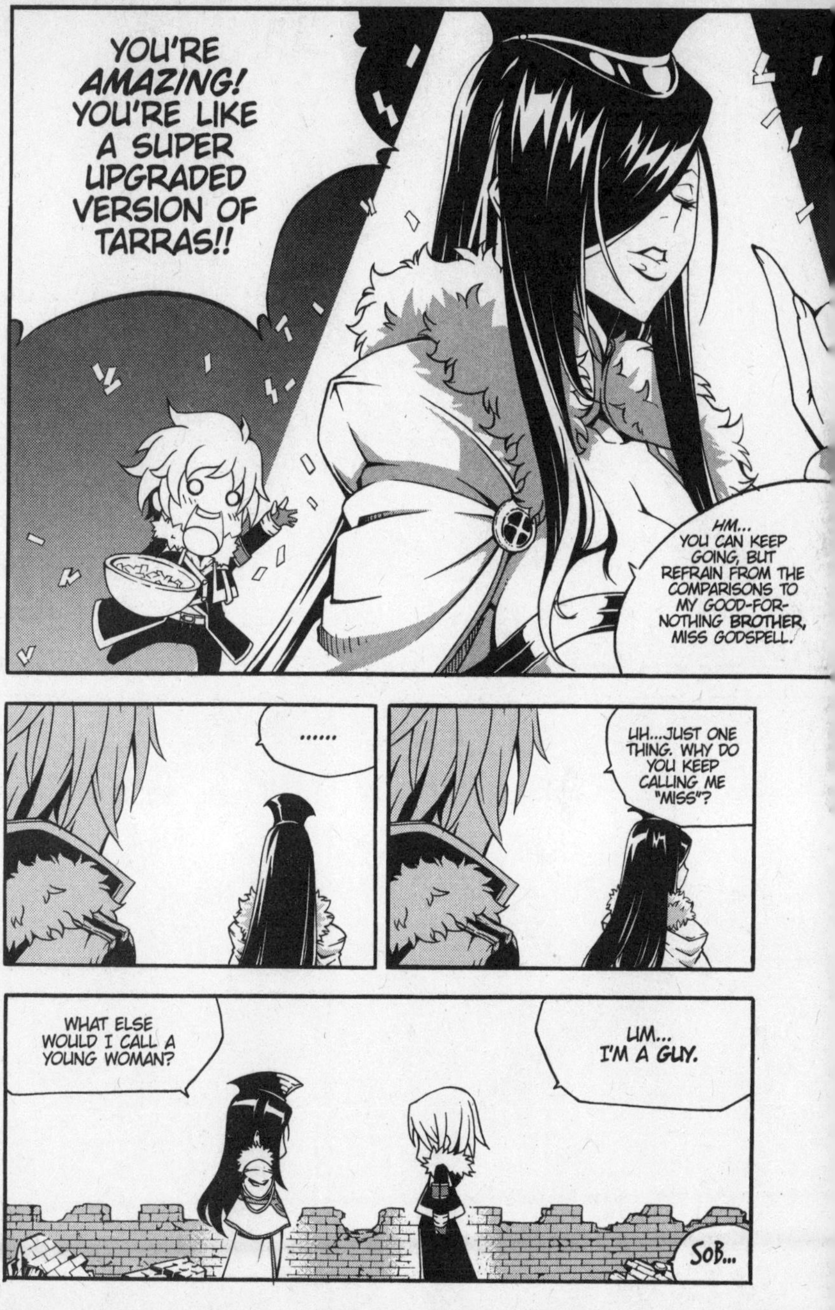
YOU'RE AMAZING! YOU'RE LIKE A SUPER UPGRADED VERSION OF TARRAS!!
HM... YOU CAN KEEP GOING, BUT REFRAIN FROM THE COMPARISONS TO MY GOOD-FOR-NOTHING BROTHER, MISS GODSPELL.
......
UH...JUST ONE THING. WHY DO YOU KEEP CALLING ME "MISS"?
WHAT ELSE WOULD I CALL A YOUNG WOMAN?
UM... I'M A GUY.
SOB...

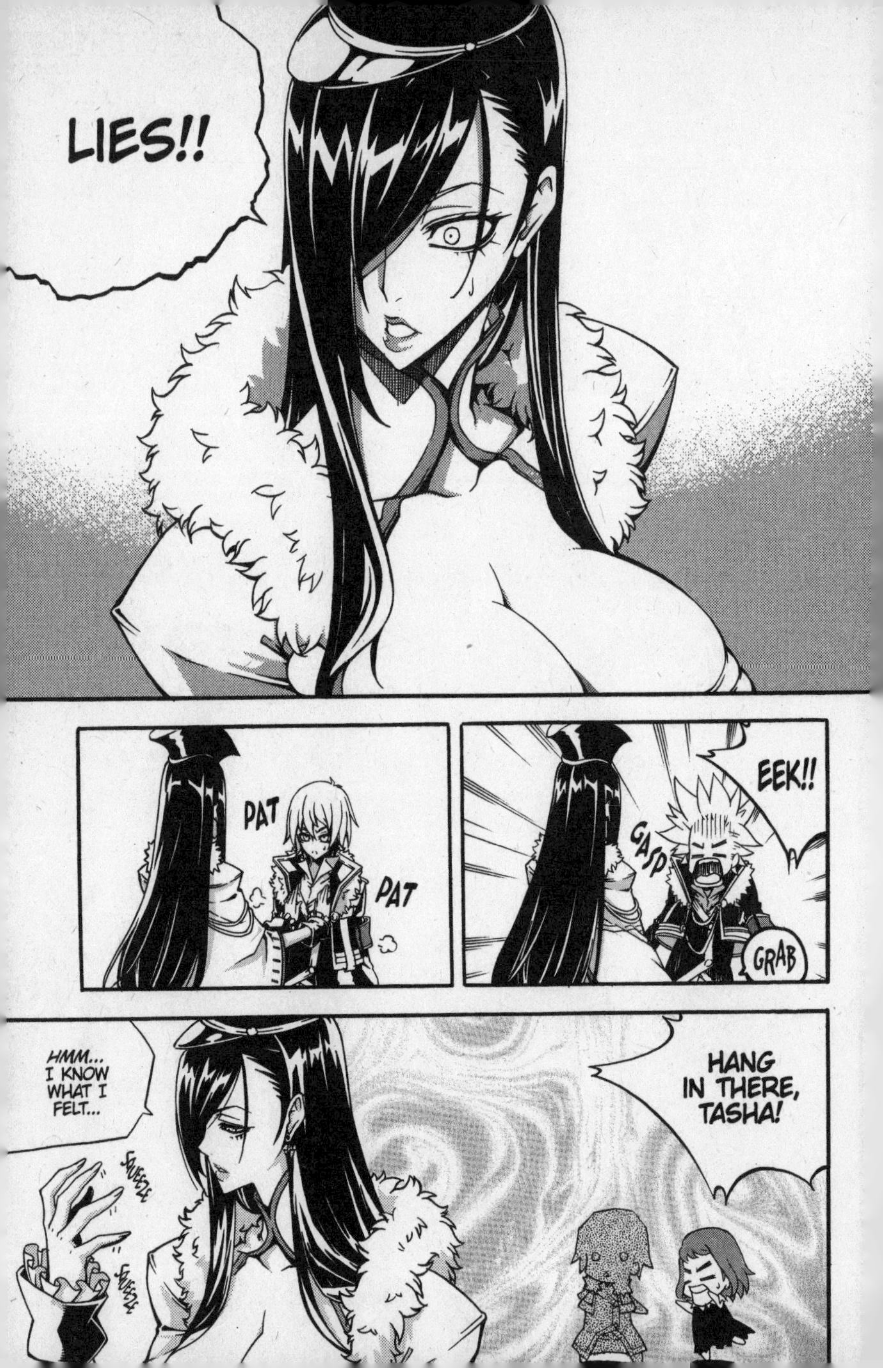
LIES!!
PAT
PAT
EEK!!
GASP
GRAB
HMM... I KNOW WHAT I FELT...
SQUEEZE
SQUEEZE
HANG IN THERE, TASHA!

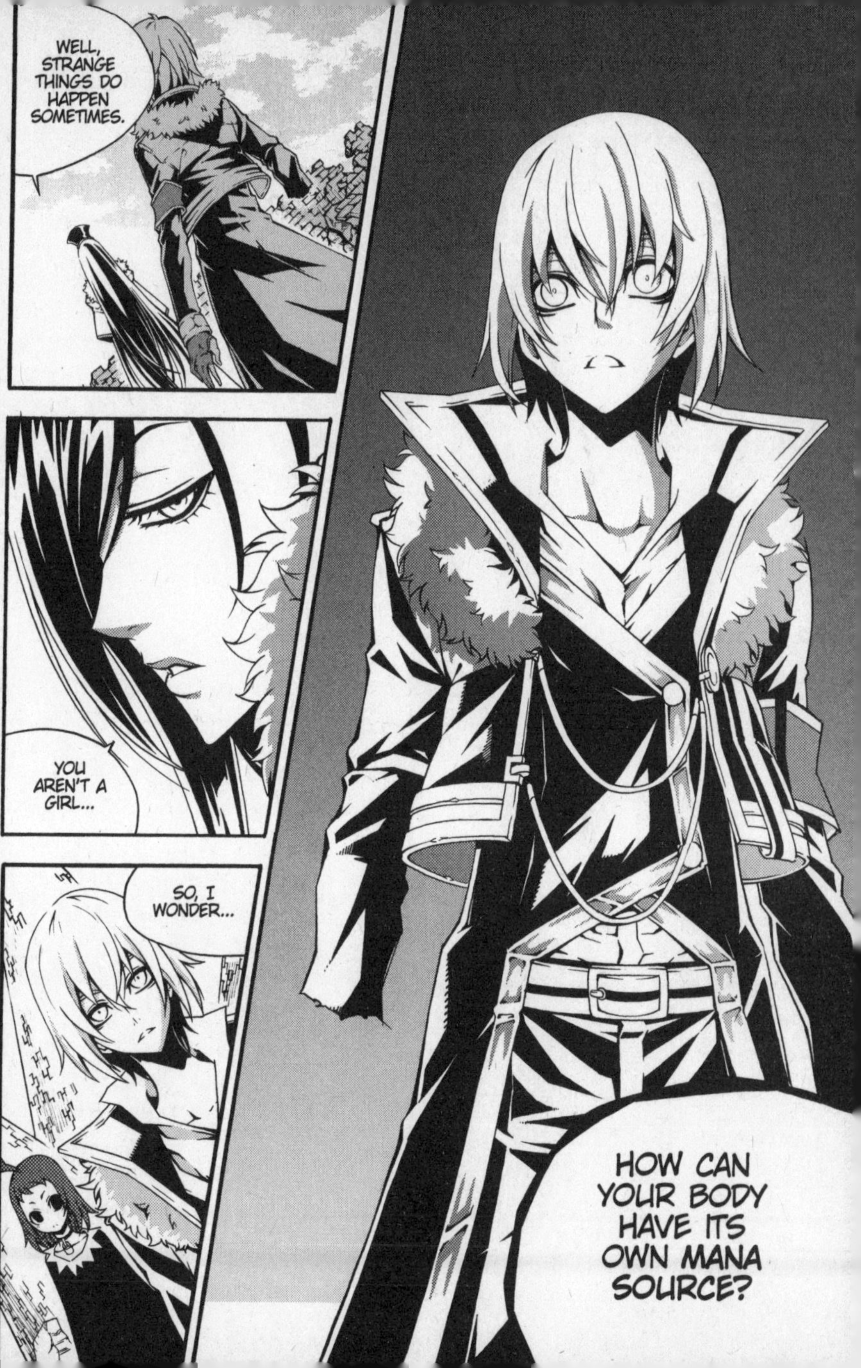
WELL, STRANGE THINGS DO HAPPEN SOMETIMES.
YOU AREN'T A GIRL...
SO, I WONDER...
HOW CAN YOUR BODY HAVE ITS OWN MANA SOURCE?

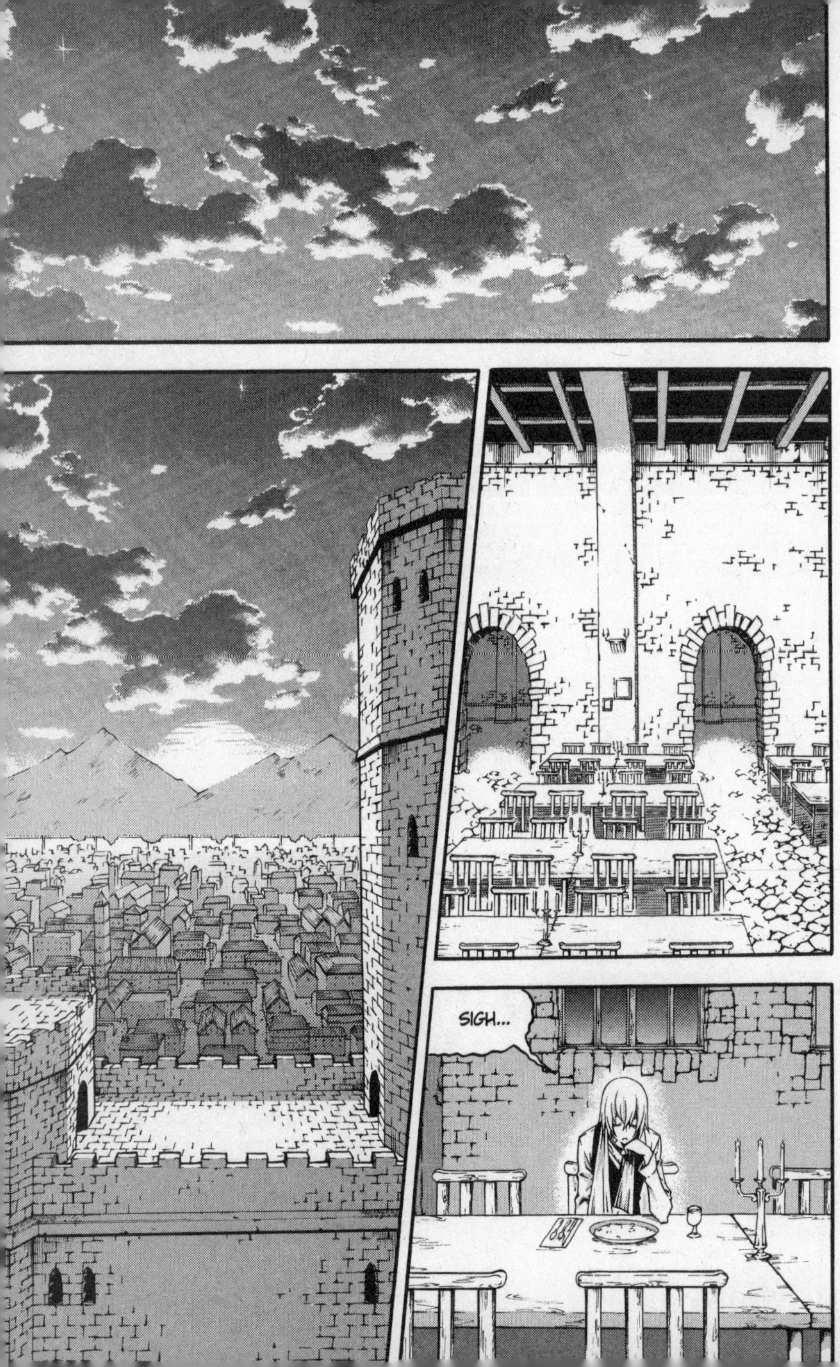
SIGH...

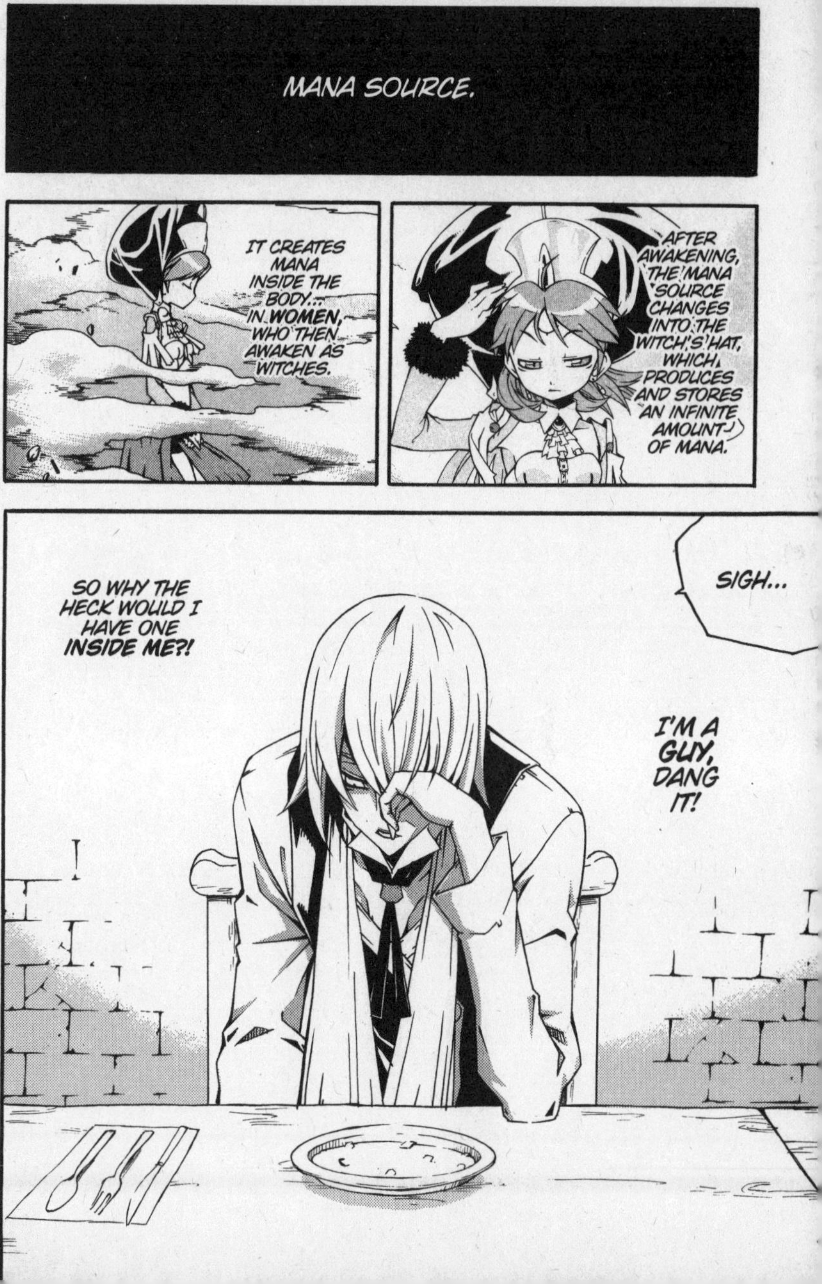
MANA SOURCE.
IT CREATES MANA INSIDE THE BODY... IN WOMEN, WHO THEN AWAKEN AS WITCHES.
AFTER AWAKENING, THE MANA SOURCE CHANGES INTO THE WITCH'S HAT, WHICH PRODUCES AND STORES AN INFINITE AMOUNT OF MANA.
SO WHY THE HECK WOULD I HAVE ONE INSIDE ME?!
SIGH...
I'M A GUY, DANG IT!

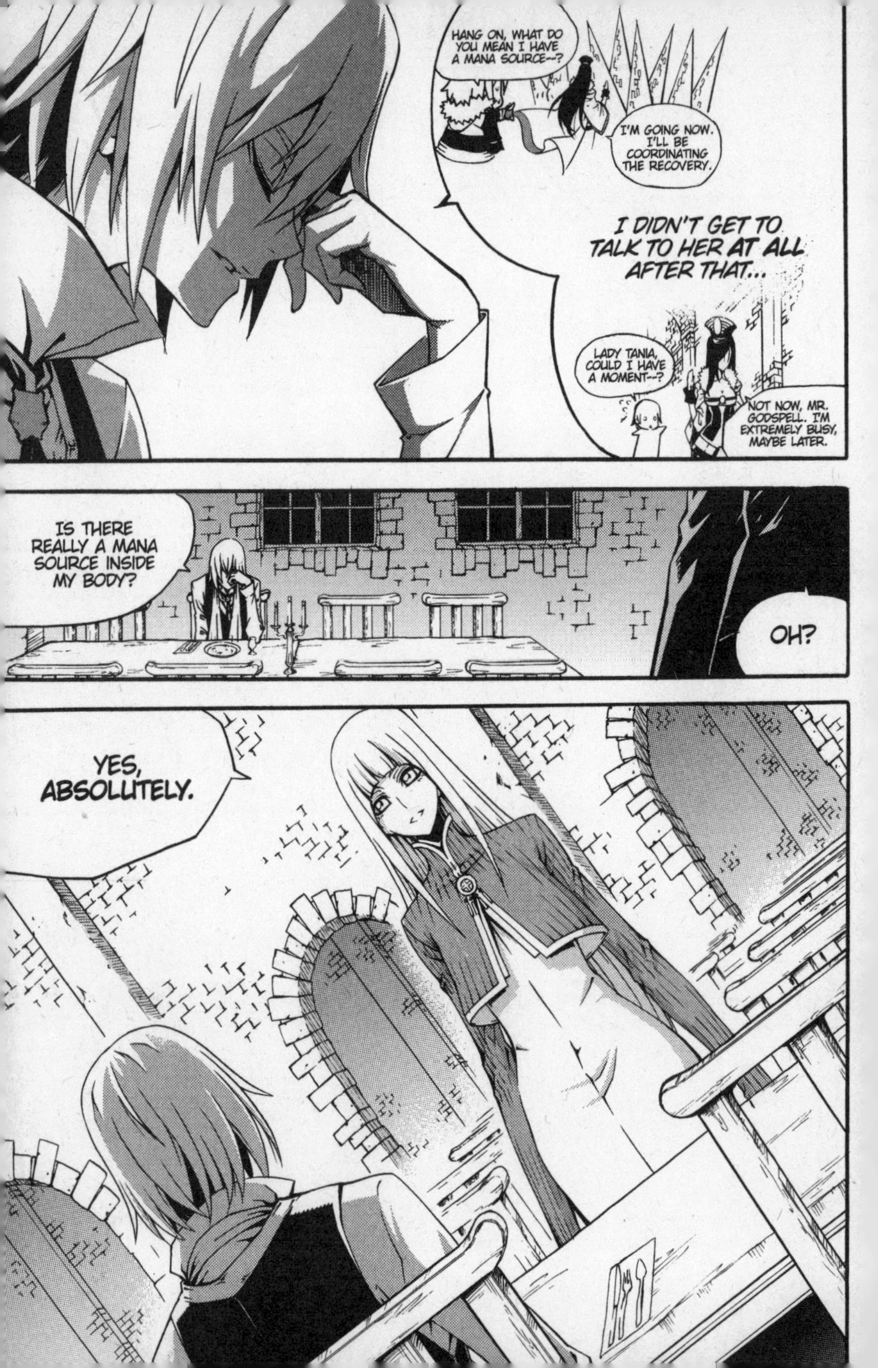
HANG ON, WHAT DO YOU MEAN I HAVE A MANA SOURCE--?
I'M GOING NOW. I'LL BE COORDINATING THE RECOVERY.
I DIDN'T GET TO TALK TO HER AT ALL AFTER THAT...
LADY TANIA, COULD I HAVE A MOMENT--?
NOT NOW, MR. GODSPELL. I'M EXTREMELY BUSY, MAYBE LATER.
IS THERE REALLY A MANA SOURCE INSIDE MY BODY?
OH?
YES, ABSOLLUTELY.

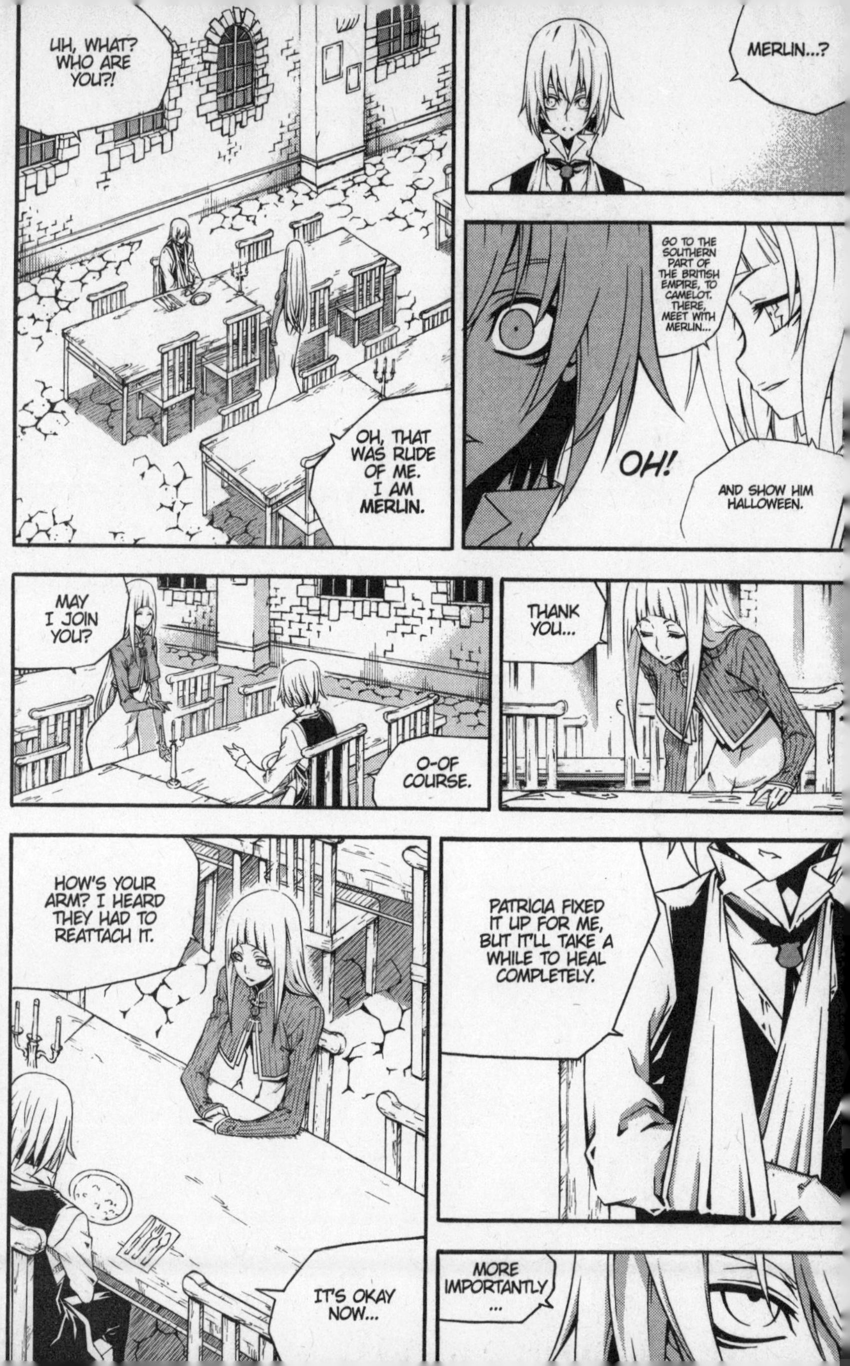
UH, WHAT? WHO ARE YOU?!
OH, THAT WAS RUDE OF ME. I AM MERLIN.
MERLIN...?
GO TO THE SOUTHERN PART OF THE BRITISH EMPIRE, TO CAMELOT. THERE, MEET WITH MERLIN...
OH!
AND SHOW HIM HALLOWEEN.
MAY I JOIN YOU?
O-OF COURSE.
THANK YOU...
HOW'S YOUR ARM? I HEARD THEY HAD TO REATTACH IT.
IT'S OKAY NOW...
PATRICIA FIXED IT UP FOR ME, BUT IT'LL TAKE A WHILE TO HEAL COMPLETELY.
MORE IMPORTANTLY ...

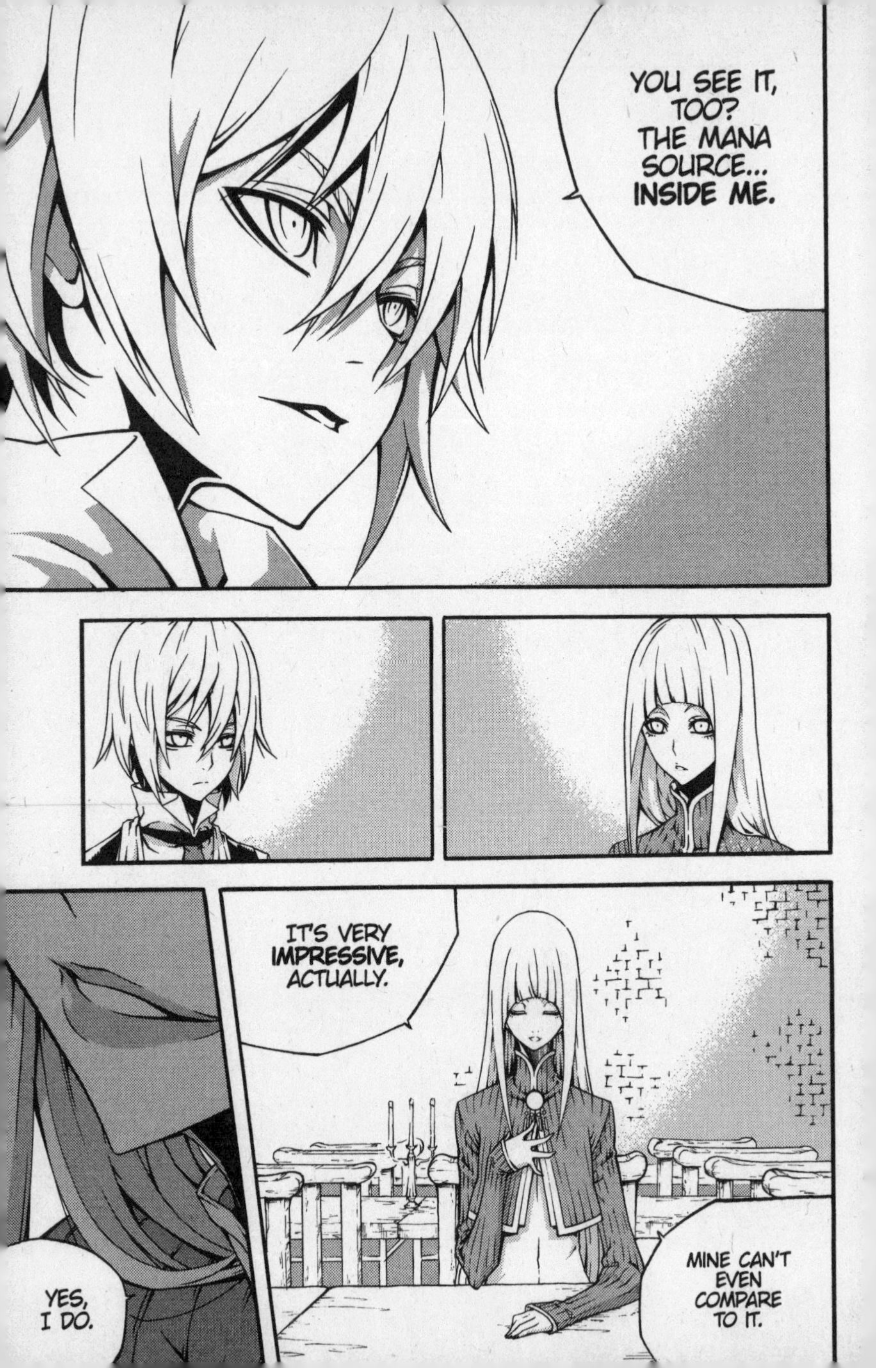
YOU SEE IT, TOO? THE MANA SOURCE... INSIDE ME.
IT'S VERY IMPRESSIVE, ACTUALLY.
YES, I DO.
MINE CAN'T EVEN COMPARE TO IT.

I GUESS IT'S TRUE, THEN.

BUT IT'S STRANGE...

YOU'RE A WH, AREN'T YOU?

WHAT ABOUT *THEIR* WITCHES?

ANY WITCH CAN SENSE A MANA SOURCE...

SO WHY DIDN'T YOU KNOW ABOUT THIS?

WELL...

YESTERDAY WAS THE FIRST TIME SOMEONE TOLD ME.

JUST YESTERDAY? SO, YOU MUST BE NEWLY AWOKEN.

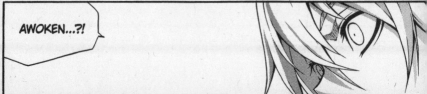

AWOKEN...?!

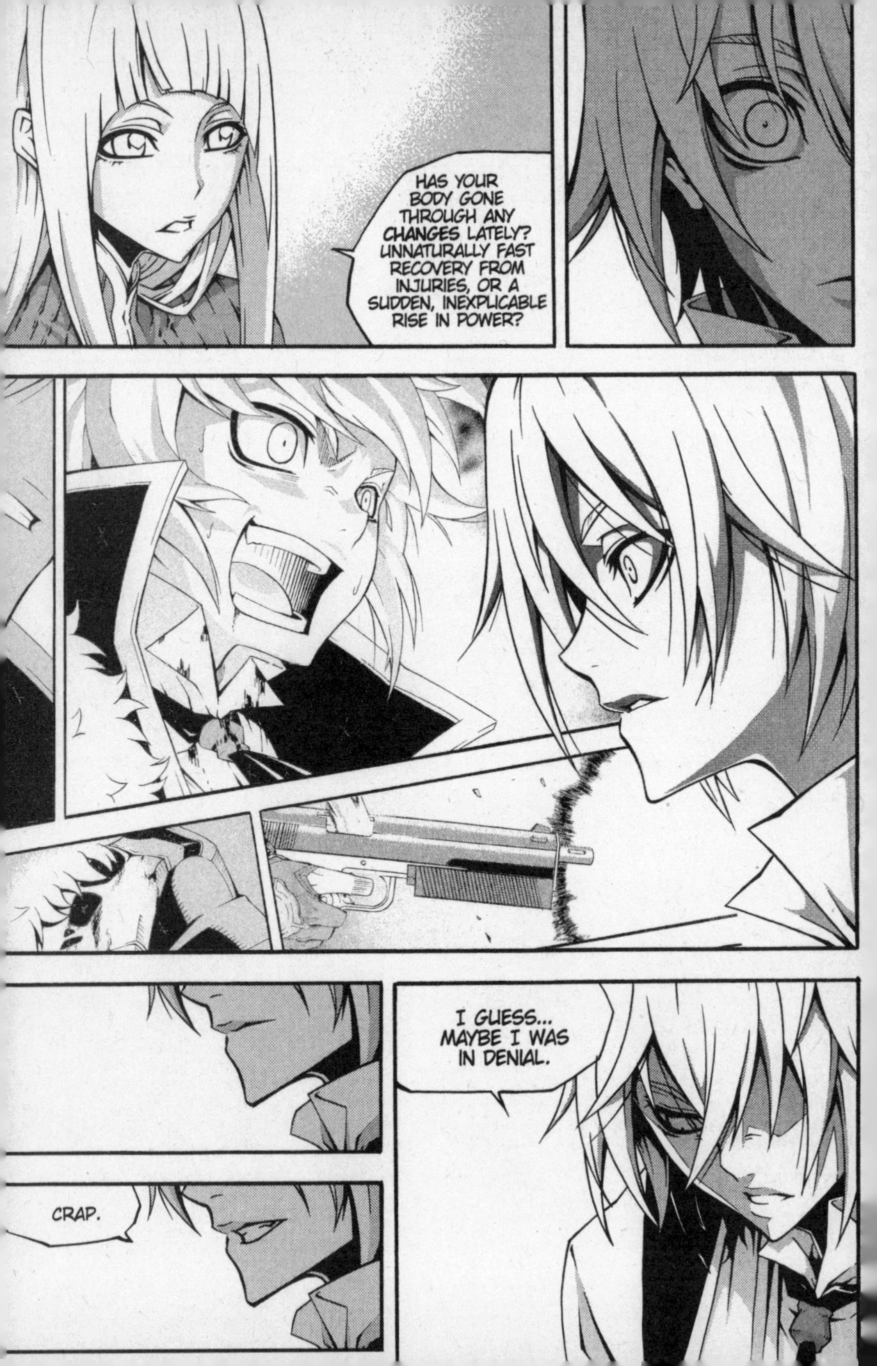
HAS YOUR BODY GONE THROUGH ANY CHANGES LATELY? UNNATURALLY FAST RECOVERY FROM INJURIES, OR A SUDDEN, INEXPLICABLE RISE IN POWER?
CRAP.
I GUESS... MAYBE I WAS IN DENIAL.

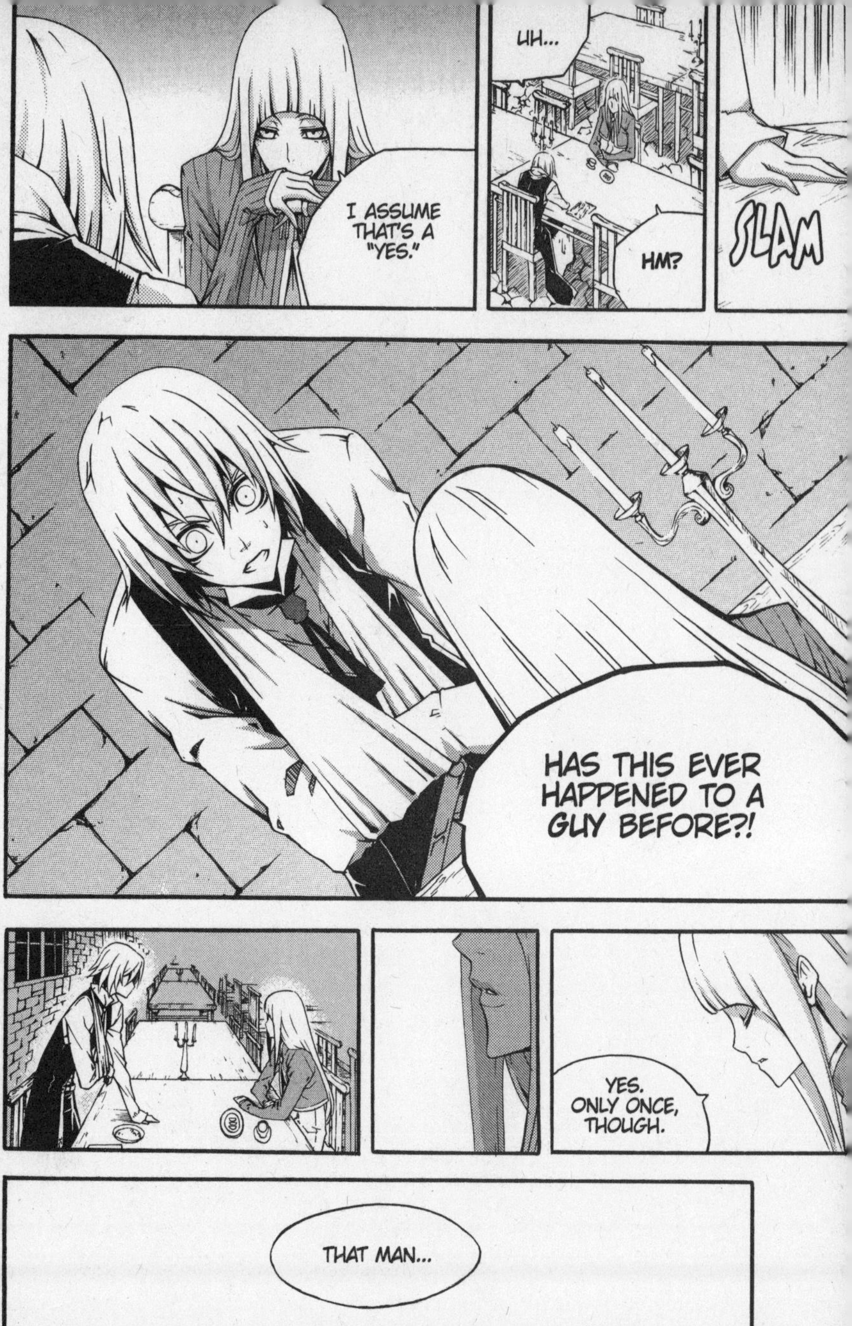
I ASSUME THAT'S A "YES."
UH...
HM?
SLAM
HAS THIS EVER HAPPENED TO A GUY BEFORE?!
YES. ONLY ONCE, THOUGH.
THAT MAN...

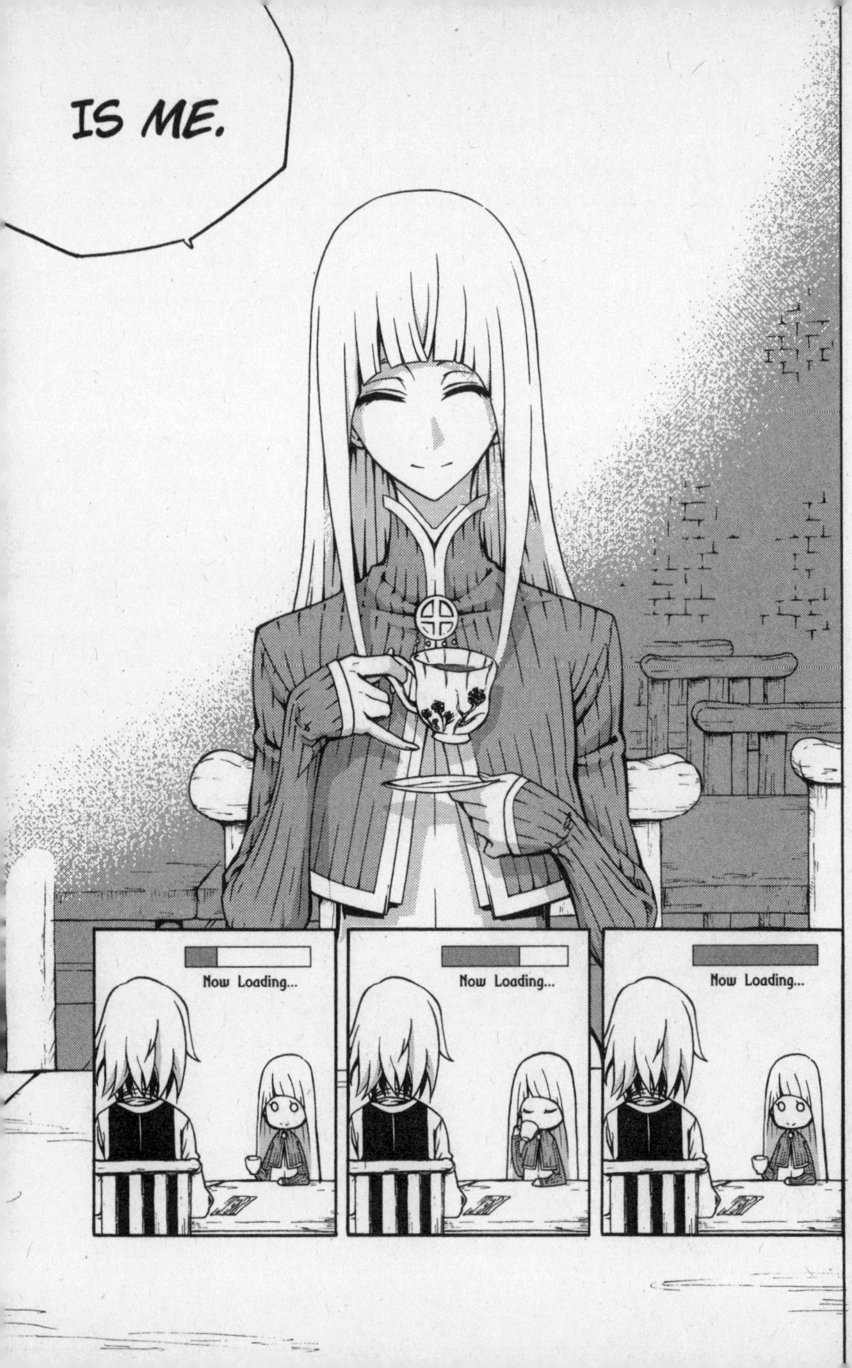

IS ME.
Now Loading...
Now Loading...
Now Loading...

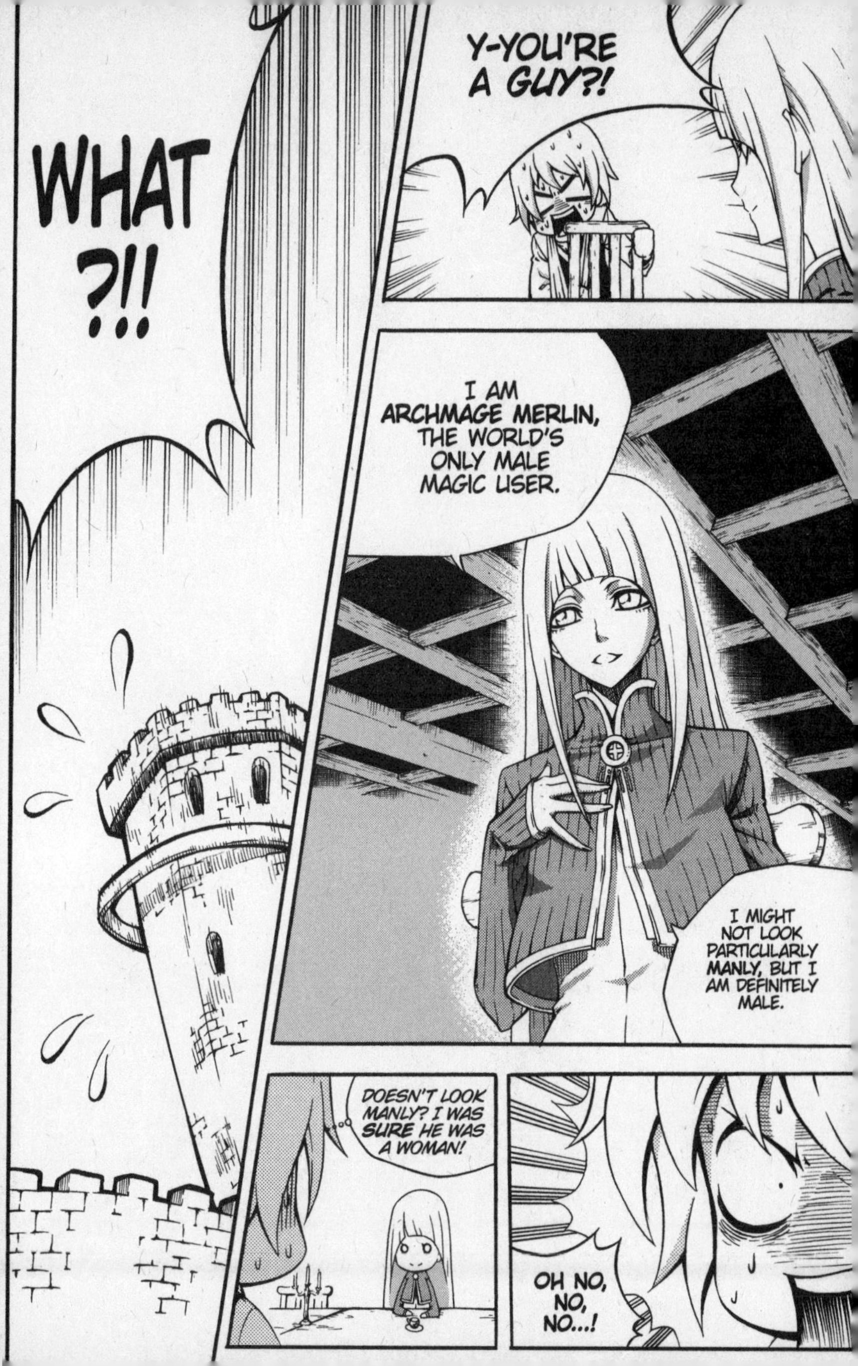

WHAT ?!!
Y-YOU'RE A GUY?!
I AM ARCHMAGE MERLIN, THE WORLD'S ONLY MALE MAGIC USER.
I MIGHT NOT LOOK PARTICULARLY MANLY, BUT I AM DEFINITELY MALE.
DOESN'T LOOK MANLY? I WAS SURE HE WAS A WOMAN!
OH NO, NO, NO...!

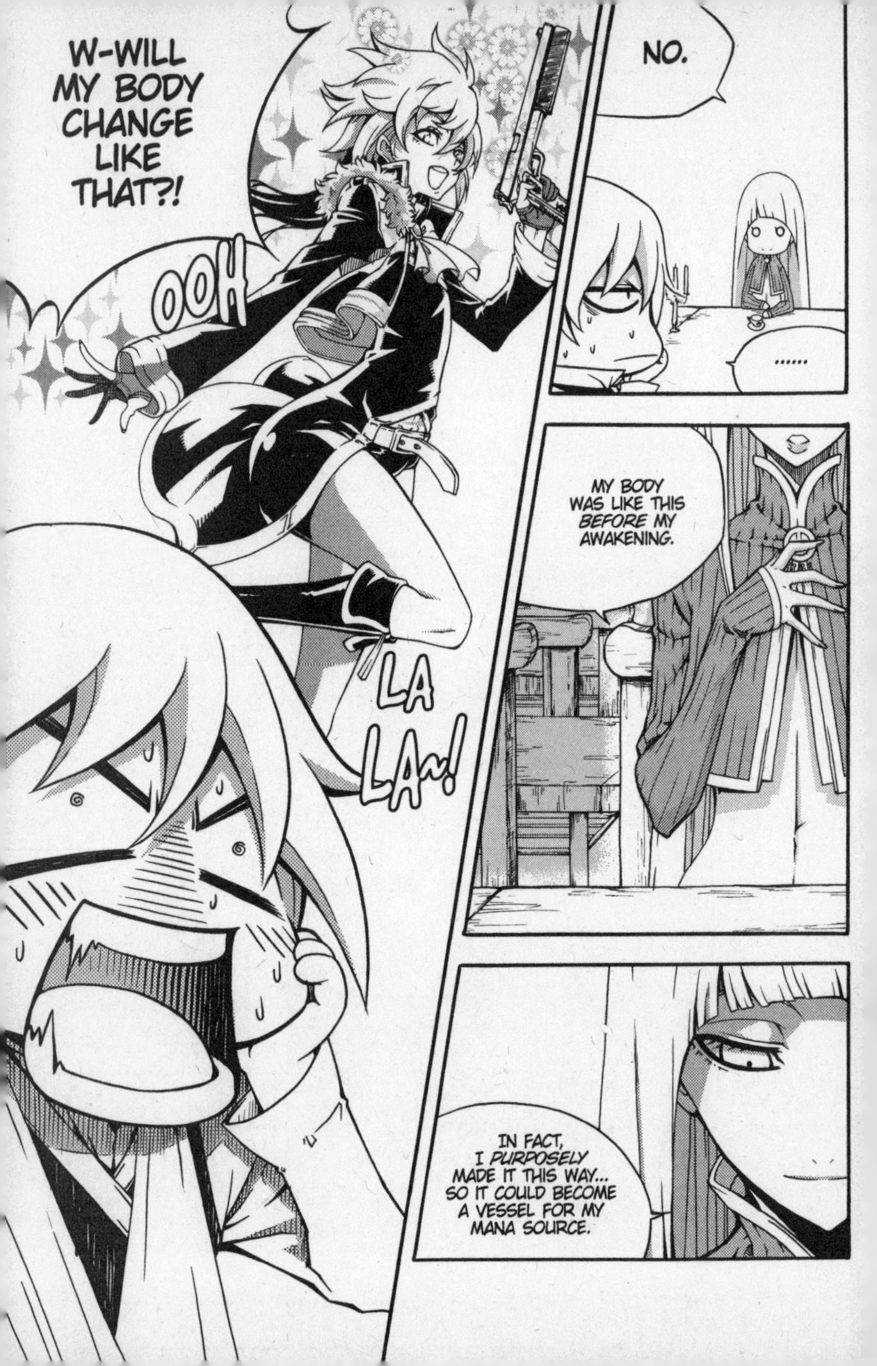

W-WILL MY BODY CHANGE LIKE THAT?!
OOH
LA LA~!
NO.
......
MY BODY WAS LIKE THIS *BEFORE* MY AWAKENING.
IN FACT, I *PURPOSELY* MADE IT THIS WAY... SO IT COULD BECOME A VESSEL FOR MY MANA SOURCE.

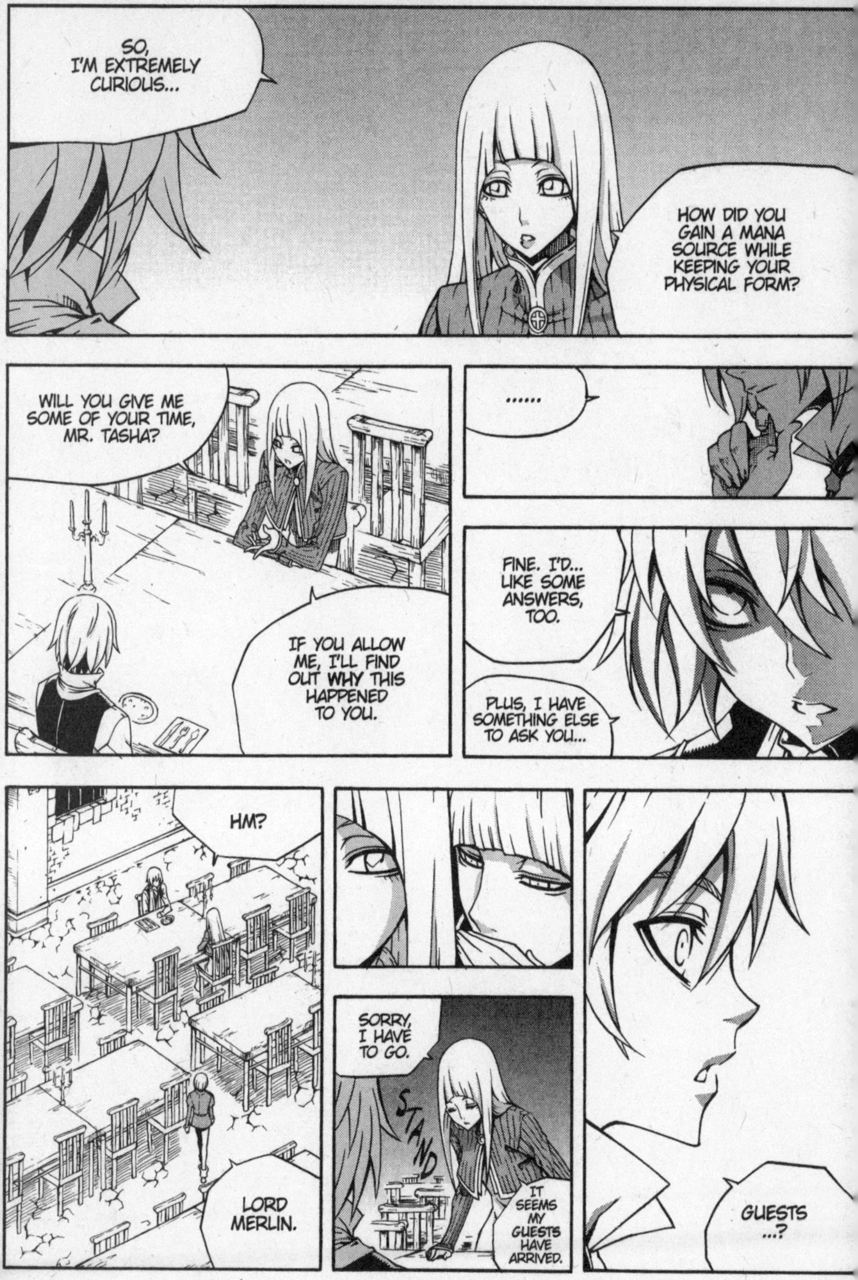
SO, I'M EXTREMELY CURIOUS...
HOW DID YOU GAIN A MANA SOURCE WHILE KEEPING YOUR PHYSICAL FORM?
WILL YOU GIVE ME SOME OF YOUR TIME, MR. TASHA?
IF YOU ALLOW ME, I'LL FIND OUT WHY THIS HAPPENED TO YOU.
......
FINE. I'D... LIKE SOME ANSWERS, TOO.
PLUS, I HAVE SOMETHING ELSE TO ASK YOU...
HM?
LORD MERLIN.
SORRY, I HAVE TO GO.
STAND
IT SEEMS MY GUESTS HAVE ARRIVED.
GUESTS ...?

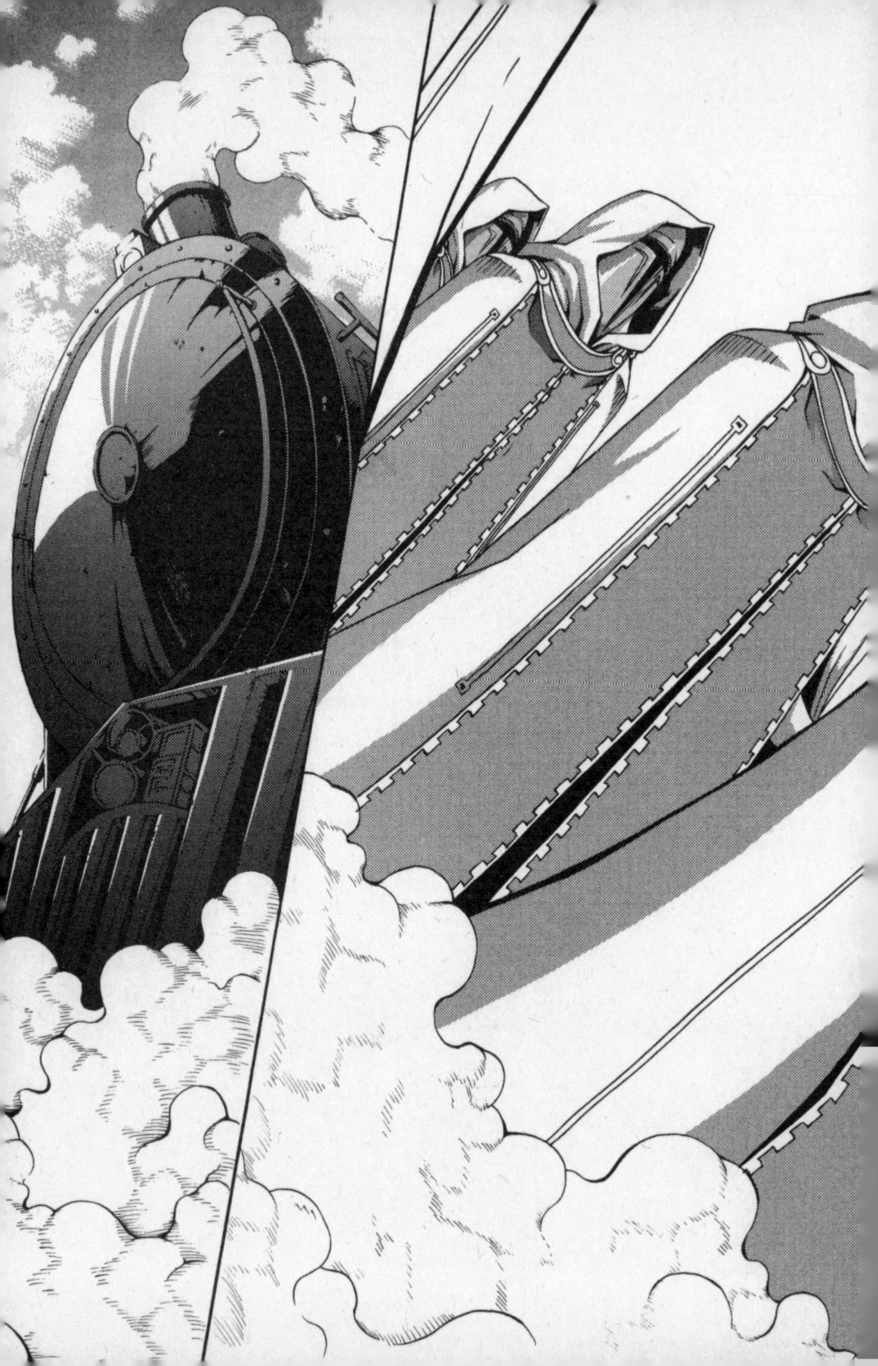

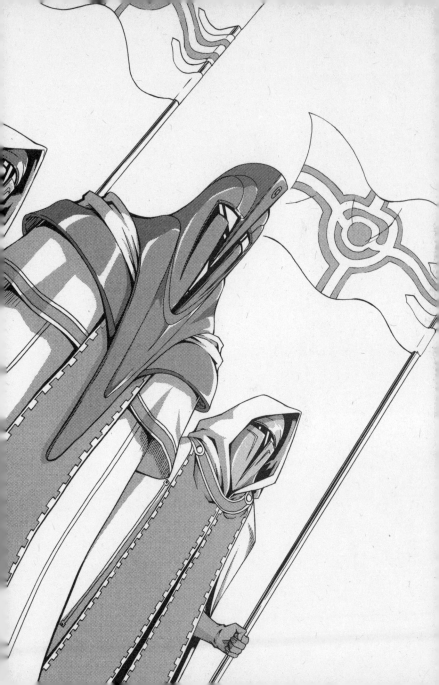

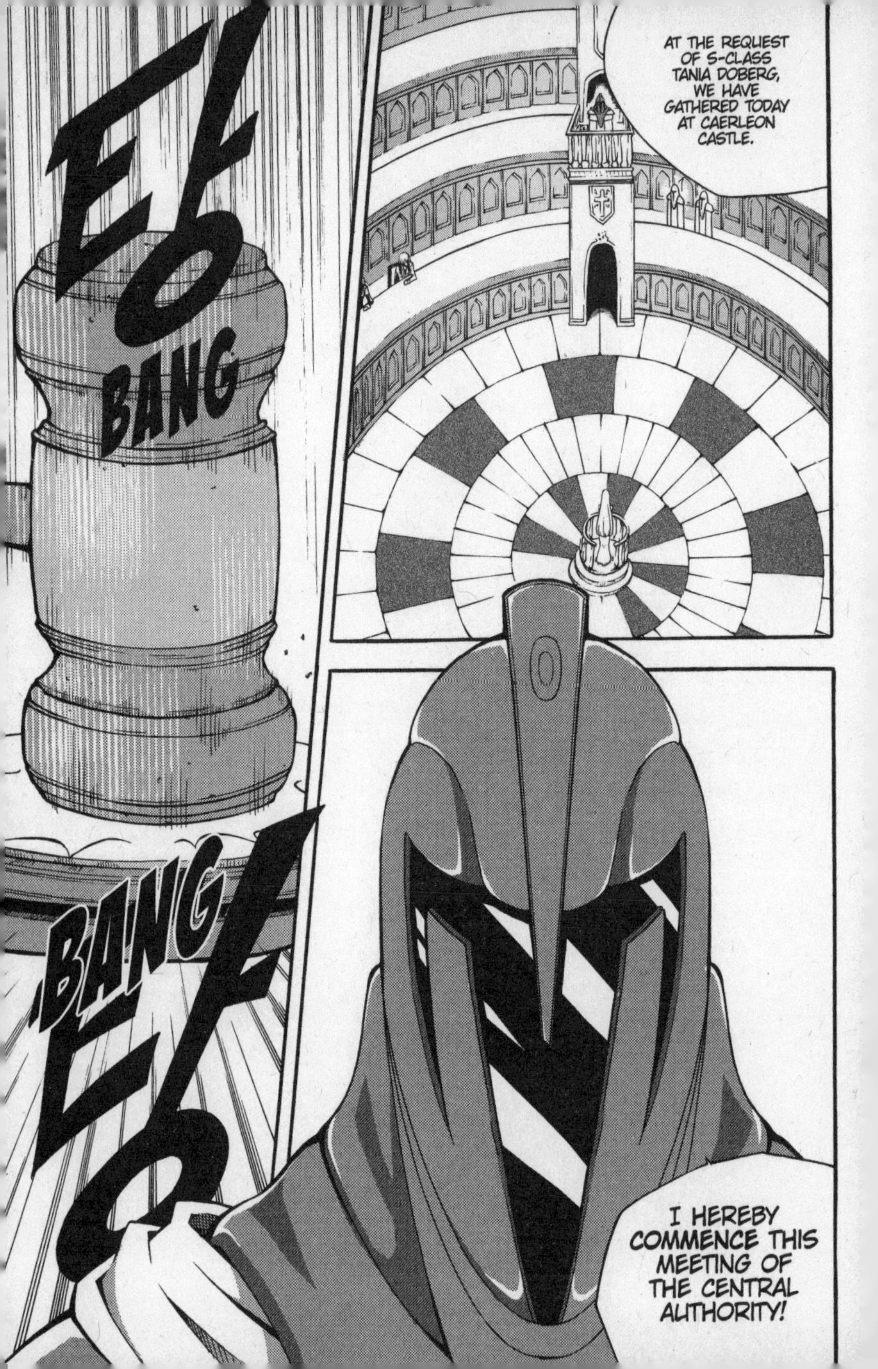
BANG
BANG!
AT THE REQUEST OF S-CLASS TANIA DOBERG, WE HAVE GATHERED TODAY AT CAERLEON CASTLE.
I HEREBY COMMENCE THIS MEETING OF THE CENTRAL AUTHORITY!

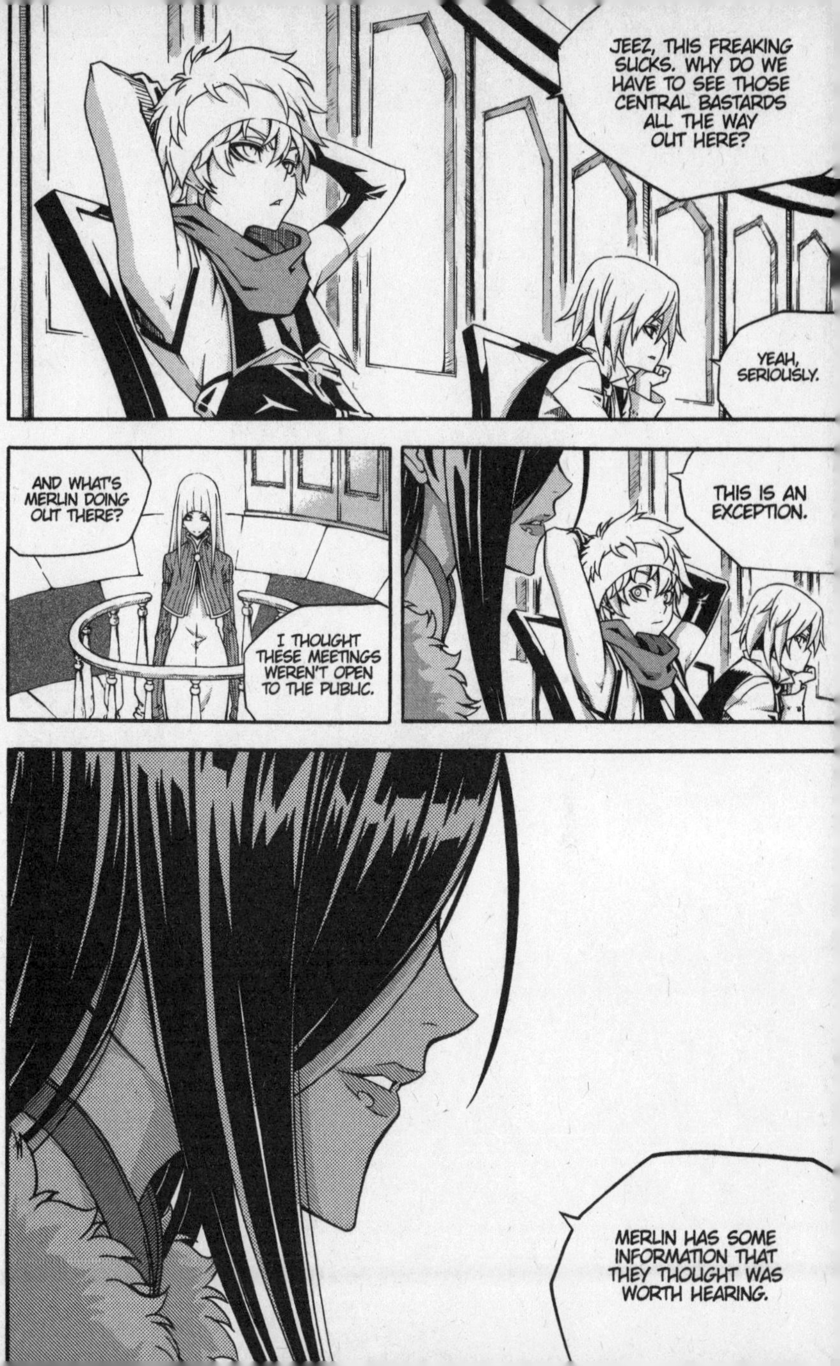
JEEZ, THIS FREAKING SUCKS. WHY DO WE HAVE TO SEE THOSE CENTRAL BASTARDS ALL THE WAY OUT HERE?
YEAH, SERIOUSLY.
AND WHAT'S MERLIN DOING OUT THERE?
I THOUGHT THESE MEETINGS WEREN'T OPEN TO THE PUBLIC.
THIS IS AN EXCEPTION.
MERLIN HAS SOME INFORMATION THAT THEY THOUGHT WAS WORTH HEARING.

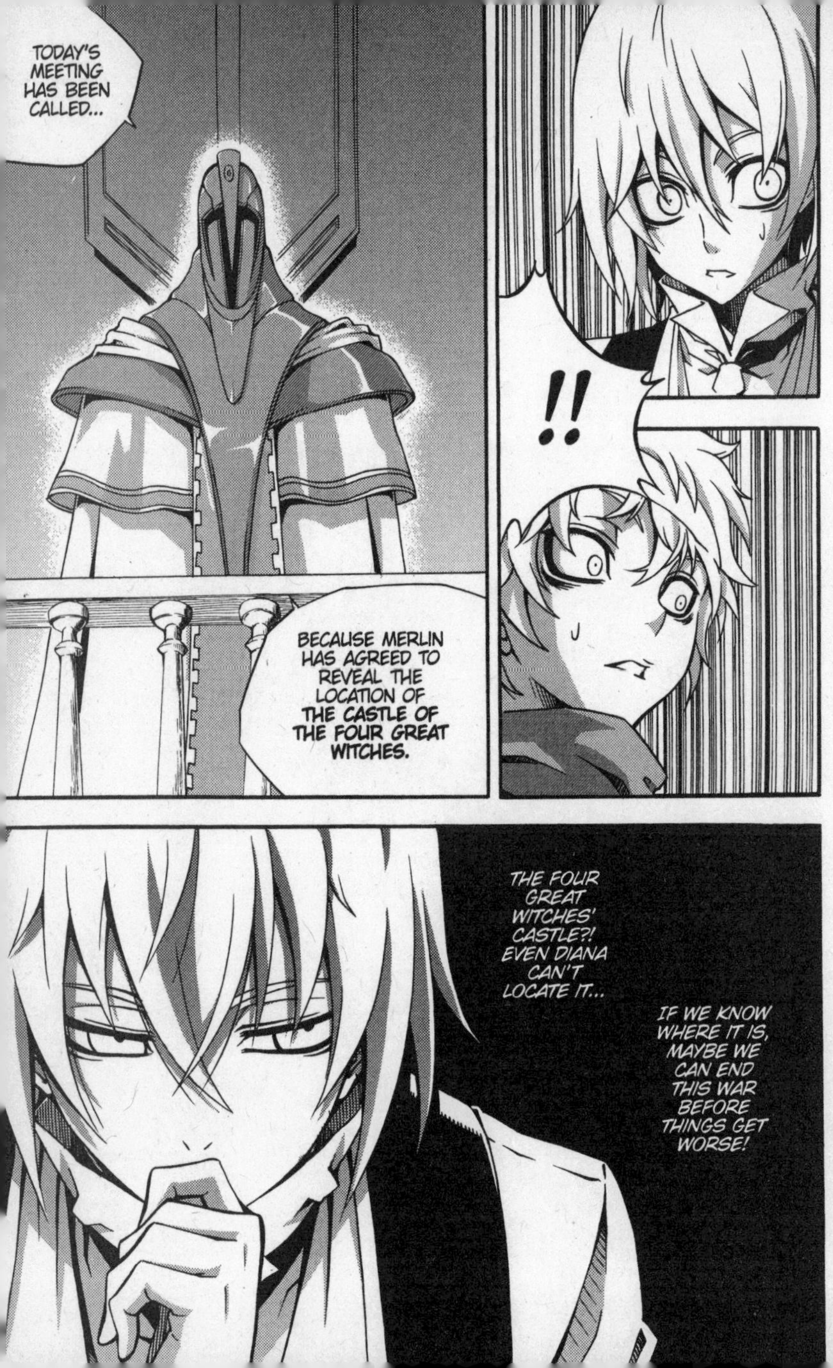
TODAY'S MEETING HAS BEEN CALLED...
!!
BECAUSE MERLIN HAS AGREED TO REVEAL THE LOCATION OF THE CASTLE OF THE FOUR GREAT WITCHES.
THE FOUR GREAT WITCHES' CASTLE?! EVEN DIANA CAN'T LOCATE IT...
IF WE KNOW WHERE IT IS, MAYBE WE CAN END THIS WAR BEFORE THINGS GET WORSE!

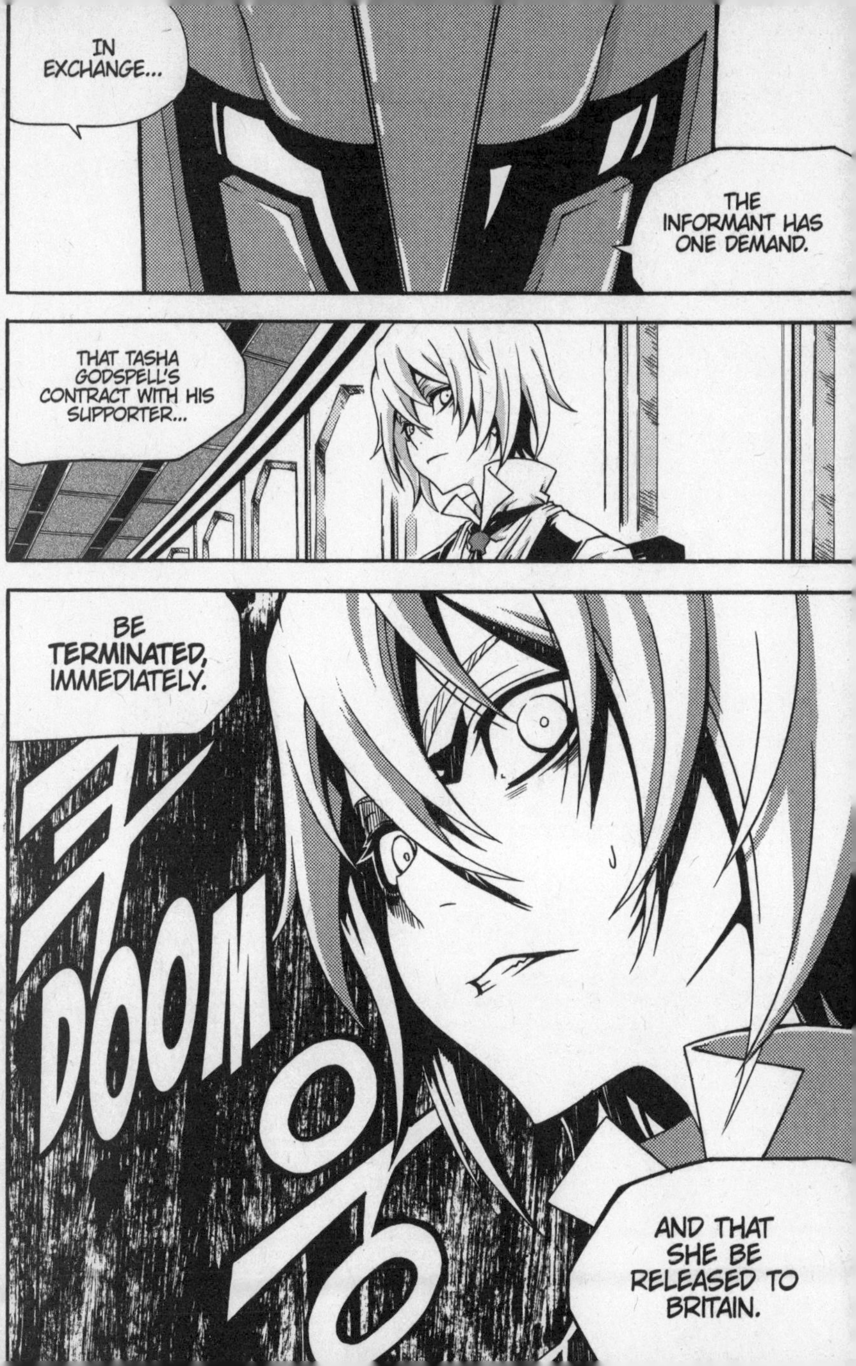
IN EXCHANGE...
THE INFORMANT HAS ONE DEMAND.
THAT TASHA GODSPELL'S CONTRACT WITH HIS SUPPORTER...
BE TERMINATED, IMMEDIATELY.
DOOM
AND THAT SHE BE RELEASED TO BRITAIN.

REACTIONS TO
THE NEW CHARACTER

I AM ARCHMAGE MERLIN, THE WORLD'S ONLY MALE MAGIC USER.

51. Termination of Contract

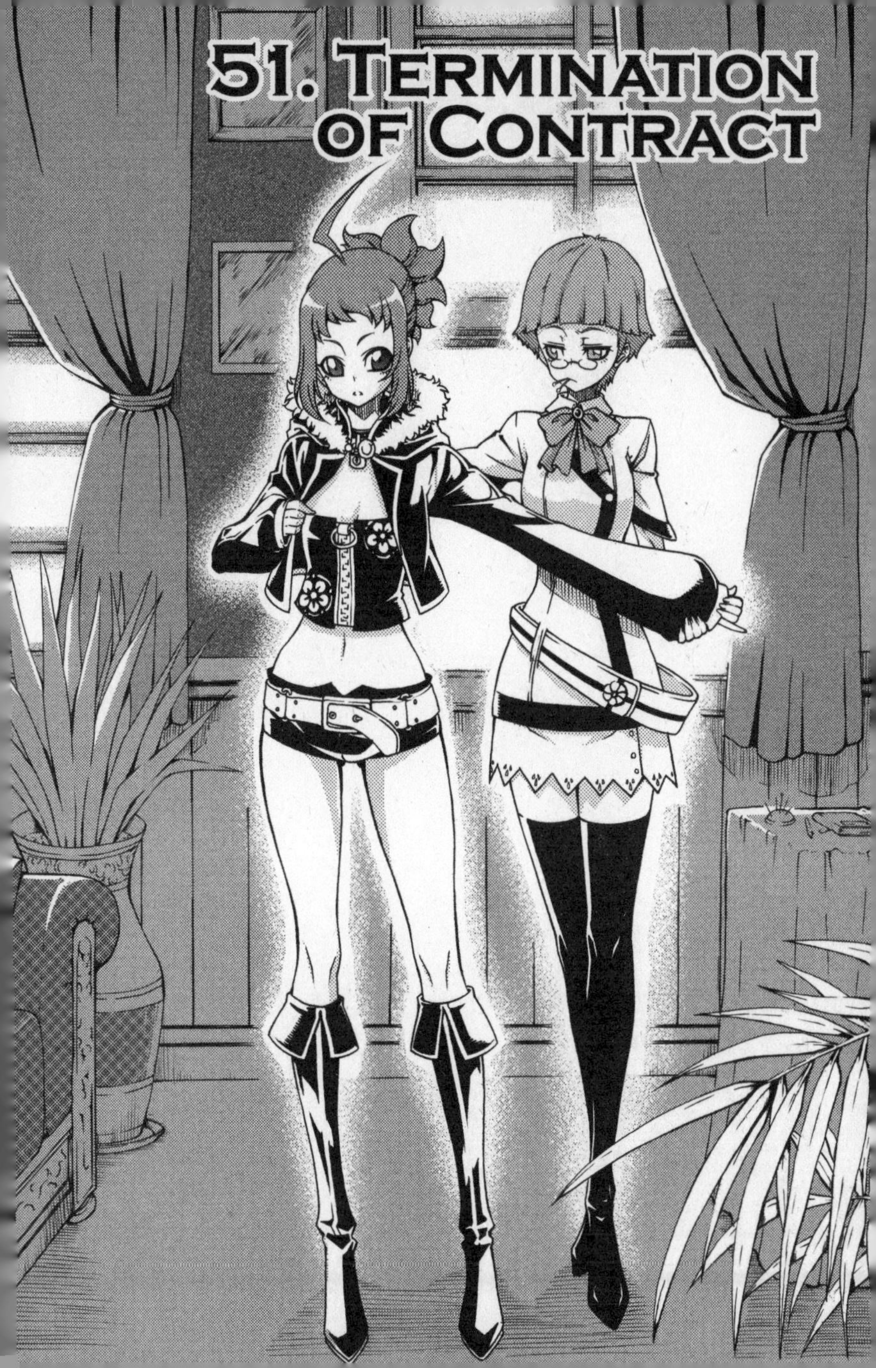

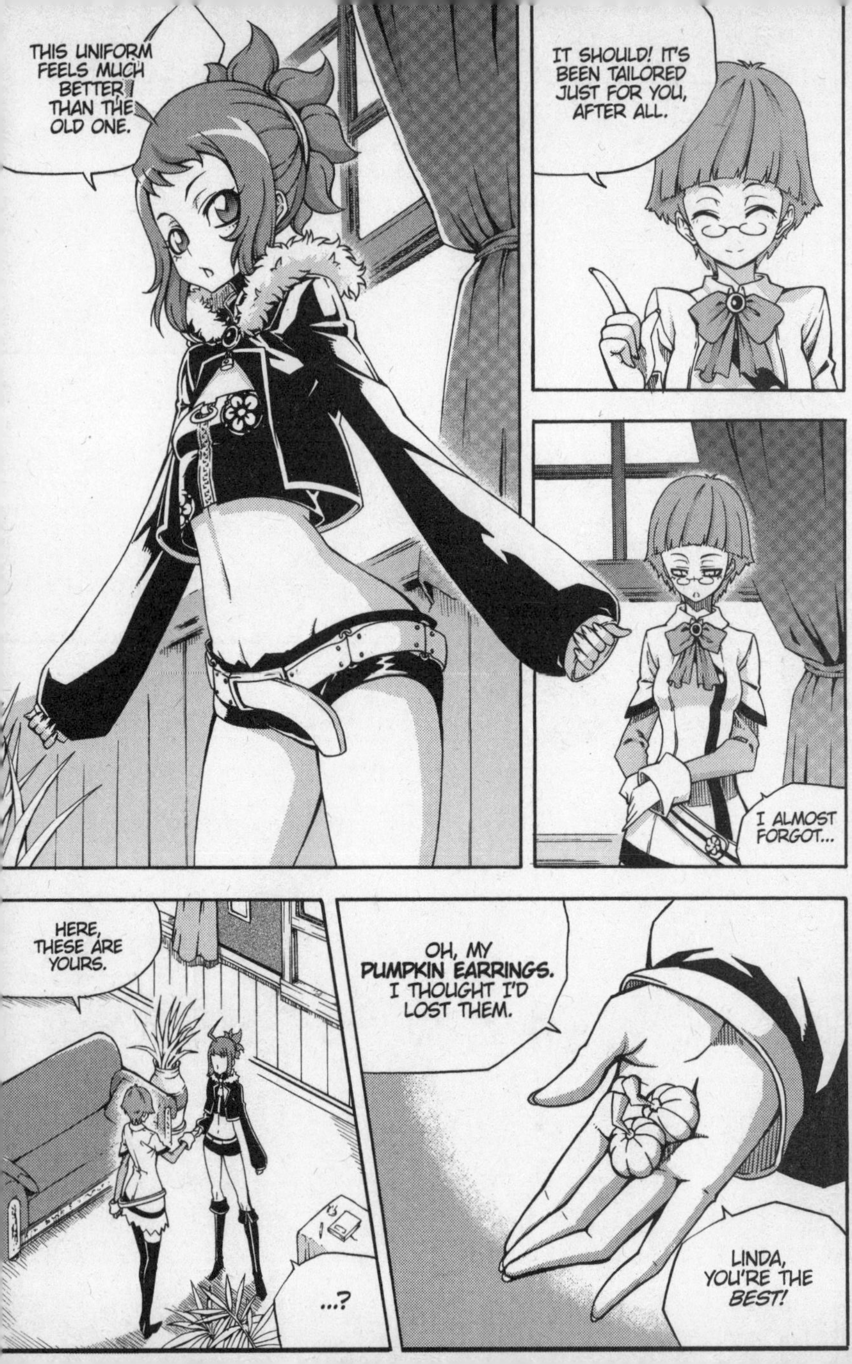
THIS UNIFORM FEELS MUCH BETTER THAN THE OLD ONE.
IT SHOULD! IT'S BEEN TAILORED JUST FOR YOU, AFTER ALL.
I ALMOST FORGOT...
HERE, THESE ARE YOURS.
...?
OH, MY PUMPKIN EARRINGS. I THOUGHT I'D LOST THEM.
LINDA, YOU'RE THE BEST!

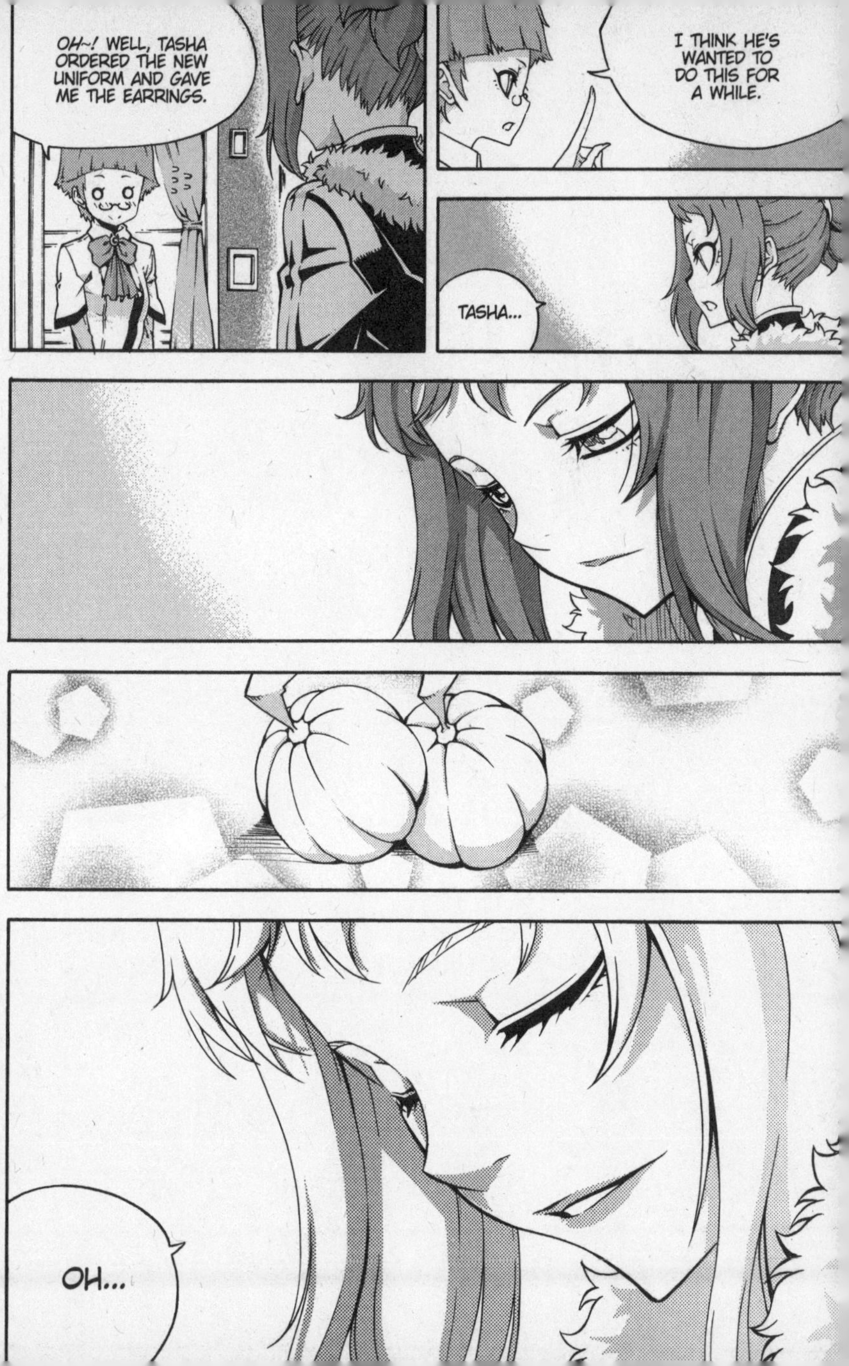
OH~! WELL, TASHA ORDERED THE NEW UNIFORM AND GAVE ME THE EARRINGS.
I THINK HE'S WANTED TO DO THIS FOR A WHILE.
TASHA...
OH...

OH, TASHA...
SLAM
NO! WHAT ARE YOU TRYING TO *PULL*?!
YOU THINK YOU CAN JUST *GIVE* HALLOWEEN AWAY?!

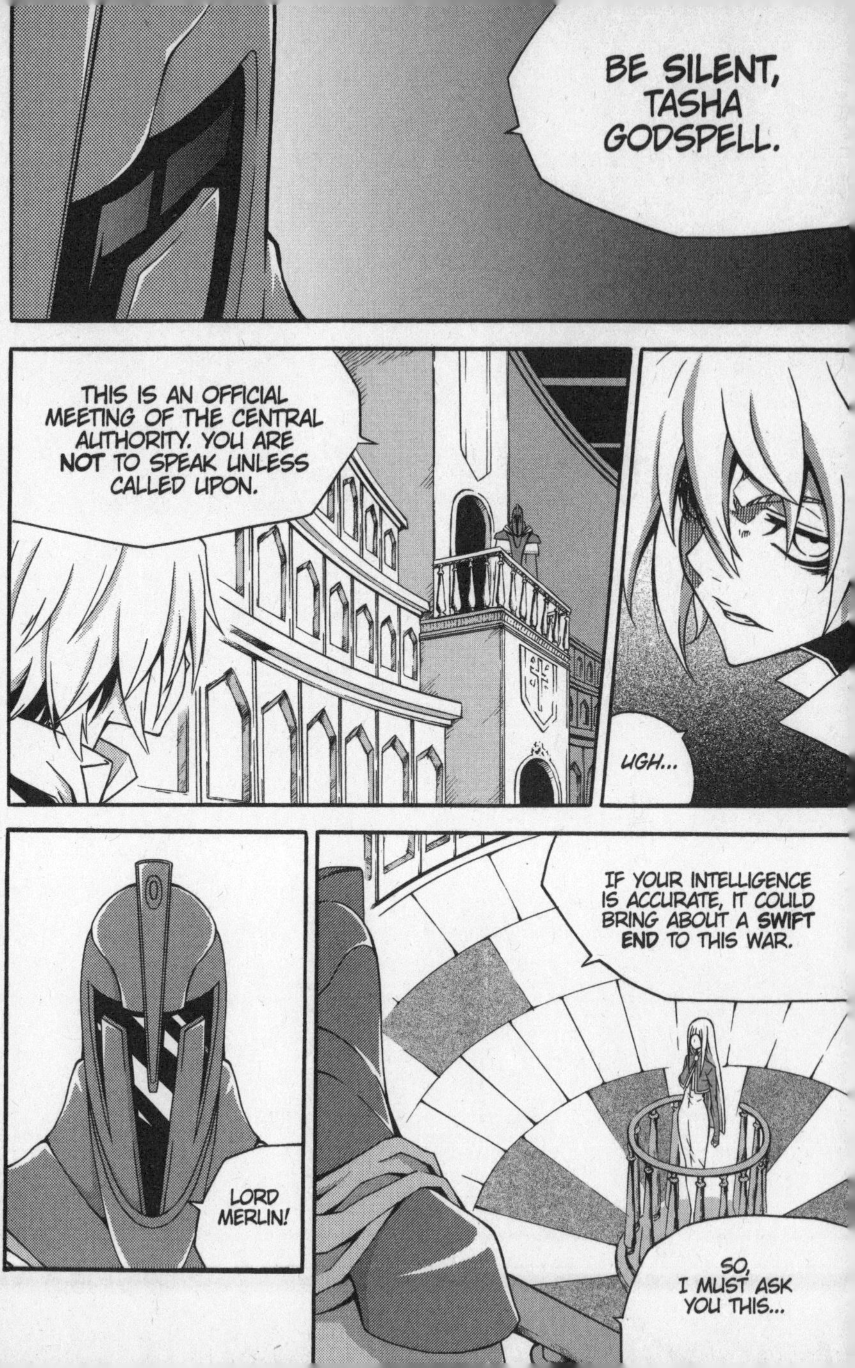
BE SILENT, TASHA GODSPELL.
THIS IS AN OFFICIAL MEETING OF THE CENTRAL AUTHORITY. YOU ARE NOT TO SPEAK UNLESS CALLED UPON.
UGH...
LORD MERLIN!
IF YOUR INTELLIGENCE IS ACCURATE, IT COULD BRING ABOUT A SWIFT END TO THIS WAR.
SO, I MUST ASK YOU THIS...

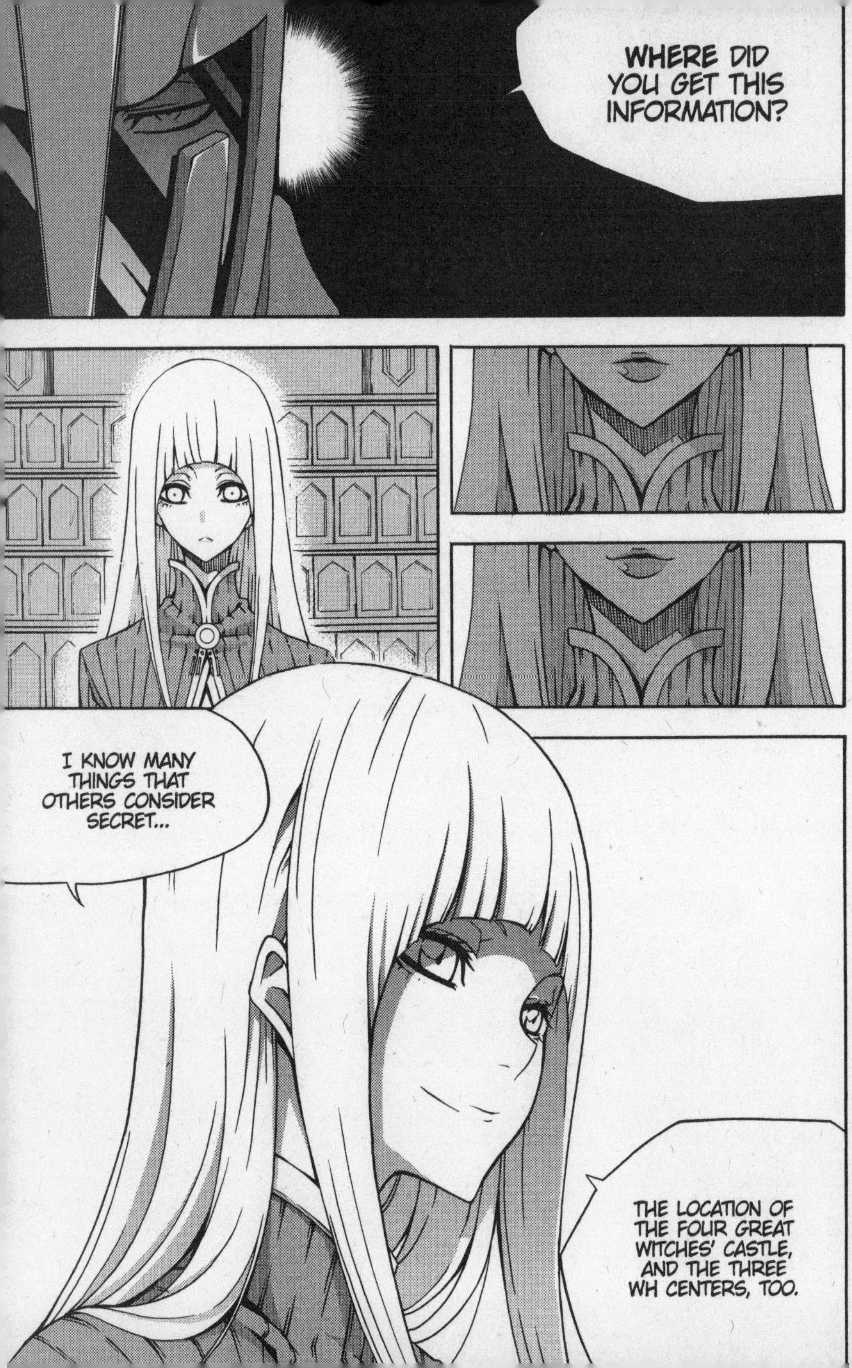
WHERE DID YOU GET THIS INFORMATION?
I KNOW MANY THINGS THAT OTHERS CONSIDER SECRET...
THE LOCATION OF THE FOUR GREAT WITCHES' CASTLE, AND THE THREE WH CENTERS, TOO.

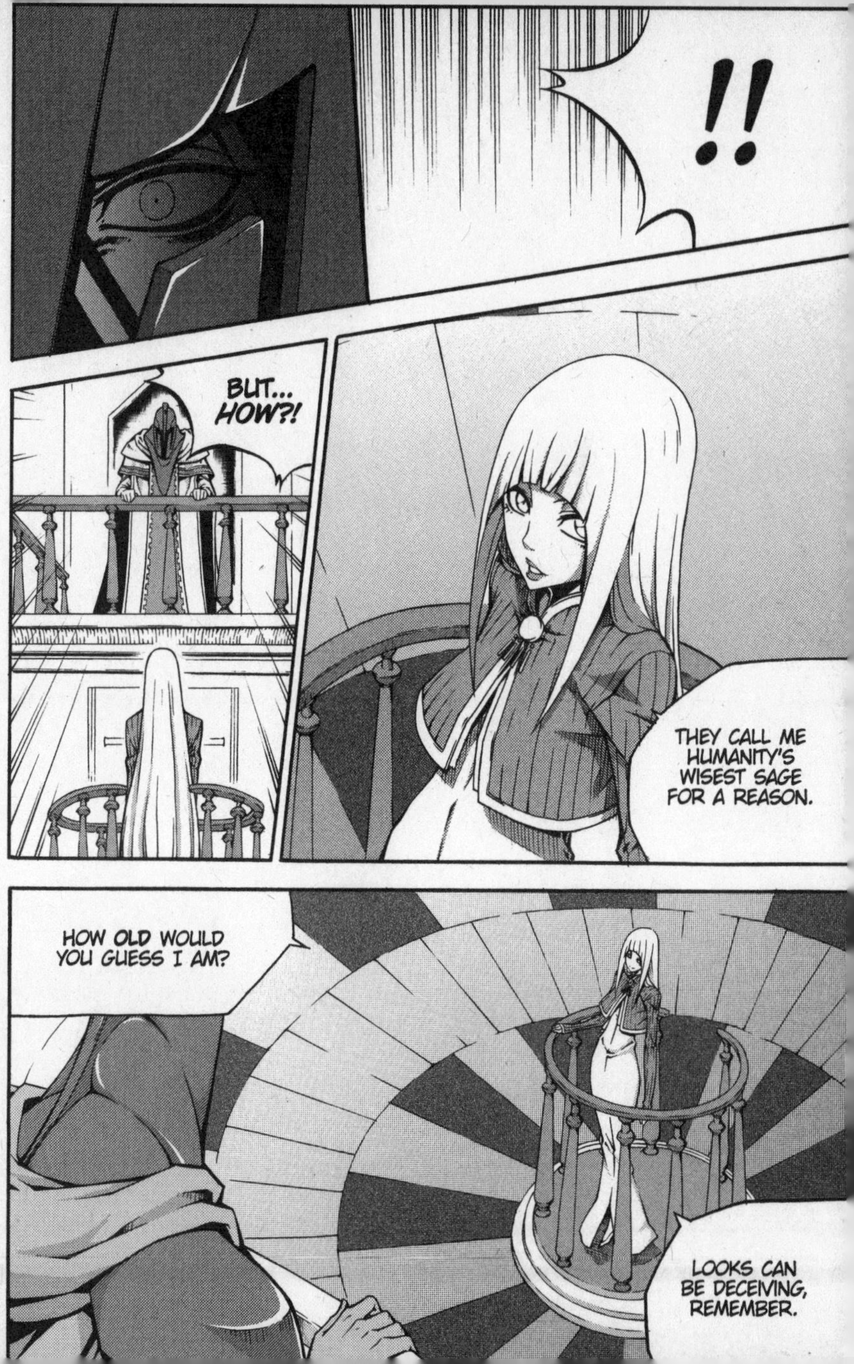
!!
BUT... HOW?!
THEY CALL ME HUMANITY'S WISEST SAGE FOR A REASON.
HOW OLD WOULD YOU GUESS I AM?
LOOKS CAN BE DECEIVING, REMEMBER.

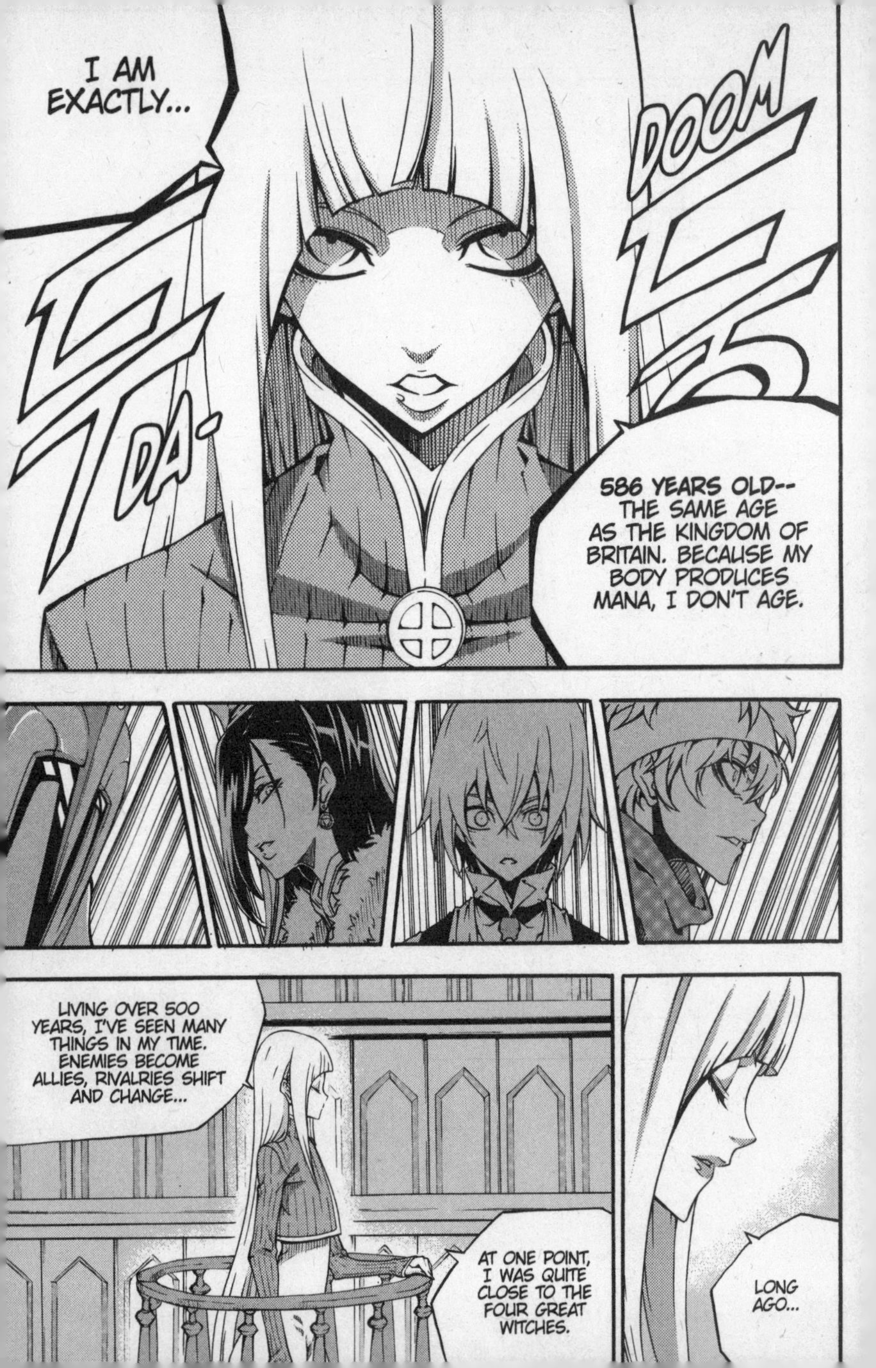
I AM EXACTLY...
DA-
DOOM
586 YEARS OLD-- THE SAME AGE AS THE KINGDOM OF BRITAIN. BECAUSE MY BODY PRODUCES MANA, I DON'T AGE.
LIVING OVER 500 YEARS, I'VE SEEN MANY THINGS IN MY TIME. ENEMIES BECOME ALLIES, RIVALRIES SHIFT AND CHANGE...
AT ONE POINT, I WAS QUITE CLOSE TO THE FOUR GREAT WITCHES.
LONG AGO...

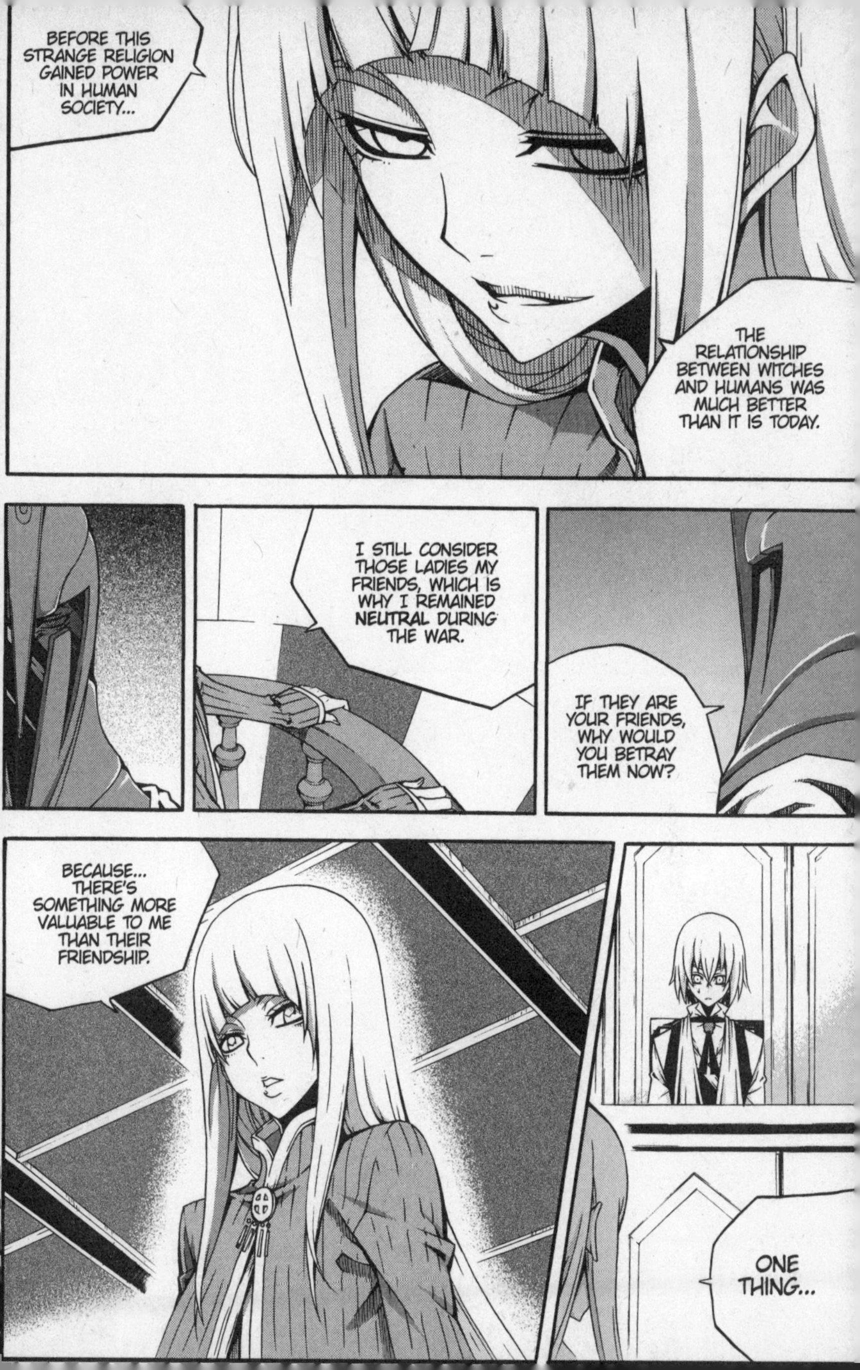
BEFORE THIS STRANGE RELIGION GAINED POWER IN HUMAN SOCIETY...
THE RELATIONSHIP BETWEEN WITCHES AND HUMANS WAS MUCH BETTER THAN IT IS TODAY.
I STILL CONSIDER THOSE LADIES MY FRIENDS, WHICH IS WHY I REMAINED NEUTRAL DURING THE WAR.
IF THEY ARE YOUR FRIENDS, WHY WOULD YOU BETRAY THEM NOW?
BECAUSE... THERE'S SOMETHING MORE VALUABLE TO ME THAN THEIR FRIENDSHIP.
ONE THING...

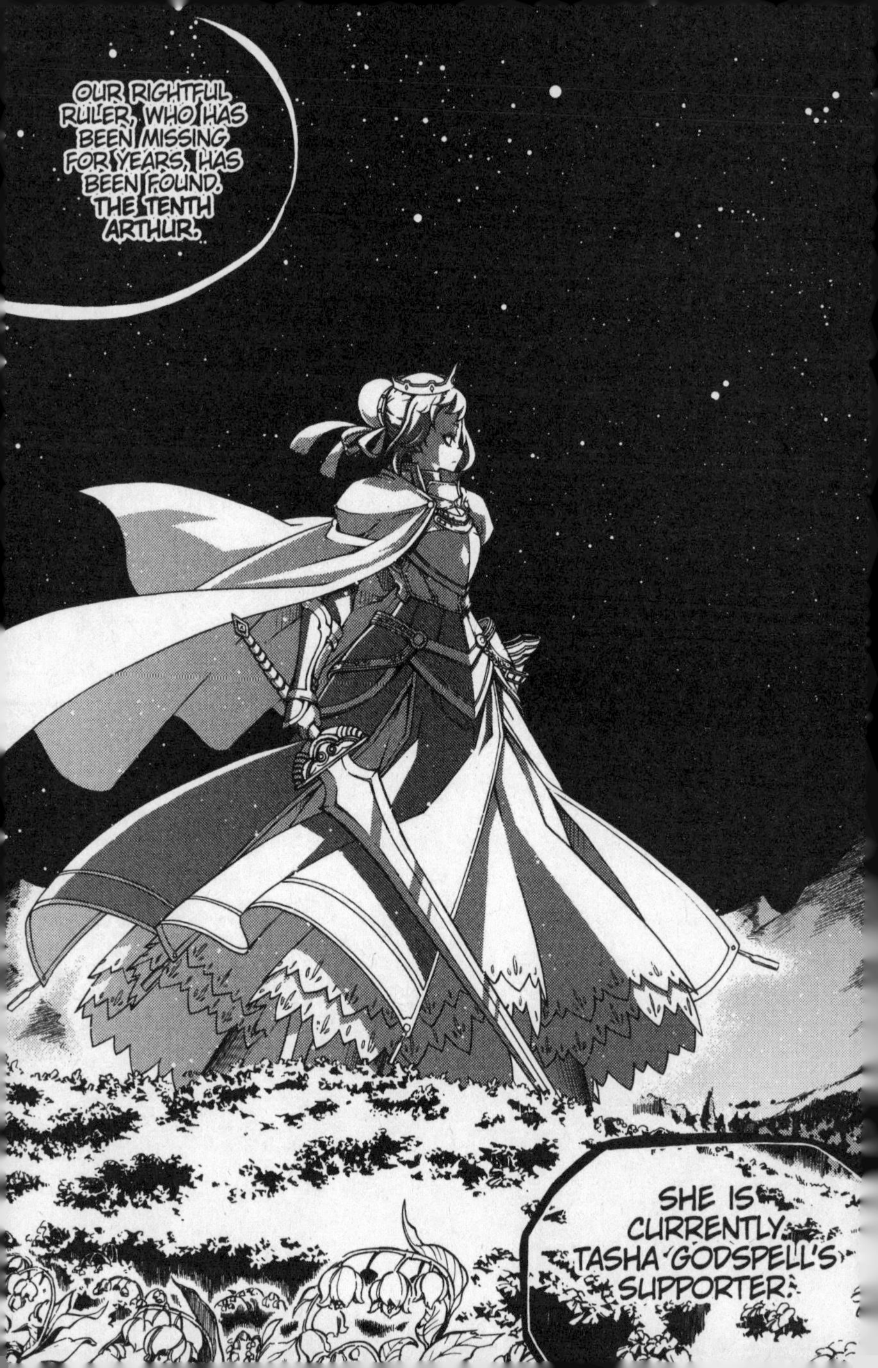
OUR RIGHTFUL RULER, WHO HAS BEEN MISSING FOR YEARS, HAS BEEN FOUND. THE TENTH ARTHUR.
SHE IS CURRENTLY TASHA GODSPELL'S SUPPORTER.

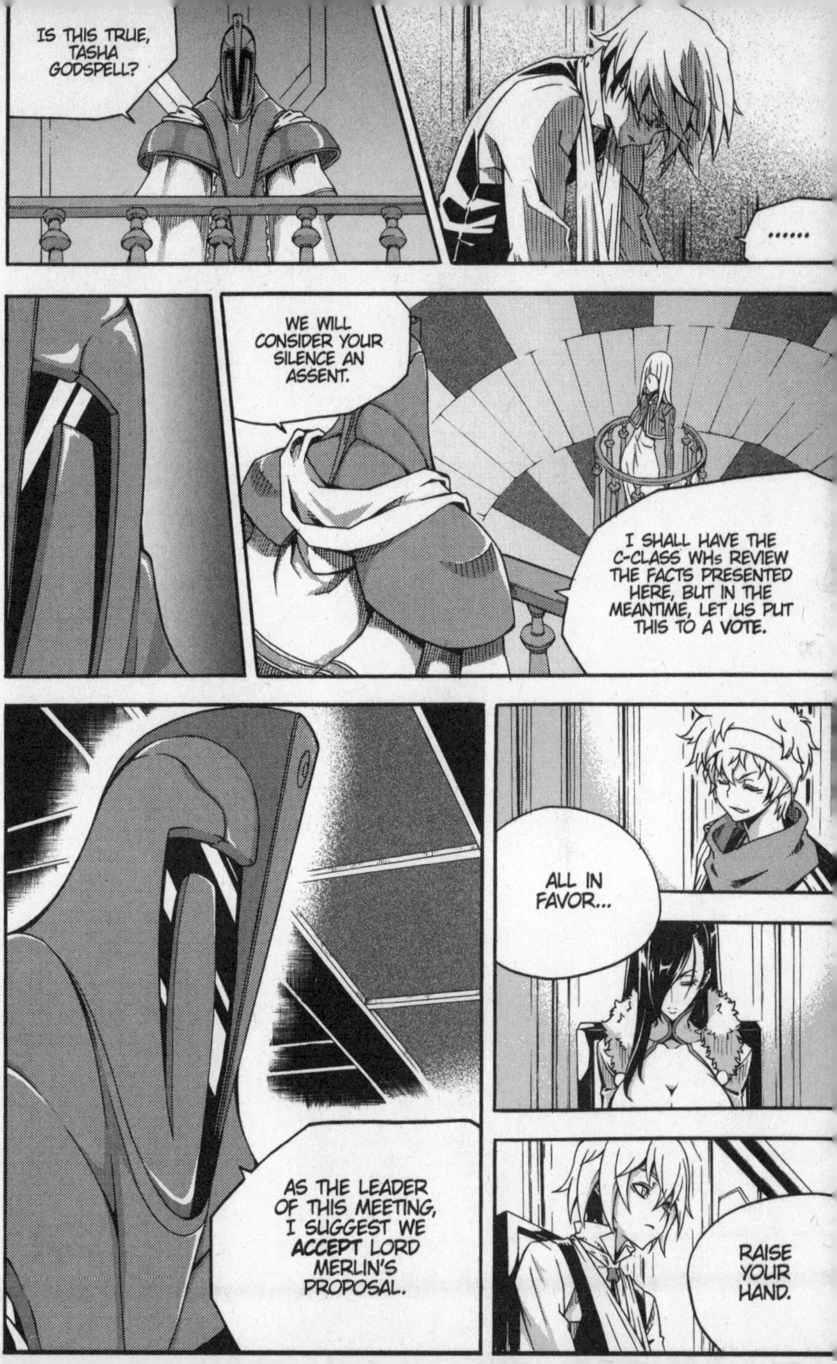
IS THIS TRUE, TASHA GODSPELL?
......
WE WILL CONSIDER YOUR SILENCE AN ASSENT.
I SHALL HAVE THE C-CLASS WHs REVIEW THE FACTS PRESENTED HERE, BUT IN THE MEANTIME, LET US PUT THIS TO A VOTE.
AS THE LEADER OF THIS MEETING, I SUGGEST WE ACCEPT LORD MERLIN'S PROPOSAL.
ALL IN FAVOR...
RAISE YOUR HAND.

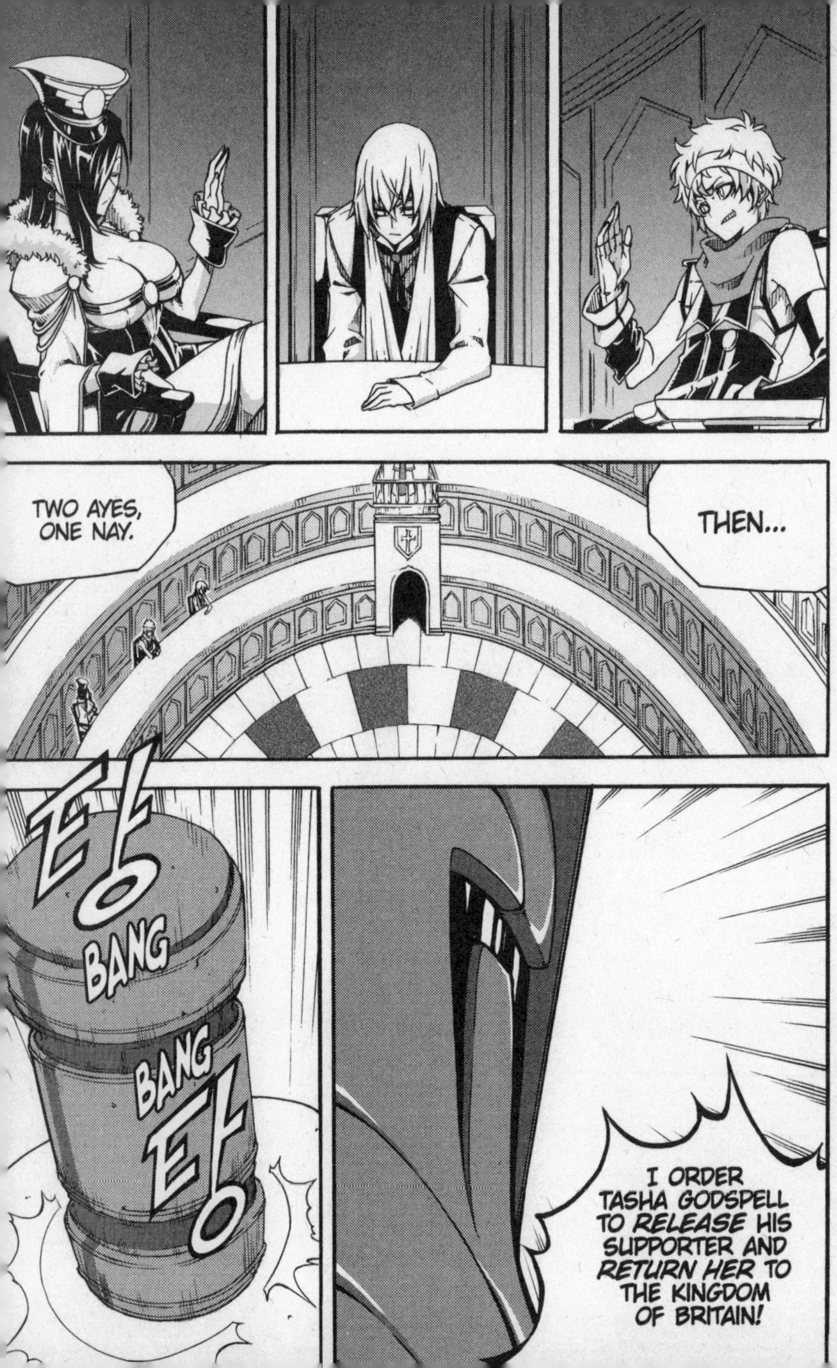
TWO AYES, ONE NAY.
THEN...
BANG
BANG
I ORDER TASHA GODSPELL TO *RELEASE* HIS SUPPORTER AND *RETURN HER* TO THE KINGDOM OF BRITAIN!

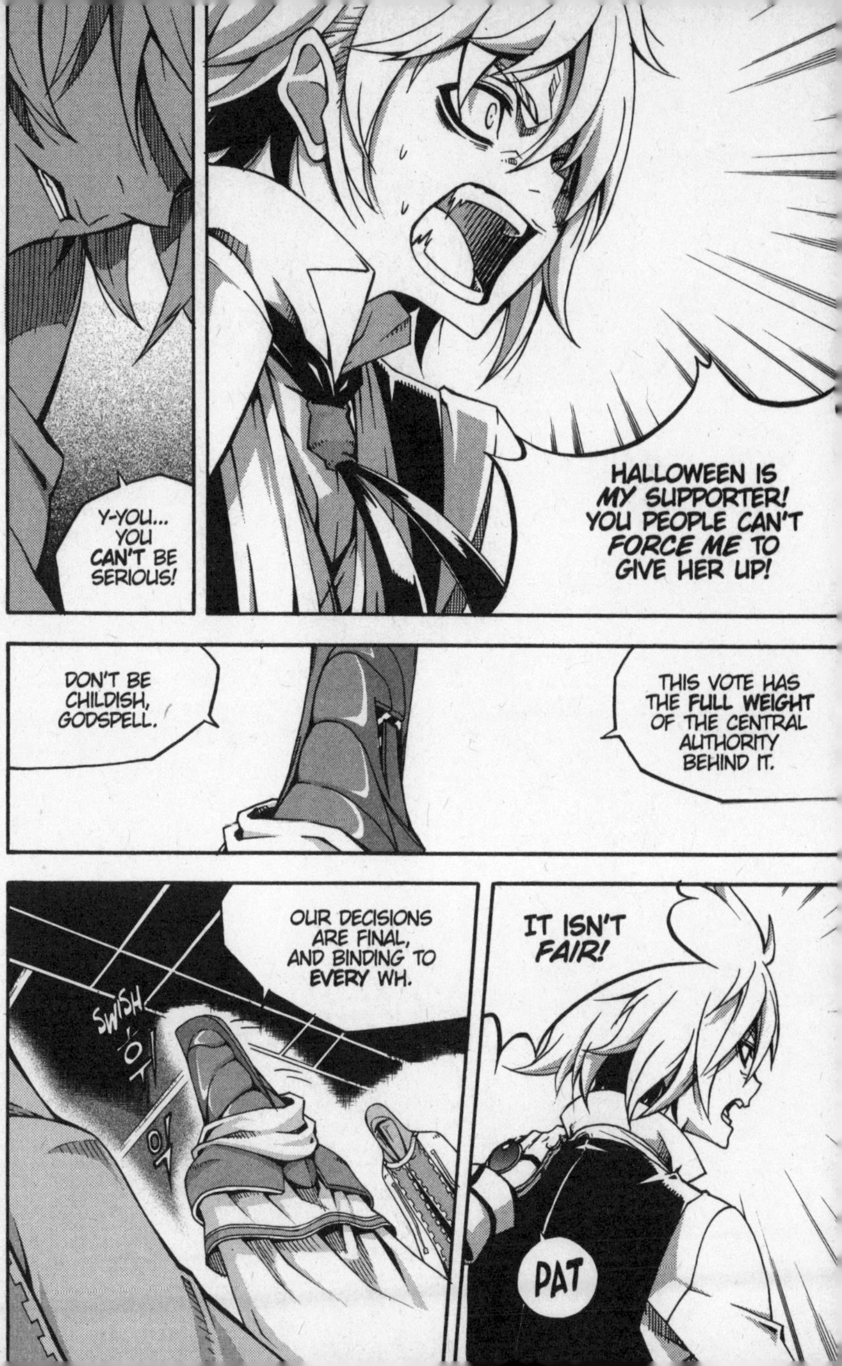
Y-YOU... YOU CAN'T BE SERIOUS!
HALLOWEEN IS *MY* SUPPORTER! YOU PEOPLE CAN'T *FORCE ME* TO GIVE HER UP!
DON'T BE CHILDISH, GODSPELL.
THIS VOTE HAS THE FULL WEIGHT OF THE CENTRAL AUTHORITY BEHIND IT.
SWISH
OUR DECISIONS ARE FINAL, AND BINDING TO EVERY WH.
IT ISN'T *FAIR*!
PAT

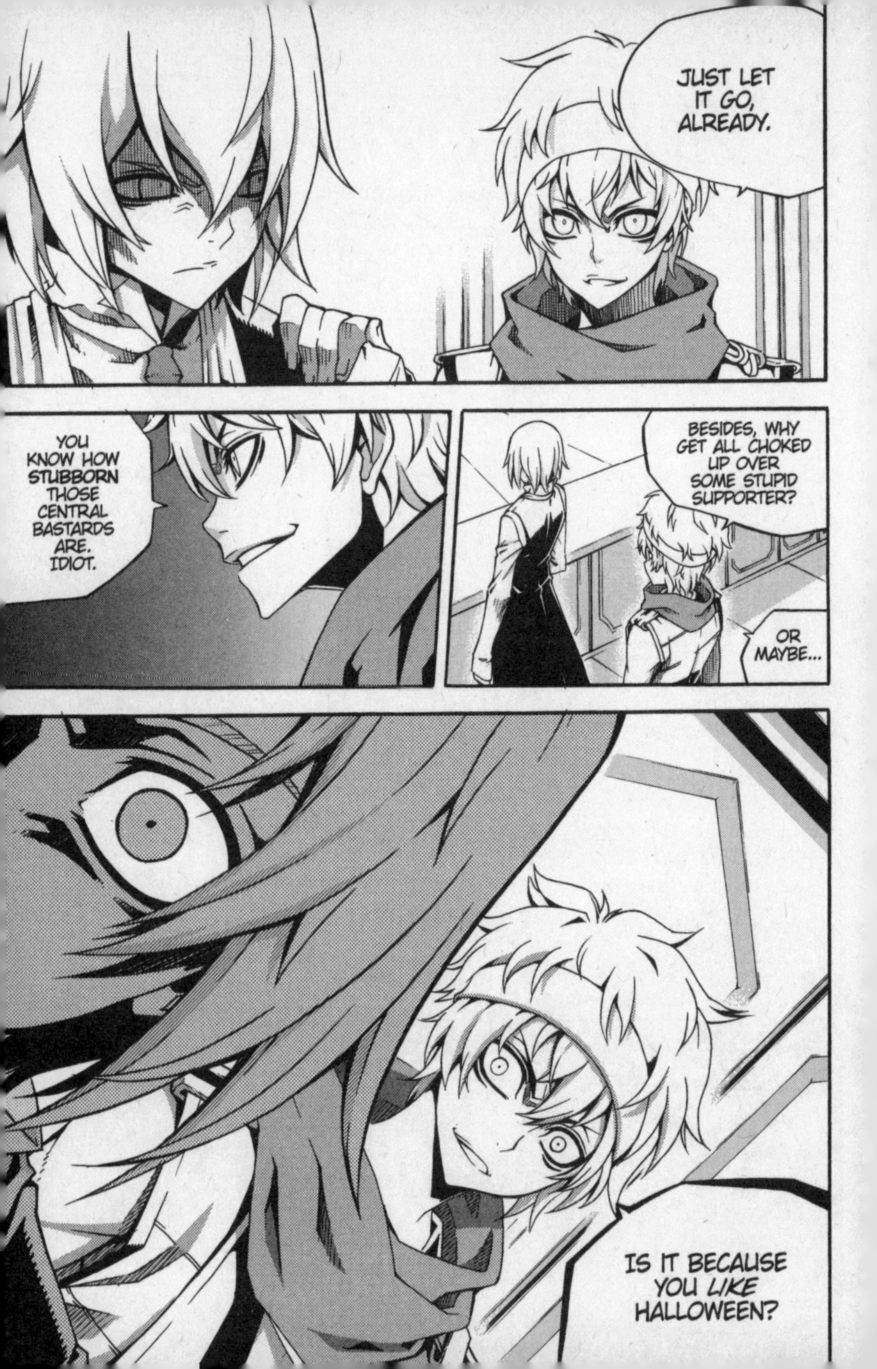
JUST LET IT GO, ALREADY.
YOU KNOW HOW STUBBORN THOSE CENTRAL BASTARDS ARE. IDIOT.
BESIDES, WHY GET ALL CHOKED UP OVER SOME STUPID SUPPORTER?
OR MAYBE...
IS IT BECAUSE YOU *LIKE* HALLOWEEN?

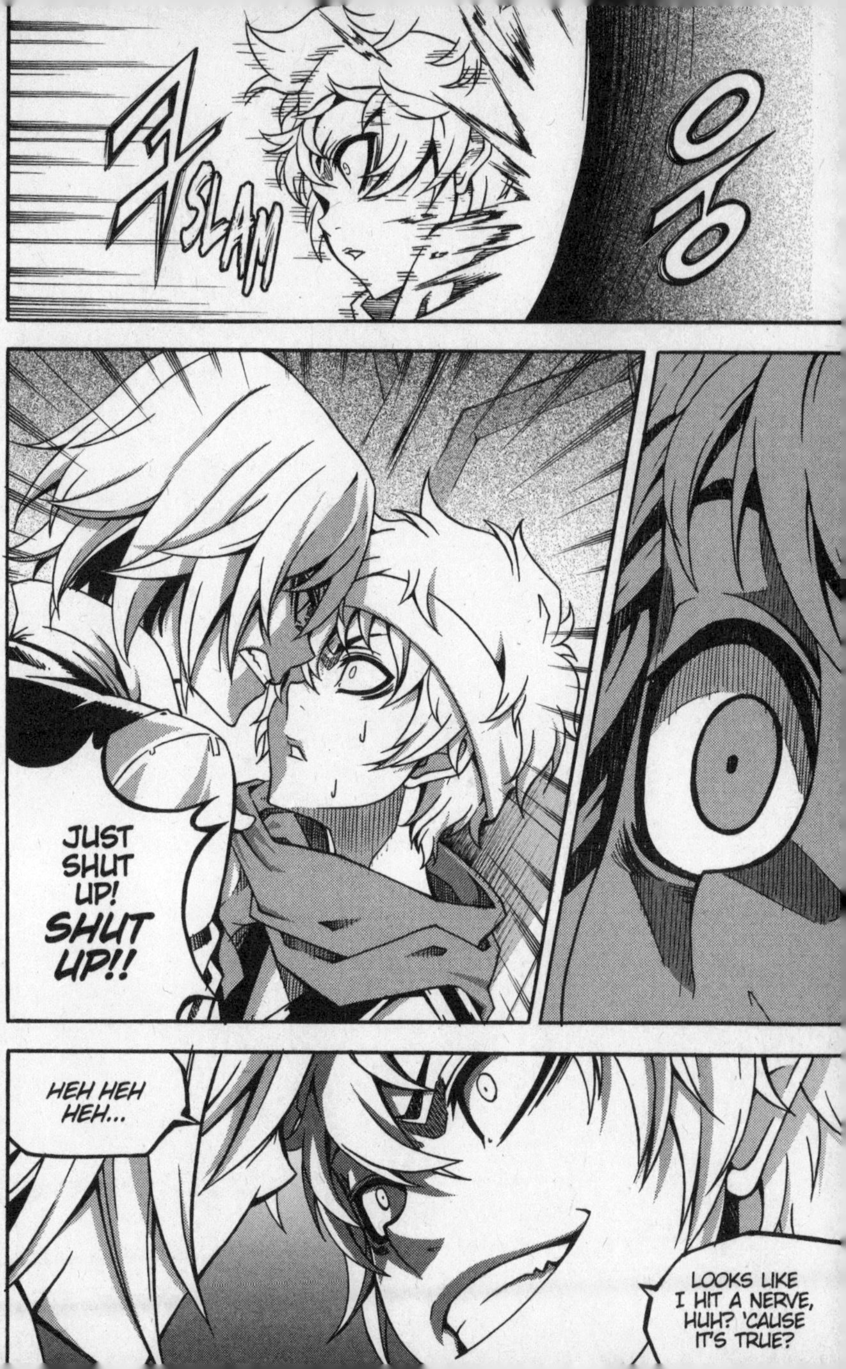
SLAM
JUST SHUT UP! SHUT UP!!
HEH HEH HEH...
LOOKS LIKE I HIT A NERVE, HUH? 'CAUSE IT'S TRUE?

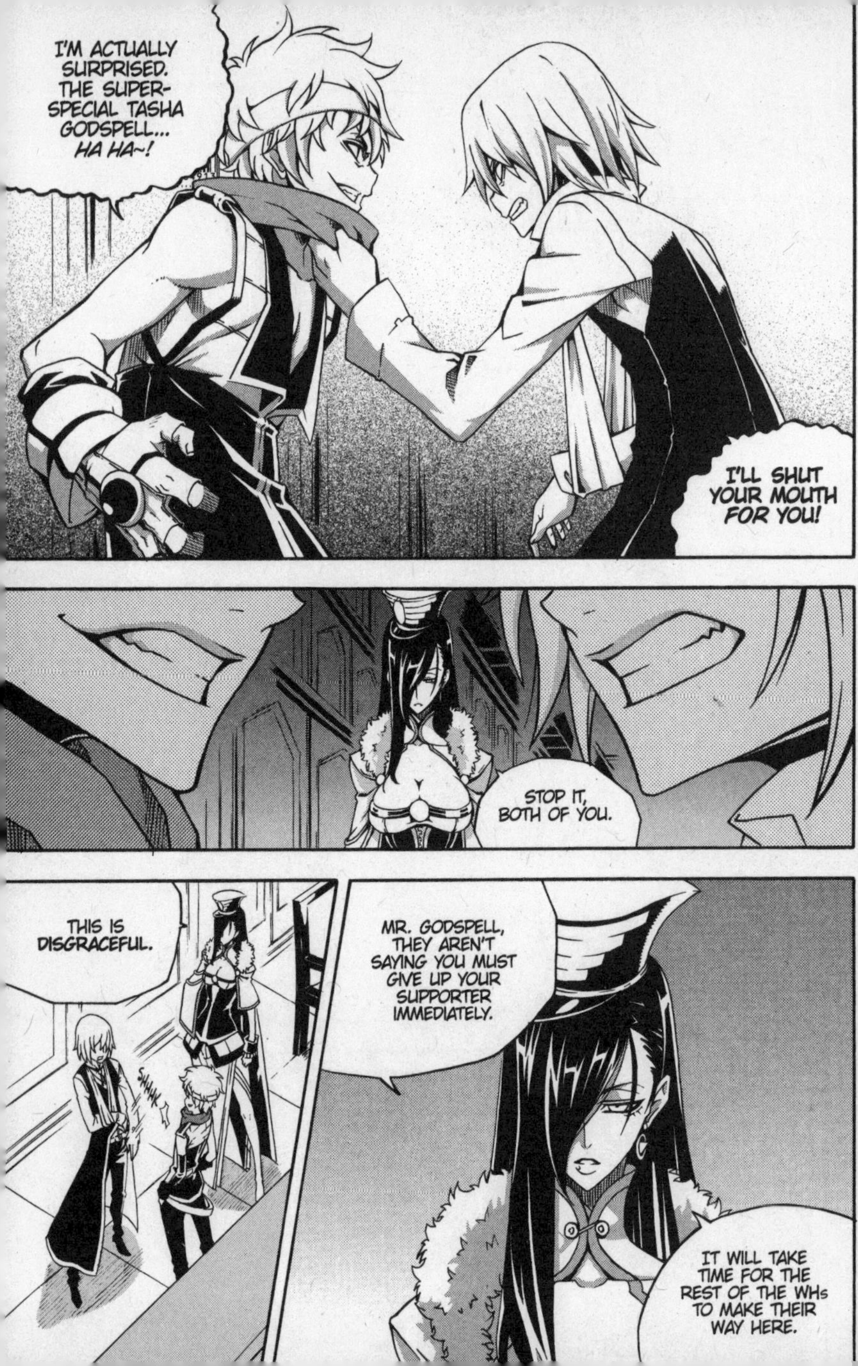
I'M ACTUALLY SURPRISED. THE SUPER-SPECIAL TASHA GODSPELL... HA HA~!
I'LL SHUT YOUR MOUTH FOR YOU!
STOP IT, BOTH OF YOU.
THIS IS DISGRACEFUL.
MR. GODSPELL, THEY AREN'T SAYING YOU MUST GIVE UP YOUR SUPPORTER IMMEDIATELY.
IT WILL TAKE TIME FOR THE REST OF THE WHs TO MAKE THEIR WAY HERE.

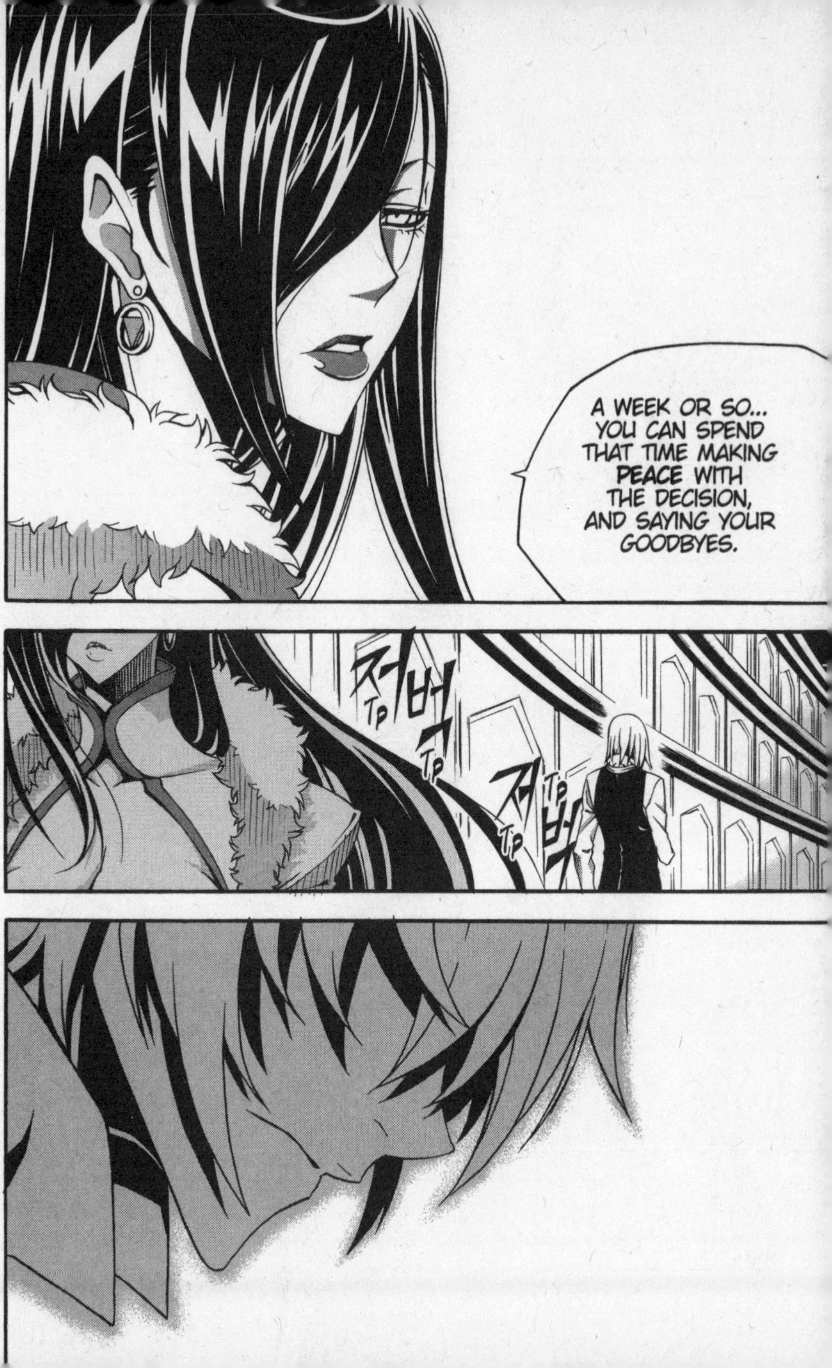
A WEEK OR SO... YOU CAN SPEND THAT TIME MAKING PEACE WITH THE DECISION, AND SAYING YOUR GOODBYES.
저벅 Tp Tp
저벅 Tp Tp

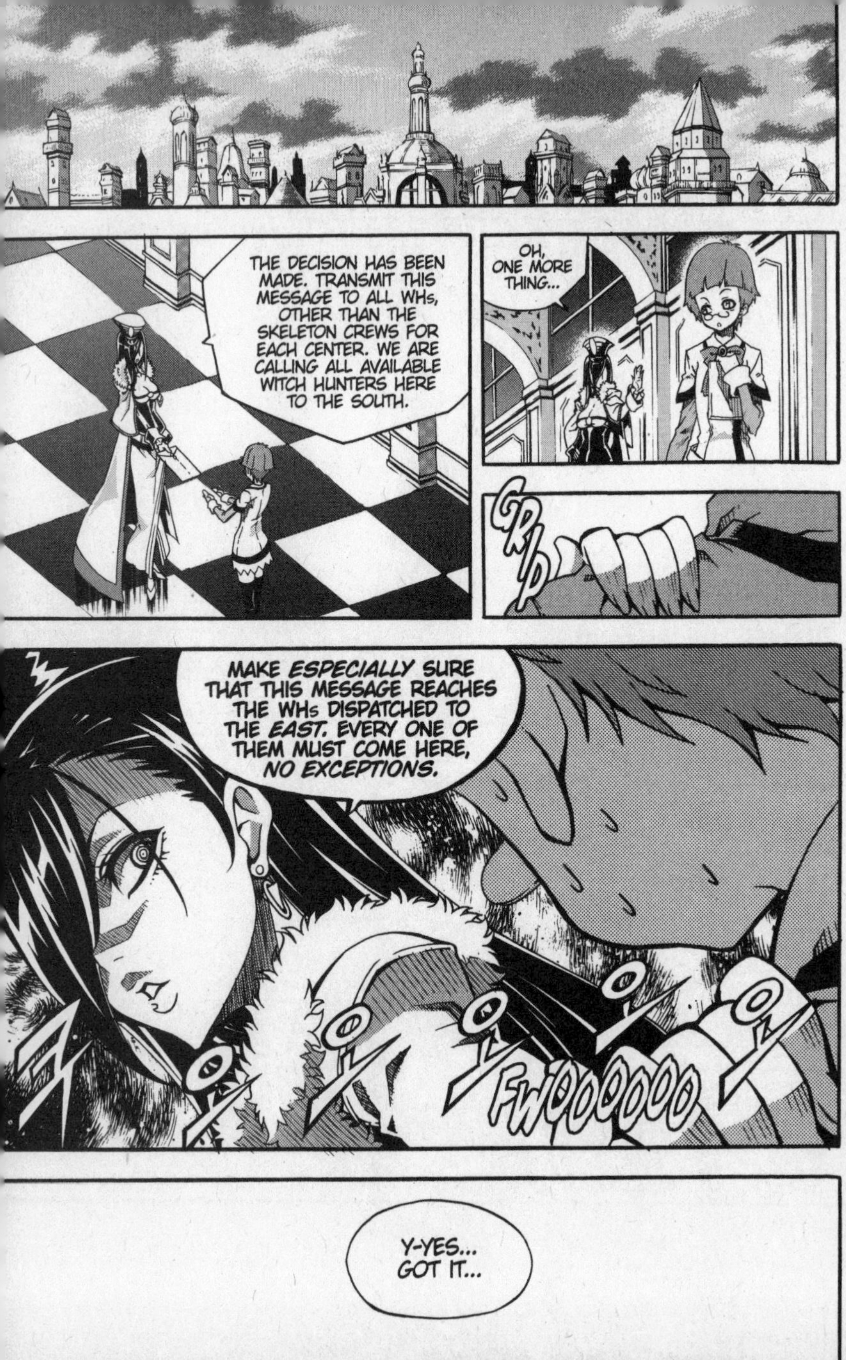
THE DECISION HAS BEEN MADE. TRANSMIT THIS MESSAGE TO ALL WHs, OTHER THAN THE SKELETON CREWS FOR EACH CENTER. WE ARE CALLING ALL AVAILABLE WITCH HUNTERS HERE TO THE SOUTH.
OH, ONE MORE THING...
GRIP
MAKE *ESPECIALLY* SURE THAT THIS MESSAGE REACHES THE WHs DISPATCHED TO THE *EAST*. EVERY ONE OF THEM MUST COME HERE, *NO EXCEPTIONS.*
FWOOOOOO
Y-YES... GOT IT...

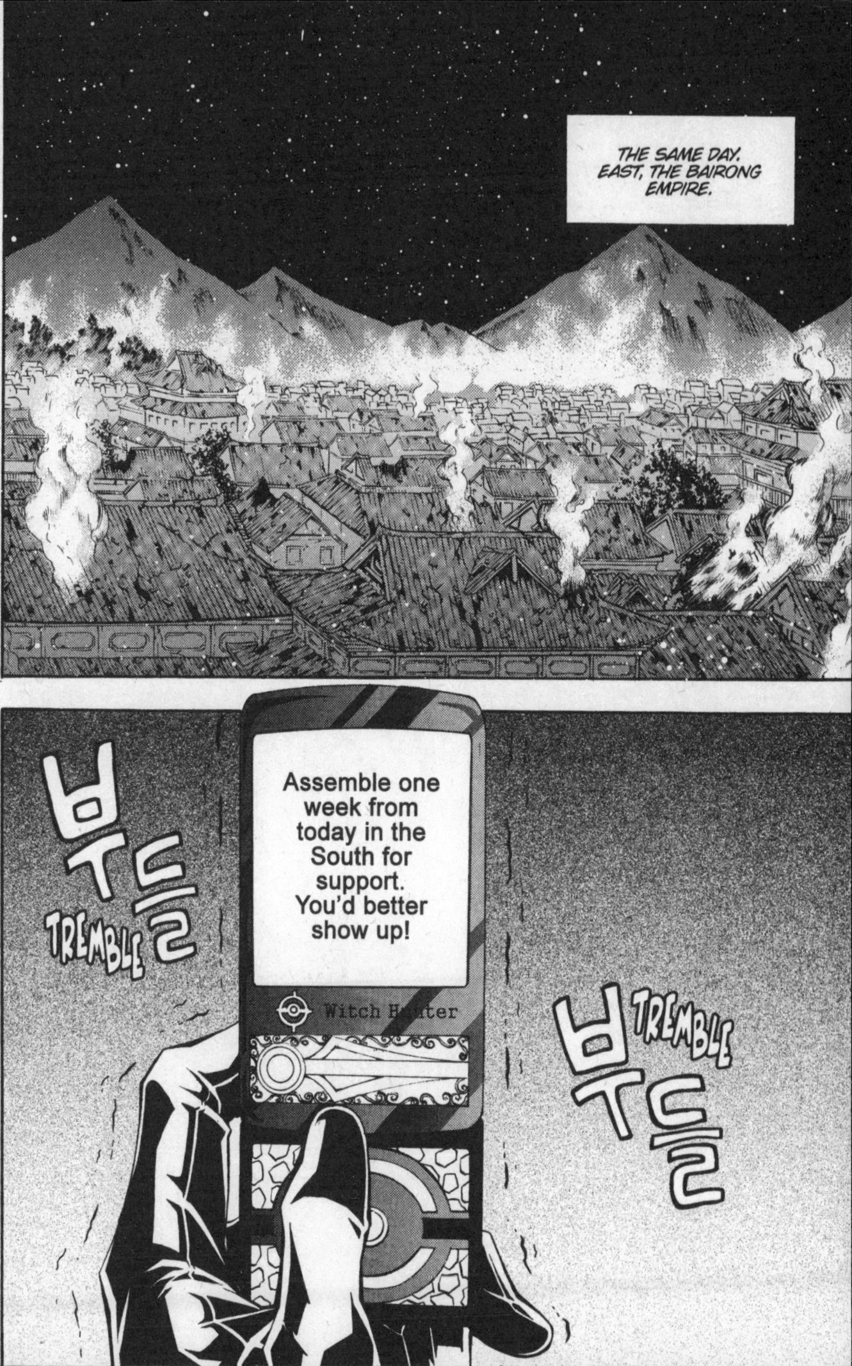
THE SAME DAY. EAST, THE BAIRONG EMPIRE.
부들
TREMBLE
Assemble one week from today in the South for support. You'd better show up!
Witch Hunter
부들
TREMBLE

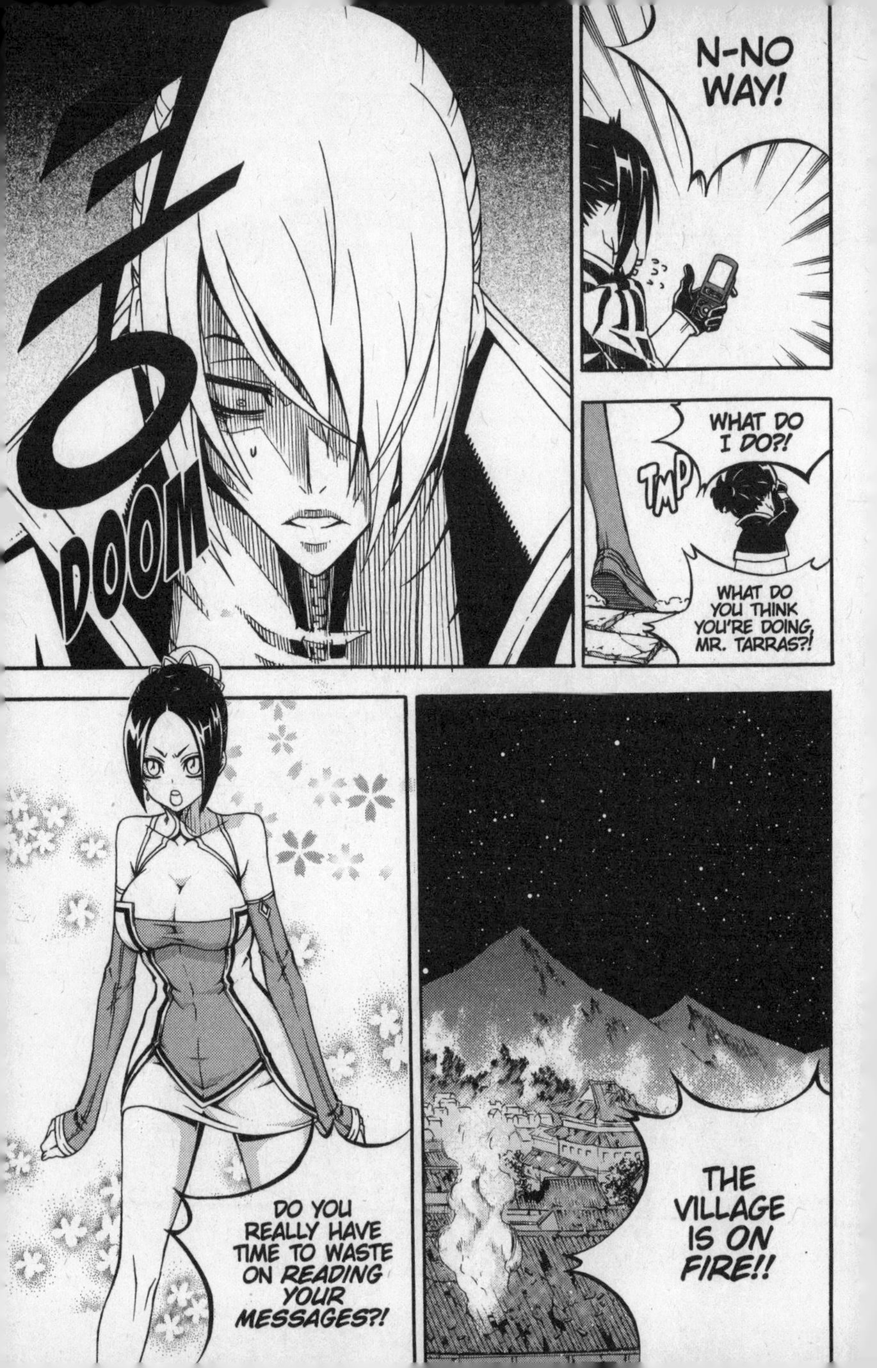
DOOM
N-NO WAY!
WHAT DO I DO?!
TMP
WHAT DO YOU THINK YOU'RE DOING, MR. TARRAS?!
DO YOU REALLY HAVE TIME TO WASTE ON READING YOUR MESSAGES?!
THE VILLAGE IS ON FIRE!!

THAT'S NOT IMPORTANT RIGHT NOW!!

ROAR

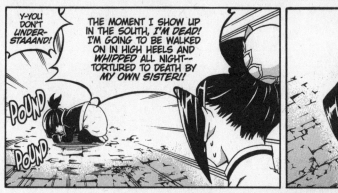

Y-YOU DON'T UNDER-STAAAND!

THE MOMENT I SHOW UP IN THE SOUTH, *I'M DEAD!* I'M GOING TO BE WALKED ON IN HIGH HEELS AND *WHIPPED* ALL NIGHT-- TORTURED TO DEATH BY *MY OWN SISTER!!*

POUND

POUND

HEY.

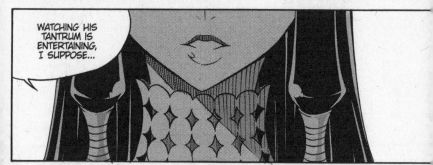

WATCHING HIS TANTRUM IS ENTERTAINING, I SUPPOSE...

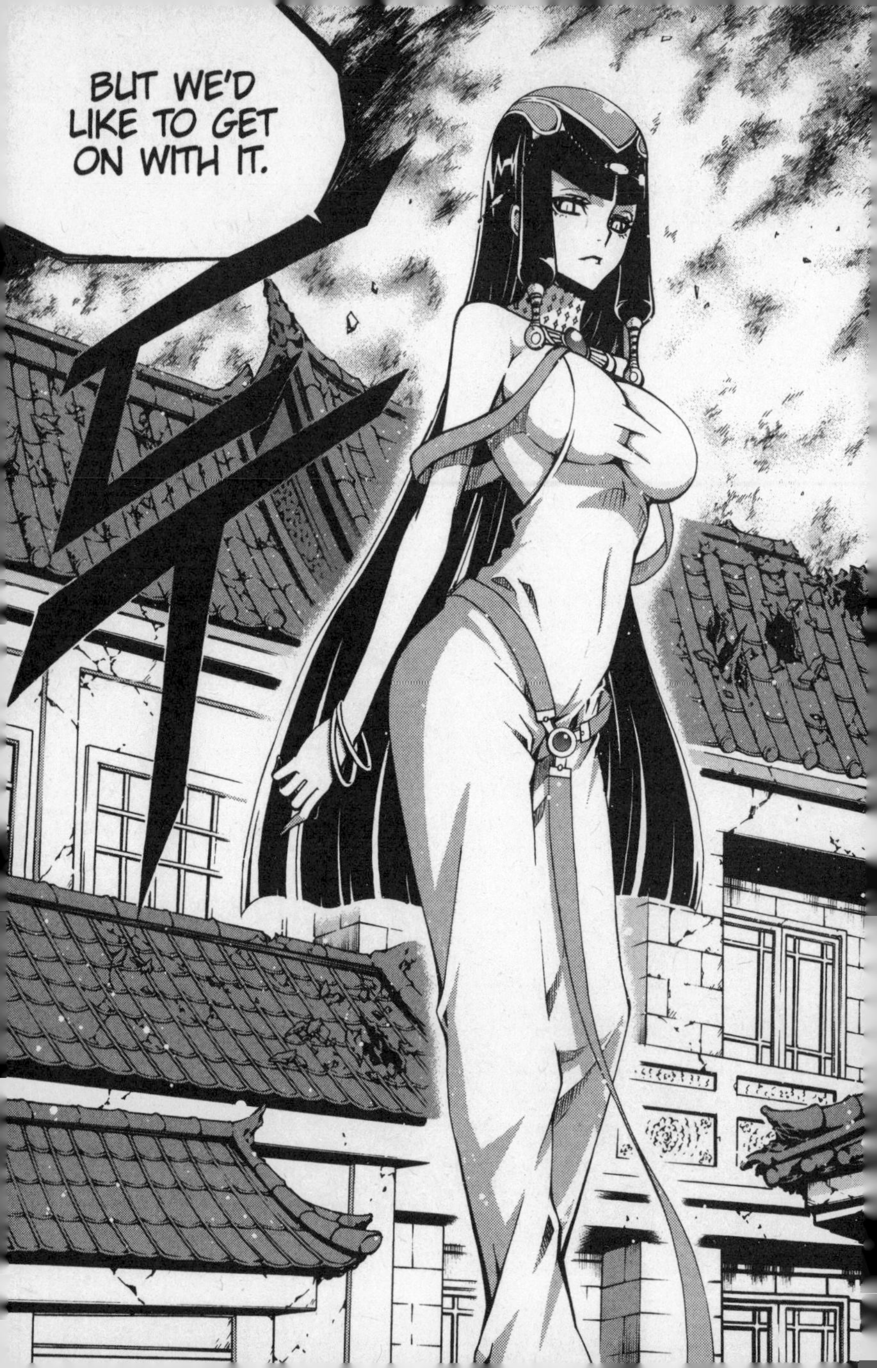
BUT WE'D LIKE TO GET ON WITH IT.

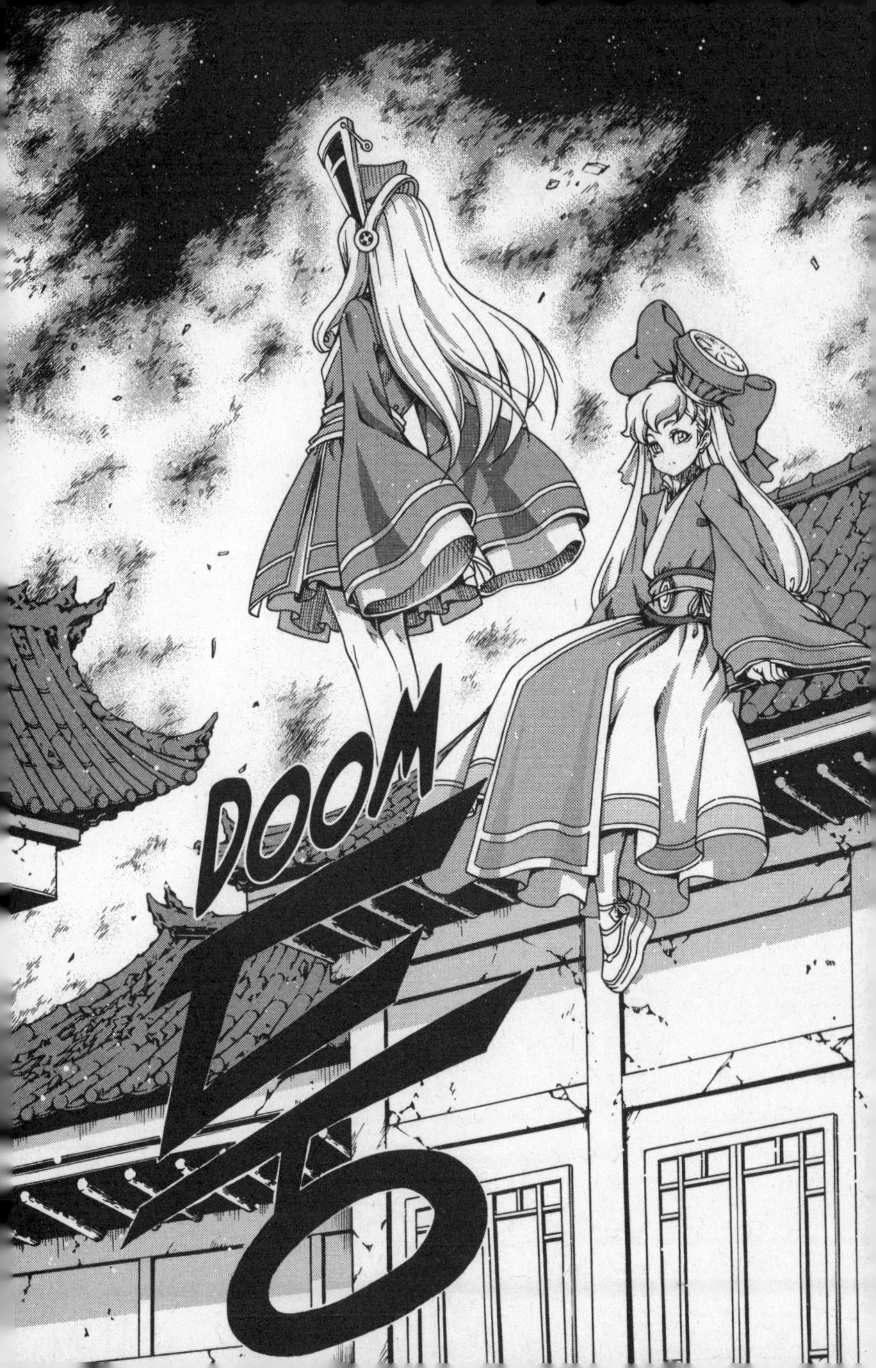
DOOM

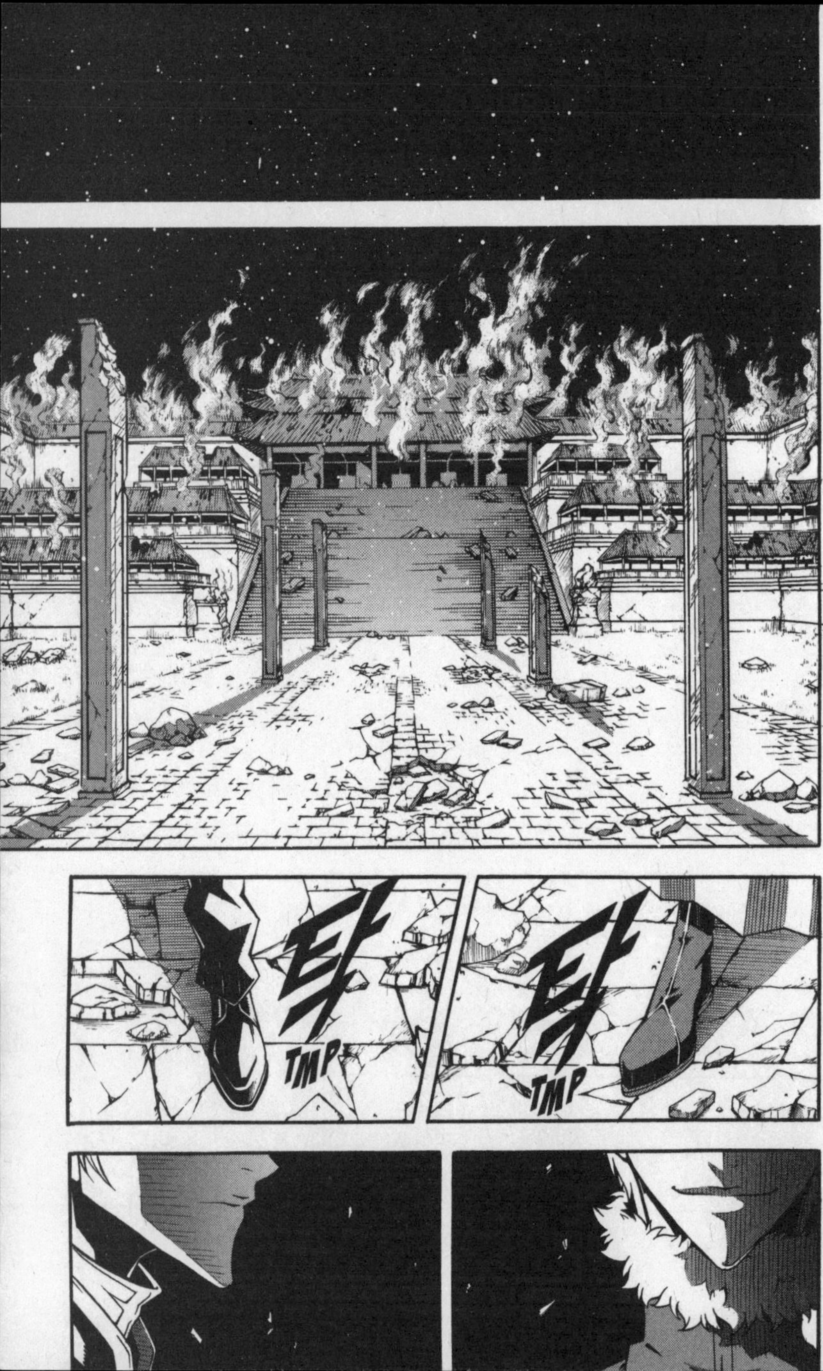

탁
TMP
탁
TMP

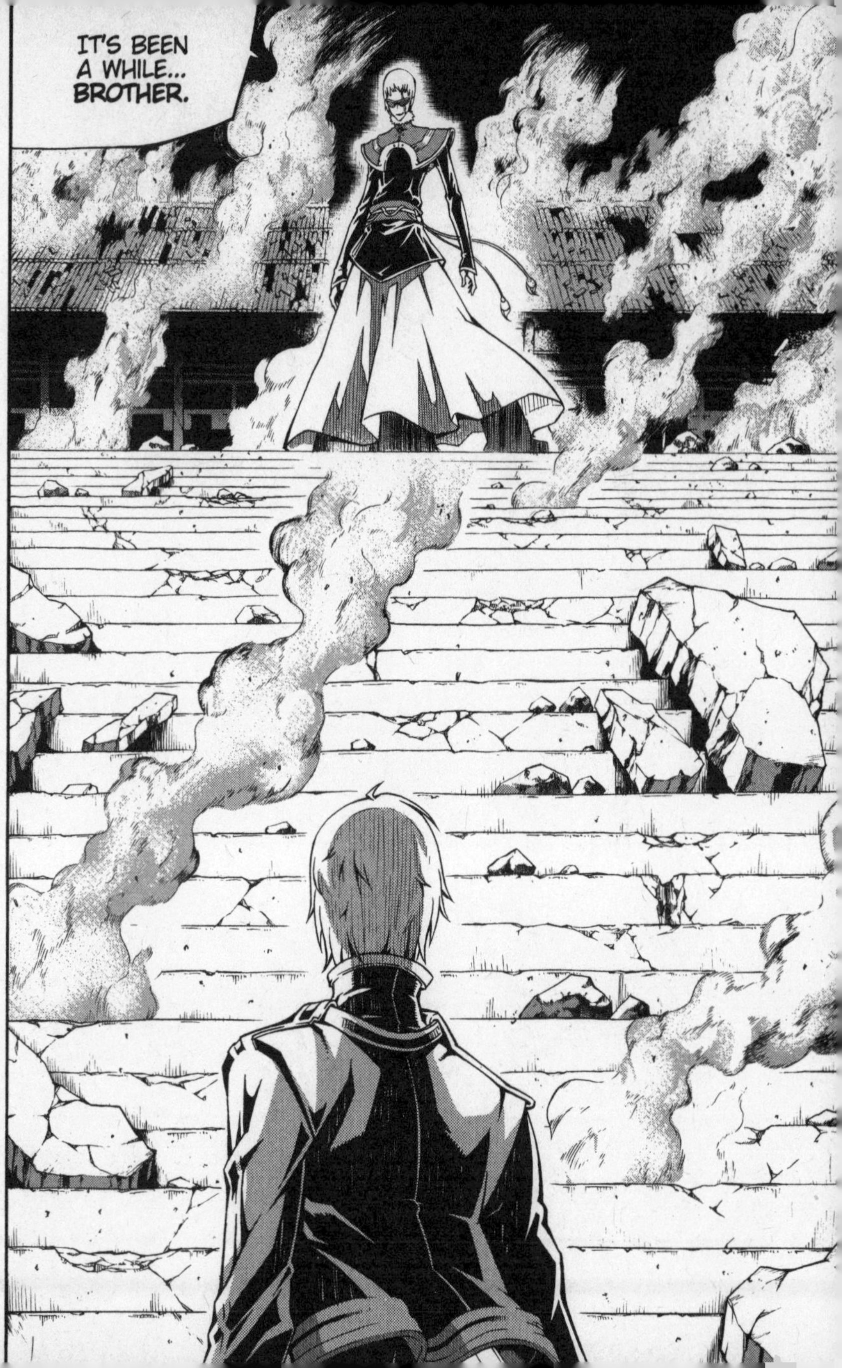
IT'S BEEN A WHILE... BROTHER.

BROTHERS

SO, THIS IS WHERE YOU'VE BEEN HIDING, YUE.
LEE...
......
DAMN... WHERE'D HE GET THOSE COOL SHADES?

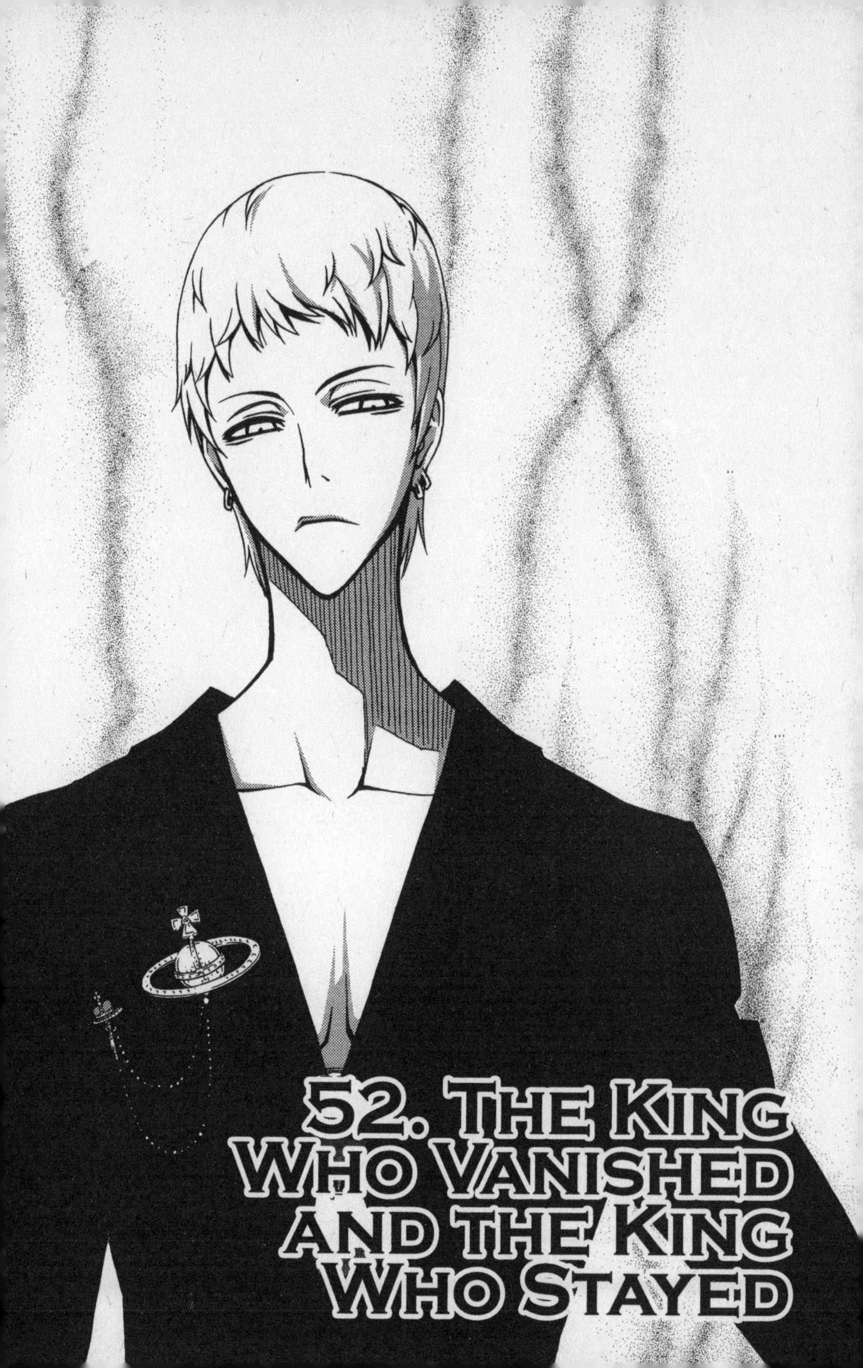
52. The King
Who Vanished
and the King
Who Stayed

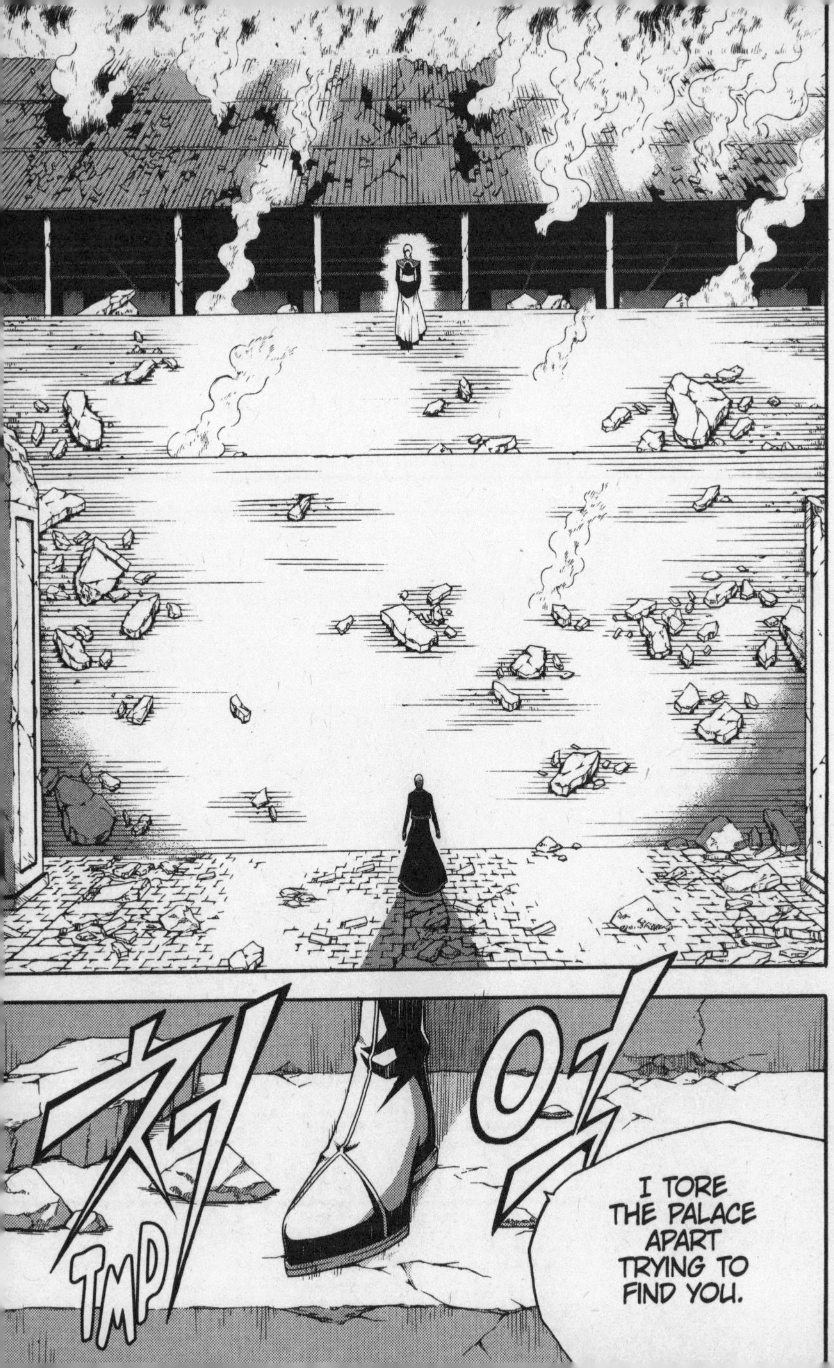
TMP
I TORE THE PALACE APART TRYING TO FIND YOU.

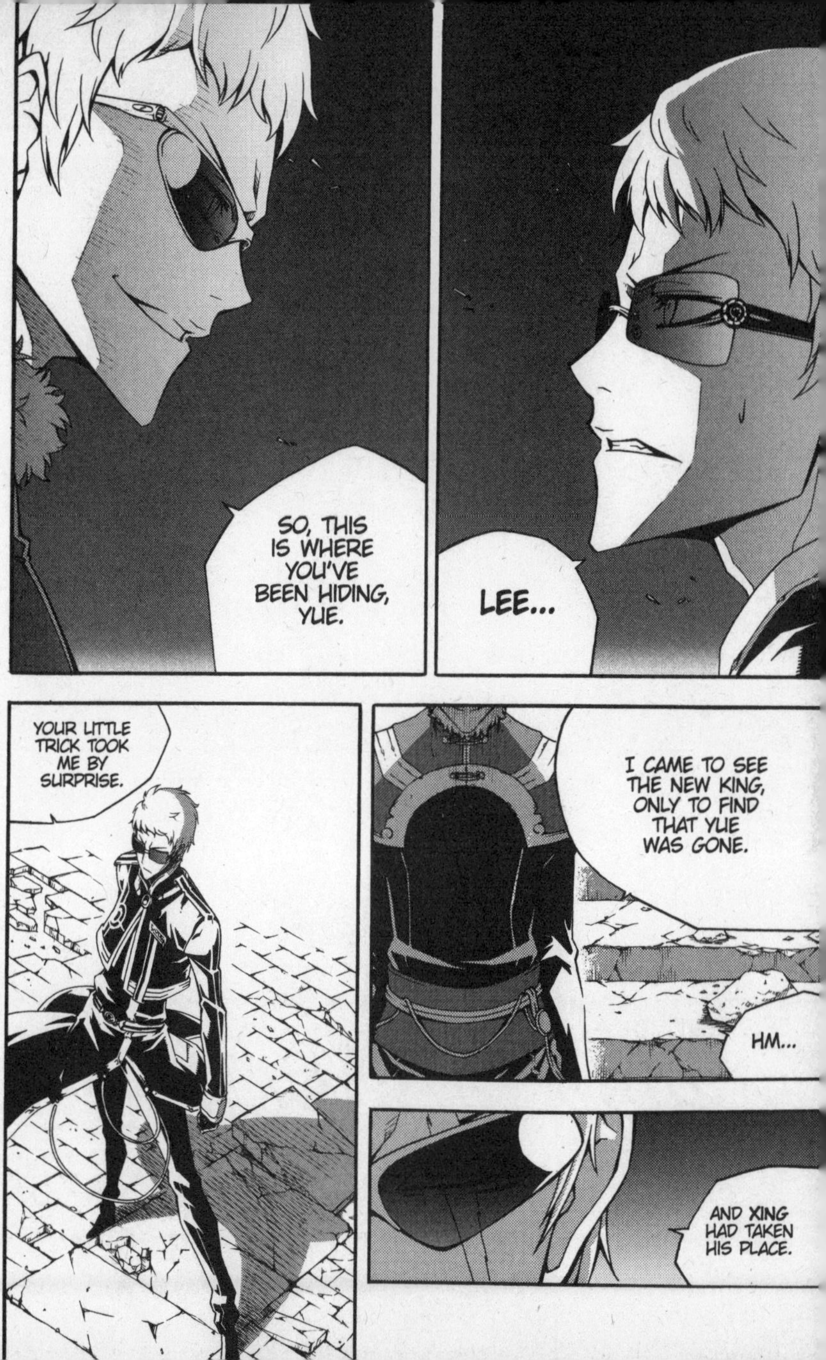
SO, THIS IS WHERE YOU'VE BEEN HIDING, YUE.
LEE...
YOUR LITTLE TRICK TOOK ME BY SURPRISE.
I CAME TO SEE THE NEW KING, ONLY TO FIND THAT YUE WAS GONE.
HM...
AND XING HAD TAKEN HIS PLACE.

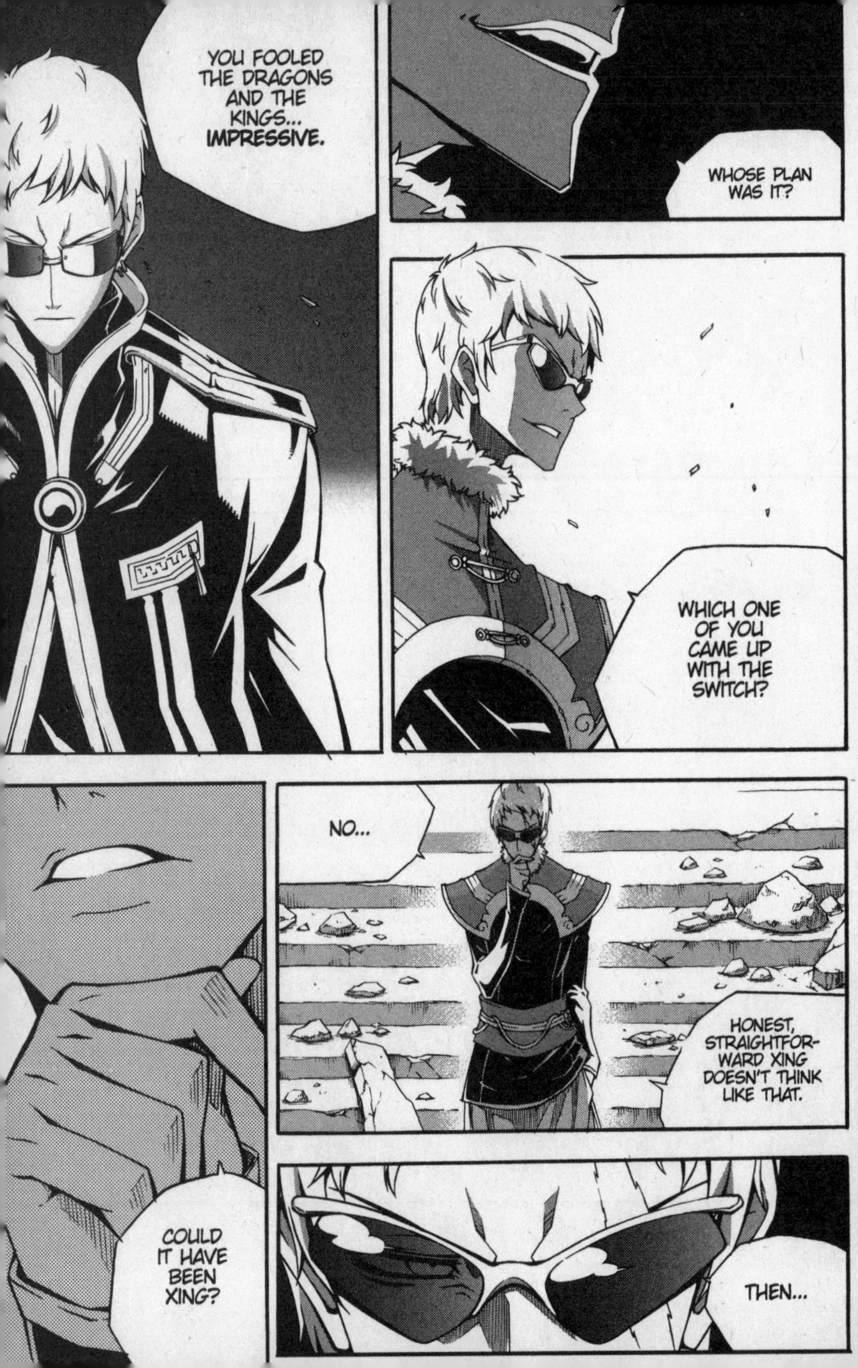
YOU FOOLED THE DRAGONS AND THE KINGS... **IMPRESSIVE.**
WHOSE PLAN WAS IT?
WHICH ONE OF YOU CAME UP WITH THE SWITCH?
COULD IT HAVE BEEN XING?
NO...
HONEST, STRAIGHTFOR-WARD XING DOESN'T THINK LIKE THAT.
THEN...

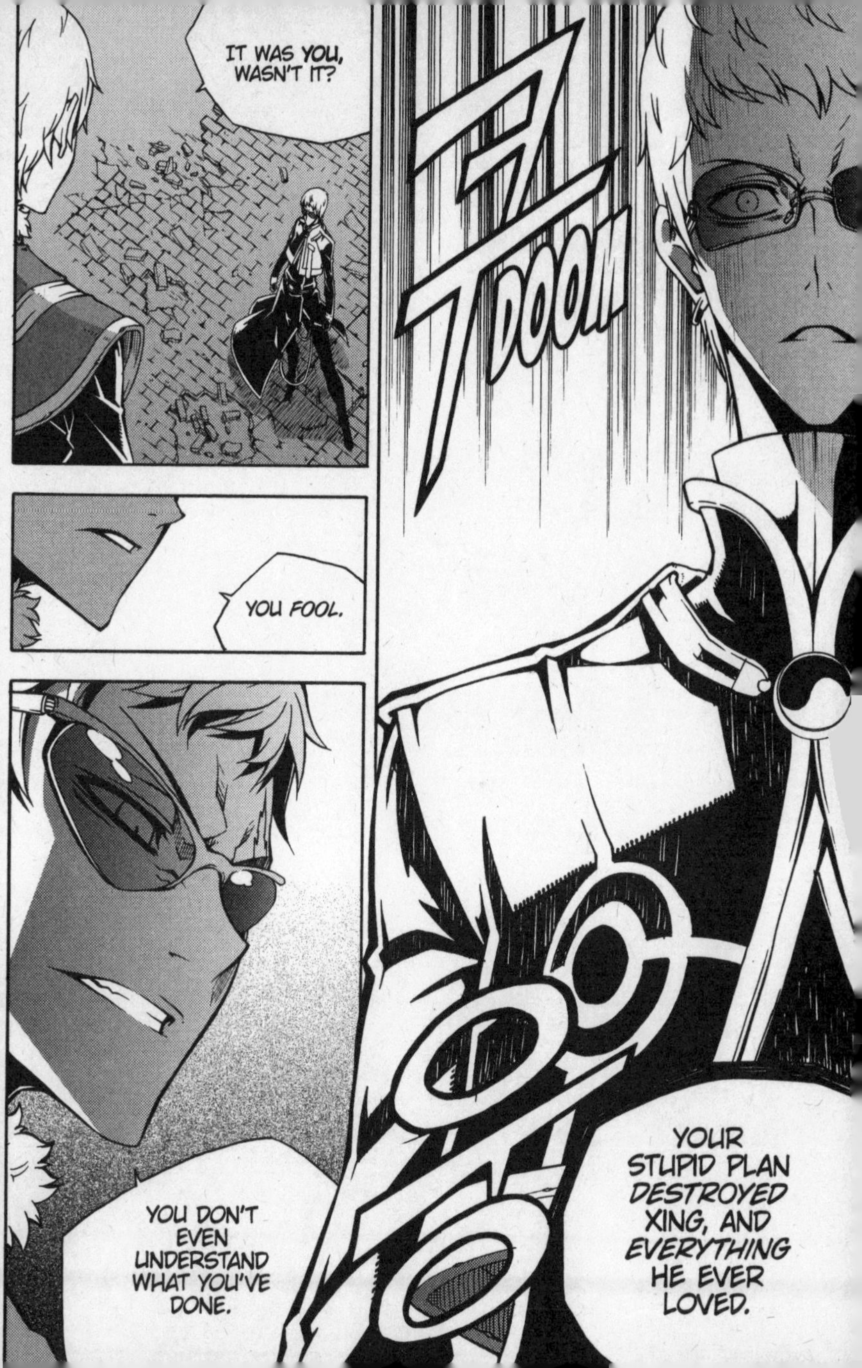
IT WAS YOU, WASN'T IT?
YOU FOOL.
YOU DON'T EVEN UNDERSTAND WHAT YOU'VE DONE.
DOOM
YOUR STUPID PLAN DESTROYED XING, AND EVERYTHING HE EVER LOVED.

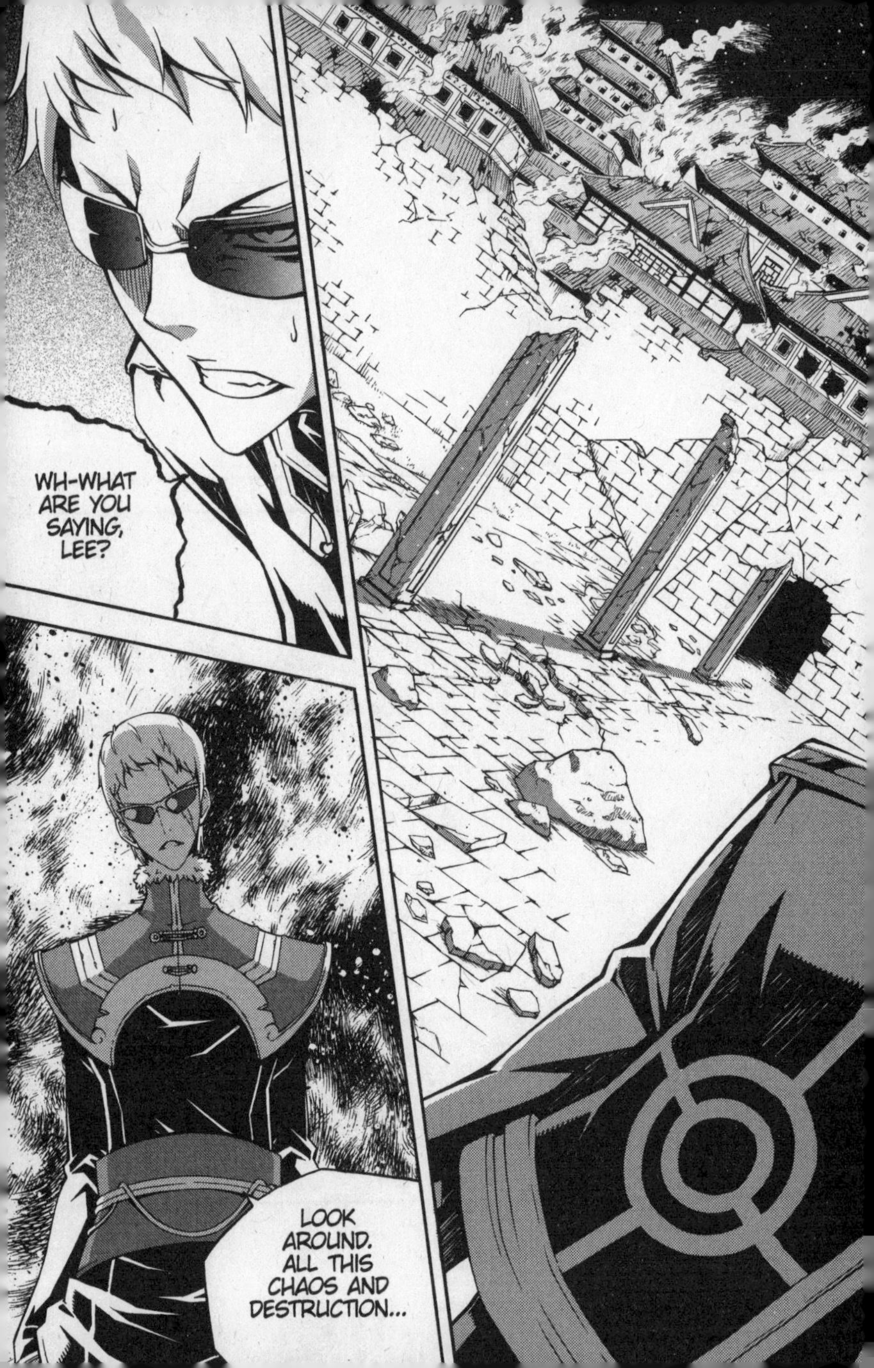
WH-WHAT ARE YOU SAYING, LEE?
LOOK AROUND. ALL THIS CHAOS AND DESTRUCTION...

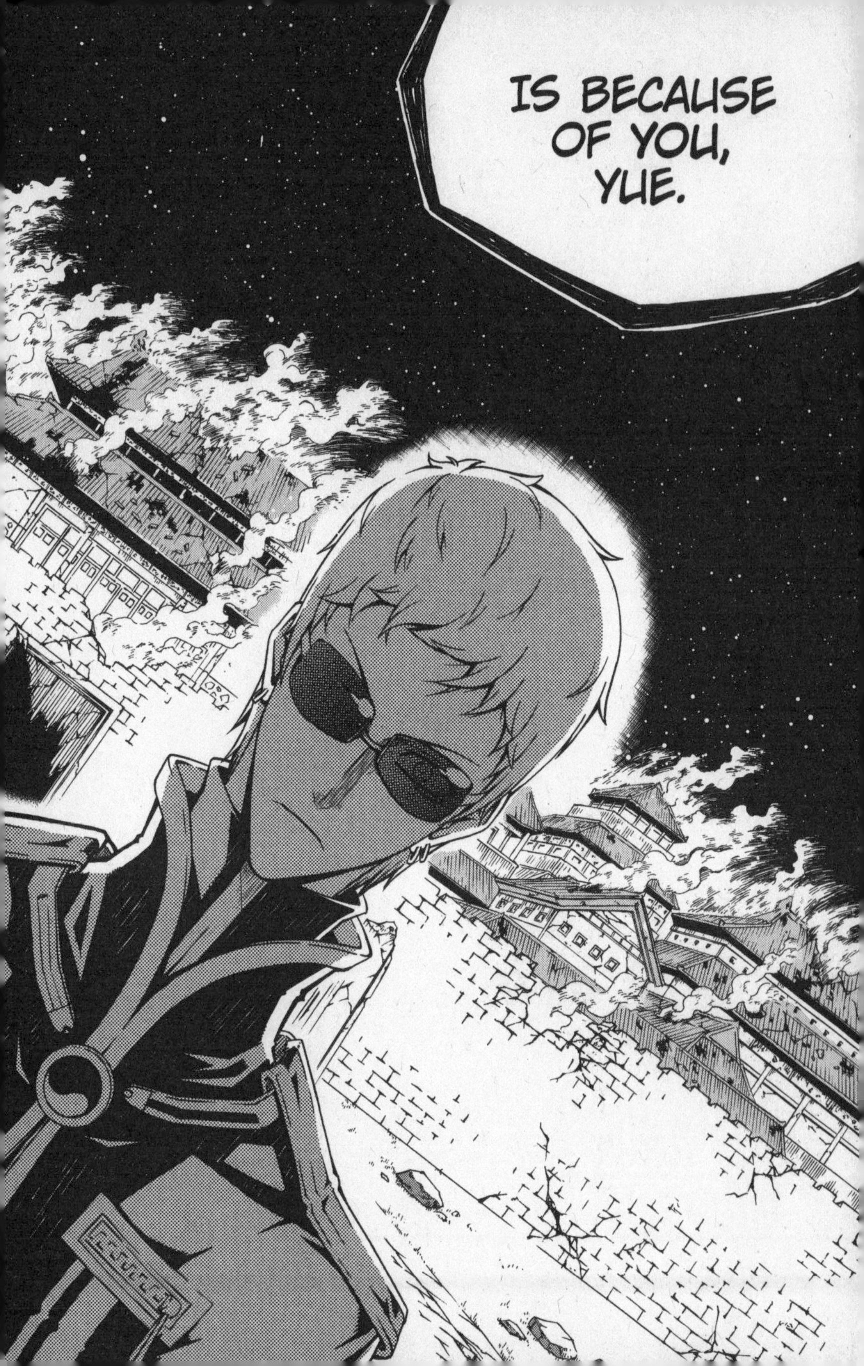
IS BECAUSE OF YOU, YUE.

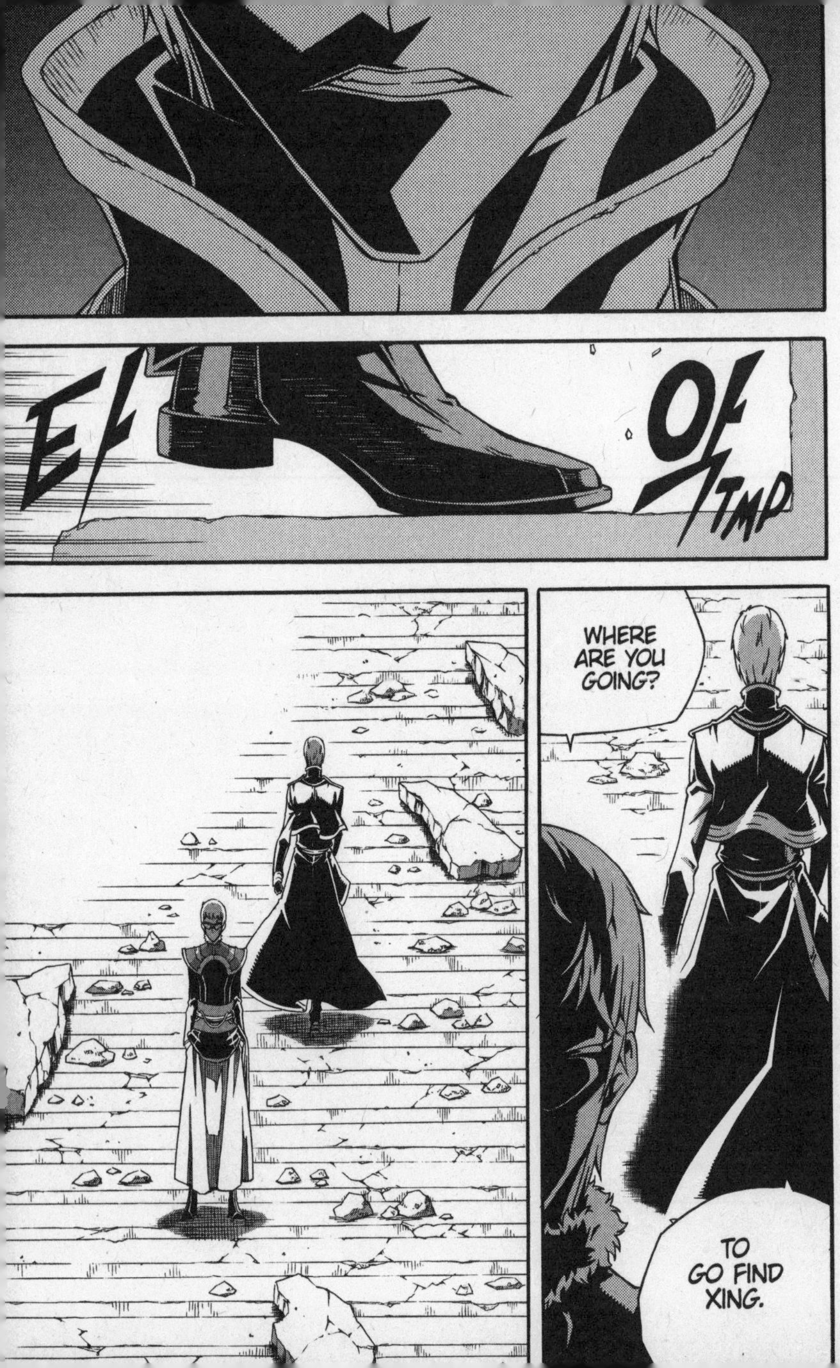

TMP
WHERE ARE YOU GOING?
TO GO FIND XING.

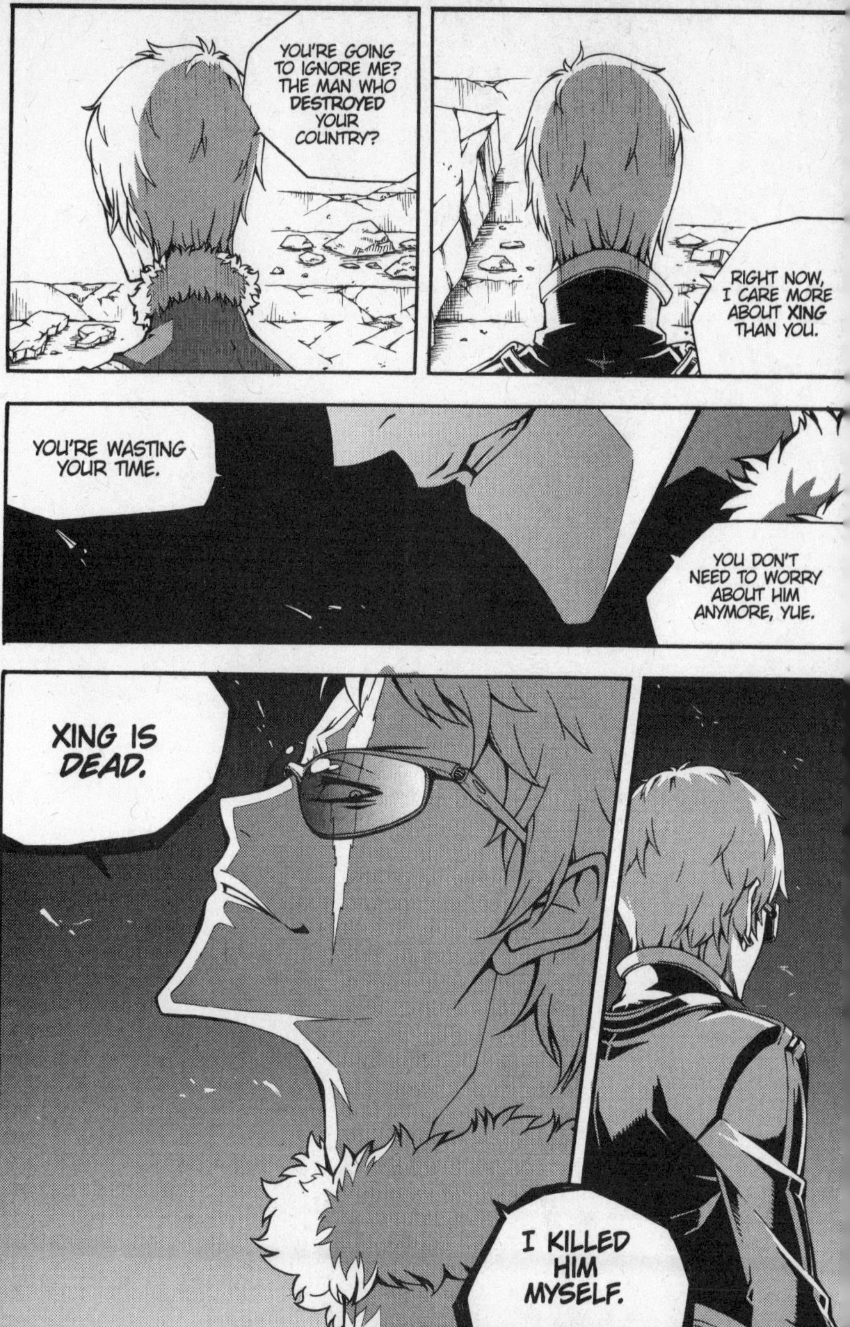
YOU'RE GOING TO IGNORE ME? THE MAN WHO DESTROYED YOUR COUNTRY?
RIGHT NOW, I CARE MORE ABOUT XING THAN YOU.
YOU'RE WASTING YOUR TIME.
YOU DON'T NEED TO WORRY ABOUT HIM ANYMORE, YUE.
XING IS DEAD.
I KILLED HIM MYSELF.

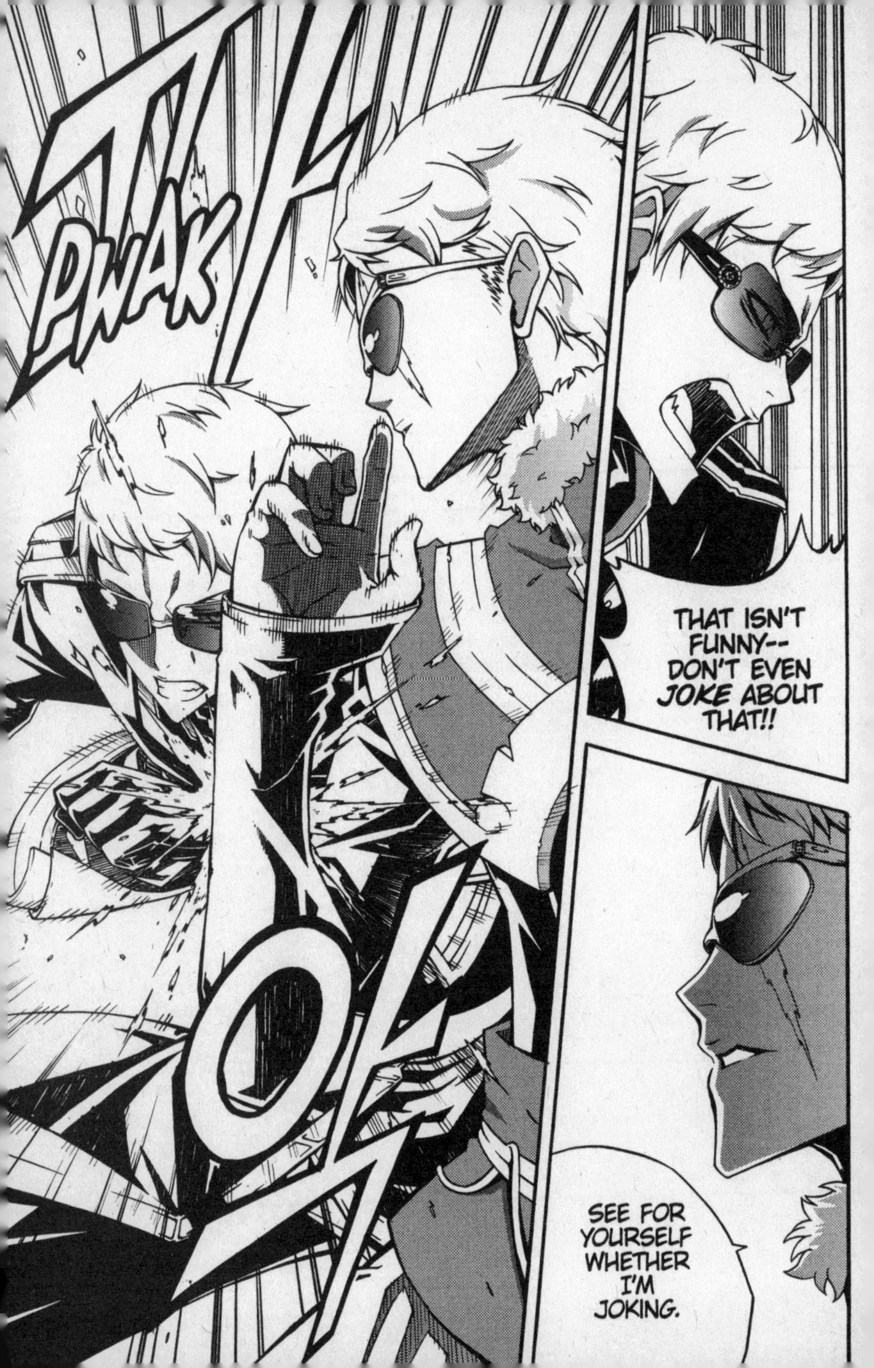
PWAK
THAT ISN'T FUNNY-- DON'T EVEN *JOKE* ABOUT THAT!!
SEE FOR YOURSELF WHETHER I'M JOKING.

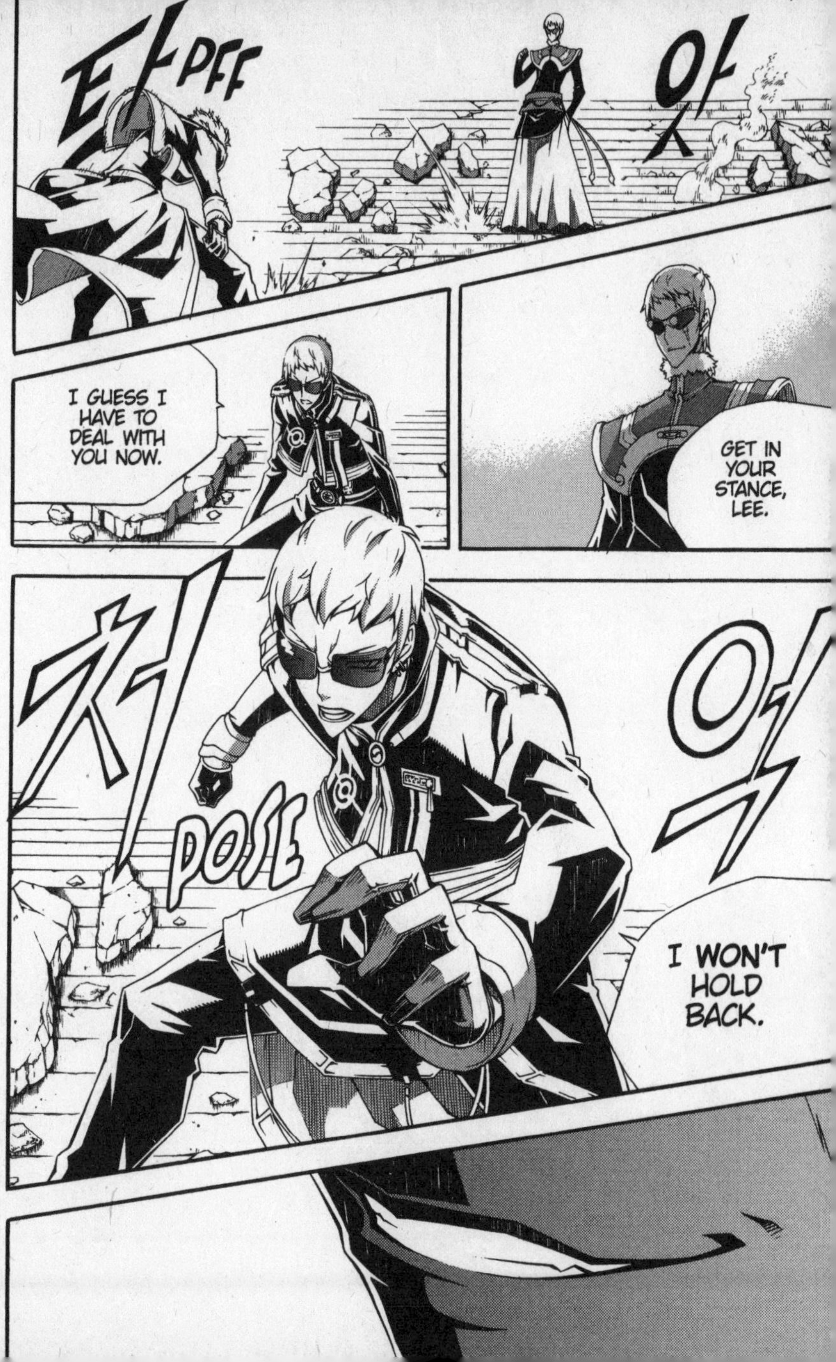
PFF
I GUESS I HAVE TO DEAL WITH YOU NOW.
GET IN YOUR STANCE, LEE.
POSE
I WON'T HOLD BACK.

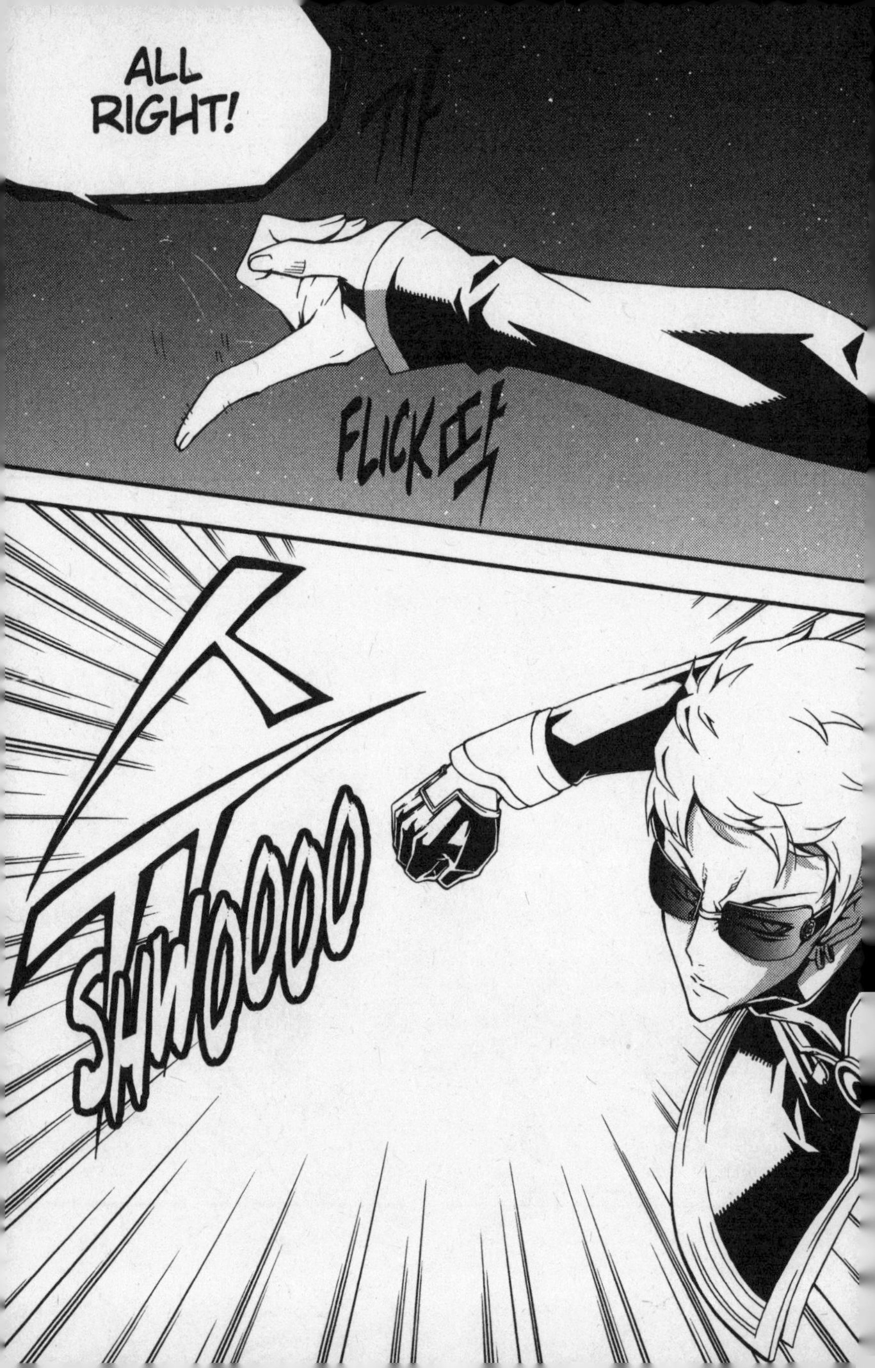
ALL RIGHT!
FLICK 딱
SHWOOOO

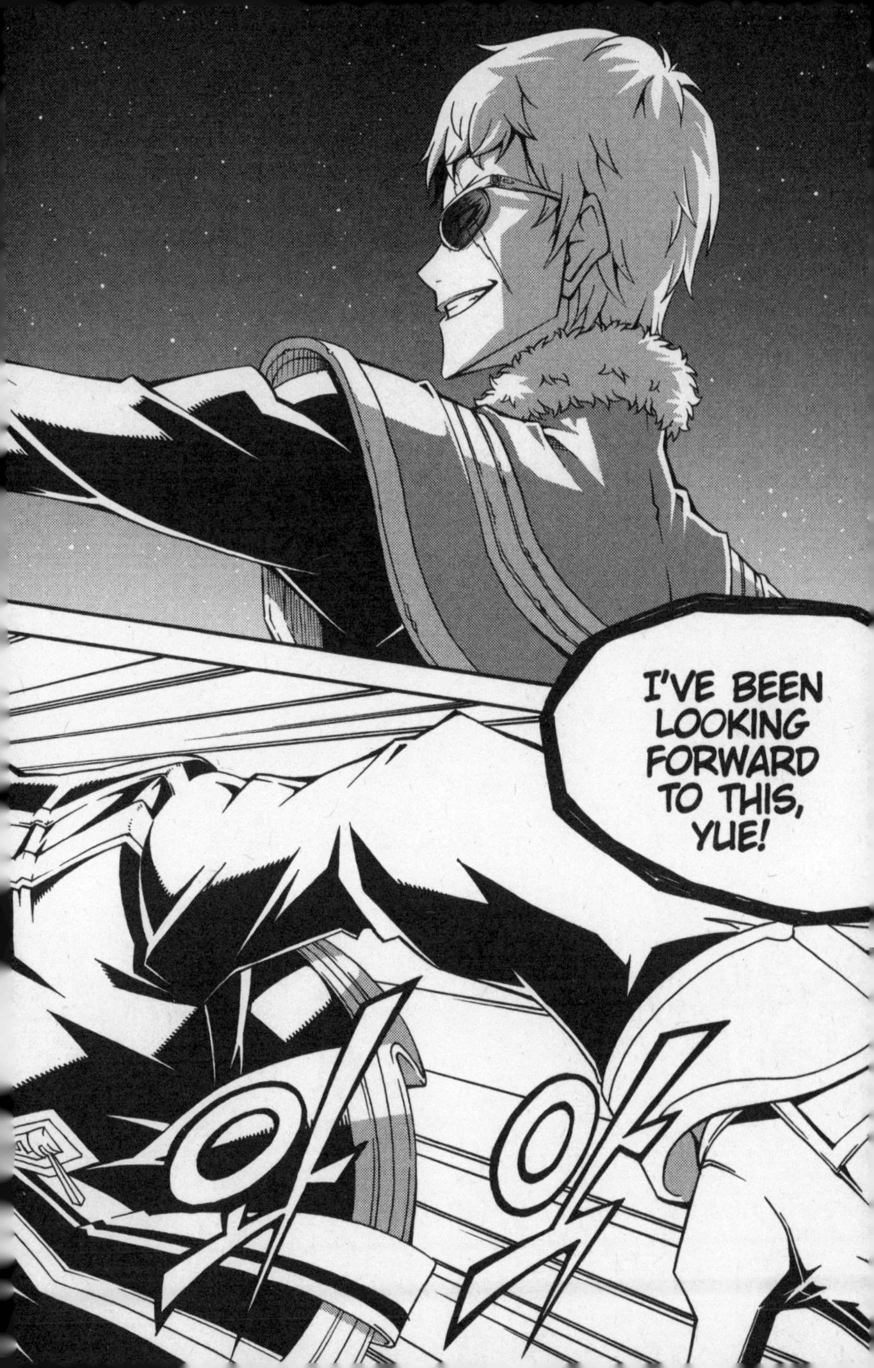
I'VE BEEN LOOKING FORWARD TO THIS, YUE!

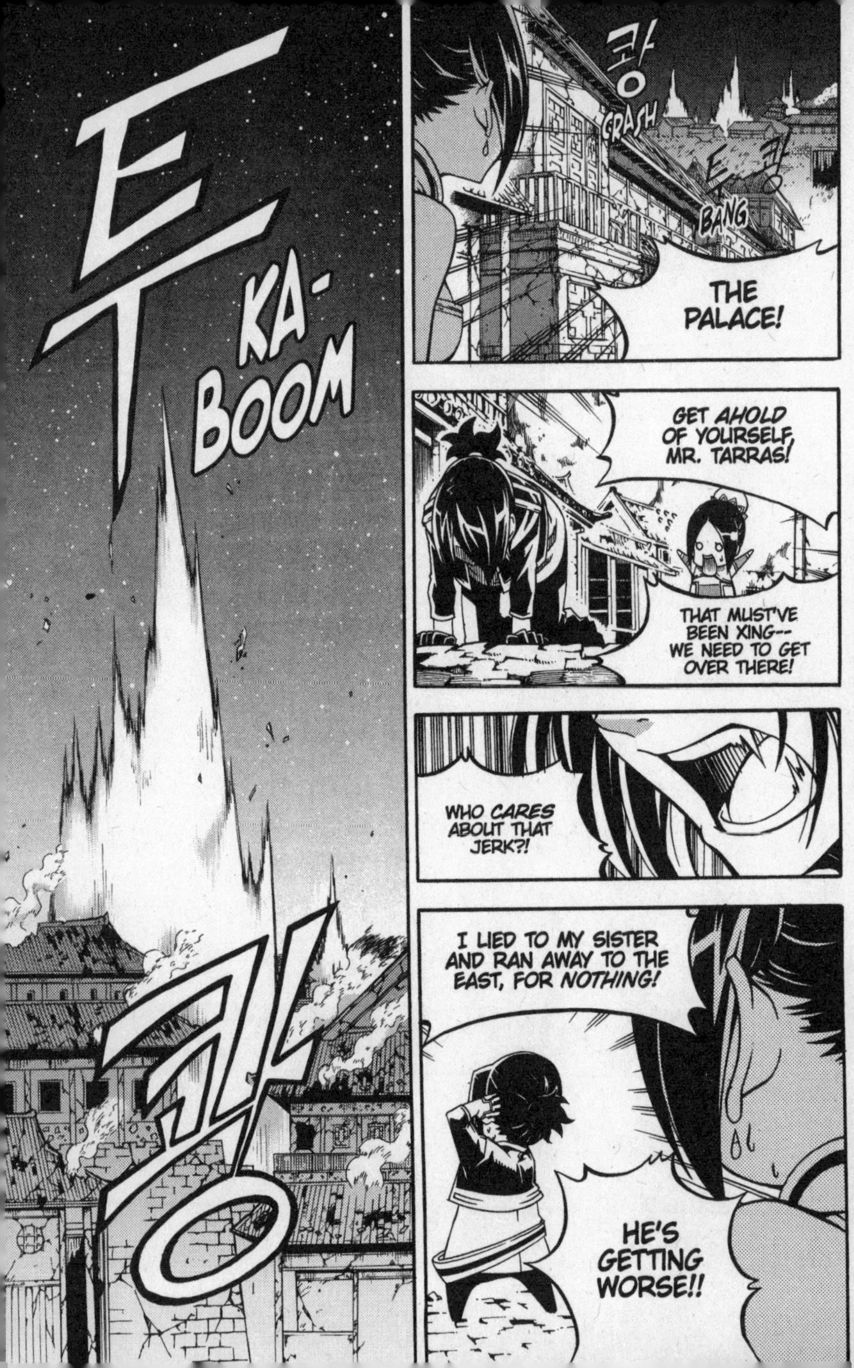
KA-BOOM
CRASH
BANG
THE PALACE!
GET AHOLD OF YOURSELF, MR. TARRAS!
THAT MUST'VE BEEN XING-- WE NEED TO GET OVER THERE!
WHO CARES ABOUT THAT JERK?!
I LIED TO MY SISTER AND RAN AWAY TO THE EAST, FOR NOTHING!
HE'S GETTING WORSE!!

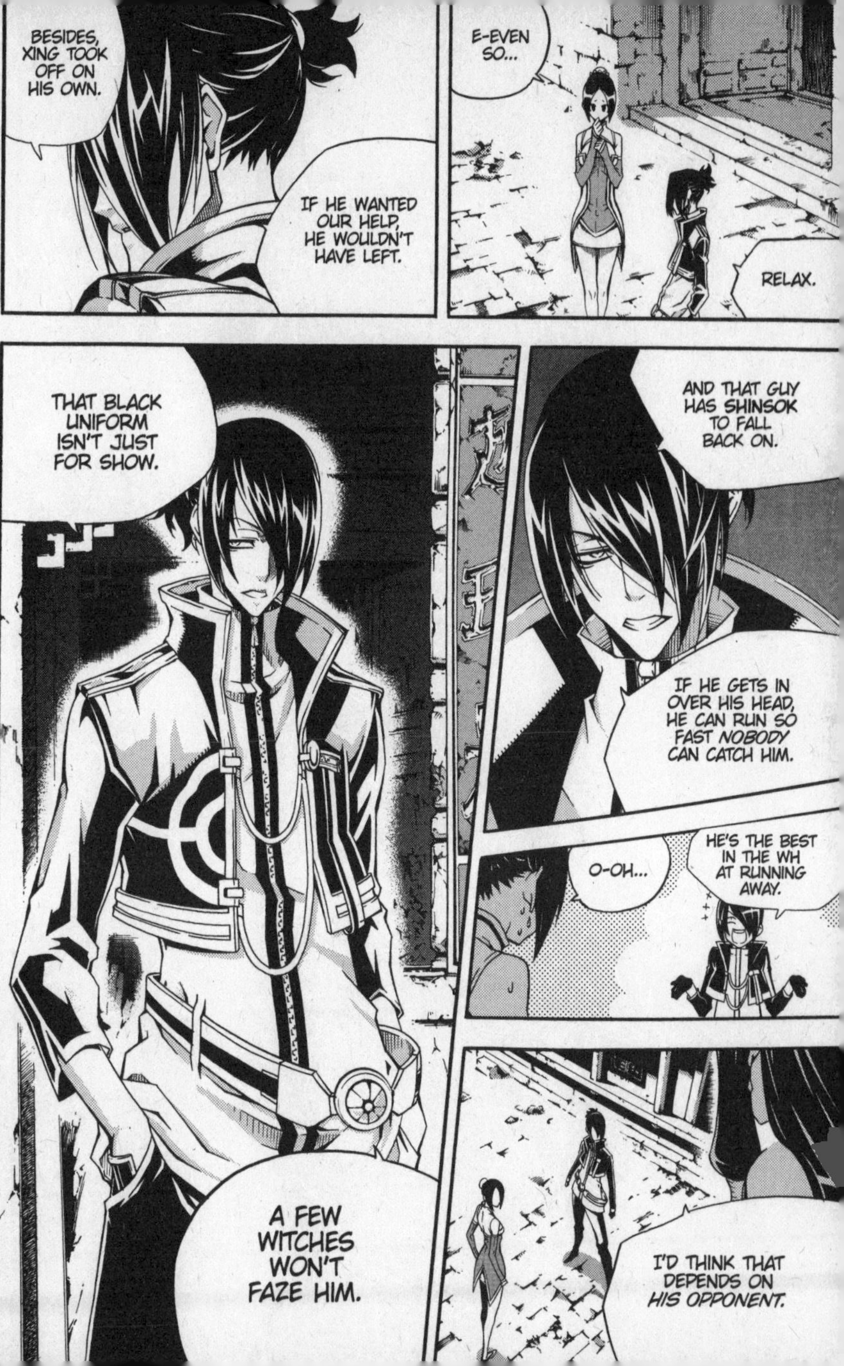
BESIDES, XING TOOK OFF ON HIS OWN.
IF HE WANTED OUR HELP, HE WOULDN'T HAVE LEFT.
E-EVEN SO...
RELAX.
THAT BLACK UNIFORM ISN'T JUST FOR SHOW.
A FEW WITCHES WON'T FAZE HIM.
AND THAT GUY HAS SHINSOK TO FALL BACK ON.
IF HE GETS IN OVER HIS HEAD, HE CAN RUN SO FAST *NOBODY* CAN CATCH HIM.
O-OH...
HE'S THE BEST IN THE WH AT RUNNING AWAY.
I'D THINK THAT DEPENDS ON *HIS OPPONENT*.

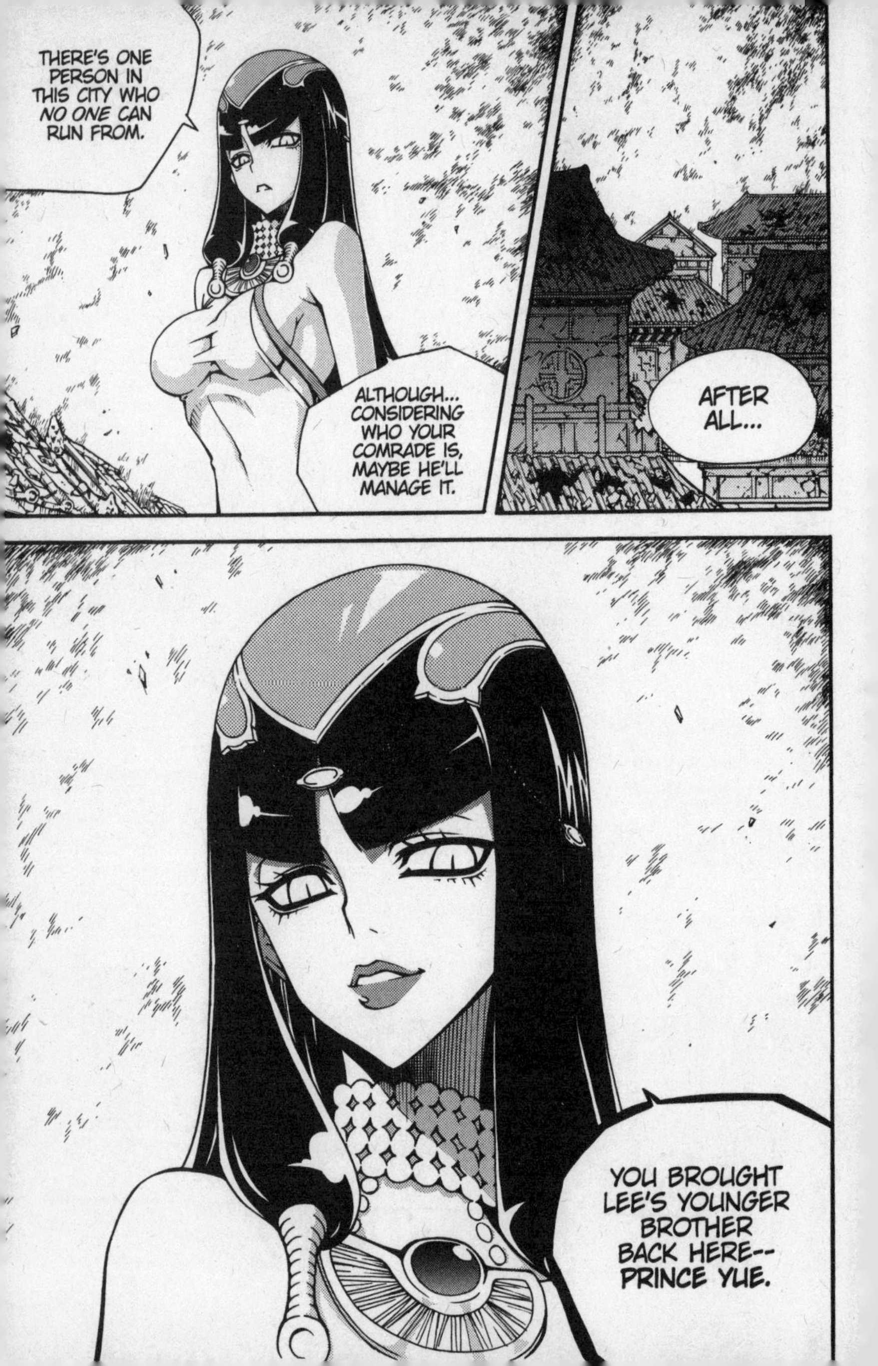
THERE'S ONE PERSON IN THIS CITY WHO *NO ONE* CAN RUN FROM.
ALTHOUGH... CONSIDERING WHO YOUR COMRADE IS, MAYBE HE'LL MANAGE IT.
AFTER ALL...
YOU BROUGHT LEE'S YOUNGER BROTHER BACK HERE-- PRINCE YUE.

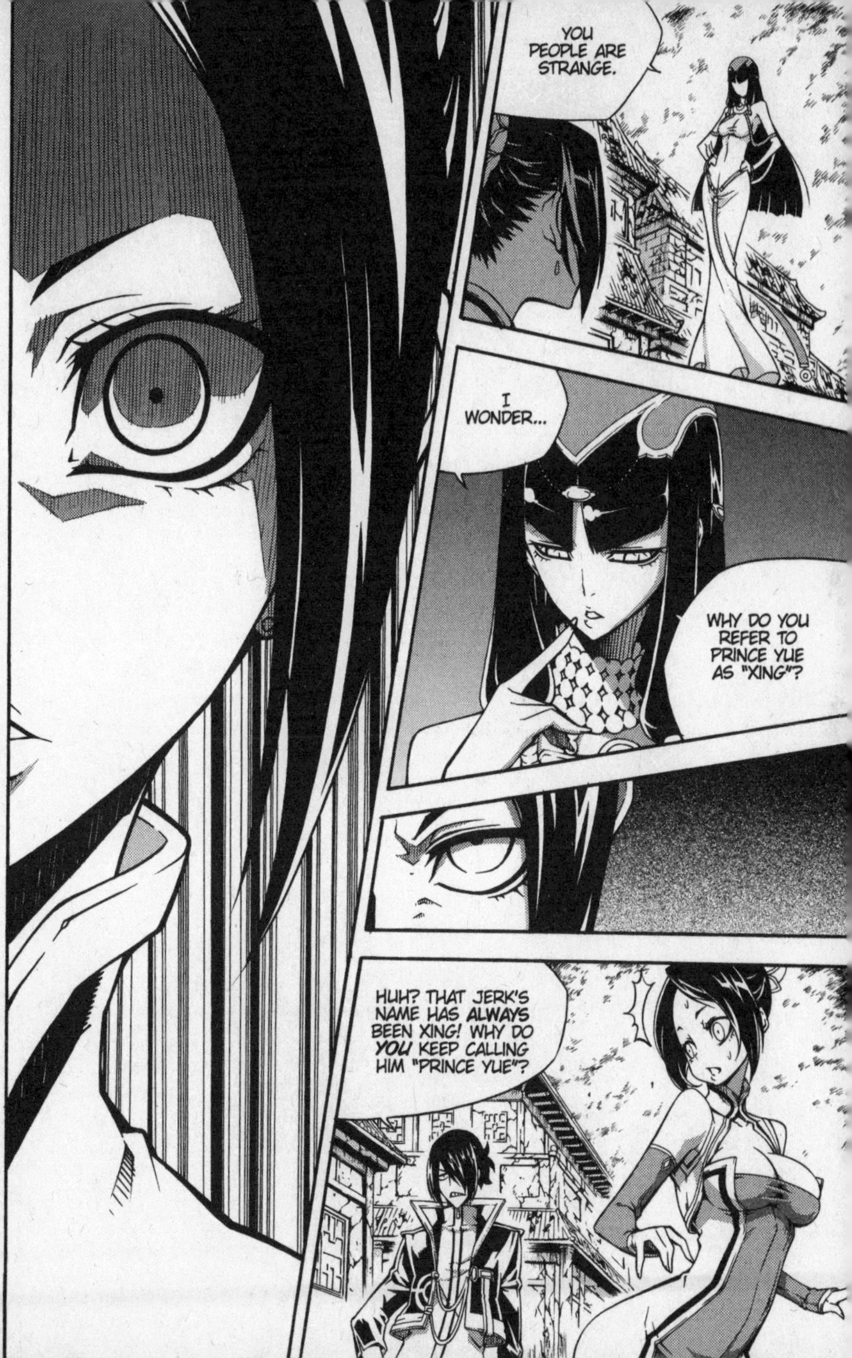
YOU PEOPLE ARE STRANGE.
I WONDER...
WHY DO YOU REFER TO PRINCE YUE AS "XING"?
HUH? THAT JERK'S NAME HAS ALWAYS BEEN XING! WHY DO YOU KEEP CALLING HIM "PRINCE YUE"?

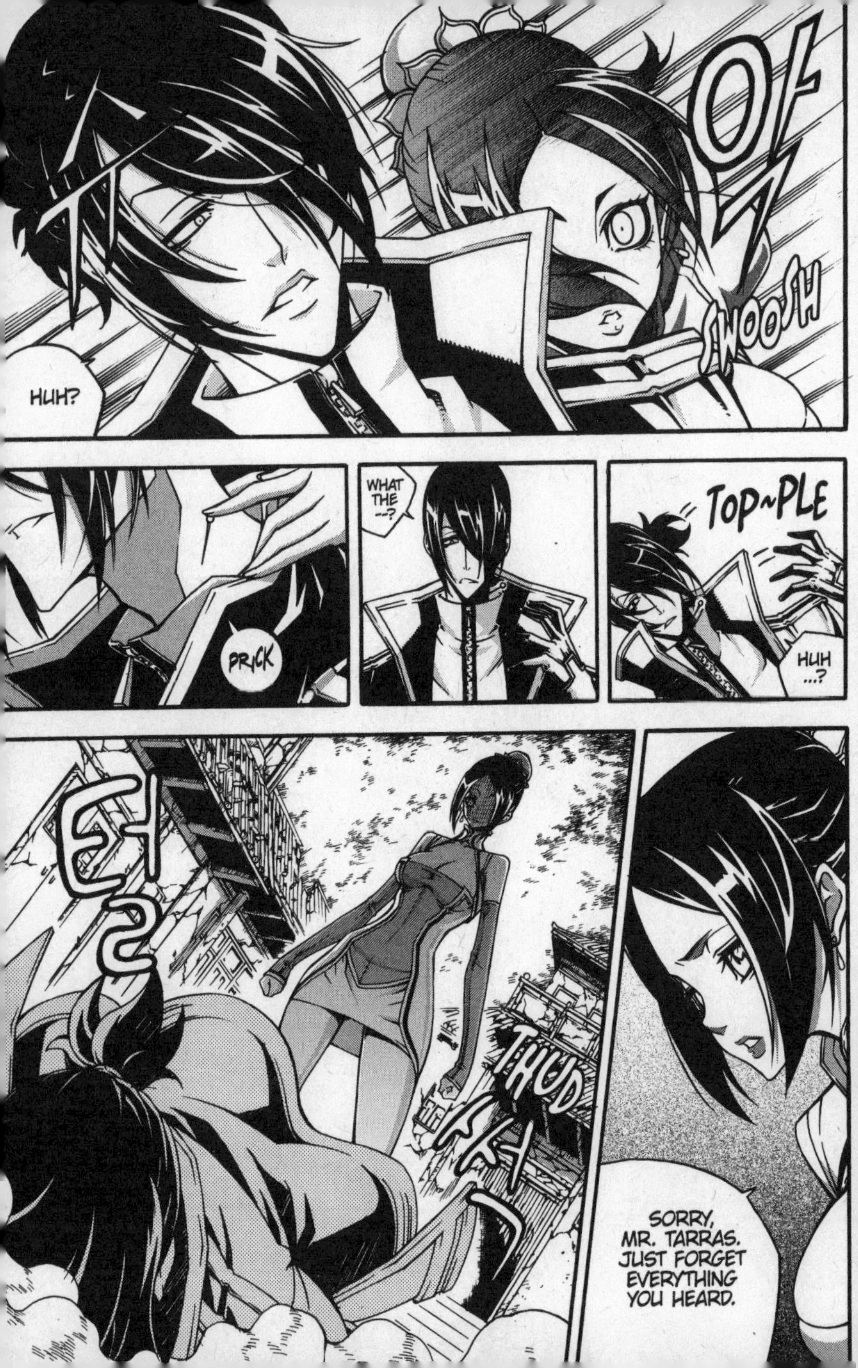
HUH?
OOF
SWOOSH
PRICK
WHAT THE --?
TOP~PLE
HUH ...?
EH?
THUD
SORRY, MR. TARRAS. JUST FORGET EVERYTHING YOU HEARD.

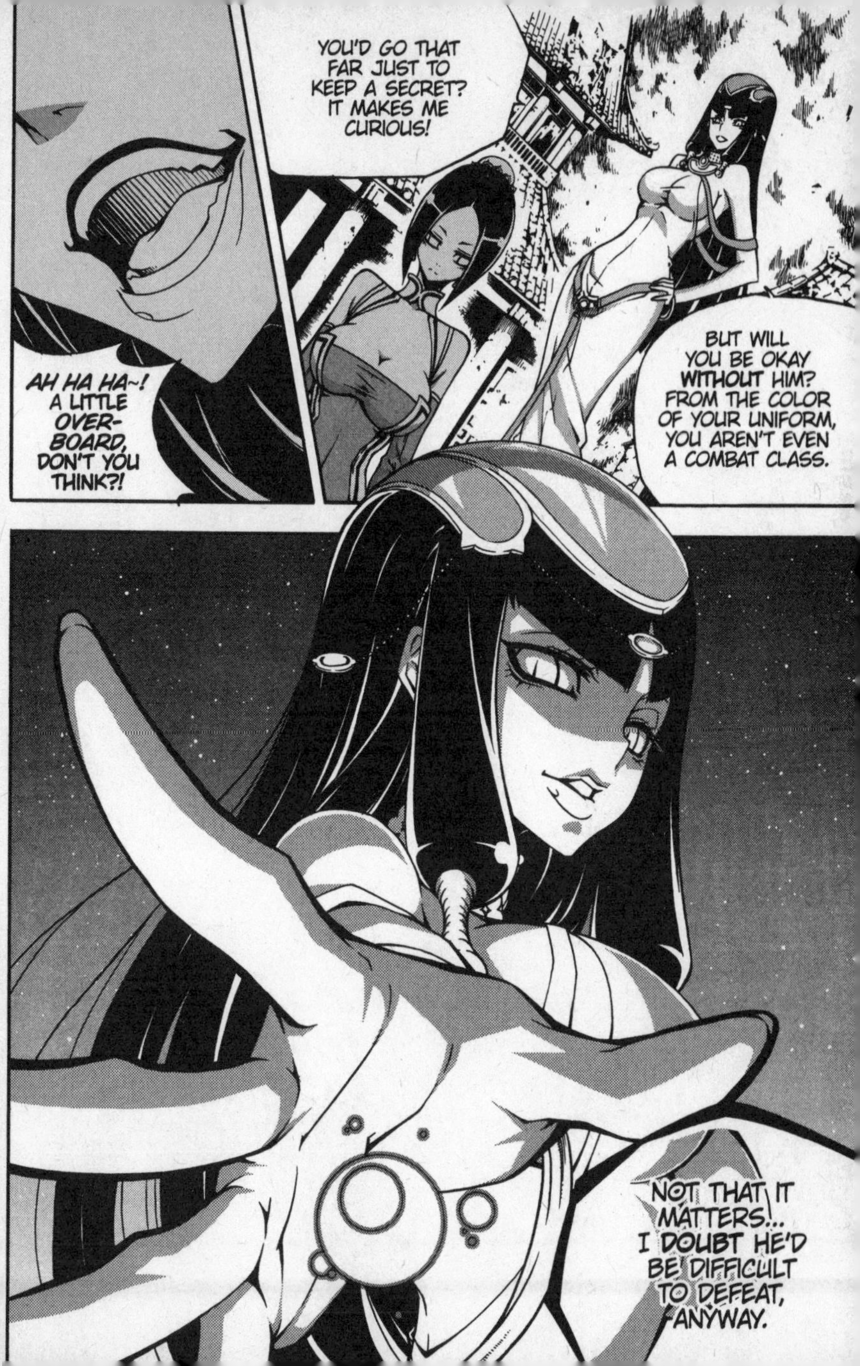
AH HA HA~! A LITTLE OVER-BOARD, DON'T YOU THINK?!
YOU'D GO THAT FAR JUST TO KEEP A SECRET? IT MAKES ME CURIOUS!
BUT WILL YOU BE OKAY WITHOUT HIM? FROM THE COLOR OF YOUR UNIFORM, YOU AREN'T EVEN A COMBAT CLASS.
NOT THAT IT MATTERS... I DOUBT HE'D BE DIFFICULT TO DEFEAT, ANYWAY.

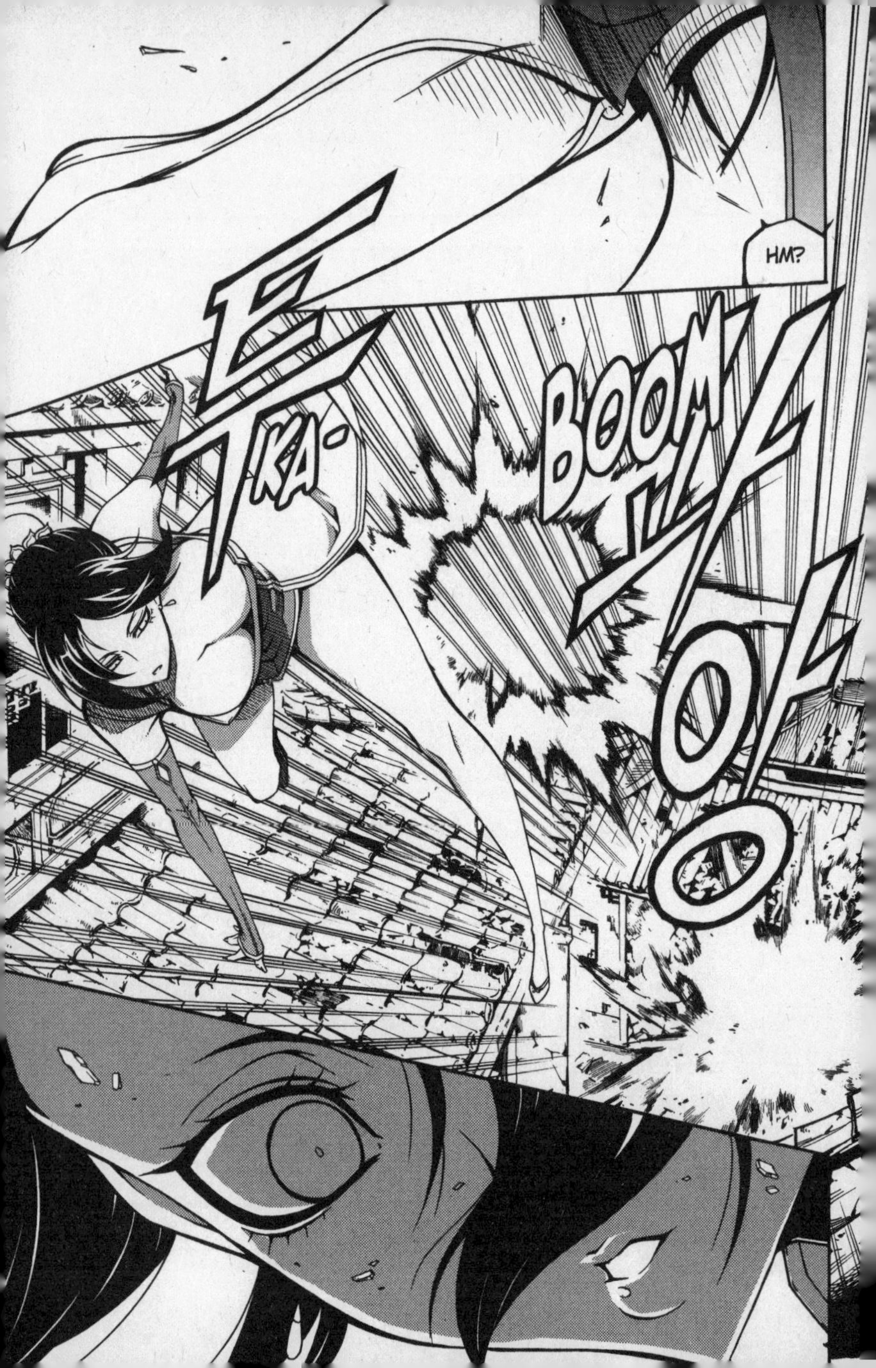
HM?
KA-BOOM!!
VOOOO

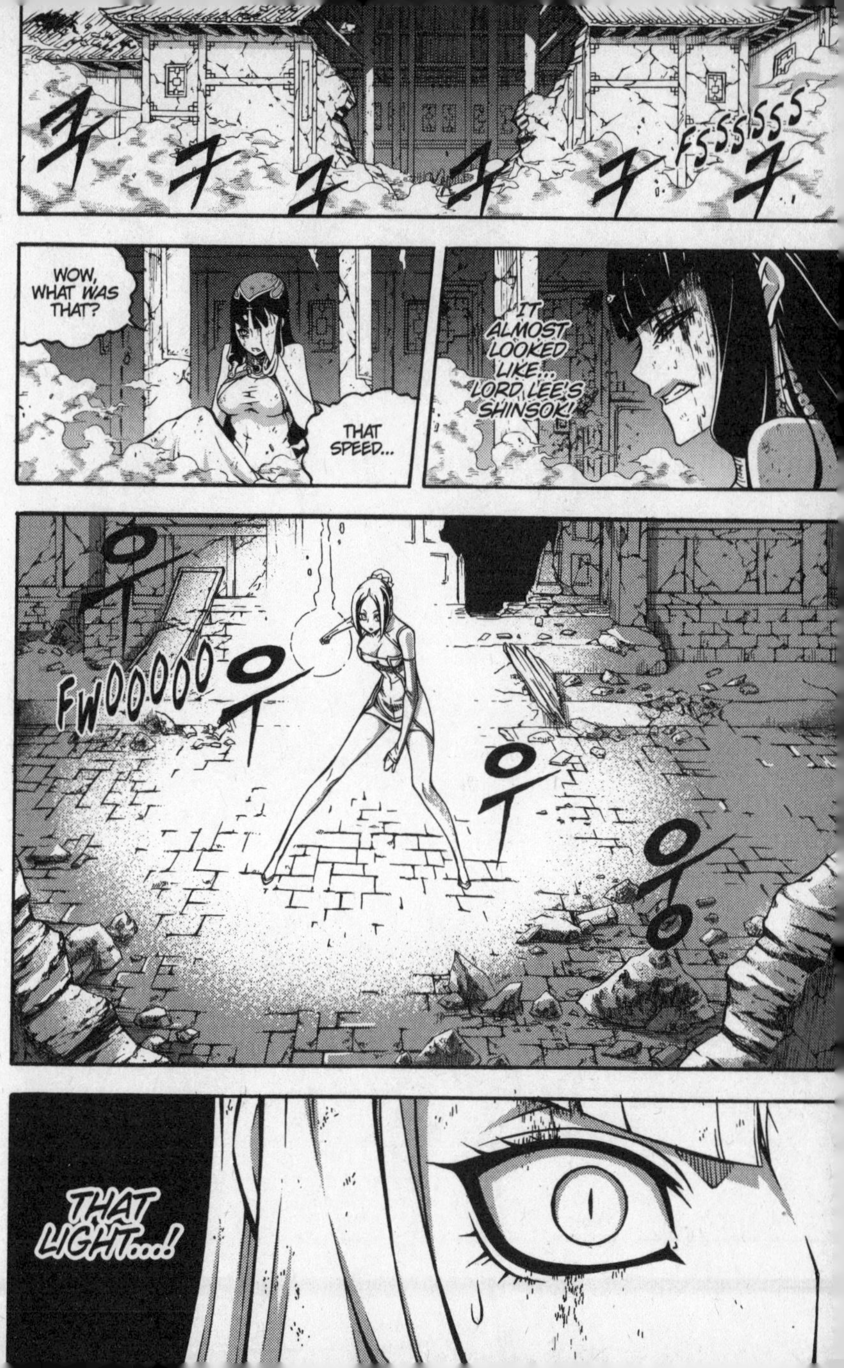
FSSSSSS
WOW, WHAT WAS THAT?
THAT SPEED...
IT ALMOST LOOKED LIKE... LORD LEE'S SHINSOK!
FWOOOOO
THAT LIGHT...!

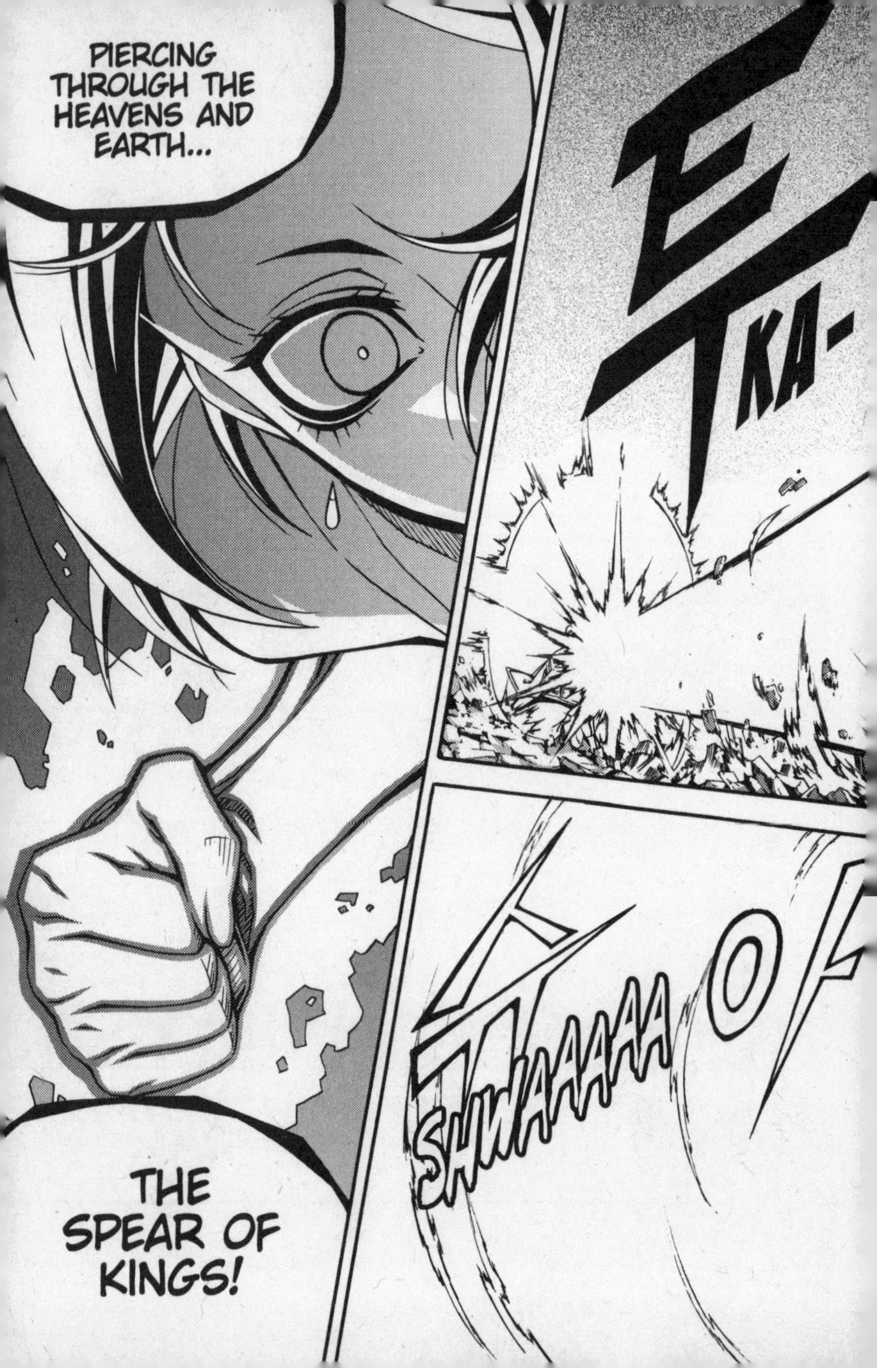
PIERCING THROUGH THE HEAVENS AND EARTH...
THE SPEAR OF KINGS!
KA-
SHWAAAAA

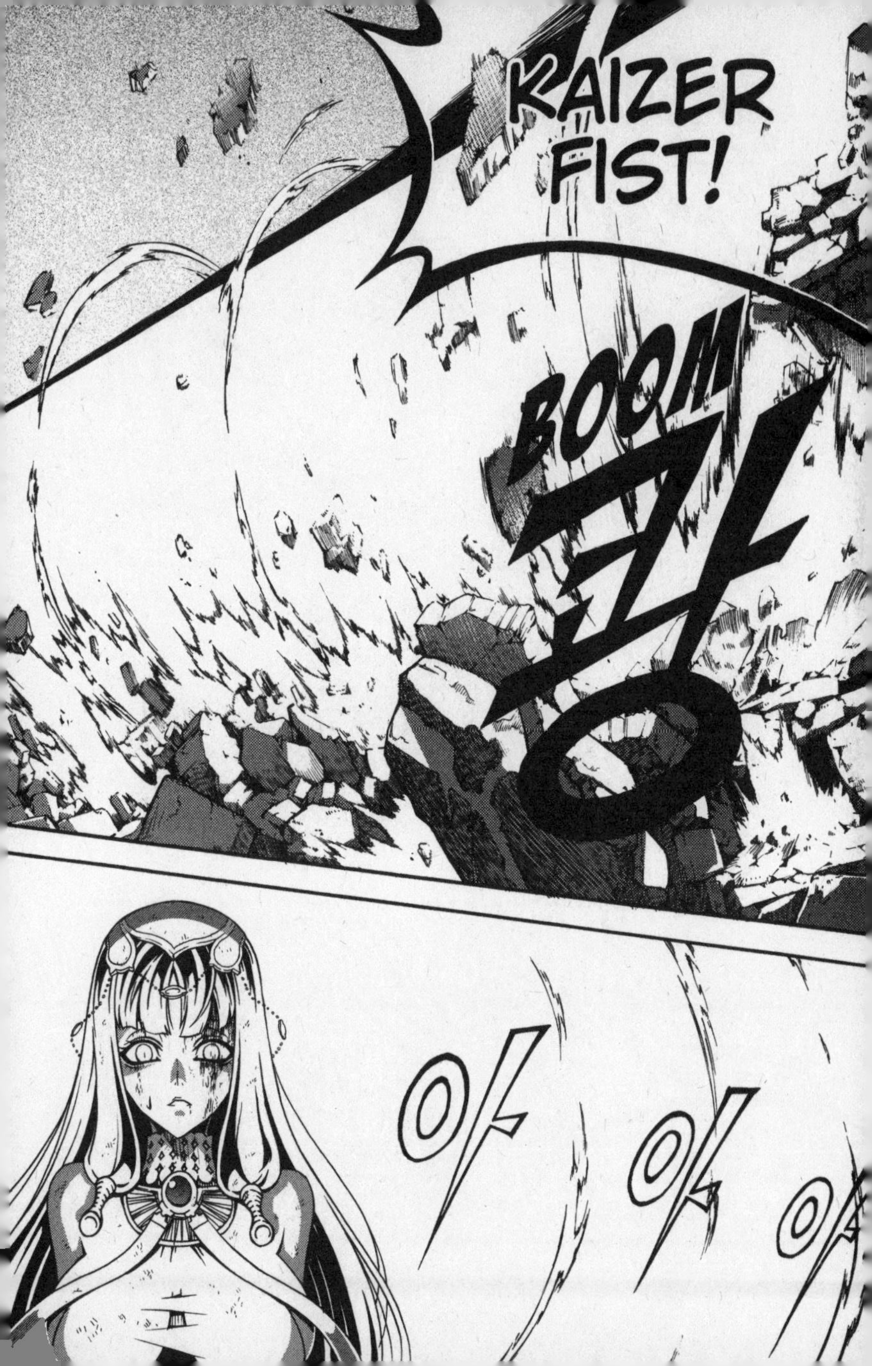
KAIZER FIST!
BOOM
OH

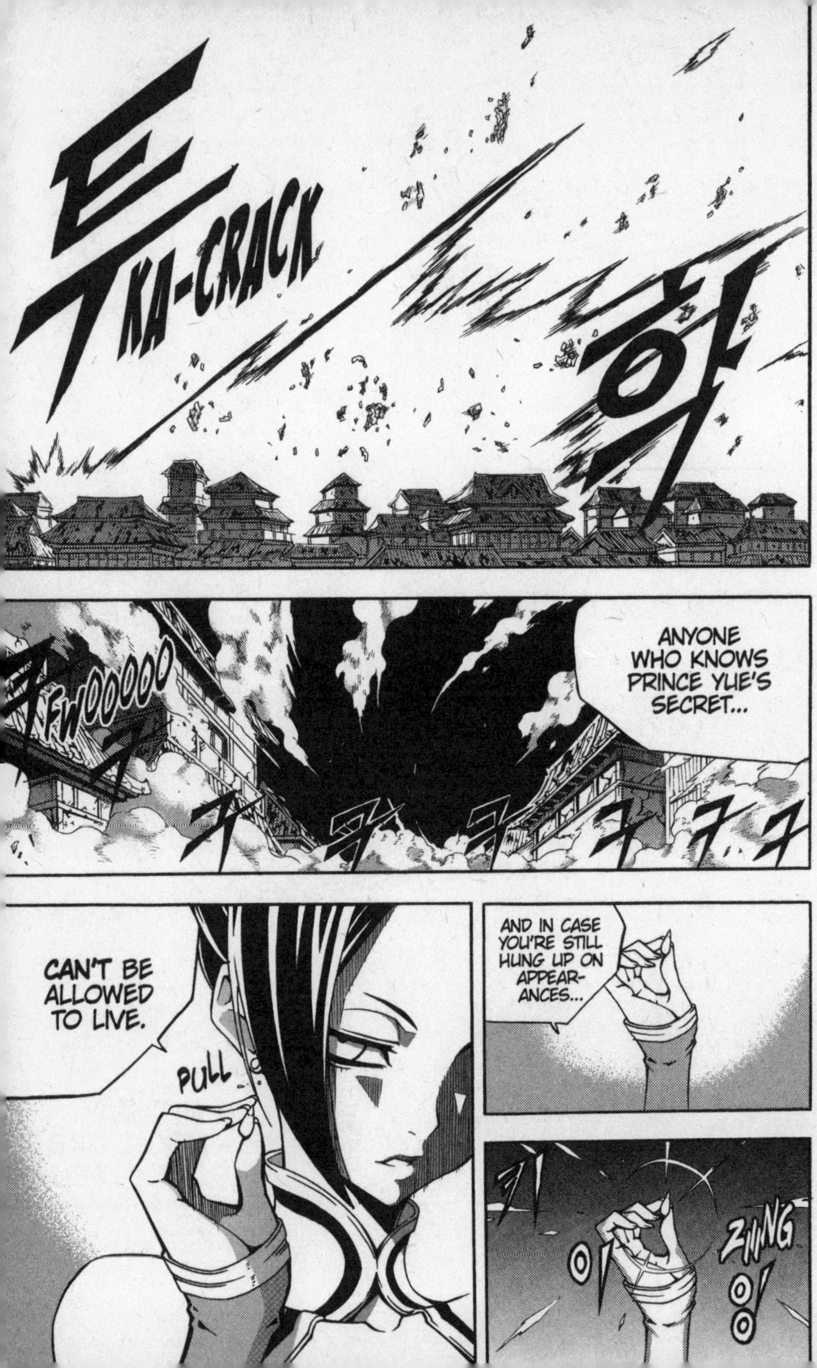
KA-CRACK
FWOOOOO
ANYONE WHO KNOWS PRINCE YUE'S SECRET...
CAN'T BE ALLOWED TO LIVE.
PULL
AND IN CASE YOU'RE STILL HUNG UP ON APPEAR-ANCES...
ZIING

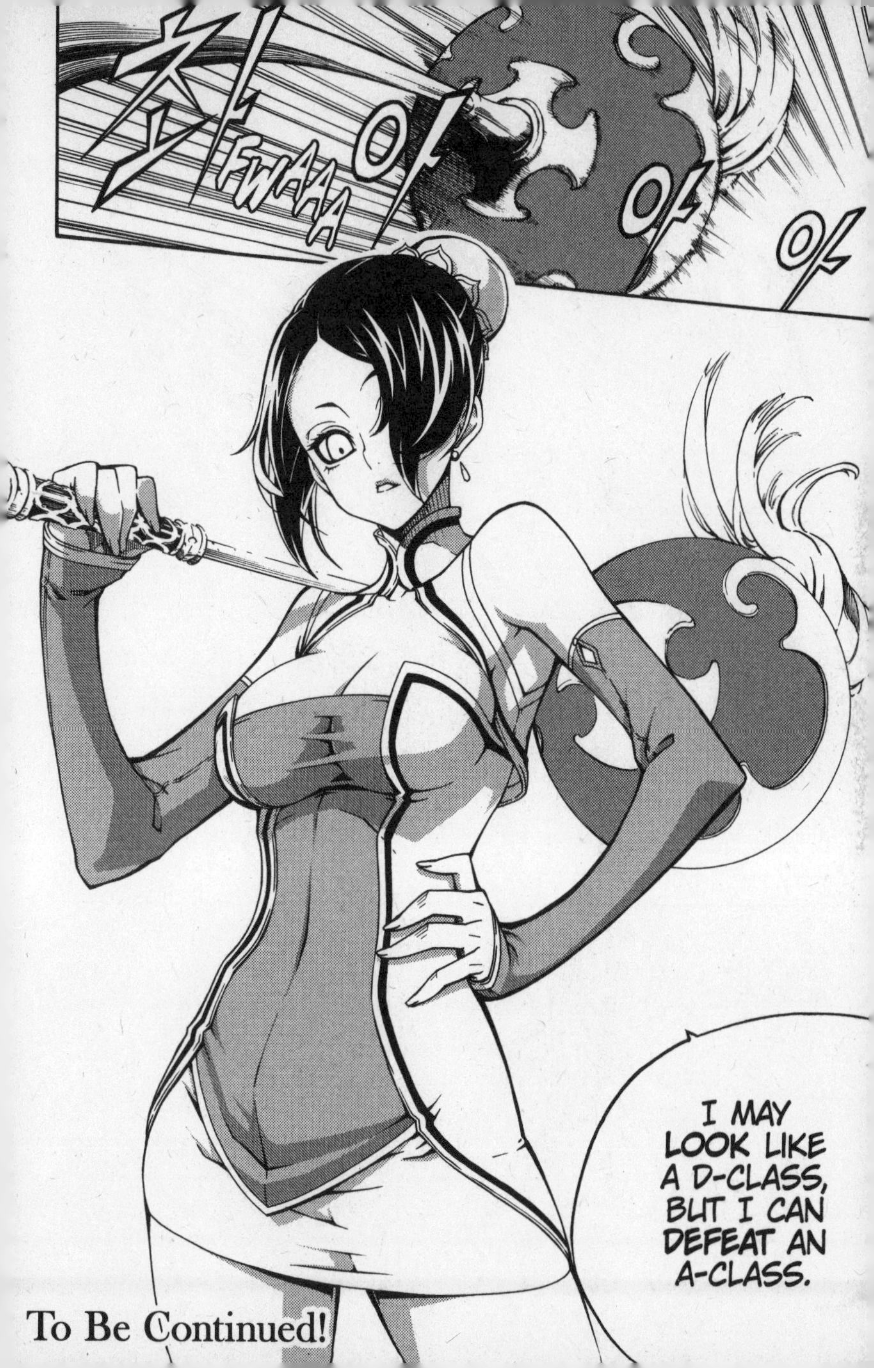
FWAAAA
I MAY LOOK LIKE A D-CLASS, BUT I CAN DEFEAT AN A-CLASS.
To Be Continued!

PLEASE BE MINDFUL OF WHERE YOU LEAVE YOUR ITEMS!

KA-BOOM
MAGNIFICATION
OOPS...?

RYUHWAN

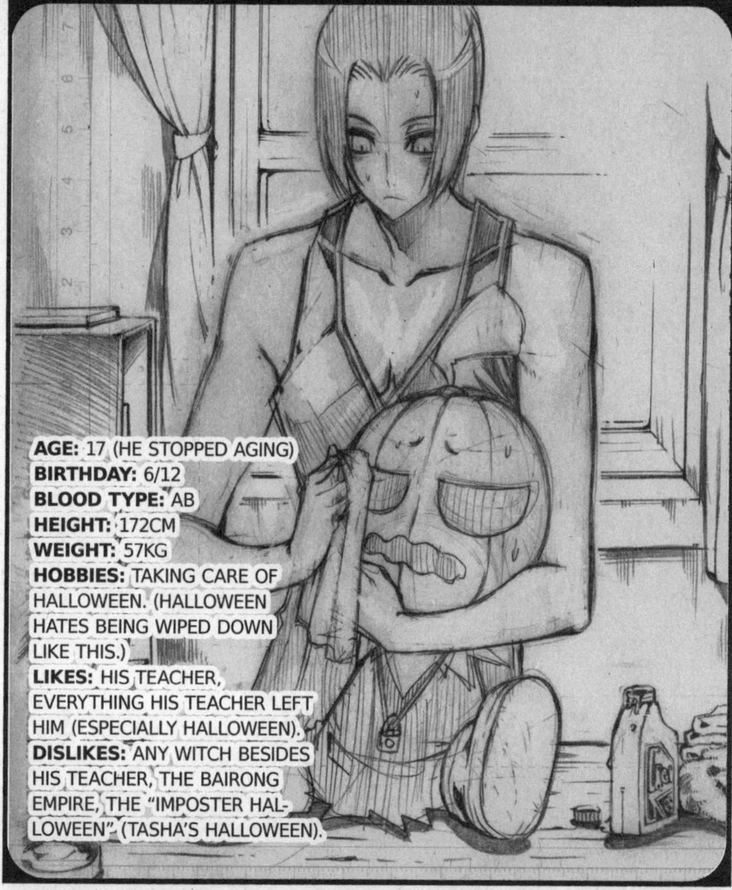
AGE: 17 (HE STOPPED AGING)
BIRTHDAY: 6/12
BLOOD TYPE: AB
HEIGHT: 172CM
WEIGHT: 57KG
HOBBIES: TAKING CARE OF HALLOWEEN. (HALLOWEEN HATES BEING WIPED DOWN LIKE THIS.)
LIKES: HIS TEACHER, EVERYTHING HIS TEACHER LEFT HIM (ESPECIALLY HALLOWEEN).
DISLIKES: ANY WITCH BESIDES HIS TEACHER, THE BAIRONG EMPIRE, THE "IMPOSTER HALLOWEEN" (TASHA'S HALLOWEEN).

I DESIGNED RYUHWAN TO BE TASHA'S RIVAL. I ALWAYS WANTED TO CREATE A CHARACTER LIKE THIS--FOR EVERY WHITE KNIGHT, YOU NEED A BLACK KNIGHT, AFTER ALL. SINCE TASHA AND RYUHWAN HAVE THE SAME COMBAT STYLE, THEY HAVE A SIGNIFICANT EFFECT ON EACH OTHER. RYUHWAN'S FUNCTION IN THIS STORY IS TO TRIP UP TASHA IN WHATEVER WAY HE CAN.

EUNRYU

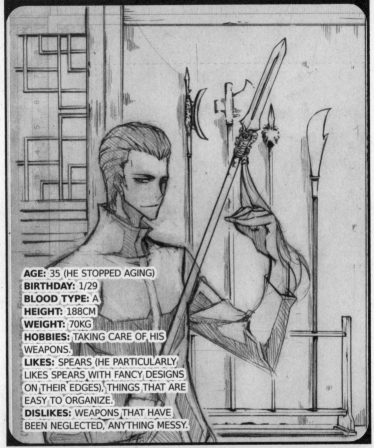

AGE: 35 (HE STOPPED AGING)
BIRTHDAY: 1/29
BLOOD TYPE: A
HEIGHT: 188CM
WEIGHT: 70KG
HOBBIES: TAKING CARE OF HIS WEAPONS.
LIKES: SPEARS (HE PARTICULARLY LIKES SPEARS WITH FANCY DESIGNS ON THEIR EDGES), THINGS THAT ARE EASY TO ORGANIZE.
DISLIKES: WEAPONS THAT HAVE BEEN NEGLECTED, ANYTHING MESSY.

EUNRYU IS ORIGINALLY FROM THE BAIRONG EMPIRE. I'VE MENTIONED THIS NATION MANY TIMES IN THE STORY, WHICH IS WHY I THOUGHT I SHOULD INTRODUCE MORE CHARACTERS WHO CAME FROM THERE. EUNRYU IS A CHARACTER WHO SHOWS THAT THERE'S A HIDDEN INFLUENCE AFFECTING THINGS IN THE STORY. HE WAS SUPPOSED TO BE A MIDDLE-AGED CHARACTER (I WANTED TO SHOW THE BEAUTY OF AGE), BUT HE CAME OUT LOOKING A BIT YOUNGER THAN I'D PLANNED (THAT'S MY LACK OF SKILL... ^ _ ^:).

I CAME UP WITH LANCELOT THE MOMENT I STARTED WORKING ON *WITCH BUSTER*. I'VE ALWAYS LIKED THE STORIES OF KNIGHTS THAT APPEARED IN CELTIC LEGENDS, AND OF COURSE I WAS A FAN OF ARTHUR AND HIS KNIGHTS OF THE ROUND TABLE. THAT'S WHY THEY APPEAR A LOT IN MY STORY. LANCELOT IS ONE OF THE MOST FAMOUS KNIGHTS OF THE ROUND TABLE, BUT HE'S JUST AS INFAMOUS AS HE IS FAMOUS! MY LANCELOT HAS BEEN SHAPED IN THE SAME WAY--A GOOD PERSON WITH NO CHOICE BUT TO BE BAD, A CONFLICTED CHARACTER...ISN'T HE COOL~?!

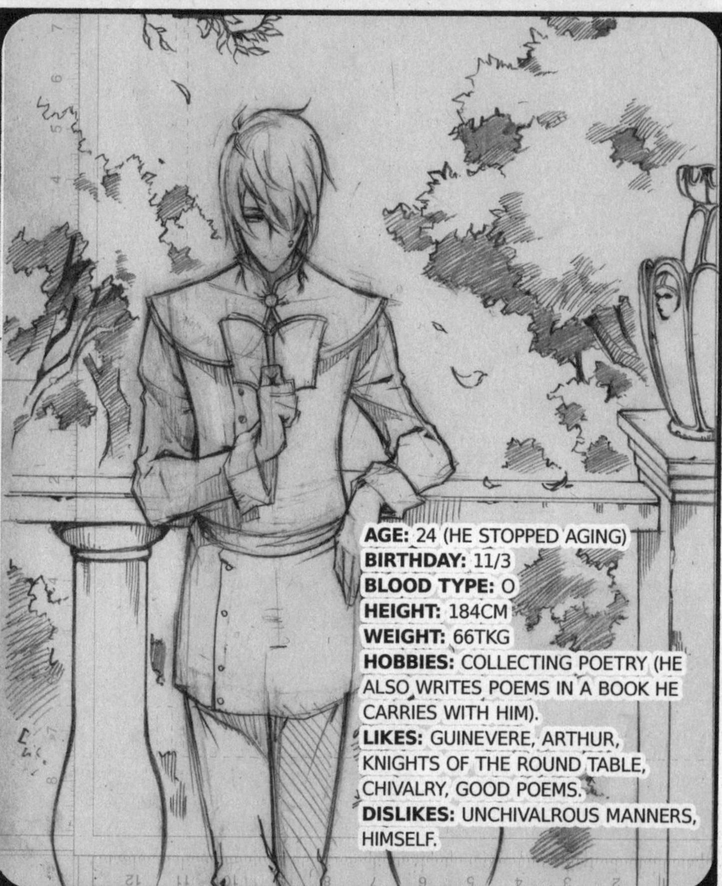
AGE: 24 (HE STOPPED AGING)
BIRTHDAY: 11/3
BLOOD TYPE: O
HEIGHT: 184CM
WEIGHT: 66TKG
HOBBIES: COLLECTING POETRY (HE ALSO WRITES POEMS IN A BOOK HE CARRIES WITH HIM).
LIKES: GUINEVERE, ARTHUR, KNIGHTS OF THE ROUND TABLE, CHIVALRY, GOOD POEMS.
DISLIKES: UNCHIVALROUS MANNERS, HIMSELF.

LANCELOT DU LAC

AFTERNOTES...

NO PARTICULAR TOPIC~!

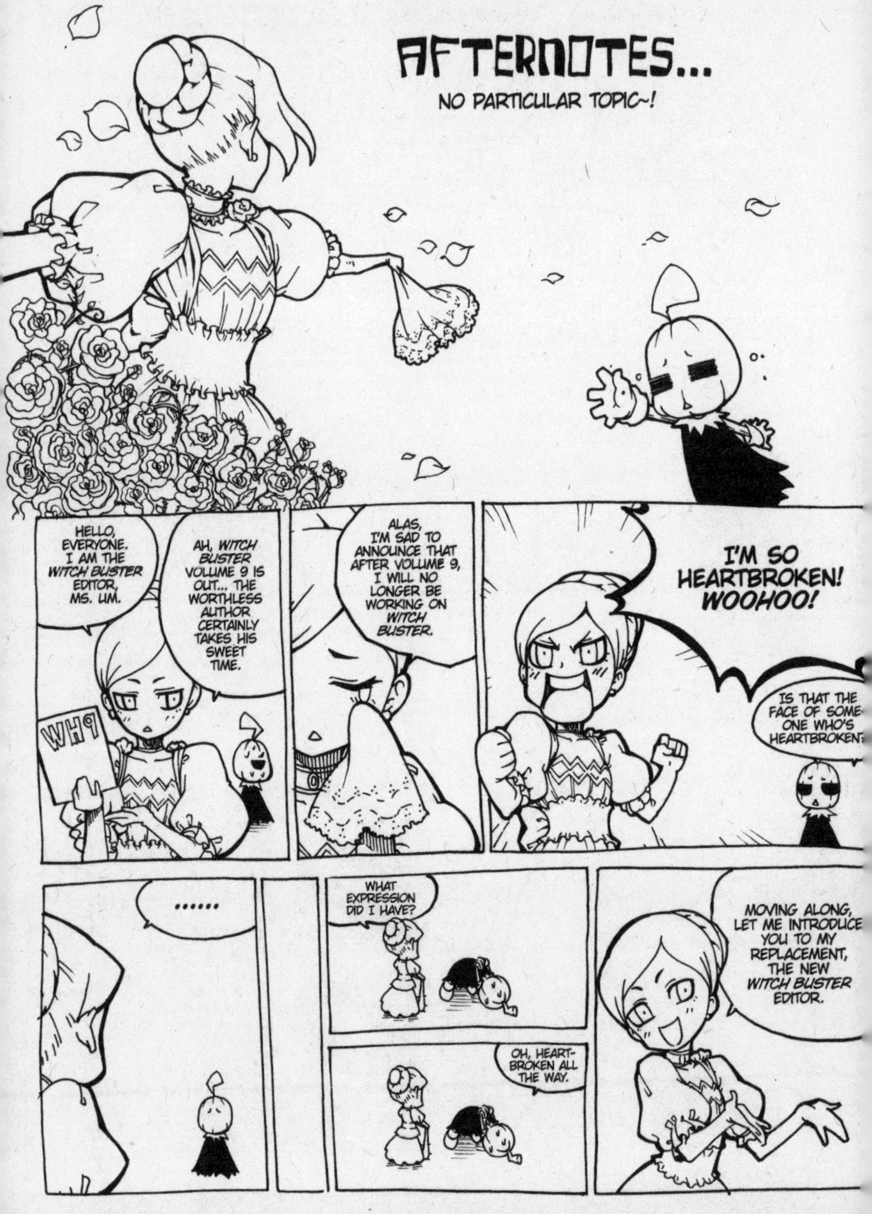

HELLO, EVERYONE. I AM THE *WITCH BUSTER* EDITOR, MS. UM.
AH, *WITCH BUSTER* VOLUME 9 IS OUT... THE WORTHLESS AUTHOR CERTAINLY TAKES HIS SWEET TIME.
WH9
ALAS, I'M SAD TO ANNOUNCE THAT AFTER VOLUME 9, I WILL NO LONGER BE WORKING ON *WITCH BUSTER*.
I'M SO HEARTBROKEN! *WOOHOO!*
IS THAT THE FACE OF SOME-ONE WHO'S HEARTBROKEN?
......
WHAT EXPRESSION DID I HAVE?
OH, HEART-BROKEN ALL THE WAY.
MOVING ALONG, LET ME INTRODUCE YOU TO MY REPLACEMENT, THE NEW *WITCH BUSTER* EDITOR.

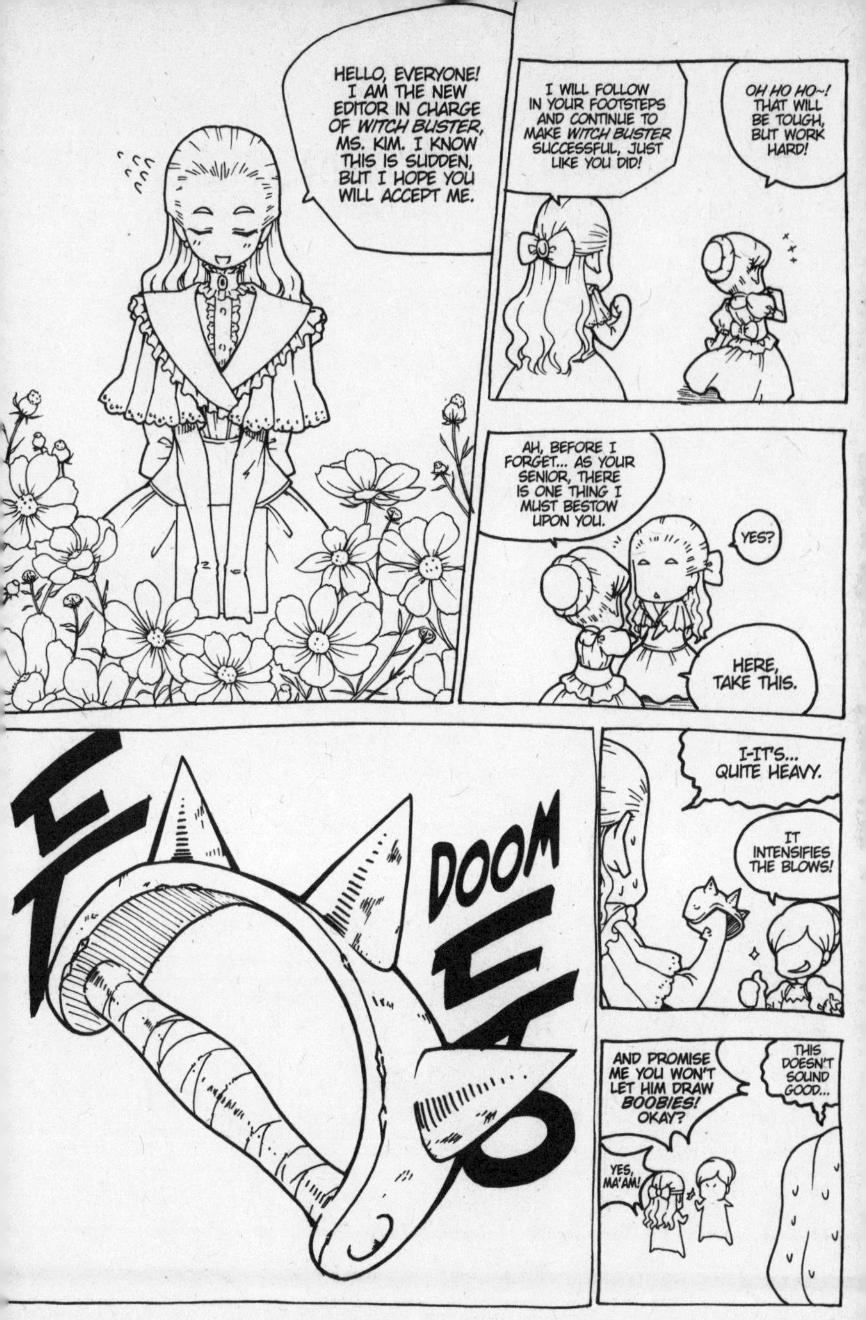
HELLO, EVERYONE! I AM THE NEW EDITOR IN CHARGE OF *WITCH BUSTER*, MS. KIM. I KNOW THIS IS SUDDEN, BUT I HOPE YOU WILL ACCEPT ME.
I WILL FOLLOW IN YOUR FOOTSTEPS AND CONTINUE TO MAKE *WITCH BUSTER* SUCCESSFUL, JUST LIKE YOU DID!
OH HO HO~! THAT WILL BE TOUGH, BUT WORK HARD!
AH, BEFORE I FORGET... AS YOUR SENIOR, THERE IS ONE THING I MUST BESTOW UPON YOU.
YES?
HERE, TAKE THIS.
DOOM
I-IT'S... QUITE HEAVY.
IT INTENSIFIES THE BLOWS!
AND PROMISE ME YOU WON'T LET HIM DRAW *BOOBIES!* OKAY?
THIS DOESN'T SOUND GOOD...
YES, MA'AM!

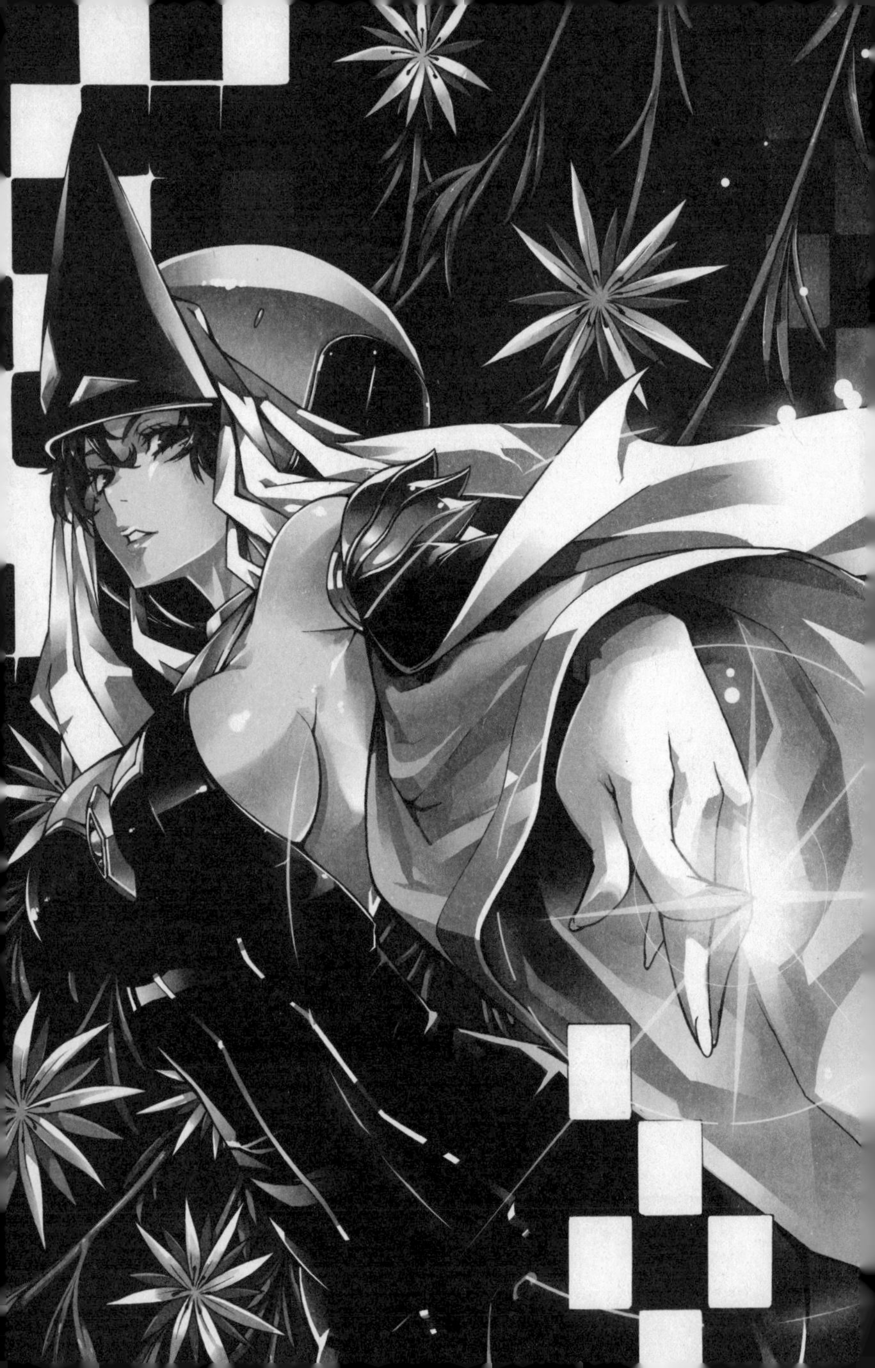

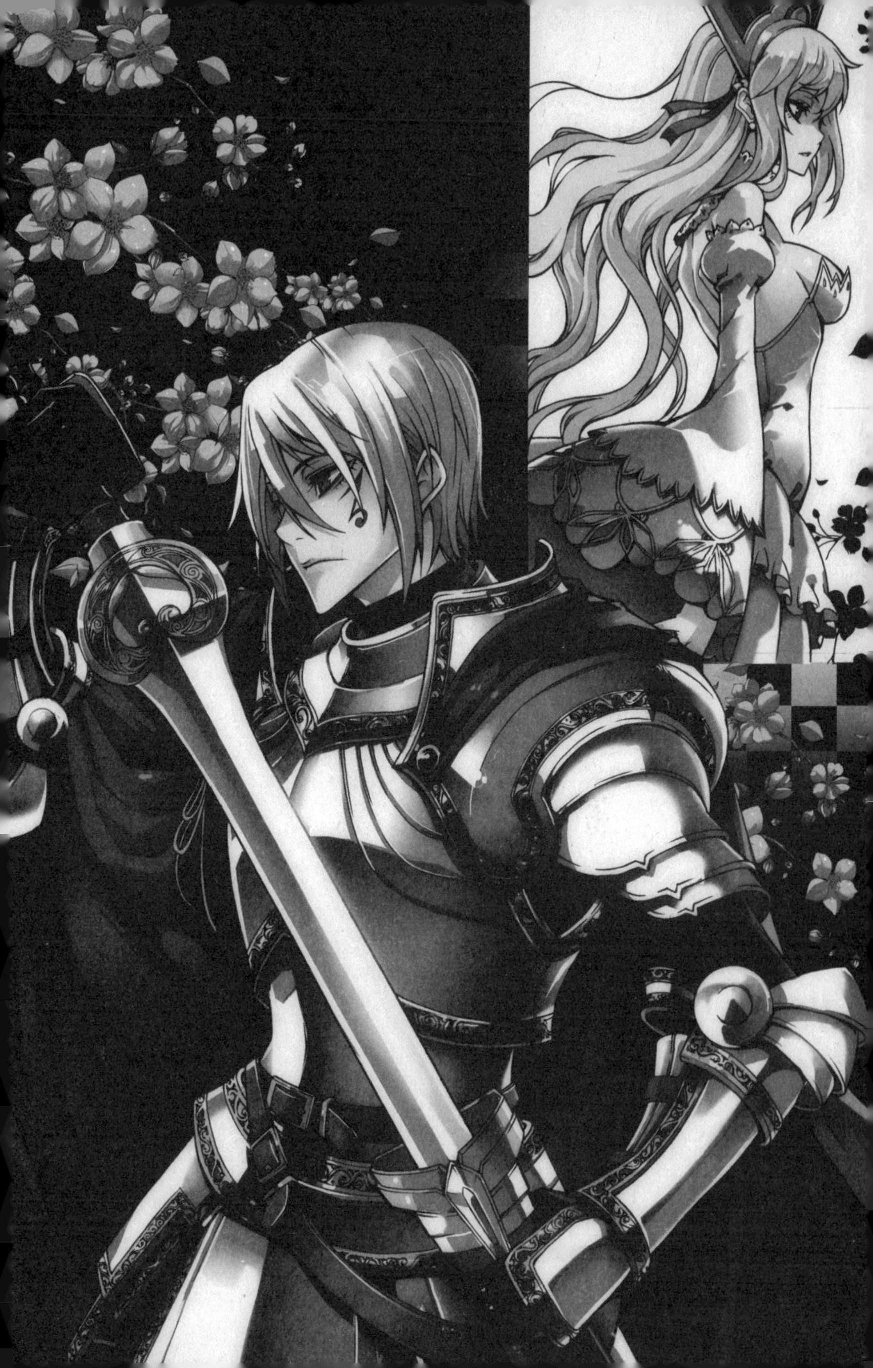

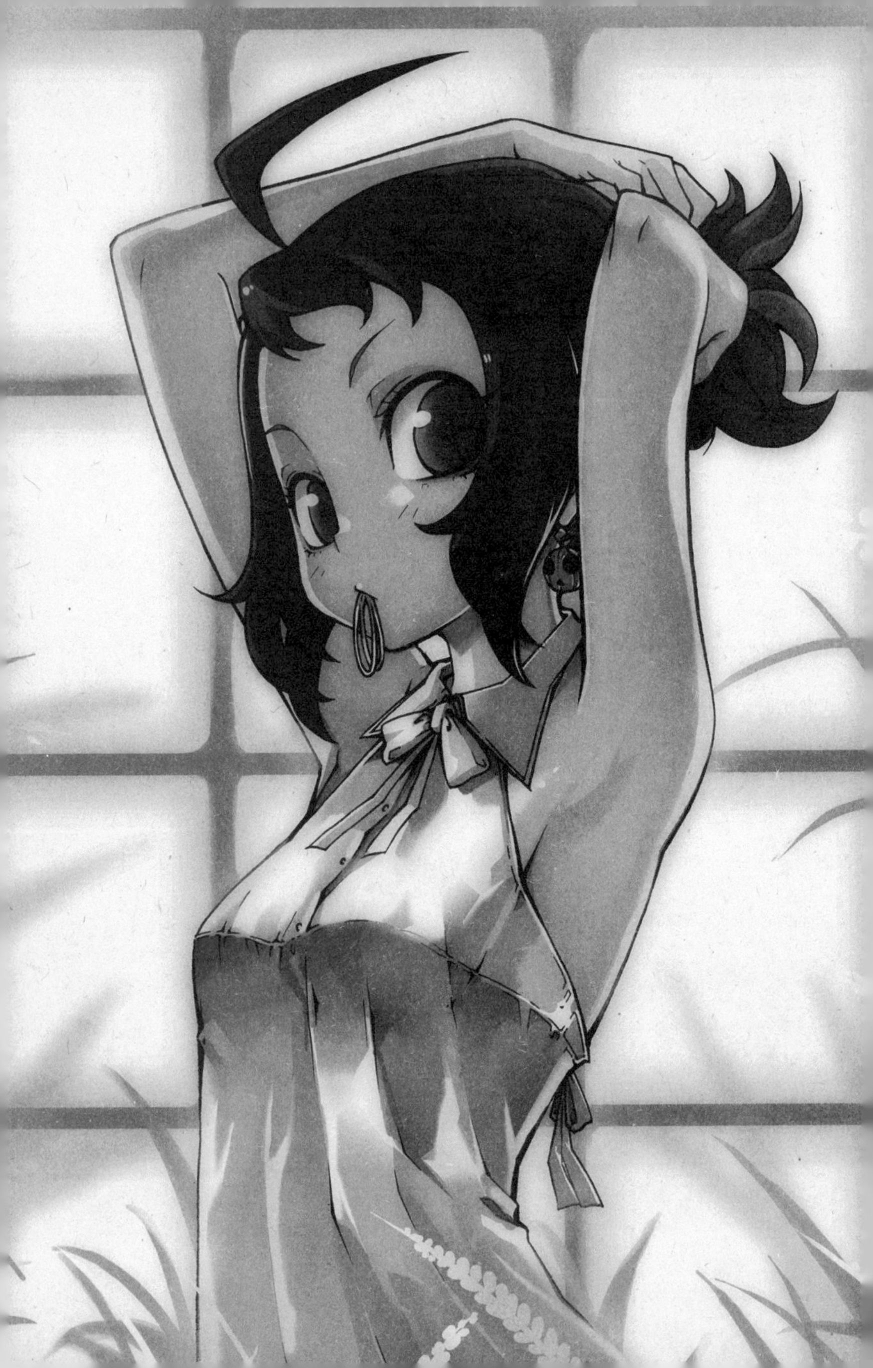